A. A. Milne: His Life

A. A. MILNE

— *His Life* —

Ann Thwaite

ff

faber and faber
LONDON · BOSTON

First published in 1990
by Faber and Faber Limited
3 Queen Square London WCIN 3AU

Phototypeset by Input Typesetting Ltd, London
Printed in Great Britain by Richard Clay, Bungay, Suffolk

A CIP record for this book is available
from the British Library

ISBN 0–571–13888–8

In memory
of my devoted parents
A. J. and H. M. Harrop,
particularly because he
gave *Winnie-the-Pooh*
to her when it was first
published and read it to
me years later at just
the right moment

'Well, how does one know anything about anybody?'

A. A. Milne, *The Fourth Wall*, 1928

'One writes in a certain sort of way because one is a certain sort of person; one is a certain sort of person because one has led a certain sort of life.'

A. A. Milne, *It's Too Late Now*, 1939

'If in the end [he] still remains something of a mystery, [we] should not be surprised: for every human being is a mystery, and nobody knows the truth about anybody else.'

A. A. Milne, *Chloe Marr*, 1946

'Life holds no more wretched occupation than trying to make the English laugh.'

Malcolm Muggeridge,
Tread Softly for you Tread on my Jokes, 1966

Contents

Acknowledgements for Illustrations

I AM GRATEFUL to the Milne family for permission to use 1, 5, 7, 14, 27, and 28; to the Harry Ransom Humanities Research Center of the University of Texas at Austin for 2 and 12; to Trinity College, Cambridge, for 6 and 21; to Andrew Birkin for 8; to the National Portrait Gallery for 15; to the *Sunday Times* for 19; to Peter Ryde for 20; to Mr and Mrs Gilbert Adams for 22; to the Theatre Museum, London, for 26 and to Anglia TV and Keystone Press Agency for 29. The photos of Cotchford and Poohsticks Bridge are my own copyright.

The illustrations in the text (pages 46, 241, 486), and Plate numbers 13 and 23, are by E. H. Shepard from *When We Were Very Young*, *The House at Pooh Corner* and *Winnie Ille Pu*, published by Methuen Children's Books, reproduced by permission of Curtis Brown, London.

A. T.

Illustrations

Illustrations in text

Introduction

I AM OFTEN asked how I came to write this book. I had discovered I was a biographer fifteen years before I began it, when I started work on my life of Frances Hodgson Burnett, another distinguished writer for children, author of those two very different bestsellers, *Little Lord Fauntleroy* and *The Secret Garden*. Even so, when my second biography, *Edmund Gosse: A Literary Landscape*, was finally published, nine years after I had begun work on him, I had a strong feeling that I could not go through all that a third time, that I would prefer to concentrate on my own life in future. But it turned out that my own life had become irreversibly that of a biographer. The varied routines of researching into someone else's life had become a necessary part of my own. I could no longer imagine living without the treasure-hunt element, the feeling of always being on the look-out for something. I was addicted to long silent hours under the great dome of the British Library or in manuscript libraries and rare-book rooms in far-flung American universities. I had got into the habit of taking out random books from the biography stacks in the London Library on the off chance that the right name would be there in the index. I was even addicted to humping about the decaying bound volumes of *The Times*.

The problem then was: who was to be my new subject? It is the modern biographer's main problem, it seems to me, that of finding someone worth all the hard work. Nearly everyone has already been 'done'. I have no interest in writing the life of someone, even someone I am extremely interested in, where a decent or recent biography already exists. Part of the pleasure for me has always been in the feeling that I am reading letters for the first time since they were read by some long-ago recipient, that I am adding (in some small way) to the published record, making accessible material that is otherwise completely unavailable to the general reader.

After *Edmund Gosse* I was approached by a number of publishers, but only Craig Raine, writing from Faber, suggested a name. 'How about A. A. Milne?' he asked. With both Frances Hodgson Burnett and Edmund Gosse, the initiative had been entirely my own. And my own inclination in 1984 had been to write a life of P. H. Gosse, the father of *Father and Son* — that remarkable character, marine biologist, fundamentalist preacher, friend of Darwin and Kingsley. I had put the suggestion, under my contractual obligation, to Secker and Warburg, my original publishers, and they had turned it down. Edmund Gosse was quite obscure enough. P. H. Gosse, even more than his son, was a totally uncommercial proposition.

It would probably be difficult to think of anyone more different from P. H. Gosse than A. A. Milne. And yet I could see immediately that Milne was exactly the right subject for me. He is, of course, best known as a children's writer, and writing for children and children's reading had been my concern for twenty-five years, indeed my only professional concern until I started work on Edmund Gosse. I had been brought up on A. A. Milne. I knew many of his verses and stories more or less by heart. My London childhood had been a slightly down-market version — a decade later — of Christopher Robin's own. Even my double name (I was always known as a child as Ann Barbara) certainly owed more to Christopher Robin than to Princess Margaret Rose. There are photographs of my six-year-old brother (*circa* 1937) clutching his own Kanga and Roo. My father's only children's book, *Round the World with Willa Webfoot*, based on our own adventures, had owed a great deal to Milne. Fortunately for us, in a sense, it had not been a success.

There was every reason for me to be as interested in Milne as I had been in Mrs Burnett and Gosse. Milne himself mentions Gosse from time to time. A writer who had stooped to write advertisements (as Milne never would) 'would deem it necessary to slink past Sir Edmund Gosse with his hat over his eyes', he wrote in 1927. So has the world changed; writers rarely wear hats. Milne saw Gosse as the final arbiter of taste, of literary acceptability. But if Milne is hardly in the same class as Edmund Gosse or his formidable father, he is no less interesting and he has one great advantage. He is much more famous. 'Thank heavens,' one of my daughters said on hearing of my new subject, 'Mum's going to write about someone everyone has heard of.' She'd grown tired of explaining Mrs Burnett and Edmund Gosse.

Pooh and the other animals, if not Milne himself, seem to pervade our daily lives. People call their pets, their friends, their shops after them. People know about them. On an 88 bus in Regent Street, I overheard a woman correcting her companion as they looked down at Hamleys' shopwindow: 'Those aren't proper Pooh bears,' she said. 'They have to be like E. H. Shepard's pictures before you can call them Pooh bears.' That same week on Radio Four I heard a child from an academy of speech and elocution in Galle, in Sri Lanka, reciting Milne's poem 'When I was One/I had just begun', and in Dorset a friend reported overhearing a girl exclaiming to her mother in disbelief: 'Samantha hasn't heard of Poohsticks!' '*Winnie-the-Pooh* changed my life,' a woman said, concluding an interview with me on the CBC in Edmonton, Alberta. I couldn't ask her how as she had already turned to the next person to be interviewed. Milne's children's books are known in a way equalled only perhaps by *Alice's Adventures in Wonderland*.

At the heart of A. A. Milne's life, I knew, was his complicated relationship with his son, and there were obvious parallels between the experiences of Vivian Burnett, the original Fauntleroy, and those of Christopher Robin Milne. Both of them had been dogged all their lives by identification with their fictional counterparts. In *Edmund Gosse* I had had to explore, as sensitively as I could, a particularly difficult father/son relationship. My biographical experience seemed to have been preparing me for A. A. Milne.

My first reaction to the suggestion that I should write a biography of him was to feel that surely, if it were feasible, there would be one already. Indeed, some people had the impression that it *had* been done already, such a major part does Milne play in his son's memoir *The Enchanted Places* (1974). But 'mine was a personal memoir, not a biography', Christopher Milne wrote in his second book *The Path Through the Trees* (1979): 'I decided therefore to confine myself to my own memories.' I had read and enjoyed those books years before but now, of course, I looked at them again. In the second one, Christopher Milne denies that he had written the first book – as he says in the introduction to it – for 'Pooh's friends and admirers'. He had written it rather, he admitted, for himself, to explore his own childhood and to come to terms with his relationship with his father. Each session at the typewriter 'had been like a session on the analyst's couch'. The writing of his book had lifted him from under the shadow of his father and Christopher Robin – 'able to look them both in the eye.'

Christopher Milne had another reason for writing *The Enchanted Places*, he said. It was to forestall other writers.

For if I did nothing, then sooner or later someone would come to me and propose himself as my father's biographer. And of course he would hope to see what in fact didn't exist and hear what I didn't wish to tell. Could I refuse to have anything to do with him? Or could I agree to answer certain questions and not others? To say 'No' would be hard enough, but to say anything but 'No' would be in the end to open my private world to a complete stranger and allow him to trample all over it, picking from it what he pleased and interpreting it how he wished. There was only one way out. 'Yes, I will write my own account in my own time and in my own words.' I had only to say this . . . to become immediately and utterly safe. For here was my reply, my impregnable defence. And twice in the course of the next two years I was to shelter behind it.

When I read that, I knew I had to have Christopher Milne's agreement to this enterprise before I signed any contract with Faber. With both my earlier subjects, I had presented their families with a *fait accompli*: I was going to write the biographies whatever their feelings about it. But in those cases I was dealing with grandchildren. Mrs Burnett and Edmund Gosse had died in the 1920s. With Milne, it was different. He had died only in 1956. Not only Christopher, his son (who apparently disliked so strongly the idea of a stranger's book about his father), but also many relations and friends who had known him, were still alive. It seemed unlikely that I would get it, but I needed Christopher Milne's approval and, indeed, his permission to quote from any material that was relevant. He seemed to think that few papers existed; but letters, of course, go out into the world and many of them survive whatever the family – or indeed their writer – feel about their existence. The famous bonfires of Thomas Hardy and Henry James could not destroy the letters they had written themselves. However many of A. A. Milne's letters to his family had been destroyed or had simply disappeared with the passage of time, I knew many others would turn up. Indeed they did, and I wanted to be sure I could use them.

Fortunately for me, the very act of writing *The Enchanted Places*, and indeed its sequel, which Christopher Milne had thought would reinforce his ability to say 'No' to potential biographers, eventually allowed him, after some years (because of that coming to terms with his father and his childhood) to say 'Yes' to a complete stranger, as

I was. It must have helped that we shared an agent, Curtis Brown (whose eponymous founder makes a good many appearances in these pages). I left Curtis Brown to make the preliminary approaches. For reasons he did not disclose, Christopher Milne decided I could go ahead; and I am extremely grateful for his confidence in me. He warned me that he would be of very little help, that he would answer, if he could, straightforward, factual questions, but that basically he had already said all he wanted to say about his father. I would find his feelings and memories in his own books. He then said something that I found extremely helpful when, after the years of research, I came to write this book. He told me I must write the biography as if he weren't going to read it.

This made me much less inhibited than I might have been – but, of course, I could not help feeling, as I wrote some passages or quoted some letters, how extremely interested A. A. Milne's son *would* be. In particular, I felt this as I used one of my main discoveries – a large cache of letters from Milne to his beloved brother, Ken, most of them written in the 1920s when the children's books were coming out and when the two brothers saw comparatively little of each other as Ken was dying of tuberculosis in Somerset. Milne wrote from London chiefly to entertain him and to keep him in touch with what was going on. They were a marvellous find for a biographer, full of all the things I most wanted to know. These letters, in the library of the University of Texas at Austin, had been returned to Alan Milne by Ken's widow on Ken's death. On Alan's own death, his widow should have returned the letters to Ken's children. Milne himself knew the position about letters and says so clearly in a 1923 play: 'When once a letter has gone through the post, it isn't the property of the writer any longer.' The material in it is still in the writer's copyright but the actual object, the letter itself, belongs to the recipient. Daphne Milne also sold to Texas a large amount of manuscript material – which Christopher imagined she had destroyed – and a great many books. Her motive, I am sure, was not mercenary. (She certainly did not need the money, though she had a perpetual dread that she might not be able to pay the Inland Revenue out of income, large as that income was.) She liked the idea of her husband's papers being in the custody of a university library. It gave them the status she felt they deserved. The Wren Library at Trinity College, Cambridge – Milne's own college – had welcomed Milne's gift in his will of the manuscripts of the *Pooh* books. But, certainly, in

1959, they were not in the least interested in the rest of the papers. The Humanities Research Center at Austin was. And there they remain, along with so much else relating to English literature.

Apart from giving me sufficient encouragement to allow me to sign my contracts with a clear conscience, the other major thing Christopher Milne did for me was to introduce me to his cousins, the children of Milne's brother, Ken. I am grateful to all four of them – they know how much I owe to them and how difficult it would have been for me to write the book without them. I shall name them all, along with so many other helpful people, in my Acknowledgements. Here I would like to single out the eldest of them, Marjorie Murray-Rust, of Stalbridge Weston in Dorset, with whom I stayed many times, and who shared with me so generously so many relevant treasures, from her bookshelves, storage-boxes, photograph albums and, above all, her memory. She had known her uncle for fifty years, from before she could remember, when he first wrote about her in *Punch*.

'How can you write a book about someone you never met?' A. A. Milne's cook's daughter asked me through a window in Hartfield, not allowing me into her house. 'People do it all the time,' I said feebly, thrown by the unexpected question. In fact, I really believe it would have been more difficult if I *had* met him. Milne, as many people have remarked, was a difficult man to get to know. If I had met him, I doubt if I would have come to love him. I doubt if he would have let me. But a biographer must feel, at least at times, what Tennyson called 'a discriminating love'. If I had met him, my own limited impression would have perhaps got in the way of a wider knowledge. Christopher Milne compares himself, rather unfairly, with an archaeologist who, having excavated a handful of sherds, goes on to deduce how the completed pot must have looked. 'No one could dispute the fragments, but somebody else, holding fragments of their own, might dispute the vase.' His cousin, Angela Killey, said to me that I now know far more about A. A. Milne than those who knew him.

It is certainly true that I have brought together many more fragments than had at one time seemed possible, but those who knew him will not let my picture distort their own memories. Clive Bell, Virginia Woolf's brother-in-law, a contemporary of Milne's at Trinity College, Cambridge, wrote in his book *Old Friends* that old friends and relations will always dispute the conclusions of biographers. 'Mrs Thrale, who knew Johnson far longer and far more intimately than Boswell knew him, doubtless said as much. And of course Mrs Thrale was right. Only she forgot that it was Boswell's business to write a biography, to depict a man in all his activities and in his relations to all sorts of people, while it was her privilege to record a personal impression.' Milne was no Dr Johnson and I am no Boswell, but the principle holds. Those readers who knew a different A. A. Milne from the one they find in this book must bear that in mind.

People have often asked me whether I would not rather be writing a biography of a woman. I find that surprising. I am interested in people – men *and* women – and the way they live their lives. I am particularly interested in writers, the literary landscape and the world of the theatre. But it occurs to me that the lives of Gosse and Milne shared many of the characteristics of the lives of women. They were both for men of their time unusually concerned with childhood, their own and their children's. Their lives as writers were home-based. They were both of them, though so different in temperament, interested in words rather than actions and in people rather than power. The worst time of Milne's life was the only time when he lived as a man among men, the life of a man of action on the Somme in 1916.

Two final points. None of the dialogue in the book has of course been invented by me. All is recorded or imagined by A. A. Milne himself. And Milne's punctuation is also, of course, his own. In 1912 he wrote to Clement Shorter at the *Sphere*: 'I do feel strongly that punctuation is a matter entirely for the author. It is not an exact science like spelling.' And, again, in 1917: '*Don't* let the printers interfere with my punctuation . . . Right or wrong, it's my own.'

Biography is not an exact science either. It is, in fact, a very subjective activity. Right or wrong, this story of A. A. Milne is my own. I myself feel quite sure that he would be glad to have his children's books, which have come to be the only thing that most people know about him, put in context. There is no question, as there is with the biographies of the majority of writers, of making any attempt to illuminate the most important texts. That, as is shown by that academic *jeu d'esprit*, Frederick Crews' *The Pooh Perplex*, would be a foolish enterprise. All the jokes have been made already and the texts remain, undiminished.

But context *is* important and revealing. Milne himself demonstrated this vividly on one occasion. It is not very interesting, he said, to read in a letter: 'It has been raining steadily all day.' But if the letter is signed Noah and dated 3000 BC, then it is different.

Ann Thwaite
Low Tharston
Norfolk
1989

— I —

'I can do it'

THERE WERE THREE boys in the room. The eldest was nearly five
– David Barrett Milne – and it seemed high time that he learnt to
read, though he was not very inclined to learn anything: the wicked
Barry, as his youngest brother would call him. The second boy was
Kenneth John. He was three and three-quarters and it was reasonable
for him to join in the reading lesson. The baby, aged two and a half,
was Alan Alexander and he was supposed to play with his toys in
the corner.

Their father came in to see how they were progressing. He pointed
to a word on the wall chart and said, 'What's that?' Barry and Ken
frowned at the word. It was on the tip of their tongues. Bat or Mat?
And from the corner a complacent little voice said, 'I can do it.' No
one took much notice. Papa asked again: 'What's that?' Still Barry
and Ken were silent, frowning. But Alan said, 'Cat.' As it was. One
can imagine the small eldest brother jumping about enraged, as
Eeyore does, stamping on the sticks. 'Education! What *is* Learning?'
A thing *Alan* knows.

This is the earliest story about the infant A. A. Milne and he tells
it himself in his autobiography, saying *he* did not think it particularly
remarkable, but that it seemed to make a great impression on his
father and that he himself had, as a result, heard the story more
times than he cared to remember. Of course it started the small boy
off on a good path. He liked, as others have done, the approval
which links pleasure with virtue. As he said of himself, years later:
'In Papa's house it was natural to be interested; it was easy to be
clever.'

His father, John Vine Milne, gave his own version of the story in
1928, in an *Evening Standard* series on fathers and sons called
'Makers of Men'. This was at the height of A. A. Milne's fame, just
before the publication of *The House at Pooh Corner*, the last of the

four classic children's books. It is interesting to notice that John Vine Milne was described as 'Father of the humorist and playwright, who wrote *Mr Pim Passes By, The Dover Road, The Truth about Blayds* and other plays.' That was the way A. A. Milne was still thought of in the 1920s. There is no mention of the children's books. And that was the way Milne liked it.

The second story is more complex. Milne tells it himself: 'We were walking along Priory Road, when a coal-cart stopped in front of us, and the coal-man staggered through the gate of a house with a sack on his shoulders. I said, "Why do they both?" Nobody knew what I was talking about, and nobody ever did know, and nobody knows now. But Papa, hammering away at it, decided that what I meant was: Why do you have to employ both a man *and* a horse? Why shouldn't the *horse* deliver the coal, or the *man* pull the cart? "Isn't that what you mean, darling?" Having a lot of other questions to ask, naturally I said, "Yeth"; whereupon Papa gave me a lecture on the Economics of Co-operation. In after years he got to think that I had given him the lecture; and that, since I was only three at the time, I must have been pretty well advanced for my age. However it was, "Why do they both?" joined "I can do it" in what one might call the family *incunabula*. It seemed to Papa that the future of his youngest son was assured.'

In the earliest photograph that survives of the three boys and their father – taken probably in 1886 when Alan was four – the youngest son looks complacent, as well he might with such strong parental faith in his future. Smug might be a better word. There is a slight smile on his lips. All the others are solemn, holding their poses. Alan has been typecast from birth as the good one, like the third son in the fairy stories, destined to inherit his father's kingdom. He and Ken look much the same size, in spite of the fact that Ken is sixteen months older. They could be twins; things might have been easier for Ken if they had been. The bearded father, if not a king, looks to our eyes as if he might well be, having a certain resemblance to the future King George V. John Vine Milne has a hand restraining Barry, the bad boy of the family, and his other arm protectively round Ken, as if to console him for not being Alan. It is the year of *Little Lord Fauntleroy* and all three boys are wearing black velvet suits, with buttoned knickerbockers and large lace collars. Their flaxen hair curls picturesquely on their shoulders, though Barry's does not, in fact, look particularly flaxen, or, indeed, particularly picturesque.

Looking back, A. A. Milne felt sure that it was not the way their father would have dressed them. It was not, anyway, a style Alan cared for and he knew their father had always wanted them to be strong, independent, and adventurous – 'manly little fellows', in the language of the day. They were indeed, and their outward appearance, like that of Cedric Errol, belied their inner competence. It was certainly their mother's idea, dressing them as Fauntleroys, sensible woman though she was in other ways. Not that there was anything eccentric about it. Many of the nice little boys in the neighbourhood were wearing similar suits. You can see small Ernest Shepard in his on the cover of his memoir of his childhood, *Drawn From Memory*. It was the hair that was the real problem. It was not cut until they were ten. It gave the wrong impression.

'If I were a psycho-analytical critic,' Milne wrote in 1939, 'and if I thought this Edwardian writer, Milne, were worth one of my portentous volumes, I should ascribe everything which he had done and failed to do, his personality as revealed in his books and hidden in himself, to the consciousness implanted in him as a child that he was battling against the wrong make-up.' The word 'portentous' obviously makes his biographer wary, but it is a comment worth thinking about. It is difficult to know whether Milne was thinking merely of his appearance – that his outer contradicted his inner self – or of more fundamental psychological issues.

Milne deflated the story about his infant precocity at reading by saying that he could see it had the makings of a good story if told about the right person – a two-year-old Abraham Lincoln, perhaps. But, as far as he was concerned, after a lifetime of refusing to do things other people wanted him to do (lecture, open bazaars, make speeches, go to Hollywood) he felt his first recorded remark should have been not 'I can do it', but rather, 'I won't do it'.

As a child he was eager, right from the beginning. There is no doubt about that. He was born, blond and blue-eyed, on 18 January 1882 at Henley House, Mortimer Road, in the registration district of Hampstead in London. He was registered Alexander Sydney. How easily he might have been A. S. Milne. His father had to go back later, when they changed their minds and decided he was Alan Alexander. (Alexander was his uncle's name and his uncle lived in the same household at that time – but there would have been no confusion, as the uncle was always called Ackie.) Mortimer Road has been renamed Mortimer Crescent and it is not far north of smart Hamilton

Terrace. A. A. Milne once said he was born 'at the Kilburn end of Maida Vale'. The name 'Kilburn' has, to London ears, very different associations from Hampstead, or indeed from St John's Wood, as some would call the area now.

The streets had been laid out in the period 1855 to 1870 and were, when Milne was born, on the very edge of London. A penny bus to the Crown Inn, Cricklewood, would take them among fields. It was to a farm at Hendon, only a mile or two to the north, that Barry, his elder brother, once went to convalesce from scarlet fever. The country was almost on their doorstep. It was a very respectable neighbourhood. In Mortimer Road there was a solicitor's family and a retired colonel. At Mayfield House there was a stockbroker with five children, a footman and five women servants. Rather less respectable, but more interesting, only a few doors away was Annie Besant, described in the 1881 census as 'a political author', then aged thirty-three, a member of the Fabians and the National Secular Society, working away on her 'free thought' pamphlets and not yet under the influence of Madame Blavatsky.

Next door to Henley House there was a huge convent, St Peter's House, run by the Sisters of Mercy. There were twenty-five nuns with no fewer than fifty-four staff of various kinds – even a dairymaid – and twenty-five girl scholars, who must have been of some interest to the boys of Henley House. No trace of Henley House remains. The site of the house and its neighbours is now covered by Camden Council housing, blocks of undistinguished flats. Five minutes' walk away, a small boy, who would one day be his illustrator E. H. Shepard, had been born just over two years before Alan. His name would be permanently linked with A. A. Milne, but they did not meet until, years later, in the new century, they were both working for *Punch*.

Leaving Mortimer Crescent today, you can walk down Greville Road, past Clifton Hill where the fashionable Victorian painter William Frith lived (it was already, when Alan was born, twenty-four years since his *Derby Day* had attracted crowds to the Royal Academy) and you can see, on the corner of Greville Road and Carlton hill, just the sort of enormous building that Henley House was. This one is, in fact, two houses, joined together but not identical twins. It is a brave mixture of brick and stucco, with contrasting towers and large light rooms, three main floors and a basement. That the Milnes lived in such a big house does not indicate that they were rich. Far from it. Henley House was a school. The building swarmed with boys.

It was 'one of those private schools, then so common, now so unusual', wrote Milne in 1939, 'for boys of all ages'. This was in the days before registration or inspection (in which, in his role as secretary of the Association of the Principals of Private Schools, J. V. Milne was to be much involved). Many schools, if not exactly in the Dotheboys Hall class, were still run by drinkers, bullies and fools who were simply interested in making money. Henley House itself was a good school within its limitations. The 1881 census, for the year before the headmaster's youngest son was born, showed there were thirteen boarders, the youngest six years old, the oldest sixteen. One boy's parents were in Paris. Another came from Montego Bay in Jamaica. The Milnes themselves had strong Jamaican connections.

The day boys, of whom there were usually between forty and fifty, came from the upwardly mobile families of North London who could not afford the public schools and found the new Board Schools (established by the 1870 Education Act) inadequate and unsatisfactory. There was no free secondary education at all in Britain at this time. If parents wanted their children to stay on at school after the compulsory school-leaving age of twelve, there was no alternative but to pay for it. The fee-paying endowed grammar schools were considered by many to be 'hopelessly inefficient and old fashioned', offering a rigid classical education to those who neither wanted it nor needed it. The private schools attempted to fill the gaps in the secondary system, as well as providing a preparatory school for a few boys who would go on to the élite public schools.

The most upwardly mobile boy of all was editing the Henley House School Magazine in the term that Alan Milne was born. He was, in the words of H. G. Wells, 'one of those unsatisfactory, rather heavy, good-tempered boys who, in the usual course of things, drift ineffectively through school to some second-rate employment. It was J. V.'s ability that saved him from that.' When he was about twelve, the boy got hold of a 'jelly-graph for the reproduction of MS in violet ink, and with this he set himself to produce a mock newspaper. J. V. with soundest pedagogic instinct, seized upon the educational possibilities of this display of interest.' The first professionally printed issue of the magazine bore the words in bold type 'Edited by Alfred C. Harmsworth', a name that would become even more familiar to the great British public when it had been transformed into Lord

Northcliffe. Harmsworth's path led to *Answers, Comic Cuts*, the *Evening News*, the *Daily Mail*, the *Daily Mirror* and eventually *The Times*, and peerages and baronetcies for himself and three of his brothers, also boys at the school. J. V. Milne was always impressed by his Old Boys, but his youngest son would coin the memorable dismissal: 'He killed the penny dreadful by the simple process of producing a halfpenny dreadfuller.'

The fifteen-year-old editor's first column ended: 'I may here state that this paper is conducted and, except where stated to the contrary, contributed to entirely by the boys, and that it is all done during play hours. Space forbids me to give utterance to more of my sage remarks.' There is a certain irony in the comments in the next column about young Harmsworth's football prowess. 'Is a most useful back and a very fast runner. Always a man that can be depended on.' Alan Milne would find years later that this was not so.

Henley House School Magazine is an unusual magazine and it gives us a vivid picture of an unusual school. For Henley House was no ordinary private school. It was not the sort of school that left its pupils knowing little but 'the counties and chief towns, dates of the kings, French irregular verbs and English parsing'. Alan Milne had been born into a child-centred world, a world where children really mattered, where they were not tied down by the sort of hideous and trivial rules that made Victorian schoolchildren, in more conventional establishments, hardly dare to move, let alone speak. ('Never speak unless spoken to', 'Never drop your pencil-box', 'Book-bags must be hung by both loops'.) Henley House, was, as its headmaster hoped, more of 'a meeting place for friends' than a shop where education was sold. 'You will find no rule, for instance,' the boys were told in the school magazine, 'that you may not put soup down your neighbour's back, or that you may not go to church in your football dress.' Rules and discipline were reserved for more important things. J. V. Milne would stand no lying, cheating or bullying. 'He was an enlightened man whose ideas on teaching were far ahead of the day.'

Alan remained his parents' youngest child. 'My only regret was that we had no daughters,' J. V. Milne said in 1928. 'But my wife always used to say, "Sons are good enough for me".' The father spoke of the boys' closeness to their mother – how they clustered round her each evening in the drawing-room, how they would have gone to her in any trouble, before coming to their father. But Alan, in his autobiography, gives quite a different picture. His father, he said, 'was the best man I have ever known: by which I mean the most truly good, the most completely to be trusted, the most incapable of wrong. He differed from our conception of God only because he was shy, which one imagined God not to be, and was funny, which one knew God was not. . . . As a child I gave my heart to my father. We loved Mama too, though not so dearly . . . I don't think I ever really knew her.'

Mama, born Sarah Maria Heginbotham and known as Maria, is very much in the background. Alan admired her competence. She had been brought up to do things for herself. 'She could do everything better than the people whom so reluctantly she came to employ: cook better than the cook, dust better than the parlourmaid, make a bed better than the housemaid, mend better than the sewing-maid, wash clothes better than the laundress, bandage better than the matron.' She was not just extremely competent. She was talented. There survives, in Ken's family, a settle wonderfully carved by her, and her schoolgirl tapestry version of the Last Supper would make Alan reflect on the immutability of art: 'It is always better to be an artist, however little.'

But the boys could never imagine their mother had been a teacher. They never thought she *knew* anything. Women, it seemed, didn't. (Is it pure chance, or is it deeply significant, that the only female creature in Milne's Forest is Kanga, the competent mother, doling out Strengthening Medicine, otherwise known as Extract of Malt?) 'When I was a child,' Milne wrote in 1939, 'I neither experienced, nor felt the need of, that mother-love of which one reads so much and over which I am supposed (so mistakenly) to have sentimentalized.' It had certainly been there; no wonder he had not felt the need of it. 'She treasured everything relating to her dear sons,' her husband wrote after her death. It had always been so.

Maria Milne 'was simple, she was unemotional, she was common-sensible. Nothing upset her.' In spite of the fact that her husband *was* very easily upset, Maria had the Victorian woman's complete faith in the rights of a father. It was he who was bringing the boys up. She had her way with their clothes and their hair (with what important consequences, as Alan suggested), but everything else was the province of John Vine Milne. She never stopped the boys from doing anything, 'knowing that a mother's job is not to prevent wounds, but to bind up the wounded.'

John Vine Milne and Sarah Maria Heginbotham had married in

Buxton, Derbyshire, near the bride's birthplace, on 27 August 1878, less than three and a half years before their third son was born. At the time of the wedding, John was thirty-three and his wife already thirty-eight. It was late to begin a family. He had been born in Jamaica, the son of a Congregational Minister called William Milne, who had himself been born in Scotland and had gone to Jamaica as a missionary and there married, in 1843, Harriet Newell Barrett. A. A. Milne called his grandfather, William, a Presbyterian but the evidence of his parents' marriage certificate is otherwise. There is other evidence from that certificate that Alan had not heard much about the earlier generation or, if he had, had not remembered what he had been told. He guessed that his mother 'came, as novelists say, of "good yeoman stock" or, more simply, was a farmer's daughter'. But his maternal grandfather, Peter Heginbotham, was actually a 'manufacturer', a word that can cover all manner of activities and all levels of income, but which can have nothing to do with farming. Of course *his* father may well have been a farmer.

We know nothing of Peter Heginbotham's status, but we do know that his daughter, Sarah Maria, had to make her own way in the world. So did young John Vine Milne. His grandson called William Milne 'the world's most unworldly muddler'. He fathered ten children, only four of whom survived to become adults. 'His income was never more than eighty pounds a year; his children, when they were not dying, lived exclusively on porridge, and were educated for twopence a week at the village school; but he could come home triumphantly from a chapel meeting to tell his underfed family that he had promised twenty pounds for the new pews. And somehow twenty pounds would be paid. It was for the Lord. Yet he was neither sanctimonious nor fanatical. He just believed quite simply that nothing which happened in this world mattered to a good man; to a man, that is, who believed in God and would return to Him. It mattered not if his sons were dukes or dustmen, so long as they were good.'

In 1874 his eldest son John was hovering somewhere between duke and dustman, as an apprentice in an engineering firm. 'For years now his over-mastering concern had been with education: the education of himself and of others. After twelve hours in the engineering shop, he would walk back to his room, spend an hour getting clean, and then settle down to the real work of the day, the achievement of a degree. B.A. (London) was his goal. It might seem that that first hour was being wasted: one can read Latin and Greek as well with dirty hands as with clean; but to him the daily struggle to rid himself of the filth of the machines was a ritual which symbolized his approaching escape from the world of manual toil into the more gracious world of the intellect. If he lost the integrity of his hands, he would lose the integrity of his mind. It was too late to be a duke, but he was damned, he would indeed be damned, if he were a dustman.'

John Vine Milne turned out to be a good teacher, keeping one step ahead of his pupils and growing a beard to help him with the problem of controlling boys who were often bigger and not much younger than himself. 'But in the rough schools to which his lack of academic qualification condemned him a beard was not enough; he needed, and had, the two great qualities, courage and a sense of humour.'

By 1874 he had passed the Intermediate and was working for his Final BA. He had moved from a school at Braintree in Essex to a boys' school in Shropshire. At a girls' school near by Sarah Maria Heginbotham was teaching. There were musical evenings at the girls' school and John Vine Milne was musical. ('Deep down inside him there was a great musical artist struggling to be free.') He played the flute.

He was always a man more at ease with children than with adults. But he acquired something of a reputation in the area when he preached a sermon to the schoolboys, saying there was no such place as Hell and no Everlasting Fire, only a week after the Headmaster had preached a sermon saying Hell was the very place where the boys would be heading if they didn't work. Young Mr Milne suggested there were lots of other reasons for working and lots of good places you could get to if you did. And then he handed in his resignation. But the Headmaster would not accept it. John Vine Milne was far too good a teacher for him to let him go.

But lose him he did eventually, of course. It was soon after this episode that John found the courage to propose to Maria. She seems to have turned him down in the beginning. She was thirty-six; there had been some painful experience with another man. She was used to being on her own. But at last she accepted him and she never regretted it. The only letter of hers that survives (written when she was seventy-three, at the time of Alan's marriage) is a moving tribute to thirty-five happy years of 'well-chosen partnership'. The phrase is hers. At the end of that long partnership, the woman friend who received that letter wrote to tell the widower how much she had enjoyed 'seeing what sweethearts you were to the very end'. And John Vine Milne wrote back, 'In my wife I had a wonderful gift.'

After their wedding they took over Henley House from a man called John Leeds who had been running a private school (nine boarders aged seven to eighteen in the 1871 census) with no great success. They had bought the goodwill, which consisted of 'twenty or thirty inky desks and half a dozen inky boys'. In the autumn term of 1878, the school opened under its new management.

Academic critics have problems with children's literature. There is often so little to say about it without sounding pretentious or absurd. One way of approaching *Winnie-the-Pooh* has been to try and 'identify' the people behind the characters, the objects of Milne's satirical observation. It is inevitable that Owl has been equated with John Vine Milne. After all, A. A. Milne's father was a schoolmaster, wasn't he? And there is Owl looking extremely wise and thoughtful on his first appearance in Chapter IV. 'And if anyone knows anything about anything,' said Bear to himself, 'it's Owl who knows something about something,' he said, 'or my name's not Winnie-the-Pooh,' he said. 'Which it is.' Sound reasoning in Pooh's particular fashion. John Vine Milne knew a great deal about a great many things (even if Alan, in the way of grown-up sons, came to decide that 'even if Father knew everything, he knew most of it wrong') but there is absolutely no justification for the identification with Owl. There was never anything pretentious or pedantic about J. V. Milne. He never pretended to knowledge he did not possess, as Owl did. He never used long words (such as 'encyclopaedia' or 'customary procedure') just to impress. Owl rarely admitted he was wrong; or ignorant – perhaps only in his failure to identify the Spotted or Herbaceous Backson. And *he* could hardly be said to have a sense of humour.

The middle son, Ken, is on record as having said at the age of three that his father had 'too much laugh' for a schoolteacher. And Alan tells a story which splendidly demonstrates not only his father's sense of humour, but also his willingness to admit he had made a mistake. One day the Matron had, unknown to anyone else, asked a boy to fetch her glasses just as everyone was about to have dinner. J. V. Milne admonished the boy for his lateness and, without letting him explain, told him to push in his chair and eat his first course standing, the regular mild punishment for lateness.

When at last told he might take his chair, the boy got the chance to explain. 'Please, sir. Matron sent me upstairs for her spectacles just as I was coming in.'

Awed silence. 'Sucks for J. V.,' the boys are thinking. 'He'll have to apologize.' The younger assistant masters look up anxiously. Do schoolmasters ever apologize? Isn't it bad for discipline?

'Then in that case,' says J. V. Milne, wishing to get it quite clear. 'It wasn't your fault you were late?'

'Please, sir. No, sir.'

'Oh!' Everybody is waiting. 'Oh, well, then, you'd better take two chairs.' And everybody laughs and is happy.

There was a great deal of laughter and happiness at Henley House. At one stage the boys were asked in a typical test paper ('not tests of what a boy has learned, but intended to make him think') to name the things in the world that appeared to them most beautiful. The responses were on the whole predictable: moonlit nights, picturesque ruins, lakes with swans swimming, a field of flax in flower, the sun setting at sea. But the reply which brought the warmest response from the headmaster was – 'a boy with a smiling countenance'. He annotated this '*Et moi aussi*'. J. V. Milne's delight was in the happiness of his pupils – true happiness, of course, not the spurious happiness of the indulged.

It was a family school and a school with an unusual method of awarding prizes. It was not quite a case of '*Everybody* has won, and *all* must have prizes', but a boy was competing only against himself and not against the other boys. As long as he received 75 per cent of the possible marks, he received a prize. 'There was no danger of emulation becoming envy.' In December 1882 the boys received their prizes from Mr Milne's two children, Barry and Ken, aged three and a half and two years, sitting on a table surrounded by books. Alan was presumably there too, aged eleven months, sitting on a friendly knee.

It was a school full of love. 'Without affection,' J. V. Milne once wrote, 'the schoolroom is a hard, forbidding place. With love, it becomes the next best place to home.' For the Milne boys, of course, school and home were inextricably entwined. As soon as he is old enough to think about it, Alan can hardly wait to be a proper Henley

House schoolboy. But it takes time. If in the CAT story he has already embarked on his formal education, so, in all his earliest memories, there is an element of a more informal education, the element of discovery.

The Milnes always took lodgings in the country for the long summer holidays. In 1884 they went to Shropshire and Alan described what remained, all his life, of that holiday the year he was two: 'There is a legend, in which my faith has grown with each succeeding year, that while there I took part in a family ascent of the Wrekin . . . There I am, trotting along – a little behind the others, of course, but definitely not being carried; just taking the hand of one of the laggards – and there, stretching in front of us, is the long, gentle slope to the summit. I do not claim to remember the actual dawn . . . though no doubt it was there as usual; and it is this reticence which makes me feel that my memory, as far as it goes, can be trusted.' The Wrekin, it should be added, is, at 1,335 feet, a fair climb for a two-and-a-half-year-old. It was this legend (or this memory) that would often encourage Alan in later years to impressive feats of physical stamina. Psychological conclusions may also be drawn, by those who have a taste for such things, from the fact that he remembered with such vividness and satisfaction the long, gentle climb to the summit, but not the summit itself, not the sunrise.

The attitude of the admired father to physical stamina and endeavour can be confirmed by the fact that John Vine Milne rode back to London from this particular holiday in Shropshire – a distance of 182 miles over rough roads – on a tricycle, the tricycle having, at this point, come into temporary respect as something more than 'an accelerated bath chair'. Five years later J. V. bought a bicycle, reversing *Punch*'s advice: 'When young, try a bike; when old buy a trike.'

Another early memory was of a total eclipse of the moon. Alan had an unshakeable memory of being whisked out of bed by his father, wrapped in an eiderdown and carried, full of excitement, to the landing window (bordered by coloured glass) to see – something that was not there, that had been eclipsed. This, he was told, was an experience he would never forget. And he never did, using it many years later, at the time of his rift with his son, to demonstrate sadly 'those failures in community of idea which are so frequent between parent and child'.

This failure of understanding of how the thing would appear to the child was rare at Henley House. Indeed, any sort of failure was rare in Alan's childhood experience. The bright CAT-reader was reading a great deal more before he was four, and he was writing elegantly, too, before he was five. He was by then attending the kindergarten of Wykeham House, a school not far away at 96 Boundary Road, next door to Alfred Harmsworth's family. It was run by Miss Alice and Miss Florence Budd. He was taken there each day with Ken by their beloved Bee, Miss Beatrice Edwards, described later by Alan as a governess rather than a nanny, though no doubt (with their mother very much involved in the life of the school) she was both teacher and nurse.

All three boys wanted to marry Bee, such was her charm. Barry, as the eldest, claimed her, leaving her sisters, Trot and Molly, to the younger boys. 'Trot had been an occasional visitor to our house, so that when Ken proposed to her and accepted himself, there was no surprise in the family.' That left Molly, known only from a photograph, to Alan.

As they walked to Wykeham House, they chose houses for themselves in Priory Road. So Alan recalls, but it is a very odd route to Boundary Road, which has always been in the opposite direction. Molly and Alan would live in a house covered with Virginia creeper, the prettiest in the road. Ken chose one with a buff-tip caterpillar in the front garden. It was much more fun choosing houses than learning a psalm by heart.

J. V. Milne thought highly of Wykeham House. When a boy, after only one term at Henley House, passed the Cambridge Local Examination with Third Class Honours, his headmaster wrote in the school magazine that it reflected the greatest credit on the soundness of the preparation he had received from Miss Budd. Alan was six then and still at Wykeham House, but in later years all he would remember of the sound preparation he had supposedly received was learning Psalm 23 by heart and singing 'All things bright and beautiful'. And the fact that, with hindsight, the older Miss Budd looked like the Duchess in *Alice in Wonderland*. The hymn remained because, as town children, they were not allowed to sing the verse about gathering rushes every day. Those lines were obviously untrue and the two Miss Budds could not allow them. ('We do *not* make a habit of gathering rushes.') There is a trace of such rigid adherence to truth in the second of the impressive letters the small Alan wrote

at 96 Boundary Road. Three of these very early letters survive. The
first two are worth reprinting in full.

96 Boundary Road
Nov 20th 1886

My dear Mama

We went to Hamstid Heft yestoday. We had a sanambil. We had piggy-
backs.

I want sme tools ples Mama

lost of OOOOOOO O O OOO
OOO OO O OOOOO OO O OOOOOOOO OO OO OO

You loving
Alan

Towards the end of his life, A. A. Milne commented on this letter:
'This must have been the first letter which I ever wrote . . . It was
written at the age of four from my kindergarten school. I never did
like collaboration, and it is clear that I spurned it on this occasion.
All around me (I like to think) were other little boys and girls
writing to their dear mammas; asking their companions how to spell
Hampstead Heath, or waiting glassy-eyed for some suggestion from
the mistress as to what constituted "a letter". I just sailed ahead,
tongue out, arms outspread. We had had a sanambil, and I had
decided to be a carpenter. The family would expect to be told.

'If anybody else has ever had a sanambil, I should like him to get
in touch with me. The word is clearly written, the "bil" heavily inked
over; as if I had played with the idea of some other ending, but
realized in time that this combination of letters was the most in-
formative. Could I have meant a "scramble"? One from whose pen
"piggy-backs" flowed so faultlessly would surely have made a better
beginning of it. Well, we shall never know now; but I like to think
of it as one of those pleasant Victorian games, now gone with so
much else of those days which was good.'

Dec 15th 1886

My dear Mama.

We are not going to have any more lessons after Tuesday Dr Gibson is
coming to give away the prizes. We are to come at a quarter to four on
Wednesday and I think I shall have a prize.

With love and kisses.

Your loving
Alan.

This second letter, amazing in its competence, was written only three weeks later. He was not five until 18 January 1887. He seems to have made rapid strides away from wild surmises. A teacher at his elbow could have helped him achieve the faultless spelling, but the improvement in writing must have been his own. Seldom has an under five been more prizeworthy. It was not an odd flash in the pan, either. The third surviving letter (22 May 1887, aged five years and four months) is equally impeccable, but calculated to distress his mother, who was away caring for an invalid Aunt Barrett: 'I hope you will soon come home. My tooth does ache so.'

Alongside Alan's writing, there is his reading. *Alice*, which would later mean so much, meant very little to him when he was young. 'All my delight in her has come since I left school.' *Uncle Remus* was his favourite book when he was really small. 'But it was read aloud to us by a much-loved father with a genius for reading aloud. How much of my happy recollection is a nostalgic memory of happy evenings round a happy fire-side in a happy home?' When Bee read *Remus* one night it was painful. She stumbled through the dialect making a complete mess of it, taking all the suspense out of 'And as for Brer Fox, he lay low'. Their beloved Bee had feet of clay. It was a relief when their father was free to read the following night. Another favourite book was George Macdonald's *The Golden Key*, which Milne called 'the most completely moving and exciting story we had ever read'.

They had *Reynard the Fox* too, very early on. When, forty years later, Milne saw Shepard's drawing of Winnie-the-Pooh, 'standing on the branch of a tree outside Owl's house', he claims to have 'remembered all that *Reynard the Fox* and *Uncle Remus* and the animal stories in *Aunt Judy's Magazine* had meant to us'. It seems strange that Milne should pick out that particular illustration, in which the only animal is Pooh who, in the picture if not in the story, is patently a toy. But that is what he says; and certainly the tree, for all its ill-spelt notices and strange bell-pull, looks an excellent one for any climbing animal to climb.

On Sundays they had *The Pilgrim's Progress*. Even in that unusual household, the Milne boys, like all good Victorian children, did not read secular books on Sundays. 'Sunday was reserved for religion and Papa had somehow got it into his head that Bunyan's *Pilgrim's Progress* was a religious book. We didn't tell him the truth. We listened, rapt, and hoped that he would never find out. For it was the only excitement of Sunday, apart from the possibility, on the way back from church, of finding a religious-minded caterpillar out for a walk.'

Later on, when Alan came to read voraciously for himself, *Treasure Island* and *Masterman Ready, Bevis* and *The Swiss Family Robinson* all seemed likely to encourage a taste for the outdoor life, for desert islands and self-sufficiency. In fact, the only islands A. A. Milne would visit would be the Orkneys, Sicily and Capri; most of his time outdoors would be spent on cricket fields, golf courses, in gardens and in Ashdown Forest.

What these books gave him, rather than a taste for exploration, was a feeling for the joy of being your own master. That was something Alan was always to be. On a desert island 'you did what you liked, ate what you liked, and carried through your own adventures. It is the "Family" which spoils *The Swiss Family Robinson*, just as it is the Seagrave family which nearly wrecks *Masterman Ready*. What is the good of imagining yourself (as every boy does) "Alone in the Pacific" if you are not going to be alone? Well, perhaps we do not wish to be quite alone; but certainly to have more than two on an island is to overcrowd it, and our companion must be of a like age and disposition.

'For this reason parents spoil any island for a healthy-minded boy. He may love his father and mother as fondly as even they could wish, but he does not want to take them bathing in the lagoon with him – still less to have them on the shore, telling him that there are too many sharks this morning and that it is quite time he came out.' Ken would be the perfect companion, of course, 'of like age and disposition' as he was. The only use for parents really, Alan thought in some moods, was to be there to come back to in the end.

When they thought of a desert-island adventure, there were real problems. It was actually as unimaginable that Papa would let them go without him as that they should go without permission. But how would they ever get away? A desert island implied a schooner. It was nerve-wracking enough catching a train to Sevenoaks. They always arrived at Victoria an hour too early. If they had been taking passage on a schooner, no doubt they would have arrived a whole day ahead of schedule. It did not bear thinking about: the fuss there would be over getting away. Schooners were out; a desert island was an impossibility.

It was this sort of thinking that led Alan and Ken to a shared fantasy, which began when they were only about five and six and lasted them for many years. The fantasy was, quite simply, that they would wake up one morning and find that everybody else in the world was dead. It sounds callous but is in fact, Milne suggests, just a variant 'of the desert-island dream which every small boy has'.

Each night after lights out the brothers would talk about it. They imagined waking up and stepping over Bee's dead body, knowing no one would ask if they had washed. Having checked that there really were no survivors, they would go out into the world. In a week they might wish everyone alive again, but for the moment they were intoxicated with their freedom.

And what did the boys want to do with it? It is rather an anticlimax that their main dream was to have easy access to every sweet shop in the neighbourhood – stepping this time over the bodies of the dead proprietors. There was that little shop in West End Lane that had marzipan potatoes, for instance. They also imagined driving a horse bus. (Animals were to be spared the Plague, or whatever it was.) 'When one sat on the box seat and talked to the driver, he didn't seem to be doing much. Well, now we would know. So many things to eat, so many things to try.'

They dreamed of freedom. But they were already, by the standards of their time, extraordinarily free. 'Almost as babies,' Alan would recall, 'we were allowed to go walks by ourselves anywhere, in London or in the country.' They kept to the rules and their parents knew they could be trusted. It is peculiarly ironic that A. A. Milne should have been described by his fiercest critics as being metaphorically 'locked in the nursery'. The room that was their headquarters, so to speak, in the basement of the Milnes' side of Henley House, was not even called the nursery; it was known simply as the Kids' Room. Milne's ideal of childhood has, in fact, little to do with nannies and nursery tea, much more to do with a love of adventuring. It is no wonder that there is no nanny or nursery in the Forest. The child is brave, godlike, omnipotent. And the toys, who are the real children, explore a world where they are not bound by nursery rules, where only friendship and hunger and a desire for adventure affect the pattern of their days.

There were organized expeditions too, of course. *Beauty and the Beast*, in 1889, gave Alan Milne his first taste of the theatre, which would later, at times, dominate his life. It was Beauty, not the Beast, who entranced him. 'I just gazed and gazed at Beauty. Never had I seen anything so lovely. For weeks afterwards I dreamed about her. Nothing that was said or done on the stage mattered so long as she was there.' He thinks he heard nothing at all of the dialogue; he was just waiting for Beauty to come back. And later he would think of this and the possible waste of all that dialogue he wrote himself in his first children's play, showing, as it might have done, such 'wonderful insight into the child's mind'; because he knew perfectly well that the children in the audience were mostly not listening to it, but just waiting for something to happen or some favourite character to return. This proved, paradoxically, that he did retain that knowledge of the child's mind which he would sometimes want to deny.

Alan discovered also as a child the attraction of the music hall, the power of 'cheap music'. He was on holiday in Ramsgate with a slightly disreputable relative, known as Cousin Annie, who introduced the three boys to a more raffish world than they were accustomed to. She was some sort of a cousin on their mother's side; she worked in a shop in South Audley Street and lived in a flat above it. Milne's comment on that fact, written fifty years ago, shows how much change there had been in the previous fifty years. 'Today nothing could be more delightful, but in those days the social degradation of the one was as regrettable as the moral degradation of the other.'

Then there was the Crystal Palace. Visiting it thirty years later, Milne recalled a joyful visit in 1888:

> Aunt Alice pays; the turnstile clicks,
> And with the happy crowds we mix
> To gaze upon – well, I was six,
> Say, getting on for seven;
> And looking back on it today,
> My memories have passed away –
> I find that I can only say
> (Roughly) to gaze on heaven.

Aunt Alice (becoming so, conveniently, to rhyme with Palace) was probably Aunt Mary. She was married to Alexander Milne, whose name A. A. Milne carried. He was John Vine's younger brother, for years part of the Henley House staff, and a regular member of the cricket team at a time when small private schools fielded mixed teams of staff and boys. He left in 1886 for University School, Hastings, a school he would run on much the same lines as Henley House. After his death, Alan would call him 'the best and bravest of men'. The first Milne light verse in print was by Ackie, as he was always called. Alan grew up in an atmosphere where it was the most natural thing in the world to put your thoughts into verse. He would write:

> That evening when the day was dead,
> They tucked a babe of six in bed,
> Arranged the pillows for his head,
> And saw the lights were shaded;
> Too sleepy for the good-night kiss,
> His only conscious thought was this:
> 'No man shall ever taste the bliss
> That I this blessed day did.'

'Heaven it was which came to pass within those magic walls of glass – the wonders of that wonder-hall!' It was a Mecca for Victorians, large and small. Many enjoyed their day out at the Crystal Palace. But Alan felt something that can only be called pure happiness. 'Childhood,' he would write, 'is not the happiest time of one's life, but only to a child is pure happiness possible.'

— 2 —

His Father's Pupil

ALAN SEEMS TO have started at Henley House officially in September 1888 – four months before he was seven. He had been insistent it was time for him to leave Miss Budd and join Ken. He was always eager to tread on Ken's heels. They appeared together in the end of term concert on 11 December, a marvellously elaborate occasion. It was held in Kilburn Town Hall and the platform was 'handsomely decorated by palms and flowers'. 'School music' started at eight o'clock with some Mozart by young Lionel Cooke. 'He was followed by Barry Milne "Spring Flowers" (Cole); Kenneth Milne "Sonatina" (Kuhlau); and Alan Milne, aged nearly seven, with "Melodious Exercises". These four little boys did what some older boys would find difficult – simply played their best, carefully and with confidence.' This was as the hall was filling, and the constant arrival of visitors must have been rather distracting for the poor little boys, but they obviously acquitted themselves well.

Then they could relax and enjoy such treats as Mr Wilberforce Franklin singing the Toreadors' Song from *Carmen* and Mrs Robinson reciting in fine style 'The Charge of the Heavy Brigade'. 'Some little boys,' and Alan was surely among them, 'were seen right in front hanging on the speaker's lips.'

They said afterwards that it was the best thing of the evening. How they followed the whirlwind rush of brave soldiers. They were no longer in a Town Hall, but out in the open, anxiously watching the flashing swords. Hurrah! our men have come through, like the heroes they are, and a sigh relieves the little breasts.

The recitations were followed by the headmaster's introduction to 'an old friend' – a base sycophant, J. V. Milne suggested, who had no ideas of his own and merely repeated what he heard. This was the phonograph, an early ancestor of the tape recorder, invented by

20

Thomas Edison eleven years before and just the sort of thing J. V. Milne loved, encouraging it to repeat 'Baa Baa Black Sheep' and other familiar stuff. Its performance that night was followed by more serious fare to demonstrate the talents of Henley House – first some scenes from Molière's *L'Avare*, about which 'several Parisian friends were warm in their praises'. And then there was a German play, though few in the audience could understand a word that was said. There must have been some yawning from the little boys in the front row.

The evening ended with a '*conversazione*'. Among the Old Boys present was none other than Mr Alfred Harmsworth, already at twenty-three the publisher of *Answers*, his first success. He came with his new wife and cast a benevolent eye over his old school, remembering, perhaps, as he had written himself in his own school magazine: 'listening to the clock's slow ticking, at this sickening Virgil sticking'. J. V. Milne was enormously proud of him already and glowed when he paid tribute to the 'generous and thoughtful way' he was educated at Henley House. H. G. Wells would lament how little Harmsworth's education had prepared him for anything but 'a career of push and acquisition'. But he could not deny that, without his headmaster's encouragement, Harmsworth might well never have found his *métier*.

That summer, on holiday in Kent, the Milne boys met Harmsworth at Penshurst and he showered them with pennies to buy themselves sweets, pouring the coins into the boys' hands with such disregard for their number that they thought he must already be the millionaire he was afterwards to become. 'Isn't he rich?' the boys said to each other. 'I say.'

On this Kent holiday they stayed in Sevenoaks, which was why Alan could always remember which year it was. He was seven at Sevenoaks, which is much neater than being six at Cobham or eight at Limpsfield. It was at Sevenoaks that the boys acquired Brownie, a Gordon setter, who must surely be the original of the dog in 'Puppy and I', one of the first poems Milne wrote for the collection *When We Were Very Young*. Many people seem to assume that all the material in the children's books came from the 1920s, from Christopher Robin's childhood, but A. A. Milne made it quite clear that he wrote, as all the best children's writers write, 'from a combination of memory, observation and imagination'. He spelt it out in his introduction to *Very Young Verses* (1929), his selection from the two books of children's poems, ('some of the things in these books were things I remembered doing myself years and years ago') and also in 'The End of a Chapter' in *By Way of Introduction*, published the same year. One of the things he remembered was avoiding the lines on the pavement, for fear of the consequences. 'As a child I played lines-and-squares in a casual sort of way. Christopher Robin never did until he read what I had written about it, and not very enthusiastically then.' Alan remembered Barry teasing him about what might come out of the gratings. Brownie, the dog at Sevenoaks, was just such a 'heaven-sent gift' as the puppy in the poem. 'I met a Puppy as I went walking; we got talking Puppy and I.' So it was and so they did. Brownie attached himself to Alan, having apparently been abandoned as 'gun-shy'. A clap of thunder would send him under the table, but that did not alienate the Milnes, who were gun-shy themselves. Indeed, they could be other kinds of shy as well.

Alan remembered his father 'twittering with nervousness' before some big entertainment, such as the '*conversazione*' in the Town Hall. He was the sort of person easily startled by a sudden 'Hullo' when outside his own four walls. Alan made his father's shyness with adults memorable when he described in detail the everyday ordeal of meeting an acquaintance – a pupil's parent perhaps – in the street. 'As soon as the acquaintance was sighted, Papa would cut short his conversation, or ours, and prepare for the ordeal. The funny story, the explanation of the Force of Gravity, our answer to a catch-question had to wait . . . "Good morning, Mr Roberts, good morning to you, good morning." Mr Roberts had returned the greeting and passed, but Papa's greeting went on. His hand still went up and down to his hat in nervous movements, he still muttered "Good morning to you". We waited. We turned the corner. "Well, now then," he would say, "what's the answer? A goose weighs seven pounds and half its own weight. How much does it weigh? Now *think*." Had the meeting been agony to him, or only an embarrassment for his family?

It certainly could be embarrassing. Really it *was* much better being on their own, just Ken and Alan. Not Barry. Alan and Ken shared everything. 'We were inseparable; sometimes, when fighting, so mixed up as to be indistinguishable. We never ceased to quarrel with each other, nor to feel the need of each other. Save for the fact that he hated cheese, we shared equally all belief, all knowledge, all ambition, all hope and all fear.' Occasionally, on holiday, they even shared a bed, and Alan remembered once asking an elderly visitor if she didn't agree that sharing a bed with somebody else was the most horrible thing that anybody could be asked to do? There had been 'a fight every morning when one of us found the tide of clothes had receded in the night, leaving him bare and beached'. Alan would spend very little of his life in the warmth of a shared bed – but his relationship with Ken, their love for each other, their importance to each other, continued without any breaks until Ken's too-early death. It was the most satisfactory relationship of his life, and it was a great credit to Ken that this was so. It must often have been very difficult, being A. A. Milne's elder brother.

'All through Ken's schooldays, it was a reproach to him that his younger brother was intellectually his superior.' But 'Ken had one advantage of me,' Alan wrote after his death, 'He was definitely – nicer: ... kinder, larger-hearted, more lovable, more tolerant, sweeter tempered ... If you knew us both, you preferred Ken. I might be better at work and games; even better-looking ... but "poor old Ken" or "dear old Ken" had his private right of entry into everybody's heart. If, in later years, I have not seemed insufferable to my friends over any success which has looked in on me, I owe it to him, in whose company complacence found nothing on which to batten. And if I have taken failure less well than I should have done, it is because I am still sixteen months behind him in humility, and shall never catch up.'

They did everything together, enjoying their extraordinary freedom. They had a habit of getting up extremely early, grabbing a handful of oatmeal from the bin in the kitchen (it was practically all that remained of their Scottish inheritance) and going out into the world while everyone else was still asleep. If they couldn't be *dead*, that was the next best thing. It was understood, at least by Alan and Ken, that they could do what they liked as long as they did not wake their parents. Once they bowled iron hoops all the way from Kilburn to the Bayswater Road and were back in time for breakfast, their favourite meal. Another day, Alan claimed, they got up at five-thirty and had a fight with long bamboo poles ('a present from Jamaica'), which hung in the hall above the aquarium as an oarsman might hang his oars. Tiring of that, they had another handful of oatmeal (the cook still wasn't up), 'went a quick walk round Mortimer Road and Greville Place, crossed the gymnasium on our stomachs, kicked a stone across the playground, hopping on one foot, and were in our places for "prep" at seven o'clock.'

Alan was a particularly diligent schoolboy. Forty years later his father told some rather embarrassing stories (how the middle-aged A. A. Milne must have hated them) in that 1928 newspaper article. 'Long after he began agitating to attend classes, permission was withheld and, when finally it was given, his delight was supreme. He made such strides at school that his mother became anxious. "Something will have to be done to stop Alan," she used to say to me. "You know these promising children wear themselves out and end by being dull men." ' It was a popular idea of the period. But there was no stopping Alan. When they cancelled some of his subjects and encouraged him to play, he pined. He became 'mopy and listless', until finally his health began to suffer and they had to let him return to a full timetable. So said his father in 1928.

In August 1889, when Alan was seven, the school magazine records the following: 'A little boy was asked how many things he had enjoyed that day. This was his answer: '1, Hampstead Heath; 2, spinning tops; 3, dinner and breakfast and tea and was about to enjoy supper; 4, getting clear of work; 5, getting credit (for extra good work); 6, geometry, and algebra, and grammar; 7, preparation.'

'Happy boy!' is the editorial comment. One day the happy boy would write the following lines:

'When you wake in the morning, Pooh,' said Piglet at last, 'what's the first thing you say to yourself?'
'What's for breakfast?' said Pooh. 'What do *you* say, Piglet?'
'I say, I wonder what's going to happen exciting *today?*' said Piglet.
Pooh nodded thoughtfully.
'It's the same thing,' he said.

The inhabitants of the world might not have been struck down dead. But life was full of excitement and good breakfasts (not to mention dinners, teas and suppers). Alan would say that breakfast was the best meal of the day, 'the only meal which could never be a disappointment' except at Westminster.

Less than three years later, before he was ten, Alan became one of the youngest boys ever to pass the Third Class of the College of Preceptors examination. He was placed in the First Division, gaining 90 per cent in English, 90 per cent in Arithmetic and 95 per cent in Algebra. He scored a total of 560 marks. Even though his father believed that 'the certificate given by one's own conscience is much more precious than that given by examining bodies', naturally his parents were proud of him. In the same examination, Ken, sixteen months older, was placed in the division above Alan (the Third Division of the Second Class) so that was all right. Barry, the eldest brother, was in the same class as Alan, but only made the Second Division, with a total of 335 marks. That was not all right. In fact, it was humiliating to be beaten so soundly by a brother two and a half years younger. Barry would get his own back and show Alan how clever he was forty years later.

'A child,' A. A. Milne once wrote, 'knows most of the game – it is only attitude to it that he lacks. He is quite well aware of cowardice, shame, deception, disappointment.' Perhaps it was the disappointment, the shame, of not being cleverer than those two bright younger brothers that would one day lead Barry, the eldest one, the wicked one, into a betrayal that eventually lost him entirely the friendship of the youngest, his one surviving brother.

The examination marks appeared in the Henley House School Magazine, for all to see. On the next page there is a more vivid and revealing paragraph about Alan, among half a dozen anonymous portraits of 'some school characters'. 'He does not like French – does not see that you prove anything when you have done. Thinks mathematics grand. He leaves his books about, loses his pen; can't imagine what he did with this, and where he put that, but is convinced that it is somewhere.' Sixty years later he would write: 'One of the advantages of being disorderly is that one is constantly making exciting discoveries.' The 1892 'report' went on: 'Clears his brain when asked a question by spurting out some nonsense, and then immediately after gives a sensible reply. Can speak 556 words per minute and write more in three minutes than his instructor can read in thirty. Finds this a very interesting world and would like to learn physiology, botany, geology, astronomy and everything else. Wishes to make collections of beetles, bones, butterflies, etc. and cannot determine whether algebra is better than football or Euclid than a sponge cake.'

A. A. Milne commented in his autobiography that this was a portrait of an enthusiast. 'So if at this time I was still an enthusiast, it was because I was still at my father's school, and he was an enthusiast. And if I disliked French, and thought mathematics grand, it was because he, who could teach, taught me mathematics, and did not teach me French.'

This mention of football in the report is the first reference to Alan's love of games. It would be cricket and golf he would most love, not football, but games in general (both watching and playing) were an important part of his life. His father had written in the school magazine when he was eight: 'Success in life is won by qualities that are developed by good school games, as well as by studies. I really do not know which I should choose if I were offered this choice for my sons: either to be clever at books and good at nothing else, without pluck, without agility, without interest in anything outside themselves; or to be hopeless duffers at books and plucky athletes. Aim to be good at both studies and games. It is truly said that the mere athlete is half man, half beast; and the mere student is half man, half ghost.' J. V. Milne was a great believer in *mens sana in corpore sano*.

He also believed in making boys face up to the realities of life and death. The school magazine would contain sad stories of the poor, as well as the cricket results, and, in the Easter 1891 issue, he told of the suicide of a boy of eleven. 'His book shows that he had been occupied upon the third declension of substantives. There was a blot upon the last word declined and then the words "I am sick of life".' J. V. Milne commented: 'This age is certainly a rather hard one for boys. All the examinations are being raised. I am afraid that poor boy did not get enough hearty play.'

It was football that was the subject of one of Alan's earliest surviving pieces of prose. He said that, of all his memories of his days at Henley House, the one most clear to him was of sitting at his desk, in the big schoolroom, biting the end of his pen into splinters and realizing that one sentence he had written, which sounded so splendid, was a gross exaggeration. His subject was a playground football match, Boarders versus Day-boys. 'The Day-boys have thousands of chaps crowding round so that you can hardly move. There are never more than eleven boarders.' 'Thousands' would obviously have to be altered. 'Reluctantly I got it down to hundreds. Hundreds? There were only thirty-five Day-boys in the school, and some would not be playing. Perhaps "twenty" would be the truth. But must one keep to the strict truth? Never! So, in my last clean copy for the printer, the Day-boys had "about fifty chaps" . . . and in all that I have written since I have held to my creed that Art is exaggeration – but in fifties not in thousands.'

The paragraph, as it was printed, reads extremely well. The writer was delighted that the Boarders, 'in spite of their numbers, always won and the Day-scholars took their lickings quietly.' 'Sometimes one of the masters plays for them, but they *don't* win. Hurrah for the Boarders!'

In two issues earlier there is a long piece: 'My Three Days' Walking Tour by Alan A. Milne. Aged 8¾ years'. It always helps to know the editor. By this time, with Harmsworth gone on to greater things, his father was editing the magazine. The article is more remarkable for its content than its style. There is an appropriateness in the fact that in his very first appearance in print, A. A. Milne should write about Ashdown Forest, which was thirty-six years later to be the setting of his most famous stories. They took the train to East Grinstead and then – but let 8¾-year-old Alan tell part of the story:

After a little while it cleared up, and we walked to Ashdown Forest, where it again poured with rain. As it was so wet, we were not able to go through the forest, which was mostly a common, six or seven miles long and three miles broad. Here we looked on a map which we had brought, and found that we had two more miles to walk and then we should have a lovely dinner at the 'Roebuck' inn, at Wych Cross. When we got there we found that it had been turned into a Vicarage! but the Vicar kindly gave us some bread and cheese and milk. We then again started; but it began to rain, and we sat under a furze-bush, with our mackintoshes over us for shelter. After it cleared up we walked to Nutley, and there we had a lovely tea of eggs. As it still poured with rain, we took a waggonette to Buxted Station, and from there we took train home. Altogether, it was only eleven miles' walk.

The other days were rather less wet, fortunately. There was a lot of walking, punctuated by some rather monotonous eating. At Hever they had ham and eggs, a dish which would always bring back his childhood to Alan. In Tunbridge Wells, they had ham and eggs again. When they eventually got to Mark Cross, 'we were not able to have anything but ham and eggs once more which made Ken feel bilious and he said he wanted to go home.' They walked to Mayfield and took a train back. They had walked forty-four miles altogether in their three days.

Let that account stand for all the other country walks they did together, Ken and Alan. On this occasion, in fact, Papa was with them – and so, for part of the time, were Barry and another boy. But often they would be on their own. 'Alan and I often used to get up at 5 o'clock and go out and walk five or eight miles,' Ken wrote at one point.

They would explore London on their own too. On one occasion they took their collection of minerals down to the Geological

Museum, then in Jermyn Street, and had a happy hour showing the curator their assorted specimens, Blue-John Spar and the like. Afterwards they had twopence to spend – they spent a penny on a box of fusees (a very special sort of match, which flared up excitingly) – and were contemplating the window of Callard and Bowser's in Regent Street, where they intended to spend the other penny, when an elderly gentleman, passing by, put a shilling on top of the match-box Alan was holding. They looked at the coin in amazement. They had promised never to take money from strangers, but there it was. They spent their own penny, giving the shilling in payment. Then they put sixpence in the missionary-box on the Callard and Bowser counter, gave threepence to a crossing-sweeper and stowed the remaining three pennies away in the drawer with their mineral collection.

Alan told this goody-goody story years later without embarrassment. Were they too good? he asked. Certainly they would often try to live up to the way they looked and to what was expected of them. But he could tell the story without blushing. 'I am (oddly enough) more ashamed of the bad things I have done than of the good things I have done, of the promises broken than of the promises kept. I like to think of that threepence in the drawer, *tabu* even in the darkest days before the Saturday pocket-money.' 'Much has been said,' J. V. Milne wrote in the *Evening Standard* in 1928, 'about sparing the rod and spoiling the child. I don't know. The rod may be necessary in some cases. But I can truthfully say that I can never remember an occasion, in school or out of school, when it was necessary to punish Alan. And I do not think this omission has done him any harm.'

They were good, Alan and Ken, but they were not milksops. They were tough, in fact. They could walk, and later cycle, enormous distances. Most of their playground games were rough or dangerous or both. There was a particularly gruelling form of follow-my-leader. There was a swing in the playground, which served as a flying trapeze. 'The swing was set in motion, we ran at it from the far end of the playground, took off from a spring-board, jumped, caught it, swung off at the other end, and left it swinging back for the next boy. Every game has its ecstatic moments: indeed, life offers quite tolerable diversions apart from games; but for a prolongation of ecstasy one must return to the flying trapeze.'

There was another version that could be used when the weather was bad. This was an iron bar half-way across the big schoolroom, across which curtains could be pulled to divide the room. The boys would jump up to the bar from a convenient desk and swing off it on to a more distant one. One evening Alan missed the bar and crashed to the ground. His mother was calm and merely looked up from her sewing machine to suggest he should be checked by the doctor. But John Vine Milne ever afterwards thought of it as a great crisis in Alan's life. 'At first we feared for his spine,' he used to say. It became a family catch phrase. And the reason for the accident was forgotten. Alan was never punished.

The boys didn't always avoid trouble, all the same. On one such occasion they were on holiday. It was that Sevenoaks holiday when Alan was seven and Ken was eight, and they were still in their velvet suits (or in starched sailor suits, which were even more uncomfortable), with their fair hair still curling to their shoulders, 'too winsome for words'. They were exploring a ruined house when they were set upon by a gang of small desperadoes. When outside the protection of Henley House and their roles as sons of the headmaster, they were not surprised to be attacked, looking as they did. ('Any old lady could be trusted to adore us, any normal boy to have the urge to kick us.') So they had their wits about them. Alan managed to slip through a window while Ken engaged the potential attackers in some blustering talk. He had a sudden inspiration. He told them he was staying in a village three miles off and, if given two hundred yards' start, would never be seen again. The lust of the chase appealed to the gang. They had no doubt at all they would overtake him and beat him up at leisure. Happily they gave him to 'just short of the cottage down the road' and set off after him with loud halloos. So Ken dashed into the cottage down the road – the cottage where they were staying – and joined Alan in the kitchen, 'to the relief of the cook who was being hurriedly organized for rescue'.

On another occasion, Ken was not so lucky. Nearer home one day the two boys intervened when they saw a small friend being beaten up by a larger boy. It was Ken's idea. Alan had thought they were going to be late for tea anyway. And it was Ken who got the big boy's blow on his own nose and fell to the ground, his clothes covered with blood and dust. It was Alan who picked him up and staunched the blood. 'Poor old Ken!' as Alan was often to say.

There was sweet, small Alan, unscathed, not even dirty. He had been lucky. He was often lucky. And although he would sometimes later want to deny it, want to show that fortune had not smiled on him particularly, that he had won fame and riches by his own long efforts (as indeed he had), he admitted that he had been lucky in his parents. He was talking to his own son: 'You know I often tell myself that everything we are is that way because that was how our parents made us. Every talent we have has been inherited. And this is something worth remembering if ever we feel ourselves getting a bit swanky. The credit is not ours: it is theirs. Not even theirs really, but their parents. And so on, back and back. And even if I say "I had this talent and he had it too, but he wasted his and I used mine. Surely that is to my credit," the answer is no. For if we make use of a talent, it is only because we have another talent, a talent for using talents, a talent for hard work, if you like; and this too was inherited.'

Not long afterwards, he wrote: 'We may "carve out" careers for ourselves but our parentage gave us the implements with which to do it. Everybody's luck, good or ill, begins on the day he was born.' It was a constant theme. In an interview in the United States in 1931 he said, 'It's too late to bother about what a person is. That was all arranged for fifty years ago.' He had been conceived exactly fifty years earlier. *It's Too Late Now* was the English title (much misunderstood) of his autobiography.

It is surprising, with this attitude to inheritance, that Alan didn't go to more trouble to find out about his ancestors. He knew little about them. He wrongly thought his mother's father was a farmer. As for his father's grandfather, the father of the improvident minister, he had the idea that he was a stonemason in Aberdeen; he thought of him, not as a carver of granite tombstones, but rather as 'the man who sat by the roadside, chipping stolidly at little heaps of granite, and trying not to get too much of it in his eyes'. That was enough to make anyone feel lucky – *not* to have such imagined, backbreaking, eyeblinding toil.

This idea of his ancestry gave him even more reason to be glad. It spared him from the arrogance of the 'well-born'. It gave him a natural sympathy with the underdog. 'The Milnes were proud of the fact that Grandfather was poor and Great-Grandfather even poorer.' As for J. V. Milne, he always valued people for what they were, not for their birth or background. He had been known to say that George IV was no gentleman, and to criticize his pupils if they characterized street-boys as 'cads'. He would chide his pupils for judging people by their possessions or despising manual work. He valued carpenters more than clerks and quoted approvingly an article in his daily paper which talked of 'the pernicious class distinctions from which we suffer in England'.

As an adult, A. A. Milne felt 'the keenest sympathy for Kipps, for young Copperfield, for Oak when he was penniless, for Henchard when he was ruined'. Alan grew up to hate being in command as much as he hated to be commanded. He really only felt happy in relations between equals – in side-to-side relationships. His son would feel the same. Expressing his own uneasiness with the establishment, Christopher would look back on *his* childhood and see that he had been born with all the 'right' labels. In a world where 'British was best', 'I was British'. 'In the class hierarchy: upper, middle and lower, again I was lucky. I was upper.' In religion, Christian. 'These three labels determined the sort of life I led. No one argued the possible superiority of other nations. No one disputed the justness of the social order. No one defended the heathen.' Christopher, in his turn, would eventually feel a surge of fellowship for those of other races, other classes, other religions.

But the uninformed reader of that passage might imagine, as many people have imagined, that A. A. Milne was himself just such a confident, upper-class English gentleman and member of the Church of England. In fact, he was conscious, even as a boy, that none of these labels really fitted. He could hardly be called upper-class with a great-grandfather whom he thought of as a hewer of stones. In his middle age, at the height of his fame, Lytton Strachey, snob that he was (as reported by the arch-snob Virginia Woolf), saw Milne as obviously middle-class, when putting the young John Lehmann in the same category. (You could tell it by their eyes, or their ankles or something.) As a boy, Alan Milne didn't even feel he was really English. There was all that Scots blood and, worse, his father had been born in Jamaica. Alan was not sure whether this was 'a fact to be circulated or suppressed'. 'It seemed to leave Papa not quite an Englishman and us, in consequence, a little suspect.' Nor, as he grew older, did it seem to be particularly natural to be fond of an Englishman, just because he was English – rather than a Frenchman, a German or an American. 'One might love anybody or hate anybody.'

As for the Church of England, the nineteenth-century Milnes certainly did not belong to that. They were Nonconformists, whether Congregationalists or Presbyterians. The boys, Alan and Ken, when they were Westminster schoolboys, staunchly refused to turn to the altar in the Abbey or bow their heads in the Creed, having an acquired revulsion from such popish practices. Alan would leave Westminster with conventional views (as far as he had any) on religion and politics, the conventional love of games and conventional ideas about good form. But forty years later all that remained was the love of games. So he said himself. There would always be something unexpected about him, whatever his outward appearance might indicate.

If, as A. A. Milne suggested, he was to go through a comparatively conformist phase at Westminster – public schoolboys often adopt a protective colouring – there is no question that the unconventionality Milne claimed in later life owed a great deal, not only to his father, but to one particular teacher. This is often the case, of course. It is commonplace for famous and successful people to look back at their schooldays and attribute their fame and success to some particularly influential teacher. It is not commonplace for the teacher himself or herself to become even more famous and successful than the pupil. In Milne's case this was so. The teacher was H. G. Wells.

H. G. Wells came to Henley House in January 1889, the month that Alan Milne was seven, just a term after the boy himself had become a full member of the school. Wells was then only twenty-two; he had left school at fourteen and was still not fully qualified, though he was already immensely well read. Anyone who has read Wells's autobiography will remember his derogatory remarks about his own brain. 'If there were brain-shows, as there are cat and dog shows, I doubt if it would get even a third-class prize . . . I cannot do any but the simplest sums in my head and when I used to play bridge, I found my memory of the consecutive tricks and my reasoning about the playing of the cards, inferior to nine out of ten of the people I played with. I lose at chess to almost anyone . . .' But it was not, of course, his lack of a particular kind of brain (Alan's own kind), which meant that, when he applied for a job educating the boys of Henley House, he had still not completed his own education. There had been a struggle to live.

What Wells did have, unsurprisingly, was a compelling way with words and an enthusiasm for education (for *real* education, not merely the passing of examinations) which matched J. V. Milne's own. Wells looked conventional enough. Indeed, turning up for his interview in the drawing-room of Henley House, he wore a top hat, which he regarded as 'a symbol of complete practical submission to a whole world of social convention'. He did not know at that stage that he had no need at all to disguise his humble origins from the Milnes. Wells handed over a great handful of 'advanced certificates' from the Science Schools at Kensington. He had certificates in every possible science (even palaeontology) and almost every possible branch of drawing (Freehand, Model, Geometrical and Perspective). The list of his certificates in the school magazine reads rather like the subjects available at the Mock Turtle's school in *Alice*, and would be bound to impress the parents. Parents were one of J. V. Milne's constant problems at Henley House. He depended on their money. 'One never knows what parents will find to object to,' J. V. Milne would sigh, when Wells talked about dissecting rabbits.

'I thought I could make a school different from all the other schools, but I had to work for what the parents required of me . . . It is not only the boys one must educate, but the parents . . . After all the Parent is master. One can't run a school without boys . . . This is as good a school as you will find . . . At least I can cultivate their characters and develop something like a soul in them, instead of crushing out individuality and imagination as most schools do.'

That was Mr Mackinder explaining *his* school in H. G. Wells's *Joan and Peter*, his diatribe against the English educational system, published in 1918. There is no doubt that Mackinder is based on J. V. Milne. He is a shy little man 'with a hedgehog's nose'. His drawing-room, too, must surely be the Milnes' drawing-room. Alan recorded that it was said from time to time that his Mama had the most beautiful drawing-room in Kilburn. 'If the curtain rose on it in the First Act of a period play, it would be received with a round of applause, and Motley or Mr Rex Whistler would walk away with the notices.' Wells saw it as the most drawing-room-like drawing-room he had ever been in. It was as if someone had said to a furniture dealer: 'People expect me to have a drawing-room. Please let me have exactly the sort of drawing-room people expect.' Parents had, fortunately, as much reason to be impressed by the Henley House examination results as by the drawing-room, for all J. V. Milne's cultivation of their boys' individuality and imagination. One year the headmaster was able to boast that of the 789 boys taking the examinations of the College of Preceptors in London, only four succeeded in gaining First Class certificates, and three of those four came from Henley House.

H. G. Wells had applied for a job teaching science (which included mathematics), drawing and scripture for £60 a year. He stipulated that he should not take scripture, as he felt he could not teach things in which he did not believe. He also gave up the offer of free board and lodging, in order to continue working for his external B.Sc. and his teaching diploma from the College of Preceptors. It was agreed he could continue to live in Fitzroy Road with his aunt and the cousin he was soon to marry. 'The arrangement worked very well for us both. He liked my putting in that conscience clause at the risk of not getting a job I evidently wanted.' Wells did have his midday meal at Henley House each day and enormously enjoyed it. There were table napkins and flowers on the table. 'In my world hitherto there had been no flowers on the meal-table anywhere. And at the end of the table, facing me, sat Mrs Milne, rather concerned if I did not eat enough, because I was still, she thought, scandalously thin.'

In class, Wells was face to face with Alan, and with Ken too. The young teacher who claimed he could not do any but the simplest sums in his head was able to record that he 'took a class of small boys between six and eight straight away from the first four rules to easy algebra . . . In those days that was a new and bold thing to do. We got to fractions, quadratics and problems involving quadratics in a twelve month.' Alan sat in the front row, aged seven, and lapped it all up. It is interesting that he himself claimed it was his father's teaching that had turned him into a mathematician. Wells certainly takes the credit for it in his autobiography, and J. V. Milne gives his own version in the *Evening Standard* article: 'Before he went to Westminster, Mr H. G. Wells, at that time a master in my school, had drawn my attention to the fact that Alan was very good at mathematics. He predicted a brilliant career for him in this branch of learning, saying, if he liked to give his attention to it, he was sure he could one day be Senior Wrangler' – using that mysterious Cambridge term, which had a particularly exciting resonance for both men, with their struggles for London external degrees.

There is evidence that Alan was not as consistently good at mathematics as Wells suggested. When his mother was away in February 1890 (Alan was just eight), he wrote to her that he had 'nine marks for Latin, nine for Euclid and 0 for Algebra', adding piously, 'I hope to get more next time.' When Alan came to write to Wells from Cambridge twelve years later, soliciting a contribution to the undergraduate magazine *Granta*, it would be Wells's geology classes he mentioned. 'Do you remember a small-sized boy with long hair to whom you taught at one time all the geology he never knew? He sat at the front desk in what was known as the "first class room" and hazarded ideas on the strata of Primrose Hill . . . I am the long-haired kid . . .'

H. G. Wells and J. V. Milne had taken an immediate liking to each other, and Alan himself years later would describe Wells as 'a great writer and a great friend', though he did not consider him a great teacher: 'He was too clever and too impatient.' J. V. Milne had a higher opinion of the young Wells as a teacher: 'I have particularly admired his teaching of science, where his extensive reading and his power of expression enabled him to handle his subject in a manner at once exact and humorous. The proof of his success was the enthusiasm aroused in his classes, which was not dependent upon mere experiment.' The headmaster's reference is an interesting gloss on the statement in Wells's autobiography that, having been provided with a mere sovereign to meet the costs of any apparatus and equipment, he decided to make do on the whole with his drawing skill and the blackboard.

A. A. Milne says he was 'indebted to Wells for many things; most of all for the affection he always felt for my father'. 'Milne was a man who won my unstinted admiration and remained my friend throughout life,' Wells wrote after J. V. Milne's death. 'I found Milne a really able teacher, keen to do his best for his boys and with a curious obstinate originality, and I learnt very much from him about discipline and management. Finance, I knew, was worrying him a good deal, but he watched his boys closely and would slacken, intensify or change their work, with a skilled apprehension of their idiosyncrasies. He would think of them at night. The boys had confidence in him and in us and I never knew a better-mannered school. He was friendly and sympathetic with me from the outset. He was a little grey-clad extremely dolichocephalic man with glasses, a pointed nose and a small beard, rather shy in his manner; he had a phantom lisp and there was a sort of confidential relationship between his head and his shoulders.'

Wells himself was not thinking of the boys at night as he slaved over his books in Fitzroy Road. In the May 1890 issue of the magazine, J. V. Milne proudly printed the exam results of 'our popular Science Master, Mr H. G. Wells'. He had not only passed the diploma of Licentiate of the College of Preceptors in almost every possible subject but had won 'the £10 prize for Theory and Practice of Education, the £5 prize for Mathematics and £5 for Natural Science', as being the best candidate in those subjects. 'It is rather rough on the other gentlemen,' Milne wrote, 'that all three prizes should thus be carried off by one man, and shows a want of consideration quite foreign to Mr Wells' character.' In December 1890, the magazine recorded: 'Mr Wells has passed his B.Sc. and is now "up" for Honours.'

The two men talked about the theory and practice of education whenever they could find a quiet moment. J. V. Milne at this period was on the board of the College of Preceptors and was very active in the Association of Principals of Private Schools. He edited their magazine, *The Private Schoolmaster*, and in February 1888 he had been re-elected secretary at the annual general meeting. It was a time when the private schools saw their future threatened by the increase in state control of education and the establishment of a Ministry of Education, which would require registration and inspection. These schools feared their market was about to disappear as the state began to supply education for the middle and lower middle classes. They worried about interference and more emphasis on examinations. J. V. Milne said that 'the great majority of private schools would welcome registration but for the fear of government interference – an interference increasing until it became intolerable.' Parental interference was bad enough. 'Education is something more than passing boys, than prizes, than scholarships . . . Examinations test knowledge not wisdom . . . Give the schoolmaster *more* liberty – he is the best judge of the education required by the pupils.'

H. G. Wells saw that this man he admired so much was suffering from a degree of self-delusion. The changes in society, the growth of knowledge (particularly in the sciences), were too vast for the individual small school to handle without some guidance from outside. Wells thought Britain's chief hope was in the proper teaching of science and economics and in radical changes in the whole system of secondary education, including the end of the whole 'obsolete sham' of learning Greek and Latin.

By 1902 J. V. Milne would be converted to the need for registration. 'It will not work wonders . . . but it will at least exclude a Squeers,' he declared, adding hastily, for the reputation of the profession, that, of course, 'Mr Squeers was a monster who never existed and is no more representative of teachers than he is of Yorkshiremen.' By then J. V. Milne had himself moved with the times. He had left

Henley House and in January 1894 opened Streete Court at West-gate-on-Sea, a creeper-clad preparatory school of the type we know today, with all his pupils under fourteen and destined to move on to other schools in due course. It was there that Alan would spend his holidays from Westminster, refreshing interludes from labouring away at the very sort of education his former master, H. G. Wells, would so roundly condemn.

For all his preoccupation with his own examinations, there was no question that H. G. Wells entered fully into the life of Henley House School. Henley House boys went out and about, as schoolchildren do today, and it was often Mr Wells who took them. One day they would be examining the strata of Primrose Hill, just down the road. Another day there would be a botanical expedition to Northwood Common or a visit to the Zoo. 'Mr Wells, our science master, had long before promised us this treat if we wrote a good essay on Natural History,' and the popular master was so compassionate that he allowed some boys to go whose essays had not really been very good at all.

There were all sorts of other expeditions: visits to the Oxford and Cambridge cricket match at Lord's, to Queen's Park v. Blackburn Rovers at the Oval, to lectures, exhibitions and museums, to the Tower and the Royal Arsenal at Woolwich. There was an annual picnic in Epping Forest ('vociferous cheers for Mr and Mrs Milne') and regular paperchases (hare and hounds). Alan and Ken had joined in picnics and paperchases from when they were very small. There is a touching account of one occasion when, 'manly little fellow' though he was, Alan ran out of puff and his father had to rescue 'the weary hound' on his tricycle. Some of the expeditions were for 'merit'. If a boy earned a day off by good work and good behaviour, he went out. If not, he stayed at Henley House 'and spent a quiet, and, we trust, improving day in the schoolroom'. The sort of boys who stayed at school (Harmsworth had often been one of them) were the sort who were always making excuses for work not done. The headmaster got so tired of them that he proposed a list of numbered excuses so the boys, instead of having to rack their brains or waste the master's time by going on and on and on, could just say 'Number six, sir' or 'Number three, this time, sir – ' running his eye down the list. It might save a lot of trouble. But 'care should be taken to avoid monotony'.

Alan's diligence and cleverness always earned him a place at any treat. In March 1889 Mr Wells took him with a group of juniors to the South Kensington Museum. All went well until one boy sent round the attractive message: 'There's a refreshment room upstairs!' Then the sharks and stick insects and the megatherium were forgotten while boys sought sustenance for themselves. One boy, according to Wells, 'made himself conspicuous by walking about the museum with a vast sheet of some doughy substance, set with almonds and plums, the corner of which he gnawed and mumbled after the fashion of a toothless dog, until arbitrary power intervened to prevent this undesirable exhibition.'

Alan and Ken continued to live a vivid life of their own, inside and outside Henley House. They took their father's advice for the holidays: 'Keep out of doors as much as you can, and see all you can of nature: she has the most wonderful exhibition, always open and always free.' They reared silkworms. They attempted to rear newts (called Robinson, Crusoe and Cleaver, for reasons some will understand), but the creatures met a sad death down the plughole of the bath. They had hedgehogs and toads. They had mice. One could have been a dormouse; certainly his grave was in the geranium bed. The boys proved that you do not need to live in the country to commune with nature and that they had taken to heart Mr Wells's very sound advice that natural history was not simply the collecting of things and certainly not the mere naming of them.

In the Henley House School Magazine, H. G. Wells, aged twenty-three, criticized 'vituperative naturalists with a classical bias' who insisted on 'calling a harmless sunflower, *Helianthus annus* and fixing *Lepus cuniculus* on the inoffensive "bunny".' At the same time, the other future writer, aged seven, was involved with Ken in a strange, vaguely scientific enterprise, concerning a toad. They had found the toad and decided to stuff it, initially perhaps to dissect it 'to show his supper'. Alan wondered long after whether they had really killed it themselves. He never 'took any pleasure in killing, and hated those who did'. At any rate, on this occasion, they cut the toad open and removed its inside. 'It was astonishing how little, and how little like a toad the remnant was.' With the skin in their hands, their surprise was that a whole toad could have got into it. 'However, we took it home and put it in the mineral drawer, where gradually it dried, looking less and less like a toad each time we considered it. But a secret so terrific, a deed so bloody, had to be formulated. The initial formula was Raw Toad (as you would have believed, if you had seen what we saw). Raw Toad was R.T., which was "arte", and Latin for "by with or from art". Artus was a limb (or wasn't it?) and the first and last letters of limb were L.B. Lb. was pound; you talked about a "pig in a pound"; pig was P.G. and (Greek now, Ken had just begun Greek) πηγη was fountain. So, ranging lightly over several languages, we had reached our mystic formula – "F.N.". Thumbs on the same hymnbook in Dr Gibson's church, we would whisper "F.N.", to each other and know that life was not all Sunday; side by side in the drawing-room, hair newly brushed for visitors and in those damnable starched sailor suits, we would look "F.N." at each other and be comforted. And though, within six months (the toad still unstuffed and crumbled into dust), we were sharing some entirely different secret, yet, forty years later, the magic letters had power to raise sudden memories in two middle-aged men, smoking their pipes, and wondering what to do with their sons.'

Sometimes the real world touched the boys, for instance at Stanford-in-the-Vale in Berkshire in the summer of 1891. It was the year Ken had his hair cut, at last, and Alan felt, for the first time, divided from him and alone. Shades of the prison-house began to close, perhaps, though Westminster was still only on the edge of their consciousness. Certainly Ernest Garrett had won a £70 per annum Challenge Scholarship at the beginning of 1890 (and as it was a last-minute decision to enter him it was done 'wholly without cram'); and in January 1891 he wrote a letter to his old headmaster saying he had won the Senior Cheyne Prize for Arithmetic and had already got his remove into the sixth. He ended up: 'I am glad to hear that the kids are getting on all right.' J. V. Milne had probably decided by then that if E. P. Garrett could do it, so could Ken and Alan, kids though they were. Ken would be put in for the scholarship examination when the time came, and, in the meantime, he would have his hair cut.

Alan had always assumed that they would be shorn at the same moment. It was ridiculous for the only two living members of the F.N. Society to have hair of such wildly different lengths. But his mother could not be persuaded. There was a cousin coming over from Jamaica, who had never seen the boys, and Sarah Maria wanted her to see the last lamb unshorn. Before leaving London for Berkshire the boys were to have a final photograph taken of them together: 'A last photograph of the little Lords Fauntleroy.'

Alan's hair is being brushed and combed in preparation for the photograph. Ken is already groomed and has darted into the studio to see what there is to see. He darts back to tell Alan what he has seen. There is a suit of armour in the studio: 'Quick, Alan, come and look.' And it is at this moment that Alan has what he later called 'my first philosophical reflection': 'It is the first day of the holidays. Time cannot go too slowly for me; not a minute now that is not precious. To-morrow we are riding down to Stanford-in-the-Vale. Six glorious weeks; there they are waiting for us; nothing can shake them. However troublesome my hair, Stanford will still be in the vale, waiting; the armour, as immovable, in the studio. There is no hurry.

'But there was. I can remember thinking, "it may be a little time, it may be a long time, but some time I shall see that armour. And when I have seen it, I have seen it, and it is over. And the holidays will be over; and I shall wish that I hadn't seen that armour, and that I still had it to see, and that I were here, having my hair pulled, with everything in front of me, armour and holidays. And one day I shall be old, and it won't matter how long she took over my hair, because I shall be old, and it will all be over. But oh! I want to see that armour *now*!" I saw it. It was a little disappointing.'

They cycled down to Stanford-in-the-Vale the following day, Ken quite unrecognizable with his new short hair and Alan increasingly irritated by his old long hair. 'There was great excitement that night in Stanford-in-the-Vale. The most notorious character in the village was being "burnt in effigy". Papa explained to us what this meant, and, as discreetly as he could, why it was being done. It was because he was a very bad man, who had run away from his wife. But if he was a very bad man, I said, wasn't it a good thing for his wife if — Ken interrupted to say that he had got somebody into trouble. What sort of trouble? "I suppose he sneaked on somebody." Papa interrupted to say that we couldn't know the truth of it, but evidently the village felt very strongly about it. Ken hoped that *he* would never be burnt in effigy. I hoped I wouldn't either. Papa thought we probably shouldn't if we told the truth, and worked hard. So we decided to go on doing this.

'Meanwhile, noses pressed against an upper window, we watched the village's retribution on the sinner. Three times they paraded his effigy round the green, the men banging pans and kettles, the women screaming, the boys making every sort of noise they could. Then they turned on to the grass, and gathered round into a circle as if for prayer; and there was a moment's silence; and suddenly a flame shot up to heaven.'

Years later, Alan would read *The Mayor of Casterbridge* and come across his admired Hardy's account of just such a procession, a skimmington, a skimmity ride, with the effigies of Farfrae and Lucetta carried through the streets by a noisy crowd. The *Oxford Dictionary* gives a seventeenth-century reference and says such effigies and pro-cessions were 'formerly common in villages and country districts, usually intended to bring ridicule or odium' on adulterers. The one that Alan saw as a small boy in Berkshire in 1891 may well have been one of the last in England, and links him to a world far removed from Victorian drawing-rooms or the nurseries of the 1920s.

It was in the same year, aged nine, that Alan read his first Dickens novel, *Oliver Twist*, and some other stories which were the stuff of nightmares. 'In those days children were usually given this unfortu-nate introduction to Dickens . . . The young can assimilate a good deal of blood-letting in their romances, but they should be spared the realism which lets the wolfish faces at the window into their innocent dreams . . . In comparison with a tale which I read when young of gypsies kidnapping a child, all the corpses of *Hamlet* would have been a subject for a pleasant reverie. One cannot imagine oneself being poisoned or stabbed in Buckingham Palace, but one can easily imagine oneself being carried off by the gypsies on the common.'

It is interesting to consider Milne's own poem 'Disobedience' ('James James Morrison Morrison'), one of the most memorable poems in *When We Were Very Young*, in the light of what he says here about his own childish reading. *Oliver Twist* was apparently terrifying. So was the possibility of being abducted by gypsies. But what of the possibility of one's own mother's total unexplained disappearance? We know Alan considered himself rather detached from his mother, as a child. We know he fantasized about the deaths of both his parents (with the chance of resuscitation after a week or so). But the point about the poem, and about the fantasy that Alan and Ken shared, is that the child is totally in control. Bruno Bettelheim considered 'Disobedience' to be 'a delightfully funny story – to adults . . . What seems funny to the adult is that here the roles of guardian and guarded are reversed . . . To the child, it gives body to his worst nightmarish anxiety about desertion.' He thought the child can only take pleasure in its warning to parents never to go out without him, never to go down to the end of the town, without consulting him. But it seems to me that most young children find it enormously pleasurable (beyond the delights of language and rhythm) because, while bringing a common fear out into the open, it shows the child in charge, in control, able to cope. It is not frightening for the same reasons that Maurice Sendak is not frightening in *Where the Wild Things Are*, however much some adults worry that he is. Max copes just as James James does – although he is only three.

If Alan looked back on most of his childhood with pleasure – and he did – the year 1892 was one he would look back on with particular pleasure. It started well with a really splendid present from Ackie – his uncle, Alexander Milne – for his tenth birthday in January. His immediate letter of thanks does not survive, but Ackie obviously asked his nephew to tell him how he spent the ten shillings, and that letter is a classic schoolboy document:

Henley House
Mortimer Rd
Kilburn   Feb 14th 1892

Dear Ackie

Thank you very much for those crests you sent us. One of the boys has given us an awful lot, and now we have got 15 H.M.S. crests. We have had 4 matches this term and lost 3 and drawn 1.

H.H.S.

Paradise House	3	5	(Hot Potatoes)
Philological F.C.	1	5	
(all men) Emanuel F.C.	1	4	

with a lot of swizzling on their part)

Kensington Park FC	2	0	(Hot Potatoes)

We played Kensington Park F.C on Saturday on Wormwood Scrubs (an awful large common about 12 matches going on at once one which was Rugby.) We watched some of it and it was awfully interesting.

We have spent my 10/- already. Behold the Bill

Birthdays	3/6	Knife	–/6*
Alarum clock	1/4	VERY PRIVATE	–/3*
++Lock with Key	1/–	Sundries	–/4¾
Game	–/6	Gave Barry one farthing	
Stationery	–/6	TOTAL	10/–
Pistol & caps etc.	1/–		

		+Lock & Key for Sacred Cabinet
Tuck	1/–	*In Sacred Cabinet

+We are badly in want of Money (Ahem!).

> I am doing Greek now and enjoy it very much.
> Also mechanics which I like extremely

> > I remain
> > > Your loving nephew
> > > Alan

+ P.S. Smallest contributions thankfully received.

It seems hardly tactful to suggest that he and Ken are in desperate need of money such a short time after such a munificent gift. There is a telling contrast between the generous 3/6 Alan spent on 'birthdays' and the mean farthing he gave to Barry. The 'sacred cabinet', which acquired a lock and key, further to guard its secrets (including whatever it was that was identified only as VERY PRIVATE) was presumably the same drawer which housed the geological collection, the '*tabu* threepence' from the old gentleman, and the desiccated remains of the F.N. toad.

Above all, 1892 was the year when, at long last, Alan's childish hair was cut and he could begin to look as old and as strong as he felt. There had been a dreadful occasion a year or two before when a visitor to the school, misled by the hair into thinking him still an infant, had presented the boy with a toy butcher's shop – and that on a day when he had been doing an algebra exam. And there was another occasion when he had missed part of a debate on Lord Salisbury's foreign policy, because his hair had taken so long to dry. He had had a lot to put up with. But in 1892 the cousin from Jamaica arrived in England at last. She admired his curls but hardly with sufficient warmth. They were apparently not the main reason for her visit to England. As she took a cursory glance at his pretty fair head, Alan thought to himself bitterly: 'There's gratitude. After all I've done for her.' They were at Seaford for the summer holidays and it was at Seaford the deed was done. He carried the precious curls back from the barber's in a paper bag for his mother. Obviously she had not been able to bear to witness the cutting.

The other great pleasure at Seaford was butterflies. A wave of Clouded Yellows came over from France. That was exciting enough but 'the kings and queens of the British butterfly world were, and I suppose still are, the Swallow-Tail, the Purple Emperor and the Camberwell Beauty. A few Swallow-Tails were to be found in Norfolk, where we never went; a few Purple Emperors at the tops of oak-trees (where we never went); a few Camberwell Beauties, no doubt, at Camberwell – where, also, we never went. We realized that these great butterflies were not for us. One day, while we were at breakfast, Papa called to us to come into the garden and see something. We went . . . and there on the flagstones just outside the garden-door was, incredibly, a Swallow-Tail. Left to ourselves Ken and I could have caught it, but the competition was too severe. Barry rushed for a net, anybody's net. The Jamaica cousin's son, who derided our English butterflies, and told us stories of West Indian butterflies like eagles, thought that he might start a collection with a Swallow-Tail, and dashed for his hat. Even Ken and I, each secretly longing to be the captor, however certainly we shared the spoil, got into each other's way. It was all too much for the butterfly, which went back to Norfolk.' Alan always hoped that one day he would read a letter in *The Times*, asking if the Swallowtail had ever been seen as far south as Sittingbourne. Then he would tell them.

At Seaford Alan and Ken wrote their first articles for the public prints. Alan sent 'How to make a Butterfly-net' to *Chums* and Ken sent 'Common Butterflies and their Haunts' (information largely derived from Morris's *British Butterflies*, which he had had for his twelfth birthday) to the *Boys' Own Paper*. Neither article was ever heard of again. The Henley House School Magazine had given them a taste for publication. Alan's first poem to appear in print was in the August 1892 issue. It is called 'The Lay of the Lazy Boy', but the adjective is rather misleading. The boy wakes at half past four, which is 'an awful bore'; he had meant to wake at half past three. So he goes back to sleep.

The magazine also records that Alan's chest measurement had increased by two and a half inches in the course of the term after exercises with Staff-Sergeant Drake, and that Milne III's running was an outstanding feature of the school sports at the Paddington Recreation Ground. He also came second to Barry in the One Mile Bicycle Handicap, with Ken coming in third – a race that left 'the handicap-value of being the Headmaster's son' beyond dispute. Alan had had to borrow a bicycle for the race, but at Christmas 1892 the boys' lives were totally transformed. 'The first detachable pneumatic tyre appeared, and a boy could now mend his own puncture by the wayside. Papa took advantage of the occasion to make the most splendid benefaction in history: he gave each of us a new Dunlop-

tyred bicycle . . . There may have been other boys with such bicycles
in England but in our journeys we never came across them.' They
were envied wherever they went – and they went everywhere. 'We
rode behind buses up Park Lane, ringing our bells impatiently and
then swinging magnificently past them; we darted between hansom
cabs. Look at us! Look at us! Did you ever see bicycles like this?' It
was two years before the rest of the world caught up with the Milne
boys, apparently.

There was an election and Gladstone was returned, old, deaf and
half-blind, for his final term of government. J. V. Milne would never
speak of party politics, for fear presumably of parental reactions, but
he worried that his pupils shouted 'Conservative!' or 'Liberal!' with
as little understanding and as much vigour as they shouted 'Oxford!'
or 'Cambridge!' at the Boat Race. Alan shouted 'Liberal!' with the
loudest of them. In his autobiography, H. G. Wells takes his old
friend to task for his lack of any realistic basic philosophy. 'Milne
and his staff taught neither human history, economics, nor social
duty and . . . launched boys into the gathering disaster of civilization
as though they were sending them into a keen but merciful prize
competition, in which "sheer hard work" was the "magician's
wand", and so forth and so on.' Certainly J. V. Milne was dazzled
by Harmsworth's success (the phrases come from an editorial about
it) and could not see that his was not a story for emulation but rather
a cautionary tale. Certainly the Harmsworths had gained no sense
of social duty or obligation from their education: Wells would call
the brothers ruffians. But there were other boys who had, and J. V.
Milne, whatever Wells may say, had a wiser sense of values than his
welcome for *Comic Cuts* suggests.

The word 'success' would come to have a special resonance for
Alan Milne. Thirty years later he would use the word for the title of
one of his plays – and regret doing so. Perhaps he would remember
his father saying that what mattered was not cleverness but character.
Men of brilliant intellect failed every day. What mattered was
strength of character, energy, courage and integrity. 'Men with these
qualities could always command success.' 'What is being successful?'
J. V. Milne would ask, and not wait for an answer. 'Is it getting
what you most desire? An infant is crawling on the floor, reaching
out to the coveted prize – a glittering, beautiful sharp knife. Is it
"successful" when it gets it?' There are some glittering prizes that
are not worth the winning.

Alan's father had taught him many things. He had taught him that manners are nothing to do with etiquette or how to behave at an evening party, but something much more fundamental. 'The essence of good manners is unselfishness and a desire to give pleasure.' If he was sometimes selfish, he would usually want to give pleasure. His early years had been full of affection, of freedom, independence and individuality. Much later these would be the wellsprings of his own books for children.

— 3 —

Westminster

CLEVERNESS might not be as important as character, but, there was no doubt about it, 'scholarships are only gained by the cleverest of the clever, the *crème de la crème*', said J. V. Milne in August 1892, anticipating Miss Brodie, that other keen teacher. He had his sights set on Westminster School for his two clever younger sons. The school's reputation was high at this stage. Indeed, one parent, writing in the *Elizabethan*, the Westminster magazine, would encourage the boys never to forget that on them 'rests the responsibility of living up to the traditions of a school which owns no superior, and acknowledges equality only with Winchester and Eton'. It was not, however, a 'fashionable' school. Another writer in the school magazine thought it quite ridiculous that the Latin Play had been cancelled because of the death of the Duke of Clarence. 'In the old days', when Westminster held 'an exalted position', it would have been a different matter.

J. V. Milne was not looking for a fashionable or 'exalted' school. He imagined Westminster provided the best education that was available. And although what it did provide was, by Alan's account, very unsatisfactory indeed (for either a mathematician or a writer), there is no suggestion that anywhere else would have been any better. 'If only I had been taught this, that, and the other instead!' Alan would say – but not: 'If only I had gone to another school.'

At Westminster in the summer of 1892 there were three Queen's scholarships and two exhibitions to be competed for. Ken was one of the boys who tried. It was an embarrassing occasion for him. He went up for the Challenge – as it was called – wearing knickerbockers, along with fifty-two boys wearing trousers. When Alan's turn came, he would know what to wear. Ken was not elected to a scholarship. No one expected him to be. In fact, his father recorded that he had gone simply to 'try what a Westminster Scholarship

Examination was like'. He and young Batsford (who would eventually be a publisher) had both done very well, qualified for places and, indeed, gained excellent marks on the scholarship papers, but were 'too young to take the scholarship'.

Ken was very nearly twelve that summer. The following January there was an unexpected by-election and he was elected a Queen's Scholar. Barry, now nearly fourteen, was still at Henley House, 'developing into a good bowler', according to his father, though there was not much evidence of the fact in the cricket score cards. He would go to a private school in Derbyshire run by an old friend of his father's from the days when they had both taught in Shropshire, and leave at sixteen to be articled to a relation, William Bowles Barrett, a solicitor in Weymouth.

Ken had only two days to be turned into an authentic public schoolboy, complete with cap and gown, stiff white shirt, white bow tie, Eton jacket, waistcoat, and trousers. He had his photograph taken to celebrate the transformation, but had worn 'naturally enough, his Eton collar outside his coat, little knowing', as he would know the next day, 'that Queen's Scholars at Westminster wear their collars inside'. The photographs were wasted; they could never be circulated among proud relatives and envious friends once the awful truth was realized. When Alan's turn comes, he will know to wear his collar inside his coat. He will not have to set off for the new school alone.

And Alan's turn would come. All Alan's energies went into making sure that it would. 'If ever in my life I said, "I can do it," I said it then. I worked in those five months as I have only worked (over any length of time) twice in my life since.' He worked during the week with the advantage, of course, of Ken's two sets of Challenge papers to pore over and guide his studies, and with all the help his father could give him. On Saturday afternoons Ken came home and coached him in the ways of Westminster. There was a lot to learn, and Ken was finding the learning hard and lonely. It will be all right when Alan is there too.

Alan learnt all the strange words: ' "Bag" was milk and "beggar" was sugar, and "blick" was ball; and the coat you wore up-Fields, whether it was a house blazer or just an ordinary coat, was a "shag"; and you always said "up" for everything – up-Fields and up-School and up-Sutts (Sutts was the food shop) and you were a Junior your first year, and then a Second Election and then a Third Election and then a Senior, and they didn't call "Fag!" as they did in *Tom Brown*, they called "Lec!" which was short for election, and if you forgot anything, you got "tanned", which was four with a very thick cane as hard as they could hit, but he hadn't forgotten anything yet, only there was such an awful lot to remember. Oh, and Juniors weren't allowed to wear gowns in College, and Second Elections had to, and Third Elections could get leave from Seniors not to, and Seniors did what they liked. And when the Headmaster crossed the Yard to go up-School in the afternoon, you had to be standing outside College door, if it was your turn, and then shout "Rutherford's coming" down College, spreading it out as long as you could, like this, and you had to remember when it was your turn, because if you forgot you got tanned. And then in the morning – '

At the time Alan listened eagerly; he couldn't have enough of it. Looking back later, he thought how strange it was that all Ken's talk concentrated on 'this meaningless, artificial life in College, in which all morality was convention'. You couldn't say that it must be wrong because it was silly, but rather you had to say, 'That *must* be right because people have been doing it for three hundred years.' It was this sort of thing that was one of the reasons, when the time came to send his own son to public school, that Alan chose a new school, Stowe, where 'the rules of conduct are based on reason not custom'.

Alan took the Westminster Challenge papers in the summer of 1893. His age in the school records is given as eleven years two months; presumably the application forms were filled in in March. J. V. Milne had the boys' entrance papers beautifully bound in leather with watered boards, inscribed 'Westminster Papers, 1893'. They show there was a great deal more in the Greek and Latin papers than Alan himself suggested in his autobiography. Alan said his Greek translation was his most disastrous effort. He claimed he knew little beyond the Greek for 'fountain' and the Greek for 'and'. (There were plenty of 'ands' in the unseen translation, but the absence of fountains was remarkable.) One suspects he was exaggerating, but perhaps he was not, for his mathematics were brilliant enough to make up for some deficiencies in the rest. It is interesting to see that only a few years later the Headmaster of Westminster was already worrying over the fact that Greek was becoming rare in the preparatory schools. 'This is one more concession to the principle that the able and willing must shorten his stride to that of the indolent and incapable.'

The arithmetic problems were just the sort of thing Alan enjoyed, and would do at times for recreation for the rest of his life. They were more difficult versions of the sort of problem ('A goose weighs seven pounds and half its own weight . . .') his father had challenged the boys with on their walks years before.

There was also Euclid and Algebra and, as if that wasn't high enough, another paper called Higher Mathematics. Alan had 'done' Trigonometry, Analytical Conics, Statics and Dynamics. He felt there was nothing he could not do. Then there was a General Paper (not more than seven questions to be attempted), which covered a variety of areas of knowledge:

1) Trace carefully either the career of John the Baptist or Joshua's conquest of Palestine.

2) Give a short account of Athens under Pericles.

3) What do you know of the Mutilation of the Hermae, the Gerousia, the Olympic Games, the Helots, Ostracism?

4) Who were the following: Warwick the King-maker, Christopher Columbus, Marie Antoinette, Isaac Newton, Prince Bismarck, Peter the Great?

5) Through what straits and seas would a steam ship successively pass
   a) between the mouth of the River Don and Southampton?
   b) between Venice and Bombay?

6) Explain fully Trade Winds, Land and Sea Breezes, Forced Draught, the Solar System, Centre of Gravity.

Finally there were ten quotations. The boys had to 'identify allusions' and name the authors.

It was the sort of examination that made H. G. Wells lament the state of English education. But it was an examination paper eleven-year-old Alan Milne relished. He would always say that, given the right conditions, the right teaching, there is nothing small children are not eager to learn. 'And then we send them to your schools and in two years, three years, four years, you have killed all their enthusiasm.' It was an unpopular speech at a dinner of headmasters thirty years later. How soon would his own enthusiasm be killed?

In July, when he had taken the Challenge and was waiting for his results, his father said that from now on he was to do just as much or as little work as he liked: 'He meant this to apply to the rest of the summer term, but it really applied to the rest of my life.' Alan was playing on the apparatus in the playground of Henley House when someone waved a telegram at him from the drawing-room window. He had done it. He would start at Westminster in the autumn, and he would start as he meant to go on. He asked Ken to check on the holiday task for the class he would be going into. In between school hunting with his father that August, he read Prescott's *Conquest of Mexico* and learnt a poem of William Allingham's by heart.

The expeditions with his father, which had started the previous year, resulted in the finding of Streete Court at Westgate-on-Sea, but the thing that Alan remembered about them was fear – 'the only unreasoning fear I can remember as a child'. His father, having enjoyed his company on the way from Kilburn to Paddington or London Bridge, would go off by himself to buy the tickets for the rest of the journey. Perhaps *this* was the origin of 'James James' – certainly J. V. Milne was not going off to the other end of the town, but he was not consulting Alan, and Alan would wait in a strange waiting-room in some unfamiliar terminus, dreading that something would happen to his father in his absence and that he would never see him again. If Ken had been there, of course it would have been different. ('Alone I felt lost.') Once he asked if Ken could go too, but his mother explained that that would make the expedition rather expensive. Alan said this was his first realization that they were poor – 'so poor that, for want of a few shillings, I had to endure these agonies.' A simpler solution would surely have been for Alan to tell his father his feelings and to stay by his side. But he always found it difficult to talk about his feelings.

Poverty is, of course, relative. One can't help remembering the splendid bicycles the boys had all had for Christmas the year before. But they had known for a long time that, as their father put it, 'It cost a lot of money to send a boy to public school and then on to university; that, as there were three of them and I was not a rich man, I should not be able to do so; but that if they worked hard they might win scholarships to take them there.' In fact, J. V. Milne inherited a little money just at this time. An unexpectedly rich second cousin had died intestate, but there was not a great deal as there were thirty second cousins to share it. That thousand pounds may have accounted for the bicycles. Certainly it made the Milnes rather more confident about taking on Streete Court, though they could only afford to rent it. The rent was £350 a year, for 'an extremely desirable residence, Elizabethan in parts, and enclosed in its own ornamental grounds of upwards of seven acres in extent'. It would provide Alan and Ken with a perfect holiday home.

Alan started at Westminster School in the autumn of 1893, on the first day of what was known as the Play Term – the annual Latin Play was performed at the end of the term, just before Christmas. There were four Queen's Scholars in Alan's election. Saxon Sydney-Turner, with his literary leanings, was, like Alan, short and thin, with pale straw-coloured hair. He would eventually make his career in the Treasury, but would be best known as a central member of the Bloomsbury Group, a close friend of Lytton Strachey, the Woolfs and the Bells. He was just over a year older than Alan. Then there was Frederick Barrington-Ward, who was about the same age as Sydney-Turner. He would become a barrister and a Fellow of All Souls. Fourth was Reginald Phillimore, who was already fourteen and would one day become Surveyor-General of India. He was the younger brother of a boy who had been Edward Marsh's close rival at Westminster. Marsh had left school two years before. Twenty years later he would be one of Alan's closest friends, or as close as any friend of Alan's ever was.

There were thirty-five Queen's Scholars out of the 225 boys in the school in 1893. Alan was the youngest Queen's Scholar there had ever been – or so his father boasted. He was just eleven and a half when he was elected, and the average age of the form he joined was over fourteen. If it was true that Alan was the youngest Queen's Scholar, Eddie Marsh was even younger when he entered Westminster ten years earlier as a day-boy exhibitioner. Westminster would be a bond later between the two clever young men about town. They would compare notes on Rutherford, the Headmaster, who had spoken so strongly to Eddie's mother, saying the boy's 'literary inclinations' were to be regretted and warning her that Cambridge 'might lead him to only a literary career, which I deprecate strongly.'

Alan was less under Rutherford's influence than Eddie, as a classicist, had been. The Headmaster was a brilliant teacher, with 'an ardour which seemed to lift an ordinary school lesson right out of the narrow bonds of the classroom and into life itself.' He was remarkable for his 'pointed Johnsonian pronouncements, delivered in a broad Scottish accent – "I thought people were *born* knowing the date of the Battle of Leuktra!" ' All his emphasis was on Greek. In comparison, even Latin and Divinity were poor relations. And as for Mathematics . . .

Even with Ken's preparation and guidance, Alan found Westminster immensely confusing that first term. No one was in the least interested in asking him questions about the conquest of Mexico; no one asked him to recite 'Up the airy mountain,/Down the rushy glen.' His attempt to endear himself to his new form master was a flop. But he was not discouraged. He would find other ways to show his brilliance and get the chance to join Ken in the form above.

And in the meantime he had to apply himself to all that stuff about what you could do and could not do. As a Junior, he had to go and return from Hall only through the Cloisters and enter the Hall only by the west door under the gallery. He must not go to bed before Prayers without permission or use the letter-box in the Juniors' room without leave first obtained from a Senior. There were privileges, of course, as well as rules. Queen's Scholars were the only boys in the world allowed to take the air on the terrace of the House of Commons. They were also entitled, in limited numbers, to visit the Strangers' Gallery of the House.

The school itself was confusing. There had been constant talk for years of moving it out of the maze of buildings in the precincts of the Abbey and into new premises, as had happened to St Paul's. The talk of removal had stifled every plan for the existing site and buildings. The school was no longer an integral part of the Abbey, governed by the Dean and Chapter, as it had been for centuries. It now had its own governing body. But of course its proximity to the Abbey remained important. In 1898 Alan would attend Gladstone's funeral and walk out of the Abbey just behind Sir Henry Irving. The daily chapel service was held in Poets' Corner. This must have had some effect on Alan, and made up a little for the low standing that English literature had in the school.

When the boys walked the half mile to Vincent Square for games, they had to go through narrow streets and slums, such as Thieving Lane and Black Dog Alley, 'which were considerably behind almost any part of London from a sanitary point of view'. The sanitary arrangements in College were not very satisfactory either. There were no baths; it was enough, Alan suggested, that the place was designed by Sir Christopher Wren: 'One cannot have everything; probably there are no baths in St Paul's Cathedral.' Showers of a sort were installed before Alan left the school, but when he started there wasn't even any hot water. In each cubicle, when they came in from games, there would be a jug of cold water. He would stand shivering in the shallow tin bath and make a feeble attempt at getting clean after a muddy game of football. They had just fifteen minutes to wash and change back into their stiff white shirts, Eton collars and the rest. If it was Alan's turn to shout 'Rutherford's coming!' he had five minutes less. In spite of the surrounding slums, the lack of hot water and the unpalatable food, Alan was never once, in all his seven years at Westminster, 'out of school' for illness. His father may have been just a little put out by this, used as he was to unreasonable parents who 'demand that their children will suffer no accident, and catch neither measles nor mumps, and who put down a common cold to gross neglect'.

The food was bad at Westminster. It was little consolation that they were eating it in College Hall, whose external walls dated from 1380 when it was built as the Abbot's refectory. For the rest of his life, Alan could not 'think of College meals without disgust and indignation'. Each day's meals were almost identical, and almost everything was awful. Breakfast, Alan's beloved meal, consisted only of tea, bread and butter, with the bread the dullest sort of bread and the butter unsalted. Alan would always hate unsalted butter. He called it a sort of 'inferior vaseline – the sort of thing you put on the axles of locomotives.' Not the sort of thing to make you bounce out of bed: 'Tea was tea, and I was never fussy about tea, but the milk had been boiled, and great lumps of skin floated about on the top of it. It made me almost sick to look at that milk, to smell that milk, to think of that milk; it makes me almost sick now to remember it. Well, that was breakfast, "the most divine meal of the day, the only meal which could never be a disappointment." At one o'clock we had the usual "joint and two veg," followed by pudding. The plates of meat had been carved well in advance, and brought to the right degree of tepidity in some sort of gas-cooler. If it were the fruit season, we had rhubarb. Not liking luke-warm slabs of beef (or rhubarb), I made no sort of contact with the midday meal. There was one terrible occasion when Rutherford came into Hall, and, observing my lack of interest in the meat, ordered me a glass of "milk". I managed to get my lips to it without being sick, and prayed earnestly to Heaven that he should move away before the shameful catastrophe happened. He moved; and thereafter I made a great show of business with knife and fork whenever he came into sight. The last meal was tea at 6.15. Tea was breakfast over again, with a few of the slabs of meat, now officially cold, for anybody who wanted them. Very few people did.'

They were allowed to supplement breakfast and tea with anything they liked to buy – but there was a limit to the amount they could afford. They had only £5 each a term for all their expenses. It had to be accounted for to their father to the last penny. He would never take their complaints about the food seriously. All boys complained about school meals. Even at Henley House boys had occasionally been known to complain, with no good reason. As a parent, J. V. Milne, having suffered so much himself from complaining parents, was going to keep a very low profile. 'I lay awake every night thinking about food,' Alan recalled. 'I fell asleep and dreamed about food. In all my years at Westminster, I never ceased to be hungry.'

The food, the hunger, were not the worst things at Westminster. The worst thing was the fear – the fear of being tanned. Corporal punishment was an everyday occurrence. It was particularly hard for Alan and Ken, coming from the atmosphere of Henley House, where their father found hitting a boy 'so utterly distasteful' 'that nothing but the conviction that the boy was being lost could compel him to resort to it.' Although a cane hung in J. V. Milne's study, H. G. Wells said it was 'a symbol of force as the ultimate sanction, but it was never used in my time, and I do not think it had been used for some years before.'

At Westminster it was another matter. As Ken had described it so vividly to Alan, a tanning was being thrashed four times 'with a very thick cane as hard as they could hit'. It was not only the actual pain but the perpetual fear of it, and the random injustice of it, which seemed to Alan later 'such an unnecessary hardship'. There were so many things you could be tanned for; there were so many bizarre and complicated demands. The four most senior boys in College – the Captain and the three monitors – were allowed to use the cane. All four had to agree to its use – and the accused could appeal to the Headmaster; but in practice he never did. Masters did not tan. It was boys who wielded the cane and seemed to enjoy the wielding.

Sometimes when they had nothing better to do and they felt it had been rather a long time since the last tanning, the order would go forth for 'all people talking up-Library' to come to the monitors' room. Then, said Alan, 'the custom was for four volunteers to take over the company's liabilities.' There would be a sort of rota; they would take it in turns. There would usually be one boy (who had been 'reading school stories, and was determined, at whatever cost, to be popular') who would take more than his fair share of tanning.

Years later, Alan Milne would hear fellow club members, or would read of magistrates in the paper, saying that they themselves were thrashed at school. He would hear them approving of corporal punishment and seeking to justify it by their own experience. 'To their opponents it seems, rather, a condemnation, as accounting for a stupidity and insensitiveness, otherwise inexplicable. The curious, but not infrequent, boast "Thrashing never did *me* any harm," invites the retort: "Then what did?" '

At least there was no unlicensed bullying in College, and the authorities kept an eagle eye on the possibility of homosexuality. 'Each boy slept in a separate, and entirely sacred, cubicle in the long dormitory.' The small boys slept secure in the knowledge they would not be disturbed. It was an offence, punishable by tanning, to enter another boy's cubicle even in daylight, and certainly not after lights out at nine-thirty. It was even an offence for Junior boys to be seen with Seniors around the school. There would be one scandal, but not until Alan's last year.

Alan felt it was fortunate that Ken was only such a short distance ahead of him. Alan was in fact a Junior for only two terms. He started off in Upper Remove, the top form of the Lower School, fagging for Ernest Garrett, who had been at Henley House. At this stage, Alan was not allowed to 'think'. 'One important and excellent rule,' according to a history of Westminster published just after Alan left, 'is that no junior is allowed to "think", i.e. he may not begin a statement with "I think" or "I thought".' Why this should be considered excellent is not explained. But Alan duly stopped 'thinking'. In that first term, in the autumn of 1893, he concentrated on Latin and Greek, reading Caesar's *Gallic Wars* (not for the first time), a history of Greece, and Xenophon, with the help of the Headmaster's own Greek grammar. Then, as now, it was the habit of teachers to assign their own books. The only history he learnt at school was the history of Greece and Rome.

Alan remembered that it was in January, in his second term, that he was promoted to the Under Fifth. But in fact it was at the beginning of the summer or election term. He was twelve and a quarter; the average age was fourteen and five months. But that did not worry Alan. He was in the same form as Ken. From now on they could do everything together, as they had always done in the past. They would be together for the next four years.

Alan had gone home to Westgate-on-Sea for the Easter holidays with the Headmaster's brief summing-up: 'Keen, intelligent and

improving fast.' What more could one want? His father who naturally took headmasters' reports very seriously, beamed. They cycled
happily up and down Kent. (In 1897, when Alan was fifteen, he and
Ken would achieve their ambition of cycling one hundred miles in a
day, ending up in a field long after dark.) They explored the surround-
ings of Streete Court. After the cramped playground at Henley House,
the seven acres seemed vast. Near the school 'there was "excellent
stabling" which housed a pony: an excellent pony, as willing to take
us for a ride as it was to mow the cricket-field or fetch the luggage
from the station.' There were two tennis lawns, a croquet lawn, and
a woodland border full of birds' nests ('Slow white petals from the
may-tree fall . . . I could hear from the may-tree the blackbird call.')
There was a kitchen garden full of fruit trees and gooseberry bushes,
a duckpond full of ducks, and hives which would eventually be full
of honey. There was even a peacock. They loved it all.

It was the first time Alan and Ken had been in the country in the
spring. Looking for birds' eggs was considered, in those days, the
thing to do. They did have some qualms as they removed one egg
from each nest, but somebody had assured them that birds can't
count. They had a special delicate bradawl for boring a single hole
and a special pipe for sucking out the contents. They had a cabinet
divided into squares. They had cottonwool, labels, gum and 'Kear-
ton's book for recognizing the eggs,' but somehow, fortunately, the
only eggs they could find were those of blackbird, thrush, starling
and sparrow.

Alan and Ken enjoyed their first summer term at Westminster
together, in spite of the food and the fear of being tanned. They were
reading Martial that term, much more amusing than Caesar. A. A.
Milne said once when asked if he were happy at school: 'Yes, I was
happy at school, but only because I had to be at school and must
get therefore what happiness I could out of it.' Their mother sent
boxes of flowers from Streete Court. Alan said later that the flowers
brought with them 'a nostalgia almost unbearable, whose subli-
mation dwelt in those sprays of wistaria which lay, a little crushed,
on the top of the box, and conveyed somehow all that I felt, but
could not express of Home and Beauty.' He is, of course, using
'nostalgia' here in its basic sense, close to its Greek root. It is not a
sentimental longing for an imagined past but the pain of being away
from home, the pain, in fact of having left childhood. He would one

day be described by a critic as being 'drugged by nostalgia' – but there was never anything soporific about Milne's nostalgia.

Alan Milne would never claim (as Osbert Sitwell did after Eton) that he was 'educated in the holidays' from Westminster. The holidays were for bicycle rides and bird's-nesting, sliding down banisters, throwing balls about at Streete Court. But, as time went on, it would seem that more and more of the education that really mattered to Alan was going on outside the classroom, in his free time in the library on weekdays and on the unstructured Sundays. He would look back on 'all the wasted hours in form and lecture-room'.

Westminster ruined Alan as a mathematician, indeed as any sort of scholar. It was the crushing, unjust report the boy received, aged twelve, in the summer of 1894, that confirmed him as a 'divergent', a dissident. The report was brief. 'Has done ill, showing little or no ambition, even in mathematics.' 'When he read this, Father turned his face to the wall, and abandoned hope. I, on the other hand, turned my face to the lighter side of life, and abandoned work.

'For (I would point out) I was twelve. I was in the top mathematical set of the school, and in the term's examinations I had come out top of that set. Nobody could specialize in mathematics until he reached the Sixth, at which point he diverged into the Mathematical Sixth . . . With the exception of those three boys, aged 16 to 18, I was top of the school in mathematics, at the age of twelve. And I was told that I had "done ill".

'It was useless to point out to Father that the report was written before the result of the examinations, and that the examinations proved that the report was ridiculously wrong. Headmasters' reports *couldn't* be wrong. If Dr Rutherford said I had done ill, I had done ill.

'Well, that was that . . . Father's happiness appeared to depend, not on my own efforts, but on an entirely haphazard interpretation of them. I stopped working. It is clear to me now that I never was a mathematical genius, but just a clever little boy who could learn anything an enthusiast taught him; who liked learning chiefly for the victories it brought him. There were neither enthusiasts nor victories in sight. Only Ken. Together we settled down happily to idleness. My "education" had begun.'

If Alan had been continuously praised and encouraged by his school, he might well have settled into a life of what can be called 'convergence', working steadily towards a brilliant mathematical future. A. A. Milne, as we know him, might not have existed. As it was, at twelve he decided not to try to be a Senior Wrangler (if indeed he really knew what a Wrangler was – it certainly struck him first as a good rhyme-word for 'strangler'). In future, he would please only himself and Ken. It was obviously impossible to please either the school or his father. So what was the point of trying? He was no longer an enthusiast. And it would save him a good deal of anxiety, for no ardent mathematician could have breathed happily in that classics-orientated atmosphere.

If one was to take Alan's own account of his life at Westminster as the whole story one would think he was totally disillusioned and corrupted by that report. Certainly he would now give most of his attention to what Ian Hay called 'the lighter side of school life'. But Alan was so conditioned and so well trained that he still had to be best – and he was still capable of being best at mathematics, at Westminster if not at Cambridge, without making much effort at all. In his play *The Lucky One*, Milne wrote of one of the brothers: 'Gerald has always been so good at everything, even as a baby.' A recent study of schoolboys has an example of two brothers close in age, where the younger had overtaken the older academically, and the older 'stuttered, blushed and had facial tics'. Ken didn't, and this must be to Alan's credit as well as his own. In fact, Ken's performance academically was not a great deal inferior to Alan's. The only problem was that he was sixteen months older.

If he could not stop himself being good at nearly everything (apart from French), Alan could at least stop himself being good. He learnt to cheat. It was not done, of course, to cheat in such a way as to give yourself an advantage over another boy – but cheating to outwit a master was another matter. The French master's method of teaching involved continual testing and he over-estimated his class's ability at the language. Each lesson he would dictate twenty-four questions and ask the boys to write down their answers. Any boy who got less than twenty correct would be sent 'up-School' and have to work in the afternoon instead of playing games.

'When we had written down our answers, we changed papers with the boy next to us, so that each boy was correcting somebody else's paper. This, which was supposed to prevent cheating, made cheating more certain, for one was now doing it with an easy conscience on another boy's behalf. We sat alphabetically, and I was next to a boy called Moon. Leonard Moon was almost then, and was to become, the hero of every Westminster boy. He was just getting into the school elevens; he became a double Blue, made a century against the Australians, played cricket for Middlesex, played football for Corinthians and the South of England, was extraordinarily good-looking, and was, with it all, an extremely modest, charming person. Could I let this paragon, who was even worse at French than I, go up-School? Of course not. Could I, as a loyal Westminster, handicap the school by denying him his cricket and football practice? Unthinkable. When his name was read out, I said "Twenty-one" firmly. And when my own name was read out, and he said "Twenty-two", it was equally unthinkable that I should rise in my place and say, "Sir, I suspect this charming boy on my left of uttering falsehoods. I doubt very much if I got more than seven answers right. I insist on a recount." Instead I looked modestly down my nose. In a few weeks I had settled down happily to a life of deception.'

Alan and Ken regularly deceived their father about the way they had spent the term's £5. He insisted on meticulous accounts for everything they spent. Of course they could never remember exactly what they had spent and they knew he would hardly approve if they simply wrote in their account books each term 'Extra Food up-Sutts: £5.' There were other things they had to spend money on – haircuts (money well spent), train fares home for the half-term exeat, a few subscriptions. There was always the possibility that a master might get married and need a contribution to a wedding present, or a canon be buried and need a wreath. And these possibilities accounted for a delightful amount of food. They married off masters and killed off canons without a qualm. Their father accepted their accounts without suspicion. Alan and Ken exchanged the most fleeting of glances. They were accomplished fiddlers. 'Little Lord Fauntleroy seemed very far away.'

The boys also became extremely accomplished at writing letters to each other under a master's nose when they were supposed to be working. Sitting together in the Mathematical Sixth (with Alan now fourteen), there were long letters making plans for the next holidays, often for some splendid cycling tour. 'Interest was added to these letters by our custom of omitting every other word, leaving blanks which the addressee had to fill in. Our minds were sufficiently in tune for this to be possible without being easy.' They were clever at not being caught and the idleness had no effect on their performance in the examinations, at least in mathematics.

The Report of the Secretaries to the Board for Oxford and Cambridge School Examinations in the summer of 1896 is full of remarks like this:

To Solution of Triangles. Twenty boys took this paper, of whom K. Milne and A. Milne sent in very good work.
Algebra. Progressions. Seventeen boys at an average 56%. A. Milne and K. Milne both did remarkably well, obtaining 97 and 93 marks respectively.
Books I-IV with alternative questions. 17 boys at 34%. A. Milne and K. Milne sent in good work with well-drawn figures. Most of the other work was fair.

Edgar Hackforth was the only other boy who was mentioned favourably in this report. He would go on to Trinity and be 8th Wrangler in Part I of the Mathematical Tripos in 1900. At the height of Alan's fame as a writer, Hackforth would be living in Purley and working in Whitehall as Deputy Controller of Health Insurance in the Ministry of Health. It was exactly the sort of career Alan's father had had in mind for him, if he were not inclined to be a teacher.

Were all these years of mathematics in Alan's case simply to make him able 'to count the words in an article and to estimate the number of guineas due to him'? Was he in any real sense training his mind?

To some people at Westminster in the 1890s the worst offence you could commit was not being keen on school games. There were plenty of boys who were not. This, to us, may suggest a rather healthier atmosphere than one in which games were the only thing that mattered. Cricket was not in a very good state. 'It is the custom at Westminster,' the school magazine said, 'to review the past cricket season with regret and look forward to the future with expectation' – expectation which was usually to end in regret. Football matches were largely ignored, except by the few boys actually involved. An editorial in Alan's first term took the school to task. The proper place for a Westminster boy on Saturday afternoons is Up-Fields. Those who are not seen there are a 'miserable and skulking lot'. They 'retire to their private amusements, into the cloak of their selfish individualism' and 'forgo all claim to be counted members of a public school'. They were accused of spending Saturday afternoons 'knitting stockings' – presumably the most contemptible occupation the writer could imagine.

The same theme was pursued with even more vigour in 1895. Slackness in the senior school was considered 'little short of criminal'.

'Only the other day a certain member of the Shell, when asked who was captain of football, replied "How should I know?" ' Or another 'brilliant specimen', when asked three days before the Charterhouse match, 'Are you going to Godalming?' was heard to reply 'What for?' The writer grieved over 'an ignoble quartette' (sic), who had played fives instead of watching a school match one Wednesday afternoon. The offence was considered particularly heinous because all four boys were monitors.

The tone of the editorials was not typical, though they may tell us something about the school. Alan would praise Westminster for its tolerance, if for little else. His own attitude to games was always reasonable. He would never have written such editorials. Though he got so much pleasure from games himself, he was not fanatical about them and usually tolerant of other people's intolerance. 'There is nothing so uninteresting to the athletic as the record of some other undistinguished performer's achievements; nothing so unintelligible to the unathletic.' He would play golf and know that 'a bore is a man who insists on telling you about his last round when you want to tell him about yours.'

At school it was athletics, cricket and football. In his last year he would win the Open Challenge Cup for Long Jump and was one of the fastest sprinters. With cricket, his breakthrough came in 1896 when the Captain of Cricket decided to encourage the young and promising. Two boys from each house were selected for coaching. Ken was actually a better cricketer, Alan says, but as usual Alan came off best. 'Because I was so small and looked so young (and promising), because I ran about so actively at football,' when one Milne was chosen for the coaching, it was Alan not Ken. 'I must record again that Ken, once more outdistanced through no fault of his own, or merit of mine, remained sweet-tempered about it. All the rivalry between us came from me. As soon as we became competitors on anything like equal terms, I had to prove myself the better man of the two. Being given the chance at cricket, I took it. And when, in Junior House matches that year, I had gone in first and got out for twenty or thirty, and Ken, going in later, was approaching the twenties, I could bear to watch him no longer, but had to look away until he got out. He never knew this, he would never have suspected it of me, he could never show any such ungenerous feeling himself. He was, after all, "the better man of the two". I like to think now that one Wednesday afternoon in his last term, when I was playing in Big Game, and telling myself that this was something which Ken had never done, he, in a Form Match, was doing something which Alan had never done, nor was ever to do; he was making a century. Doubtless the opposition was not strong, but it was a hundred, and the only hundred the Milnes of Kilburn have ever made.'

It may have been Ken's greatest moment of glory at Westminster. Whatever the opposition, it was a considerable achievement. There was rarely time for scoring a hundred runs and any centuries that were made must have been largely composed of fours, if not sixes. Alan was not there to feel ashamed of feeling jealous. And soon Ken was not there at all. He left in the summer of 1898, at nearly eighteen, and, having no idea what he wanted to do, he was articled, as Barry had been, to William Bowles Barrett, solicitor, of Weymouth. Alan had to start learning to live without him, something he would always find hard. In the summer of 1899, he concentrated more than ever on his cricket.

'I was a taught batsman rather than a natural one,' Alan would say. He owed a lot of pleasure in years to come to that coaching at Westminster. The professional had a perfect length. He dropped the ball on 'the usual half-crown or postage-stamp' and mechanically told the boys to 'Come out to it.' 'Without any difficulty,' Alan said, 'we came out to it. I could come out to anything that was straight and not too high; the difficulty lay in staying in.' As Alan replaced the stumps he could see the coach making his own forward motion with a bent left elbow, suggesting that if he had only come out to it like that his stumps would still be intact. 'He continued to drop the ball on the same postage-stamp, we continued to play forward for it ... and in a little while we were being spoken of as a candidate for our house eleven.'

Alan was a bowler as well as a batsman. There is a great deal to be said for being an all-rounder, he considered. In his last two years at Westminster, he played for the school. The school records have his top score at 38, in a match against the Town boys: 'A very plucky innings. He was suffering from a badly damaged finger, which he hurt while fielding.' In his autobiography, written exactly forty years later, Alan's memory adds only one to his total, but the damage had been done to his *thumb*.

One of Alan's saddest moments at school was in that same summer of 1899 when he was out without scoring a single run in a memorable two-day match against Charterhouse, which Westminster, against all expectation, won with five minutes to spare. Alan had taken just one wicket in the first innings. But at least he had not done anything as foolish as a boy called Plaskett at the other end of the wicket when he was batting. He told the story in a letter to Ken's granddaughter fifty years later.

Playing against Charterhouse in 1899 (the year Canute died, if your History book goes back as far as that) I was in with a boy called Plaskett. And he hit his first ball up in the air towards the bowler, and we ran; and in comes the bowler in the middle of the pitch just as he was getting ready for his c. & b.; and Plaskett was so nervous and excited that he leaped in the air, rather as if he was up at the net, and knocked the ball away. He didn't wait for an appeal, but ran straight back to the pavilion, and hid in a locker. Luckily for him he took 6 wickets for 58 in the next innings, and we won the match. Otherwise he would have had to emigrate. Now you know all about Obstructing the Field.

If cricket, Milne thought, was not the greatest game in the world to play and not always the most exciting to watch, it was certainly 'the greatest to love'. Watching cricket, he considered at the end of his life, had given him 'more happiness than any other inactivity in which I have been engaged'. He and Ken would share a pleasure in the game, as long as Ken lived. They would endlessly choose Test sides for England and buy early newspapers to get the lunchtime scores and thank heaven in September that it was 'only seven more months to the cricket season'. Football was never such a pleasure again as it had been on Saturday evenings in the long stone corridor at Westminster during his first winter at the school (played with a tennis ball, four or five a side), reminding him of playground games at Henley House. But Alan did play for Westminster and later for his Cambridge college.

If Westminster ruined Alan as a mathematician, as he said, it did little to prepare him for being a writer. 'With the English language,' he said, 'we never had any official dealings.' English literature was unknown territory to English schoolboys at this time. John Drinkwater, playwright and poet (whom Alan later was to know and like), said that he left his school not knowing 'whether Milton lived before or after Shakespeare . . . whether Charles Lamb was alive or dead, or what was the difference between a sonnet and a saga.' Drinkwater said that was no exaggeration but the plain truth. If Alan's ignorance was not quite so abysmal, it was still considerable. Alan was already well read in Shakespeare – Henley House had seen to that – but he had to wait until he was in his sixth year at Westminster before he could join the Literary Society and read Shakespeare plays regularly each week, with an occasional Congreve, Sheridan and Goldsmith to encourage his interest in English drama.

Apart from the letters home each Sunday and the illicit letters to each other in class, the boys wrote nothing in English. 'In my seven years there I never wrote so much as one essay for authority.' Obviously the authorities at Westminster did not share J. V. Milne's passionate belief in the importance of writing. 'Boys who will take the trouble to form the habit early in life of clothing their thoughts with appropriate language, will find that they gain clearer ideas. They will know what they know . . . The ability to think consecutively, and to write clearly and to the point, is only attained by study and practice . . . In former days every gentleman was required to be skilful with the sword; in the present day he must wield the Pen.' Westminster seemed to be still living in the days of the sword.

But at least Alan could *read*. Right from the beginning there had been the library, open each evening from 5.15 to 6.15 during the period for 'Occupations'. 'Occupations' covered a lot of things and at first, enthusiast that he was in those early days, Alan tried the Glee Society, Drawing and Gym. But he realized that he wasn't doing these things because he wanted to do them, but only because he felt he ought to improve himself. After that disastrous report, he stopped trying to improve himself and spent 'every evening happily up-Library'. 'Nobody asked you what you were reading, or minded what you read, but the books were there and you were there . . . Of all Westminster institutions this seems to me to have been the best . . . It was wonderfully reassuring to feel through the darkest hours of school that David Copperfield or Becky Sharp or Mr Bennett was waiting for you round the corner, and that nothing could endanger that meeting.' Forty years later, when A. A. Milne came to dramatize *Pride and Prejudice*, he would remember his first reading of it at Westminster. It remained one of his favourite books. The boys were not officially allowed to take books out of the library but, with his new-found ability to do things which were against the rules, Alan would often slip a book up his waistcoat on a Friday and return it the following Monday. Sundays were excellent for reading. As long as the boys turned up for two Abbey services, no one minded what they did the rest of the day. No master spoke to them all day.

The darkest hours of school, the actual classes, could certainly be dark. Alan tells a painful story of being a mathematician in a classical school.

I remember once at school having to do a piece of Latin prose about the Black Hole of Calcutta. The size of the Black Hole was given as 'twenty foot square'. I had no idea how to render this idiomatically, but I knew that a room 20 ft square contained 400 square feet. Also I knew the Latin for one square foot. But you will not be surprised to hear that my form master, a man of culture and education, leapt upon me.

'Quadringenti,' he snapped, 'is 400, not 20.'

'Quite so,' I agreed. 'The room had 400 square feet.'

'Read it again. It says 20 square feet.'

'No, no, 20 feet square.'

He glared at me in indignation. 'What's the difference?' he said.

I sighed and began to explain. I went on explaining. If there had not been other things to do than teaching cultured and educated schoolmasters, I might be explaining still.

The thought that Westminster had managed to produce Ben Jonson, Warren Hastings, Gibbon and Christopher Wren, without particularly trying, seemed to Alan to be used to justify a good deal of indifferent teaching. There was no master he would remember as he would remember his father and H. G. Wells. It was Henley House, not Westminster, that had laid the foundations for his life as a writer. And it would be at Streete Court in the holidays from Westminster that he first discovered the real pleasure of writing.

The most revealing glimpses of Westminster, outside Alan's own account, come from the Captain's handwritten report on Play Term 1899, the first term of Alan's last year at school. 'There was much internal trouble,' Arthur Gaye wrote. 'During the early part of the term, things went on well: my experience as a monitor served me well as Captain, and two of my monitors' (one of these was Alan) 'were quite above reproach, of the other more hereafter. After about a month, however, the first blow fell. In Library a Second Election was seen to draw a picture of a most obscene nature, implicating a fellow Second Election and a Junior. The discovery was made by the master superintending Library "Occupation". He sent the picture to the Headmaster and after Preparation I first learned of the affair.' The boy appearing in the picture 'had been guilty of gross immorality' and was expelled. So was the author of the drawing though, after his parents appealed, he was allowed to return a few days later. The

Junior involved, who had turned 'Queen's evidence', was allowed to remain 'on condition of good behaviour'.

Soon after this event Arthur Gaye, Alan Milne and the other reliable monitor went up to try for scholarships at Trinity, Cambridge, but unfortunately, Gaye reported, he was the only one who was successful. In the absence of the three, the 'unreliable' monitor, a boy called Jacob, was left in charge and proved totally incapable of keeping order. There was a good deal of ragging and a wall was badly stained as the result of someone throwing a mug of beer at another boy. (They drank beer at Westminster and put Alan off it for the rest of his life.)

Worse was eventually to follow as far as Alan was concerned. There was a new matron, Miss Dawson, who seemed to have no appreciation of the Latin Play, the play regularly performed each year just before Christmas, on the last Thursday, Monday and Wednesday of term. Every small detail was hallowed by tradition and one can understand why Miss Dawson was less than enthusiastic; the large dormitory of College was entirely taken over, with stage and auditorium erected within it. The play dominated the whole term from the moment, in the first week, when the Master of the Queen's Scholars put up a list of passages to be learnt by those auditioning for parts. To reduce the amount of disruption in the school a short rehearsal period had been introduced in 1897, which meant that rehearsals had to take place almost every evening. The dormitory was in 'a state of chaos', and the stress was tremendous. Alan had been in the topical Epilogue twice before – as a paperboy in 1893 and as a monkey with Ken in 1894. But now in 1899 he had his first real part – as Geta in Terence's *Adelphi*. Apart from the normal pleasures of performance and excitement, there was the additional joy that each performer received thirty shillings (a considerable sum at that time, when 'thirty bob a week' was the wage of a London clerk trying to keep a whole family). This came from the 'cap' passed round among the audience, which consisted of 'all titled persons and MPs who have sons in the school' (not apparently such parents as the Milnes) and a large number of other distinguished people. Henry James had been in the Dean's party, for instance, in 1897, soon after finishing *The Turn of the Screw*.

At four o'clock on the first day of the Play Juniors were required to be in the dormitory to dust chairs and so on. Everything was laid down. 'A sufficient number of Plots, Topics and Casts must be arranged for the Plot-boys to distribute in the evening. Casts should be placed inside Topics and Topics inside Plots.' 'Copies of the Prologue and Epilogue should be distributed among the Gentlemen of the Press,' whose Latin was obviously not thought to be up to taking it in on the ear. To encourage good notices, presumably, the instructions laid down that 'the Press must be well supplied with drinks during the Play.' And after supper was over the Captain of College had the job of 'keeping order and restraining the drunken.' The play was widely reported in the national press and gave Alan his first taste of reading his own reviews.

Alan had his moment of glory. He could still, forty years later, remember his opening speech as Geta, Sostrata's faithful slave: '*Nunc illud est, cum si omnia omnes sua consilia conferant, atque huic malo salutem quaerant, auxili nil ad ferant.*' He had to be full of righteous indignation and go on and on in that way for some time, pacing up and down in front of the footlights. Electricity had been installed in Wren's dormitory the previous February and it was colder than ever without the heat from the gaslights. Alan as Geta kept his eyes firmly on the audience – and then registered a tremendous start of surprise when he realized he was not alone. '*Heu, perii!*' he thought he probably said, meaning roughly 'We're sunk.'

He loved to remember his performance, forgetting that the school magazine had thought him 'somewhat stiff' and a bit inaudible. His first performance on a sort of stage had been long before at Henley House one Christmas holidays when the boys had dramatized *The Golden Key*, working out scenes and leaving the dialogue for spontaneous improvisation. Alan had played the female lead but never felt drawn to be an actor. And, as he said himself, the Latin Play was hardly likely to give anyone a passion for the theatre, though in 1899 the *Adelphi* was generally judged a great success. The cast had a perfect knowledge of the text and 'did not fall far short of attaining all-round excellence'.

On the last night, Alan and the others celebrated. Arthur Gaye's report as Captain tells us what happened. 'It had always been customary for certain actors and leaving Seniors to sit up in Saigne's after the Play and drink claret-cup and sherry and even smoke. This was no doubt very wrong, but the custom had always been defended by the fact that term was over and we were no longer bound by the rules of College. Matrons had countenanced it and this year we had no hesitation in doing as our predecessors had done. The new matron, who had resented everything connected with the Play, promptly showed up all concerned to the Headmaster, namely three monitors, including myself' and Alan Milne, 'a senior and two Third Elections. He was for expelling the Third Elections, who had been in trouble before, while he was undecided about the rest. In correspondence' (term had now ended and all the boys had dispersed for the holidays) 'I pointed out that it would be most unfair to punish the younger culprits without doing likewise to the older, who were the more to blame. He finally agreed and very generously pardoned us all. Such leniency will not be shown again.' Gaye ended his report, which was obviously going to be seen by the masters: 'I deeply regret that it did not occur to me to stop [the custom] this year.' In fact, as one can imagine, there was a good deal of resentment among the boys that the authorities had not turned a blind eye, as they had in previous years.

Alan spent an uncomfortable Christmas holidays, not knowing what the Headmaster had decided. His whole future was uncertain as he had failed, against all expectation, to get a university scholarship the previous term. His pre-eminence at Westminster as a mathematician was totally unchallenged since Edgar Hackforth's departure for Cambridge, in spite of his lack of devotion to his subject. In the report of the Oxford and Cambridge School Examinations in the summer of 1899, A. A. Milne was mentioned particularly for his papers on Euclid and on 'Geometrical Analytical Conics': 'Milne's work was exceptionally good, no one else solving half as many problems.' The list of principal school prizes that summer shows A. A. Milne won both the Jones Prize for Geometry and the Marshall Memorial Prize. The Gumbleton Prize for English Verse was won by Saxon Sydney-Turner. Incidentally, Arthur Gaye, the Captain who already had his Trinity scholarship secure, followed a very similar path to that of Edgar Hackforth. He went into the Civil Service and became Commissioner of Crown Lands.

Fortunately there was so much going on at Streete Court that Christmas that Alan could ignore, at least some of the time, his problems at Westminster. He must surely have confided in Ken, home from the solicitor's office in Weymouth for the holidays, but presumably, while Arthur Gaye's correspondence with the Headmaster was going on, the parents of the erring boys had not been informed of the disgrace they were in. The Milnes were in charge for the holidays of a family – two boys and two girls – whose parents were in India. The boys, aged twelve and eight, were pupils at Streete Court. The two girls, aged fourteen and ten, were at a neighbouring girls' school. It was a time of national tension. Indeed the unexpected reverses in South Africa had spoilt the many references to the war which were to have been introduced in the Epilogue to the Latin Play at Westminster. But at Streete Court there had never been such an enjoyable Christmas. 'They were nice children,' Alan said of the Anglo-Indian family. There were great games. Then Ken had to go back to his office in Weymouth.

A couple of days later Alan came across the older girl, Ghita, writing. It was an important moment in Alan's life, for Ghita was trying to write a poem for Ken and she asked Alan to help. He looked at what she had written. 'The theme, one of cheerful insult, was good, but the execution was poor. I took some of the bones out, moderated the scansion and arranged for a few rhymes. The result was copied out by Ghita and sent to Ken. In a few days he replied to her with a set of verses which surprised me: verses in the real Calverley tradition.' C. S. Calverley was then, and was to remain, one of Alan's heroes. 'He was the supreme master of one of the loveliest of arts: the Art of Light Verse.' Before this Alan had no idea that Ken could do it. At the bottom of the page, Ken had written to Ghita: 'All my own unaided work – and I bet yours wasn't.'

So Alan wrote back and admitted he had had a hand in Ghita's verses. He then sent some of his own, his first real attempt at light verse, to show what he could do. Ken wrote back from Weymouth: 'Good heavens, you can do it too.' And for the next two years they collaborated, the verses winging their way back and forth between Westminster and Weymouth, and eventually between Cambridge and Weymouth – with occasional appearances in print over the initials A. K. M., which belonged to neither of them and to both of them. It is worth looking in detail at part of one poem they wrote together, which already shows an extraordinary facility. The first line refers to the fact that the poem was requested by Ackie, their uncle, for his school magazine in Hastings.

> You ask for a poem, my ownest own editor –
>   Don't be alarmed at the epithet, pray:
> It occurs in Lord Tennyson's *Maud* – have you read it? – a
>   Poem of merit authorities say.
>
> Shall I write you a parody, smart and satirical,
>   After the manner of *Punch* and the rest –

Or something in dialect, pretty and lyrical,
   Safe to remind you of Burns at his best?

Perhaps you would fancy an 'Ode to an Eider-duck'
   Telling his praises with never a pause:
How he was born a duck, lived – yes, and died a duck,
   Hampered by Nature's inscrutable laws.

Or a rapturous ode on the worth of some Lycidas –
   Blenkinsop Brown he was called when alive,
And reckoned as likely as not an explicit ass:
   Trivial facts not allowed to survive.

'And so on. I was spending some of the holidays with Ken at Weymouth and we wrote this literally together; not, as more usually, by correspondence. The general idea, of course, was old and obvious. As I remember, Ken was responsible for the initiation of the first and fourth verses and I for the other two, but we worked them all out together. It is the third verse to which I invite your attention.

'In the first "final" version – as we thought a few days before it was finished – the last two lines were:

How he was born a duck, lived a duck, died a duck –
   Fettered by Nature's miraculous laws.

'I am still uncertain whether we improved the first of these lines, but I know that we argued about it for hours. There is a charming monotony about this earlier version, which echoes the monotony of a life from which no duck can escape; but I like the break in the rhythm of the other – ("*How he was born a duck, lived – yes, and died a duck*") – and I like the hint of astonishment that even in death he was not divided from himself. I should say, though I cannot certainly remember, that Ken preferred the first version and I the second; modest Ken standing aside and letting the tragedy reveal itself, the more egotistic Alan intruding the writer's personality in comment on that tragedy. The comment had to come, in any case, in the fourth line:

Fettered by Nature's miraculous laws.

'We thought this was very funny and ironic, until the more scholarly Ken pointed out that the one thing which Nature could not be was miraculous; it was a contradiction in terms. I agreed reluctantly, feeling that I ought to have seen this for myself, feeling it still more strongly when he suggested the perfect word "inscrutable". Now it was my turn to assert myself. I said that we ought to improve "fettered". If you were fettered, you were without hope; you knew you couldn't escape, and you threw your hand in. It was much funnier to think of the duck continually trying to be a skylark, and continually being prevented, but always hoping. Some word like "thwarted", or "obstructed" . . . or – Got it! *Hampered. "Hampered by Nature's inscrutable laws"* – we said it over and over to ourselves, loving it.'

Alan went back to school in time for his eighteenth birthday. He had always at Westminster felt unlucky that his birthday came in the middle of January in perhaps 'the unhappiest week of the year, as the Lent Term was the dullest term; to have one's birthday dropped into such a week was to rob it of all its natural delight.' This year, 1900, there was at least a feeling of relief that he had been reprieved, that the celebrations on the last night of the Latin Play had not led to disaster. But there was still the problem of his future. This term would decide his university, if indeed he was to get there at all. After his failure the previous summer, he was not absolutely sure he would. His father had long recovered from the blow of the twelve-year-old's report and had regained his confidence in his youngest son's abilities, but he had made it clear, though Streete Court was now flourishing, that Alan needed to win some financial support. There were closed scholarships and exhibitions for Westminster boys at Christ Church, Oxford, as well as at Trinity, Cambridge. Someone suggested Oxford would be more suitable for his 'particular mathematical talent, which, as far as it existed, was for "pure" not "applied" mathematics'. But Alan had always shouted for Cambridge in the Boat Race and when, in January 1900, he scored a goal for Westminster in a splendid match against Selwyn College, Cambridge, his mind was almost made up.

It was the chance arrival at Westminster of a copy of *Granta*, the Cambridge undergraduate magazine, that decided the matter. R. C. Lehmann had been one of the people who had started it eleven years earlier, and he and all the Cambridge humorists Milne admired had written for it: Barry Pain, E. F. Benson, F. Anstey (whose *Vice Versa* had been published in the year Alan was born) and Owen Seaman. Seaman was already a member of the *Punch* table and soon to be assistant editor. The Milnes were great admirers of *Punch*. Indeed some of Ken's letters home (Ken's not Alan's) had been declared by his father to be 'good enough for *Punch*'. *Granta* had called itself the Cambridge *Punch* until it got the idea of calling *Punch* the London *Granta*.

Alan must have been showing Arthur Gaye the fruits of his light-verse writing with Ken. When they were looking at *Granta* together, Gaye suddenly said to Alan: 'You ought to go to Cambridge and edit that.' So Alan said, quite simply: 'I will.' 'It has an heroic sound,' he commented years later. 'But to anybody who has said "I can do it" at the age of two, saying "I will" at the age of eighteen is easy.'

Alan succeeded, that Lent term, in winning a subsizarship to Trinity College, Cambridge. It was a sort of minor scholarship, open only to Westminster boys, and worth £40 a year for three years. He was also awarded a Sanwaies exhibition, which was worth an additional £23. He had not yet passed Little-go, the qualifying examination for Cambridge, and needed for that to brush up his classics (almost entirely neglected for the past four years); but most of the time he played games, wrote long letters and verses to Ken in Weymouth, talked and tried not to get too involved in the College rows.

Alan joined the Debating Society when Ken left school: he seemed to have so much more time, and he didn't know quite what to do with it. As an adult, he hated public speaking and his first experience of it at Henley House had been ignominious. (Asked to speak on Gymnastics at the age of eight, he had managed only a phrase muttered in his ear by his neighbour: 'Gymnastics strengthens the muscles.') At Westminster in his last year he spoke a great deal. The most interesting proposal, seconded by Alan Milne, was that 'the railways should be entirely under government control', nearly fifty years before nationalization. The motion was narrowly defeated in spite of a strongly felt speech by Alan, full of typical exaggeration. It was, he said, ridiculous 'that a man residing, say, in Thanet,' in other words at Streete Court, Westgate-on-Sea, 'should take five or six hours to travel his seventy miles in what was little better than a cattle-truck,' while a man living in the Midlands could travel at three times the speed in superb carriages. 'This state of affairs would surely be done away with, were the State to take control of the railways.'

The Debating Society was not a very well-ordered organization. Indeed, hardly had Alan joined the previous year than he had resigned as part of a mass walkout of Queen's Scholars after the Secretary, a Scholar, had been suspended by the President, a Town boy, nominally for disputing a ruling of the chair, but really for protesting at the abusive language used to describe some Scholars who were being proposed for membership.

Alan's last term was also not without trouble. Arthur Gaye reported that 'things looked hopeful at the start' but the Third and Fourth Elections became increasingly unruly. 'I tried kindness. I tried severity: they grovelled outwardly and resorted to covert abuse of College law. I much regret now that I did not allow the leader of the gang to be expelled,' as the Headmaster had first proposed after the drunken celebration two terms earlier. 'I twice yielded to misplaced humanity and begged him off; I had done well to have remembered before the fable of the frozen serpent.' Gaye, who would himself be leaving for Trinity with Alan, warned the Headmaster not to give the culprits any power the next year. 'The issue at stake is incalculable.'

It is interesting to see from the College records that the gloomy forebodings of Alan's friend were justified, according to the Captain of College in the following year, but that in the autumn term of 1901, when the unruly scholars of two years earlier were themselves in power, in spite of Gaye's warnings, they wrote in the book: 'The entries of the last two years were full of gross exaggerations.' They said that Arthur Gaye was himself to blame for 'culpable mismanagement'. Whatever the rights and wrongs of the case, Alan's last year at Westminster was not idyllic. He had had his fair share of success, and he had celebrated, like everyone else in England, the Relief of Mafeking. But he was very glad to leave in the summer of 1900, having been, as he said himself, 'a Westminster boy for far too long'.

It was difficult, Alan saw, to estimate his debt to Westminster. 'It is not enough to reckon up my assets and liabilities on leaving. As the landlady suggested when the lodger complained of the fleas, I may have brought them with me.' 'When I read that Shelley was despised and persecuted at Eton, I reflect that he still came out Shelley.' Alan had not been despised and persecuted at Westminster (and he knew he was not a Shelley). In fact he had done rather well. But there was no doubt that that one crushing report when he was twelve had changed his idea of himself and his relation to the school. It had turned him permanently into someone who would never accept without questioning the judgement of the establishment. It had not been fair. The establishment was often unfair. It had confirmed some divergence in him which had been sown when he was much younger, fighting inwardly against his outward appearance, against the way that he was expected to behave. Westminster had made it impossible for him to be a civil servant, to be one of those people who, in words his father used, 'go to their business in the morning and return to their puddings in the evening.' Westminster had, in spite of itself, made it more likely that Alan would be a writer.

It had made him see that it might be possible to do what he wanted to do and not to put much effort into things he didn't want to do. He had been able to work at his own pace, not often to feel that impatience he would later often feel, 'waiting, waiting, waiting' for fools to catch up. He had already a good sense of his own particular skills and talents, undeveloped as they were. He was still nominally a Christian but he had begun to think for himself, to realize that his conscience was not always an inspired voice, but rather the voice of those who had taught him – not necessarily the voice of truth, but of what others thought true.

Westminster had also confirmed in him a dislike of rows and a natural puritanism or prudishness he would have all his life. The boys had allowed him not to laugh at dirty jokes and he was grateful for that. 'They were all rather nice about it, apologizing if I were present in the way one would apologize for telling a story from Aberdeen in the presence of a Scotsman.' Alongside his enormous enjoyment of the lighter side of life, there was something in him already of what Frank Swinnerton would call 'the sternness of a Covenanter'. He could never bear to give the Devil any really good tunes.

Alan Milne's affection for Westminster seemed to increase as the years went by. He would take a particular interest in it when Ken's sons in their turn became scholars, King's Scholars, as they were by then. He would not send his own son there. Westminster's importance to him was mainly perhaps that he had shared so much of it with Ken, as he had shared so much else. When Alan Milne died he left the school a large share of his estate.

— 4 —

Cambridge

A. A. MILNE WENT UP to Trinity College, Cambridge in the Michaelmas term of 1900. He went up before full term in order to pass his qualifying Little-go, having failed an earlier attempt while still at school. It was quite common, if rather nerve-wracking, to take the examination at the last moment like this. He was given rooms on P staircase in Whewell's Court and kept them for seven terms until, to his pleasure, he was able to move into Great Court for his last two. Whewell's Court, across Trinity Street from the Great Gate, is that 'gloomy but imposing' collection of Victorian Gothic buildings, which would have the advantage for Milne of being almost exactly half-way between the hall of Trinity and the *Granta* office at 43 Sidney Street, just opposite Sidney Sussex. A guidebook of the period says the rooms of Whewell's Court were 'comfortable and picturesque habitations'. Milne's bedder hung up the navy blue velvet curtains Mrs Milne had lovingly made at Streete Court and admired the curious cushions. Both curtains and cushions were embroidered in gold thread with the arms of Westminster and Trinity.

Alan Milne signed the Admissions Book on 30 September ('native place, London; present address, Streete Court, Westgate') together with an interesting collection of bright young men. Several of his fellow undergraduates were from the Empire – India, Ceylon, Australia, South Africa. Most were from the major English public schools: Eton, Oundle, Charterhouse. There were a Rothschild and a Sassoon from Harrow. There were several he knew already, who had been with him at Westminster, including Arthur Gaye, the boy who had suggested he should edit *Granta*. And already in residence, just starting his second year, was Saxon Sydney-Turner, whom Alan Milne had known since he was eleven when they had been elected Queen's Scholars together.

Cambridge had gone to Sydney-Turner's head when he had arrived at Trinity the year before with a group which included Lytton Strachey, Thoby Stephen and the two men who married his sisters, Virginia and Vanessa: Leonard Woolf and Clive Bell. If he hadn't been at school with Sydney-Turner, it is doubtful whether Milne, in such a large college, would have met these remarkable young men. Strachey described Sydney-Turner as 'a wild and unrestrained freshman, who wrote poems, never went to bed, and declaimed Swinburne and Sir Thomas Browne till four in the morning in the Great Court at Trinity.' By the time Milne joined him, he had become pale and quiet, 'ghost-like and shadowy', in Leonard Woolf's words. 'He rarely committed himself to any positive opinion or even statement. His conversation – if it could rightly be called conversation – was extremely spasmodic, elusive and allusive . . . Saxon quite naturally talked, looked, acted, *was* a character in an unwritten novel by Henry James.'

Certainly Sydney-Turner was not the sort of person Alan Milne would have been likely to become friends with if they had met for the first time at Trinity. (Milne had barely then heard of Henry James and would never enjoy him.) But they had slept in the same Wren dormitory for years, eaten the same awful food and read Shakespeare plays together at Westminster. Woolf suggests how important these school connections were. He himself had felt very lonely at the beginning; most St Paul's boys went on to Oxford. He had met Sydney-Turner by the purest chance as they looked at the notices after dining in Hall, and it was through Sydney-Turner he met Russell Gaye, Arthur Gaye's eldest brother. Gaye rarely talked to anyone (he would eventually kill himself) but he 'admitted Saxon and me into a restricted acquaintanceship because Saxon was at Westminster' with him. So it was with Alan Milne.

Leonard Woolf and Alan Milne had, in fact, a good deal in common, but they were never to progress beyond that sort of 'restricted acquaintanceship'. Woolf, too, had known (after his father's death) what it was to think carefully before spending a sixpence and to know that his future depended on his brain and his ability to win scholarships. Like Alan and Ken, Leonard Woolf and his brother, Herbert, had as boys cycled all over England. Both young men liked cricket and Jane Austen. They both considered Thomas Hardy the novelist who mattered most to them and both would recognize Samuel Butler's The Way of all Flesh, when it was published in 1903, as a book of special significance to them. Woolf hailed Butler as 'a leader'. Butler and Hardy, 'so amazingly different from each other', 'were very definitely on our side'. Milne would go so far in 1922 as to call *The Way of all Flesh* 'the best novel in the English language'. Woolf and Milne were definitely on the same side. They shared not only an increasing radicalism, but also an ingrained puritanism. Lytton Strachey would tease Woolf, suggesting he should form a League for the Advancement of Social Purity. Milne could have been a founding member. He would sympathize with what Strachey described as Woolf's 'fractional yet uncontrollable recoil from an obscene bit of gossip'.

It is interesting to speculate how different a writer Milne might have been if he had become more involved with these friends who would one day form the very core of what has become known as 'Bloomsbury'. Alan Milne's brain was, in fact, very like that of Sydney-Turner – brains that would, when crossword puzzles were invented twenty years later, make them both champion solvers. Woolf also could explain convincingly, though he was a classicist, the particular appeal of mathematics: 'The curious ecstasy which comes from *feeling* the mind work smoothly and imaginatively upon difficult and complicated problems.' Alan Milne, as a Queen's Scholar at Westminster, had escaped the intense philistinism Woolf had found at St Paul's, the contempt for all things intellectual. At St Paul's not only the boys but also nearly all the masters despised the intellect and the arts and everything connected with them. So Woolf said. And yet this was the same school, at the same period, where the young E. H. Shepard had later resented his lack of general education because he was encouraged to do nothing but draw and paint and to put all his energies into winning a scholarship to art school.

Leonard Woolf had found the passage from boyhood to manhood 'in many respects the most difficult period psychologically' of his life. 'The metamorphosis is much more commonly painful – and more painful – than novels or autobiographies admit or depict.' Milne, in his autobiography, certainly never depicts any pain. And he admits to it only in one fleeting sentence, and this to the pain of love rather than of lust or the first discovery of sex: 'How hard to realize that one's father, the elderly Olympian, may also have endured the agonies and ecstasies of love, as we have endured them!'

In a letter to *Granta* Alan Milne would use the phrase, 'we have had for once the bad form to be serious', and it was this dislike of being serious that not only makes it very difficult sometimes to know what he was really going through, but also made it difficult for him to sustain the sort of friendships that would nourish Leonard Woolf and the others for the rest of their lives. Woolf actually said, 'We were very serious young men', though Strachey's 'cynical wit and humour' disguised a mind that was 'fundamentally and habitually ribald'. Neither seriousness nor ribaldry appealed to Alan Milne.

He seems to have taken in his stride his separation two years before from his beloved brother. (Of course, they were still in constant contact through the post and in vacations.) He seems to admit lightly, without anguish, that the same body can be inhabited by jealousy, ambition, pride and selfishness – and by a spirit that is still eager, gentle, inquisitive, generous and vulnerable. Woolf wrote of his own puberty. Milne said nothing of his. It is as if we are meant to realize that his dislike of what he calls 'lavatory jokes' extends to a dislike of any mention of the more exciting activities of the body. One can't help imagining that he must have gone through similar agonies to those Woolf describes: 'How dense the barbaric darkness was in which the Victorian middle-class boy and youth was left to drift sexually is shown by the fact that no relation or teacher, indeed no adult, ever mentioned the subject of sex to me. No information or advice on this devastating fever in one's blood and brain was ever given to me. Love and lust, like the functions of the bowels and the bladder, were subjects which could not be discussed or even mentioned. The effect of this was, I believe, wholly bad, leading to an unhealthy obsession and a buttoning up of mind and emotion.'

I quote this particular passage from Leonard Woolf's *Sowing* because it uses the very phrase Christopher Milne used in his autobiography: 'My father's heart remained buttoned up all through his life.' This 'buttoning up', I think, was not a 'natural' aspect of Alan Milne's character but, at least in some sense, a consequence of being born a Victorian. His father, who was in so many ways ahead of his time – so natural, so warm – revealed in a letter written several years after his wife's death that he also was inhibited: 'Sometimes memory goes back and I wish that I had in some way *shown* my love more plainly. It was always there. If I could only see her for an hour and ask forgiveness for this neglect.'

Milne's contact with girls before he went up to Cambridge had not been extensive. There were the four girl cousins, his uncle Ackie's children, in Hastings; Ken and Alan had often cycled down to see the family in the holidays. There had been the girls at Streete Court, whose parents were in India. Then, on one holiday in 1898, Alan had felt the first stirrings of sexual interest and writes about it with typical self-mockery: 'Father and I took what he thought was going to be a pleasure-cruise to Norway that summer. I was sixteen, just beginning to fancy myself at cricket. I was also just beginning to grow up. I was, in fact, unbearable.

'There was a very attractive young woman on board who had all the men round her. I was on the outskirts of the crowd, hoping for, and sometimes getting, a smile. In my pink-and-white tie (second XI) and green and blue cap (College colours) I could probably have got a smile from anybody. When she sat swinging her legs on the deck rail, gaily holding her own against all our compliments, mine wordless but by far the most sincere; when at moments she caught my eye, or her eye caught my tie, and she gave me that warm, sudden smile which meant – that we two had some secret which the others did not share; then I felt that I could have died for her, or thrown my cap overboard (though I was more doubtful about this) if she had desired it. Was I in love for the first time? I don't know. The sea moderated, her ladyship emerged from the cabin in which, solitary, she had been praying for death, and her ladyship's maid, that adorable creature, returned demurely to her duties. It was a great shock to all the men. They went about pretending that they had always known it, but had wanted the little thing to have a good time while she could. My distant adoration left me less compromised. Without any embarrassment I transferred my affections to the charms of deck-cricket and a girl called Ellen. Ellen was my own age. I remember her surname, but shall not mention it here in case she is no longer my own age; I also remember her face. Do you suppose she remembers *my* name or *my* face? Of course not. O faithless Ellen! I haven't given you a thought since 1898, but it seems that I can never quite forget.'

Milne used this incident in some verses he wrote in April 1940, when he imagined that without the distracting charms of Ellen, metamorphosed into Matilda, he might have been able, at a time when Norway was much in the news, to have contributed some first-hand knowledge of the subject:

> We reached Stavanger. Did I shout
> 'Behold Stavanger! Key to Norway'?
> I did not. No, I lay in wait,
> In sight of Cabin 28,

> And caught Matilda coming out
> And kissed her in the doorway.

The whole thing seems likely to have started with that Norway/
doorway rhyme and it seems unlikely that he actually kissed her. In
1898, and indeed for many years afterwards, it was not 'good form',
in Alan Milne's circles, for a young man to kiss a girl without
intending marriage. At Cambridge it was impossible for a young
woman to be alone in the same room as a young man (even her
brother) without a chaperon. It *was* apparently possible to take a
girl out on the river. Perhaps it was considered sufficiently public.
Clarissa, a typical Milne girl (precursor of Dahlia and Myra and
Celia), goes canoeing in *Granta* and there was (one imagines and
hopes) a real-life counterpart. She is a self-confident, not entirely
respectful girl ('pert' could be the word), not very well educated but
bright, *very* good at lawn tennis and prepared to watch cricket under
a pink parasol. Indeed at tennis she can beat single-handed both
Jeremy and 'I', if not the jelly-fish – characters who will appear later
in this story.

It would be twenty-five years before A. A. Milne could write:
'What I feel is that love and marriage are two different things.' At
this stage, at least in his writing, love and marriage constantly go
together. All the girls in the verses and sketches Milne wrote at
Cambridge are nubile in the most exact sense – all love is seen as
courtship.

One of Milne's first poems published over his own initials was
called 'In Case of Rejection – What to do when a marriage-proposal
fails'. In a prose piece, 'Could you marry me now, do you think?'
he asks Clarissa, having changed his hair-style and acquired a pink
waistcoat. Marriage seemed to be much on his mind, though it would
be more than ten years before he would marry. Ken, in Weymouth,
was falling in love with Maud Innes, the sixth of the eight daughters
of a builder and developer, who had stories of Thomas Hardy from
his days as a young architect in the town. They would be engaged
in the summer of 1902, Alan Milne's second summer at Cambridge.

When the brothers were together in the Easter vacation of 1901,
they prepared a sort of autograph confessions book called 'Bookworms and Beauty', in which they intended to ask their friends to
write. In those sexist times the bookworms were male and the beauties female. Unfortunately only the 'instructions' pages survive. The
one for the 'ladies' goes like this:

To the Ladies

1 All women are beautiful: some are more beautiful than others: candidates for admission must be more beautiful than others.
2 All women are young: some are younger than others: candidates for admission must be younger than others.
3 All ladies are ready to oblige: some are readier than others: those who consent to write their names in this book will be readier than most.

> If (pardon me) I think you fair,
> And hope to find you tender-hearted;
> Thus pray forgive me that I dare,
> (As others do) to think you fair,
> And turn, oh turn not to despair
> The hope wherewith I fondly started!
> So could I care to think you fair,
> And hope to find you tender-hearted.
> A. K. M.

The writing is Ken's, but the initials on the verse show they were still writing together. They were still writing – and they expected their friends to be writers too. The instructions for the Bookworms (who were to be male friends aged between four and forty, of 'literary tastes and talents') included the suggestion that they should write down the dates of such interesting events as 'i) The sending off of your first MS, ii) Its return (You may just as well forgive the Editor: he has probably forgiven you), iii) Your first appearance in print. (Contributions either to your local rag, or to such papers as "Hearth and Home" and the "War Cry" may be ignored.)'

'We all wanted to be writers,' Leonard Woolf wrote later. It was a time 'of conscious revolt against the social, political, religious, moral, intellectual and artistic institutions, beliefs and standards of our fathers and grandfathers . . . The battle, which was against what for short one may call Victorianism, had not yet been won, and what was so exciting was our feeling that we were part of the revolution, that victory or defeat depended to some small extent upon what we did, said or wrote . . . We were not part of a negative movement of destruction against the past. We were out to construct something new; we were in the van of the builders of a new society which should be free, rational, civilized, pursuing truth and beauty. It was all tremendously exhilarating.'

If Alan Milne could not have put it quite like that at the time (not recognizing yet a hunger in himself to be more serious), later, looking back, he would acknowledge that he had exactly those feelings as the country mourned the death of the old Queen and prepared for the Coronation of Edward VII. He was certainly exhilarated. Milne describes himself at Cambridge (and there is no contrary evidence) as not just light-hearted, but light-headed. 'We were very young in those days and young, it still seems to me, in the right sort of way . . . laughing too easily, if you like, too loudly, if you will have it so, but laughing . . . Life for us was not "rather a problem" and at twenty most to be enjoyed.' Writing in 1924, just before the publication of *When We Were Very Young*, he would say, 'Does any of that divine youth hang over us still? If it be so, let us thank Cambridge and the *Granta* for casting the spell on us.' Cambridge confirmed in him a belief in play, in pleasure, in making people smile and laugh. He always saw the point of enjoyment and he cultivated his awareness of quiddity, of the oddity of life. He did not give an impression of frivolity but rather of a sort of shy confidence, a paradox often commented on by people trying to describe him.

He gave the impression that there was more going on below the surface than he revealed. Woolf and his friends would muse on 'the withdrawal of the self into the inner recesses of one's being behind the façade, and the series of psychological curtains which one interposed between oneself and the outside world'. Alan Milne would go out and play football for the college and seem, as he had often seemed at Westminster, to be a conventional games-playing mathematician, but the psychological curtains would get thicker as the years went by. E. H. Shepard would use the word 'cagey'. A. A. Milne was always reluctant to give himself away. Rupert Hart-Davis would use the word 'aloof'. But at Cambridge Milne was not holding himself apart.

He described himself as 'not scornful, not cynical, not superior'. He was an optimist. His father had said, 'Let a man live to be a hundred, his first twenty years will be the greater part of his life. In those years the man was made.' And so it was. Cambridge established A. A. Milne as the sort of writer he would always be, however much he might try to be otherwise, however many different forms of writing he would explore. He was not an intellectual but he had a quiet passion for using his brain. He knew he would never be Milton or Fielding, or Shakespeare. And the man within the buttoned jacket would always be, fundamentally, the same man. It was already too late for anything to change.

From the moment when Alan Milne and Arthur Gaye had looked at *Granta* together in the monitors' room at Westminster, Milne had begun to get an idea of what he wanted to do – not just to edit *Granta* but to edit it as a step to something else, preferably writing for *Punch*. He might spend his life, not in an office or a classroom, but as his own master, doing something he enjoyed doing. It was a heady prospect. 'The aim of the majority,' he would write in *Granta*, 'is to find some employment which is not without honour and not without remuneration.' He wanted honour and remuneration too, but most of all he wanted to be free to do what he wanted to do. It began to seem possible that he might try to make his living as a writer – well, as a journalist anyway. Harmsworth's success and the experience of H. G. Wells, which he had known about almost as long as he could remember, made it not quite as strange a choice as it might have been for another young mathematician.

For the moment he was still a mathematician. His bookshelves in his rooms in Whewell's Court were full of clean, uncut copies of books such as *Functions of a Quaternion*, books about hydromechanics and the dynamics of a particle and differential equations. Some of them would look not much less new at the end of his three years, when phrases from his subject ('a sphere in a uniform field', 'circular currents' and 'a couple of opposite poles') would seem most useful as the stuff of light verse.

Milne's first interview with his supervisor shows that he was not quite as much in charge of his own fate as he would have wished. The don was a Scot called Gilbert Walker, university lecturer in mathematics and a Fellow of Trinity. Milne was planning to play football every afternoon, and didn't feel inclined to work immediately afterwards, so proposed to go to Walker in the morning at some hour when he didn't have a lecture. 'And will ye come in for the for-r-r-r-noon or the after-r-r-r-noon?' Walker asked. Milne recorded, 'My three-quarter English blood boiled at the idea of saying "for-r-r-rnoon", politeness forbade me to say "morning". So I went to him in the afternoon and never ceased to regret it.'

It was pleasanter to follow football with tea, though you might find yourself with a group of young men, all from the same school when you weren't. Eating muffins was the proper thing to do between four and five, but it was confusing if you could not discriminate between the pet name of somebody's housemaster and the common synonym for a particular kind of sweet only obtainable from that particular school's 'sock shop'. After Westminster's 'seven years of starvation', food was one of the major pleasures of Cambridge. It was delightful to be ordering his own breakfast and lunch. Even in formal Hall, every evening, the food was very good. Milne tells a story that on his first evening a shy freshman was puzzled by being offered by the waiter, 'Capercailzie or beef, sir?' Capercailzie, a sort of large grouse, has two pronunciations (and indeed two spellings) and is hardly familiar in either. The shy freshman had to settle for the beef. This story, so definitely placed by Milne in his autobiography in September 1900, crops up in *Granta* on 22 February 1902. ('The following conversation occurred in the hall of a well-known College the other day . . .') But it is Milne himself using it, and merely altering the date doesn't mean it isn't true.

Another story relating to a meal sounds more apocryphal. It was the habit of the Master of Trinity, Dr Butler (that remarkable man who had long before been translated from a Cambridge curacy to be Headmaster of Harrow at the age of twenty-six), to entertain undergraduates at breakfast. Apparently he came into the dining room of the Lodge one wintry morning, looked out of the window towards the river, and said cheerfully to the assembled freshmen. 'Well, we have a little sun this morning . . .' And it was the most nervous freshman who responded, 'I hope Mrs Butler is all right.'

Alan Milne was not nervous. After Westminster he was not over-awed by the Wren library or (as Frank Sidgwick put it in a *Granta* verse) by the thought that Tennyson might have put the same spoon, dated 1798, to his mouth, or Macaulay or Thackeray known its 'curling lip'. He was beginning to feel very much at home. He played outside-left in the Freshmen's football match and appeared as 'a silent Greek maiden' in a splendid production of the *Agamemnon*, with music by Sir Hubert Parry, and a sumptuous souvenir programme published by *Granta*. Several members of the *Granta* staff were in the production.

He bought himself two pipes, silver-bound, in a morocco case, and would be a pipe-smoker for the rest of his life. He opened a bank account and established his cheque signature as Alan A. Milne, a form he would use for nothing else, so that for ever afterwards he would know at once that any letter so addressed was a bill, receipt or charitable appeal. His father had worked out the cost of Barry's articles and maintenance and decided that each of the boys should have £1,000, in suitable instalments, as a start in life. It was of course a considerable sum of money in those days – the equivalent of at least £25,000 in today's terms. It suggests how well Streete Court was doing. Alan planned to use less than £250 of it each year at Cambridge, supplementing his scholarship money, so he would have some in hand when he went down.

He seems to have managed his money quite well, though of course he felt there was never quite enough of it. He had occasion to learn the meaning of the phrase 'refer to drawer' and would write in *Granta* of his unpaid tailor's bill. In a series called 'The Complete Letter-Writer', he would give advice on how to write 'to one's father, asking for a small advance', telling a tragic tale of a young man who has pawned everything but a photo of his father in a silver frame. With Ken he would perpetrate a dreadful parody of Tennyson:

> I am broke as thy stones, O sea!
> . . . I am broke as a man can be.
> O for the touch of a five-pound note
> And the joy of a paid-off bill.

Alan Milne started bombarding *Granta* with verse from the moment he arrived in Cambridge. The editor in his first year was Edwin Montagu, also of Trinity. Montagu's name is now familiar as that of the man who finally married Venetia Stanley, the object of Asquith's extraordinary devotion when he was Prime Minister. Montagu was himself extraordinary – the radical son of a Jewish millionaire, Lord Swaythling, he distinguished himself most as Secretary of State for India. When he died the Maharajah of Alwar said, 'He was our friend, faithful and just to us.' Asquith, whom he loved, had reason to be prejudiced and described him as 'a bundle of moods and nerves and symptoms, intensely self-absorbed'. It was through him, perhaps, that Milne met many of the people he would later know in London, including Edward Marsh and Raymond Asquith, the son of the Prime Minister, whom Milne would describe as 'the most brilliant man I have ever met'.

Montagu took pleasure in claiming to have discovered Milne. 'I think my proudest recollection,' he wrote in the celebration of twenty-five years of *Granta*, published in the year he died, 'is that it was during my Editorship that A.A.M. – A. A. Milne – sometimes in collaboration with his brother, wrote for publication. I remember how I rejected – how arrogant we were! – his first contributions, telling him to persevere and that he might one day learn to write.' The Milnes' first verses were not accepted by Montagu until Alan's second term. They appeared in *Granta* on 4 February 1901 over the

initials A.K.M. and were called 'Sonnets of Love (and other things)'.
Three weeks later their prose piece 'The very latest method of self-
defence' appeared, followed by two more poems that Lent term and
just one in the summer when, in fact, Montagu had left most of the
work to a fellow undergraduate called J. C. Stobart, who was reputed
to have written the whole of the term's first issue (sixteen pages)
himself. Editors (Alan Milne would be among them) tended to think
the products of their own pens superior to the (few) unsolicited
manuscripts that arrived in the office in Sidney Street.

Milne *would* be among them, but it seemed highly unlikely at this
point. Edwin Montagu was soon to become President of the Union.
He already had the air of one who would be, at thirty-six, the
youngest minister in Asquith's cabinet. Such was the editor of *Granta*.
Milne was merely one of his occasional contributors, and of contributions that were not entirely his own.

He tells a story of stopping at a pub in Bletchley in March 1901
on the way back from a football match in Oxford. 'While I was
shyly drinking my ginger-beer, and wishing that I liked beer and
whisky more than I liked rice-pudding, which was not at all, I heard
no less a person than the Captain of the side say to no less a person
than one of the "blues" in the side: "Did you see those awfully good
verses in *The Granta* this week – a new sort of limerick by somebody
called A.K.M.?" I plunged a glowing face into the ginger-beer. This
was authorship. If only Ken had been next to me, so that we could
have nudged each other and grinned, and talked it over happily
together afterwards. Well, I would write to him tomorrow.

'It was unlucky for poor old Ken that our verses were appearing
in *The Granta* and not in the *Weymouth Times*. As we went on
contributing, it gradually became accepted that I alone was A.K.M.,
disguising myself under these alien initials, presumably from modesty.
A few friends knew the truth, but to others a brother in Dorsetshire
seemed as remote from reality as a Bunbury in Shropshire or the dog
that you go to see a man about. Our contributions came out regularly
now, and from time to time somebody would say "I liked your last
thing in *The Granta*", of which a shy smile seemed the appropriate
acknowledgement. To go on: "Well, as it happens, I have a brother
down in Dorsetshire" sounded like the beginning of a new and
irrelevant anecdote desperately in need of an audience. With an
apologetic nod the other hurried on his way.

'Ken may have guessed that this was happening, though I don't think he would have resented it, but it made little difference; for, at the end of the summer term, he announced his withdrawal from the partnership. His reason was that I could do "this sort of thing" just as well without him, and that he would prefer to try some other sort of thing without me. In short, his heart wasn't in frivolity, he wanted to be more serious. He put it, as he would, charmingly, making it seem that there had never really been a "K." in A. K. M., making it seem that I had been generously carrying him on my back for two years. This was so completely untrue that I protested violently against any idea of separation; indeed, I felt miserable at the thought of it. It was in his second letter that he confessed to a wish to be alone.

'Well, it was for him to say. If he wished it, he should write essays for the *Cornhill*, while I wrote nonsense for the *Granta*. And good luck to both of us.'

Alan Milne gives the impression in this passage from his auto-biography that Ken's decision not to write with him any longer came at the end of his first summer term. In fact their partnership continued throughout Alan's second year – the last joint poem appearing in *Granta* on 4 June 1902.

In the second term of his first year, Alan Milne was invited several times to be a 'reading visitor' at meetings of the Trinity College Shakespeare Society. This was a rather exclusive old-established society in which at this time Woolf, Stephen, Strachey and Sydney-Turner played leading parts. Edwin Montagu was also a member. At Milne's first meeting it was *The Taming of the Shrew* and Sydney-Turner read Kate. There was an even more exclusive society, the X Society, founded only the year before by the same group, the purpose of which was to read work other than Shakespeare's. On 2 March 1901 Milne was invited to take part in a reading of Webster's *The White Devil* in Saxon Sydney-Turner's rooms in New Court. He read Cornelia, the French Ambassador and the Doctor.

In his second year Milne's presence at the Shakespeare Society is recorded in Leonard Woolf's own handwriting. Woolf was then the secretary of the Society and Lytton Strachey was President. It was *The Merchant of Venice*. Woolf was inevitably Shylock and Strachey read Portia. Thoby Stephen took Gratiano, Lorenzo and Balthazar. 'Mr Milne as a reading visitor took the parts of Antonio and Nerissa . . . The evening was marked by no incident worthy of com-memoration except for one of those miraculous coincidences for which the Society is justly famous. The presenting of the letter to the

Duke was contemporaneous with, upon the opening of the door, the appearance of a corporeal epistolary messenger.'

It was not until the Lent term of his second year that Milne was elected a member of the society. It was on an evening with a memorable reading of *The Winter's Tale*. Woolf was now President and signed the minutes that recorded that 'the true love of Messrs Woolf and Sydney-Turner as Florizel and Perdita was deservedly successful and Mr Strachey as Autolycus said with a not unjustifiable bravery "I can bear my part . . ." The realistic solidarity of Mr Stephen's impersonation of the Clown was also acclaimed.' When they started reading *Richard II* the following week Sydney-Turner was the King and Milne had the unsympathetic part of Northumberland, with the second Herald and a Captain thrown in. He did not appear the following Thursday and was supposed to pay a fine of 2/6 for failing to turn up without giving two days' notice. It is doubtful whether he actually paid up; the Society's finances were never very well organized. One term the Treasurer neglected to collect any subscriptions or pay any bills: 'The Society through the carelessness of past officials is left with the heavy burden of 1/9, a debt for which the Treasurer for this term feels no responsibility.' Milne didn't miss much by not turning up. It was a continuation of *Richard II* and 'except for Mr Woolf's rendering of Richard, the reading was somewhat languishing, and dull and somnolent, many members being often found asleep at the critical moment.'

Fortunately he *was* there on 6 March. This particular evening makes one wonder why there was any need for the X Society because it was a meeting of the Shakespeare Society and they read *She Stoops to Conquer*. Milne got to read only two servants, one 'fellow' and the maid, and had little chance to make an impression. But it was a memorable evening.

The great success of the meeting was chiefly due to an unintentionally prophetic omission in allotting the parts. When Mrs Hardcastle should have opened the proceedings, there was naught but the silence that preceded a storm. Mr Sydney-Turner at once rushed out and returned with the said storm in the person of Lady Strachey, whose magnificent and dramatic impersonation of the defaulting lady gave to the proceedings a lively vigour seldom found in the meetings of the Society. Inspired by her force, all the members surpassed themselves . . .

Lady Strachey, Lytton's mother, who happened to be in Cambridge that week, was, it was thought, 'the first lady who has ever honoured a meeting of the Society'. Though 'passionately intellectual', according to Woolf, she had published a volume of *Nursery Lyrics* in 1893, which would be reissued not long before Milne's own *When We Were Very Young*. She was well known as a magnificent reader of poetry. When she was old and blind, long after that evening in Trinity, Leonard Woolf recorded how he and Virginia saw her sitting one evening under a tree in Gordon Square. 'We went and sat down by her and somehow we got on to the subject of Milton's *Lycidas* . . . She recited the whole of it to us superbly without hesitating over a word.'

Alan Milne had also, in the Michaelmas term of 1901, been proposed by Arthur Gaye for membership at the 757th meeting of the Magpie and Stump, the Trinity Debating Society. There was lots going on, but he would not put his heart and soul into any of it (he would not even play football that winter), because all his energies were concentrated on *Granta*. He had had three poems of his own accepted by the magazine that Michaelmas term (including 'To Alfred Austin, after reading his latest'), when to his absolute amazement he received a letter from Clement Jones, also of Trinity, who had succeeded Edwin Montagu, asking if he would take over as editor the following term, Lent 1902. 'This was almost the biggest surprise of my life. The most surprising thing was that he took twenty pages to elaborate his theme: the pleasure and profit to be derived from editorship and my supreme fitness for the job: when four words "Will you be editor?" would have been enough. I suppose that I was the only possible person in sight, and he had to be sure of getting the paper off his hands somehow. It was a little disappointingly easy. There is no fun in saying "I will" grandly, and then being as good as told that, willy-nilly, you've got to. Well, anyway, I was editor.' He had been in the right place at the right time. The link between Westminster and Trinity had been fortunate for his ambition; he was at the right college. (In the years up to 1914 Trinity had thirty-one *Granta* editors; Clare, the next college in the list, only four.)

The job that had fallen so easily into Alan Milne's lap was not an easy one. There were not crowds of young men eager to take it on. According to the editor who succeeded Milne, it required an iron constitution. Indeed even an iron constitution would be likely to be overthrown. 'Men may be found of a gallant spirit who set out on their task lightly and complacently, and lay down their waste-paper baskets, embittered wrecks. How callous are the majority to their sufferings. Vicious criticism is their sole reward.' It was even said, on unreliable authority, that 'no man has edited the *Granta* for two consecutive terms and kept clear of a lunatic asylum or a cemetery'. In his second term Milne would thankfully enlist Hugh Vere Hodge, a classical scholar of Trinity, as co-editor 'and make him do all the work which I didn't like'. Each successive editor was nominally the proprietor and, although the printers handled the business side of things, he was actually responsible not only for finding his own successor but for handing on a thriving magazine.

Undergraduate journalism at Cambridge at the beginning of the century was not in a very good state. At Oxford six periodicals flourished; Cambridge had problems keeping two going. In Milne's last year a desperate editor appealed to everyone to have a try. How in the name of common sense do you know that you can't write unless you try? 'One does not expect a Calverley in every generation, but it cannot be denied that at present both the quality and the quantity of literature worthy of the name emanating from this university must be seen to be below the traditional standard.' In the surrounding desert, Milne blossomed like the rose. Ten years later a newspaper profile would say he had made *Granta* 'wittier and livelier than it had been for a considerable time'. This was with his own pen rather than with his ability to discover new talent.

It was *Granta*'s history (and its connections), rather than its present, that attracted Alan Milne. The only Cambridge magazine that had survived longer was the *Cambridge Review* (known to *Granta* as 'Aunt Review'). That was said to owe its longevity and subscription list to the fact that it published the University sermon and had a devoted following among country parsons. Most undergraduate journals survived for only half a dozen issues. *Granta* was different: it had been going since 1889. It was the Cambridge *Punch*. Its links with *Punch* were so well established that when *Granta*'s hundredth issue was celebrated at a dinner at the Reform Club in London in 1893, half those present were writing regularly for *Punch*, including Milne's particular hero, R. C. Lehmann. It is difficult for us now to realize just what a pre-eminent place *Punch* held at this period. An anecdote from Anna Wickham's autobiography sums it up as the supreme goal for the young writer. As twenty-year-old Anne set off from Australia in 1904 to find fame in England with her writing, her father shouted out to her as the liner moved away from the wharf: '*Punch*, Anne, *Punch*!'

Alan Milne was hearing just such words in his ears: '*Punch*, Alan, *Punch*!' as he went back to Trinity in January 1902. 'It was the custom for undergraduates to meet their Tutor on the first day of term, not to present but to receive an address of welcome, and to be informed of any new College or University regulations which might concern them. On the first day of Lent Term 1902 our Tutor so addressed us, and then added. "Well, that's all, thank you, gentlemen. Mr Milne will remain behind." The others went out, wondering what I had done. So did I.

'He told me. In effect the conversation went like this:

"I hear you are editing *The Granta* this term?"

"Yes."

"Well, you can't."

"Why not?"

"You had no business whatever to commit yourself to anything like that without consulting me."

"Oh!" I decided to consult him. "Well – may I?"

"If you had consulted me, as you ought to have done, I should have forbidden it."

"But why?"

"You're a mathematician – "

"Well – "

"And the College pays you for being a mathematician – "

"Not very much."

"And from what I hear you will have to work a great deal harder, even as it is, in order to get the degree that is expected of you. And this is the moment which you choose to take on other responsibilities – "

"I always meant to edit *The Granta*. I simply must."

"I warn you that the College may decide to withdraw the money it pays you – "

"I simply must. I always meant to."

There is a long pause. I am not looking heroic. I am looking sulky and stubborn and uncomfortable.

"I'd rather do it," I mumble, "than have the money."

"And you think you can edit *The Granta* and do your legitimate work properly?"

"How many hours a day do you call properly?"

"I should expect at least six from anyone with any pretensions to be a scholar."

"All right. Six."

"Very well then. You will keep a record of your working hours, and show it to me every week."

So there it was. It is funny to think that my "working-hours" then were the stern laborious hours when I wasn't writing.'

It was no wonder that Alan Milne's attendance at the Shakespeare Society was irregular that term. There was a lot of writing to be done. One could hardly count on the standard of other people's contributions. 'When one more set of verses was wanted for the next number, and X.Y.Z.'s "Ode to My Tailor" filled the space exactly, the fact that I was pledged to Electrodynamics for the next two hours did not prevent me wondering whether I couldn't have filled the space as exactly, and even more delightfully, myself, if I had had the time. Naturally on these occasions one takes an exaggerated view of the possibilities. Pushing Loney's *Electrodynamics* a little to one side and rattling a pencil against my teeth, I allowed various ideas to wander through my mind, the conclusion three hours later being a set of verses signed A.B.C. which endeared itself to me as X.Y.Z.'s had never done. No doubt it was only better in my own opinion, but, as editor, whose opinion could I consult but my own? Making a note that I should have to do eighteen hours' mathematics to-morrow to get back to schedule, I went to bed. Life was very full just then.'

Milne had a very good idea already of the importance of titles. In a piece he published in his own *Granta* called 'The Complete Novel-Writer', he suggests that the important thing for a title is that it should have no meaning. In his very first issue, Milne published the first of a series under the title 'Jeremy, I and the Jelly-fish', a title sufficiently meaningless and memorable to deserve its place in A. A. Milne's own story. It was this series, written with an extraordinary confidence by someone who had only just started writing funny prose, that attracted the attention of R. C. Lehmann himself. 'Jeremy's real name was Jones, but he doesn't come into this story at all. Neither does the Jelly-fish. I mention them both because it helps the title.' Milne was always playing with what has come to be called 'fore-grounding'. The writer is right there in the middle of the story.

' "Why do you always talk in monosyllables?" she enquired.

"To tell you the truth," I said, growing confidential, "when you get paid by the column, it helps a lot." '

Looking back, Milne didn't think much of the series. The dialogues, he said, 'fill me not only with unease, but with a profound surprise that they led me anywhere. Yet they did, in fact, lead me away from the Civil Service, school-mastering, chartered account-ancy, all the professions which I might have followed, into the pro-fession of writing.' When he returned to Cambridge from the Easter vacation, there was a letter waiting in the *Granta* office. Lehmann himself recalled what had happened in his diary in May 1910 when Alan Milne made his first appearance at a *Punch* dinner, as a member of the famous 'Table'. 'It must be more than five years ago' (it was actually eight) 'since I was struck and delighted by a serial that appeared in the *Granta* under the name of "Jeremy, I and the Jelly-fish", a piece of sparkling and entirely frivolous and irresponsible irrelevance. I wrote to the Editor of the *Granta* at the end of term to inquire the name of the author, and received in reply a letter from Milne (the editor) who said, in effect, "Please, sir, it's me." There-upon we met and became friends.'

It was the sort of fairy-story happening of which every young writer dreams. It was even more exciting than it would have been later. Milne wrote in 1939: 'The undergraduate of today will find it difficult to appreciate the thrill which I received from this letter.' No one in London in 1902 apparently took much notice of Oxford or Cambridge, except on Boat Race Night. Few were concerned with talent-spotting. But now 'people in London' were talking about this new young writer on *Granta*. Of course Alan Milne was thrilled, and there was only one person in the world with whom he could share that thrill. He wrote at once to Ken, confident he would share his pleasure.

'How easy I have found it to go through the world making on equal terms friends, acquaintances, enemies, and to have the persist-ent feeling that the only side of the equation which matters is my own,' Milne wrote in his autobiography at this point in his story. 'I meet Smith, I like Smith; that is all there is about Smith. I meet Jones, I detest Jones; that goes for Jones. What do they, in return, feel about me? That is their own concern. But for some reason which I cannot explain I assume that their feelings are not so definite as mine, not so well considered. Is this because they feel less deeply than I, or because I am less worth consideration than they? I have never answered that question. The answer lies in the usual tangle of superi-ority complexes, inferiority complexes, conceits, modesties, mock-modesties and vanities of which modern man is composed.

'Through the rivalries of our childhood and boyhood I had tried to be "nice about it" to Ken. It did not occur to me that he was trying, with complete success, to be nice about it to me. He was nice without effort, simply because he was not so interested in our rivalry as I, because (I could almost persuade myself) he didn't even know that we were rivals, and that I had beaten him again. How could it be a humiliation to him who showed no signs of being humiliated? All these little "victories" and "defeats" meant no more to Ken than the winning or losing a game of beggar-my-neighbour.

'I was wrong. He wrote to congratulate me. No friend could have been more honestly delighted, no lover have paid more reckless compliments. And then for the first time he brought our rivalry into the light, showing what it had meant to him from those earliest days until now:

Whatever I did, you did a little better or a little sooner . . . And so it went on. Even after all this, I could still tell myself that I had one thing left. I should always be the writer of the family. And now you have taken that too. Well, damn you, I suppose I must forgive you. My head is bloody but unbowed. I have got a new frock coat and you can go to the devil. Yours stiffly, Ken.'

After printing this letter in his autobiography after Ken's death (to which he would refer only glancingly), Alan Milne did a most curious and revealing thing. He printed, as I do now, Leigh Hunt's familiar verses:

> Jenny kissed me when we met,
>   Jumping from the chair she sat in;
> Time, you thief, who love to get
>   Sweets into your list, put that in!
>
> Say I'm weary, say I'm sad,
>   Say that health and wealth have missed me,
> Say I'm growing old, but add
>   Jenny kissed me.

Then he added, 'Throughout his life I never lost Ken, nor he me. Time, you thief, who love to get sweets into your list, put that in!' He made only one more strange reference to the strength of the bond, the depth of the feeling between them. In August 1902, the summer of Ken's engagement to Maud Innes, the two brothers went rock climbing together in the Lake District. They were foolishly ill-prepared and rash, and had moments of wishing they had stuck to Essex. They climbed Napes Needle on Great Gable and seem to have come quite close to death.

'Say "I can do it,"' Ken said.

'I can do it,' Alan said.

And they did. 'I have told how Ken kissed me once,' Alan wrote, 'But on this occasion we didn't even shake hands.' Once every ten years or so, he said, it came back to him, that feat they had accomplished together, each one depending so much on the other. 'In addition to all the things I can't do and haven't done, I *have* climbed the Napes Needle. So have thousands of other people. But they, probably, knew something about it.'

A. A. Milne's first editorial in *Granta* was very straightforward, nothing more really than an encouragement to the young men of Cambridge to buy the paper; but it ended with a rather shocking tale about a book, published three years before by an up-and-coming MP: 'There is a pretty story about Winston Churchill and General Tucker,' Milne wrote. 'The former presented the General with a copy of his book *The River War*. Some days after, he enquired if the General had read it. "Oh! was that meant to read?" said Tucker, in surprise. "I hung it in my bedroom and have been tearing off a page each morning to shave with." ' This is a story that perhaps means little to people with electric razors and no knowledge that the old cut-throats needed wiping. Milne would seem to use it just to bring a smile, to suggest that if you weren't interested in reading light verse or the rowing notes (even if they were by Ian Hay), then at least *Granta* might be useful when you were shaving. But the story has a definite sub-text. With its image of the illiterate General, it presages for us the pacifist anti-militarist Milne.

It is not easy to quote from Milne at his funniest. That 'sparkling irrelevancy' R. C. Lehmann admired depends on a cumulative effect, on a sequence of remarks and on high spirits and on a juggling with words that never seems to flag. No art is so difficult as that of being funny. That art came naturally to Alan Milne; there is no doubt about that. ('He was *so* funny,' one of his friends told me eighty years later.) He would see the dull pebbles lying on the ground and pick them up and hold them this way and that, so that the light caught them and transformed them and they were dull no longer. 'The whole art of writing,' Milne once said, is 'to know what it would be any good putting.' He seemed to have an instinct from the beginning. Some people, of course, find this sort of prose irritating – even when it was perfected in *Winnie-the-Pooh* and *The House at Pooh Corner*. Milne has always had his detractors, and the word 'whimsical' came to be the word he hated most in the English language.

At this early stage, his greatest pleasure in writing still came from light verse, and the challenge of rhyme. One poem of five stanzas was entirely inspired by the fact that ' "Astrolabe" is the only word that rhymes with "babe".' So he said. Much as he admired Lewis Carroll, that real mathematician, Milne was not then a Carrollian inventor of words: 'wabe' and 'outgrabe' were not in the running.

> When I was the usual innocent babe
> I played on the nursery floor
> (For the sake of the rhyme) with an astrolabe;
> When I was a babe – with an astrolabe,
> As, I think, I have said before.

'Love among the bricks' has a certain interest, looking forward as it does, in a sense, to *Now We Are Six*, twenty-five years later.

> Oh do not make light of the past, love,
> Nor say that my wishes are vain.
> I never supposed it would last, love,
> Yet why not begin it again?
> Oh think, can you think, of the past, love,
> When I was a beggar for bricks!
> No, I never supposed it would last, love,
> But, why did you ever turn six?

Don't do what I do, do what I say, Milne would suggest. 'Light Verse,' he really believed, 'obeys Coleridge's definition of poetry, the best words in the best order; it demands Carlyle's definition of genius, transcendent capacity for taking pains; and it is the supreme exhibition of somebody's definition of art, the concealment of art. In the result it observes the most exact laws of rhyme and metre as if by a happy accident, and in a sort of nonchalant spirit of mockery at the real poets who do it on purpose.'

'Contributions are pouring into the *Granta* office at the rate of one poem and a half per week . . .' 'I have an idea that the art of writing light verse is dying out at Cambridge,' Milne wrote in his fourth issue. 'So many seem to think it is sufficient to scan and rhyme in an ordinary sort of way. But more than that is wanted. If you wish to see what it is that makes light verse, then don't, I implore you, look in this week's number; we are not at our best this week.'

He was often not at his best, but at least he was trying. It was a perfect training ground. Was this funny? It was certainly ingenious.

> Brown was a tutor, who loved and lost
>   An affectionate cannibal queen.
> He swore he would win her whatever the cost –
> She asked him to dine (as a matter of 'course').
> He *was* with a highly original sauce!
>   And Brown is the fellow who's been.

One tends to think of far-off summers as always glorious. Milne's first summer at Cambridge, 1901, had been pretty good. There is a glimpse of him trying to write a sonnet on Clare Bridge but it is too hot to think of rhymes for ducks and panamas and weeping willows. There is some good cricket. Fifty years later he can still hear the rattle of his ball against the spokes of a bicycle someone had left leaning against a fence, just beyond the boundary. He said it was the zenith of his cricketing career: a fast bowler, half a dozen slips, and he had found the only small gap.

But the summer term of 1902 was awful. On 10 May Milne wrote in *Granta*: 'It is still raining and there is a miserably cold wind . . . My one consolation is that my panama is away to be cleaned and won't be back for a fortnight.' And a month later: 'May week came in (as the poet says) like a lamb and went out like mint sauce, which is another way of saying it has been wet.' There had been a smallpox epidemic in England. Hundreds of people had died and hundreds more had to be treated on special quarantine ships anchored in the Thames. Vaccination was constantly mentioned in *Granta*. It was sometimes difficult to be funny.

Milne was often at this stage more effective when he wasn't trying to be. It was fortunate that he sometimes forgot that being serious was supposed to be 'bad form'. He published a good piece about 'log rolling'. *Granta*, like almost every institution in the world, suffers from 'the pressure of custom and the fear of truth'. There was too much indiscriminate praise in it, he thought. Union speakers, athletes, everyone was constantly praised. 'If everyone is praised, praise means nothing.' Milne was his own drama critic, and his honest criticism of the plays at the New Theatre (Ben Greet in *Hamlet* was quite inaudible, the scene shifters were noisy, and so on) resulted in *Granta*'s free pass being withdrawn.

'So there will be no more Theatrical Notes in future; at least, not until there is a new editor. Personally I never saw the use of them, except as a means of filling space.' As a playwright, he would never have much time for drama critics. But by far his worst criticisms of the theatre were reserved for the undergraduate audiences. 'Granta has now no official connection with the theatre but I am engaged in writing to myself as Editor a letter from myself as an ordinary member of the university, calling my notice to the behaviour of certain men who frequent the stalls' and with their audible comments and drunken laughter ruin the performance for everyone else. In the musical Naughty Nancy the actresses were almost afraid to go on the stage. At Oxford, Isis tells us, 'the hurling of plates and other trifles of that sort' at the chorus was a favourite amusement.

Twenty years later a protest in the London Play Pictorial would show that this was a continuing problem. 'That these young cubs should be allowed to perform their Wild West monkey tricks in the decent society of people who have paid high prices for an evening's entertainment is a disgrace to the colleges from which they emanate. If they were East End work lads, a posse of police would deal with them in no uncertain manner and hooligans from Oxford and Cambridge should receive the treatment that would be meted out to hooligans from Whitechapel or Poplar.' More surprisingly, perhaps, Milne in Granta also had reason to castigate similar awful behaviour at compulsory chapel services where men whisper together, giggle and joke.

Alan Milne admired a special May Week issue of Granta which had been published in the summer of 1899 when Oliver Locker-Lampson had been editor. There had been contributions from a lot of impressive names, including Edmund Gosse, Andrew Lang and the Bensons, all of whom Locker-Lampson knew through his father, Frederick. Drawing on his one literary connection (Harmsworth could hardly be called 'literary'), Milne wrote to H. G. Wells, someone 'with – well – something more than a local reputation', asking for a contribution for the May Week issue of 1902; but he had left it rather late to ask.

He certainly worked in his last year but it was no good. 'He was a Granta man' (he said that was what he would like on his tombstone). He was no longer a mathematician. Looking back, he could say with Leonard Woolf, 'I am glad too that I lived the kind of life at Trinity which was mainly the reason why I did not do well in the examinations.' 'I had been happy at Cambridge,' he wrote himself. 'The only cloud over my happiness had been the Tripos.' Looking back when he was nearly thirty, this was what he wrote:

GOLDEN MEMORIES

When Memory with its scorn of ages,
 Its predilection for the past,
Turns back about a billion pages
 And lands us by the Cam at last;
Is it the thought of 'Granta' (once our daughter),
 The Fresher's Match, the Second in our Mays
That makes our mouth, our very soul to water?
 Ah no! Ah no! It is the Salmon Mayonnaise!

The work we did was rarely reckoned
 Worthy a tutor's kindly word –
(For when I said we got a Second
 I really meant we got a Third) –
The games we played were often tinged with bitter,
 Amidst the damns no faintest hint of praise
Greeted us when we missed the authentic 'sitter' –
 But thou wert always kind, O Salmon Mayonnaise!

Even our nights with 'Granta', even
 The style that, week by blessed week,
Mixed Calverley and J. K. Stephen
 With much that was (I hold) unique.
Even our parodies of the Rubaiyat
 Were disappointing – yes, in certain ways:
What genius loves (I mean) the people shy at –
 Yet no one ever shied at Salmon Mayonnaise!

Alas! no restaurant in London
 Can make us feel that thrill again;
Though what they do or what leave undone
 I often ask, and ask in vain.
Is it the sauce which puts the brand of Cam on
 Each maddening dish? The egg? The yellow glaze?
The cucumber? The special breed of salmon? –
 I only know we loved, we *loved* that Mayonnaise!

  . . . .

'Did Beauty,' some may ask severely,
 'Visit him in no other guise?
It cannot be that salmon merely
 Should bring the mist before his eyes!
What of the river there where Byron's Pool lay,
 The warm blue morning shimmering in the haze?'
Not this (I say) . . . Yet something else . . . Crème Brûlée!
Ye gods! to think of that *and* Salmon Mayonnaise!

— 5 —

Freelance

'ONE CANNOT EXPLAIN a Third Class to one's father.' That was Alan Milne's immediate problem when the degree results were published in the summer of 1903. BA (Hons.) Cantab. can look well enough after one's name and satisfy aunts, perhaps – but J. V. Milne was a different matter: 'Father was so bitterly disappointed that for a week he did not talk to me.' It was a repeat of the aftermath of the dreadful Westminster report when he was twelve, only this time Alan felt his father's reaction rather more justified, which made it even worse. He realized it was not the moment for raising the question of what he really wanted to do – what he *would* do in the end. His father still hoped he might get into the Civil Service, serve his country well, and end up with a knighthood. Alan dutifully went along to a crammer which specialized in coaching for the Civil Service examinations; it was worrying how little history he knew.

He sat for weeks in a deckchair near the bandstand on the Westgate seafront, reading constitutional history to the strains of the *Blue Danube* waltz; or not reading it, and dreaming of what he really wanted to do; or not reading it, and admiring the prettiest of the pretty visitors to Westgate. His father could not help seeing that Alan's heart was not inclined towards the Civil Service. In a letter to H. G. Wells it sounds as if Milne actually took the exams and failed. 'I was not thought clever enough for the Home Civil,' he wrote. If there was a doubt in J. V. Milne's mind now, it was whether Alan was 'good enough to be a schoolmaster', to inherit, as the youngest son, his father's kingdom. Well, at least he would be given the chance. There was, after all, the future of Streete Court to be considered. J. V. Milne had been working things out. He suggested a year in Germany studying the latest educational methods, a few years teaching at a good public school, then the return to Streete Court as an assistant master. Eventually he would become a junior partner and finally, buying his brothers out of their share of the patrimony and providing a retirement income for his parents, have the chance to take over the school completely.

They sat talking on a garden seat by the croquet lawn at Streete Court. 'Well, dear, what do you think of it?'

'It's all right. It's very generous,' Alan said, reluctantly.

'Well, you must think it over. I don't want to hurry you.'

There was a long pause and then Alan said, 'I think I – I think I – I'd like to try to be a writer.'

'It's for you to decide.'

'Yes . . . I think I have decided.'

J. V. Milne took it very well. He reminded his youngest son, of course, how very difficult it is to make a living as a writer. 'Even Mr Wells had to do other work for a long time before he could support himself by writing.' But 'Mr Wells', as J. V. Milne would always call him, had no money of his own. Alan had what was left of the £1,000 the father had given to each of the three sons. As he put it to H. G. Wells on the 4 September 1903, just a few days after the conversation in the garden at Streete Court:

I thought I would write and tell you that I am going to try my luck at journalism. Thanks to an arrangement with my father made some years ago, I have enough money to keep me somehow in London for two years – even if I earn nothing. But I'm going to earn something. You see!

I know this sounds very foolish, but I believe it is better to go the whole hog – rather than to pretend to be a school-master during term, and play at journalism in the holidays . . . I will let you know now and then how I get on – if it won't bore you.

The money that was to keep him for two years if necessary amounted to £320. He used it up in sixteen months. But he was entirely optimistic that autumn. 'I came to London in 1903, very hopeful as one is at twenty-one.' There was something in his confidence of that childhood feeling he would put in his poem 'The Island': 'The world was made for me.' He must have known it would not be plain sailing. There had been a disappointing business the year before. After R. C. Lehmann's praise of 'Jeremy, I and the Jelly-fish' in *Granta*, he had suggested Milne should write a series of sketches for *Punch*. They were written and, Milne said, they 'went backwards and forwards between me and the Assistant Editor, Owen Seaman, for some weeks until at last they were all to his liking.' Then they were submitted to the editor, F. C. Burnand, and nothing was heard of them for seven months.

Burnand was no longer the 'prince of men' he had seemed to ten-year-old Max Beerbohm (in the year Alan Milne was born), when he had swung round in his office chair to greet the boy 'in a most fascinating manner'. He was getting old and lazy; he preferred writing his reminiscences in Ramsgate or staying in country houses to spending much time in Bouverie Street. 'The first that anybody knew of his return was the heavy thud of his boots, which he was accustomed to remove and throw outside the door of his office. Visiting contributors would find him looking rather lost and eating shrimps out of a paper bag.' As early as 1897 one of the proprietors of *Punch* had pressed Henry Lucy to take over as editor, but he had refused out of loyalty to Burnand though, as he said himself (and again it suggests the special power *Punch* had over its contributors), 'I would rather have been Editor of *Punch* than Emperor of India.' Burnand never did get round to considering those undergraduate sketches by Alan Milne. Lehmann had finally taken them away from him, unread, and sent them to another paper, which accepted them at once and then went bankrupt before they appeared.

This hardly augured well for A. A. Milne's future in journalism, and there were certainly moments when he wished he had decided on an actual job, rather than the insecurity of the freelance, in spite of the comforting £320. There were other reasons than financial ones why a job might have been useful. 'I often wish I had started as a reporter; it is all experience for subsequent books and plays,' he wrote towards the end of his life in reply to a fan letter. It would have broadened his experience, his knowledge of what his critics would be so fond of calling 'real life'; Milne would often be accused of failing to 'come to grips' with it. He did apply to the Cambridge University Appointments Board – 'a blessed institution . . . which tries to get posts for graduates with no particular qualifications, like myself.' He told Wells that

It wrote to me about a 'leader-writer for a paper in India' a little while ago, but the letter was put away in a drawer by my idiot of a servant and I only got it a month later. I have just heard from the Secretary that if I had applied he could almost certainly have got me the job and that it is worth £500 a year . . . I am darned keen on seeing something of the world besides England . . . Behold the might have been Rudyard Kipling, who has been nipped in the bud.

A. A. Milne never did see a great deal of the world beside England, and this is the only evidence that he had ever felt a real urge to do so, after his childhood fantasies. The next mention of the Appointments Board is in a domestic context. It gave Milne an introduction to the *Westminster Gazette*, but this does not seem to have led to anything either. It took him a good while to get going, though he was well set up to take advantage of any opportunities there were.

The 'idiot of a servant' mentioned in that letter to Wells was not his own personal employee. Milne had moved, in late September, into two rooms in Temple Chambers, which still exist on the right-hand side of Bouverie Street, going down towards the river. They were ideally placed, he thought, should he ever become editor of *Punch*, and near enough to set the Thames on fire, should he ever get the chance. Breakfast was provided, the rooms were cleaned and his laundry sent out. Lunch was at an ABC. Milne always remained much attached to the ABCs, those teashops run by the Aerated Bread Company, which could provide at any hour of the day such minimal sustenance as 'a cup of coffee, half a toasted scone and two portions of honey', 'a pot of tea and a Bath bun', eggs if you were feeling a little better off or even fried fish. If the fish was 'off', you could substitute 'a plate of porridge and an apple' and no one would bat an eyelid. Thirty years later Alan Milne would occasionally take his son to an ABC and have scrambled eggs on toast – he and Christopher 'and the ghost of Ken', as Christopher put it in his autobiography. For Ken was in London too, as Alan started out on his career, and they had lunch together nearly every day. Ken had, after two wretched months, discovered that the flaw in training to be a solicitor was that you became a solicitor. He knew now that he did not want to be a solicitor in private practice, worked hard to take exams similar to the ones it seems Alan failed, and found himself a civil servant in the Estate Duty Office, apparently a more congenial place than the solicitor's office that had made him miserable. It was just the sort of job of which J. V. Milne approved.

In the evenings Alan usually ate at the Cock in Fleet Street, while Ken caught a train first to a flat in Hammersmith and later to a house in Ealing, for he married Maud Innes very quietly at St Paul's Church, Portman Square on 27 September 1905. In the years to come, Alan would go and have supper with them regularly, usually on Thursday evenings and often on another night or two as well. Sometimes Ken and Alan would buy at the grocer's all the things which they would have bought so gladly when they were at Westminster: sardines, tongue, tinned fruit and soft drinks, with cherry brandy as well, because they were now grown up. Occasionally, especially when Maud was expecting a child, the two young men would actually cook a meal, with 'Mrs Beeton watching from the top of the oven'. They would serve it up triumphantly, roast with two veg – 'no better beef on any table in England'.

They got on very well together, Alan and Ken and Maud. They were all happy and high-spirited. Maud and Alan were, in fact, devoted and remained so all their lives. She had never had a brother; he had never had a sister. She *was* a sister to him – mended his socks, listened to his stories of girls, encouraged his ambitions, even spring-cleaned his flat, it seems, though that was something of a mixed blessing. She was certainly the 'Beatrice' of his sketches. He tells us, more or less, that everything he writes comes from real life: 'Whatever subject an author chooses or has chosen for him, he reveals no secret but the secret of himself.' W. A. Darlington, the theatre critic, whose admiration for Milne started as a *Punch*-reading schoolboy and developed as his lifelong friend, would describe A. A. Milne, after his death, as 'always an autobiographical writer'. His first published freelance contribution after he came to London was uncharacteristically a parody of Sherlock Holmes, which appeared in *Vanity Fair* in October 1903. But his material usually came from the day-to-day events of his own life.

H. G. Wells had discovered this 'secret' of journalism, so he recorded in his autobiography, in a book by J. M. Barrie called *When a Man's Single*. Wells realized he had wasted his time for years in trying to find 'rare and precious topics . . . The more I was rejected the higher my shots had flown. All I had to do was lower my aim – and hit . . . I reflected that directly one forgot how confoundedly serious life could be, it did become confoundedly amusing.' Milne hardly needed Wells and Barrie to tell him that; he knew it in his bones. Everything was the stuff of humour.

He sat in his rooms in Temple Chambers, day after day, playing with his thousand words. There were so many places to send them. Apart from everything else, there were *eight* evening papers in London alone, six days a week. 'By today's standards,' as John Gross put it twenty years ago, 'There is something impressive in the mere fact that so many papers existed at all.' But the existence of so many outlets created its own problems. It was much more difficult to make any sort of reputation unless one concentrated on one target. For Milne, *Punch* was the obvious target. The trouble with *Punch* was that its impressive circulation (105,000 at this point) and reputation meant it was inundated with contributions, which in turn meant it paid outside contributors very badly, to discourage them – while its style and demands were so specialized that a piece aimed at *Punch* and rejected was unlikely to find a home anywhere else.

One of the first things Milne had done, when he had decided he was going to try to make a living as a journalist, was to write to his father's old pupil, Alfred Harmsworth, who was already in 1903 a baronet and soon to be raised to the peerage as Baron Northcliffe of the Isle of Thanet. (He had taken a house not very far from Streete Court.) Harmsworth was by now less admired by Alan's parents. J. V. Milne had done so much for him as a boy; he had even taken one of his younger brothers without school fees at a critical point in the Harmsworth finances – and had been repaid when things were beginning to work out. But when his old headmaster had approached Harmsworth for a loan to enable him to buy the lease of Streete Court, to give him security of tenure until he could afford to buy it himself, Harmsworth had prevaricated. His money was tied up; there were so many claims on it. J. V. Milne asked him to forget he had ever asked, but he himself could never forget. Mrs Milne sniffed; Harmsworth became '*That* man . . .'

When Alan needed work, J. V. Milne thought it would give Harmsworth the chance to redeem himself. This first decade of the new century was 'the zenith of Alfred Harmsworth's career . . . By his own efforts as a journalist, he had won a remarkable position in English life. The support of his newspapers was courted by statesmen . . . He was rich beyond the dreams of avarice.' 'Knowing Harmsworth' was the best of all possible introductions to Fleet Street. So Alan Milne wrote to him. The answer came two weeks later. It said that in Sir Alfred's absence abroad, his letter had been forwarded to Mr Philip Gibbs, the literary editor of the *Daily Mail*, 'to whom the articles you mention should be sent'.

'I did not show this letter to Father; I did not send any articles to Mr Philip Gibbs. I felt as Father had once felt, ashamed of my own letter. Whether Harmsworth ever received it, and returned it with instructions to the office, or whether he knew nothing of it, I never heard. I told myself that I had really only written to "that man" for my parents' sake, and that I was glad that the great name I was going to make for myself would be made without his or anybody's help. I pictured him on his knees a few years hence begging me to edit *all* his papers for him. Proudly I should refuse . . .'

In fact, according to R. G. G. Price, the historian of *Punch*, some years later Lord Northcliffe did try to buy *Punch* and 'through an intermediary offered Milne a princely salary to edit it.' He was 'astonished at the young journalist's prompt refusal of the glittering offer.' J. V. Milne did not give up, however, after Alan's own abortive attempt to see the millionaire. On the 27 September 1903, Alan Milne had told Wells, 'Like a fool I wrote to Harmsworth and the result made me very sick for a bit.' Twelve days later he wrote:

I enclose a letter from my father which may interest you. I go to see Harmsworth on Wednesday. I heard the other day of a man who hoped to embark on a literary career and was introduced to Harmsworth. To his great joy the latter found him work, and it was not until some weeks after that the man discovered he was really no more than a nightwatchman at Carmelite House. Absit omen.

Milne says he was sick with indignation that his father had written. Well, it was too late now. The appointment was made. He had to keep it. He was shown into the Great Man's room and told, kindly, that Harmsworth was going to send him along to two of his editors. 'I have been careful,' Harmsworth said, 'not to let them know that your father is one of my oldest and greatest friends' (Alan could hear his mother sniff, if not snort) 'because I want you to make your own way. So now it's up to you.' Milne was taken in to Arthur Mee, who had apparently succeeded Mr Philip Gibbs as editor of 'the articles you mention'. 'He told me that, if I cared to send in contributions to *The Daily Mail* I could address them to him personally. I was in no mood to realize that this was a valuable concession; I felt that it just left me where I was before. We passed on to the next editor. I have forgotten his name, but still have a memory of shirt-sleeves and a half-smoked cigar. He was that sort of editor, and he was responsible for some twenty "comics", boys' papers and what not. Humorous writers, he assured me with his feet up, were in demand, but I must realize that his public did not want anything subtle or refined. "Funny stories about policemen, y'know what I mean, umbrellas, knockabout, that sort of thing." I assured him that I knew what he meant. I left the building. I walked across the road to Temple Chambers. Telling myself that I mustn't let Father think that his help was in vain, I sat grimly down and began to write a funny story about a policeman; not subtle, not refined. Knockabout. I wrote four hundred words. I think I can say truthfully that those are the only words I have ever written which I did not write for my own pleasure. At the four hundredth word, I stopped, read them through, and with a sigh of happiness tore them into pieces. I was back on my own again; making, as Harmsworth said, my own way.'

H. G. Wells was helpful, full of friendly advice and encouragement, but he was not an editor. He had invited Milne to his new house at Sandgate, near Folkestone, that summer, his brand-new, architect-designed house, which was itself a symbol of how far he had come since they had last met, during those ten years that Alan had been at Westminster and Cambridge. The eager bird-like young teacher had solidified. Wells was now not only extremely successful but deeply controversial. At Sandgate he was working on *Kipps* and showed Milne the manuscript. He had already published *The Invisible Man, The War of the Worlds* and that autobiographical novel *Love and Mr Lewisham*, which suggests so strongly the dangers of a self-destructive marriage and encourages the young to demand the freedom to find their own ways to happiness. He was soon to publish *Ann Veronica*, when a clergyman would say he would rather send his daughter to a house infected with diphtheria or typhoid fever than put a copy of the new Wells novel in her hands.

Rich and well established he was already, but he was, as Milne was only slowly to realize, a rather dangerous ally in that Edwardian world. Scandal never seemed far away from him. While Milne was still at school, Wells had left his young wife to live with one of his students, Amy Catherine Robbins, now transformed into Jane Wells and the mother of two new small sons. She, like Wells, was now at the centre of a Fabian storm, a storm closely related to Wells's attitude to women. How much Milne knew of Wells's involvement with Rosamund Bland and Dorothy Richardson, with Amber Pember Reeves and later with Rebecca West, we have no way of knowing. But he must have realized, as he wrote his funny bread-and-butter letters to Jane Wells after another happy weekend at Sandgate (stiff from 'the violent exercise H. G. gave me with his Caesar's Camps and Darts and things') that it was not a conventional marriage. If he read *In the Days of the Comet* (and he seems to have read everything Wells wrote, and many books more than once) he can hardly have avoided seeing it was 'obscurely phrased but absolutely unmistakable' as an 'endorsement of free love'.

Wells was an enormous influence on Milne in these years – not perhaps in literary or sexual terms but certainly politically and socially. He took Milne to the National Liberal Club only a few days after the young man had moved into Temple Chambers.

'He said that I must join a club, so that by reading every sort of London and provincial paper I could keep in touch with the needs and ways of editors. "In fact," he said, "you'd better join this. I suppose you're a Liberal. Your father's son."

'I assured him that I was a Liberal, but not for the reason suggested. Father, I implied, had ratted on us. I also told him that there was nobody in London whom I could ask to put me up for this or any club.

' "Good," he said. "Then I'll propose you and we'll get Archer to second you."

' "William Archer?" I asked in awe.

' "Yes. You'll have to meet him, of course. I'll arrange it."

'A day or two later, at some horribly early hour on a cold November morning, I breakfasted with Wells and William Archer. Archer had more gravity than any man I have met. In his grave, handsome presence it was useless to remind myself that Stevenson had once been delighted by the humour of his letters. One felt that humour in his presence would have as little chance of establishing itself as would some practical joke on a Bishop during the final blessing. Nor was it more hopeful to be intelligent. Archer, one felt, knew it all, and had rejected it. They talked: wisely, profoundly, unceasingly: together they seemed as old and wise as God. From time to time one of them would look to me for support against the other, and whichever looked first would get my support: "Er – yes," or "Oh, rather," or "Well, I suppose in a way it is." It wasn't helpful. Contemplating myself from outside I got the impression of somebody who could do nothing but eat. With every mouthful I felt younger and more stupid; it didn't seem possible that there could be any club from which Archer would not blackball me. However, when he had finished his breakfast, he filled in a form to say that he had known me intimately for several years, in the course of which I had proved to be a most entertaining companion. I was elected.

'For many years afterwards Archer and I would meet at the club. Neither of us had thought of this, and we didn't know what to do about it. He was as shy of me as I was of him. We said "Hallo!" or "Good evening" gaily, as if each of us had much to tell the other.

In the silence which followed the gaiety slowly died away. After a period of intense thought a smile would light up our faces, and we would say simultaneously: "Have you seen Wells lately?" Wells was safely in Sandgate, away from all this, and we hadn't seen him for some time. We said so – simultaneously. Then he would say, "Well – er – " and give a little nod, and I would nod back and say, "Well," and we would hurry away from each other. I find that if I start wrong with anybody I never get right again. Some years later we were fellow-guests at E. V. Lucas's house in the country, and I hoped that this would bring us together; for a man may be tongue-tied in a drawing-room, but sing his heart out under the open sky. Something, however – possibly the fact that Archer wore a bowler hat all the time – kept us spiritually in London. We returned there in the body on Monday, fortified by the knowledge that our repertory now included an enquiry as to when we had last seen Lucas.'

In fact, there were lots of things Milne might have discussed with William Archer. Archer was the man who had shared with Edmund Gosse the credit for establishing the reputation in England of the now aged Ibsen; thirteen years before, Archer had been accused by Henry James of 'extravagant malevolence' when he attacked Gosse's translation of *Hedda Gabler*. There was nothing extravagant or malevolent about Archer these days – but the theatre remained his passion, and his criticism had had a tremendous effect on standards. At this time he was already deeply involved with Harley Granville Barker in plans to form a working committee towards the establishment of a national theatre. He had, moreover, 'a deep and genuine humour'. It is sad that Milne so totally failed to relate to this man to whom Wells had introduced him – particularly as it was towards the theatre, towards being a playwright, that his talent seemed determined to take him, even in 1904, thirteen years before his first play would be produced.

'That's just the worst of it,' Milne wrote to Wells in December that year. 'Whenever I write, or begin to write, a story I think what a ripping curtain-raiser it would make; and at great labour and expense I turn it into the same – beautifully typed and got up. And that is usually the end.' As early as 1900, in the summer before Alan went up to Cambridge, Ken and Alan had written a play together and sent it to Seymour Hicks – one of the leading actor-managers of the day – and he had kept it for a whole year before returning it with 'a note of praise and congratulations' which gave them little pleasure. Then in November 1903, Alan had sent what he himself called 'a hopelessly bad one' to Max Beerbohm at the suggestion of someone who knew him, and there it was still, over a year later, unacknowledged. But he remained 'awfully keen on doing something in the play way', though it seemed 'such a hopeless waste of time when you have to wait a year in between each refusal of it'.

At least with sketches and poems, the response, if often unfavourable, was more prompt. His immediate ambition was still to write regularly for *Punch*. His first *Punch* poem appeared on 18 May 1904, just over seven months after he had moved into Temple Chambers and started submitting material. It was called 'The New Game' and extolled the unlikely Tibetan activity of 'firing jingals from a jong'. It would be tedious to look too closely at Milne's successes and failures in 1904 as he struggled to establish himself and prove that he could make a living as a writer before his father's £320 ran out. A letter to H. G. Wells on 10 July is worth quoting in full for the general picture it gives, as well as the particular detail.

My dear H. G. Wells

The Pater showed me your card; and at the risk of boring you I am giving the result of my labours so far. I would have written before, but I wanted to wait till I had done something good, or got some regular work. Neither of these things has happened yet.

First then:

Total earnings £17.8.0

made up of (I am doing the details in my head, so it may not add up right)

	£ s d
St James Gazette (6 articles)	6.16.6
Black & White (2 articles)	2.18.0
Bystander (2 contributions)	2. 2.0
Express (1 contribution)	1.15.0
Manchester Guardian (odd jobs)	1.17.6
Vanity Fair (1 contribution)	15.0
Punch (2 contributions)	16.6
Daily Chronicle (one roundel)	7.6

I called on the editor of the St J.G. a little while ago and asked – first, for higher pay – which was ignored; and secondly for regular work but he had no more to offer, tho' he told me several times how much he admired my style etc. and that if I could suggest any new feature he would be glad to welcome it. The only new features I could suggest were my own – on his staff. However I am practically certain of anything I send there being accepted; only I don't want to make him tired of me . . .

The paying power of *Punch* was rather a blow, and the proprietor is not spoken of in our family now. He is under a ban.

As for my prospex, they are

(1) If anybody on the *St J.G.* staff died, I really think I should get his place.

(2) When the war ends, *Black & White* have half promised to start a sporting page – by that famous athlete Mr. A. A. Milne.

You see how my future depends on others –

Also I am about to be introduced to Barry Pain and the Editor of the *Gentlewoman*. And through R. C. Lehmann I hope to bag £8.8.0 at one swoop in the autumn. But I will tell you about that later on, when it has come off.

If it would interest you, I will send some of my work to you; but at present Barry Pain has it all. There is something tho' in this week's (that is, last Friday's) *Black & White*. If you have not seen it I will try and send a copy.

I must stop as I have to catch a train to have dinner with my brother. The atmosphere of this place has made me a keen Liberal, tho' I used to have no views at all!

Good bye. When is the 'Food of the Gods' coming out; and under what title? I want very much to review it!, but I can't find anyone else who wants me to.

With kind regards to Mrs Wells and the family

> Ever yours
> Alan Milne

In spite of his need for ready cash, Milne was still keeping his wits about him. In another letter to Wells, later that year, he recorded that he 'took a story into the *Idler* the other day and saw the editor'.

He said that he was full up for two years ahead and that it was useless my bringing him anything etc. etc. However he said that I could leave it if I liked, and that if it was as good as Anthony Hope, Rudyard Kipling and H. G. Wells . . . all put together, it might be accepted. Two days ago I got a line saying he would give me a pound for the copyright. I declined on your behalves with scorn, asked for it back and sent him one penny stamp to defray expenses.

In the same letter, Milne challenged the impression Wells had that he was living in luxury. In fact he had moved to 'two cheap and dirty rooms' at 8 Wellington Square, Chelsea, to try to cut down on his weekly expenses. ('Your last three letters went to Temple Chambers. Ichabod.') Wellington Square in those days was not the place it is now, or that it had become even by 1939. Writing then, Milne said, 'When I tell my friends that I used to live there they think that I have come down in the world. It was not so fashionable in 1904. I lived in a police-sergeant's house; I paid ten shillings a week for the two rooms at the top of the house; and the bathroom, to which I travelled every morning, had been, until lately, a sort of conservatory linking up the backyard with the ground-floor passage. There was an incandescent mantle and a smell of gas in the sitting-room, there was some sort of music-hall singer in the floor below, there was a variety of police-sergeant's children on the stairs. I paid sevenpence for breakfast, and had my other meals out. The sergeant's wife was a big, friendly soul, motherly (as she might be with the practice she had) and embarrassingly kind. Her husband had been the champion revolver-shot of the Empire, or something like it, and the two targets, right and left-hand, which hung framed in the hall, explained why. I was very happy at Wellington Square, and life was exciting.' At the time he told Wells, 'I found 3 beetles in my sugar the other day. Now I ask you – is this luxury? (You will probably say that it was luxurious of me to have had 3 beetles when 2 would have done.)'

It was while he was living in Wellington Square that A. A. Milne worked on his first book: *Lovers in London*. The core of this shilling book was material which had brought his most substantial earnings – six and a half guineas – from the *St James's Gazette* in the list in that July 1904 letter to H. G. Wells. Wells had suggested that Milne should turn these 'Amelia' pieces into a book – and Barry Pain (introduced to Milne by Lehmann) suggested the same thing, and moreover recommended their agent to help bring it about. 'It seems rather early to start an agent,' Milne wrote to Wells, but Pinker took him on: J. B. Pinker, 'unobtrusive, thoughtful, so respected', whose clients would be 'the most distinguished in the annals of literary salesmanship: James, Conrad, Wells, Kipling, Bennett'.

By 19 October, Milne was writing to Pinker: 'I have got the book planned out and a good many chapters, which aren't suitable for separate publication, written.' But, financially, things were getting rather desperate.

I am emphatically *not* going to take up school-mastering, which is the only other thing I can do. So I want to know: (1) Can I get on as an author – as opposed to a journalist? (2) If not, had I better be looking about for a vacant reporting, sub-editing, type-setting or any other job? . . . (3) or could you mention, better, to editors or anybody that you know somebody who wants anything? But if this short story would come off as a curtain-raiser, it would be a heavenly thing and save the situation.

Two things, in fact, saved the situation which was really worrying in December 1904, at the time of the move to Wellington Square. In his optimism he had not been as careful about his money as he should have been. He had felt (with an ounce of tobacco and two boxes of matches still giving change from a sixpence) that his £320 would go further than it did. He had taken hansom cabs to Lord's cricket ground (the only way to approach Lord's, he felt) and had had celebratory meals with Ken (*not* in ABCs) when anything deserved celebrating. He had even paid an extraordinary £4 10s for a wrestling match, arriving sixteen seconds late and missing entirely the first bout of fifteen seconds. 'I have at the most £20 in the Bank, not a penny more anywhere, and no earthly prospects save journalism.' One thing that saved the situation was *Lovers in London*, published in March 1905. Pinker secured him a rash advance of £15. ('*You never had a book published by the Alston Rivers Mining and Exploration Company*,' Milne wrote to H. G. Wells, trying to make the best of the fact that he had never heard of 'the Alston Rivers Co.', the publisher Pinker had found.)

But the most important thing in the long run was that in 1905, after a period when he had been sending something in one week and getting it back the next, *Punch* started taking Milne's work regularly, both verse and prose. By September his character Lilian (whose 'Loves' had marked his first prose appearance in *Punch* in August the year before) had begun appearing in a regular series and had established an extremely popular style. When collecting his *Punch* pieces together in 1929, Milne wrote: 'I suppose that originality can be attributed with certainty only to Adam. I neither wish nor presume to claim that I am the originator of this sort of dialogue, but I fancy that I made it popular: by which I mean that I made the writing of it popular, not necessarily the reading of it. So much the worse for me. It is not easy to make a reputation in England, but it is much more difficult to lose one.' Long after he stopped writing for *Punch*, he would be congratulated at dinner parties on pieces written by his imitators, pieces evidently from the same desk as that early Lilian and Amelia and that earlier Clarissa. W. A. Darlington, the theatre critic, certainly considered that Milne had *invented* 'a new fresh form of humour' and a new kind of dialogue – inconsequent, graceful, fluid and funny. Even when, later, he would criticize the plots of Milne's plays, he never stopped admiring his dialogue. E. V. Lucas also called it a *new* kind of nonsense, 'based upon and blended with the facts of life . . . all carried out with apparently effortless ease and the utmost gaiety. The art that conceals art.'

Lilian, like all Milne's young unmarried heroes and heroines, is perpetually on the edge of marriage. But if Alan Milne himself had an 'all-devouring passion' at this stage we don't know about it. 'Lilian: her narrow escape' celebrates her refusal of the vicar's proposal. In 'Lilian: a bit of ancient history' she remembers a proposal during a round of golf and in 'Lilian: a row of asterisks' she actually proposes to the narrator. *Lovers in London* ends with a proposal – 'a treaty between England and America', for Amelia, the heroine, is an American and the narrator is a young London writer, who shows her round.

There would seem to be no biographical significance in the fact that Amelia is American. It just 'explains why she wants to go to places like the Tower,' as Milne said to Wells. The sightseeing gives some sort of shape to a book that lacks, among many other things, any plot at all. 'Most of my stories have a way of avoiding anything that approximates to a plot. They do this of their own intention, not regarding the wishes of the author.' Milne was very conscious that, if he did try to write a real novel, it might turn out like that of his own character, John Penquarto, who had looked round his diminutive bedsitting room with a feeling of excitement not unmixed with awe, counted out his rapidly decreasing stock of money, and reflected that he was as far from completing his novel as ever. The hero of John's novel was a boy called Henry who wrote a novel about a boy called Thomas who had lived in Cornwall and written a novel about a boy called Stephen who had lived . . . There seemed no end to this kind of novel; perhaps it was better not to start it and to concentrate on short pieces for the *St James's Gazette*, even if the result was a first book called *Lovers in London*. At least it was finished. At least it was published.

In an answer to an inquirer in 1915 Milne would say, 'It is out of print fortunately; I haven't even a copy myself. But I read my brother's copy the other day with mixed feelings; gladness that it was out of print, shame that I once thought it so good, pride that I had advanced so much since then. I hope you will never come across it.' And to another collector he wrote: 'Humorous Juvenilia – how awful it sounds. You're much better away from it.' It is certainly not worth seeking out. A recent American critic called it 'perhaps the silliest book ever to begin a celebrated career'. Milne eventually bought back his copyright for £5 to prevent a reprint.

Not everyone was as critical of Amelia and *Lovers in London* as Milne was to be himself. The literary editor of the *Evening News*, commissioning a weekly article ('Price 25/- = one morning's work'), said, 'Think how glad Amelia would be.' Milne blushed, 'not with embarrassment at the thought of Amelia, who didn't exist just then, but with pride to think she had become real to somebody else.' In his diary on 23 March 1905, R. C. Lehmann said: 'Wrote a notice of A. A. Milne's capital little book *Lovers in London*.' H. G. Wells was kind, too, in a letter. He could hardly fail to be.

8 Wellington Square
Chelsea

6.iv.05

My dear H. G.

I've only this evening found your letter here. Many thanks for what you say about the book. I've had very nice reviews from *Punch, Evening Standard*, and *Scotsman* (Hoots) but may I quote the *Sheffield Independent* in full to you?

> 'The only readable portion of this book is its title which might stand for something good. It is a series of jerky dialogues with the author's comments and the readers' suppositious reflections interjected so that it is difficult to distinguish one from the other or guess what the author desires to convey. The book is devoid of style, lucidity, and is unintelligible to the reader. We sympathise with those who had to see it through the press.'

He was an old man, who was once on the staff of the *Saturday*, and is now on the *Sheffield Independent* – and only allowed to review reprints of Shakespeare and children's stories . . .

Right 0 for the £5. I've seen *Peter Pan* lately, and am about to go to *Alice S.B.F.* It appears that one can see quite well in the Pit. I'm all for playwriting. But may I observe that if Mr. H. G. WELLS and MR JAMES WELCH combined find a difficulty in persuading Curzon to produce their play, how do I come in? (I say, give me a first night seat for yours, when it comes off. Let's consider that a bet.)

Have you seen *Peter Pan*? It's too wonderful to live. My heroes in real life are J. M. Barrie and the editor of the *Sheffield Independent*.

Good bye
Ever Alan

Nearly three years later, when he was much more financially secure, Milne was writing another play. He could not give up – however remote the chance of getting anything on the stage – and wrote to Wells:

I'm not going to tell you anything, because you'll only say it's young and thin (like myself); but perhaps I'll send you the first act when it's finished . . . I have just realized that the obvious time to write a play is now, when I can afford to. Later on, when I am a middle-aged family man, it will be too risky to spend months on something which probably (nay, certainly) will never get acted. These sentiments are known as 'Art for Art's sake'. The truth is that it's much easier to write a play than a novel (I mean, much more exciting) – and I am trying to make excuses to myself for taking the easy and broad and exciting path.

In the summer of 1905 Milne spent some time in the Orkneys, tutoring a boy who had missed some schooling. Milne's uncle had asked him to do it; it seemed a good chance to see Scotland and the far north. It would undoubtedly, as everything did, give him some material for his writing. One particular experience shows that he still had some longing for the sort of 'adventures' he and Ken had dreamed of as boys, though it would rarely find expression. 'I have said that once every ten years I remember with pride that I am one of the many, or not so many, who have climbed the Napes Needle. Once every twenty years I remember, not exactly with pride, but with a slight lifting of the chin, that I am one of the few, or very few, who have spent a night alone on a desert island.

'There the island was, perhaps a few hundred acres of it, half-a-mile from the mainland, its only inhabitants seafowl. We landed one afternoon and walked about it; found an eider-duck's nest, surprised a few rabbits, and rowed home to tea. At dinner that evening I said that I should like to stay there one night. Nobody knew why; I didn't know why myself, but I supposed that there 'might be an article in it'. Sometimes we fished at night. It was easy for the others to drop me on the island after the fishing and to send somebody over for me next morning. I landed with a rook-rifle, a rug and a flask of brandy.

'There was no shelter anywhere. I wrapped myself in my rug and snuggled down into the heather. As long as I lay still the world was still, but every movement of mine filled the sky with the deep-breathed sound of wings, as if a sudden storm had blown up and died away again. The night was too dark for sight, but the nearness of all that life was faintly menacing. I turned from one cramped position to another as quietly as I could . . .

'The dawn came early and with it a gentle rain. I drank the brandy. The brandy had been part of the joke; like the rifle, a concession to romance. Now I was glad of it. Rifle under the arm, I walked down to the shore. I followed the coastline until I had caught up my footsteps – how many people, I thought, have done that? I did it again. It didn't seem so original this time. I sat on a rock and looked out to sea, my rifle on my knees. Nothing happened . . .

'I decided to shoot a rabbit. Since I was using a rifle I supposed that I should be allowed to shoot it sitting. Well, it was my island and I could make my own laws: I would stalk a rabbit until I got it into a sitting posture, and then we should see. This took time, but time was what I wanted to take just then. It was appreciably nearer breakfast when we got into the required positions: the rabbit sitting up outside its hole, polishing its whiskers, I on my stomach, a suitable distance off, my finger at the trigger. I fired. The rabbit looked up at the noise, noticed me, and trotted into its hole to tell the others. I hadn't killed it, but I could tell myself proudly that I had distracted it.

'I fetched my rug and went down to the landward side of the island. The grey lifeless air melted into the grey lifeless waters, I could see no land, but soon I should hear the creak of oars, and from the mist would come the rescue for which I waited now as eagerly as any authentic castaway. Soon – in about two hours – it came. I lit a pipe, and went down to the beach to meet it.

'Naturally I made an article out of all this. It was too long for *The Evening News*, and apparently too bad for every other paper. But the experience was not wholly wasted. At dances that autumn I would tell my partner that I had once spent a night alone on a desert island . . . and get her surprised attention for a moment.'

That rabbit was, I think, the last living thing he ever tried to shoot, though it would be difficult to avoid shooting on the Somme.

Milne had written a play in the Orkneys too, and Wells spoke to Golding Bright for him. 'He thought it too flimsy,' Milne wrote to Wells, ' "although it shows – – " etc. etc. – the usual "promise".' There seemed to be a lot of 'promise' in the air. The *Daily Mail* had printed one of his articles in May and followed it up with a suggestion that he should call on the editor. After all, wasn't his father one of the Chief's oldest friends? Milne gritted his teeth and went. Things were still rather difficult. The editor said

Would I, if it was offered to me, take a post in the office: viz: editorship of the 2 columns on page 4. Only a morning's work each day: arrange my own hours: princely salary (unspecified further). I said Yes . . . And that's the end of that story: except that I have sent him several things since, all of which have been returned. So I expect it's off, but it doesn't worry me.

Owen Seaman asked me to come to see him, and hinted that I might eventually (say 1910) get pushed on to the *Punch* staff. Only he said it much more indirectly than that.

Milne decided to put that remote delightful possibility right out of his mind.

On a mild February day in 1906 Alan Milne was sitting on a bench in Battersea Park and thinking about his future. It was a time of great excitement in London. The Liberals had just secured a landslide victory in the General Election. It was a time for new decisions. 'At twenty-four,' Milne thought, 'one must be certain of fame at thirty.' Darlington would later write of Milne's 'meteoric rise', but it did not feel like that at the time. What was he to do? Milne said that when he was in doubt or difficulty, he would ask himself, 'What would Napoleon have done?' The answer generally came at once. 'He would have borrowed from Henry' or 'He would have said his aunt was ill.' This time the answer took a bit longer than usual. It seemed unlikely that he would ever succeed in getting a play produced. It seemed unlikely that he could make any sort of name for himself with scattered journalism, much of it anonymous. It was certain that he had made no impact at all with *Lovers in London*, a book so mild-mannered that it admitted it had no place for even 'an illegitimate canary'. What was there to look forward to?

The only possibility seemed to be, in spite of his earlier qualms, to write a proper novel – strong, with a plot – a six-shilling novel, which would be the talk of every dinner table in London. He decided to begin writing it the following Monday; it was to be called *Philip's Wife*. He sat down as soon as he got back to Wellington Square and wrote to Owen Seaman at *Punch* (where he had by now made no fewer than thirty appearances). He said he would not be sending any contributions for the next few months as he was going into the country to concentrate on writing a novel. He had saved just enough to allow him to do so. And the 'country' would presumably be Steeple Bumpstead where his parents, tiring of Streete Court with no heir coming along to take it over, had recently retired. He could live very cheaply at Steeple Bumpstead and write the book that would make his name.

A letter came back from Lehmann by return of post: 'Owen showed me your note. Don't come to any decision about leaving London until you hear from him.' By a strange chance, Milne's note had reached Seaman at the very moment he was taking over as editor of *Punch*. F. C. Burnand was at last, after twenty-six years, about to retire. He had actually been 'brutally dismissed', according to

Lehmann's diary, though it was to appear a resignation. Seaman asked Milne to come and see him. 'He said he needed someone to relieve him of the worst of the donkey work: somebody who came in for, say, a couple of afternoons a week and sorted out the contributions: naturally I should be on trial at first: naturally I couldn't expect to be put on the *Punch* table immediately: obviously this and obviously that: but what it came to, however he glided over it, was – How would I like to be Assistant Editor of *Punch*? It didn't seem possible.

' "The Proprietors thought, seeing that they wouldn't require your full time, that £250 a year would – er – meet the case." That didn't seem possible either.

' "As regards your own contributions, they would be paid for at double rates, and naturally we should expect you to contribute every week." I tried to look grateful, eager, but not surprised, while doing simple arithmetic in the head. It wasn't coming out. I put the arithmetic by for the 'bus, and looked grateful, eager, but not surprised.

' "Normally, of course, you would send them straight down to the printer, but I think perhaps that just at first you had better let me have a look at them before they go." Nothing that was going to happen "just at first" mattered now, I was so certain that I should get everything I wanted in the end. Hadn't I always said that I would be Editor of *Punch* one day? Or hadn't I? I couldn't remember. Anyhow I was going to be.

' "Of course," I said eagerly to everything.

' "You'd better start on Tuesday. I don't come on Monday."

' "Right," I said, wondering how I could possibly live until Tuesday.

'I left the office. It appeared on the 'bus that I should be getting £500 a year. Could it be true? Could I have misheard the figures? Should I go back and ask for it all again? Perhaps in writing this time. No, it was true. I wanted to think of all that it would mean, of all that I would write to Father, of all that I would tell Ken, but I could not think for happiness.

'Just as it had seemed wonderful to be editing *The Granta* after so short a struggle, so it seemed wonderful now to be, at twenty-four, Assistant Editor of *Punch*. In fact I had no need to be so surprised at myself. My real achievement in either case was to be not wholly the wrong person, in the right spot at the right moment. When Seaman was Assistant Editor, the Editor was travelling about the country writing his reminiscences. The new Editor proposed to live in his office chair and devote himself to his paper. The new Assistant Editor would have none of the responsibilities which Seaman had had, his position would be one of more subjection and less dignity. Clearly, then, he must be a young man; clearly he must be a young man who was already a journalist, but not a journalist bound to another paper; he must be himself acceptable as a contributor; and, not least important, he must possess, for the Editor's peace of mind, a degree of presentability such as was only conferred, it was thought, upon the whiter students of the larger colleges at Cambridge. I met all the conditions.'

On 13 February 1906, a month after his twenty-fourth birthday, A. A. Milne started work as assistant editor of *Punch*.

— 6 —

Punch

A. A. MILNE OWED A great deal, not just to his obvious suitability
for the job of assistant editor, but also to R. C. Lehmann, who had
done so much to encourage Milne's natural progression from *Granta*
to *Punch*. As Lehmann had said in his diary entry quoted in an earlier
chapter, the two men had become friends. Lehmann was a good
friend to have. He made a point of encouraging bright young men,
did all he could for them – introducing them to people and inviting
them to Fieldhead, his house at Bourne End, on the reach of the
Thames between Marlow and Cookham. It was very near the place
where Kenneth Grahame had lived as a boy after the death of his
mother. Alan Milne would himself imagine the river near Fieldhead
when he read *The Wind in the Willows* on its publication in 1908.
It was a book that would mean a great deal to him. 'And you really
live by the river? What a jolly life,' as Mole said to Rat. 'By it and
with it and on it and in it.' Milne would repeat the words in *Toad
of Toad Hall*, the play he made from Grahame's book.

It was like that at Fieldhead. We all know by now that 'There is
nothing – absolutely nothing – half so much worth doing as simply
messing about in boats.' The Lehmann household revolved round
the river. R. C. Lehmann, the hero of Cambridge (President of the
Union, outstanding oarsman, editor of *Granta*) had gone on not only
to report on 'distant Balkan wars' and edit the *Daily News*, write
for *Punch* and take a Liberal seat in parliament in that 1906 landslide
victory, but to be, as the young F. D. Roosevelt described him in a
letter home from Groton, 'about the greatest authority on rowing in
the world'. Lehmann had met his American wife, Alice, on a trip
to coach the Harvard crew. 'Always at Fieldhead,' their son, John
Lehmann, wrote in his autobiography, 'one was conscious of the
river.' The youngest of that remarkable family, he was born the year
after Milne joined the staff of *Punch*. John went on: 'As one walked

down from the french windows of the library, past the walnut-tree and between the old apple-trees on the lawn, one came to the gates into the kitchen garden, through which a long tunnel of roses, honey-suckle, clematis and vines, whose grapes never fully ripened, led to the dark laurel boskage of the garden's end . . . The play of light off water was in one's eyes, the familiar faint smell of river-water and weeds was in one's nostrils.'

Fieldhead was the sort of comfortable country house, lavishly staffed, which would appear over and over again, in Milne's *Punch* pieces, his novels, his plays. It was a writer's house, but there was nothing remotely Bohemian about it. Years later, when John was grown up and working for the Woolfs, he would contrast the 'bohemian atmosphere' of Charleston with the more formal comforts of Fieldhead. Over and over again, in the years between Milne's going down from Cambridge and the war, R. C. Lehmann's diary records Alan Milne's visits, but rarely in any detail. It is one of those irritating diaries that goes in only for names and facts. ('Townsend gave Milne and me lunch at the Savoy.' 'Omar Khayyam Club . . . George Drinkwater and Alan Milne were my guests.') He often wrote it up from his pocket engagement diary, months later, with only a little extra information. On one occasion he wrote: 'A jolly dinner full of good talk. Wish I had noted it all down at the time.' If only he had. He does, however, record 'great rejoicing' when at last in 1910 Seaman invited Milne to join the *Punch* Table, that weekly gathering over dinner, to which Lehmann had already belonged for nearly twenty years.

Alan Milne often went down for weekends in the summer. There was lawn tennis as well as the river. There were dogs. Milne would pass on to the Lehmanns a black spaniel, Chum, who was becoming too obstreperous for his parents at Steeple Bumpstead. Chum appeared on several occasions in *Punch* and has some claim to be partly responsible for Tigger, that bouncy animal. There were also delightful small girls at Fieldhead. 'We played a good deal of lawn-tennis, Helen, Rosie, Milne and I,' R. C. Lehmann wrote in his diary the day after his fifteenth wedding anniversary when Milne joined in the celebrations, 'and all the children dined.' Rosamond Lehmann, the second daughter, would remember Alan Milne curled up in an armchair in her father's library, 'very blond', 'gentle and quiet with a soft voice when he did speak, but he didn't speak very much.' He nearly always went down for New Year's Eve, staying overnight and playing paper games. The friendship of Rudie Lehmann, this radical family man, was extremely important to Milne. Lehmann was both physically and morally fearless. Speaking out against the Boer War had taken at times both sorts of courage. He had 'an enormous circle of devoted friends', many of whom Milne met. Milne would learn a great deal from Lehmann – including the way he used his own family in his writing. 'It was typical of my father's attitude towards his family,' John Lehmann wrote, 'that he used us all quite shamelessly.' Readers loved it. And John did not grumble when a mention in *Punch* of his stamp-collecting brought him stamps from all over the world. In 1910 Milne would dedicate his first collection of *Punch* pieces 'To R. C. Lehmann, my chief creditor, this trifle on account.'

Lehmann came from a background which filled his conversation with good stories – and his library, where Rosamond remembered the young Alan Milne, was hung with portraits by his uncle Rudolf Lehmann, of Wilkie Collins and Robert Browning – and a 'terrible' painting by Pen Browning. The shelves were full of the Victorian novelists and poets ('in all the darkly glowing colours of their gold-printed leather bindings'), who had been the friends of his parents. Alan was shown a piece of writing paper from Lehmann's parents' house at 15 Berkeley Square, on which Browning had written a few words in 1886 – four lines in English and two quotations in Greek – in tiny handwriting to prove his eyesight was still perfect. The library was also rich, of course, in bound volumes of *Punch*. Lehmann himself had done a certain amount to restore prestige to *Punch* at this period, shaking it out of its Victorian complacency, though with Burnand and now Seaman in charge, there was no hope of it returning to its original attitudes.

Punch had after all, as the very name suggests, been established as anarchic, anti-establishment, socially disruptive – like Mr Punch himself. Writers in early *Punch* were characterized in an 1848 cartoon as 'Chartists, deists, atheists, anarchists and socialists to a man' who derived most of their income from 'sending threatening letters to the Nobility and Gentry'. Now it had become, some thought, rather anaemic, certainly 'a mirror of middle-class public opinion, faithfully reflecting our domestic troubles and preoccupations'. And yet it still had a certain charisma and a residual faith in the possibility of bringing about change through humour. Cabinet Ministers and Field Marshals still thought it worth taking trouble to have *Punch* on their side.

Rudie Lehmann obviously saw Milne as a useful ally in the editorial offices at *Punch*, but as Penelope Fitzgerald, daughter of E. V. Knox, a later editor, once put it (admiring 'the young and radical A. A. Milne', 'the incurable dissident'), '*Punch* was no country for young men'. Seaman, the new editor, was in fact only forty-five when he took over *Punch*, but he had been around a long time. He and Milne were not only politically but 'temperamentally opposed, which was probably good for both of them', according to R. G. G. Price. Seaman was best known for his parodies. He is said to have been deeply insecure because of a background in trade (his great-uncle, appropriately named Mantle, was a linen draper in Leicester Square and his father an importer of artificial flowers in Sloane Street) – but he had been to Shrewsbury and Clare College, Cambridge (where he won the Porson Prize for Greek Iambics) and gave a good impression of being a perfect gentleman. Pearl Craigie (who wrote as John Oliver Hobbes) was sure Henry James was thinking of Seaman when he created Merton Densher. 'Henry James has sent me *The Wings of a Dove*. Clearly the man is meant to be Seaman. It is hard upon him.' Seaman had parodied James, but James did not know him well. Pearl Craigie did know Seaman well, and it is interesting that she saw him in that James character, the 'longish, leanish, fairish young Englishman, not unamenable on certain sides to classification – as for instance by being a gentleman, by being rather specifically one of the educated. The difficulty with Densher was that he looked vague without looking weak – idle without looking empty . . .' Pearl Craigie would have nothing to do with Owen Seaman, who, according to Mrs Henniker, was madly in love with her. 'I disapprove of his conduct, of his mistresses and of his manners.' Alan Milne could not avoid having plenty to do with him.

At Clare, Seaman had been a friend of Lancelot Speed, who became a quite successful artist. Speed's niece, Dorothy de Sélincourt, was Owen Seaman's god-daughter. She will appear later in this story. Milne called Seaman a 'strange, unlucky man'. 'All the Good Fairies came to his christening, but the Uninvited Fairy had the last word . . . Humour was drowned in Scholarship and Tact went down before Truth.' He was a bad loser. Milne tells a story of Seaman as a golfer, 'making an excuse for every bad shot until he got to the last green, when he threw down his putter and said: "That settles it. I'll never play in knicker-bockers again." It could have been so delightfully said – but it wasn't.' He was a difficult man to work for, though

Milne remained convinced that he had a heart of gold. It has been suggested, not very convincingly, that he inspired Eeyore. Certainly R. G. G. Price says that Seaman was good at spotting the possibility of offence where none existed. And if Milne could be called prudish, Seaman was even more so, in spite of his mistresses. He was once extremely disturbed to hear that an octopus in a cartoon was expelling ink from its anus – until his Art Editor assured him that its anus was between its eyes. In spite of all that would happen, in 1921 Milne would dedicate *The Sunny Side* affectionately to Owen Seaman.

Seaman had some odd ideas. He told E. V. Knox he belonged to a group called the Samurai, dedicated to the notion of evolving a 'higher human type'. He once said sadly of someone: 'He is the kind of man who doesn't take his humour seriously.' He thought Socialists were the very devil, and Liberals only to be tolerated if they kept quiet about it. In fact, Milne said, Seaman would go so far as to say that all Radicals were traitors and all gentlemen Conservatives. Even Rudie Lehmann could not stop him generalizing. It was, in any case, a view widely held. 'In all my contacts on dance-floors, cricket-fields and at country houses,' Milne said of the period when the Liberals were in power, 'it never failed to be assumed that I shared my companions' estimate of the Government's perfidy.' At the *Punch* Table, Lehmann did his best for Liberalism, but he had been trying to do so for so long that he had almost given up hope. E. V. Lucas had been his only ally.

There seems no doubt that it was Milne's politics, rather than his youth, that kept him off the *Punch* Table for so long. It was frustrating, but Milne was not inclined to grumble. He was so delighted with his job and the chance to write for *Punch* and know he would be paid for it. 'It will remain,' he thought in 1929, 'the most astonishing day of my life, that February day in 1906, when I entered the *Punch* office, awed but unsuspicious, a casual contributor with £2 in the bank,' ('Art is exaggeration') 'and left it Assistant Editor, with a regular salary and, as regularly, the freedom of its pages.' The *Punch* dinners, attended by all the members of the Table, were normally held in Bouverie Street, on Wednesday evenings, mainly to plan the political cartoons for the next issue. They were held on the floor below the editorial offices. Not yet invited to join the Table, Milne wrote: 'Wednesday was a busy day and I was generally in my room when the diners began to congregate. Most of them would put their heads in to say "Good-evening"; some of them would stay for a little talk; just so (one felt) would kindly uncles who had come to dine look in on the nursery to say good-night to the children.'

Fridays were even busier. It was on Fridays that Milne wrote his own pieces, which could have been written any other day. His articles had to be sent down to the printer by four o'clock on Friday and that 'made both the writing of it possible and the writing of it earlier impossible. Ideas may drift into other minds, but they do not drift my way. I have to go and fetch them. I know no work manual or mental to equal the appalling heart-breaking anguish of fetching an idea from nowhere.' It worried him to think that if he stayed at *Punch* until he was seventy, as so many people seemed to do, he would have to find about two thousand five hundred ideas before he died. He would envy the miners or bricklayers who worked with their hands and 'knew nothing of what work really meant'. In another mood, he would boast he could write something, if he had to, on absolutely anything.

Milne described how one particular piece came to be written. He had been in the country and came back to London on a morning train, which got in at noon on a Friday. Unless he could think of something on the journey . . . At first he couldn't. Then 'at Chisle-hurst or some such place, a girl got into my carriage; I whisked my dressing case off the seat, and – nothing happened.' But the article was assured. In that moment, Milne had imagined the bag opening and its contents scattered over the carriage – dirty collars, crumpled pyjamas, 'an absurd piece of shaving soap', and, worst of all, dirty socks with unmatching suspenders attached to them. Not *very* funny; but adequate. People smiled in dentists' waiting-rooms and as they buttered another piece of toast. Just the sort of thing that *would* happen, wasn't it?

When he had sent his article down to the printers, he would go out in search of a late lunch. 'Soon after four I was back in the office, criticizing a play to which I had been the night before, and writing a book review. By five o'clock I was doing the paragraphs.' The book reviews were most often what can loosely be called deck-chair or railway-carriage reading, with little indication that it was the age of Yeats, Conrad and Forster. Milne reviewed large numbers of books for 'Our Booking Office' – as many as thirty-one in 1906 and twenty-six in 1907; fewer books and more plays as the years passed. The paragraphs were cuttings from other papers with appropriate com-ments – the sort of thing still seen in *Punch*, and indeed in *Private*

Eye and the *New Yorker*. Milne is credited with having started the idea of commenting on 'the howlers, ineptitudes and inanities of the press' and with having encouraged the flood of possibly appropriate cuttings into the office. J. V. Milne in Steeple Bumpstead was always on the look-out for something suitable, and so, it seemed, was half England – even Winston Churchill, to whom Milne illogically offered three shillings rather than the customary '½ a crown and a free copy', as he was a Cabinet Minister.

By six o'clock the paragraphs were finished and it was time to go through the week's unsolicited contributions. The standard was not always high. One old gentleman wrote: 'On my seventy-seventh birthday last week a young friend of mine who is a great footballer' – (and 'footballer' was crossed out and 'cricketer' substituted) – 'said to me, "seventy-seven not out!" I think this is clever wit.' 'It was difficult in this welter of clever wit to keep one's head; difficult not to feel, on one day that anything which didn't try to be funny was funny, and on the next that nothing would ever be funny again.'

By ten o'clock (after some time off for dinner) 'the paper had been set and the pages were beginning to come up.' Seaman was maddeningly slow in reading the proofs. Milne wanted to scream: 'Time isn't a thing you do this to.' By one o'clock in the morning they were through. 'It had been interesting to cut ten lines out of somebody else's article, and annoying to have to cut two of my own.' On Saturday mornings Milne would get to Bouverie Street at ten when the pages came back for final correction. He waited impatiently for Seaman to come. 'I was playing cricket at twelve or I was catching an 11.40 into Sussex for the weekend, or I was going to Lord's, or Twickenham, or . . .' For some reason, Seaman could hardly bear to let him go.

Milne's social life was very full these days. Being assistant editor of *Punch* seemed to make him much more eligible and invitable than he had been as a mere freelance journalist. His initials were attached to his pieces from the beginning of 1908, and people started noticing and asking 'Who *is* A. A. M.?' R. G. G. Price said: 'After Milne had been writing for *Punch* every week for a few years, the older prose writers there began to seem tired and heavy.' Milne was in demand. There were horses and traps waiting for him at pretty wayside stations, and elegant cards inviting him to dine. With *Punch*'s large circulation and vastly larger readership, Milne's initials were becoming known to a fair proportion of literate England. 'Everyone reads *Punch*,' the reviews of his *The Day's Play* said in 1910.

It was in May that year that Milne at last took his seat at the *Punch* Table, just five days after the King's funeral brought to an end the Edwardian period Milne later thought would be considered peculiarly his own. He carved a neat monogram of his initials on the Table itself, as was the custom, and sat down regularly on Wednesdays to dine. Membership was a mixed blessing. Lehmann often recorded 'the damnable stodginess' or the 'stickiness' of the dinners. Anstey Guthrie was known to 'shriek and nag and niggle'. Lawrence Bradbury, one of the proprietors, could be irritable and tempestuous. Charles Graves, Robert's uncle, was rather less irritating, but was Seaman's 'leading disciple'. They often argued over the cartoons until late into the night. But there was one memorable occasion, in the scorching summer of 1911, when Rudie Lehmann delighted the Table by reading Rosamond's first attempt at light verse: 'For a child of ten it is really amazingly well done and shows not only a great command of metre and language, but a strong sense of fun.' Milne was particularly interested.

The home that Milne returned to, after the dinners were over and after his weekends away, was no longer the policeman's house in Wellington Square, Chelsea, but serviced chambers, this time in Queen Anne's Gate. In fact, as the alternative address was 31 Broadway, Westminster, Milne's rooms seem to have been on the site of the present headquarters of London Transport, in the block that includes St James's Park station. The chambers were not ideal: 'In order to get to the long living-room in front, it was necessary to pass through either of the two rooms at the back; which gave visitors an immediate acquaintance with one's bedroom or one's bathroom, as preferred. In these days,' Milne was writing in 1939, 'this might be supposed to strike the right note of intimacy at the start, but in those days one kept something in reserve. I decided, therefore, to sleep in the bathroom, or, as I chose to put it, to have the luxury of a completely fitted bath in my bedroom. The other room thus became the ante-room or library. Through this visitors were shown, little knowing that for their sakes I was sleeping with the geyser. Luckily I had got used to the smell of gas in Chelsea.'

Both his social life and his new chambers provided Milne with endless material. In a series called 'Bachelor Days', we can see him, or his *alter ego*, in thrall to a bossy 'housekeeper'. He has foolishly forgotten to tell her that he hates unsalted butter, reminder as it was of horrible breakfasts at Westminster. There was a huge lump of the stuff at his first breakfast in St James's Park Chambers.

I hate waste in small things. Take care of the little extravagances, I say, and the big ones will take care of themselves. My first thought on viewing this pat of butter was, 'It is difficult, but I will eat it.' My second, 'But I must tell the housekeeper to get salt butter next time.'

An ordinary-minded person would have stopped there. I went one further. My third thought was this: 'Housekeepers are forgetful creatures. If I tell her now, she will never remember. Obviously I had better wait until this pound is just finished and she is about to get in some more. Then will be the time to speak.' So I waited; and it was here that I made my mistake. For it turned out that it was I who was the forgetful creature. And on the fifteenth day I got up to find another large pound of vaseline on my table. The next fortnight went by slowly. I kept my eye on it every day, waiting for the moment to come when I could say to the housekeeper, 'You will be getting me in some more butter this morning. Would you get salt, as I don't much like the other?' Wednesday came, and there was just enough left for two days. I would speak on the morrow.

But, alas! on the morrow there was another new pound waiting. I had evidently misjudged the amount . . . So it went on. But what *could* I do? After eating fresh butter for four months without protest I couldn't possibly tell the housekeeper that I didn't like it, and would she get salt in future. That would be too absurd. Fancy taking four months to discover a little thing like that! Nor could I pretend that, though I used to adore fresh butter, I had now grown tired of it. I hate instability of character, and I could not lend myself to any such fickleness. I put it to you that either of these courses would have shown deplorable weakness. No, an explanation with the house-keeper was by that time impossible; and if anything was to be done I must do it on my own responsibility. What about buying a pound of salt butter myself, and feeding on it in secret! True, I should have to get rid of a certain portion of fresh every day, but . . .

I don't know if you have ever tried to get rid of a certain portion of fresh butter every day, when you are living in a flat at the very top of chambers in London. Drop it out of the window once or twice, and it is an accident. Three times, and it is a coincidence. Four times, and the policeman on duty begins to think that there is more in it (if I may say so) than meets the eye.

More months passed and more pats of vaseline. Every day made an explanation more hopeless.

After anonymous letters and a visit to Switzerland in order to be able to return and sing the wonders of salt butter, Milne ends: 'There remains only one consolation. In three years my lease is up. I shall take a new flat somewhere, and on the very first day I shall have a word with the new housekeeper. "By the way," I shall say, "about the butter . . ." '

This is typical Milne. You either find it funny or you don't, this mixture of fact and fantasy, this self-mocking chain of circumstance. E. V. Lucas called it 'enchanting ingenuity'. Others have been less enchanted. Marriage is still much on his mind. If one were married, there would be no need of intimidating housekeepers: 'Of course, it is quite possible to marry for love, but I suspect that a good many bachelors marry so that they may not have to bother about the washing any more. That, anyhow, will be one of the reasons with me.' In those pre-launderette days he was always losing collars at the laundry or getting back a tablecloth when he had sent his 'footer shorts'. He would soon stop playing football for Westminster Old Boys and take up golf for himself. It was not so dirty.

Milne went frequently to other people's weddings. At one stage, or so it felt, he was an usher three days running.

> For what seemed weeks, but was the last two days,
> I'd pottered up and down that blessed baize –
> Sorting out aunts in browns and aunts in greys.
>
> For what seemed always, but was only twice
> (Looking, if I may say so, rather nice),
> I'd lent a hand with hymn-sheets and with rice.
>
> Once more the dear old bells ring out; once more
> I linger, pink and anxious, at the door –
> This is the third time. Here she comes! Oh, lor'!
>
> Something on these occasions goes and thrills
> My fancy waistcoat at the first 'I will's':
> It *can't* be hopeless love – it must be chills . . .
>
> Something . . . And yet the fiercest unconcern
> So masks me that the vergers never learn
> How underneath my chest I yearn and yearn.

For all his jesting, another poem, 'Reverie', seems to suggest a genuine loneliness, a real disturbance of his habitual equanimity. He had met a girl at a dance ten days before and they had talked. She had been rather keen on golf; he had never been to Scarborough. They both thought well of Bernard Shaw. When she went off to dance with someone else, he asked the waiter had he ever been in love. Then he asked himself, 'Am I in love? Well, no, I hardly think so. For one, I'm much too happy as I am.' But writing a letter to her, he said, 'Had a mouse appeared, I could have loved it in my loneliness. Had but the humblest cockroach shown his head, I think I would have said "Goodnight" to it . . . Just for one moment you upset me slightly.'

H. G. Wells had certainly made him wary of the wrong marriage; Maud and Ken were a constant reminder of the joy of a good one. Their first child, Marjorie, was born in 1906 and the second, Angela, in 1909. Marjorie, in particular, provided her uncle with plenty of copy, though he insisted on calling her 'Margery', too like 'margarine' for her parents' pleasure. Margarine is apparently called so because of its pearly lustre, Milne told his niece. 'You are Margery to me: I hope I have a mind above your common-place Marjories.'

The series shows a real knowledge of how a child's mind works. At their best, and certainly as the child grows and provides original material, the sketches escape from an initial whimsicality into a convincing humour. 'Most of the stories about her are founded on fact,' he wrote in reply to a fan letter. 'Her own share in the conversation is, if not actual, at any rate true to life . . . To get a child properly on to paper one needs to know her by heart . . . She is a darling and thank you for adoring her.' The talk of a very small child has rarely been so accurately conveyed. Milne celebrates the unembarrassed egotism of children, as he would do later in such poems as 'Disobedience' and the much-reviled 'Vespers'.

'Bother' and balloons, later to be connected with Winnie-the-Pooh, make an early appearance:

'Tell Margie a story about a balloon.'

'Bother,' I murmured.

'What's bovver?'

'Bother is what you say when relations ask you to tell them a story about a balloon.' But the two-year-old is really more interested in buttons than balloons and drives her beloved uncle mad by asking 'What's 'at?', dabbing at every button on his waistcoat in turn. After he has patiently explained that, yes, every one is a button, the child asks 'What's a button?'

'You don't mean to say,' I reproached her, 'that I've got to tell you now what a button is? *That*,' I added severely, pointing to the top of my waistcoat, 'is a button.'

'What's 'at?' said Margery, pointing to the next one. And the whole process starts all over again.

As she grows, the child obviously fascinates Milne even more than she exasperates him. She calls her mother 'Maud', a term suitable only for upstairs: that is, there are certain words ('sick' and 'corsets' among them) which she can say upstairs but not downstairs. When she is angry, she shouts them from the top of the stairs. At three, she has a fairly sceptical attitude to her elders. 'Well, that's a *silly* thing to say,' becomes a favourite expression in the family. It appears in *Punch* in March 1910 but makes its first appearance in a letter from Alan to his father. Maud and Ken have brought Marjorie to tea in St James's Park Chambers; they then set off for a walk in the park.

ALAN: Come along, Marjie. You must run now.
MARJIE: Why, dear uncle?
KEN (crossly): Because you're told to.
MARJIE: What do you say, Daddy?
KEN (improving the occasion): You must always do what you're told.
MARJIE: What, Daddy?
KEN (slowly): *You must always do what you're told.*
MARJIE (with great contempt): Well, that's a *silly* fing to say.

The phrase is there again in Milne's inscription in what he liked to think of (trying to forget *Lovers in London*) as his first book: *The Day's Play*:

> To the dear authors of Marjorie
> from the author of Margery.
> ('Well, 'at's a silly fing to say.')
Sep. 22nd, 1910

Marjorie's words even provide the caption for at least one *Punch* cartoon. Drawn by F. H. Townsend in 1912 (the year Marjorie was six), the original hangs on the wall in Marjorie's own study in Dorset, seventy-six years later. The poor child was apparently always being expected to run: 'When you're asked to do anything, Margery, you should always *run*.' She has been slow bringing her father's newspaper.

MARGERY: Yes, I will, Daddy; except, of course, I can't when my legs ache.
FATHER: Rubbish. *Your* legs never ache.
MARGERY (indignantly): Hoo! What's the use of the word 'ache' then?

'It's not very funny,' Marjorie says to me in 1988.
Some more of that same letter to J. V. Milne in Steeple Bumpstead in the spring of 1909 is worth quoting:

after midnight, Friday.

Dear Father,

I must write a line before I retire, as I may not have time tomorrow.

Cornwall. Seaman has just announced that he goes away to Cap Martin (or some horribly jolly place) on the 26th for a month or a year or some incredible time. Unfortunately I have an engagement (Scarboro's dance) on the 24th. I cannot come away when Lucas is here (daren't trust him alone!) so that my only chance of seeing Cornwall with you would be a long week-end. That is, Friday Saturday Sunday Monday Tuesday. Friday and Tuesday would be spent in the train, leaving three clear days. That isn't much, is it? What say you? . . .

Wells found me in the N.L.C. yesterday and took me to the weekly dinner of a little club to which he belongs; where I met (among others) Herbert Trench (who now runs the Haymarket Theatre), H. W. Nevinson (a man whom I admire – though I disagree profoundly with some of his views – more than any man in London almost; a 20th century Don Quixote), and a Maurice Baring of whom you may or may not have heard. He was in the diplomatic, then war correspondent in Manchuria for *The Morning Post*, novelist and many other things . . . Well, Wells and Nevinson and I went round to Baring's house afterwards: the most wonderful eighteenth-century place hidden away in Westminster (just behind the school) that I have ever been in. I never dreamt that there could be such a house in such a part of London. 'North Cottage' it's called: fancy a cottage in the heart of Westminster and it's just like a cottage too: all twists and turns and narrow stairs (and a little courtyard! and a wonderful carved ceiling).

Wells was in ecstasies (as usual) over the Rabbits 'If I could do any one thing as perfectly as you do that', he said, 'I should be perfectly happy' etc. etc.

[Interval for pouring out Wincarnis which I quaff and continue] . . .

1 o'clock – no fire as I've been at the office all day – and I'm tired.

So good night to you both
Your loving Alan

Tell Mother when my 3rd bottle is finished (which is nearly) I am going to try Phospherine. I hear it's awfully good for the brain!

The Rabbits, whom Wells so admired, made no fewer than forty-six appearances in *Punch* between June 1909 and April 1914. For the rest of Milne's life, people would remember the Rabbits. In a review of *The Day's Play*, which was a collection of Milne's *Punch* pieces, the *Scotsman* went so far as to say that, with the 'conversational somersaults of the Rabbits, it would seem that the mantle of the lamented Lewis Carroll had fallen on Mr Milne.' He would often be compared with Carroll: 'The author, with his real wit and inconsequent humour, approaches more nearly to the spirit of Lewis

Carroll than any other modern humorist.' But the Rabbits have a flavour that is not really Carrollian, unique and difficult to define.

The Rabbits are totally middle-class. Like Milne himself, they have comfortable sociable lives but they are not part of Society. 'In my day,' Milne wrote in his autobiography, 'there was something called Society, into which (unless you were born there) it was almost impossible to enter; and if you were outside it, as I was, you read about it in the Society papers with awe or indulgence or an amused contempt.' If in 1939, when he wrote that, it was amused contempt, before the first war it was more often a kind of awed indulgence. Milne was not always as much of an outsider as he suggests in this paragraph. One wonders if the 'Scarboros', whose dance he mentioned in that letter to his father, were rather the aristocratic Scarbroughs. Certainly he was refusing some aristocratic invitations these days. If he was always, as he said, on the side of the underdog (the animal about to be shot, the convict, the man against the odds), he was mixing a good deal with the top dogs.

Though little evidence survives, there is enough to show that Milne's company was sought after. In a letter to Edward Marsh in 1911, Milne regrets that he is unable to go with Marsh to Lady Lytton's. 'Certainly I remember meeting Lady Lytton at the Palace and I also remember (which she doesn't) meeting her about 25 years before that . . . being only four at the time I forget what I said. It is very nice of her to ask me to dinner.' What this was all about – whether the Palace was the Palace Theatre, the Crystal, St James's or even Buckingham, we have no way of knowing, and it is difficult to imagine on what occasion in 1886 their paths might have crossed. But the letter reveals an intimacy with Eddie Marsh, which was apparently well established. Marsh had been Winston Churchill's Private Secretary and close friend since Churchill had become a minister in the Liberal landslide, just at the time Milne joined *Punch*. Marsh always appeared to know everyone and it gratified Milne, of course, that he had so much time for *him*. They were going regularly to the theatre together. 'No, my friend, you're going to come out with *me* this time,' Milne wrote.

Milne also refused an invitation from Venetia Stanley, Lord Sheffield's daughter, who would eventually marry Milne's old Trinity friend, Edwin Montagu. The refusal was because he was going down to Cornwall to stay with Charles Turley Smith, a newish friend, *Punch* reviewer and writer of some excellent school stories as Charles

Turley. When he had arrived at *Punch*, Milne was often asked 'Don't you know Turley?' He had been told so many times that he would love him that when he did eventually meet him, at a weekend party at Philip Agnew's (one of the proprietors of *Punch*), he had determined not to. But 'within a month or two I was staying with him for the first of many holidays at Mullion'. Turley, as he was always known, had 'an innocent goodness with a keen sense of humour, and intelligence with a boyish devotion to games'. Milne might have been describing himself.

It was Turley who turned Milne into a golfer. Golf was a game which, like cricket, would give A. A. Milne lots of chances to try to be funny in print – starting with 'Why do I hit the ball with a ridiculous club like this? I could send it farther with a cricket bat. I could push it straighter with a billiard cue.' Before long he was addicted. Asking Marsh once whether there was any point in taking golf clubs to Alderley, Venetia Stanley's home, he said, 'I am quite childishly mad about it now and am prepared to beat you, Winston, Ben Tillett, Harry Vardon or anybody else.' And cricket was as important as ever. Milne returned from a holiday with Turley in 1912 to find that Ken and Maud had had their third child. It was a nephew for him: Ian Innes Milne, 'fully qualified for Middlesex' and a possible left-hand bowler, even if his initials sounded rather like a parody of his uncle's own. When Turley stayed with E. V. Lucas and his family, at Kingston Manor near Lewes, Audrey Lucas recalled, 'People came out beaming from their cottages. It was the same wherever he went.' Audrey Lucas looked back to the house parties of her childhood:

Hugh Walpole and Alan Milne, who seemed generally to arrive together, would lie in deck chairs talking of the great things they meant to do. I used to sit listening avidly. They talked and talked while I gave them my mute, unobserved attention: unobserved, that is, except at such times as I would fetch from the house long, cool drinks for these thirsty prophetic conversationalists. Alan, very fair and handsome, knowing exactly how to talk unpatronizingly to a child was, with one exception, my favourite among all the visitors.

Long afterwards Audrey Lucas called Milne 'glamorous', 'to use a word now which I never used then'.

E. V. Lucas, who had joined the *Punch* Table in 1903, went on to become chairman of Methuen in the year that it published *When We Were Very Young*. Lucas and Milne were very fond of each other. After his death, Milne wrote of him in *The Times*: 'To be a writer and to have him for a friend was to feel that whatever one wrote was written in a special sense for him; so that the thought "E.V. will like that" gave me a new conceit of the last paragraph, a new confidence for the next.' 'I must tell E.V. that,' he thought over thirty years of friendship. Milne knew he was a better writer for Lucas's appreciation. 'I thrive on your praise, for there is none that I value more.' Seaman was never one to praise, but Lucas knew that 'you can't be light and gay and off-hand and casual and charming in print, unless you are continually reassured that you are being some of those things.' 'Not since its foundation in 1841 has *Punch*, in my opinion,' E. V. Lucas wrote in his memoirs, 'printed articles of such unwavering high spirits, fun and felicity of phrase as those signed "A.A.M.".' It was through Lucas that Milne came to write for years for Clement Shorter's *Sphere*; he had started by filling in once when E.V. was in Florence.

Lucas, like Milne, was a cricketer. He had often played for J. M. Barrie's famous team, the Allahakbarries. (So too had Charles Turley Smith.) The team had always had close associations with *Punch*. Milne later regretted that he had engineered an introduction to Barrie, rather than waiting for a natural connection through their many mutual friends. What had happened was that when Milne published *The Day's Play* in 1910, Lucas had suggested that, 'since I had parodied the title, I should send a copy to the author of *The Day's Work*. When I said that I didn't know Kipling, and couldn't imagine the author of the famous and recently published line "The flannelled fool at the wicket, the muddied oaf in the goal" being interested in a book full of cricket and lesser games, E.V. assured me that Kipling was "not like that" and that he would write me a charming and appreciative letter back. I should have loved a charming and appreciative letter from Kipling, but had to wait twenty years for it; for in those days I couldn't regard it as possible that young writers should introduce themselves in this way to older writers whom they didn't know. The school tie wouldn't hear of it; it was "bad form". However, each Wednesday when we met at the dinner, E.V. would say, "Have you sent your book to Kipling yet?" until at last I had to promise him that this next week I really would. So I sat down to write the accompanying letter: "Sir," I began ... It was, it had to be, one of those letters in which the case for the importance of the addressee and the unimportance of the addressor is slightly overstated ... My letter beginning "Sir" and enclosing my own modest volume expressed not only an unrestrained admiration for the great man's own work, but the assurance that it was from him alone that I had drawn my first enthusiasm for literature, and that it was to the peak whereon he sat that I was lifting my eyes, content if I could master only so much as the few first gentle slopes. (Or whatever. I don't keep copies.) When I had written this, I read it through, and decided that it was so utterly false that I simply could not let it go. I admired much of Kipling, but not like that. The only writer whom I did admire at all like that in those days was Barrie. So, not wishing to waste the letter, I sent it and the book to Barrie.'

J. M. Barrie reacted to A. A. Milne's present of *The Day's Play* with gratifying enthusiasm. He wrote on 13 October 1910 from Adelphi Terrace House:

I see no one among the young people with so light and gay and happy a touch as you show ... It set me looking for a little booklet of my cricket club ... I elect you the last member. The gaiety and irresponsibility of your work (I know it in *Punch*) are rarer gifts than you wot of now. When you know you won't be so gay. So don't know as long as you can. Something else will take their place by and by – something very good, I hope, but don't be in a hurry. Hide and seek with the angels is good enough for anyone.

I feel an affection for the man behind your book, and hope all will always be well with you – or thereabouts. Perhaps some day you will lunch with me. I wander about alone.

That last sentence could hardly be ignored. Nor could the honour of being elected the last of the Allahakbarries, founded more than twenty years before. The friendship flourished. Adelphi Terrace House was only a few minutes' walk from the *Punch* office. Welcoming Milne, Barrie would stand, always with his pipe in his mouth, with his back to the fireplace, facing the windows with their magnificent view down the Thames. Not the least of Milne's appeal to Barrie was that the Llewellyn Davies boys loved A.A.M. as much as he did. When Milne's next book, *The Holiday Round*, reached them in 1912, appropriately in the wilds of Harris, Barrie described how the book was fought over: 'George got it first, stolen by Peter, recovered by George, handed on to Roger, again borrowed by Peter, borrowed by Michael, disappeared with Gerald while Peter and Michael were hot over it, finally fell to me and just read with much glee. It is delicious and I applaud heartily.' George Llewellyn Davies turned nineteen that summer and Michael twelve.

The following summer Milne took part in the last match of the Allahakbarries at Downe House, Audrey Lucas's school, then in Darwin's house in Kent. There was the steam train from Charing Cross to Orpington and then horse brakes through the narrow leafy lanes to the school. It was beautiful summer weather ('one of those glorious deep blue days') as it was, it seems, so often in those last summers before the war. Audrey remembered, years later, 'a wonderful cold lunch out of doors'. George Llewellyn Davies, recently captain of the Eton eleven, wore perfect white flannels and a striped cap. He would be killed less than two years later. Alan Milne sat immediately in front of him in the group photograph, looking keen and confident. And, in front of him, was E. V. Lucas's brother, Percy, killed on the Somme in 1916 (not far from where Milne was himself) with George's revolver at his hip. Barrie would write sadly to Turley that: 'George's revolver and field glasses are again without an owner.'

Milne was also involved in another much-recorded pre-war occasion, though he does not mention it in his autobiography. It took place in the Royal Albert Hall on 4 December 1912. Edward Marsh wrote to Lady Gladstone: 'I've been living mainly with poets' (*Georgian Poetry* was just about to appear and to create more excitement than any book of verse since the days of Tennyson) 'and haven't got much news of the smart set. Has anyone told you of Diana Manners' floater at the Albert Hall Ball?' Commenting on this, Lord Norwich (the son of Lady Diana Cooper, as she became) said that he hardly supposed Alan Milne was a member of the Smart Set, but he must certainly have been a Bright Young Thing. On this occasion, he was undoubtedly shining brightly. Lady Sheffield, Venetia Stanley's mother, had invited him to be one of the princes partnering the twelve dancing princesses at the fancy-dress ball. Fancy dress was something that often appeared in A.A.M.'s pieces in *Punch*, Milne always portraying himself as a most reluctant dresser-up. 'Why do you want to thrust royalty on me? I'd much sooner go as Perkin Warbeck. I should wear a brown perkin – jerkin . . .' On another occasion he chooses to go as an architect as architects wear dress clothes very like his own. Deciding what to be, what to go as, was awful.

> I am going as Joseph.
> I am going as Swan and Edgar.

I am going as the Sick Duke, by Orchardson.
I am going, yes, that's it, I am going back to bed.

On one New Year's Eve at the Lehmanns' he had to sit through dinner in an ivy wreath, representing some improbable book title.

On this occasion at least the decision was made for him, even if it did involve wearing a 'silver smock, with very tight tights and a golden wig'. They dined first with a glittering party that included Winston Churchill and Raymond Asquith (whom Milne so much admired and who, like George Llewellyn Davies, would soon be dead). The dancing princesses, Venetia and Diana among them, were supposed to be dressed in virginal white. All the dresses were to be exactly alike – not a variation in any detail would Lady Sheffield allow. Diana's dress was exactly the same in every detail as those of the other princesses. But it was black. 'Little else was talked about' for weeks, Marsh told Lady Gladstone, who was abroad, but, recalling it years later, Alan Milne would remember more vividly how Eddie Marsh had looked in his golden wig, with his eye-glass screwed firmly into his eye and a fake CB round his neck. He would get a real one six years later.

Invitations poured in, often from people he did not really know. Forty years later he wrote:

Now a dinner-party in those far-off days was a solemn business. Dismiss at once from your mind, young men of today, the picture of yourself, cigarette between fingers, drinking gin-and-orange in the bed-sitting-room with your host, while your hostess bustles in and out of the kitchenette telling you that the soup is just coming in, and have you ever tried veal-loaf because it's rather fun – 'Oh, and Peter, could you do something constructive about the pineapple chunks, because the thing you're supposed to open it with doesn't seem to work.' It was nothing like that.

There would be nineteen people in the drawing-room when the Shy Young Man was announced by the butler in a loud authoritative voice as 'Mr Million'. The Hostess, possibly remembering where she had seen him before, possibly not, would advance beneath a forest of chandelier and over an acre of parquet flooring, to give him a languid hand and say 'So glad you could come, let me see, I think you're taking Miss Postlethwaite in, ah there she is, Muriel dear, this is Mr Melon' – and there, poor devil he was.

There were no cocktails in those days: nothing to loosen the tongue, nothing to occupy the hands. Had Mr Melon lit a cigarette, the ladies would have swooned and the men muttered that it wasn't cricket; 'Parkinson', the Host would have said, 'remove Mr Mullins'. Smoking was for the dining-room only, when the ladies had withdrawn. Mr Melon and Miss Postle-thwaite have to get on as best they can under their own steam. This is what was known as the *mauvais quart d'heure*. Once safely in the dining-room, they can eat; now there is nothing they can do but talk. They are both very shy, but, as Mr Melon knows only too well, the initiative is with the man.

There followed some of the most deliberately dreary dialogue ever devised. Nothing rouses the girl's interest – not a mention of the latest musical comedy nor a reference to William Archer's article in the *Fortnightly* on Ibsen's influence on the modern stage. She is monosyllabic: 'A pudding of a girl, Miss Postlethwaite, I fear.' On another occasion it might be Miss Hepplewhite, a very different matter. Nothing can stop her talking. Mr Milne/Million/Melon can hardly get a word in edgeways.

Miss H: Now what were we talking about? Oh, of course, the geraniums. You may think it funny of me, but I must say I *prefer* daffodils. I *adore* daffodils. I always think when I see them of those wonderful lines of Wordsworth's: 'My heart leaps up when I behold the dancing daffodils.' So true, isn't it?
Mr. M: I think the actual lines –

But Miss Hepplewhite is not listening, she is off on another track. 'There's something about a play which makes it so utterly *different* from a novel.' She had seen a play the other night but, alas, she cannot remember what it was called. How far they were from Clarissa, Lilian, Amelia and Myra, these Miss Postlethwaites and Miss Hepplewhites. Dining out was not much fun, but at least fun could be made of it.

And sometimes his name would be recognized. He was becoming better known. In 1912 he would appear in *Who's Who* for the first time. He was beginning to be interviewed. A man called Gerald Cumberland recalled in his memoirs, *Set Down in Malice*, being sent to interview A. A. Milne at about this time. When he left, Milne told him, 'I must see a copy of your article before it is printed.' When Cumberland eventually got it back, he could hardly recognize it, 'so heavily was it scored out, so numerous were the alterations'. When it was published 'at least seventy-five per cent of it was from Milne's pen. He wrote one or two other stabbing sentences to me, from which it appeared that, however numerous his virtues may be, he is unable to suffer fools gladly.' Cumberland was not too much of a fool to recognize something that was always true of A. A. Milne, however much it seems to contradict the general picture so many people had of him. Milne was a mass of contradictions, as his son would realize: 'shy, yet at the same time self-confident; modest, yet proud of what he had done; quiet, yet a good talker; warm, yet with a thin lip and an ice-cold eye that might, if you said the wrong thing, be pretty chilling; sympathetic yet unsympathetic to what he felt was stupidity.'

A friendlier account of him than Gerald Cumberland's appeared in the *Daily Citizen* in 1913. Angela Killey, Ken's second daughter, reading it seventy-five years later, said it was exactly right: 'That's how he was.'

Though still little more than a youth, he is not overburdened by the responsibilities of his post. He is shy but confident, nervous but by no means silent. His shyness makes him talk hurriedly and with an air of deprecation: he suggests rather than states even his firmest beliefs. He is tall, lean, and athletic. His face is brown, his hair light, his eyes blue. Like nearly all men of great humorous gifts, he is exceedingly sensitive and intuitive. A smile constantly plays about the corners of his mouth, and his eyes light up from time to time. Few men know their limitations better than he does. He knows precisely what is within his powers, and never flatters himself that he can do things just because he would like to do them. In many ways he resembles his work. He is refined, subtle, and elusive. He has little use for the obvious jest, and in conversing with him it is necessary to keep one's wits extremely active if one is to take an intelligent part in the conversation. He has no belief in 'hidden' talent – at all events, in journalism. The man with ability, he declares, soon finds his place. He himself is most conscientious in his search for new humorists, and diligently reads the heap of manuscripts that come daily to the office of *Punch* from unknown writers. Humour is rare, but when discovered it is hailed with delight.

His own humour was giving delight to more and more people. *The Day's Play* was reprinted over and over again. It was already in its fourth edition when Milne's second collection of *Punch* pieces, *The Holiday Round*, was published in 1912. My copy of that book is inscribed: 'To my dear Connie and Barry from their loving brother'. Barry's wife – but not Barry – would remain dear to Alan through everything. She would be one of only four people mentioned by name in his will forty years later – but their relationship is one that is impossible to describe, as all the many letters they exchanged have apparently been destroyed.

In 1910 the *Daily Graphic* painted a vivid picture of families up and down the land tearing *Punch* apart in eagerness 'to read of Dahlia and Simpson and the captivating Myra'. Readers lapped up the smart, mildly shocking talk of those 'very up-to-date young men and women' – proof that Victorian values were dead. 'Who does not know and love the Rabbits?' asked the *Literary World*, and even the *Evening Standard*, which suggested that the idiotic fooling of these perfectly charming people could leave one tired, said: 'We do not know which is our favourite, Simpson, perhaps, but the supremacy is frequently threatened.' They are always on holiday, these Rabbits, at least for the weekend. They have jobs certainly, or at least the men do (Simpson works on the *Spectator* and Thomas is in the Admiralty, to which Eddie Marsh moved with Churchill in 1911). But the jobs are not part of the story. There is lots of cricket and tennis – croquet and golf too – with predecessors of Betjeman's strongly adorable girls. When it rains, they don't play bridge, but rather some sort of boy scouts' tracking all over the house, all kinds of indoor games and amateur theatricals.

In one game you had to lie full-length on the floor with a glass of water balanced on your forehead and come up again without spilling a single drop. 'Personally, I shouldn't have minded spilling a single drop; it was the thought of spilling the whole glass that kept me back. Anyway, it's a useless trick, the need for which never arises in an ordinary career.' The narrator tends to be a bit of a spoilsport, a bit of a cynic which, for those who are charmed, adds to the charm.

In one play the narrator finds himself reluctantly cast as a small rat-catcher. 'Does that mean I'm of diminutive size or that I'm in a small way of business, or that my special line is young ones?' 'It means that you haven't got much to say.' The rat-catcher does say: 'My father, when I was a child, didst apprentice me to a salad binger.' To which the obvious query is: 'How does one bing salads?' The rat-catcher replies curtly, 'Ballad-singer.' It is all good clean facetious fun. The Rabbits (though certainly in their twenties and inclined to get engaged) are really rather articulate overgrown children, with the ability to enjoy themselves, whatever the circumstances.

It is the same world in which, at exactly this time, Milne's old friend from Trinity, Lytton Strachey, and his friends (who included Adrian Stephen and his sister – Virginia not yet Woolf – wearing a turban and a false beard) hoaxed the Commander-in-Chief of the Home Fleet by dressing up and pretending to be His Imperial Majesty, the Emperor of Abyssinia, and his retinue. And on another occasion they asked a stranger to hold the end of a tape 'for a moment' and then, round the corner, persuaded another stranger to hold the other end. Half an hour later they were still holding their ends and beginning to get impatient. This is Rabbit behaviour on a grand scale – 'pure lunatic audacity', as Quentin Bell called it.

One of the most remarkable things about the Rabbits is that they are all, though never described, quite clearly individuals. They are characterized entirely by the things they say. They have a great deal in common, but they are all different. They are deeply eccentric in a way that is difficult to demonstrate by quotation. But this scrap of dialogue will give some idea of the sort of things they get up to:

'Dahlia, darling,' interrupted Myra, in a fair imitation of Archie's voice. 'How often have I told you that we *can't* afford india-rubber in the cake? Just a few raisins and a cherry is really all you want. You *mustn't* be so extravagant.'

'Dearest, I do try; and after all, love, it wasn't *I* who fell in the cocoa last night.'

More N. F. Simpson than Lewis Carroll, perhaps. But 'no one can compare with Mr Milne for being silly, wittily, neatly and gracefully,' said the *Manchester Guardian*.

During the war, Milne would write to a fan, Margaret Baird, who later became a friend: 'The truth must be told you. There *are* no Rabbits. I have played cricket and the theatrical fool at one house; and sailed with a different party; and gone to Switzerland with others . . . That is the truth behind the doings of Archie and Company; the rest is imagining. There is no Archie or Dahlia or Thomas. There is no Simpson really; certainly he started out of my head. As for Myra, she is my wife now; though she too (as Joseph Conrad once said) "came out of my ink-pot" at the beginning. But when I write of her now, I think of my wife, and I like other people to think of her too.'

Christopher Milne's explanation of why his parents married – a marriage which seems to need some explanation, as many marriages do – was an explanation Alan Milne gave himself: 'She laughed at my jokes.' When they met, she endeared herself to him by showing she knew some of his *Punch* pieces more or less by heart. She had, he could not help thinking, 'the most perfect sense of humour in the world'. It is interesting to think that Milne had created Myra before he met the real-life version. Myra is undoubtedly delightful. She is the sort of girl who has brothers (as indeed his wife would have in abundance). She is Archie's sister, easy with young men and not overimpressed by them. She is confident ('Oh, I'm very good,' says Myra) and competent – she knows how to load a camera, not so easy in those days. She can captain a cricket-team and has even been known to hole in one. They have 'jolly good fun together'. ('We always have *that*,' says Myra.)

In *Punch*, in August 1909, Milne had suggested that falling in love is decidedly overrated, leading as it does to marriage. 'I should hate to be settled. It's so much more fun like this. Myra quite agrees with me.' Milne was twenty-seven and still not looking more than a week ahead. ' "It has been great fun this week and it will probably be great fun next week." That's my motto.' He 'loved being in love, and being out of love and free again to fall in love.' But in December 1910 he was taken by her godfather, Owen Seaman, to Dorothy de Sélincourt's twenty-first birthday dance. And she seemed to be Myra, one of his own characters. Later she would be at times, and for one reason or another, both Miss Middleton and Celia as well. 'We can be lovers so easily,' he said. 'Can we be friends?'

They became friends – very much in the way that Myra was friends with Thomas and Simpson and 'I' – a relationship of equality which was in fact not unusual in certain circles in England before the First World War. 'When I wanted a present for a sister-in-law or a new suit for myself, I would summon her to help me; when she wanted a man to take her to a dance she would ring me up.' A review in the *Morning Post* in 1912 talked of the Rabbits as engaged in 'a match of dialectical tennis, in which Merton serves and Girton replies, keeping the score about even'. Certainly in this sex war, the women do extremely well in a way that could astonish today's young.

George Meredith once suggested that comedy is possible only in societies where there is social equality between the sexes. The sparks must fly between equally charged poles. Thinking of the sparks flying between Cecily and Algernon in *The Importance of Being Earnest* (Milne's favourite play), one realizes that comedy need not entirely reflect the society that gives rise to it. The Rabbits were amusing to thousands whose daily conventions were entirely different, in a world that was soon to be destroyed by war.

If the girl Milne married seemed to be one of the Rabbits, Milne himself really wasn't. That was the trouble perhaps; and there would be, if not trouble, at least disappointment. No man should be judged entirely on what he writes for *Punch*, though it should be stressed that Milne himself never disowned or undervalued his *Punch* pieces. 'It is assumed too readily, I feel, that a writer who makes his readers laugh would really prefer to make them cry.' He was not the clown pining to play Hamlet. But there *was* another side to him – a more serious side. At this period, Milne was very active politically. The second 1910 election had, he said, added years to his age. He had canvassed for the Liberals street by street, arguing, even shouting, and saying over and over again, 'My point is perfectly simple.' A newspaper report at one stage gave Milne's interests as 'politics and children'. 'Miss Middleton', on the other hand, says in late 1910: 'I don't know anything about politics.' She never would.

One consistent thread in Milne's political thinking was a passionate concern for democracy, for the representation of *all* the people. The other was his pacifism. It is easy to imagine that it was the war that turned Milne into a determined pacifist, that it was the Somme that made him speak out in a very different voice, not playing for smiles: 'I think war is the ultimate expression of man's wickedness and man's silliness . . . I think war wrong as I think cruelty to children wrong: as I think slavery and the burning of heretics wrong: as I think the exploitation of the poor wrong, and the corruption of the innocent.' Milne wrote that in 1933, but it was twenty-three years earlier that he read Norman Angell and was converted to the cause that would make such a difference to the rest of his life.

Norman Angell, who earned his living as one of Northcliffe's men in Paris, had just published in 1910 his book *The Great Illusion*. Later he would be Labour MP for Bradford North and in 1933 win the Nobel Prize for Peace. 'I have been an ardent Pacifist since 1910 and still am,' Milne wrote in his last book, over forty years later. 'In 1910 Pacifism was derided. All the Wars in the memory of Englishmen had taken place outside their country, and could be followed with the eager and impersonal interest with which we now follow the broadcast of a cricket match. It was true that a few soldiers got killed, but this was just an occupational risk, cheerfully to be accepted in return for the adventure and the glory promised. If the civilians did think about war in the abstract, they told themselves that it was bracing, like corporal punishment and cold baths; and that, since it had been going on for thousands of years, it would probably be wrong, and would certainly be impossible, to stop it now. So Pacifists were dismissed as idealists, cranks, and, as likely as not, vegetarians . . . Perhaps because I became a Pacifist on impersonal grounds, before I had experienced the horrors or even the discomforts of war, I consider all war, from the wars of the Israelites onwards, to be horrible, and all weapons of war, from the sword and the club and the spear onwards, to be barbarous.' This abhorrence of violence, this total rejection of aggression, was a fundamental trait in Milne's character. It affects everything he writes. It is one of the most attractive aspects of *Winnie-the-Pooh*. The only gun must be a pop-gun, quite incapable (as Shepard's picture, with the cork hanging from its string clearly shows) of shooting anything, even a balloon.

Pacifists tend to be intellectuals. Certainly Milne was doing a good deal of thinking in 1910, and would always do so. But he was not an intellectual, his son, who should know, would insist, while admitting he was 'brainy'. One definition of intellectual can be 'a person of superior reasoning power', and that he undoubtedly was, though his reasoning power would be more likely to be devoted to crossword puzzles than to reading Hegel. Even his knowledge and love of poetry would become, in his wife's company, not more than something useful for 'solving the quotations in the *Times* crossword'.

Christopher Milne, sadly undervaluing his mother's wits, would go so far as to say that when his father made Rabbit say to Owl:

'You and I have brains. The others have fluff', he might have been thinking of the de Sélincourts. For there was no doubt that Uncle Ernest, the famous Wordsworth scholar, had immense brain, and so had brother Aubrey. And there is equally little doubt that Dorothy and brother Bob had fluff. But if there had been this unequal distribution of brain among the family, all, in their individual ways, were artistic. This turned the brainy ones into intellectuals, making them, in the eyes of the unbrainy, totally unbearable. They talked about Art in a solemn and learned manner which the others couldn't stand. One can imagine Uncle Ernest sweeping Aubrey off to the Tate Gallery or the Queen's Hall, leaving Dorothy, to whom *chiaroscuro* and *allegro vivace* meant absolutely nothing at all, upstairs in her bedroom, contemplating her wardrobe and humming her own private home-made hums.

They were a remarkable family, the de Sélincourts. Dorothy, who would soon prefer to be Daphne or Daff, had been born on 2 November 1889 (when Alan was nearly eight) in Albert Road, Battersea, the daughter of Martin de Sélincourt, then described as a 'mantle manufacturer', in the same line of business as the family of her godfather, Owen Seaman. Dorothy's grandfather was said to have fled from France as a very young man at the time of the abdication of Louis Philippe in 1848. His sons included not only Martin, the 'mantle manufacturer' (who became extremely rich, Chairman of both Swan and Edgar and the *Geographical Magazine*), but also Ernest, the Wordsworth scholar, who was one of Churton Collins's successors as Professor of English at Birmingham University, was instrumental in founding the Birmingham Rep. and later became Professor of Poetry at Oxford. Then there was the musicologist Basil, who had recently married Anne Douglas Sedgwick, an American novelist and short-story writer much admired at the time and still worth reading. Marrying into the family, she found it '*thick* in up-to-date culture', but she was not thinking of her new niece. Another uncle, Hugh, was dramatic critic of the *Star* and a book reviewer for the *Observer*. He was a friend and disciple of Havelock Ellis: he and his wife, a pianist, lived separate and totally unconventional sexual lives, of which their niece may not have been aware. There was a distinguished aunt, too – Agnes, a pacifist, who was said to know fourteen languages and had just been appointed Principal of Westfield College in the University of London.

Altogether, Milne thought, with four younger brothers and all the members of her mother's side of the family as well, that Dorothy 'had more relations than would seem possible'. The girl's education had been 'finished' in France, so her son would say, 'but where and with what it had all begun remained a mystery'.

Early in January 1913 Daphne de Sélincourt and Alan Milne found themselves buying boots.

'Any sort of boots or just boots?' she said.

'Ski-ing boots,' Milne said proudly. 'I bought mine yesterday.'

'What for?'

'Ski-ing.'

'Where? Hampstead Heath?'

'Switzerland.'

'But that's where *I'm* going!'

'Well, there's plenty of room for both of us. I'm going to a place called Diablerets.'

'Dash it, so am I.'

'What a very small – '

'Don't say it. Are you at the Grand?'

'Yes. What fun. I've got a pair of orange trousers.'

'I shall be wearing a red carnation in my button-hole. We're bound to recognize each other. What are you like with a lot of other people about?'

'Heavenly.'

'So am I. I do hope we shall like each other.'

They did, Milne said. 'The "other people about" made everything different. I proposed to her at eleven o'clock one morning in a snow-storm.'

On the day that he returned to London from Switzerland he presented her with copies of *The Day's Play* and *The Holiday Round*. Both are dated 23 January 1913 and both are inscribed: 'To my Dorothy, with the author's heart.' Lehmann records that Milne announced his engagement at the *Punch* dinner on 29 January. In *Punch* on 26 February he wrote: 'There are engagements and Swiss engagements – just as there are measles and German measles. It is well known that Swiss engagements don't count.' But this one did.

Milne wrote to Eddie Marsh:

I have some absolutely original news for you. I am engaged! Her name – though it will not convey anything to you – is Dorothy de Sélincourt. A niece of Hugh de Sélincourt, Anne Douglas Sedgwick and Lancelot Speed and future wife of A. A. Milne. Kindly step forward with congratulations. Break the news to Winston. Acquaint Asquith. Farewell.

Yours A.A.M.

Milne was overwhelmed with congratulations. Thanking Marsh for his, he wrote: 'Now I've only 999,999 more.' Later, Milne thanks Marsh for his wedding present – a hot water jug – and tells him: 'We go to Dartmoor for the honeymoon. Jokes about convicts are not being made this year.' Milne preferred to make his own jokes. He would certainly not be going fishing: 'I should hate to catch a fish who was perhaps on his honeymoon too.' He wrote to Charles Turley Smith in similar high spirits. 'I will have no other best man,' he said, though in fact he had to, as it turned out. Audrey Lucas called Turley the most delightful and most elusive of men. Milne implored Turley to come and meet Daphne. 'She adores you, having heard lots about you.' Barrie also urged him not to miss the Milne wedding 'entirely in the hope that you will stay with me'. But miss it he would.

There is no evidence of how Ken and Maud reacted to the news. One of Ken's daughters suggested that Ken would have felt 'Good for him; good luck to him, all that'; but that Maud probably felt it as 'a bit of a blow' – devoted Maud so normal, so unaffected, a little provincial perhaps – someone who, her daughter thought, *would* have been an intellectual, if she had had a better education. Maud saw Alan's anti-intellectual fiancée 'with her background of brothers and yachts and riches (all very foreign to Maud) breaking the party up'. There was something highly polished and glamorous about Miss de Sélincourt, something outrageous about the way she dressed – the orange trousers at Diablerets were typical. She was quick-witted, self-centred, a little ruthless. Ken and Maud saw little of her. Alan would continue his visits on his own; but not, of course, so often. His regular visits to Fieldhead, the Lehmanns' house, were also affected by his marriage. Daphne went with him three times but, 'I don't think his wife took to us,' Rosamond said, remembering her as 'not at all pretty or charming – rather like a Pekinese' but 'obviously very masterful'. Most people remembered her as always attractive if not pretty with 'dark eyes and a vivacious manner'. The odd thing about the reference to the Pekinese is that the Lehmanns gave a Peke puppy to Daphne in 1914 and one might think Rosamond's description was influenced by this – but there *was* something Pekinese-like about Daphne Milne's face; other people noticed it too.

Milne gave many reasons for marrying. Marriage had, as we have seen, been on his mind for years. One reason was sex, of course, but that remained unmentionable, in spite of Havelock Ellis. Then there was the question of writing letters. Milne *hated* writing letters. When he became engaged there opened before him a vista of invitations and accounts rendered, all answered promptly by his wife, 'instead of put off till next month by me'. They agreed before the ceremony

19_13_. Marriage solemnized at _____ the of S_t_ Margaret Westminster _____				
Columns.	1	2	3	4	Rank
No.	When Married.	Name and Surname.	Age.	Condition.	
309	June 4_th_ 19_13_	Alan Alexander Milne	31	Bachelor	
		Dorothy de Sélincourt	23	Spinster	

Married in the _Parish Church_ according to the Rites and Ceremonie

This Marriage was solemnised between us. { Alan Alexander Milne / Dorothy de Sélincourt } in the Presence of us,

that 'obey' should mean nothing more than 'write all my thank-you-very-much letters for me'. Milne also hated complaining to the laundry and finding plumbers. He hated all domestic duties, even if 'very little loss of blood' was involved in putting up a door-knocker. Not that Dorothy de Sélincourt would put up door-knockers. Her son would say, with some exaggeration, that her only domestic skill was tying up parcels, though she had been known to be capable of applying a match to a fire that someone else had laid. She certainly would not *do* much, but Milne lived in hopes that she would see that other people did things.

The Celia/Ronald pieces in *Punch*, in the spring of 1913, suggest what may have gone on before the wedding. 'Probably you thought that getting married was quite a simple business. So did I. We were both wrong. It is the very dickens.'

My idea was that Celia should say to me suddenly one evening, 'By the way, Ronald, don't forget we're being married tomorrow,' and I should have said 'Where?' And on being told the time and place I should have turned up pretty punctually; and after my best man had told me where to stand, and the clergyman had told me what to say, and my solicitor had told me where to sign my name, we should have driven from the church a happy married couple . . . and in the carriage Celia would have told me where we were spending the honeymoon.

	in the	*Parish*
	in the County of *London*	

	6	7	8
fession.	Residence at the time of Marriage.	Father's Name and Surname.	Rank or Profession of Father.
alist	32 *The Broadway Westminster*	*John Vine Milne*	*Gentleman*
	13 *Palace Street W*	*Martin de Sélincourt*	*Merchant*

ho	*Established Church*	*by*	*or after* *Banns* *by me,*
de Sélincourt	*Mabel de Sélincourt*	*H. F. Westlake*	
Vine Milne	*Roland D. Kitson*	*Minor Canon of Westminster*	

What it was really like, we don't know. There was no doubt in Milne's mind that the whole thing was entirely for the guests and that he himself would get little pleasure from it. He dreamt he quite forgot about the ring until the day itself and then the only cab he could find to take him to a jewellers was drawn by a camel. But the only accounts of the actual wedding are very brief and dull. On 4 June 1913, the day of the Derby at which the suffragette Emily Davison threw herself fatally in front of the King's horse, R. C. Lehmann wrote in his diary: 'To London with Alice for Milne's wedding at St Margaret's, Westminster. Later we went to the R.A.' In that one surviving letter from Alan's mother, Maria Milne, she writes to her friend Miss Pinnington in the following September: 'You will have heard of Alan's marriage in June. Their first At Homes are to be 8th, 9th and 10th of next month. They had a very fashionable and large wedding at St Margaret's, Westminster, to which we went and I afterwards went on to Brighton for a fortnight. We like our new daughter Dorothy very much and look upon it that our third and last son will make another woman happy. *They* think no couple ever married under such devotion as they. The old folks are not in it – the old folks think, dear children, talk when 35 years, happy years, have passed and you may have realized what we could tell you now. That it is just the old old story that comes with every happy experience of well-chosen partnership for life.' In fact, this partnership would have some new twists in the old story. It certainly started very happily but Alan Milne would never be able to say as his father did: 'I am very fond of Browning, but sometimes think that even his happiness in marriage was less than mine.'

The best man that June day was Roland Kitson, who had been at Westminster and Trinity with Milne. He would survive the war with the DSO and the MC, and eventually become Lord Airedale. They would go on meeting from time to time in clubs and drawing-rooms. His son, Oliver, would remember that when he was quite young Milne had once spent most of an evening talking to him while the others played bridge.

Ken's two small daughters were supposed to be among the brides-maids. Marjorie was certainly one, but three-year-old Angela was ill with peritonitis following a ruptured appendix, and lay in bed in a nursing home with her rose-strewn bridesmaid's dress from Paris forming a coverlet. Her mother felt distinctly uneasy as Marjorie walked up the aisle behind the bride. 'Well, as Celia says, it's too late to draw back now.'

— 7 —

Marriage and War

KENNETH MILNE ONCE said to his second daughter: 'Never pass judgement. No outsider has the slightest idea what goes on in a marriage.' It is good, if unoriginal, advice; all marriages are opaque and no judgements will be made. But the evidence is that Alan Milne was certainly not going to have everything as he would have wished, from the very moment that the young couple returned from the three-week Dartmoor honeymoon. ('Personally I loathed my honeymoon,' says Sheila in Milne's play *Gentleman Unknown*. Could that have been Daphne speaking?)

Alan Milne had made so much jokingly of the fact that his wife would write his thank-you letters for him that it is rather ironic that his first surviving letter after the marriage is to thank 'our dear Aunt Bessie', the wife of Wilfred de Sélincourt, Daphne's uncle. It is dated 22 June 1913 and begins: 'I am writing this letter for Daff, who is tired.' Milne thanks Aunt Bessie for the flowers they found waiting in the flat at 15 Embankment Gardens, Chelsea – arranged to welcome them by Gertrude, Daphne's personal maid, who had come with her as part of the marriage settlement. 'That you should have chosen the exact colour to suit the room does not surprise us; it were impossible that a gift so kindly thought of should lack anything.' If the effort of writing was Alan's, this sentiment was particularly Daphne's; colour schemes were what she excelled in. The way things looked would always concern her.

They had chosen Chelsea together. 'Beloved Chelsea! ... She is now but a name with which to feed romantic schoolgirls,' Milne would write in 1929. By then, he said, you could look in vain for painters' hats and writers' cloaks – but 'no motor-omnibuses can distort' the King's Road nor 'Power Stations dislimn her river'. In 1913 Chelsea was the proper place for a writer to live – as Milne had indeed felt years earlier in the policeman's house in Wellington Square.

They had chosen the flat in Embankment Gardens together – but it would be (as would all the places they lived in) always more Daphne's territory than Alan's. For all Alan's strength (and many people would testify to the strength of his character) it was Daphne who made the ground rules, who determined the style of their marriage. It was she who decided everything practical – not just the colour schemes, but the furniture and even the light fittings. 'Somehow I never regarded anybody as choosing *them*,' Milne said, 'I thought they just grew in the wall. From bulbs.' He – or his *alter ego* Ronald – stresses over and over again that the reason he got married was to free himself of all sorts of domestic bother – choosing light fixtures, insuring servants and so on. His funny piece in *Punch* on 13 August 1913, called 'The Missing Card', must not have seemed so funny forty years later when, on their gardener's death, they realized *his* insurance had never been paid and Milne had to hand over a vast sum to enable the gardener's widow to claim her pension.

In 1913 the missing insurance card would not come between them, but simply provide material for the weekly article. At this stage, and for many years, Alan Milne was utterly devoted. He would do anything for Daphne, even write thank-you letters if necessary. He thought himself extraordinarily lucky to have won her. 'If women only married men who were good enough for them,' he wrote in an early play, 'where should we be?'

The *Punch* pieces give a shadow commentary on the first months of married life. A series of adventures of the Rabbits in the south of France followed a sort of second honeymoon Alan and Daphne enjoyed at Cap Martin in February 1914. They had been lent a villa by some people called Williamson ('Anne Williamson was an American, to whom such gestures are natural'), complete with 'staff, food, the cellar and even the cigars, together with letters of introduction to everybody and the company of that delightfully wheezy bulldog, Tiberius'. It was a noble piece of hospitality, as Milne said.

Milne's first poem in *Punch* for three years reflected a golfing visit to Charles Turley Smith at Mullion in July 1914. There was a feeling of a final happiness: 'The day that's here is the day to seize.' Gazing into rock pools in Cornwall, Celia (or was it Daphne?) found herself thinking 'the most obvious thoughts'.

'The great thing is not to speak them,' Ronald said (and probably Milne had said it first). 'Still, you'd better tell me now. What is it?'

'I was just thinking that life was very wonderful. But it's a *silly* thing to say.' It might have been silly, or at least obvious, but Milne would remember the rock pool and that summer of 1914 as a time when such a statement was true as it never would be again.

We can be sure of the thoughts that were running through Milne's head, or at least those of them that were getting on to paper, in those days before the war. And there is a suggestion of Milne's own working methods, and Daphne's longing to find excuses to interrupt him, in a piece called 'A Trunk Call'.

She went out and I returned to my sofa. After an hour or so my mind began to get to work and I got up and walked slowly up and down the room. The gentle exercise seemed to stimulate me. Seeing my new putter in the corner of the room, I took it up (my brain full of other things) and, dropping a golf-ball on the carpet, began to practise. After five or ten minutes, my ideas being now quite clear, I was just about to substitute the pen for the putter when Celia came in.

'Oh,' she said. 'Are – are you busy?' I turned round from a difficult putt with my club in my hand.

'Very,' I said. 'What is it?'

'I don't want to disturb you if you're working – '

'I am.'

'But I just wondered if you – if you liked artichokes.'

There was much they did not know about each other when they got married, and not everything was as easily discussed as their taste in the more unusual vegetables. Daphne de Sélincourt had come to Alan Milne totally ignorant of the physical side of marriage, and from a background which made her nervous of men's sexuality. A friend recalled: 'Her father seemed to have had what can be described as a "roving eye" and this upset Daphne's mother very much; there was much weeping and wringing of hands. It had a profound effect on Daphne; whereas she sympathized with her mother, she also had a certain understanding of her father. Tears, she thought, were very boring and men did not like them . . . She would never weep as her mother did (should she have cause).' She *would* cry; she 'cried very readily, an easy prey to her emotions,' as her son said, but she would cry quietly and never in jealousy and resentment.

The suggestion is that Daphne started marriage determined never to care deeply enough to weep. She would be 'devoted' to Alan Milne – but everything would remain delightful, charming. There would never be scenes. There would certainly never be jealousy. The emphasis would always be on romance, not passion, on appearances, on style and elegance – on what one of Milne's critics would call 'the bright glitter of surfaces' – not on strong, spontaneous feelings. What mattered in marriage was not sex, but something that could be called 'romantic love', which found its expression in talking and listening and laughing together. There was the blessed fact of the shared sense of humour. 'I shall not bore her by repeating what seem to her to be pointless stories which I heard at the club, nor, on the other hand, will she irritate me by listening with an artificial smile to what seem to me to be delightfully humorous stories. The same people, the same accidents to ourselves or to others, will amuse us.' That is Brian in Milne's play *Mr Pim*, but it is certainly also Milne himself.

Daphne would even listen, in those early days, when Alan told her who ought to play for England – but she was not really interested in cricket. There is a family story that Daphne on a rare visit to Lord's, walking out of sight of the game behind a marquee, was heard to exclaim, on hearing a burst of clapping: 'Another goal, I suppose?'

Milne was good at listening too. He once said that 'He was a good listener' was one of the remarks he deserved on his tombstone. And there is plenty of evidence from the women in his writing that he was more than usually aware of how some women felt (and also of the dangers of generalizing about women). A girl at a party explodes:

Oh, I want a vote or something. I don't know what I want, but I *hate* men! Why should they think that everything they say to us is funny or clever or important? Why should they talk to us as if we were children? Why should they take it for granted that it's our duty to *listen* always?

Milne would make the heroine of his play *Ariadne* ruminate on the subject of bees. 'It says in my book about bees that when the queen bee has finished with her husband she kills him . . . It's a funny idea, isn't it? You'd have thought she'd have kept him to talk to her in the evenings.' Daphne 'felt and often told me so,' a friend recalled, 'that the most important thing in a marriage is talking.' That *Daily Citizen* reporter, in the year of their marriage, said that when talking with A. A. Milne 'it is necessary to keep one's wits extremely active if one is to take an intelligent part in the conversation.' Daphne was quick-witted, lively and admiring; she was herself an amusing talker. But, according to their son, she never shared with Alan Milne 'those things that were closest to his heart', and by that he did not mean merely cricket. Even at the beginning, when he was most entranced by her, Milne was far too intelligent not to realize how little they really shared.

Sex was certainly a problem, but it was always Daphne's policy to avoid problems. 'If you don't think about something, it isn't there' – that was her attitude, one of Alan's nieces said. 'She was anti-sex,' an elderly friend said to me, adding, 'I hope I don't shock you.' She was talking of Daphne as she had known her in her later years, but it could apply to those early years of marriage too. Celia and Ronald, their *alter egos*, certainly had separate bedrooms in their first flat, as Milne makes clear in a *Punch* piece about the problems of disposing of eight wedding-present clocks.

Marie Stopes had come to her own marriage, two years earlier, in a state of ignorance, in spite of having studied zoology at London University. She advised separate bedrooms in her *Married Love* in a passage which would have its appeal to Daphne Milne, who had undoubtedly been similarly ignorant. 'Be always escaping. Escape the lower, the trivial, the sordid. So far as possible ensure that you allow your husband to come upon you only when there is delight in the meeting. Whenever the finances allow, the husband and wife should have separate bedrooms.' Separate bedrooms could preserve the romance of marriage; but they could also lead to feelings of isolation and even estrangement. Many years later Milne would write: 'The doom of Holy Matrimony is the Separate Room.'

In these early days of their marriage, A. A. Milne was writing in *Punch* every week and also (from July 1913 to January 1914) contributing weekly to the *Sphere*. In May 1913 he had asked the editor, Clement Shorter, if he might again write a regular piece in the *Sphere*; the money would be useful with his approaching marriage. (Daphne, of course, the daughter of a very rich man, came with her own independent income, but her tastes were extravagant and there was no doubt that life would be more expensive.) They settled on the title 'London Letter'. 'If A Few Days Ago were called Half Hours in our Taxis one week and Behind the Bowler's Arm the next, not nearly so many people would read it, but people will read anything if it is put before them regularly enough.'

Milne was reasonably reliable as a contributor. Something would get written somehow, week after week, though just occasionally he had cause to apologize to Shorter: once it was flu; another time unbearable toothache. And then one day he wrote: 'I am so sorry I have been unable to get an article done this week; the *Punch* Almanac has been too much for me. I excuse myself with the belief that you will have more than sufficient Serbs, Bulgars and Sanjaks to take my place . . . To tell you the truth,' he wrote, feeling suddenly exhausted, 'I am beginning to wonder how much longer I can go on with these weekly essays. If I had anything to write about, it would be different.' Sometimes, he said, he wished he were a bank manager. There *is* the occasional sign of strain in both the London Letters and in his *Punch* pieces but A. A. Milne's reputation was at its highest. 'His high spirits never seem to flag.' As early as 1910 the *Scotsman* had used the word 'whimsical' – the word Milne came to hate so much – but it was then used with no derogatory overtones. 'Milne's influence between 1910 and 1914 was staggering,' Edward Shanks said in 1929. 'Scores of young writers tried to imitate him, but could not be both frivolous and thoughtful at once.'

'Everyone loves A.A.M.,' the *Observer* said, calling Celia, Dahlia and Jeremy, the archetypal Milne characters, 'those public favourites'. In *The Times Literary Supplement*, the reviewer of *Once a Week*, the collection that came out in 1914, would say that Milne had 'one of the most engaging silly senses of humour in the world', and decided (as one must decide) that it was with Milne 'more than usually futile' to try to explain what makes him so funny. The general opinion was that he was already 'one of the foremost English humorists' and that he can be read and reread. 'Fresh charms appear every day.' A widow, when asked if she did not miss her recently dead husband, said carefully, 'Well, if I'd taken him in parts, I shouldn't have had him bound'. A. A. Milne, on the other hand, was always worth the binding. His collections of *Punch* pieces were constantly going into new editions. *The Day's Play*, the first of them, was in its third edition only four months after publication.

Milne's invention seemed to be as fertile as ever and, looking back, he would think of these pre-war years on *Punch* as perhaps the happiest time of his life. His high spirits had been genuine, his delight in life not something put on to entertain his readers, but his own expression of what he thought of later as a 'simple happiness'. Life's morning radiance had not left the hills. He would echo Wordsworth's 'Those were the days' – giving the title in 1929 to a compendium of all four *Punch* books. But the whole business of the constant writing of funny articles was beginning to appal him.

It was not quite as glamorous as he had imagined, being a member of the *Punch* Table. How could he face the possibility of another forty years of those boring Wednesday dinners? Under the tablecloth there were indeed, with his own, the carved initials of Thackeray, Tenniel, Phil May and the rest, but the present company was less impressive. It wasn't even as if all the members of the Table had a sense of humour. Raven Hill had told them, with perfect seriousness, that his own picture was unquestionably the best in that year's Academy; he had looked very carefully and there could be no two opinions about it. The weekly dinners had become a 'fearful burden' to Lehmann and were becoming so already to Milne, who was never as gregarious as his mentor. The regular waiter, 'a cringing, obsequious old rascal', did not add to the pleasure of the occasion. Even the food itself could be described as 'rotten'. And the politics . . . 'In those days,' Milne said, 'politics made me extremely warm . . . I found it difficult not to get over-heated at those interminable discussions which followed the over-heating Punch Dinner.'

Was he really going to be editor of *Punch* one day, as he had often imagined, and as his new wife was convinced he would be, succeeding her distinguished godfather? There was no doubt that, in those days, editor of *Punch* was a rather splendid thing to be. F. C. Burnand, in spite of his absences in Ramsgate and his paper bags of shrimps, had been knighted in 1902. He had earned his place in the *Dictionary of National Biography*, where Milne would write about him. Under Burnand, Milne considered, *Punch* had discarded 'its air of a Family Joke and aspired to be the National Institution which it has since been proclaimed'. The editor was the controller, Milne saw, of 'the most famous humorous paper in the world'. Owen Seaman, predictably, was also knighted in 1914. He had already been made a fellow of his old college at Cambridge and had received an honorary degree from Durham. Before he died, Edinburgh and Oxford would also honour him and he would be made a baronet. It was the sort of glittering career Daphne wished for Alan. But did he really wish it for himself?

In practice, Alan Milne thought, putting into use his talent for mental arithmetic, it would mean (even if he wrote for *Punch* alone) at least another thousand funny articles. He was finding it difficult enough being absurd twice a week. The thought of being funny a thousand times, week after week after week, was almost too much to bear. Seaman, if Burnand was anything to go by, would last another twenty years. 'Nothing (I felt) which I wrote for *Punch* in 1930 would be better than what I was writing now. I had by this time mastered the technique (the tricks, if you like to call them that) of the "humorous" sketch; I couldn't expect to become "funnier" . . .' Having made a reputation, however small, by 1910, it was silly and unexciting to spend the rest of one's life trying to keep that reputation unsullied. Did he even want to edit a National Institution? He thought not. He would not be allowed to do what he liked with it. There was no possibility of returning it to its anti-establishment roots. 'With its large circulation in the Shires, the Vicarages and the Messes of England, *Punch* was almost compelled to be true Blue.' Milne's nickname among his friends was Blue (his eyes were blue; he tended to wear blue) – but his politics were the wrong colour.

The only way, it seemed, to escape from *Punch* was by writing novels or plays in his spare time, until he got to a point when he could depend on them for a living. The trouble was that his work for *Punch* and the *Sphere* left him no time 'or (more important) brain' for any other work. The day of escape seemed farther off than ever when a curtain raiser, requested by his friend Anmer Hall, came back more or less by return of post. Milne had to fight down the feeling he had had so often in the past – and would have so often again – that playwriting was almost as much of a waste of time and money as playing golf, pleasurable as they both were. It seemed 'a depraved proceeding, almost as bad as going to Lord's in the morning'. Daphne, optimistically, had already bought a new dress for the first night, and Milne was certainly not convinced that Hall was right. He sent the play to J. M. Barrie, who wrote:

I think it is a very good little play and sufficiently you to have its own particular quality. In my opinion it would act very well if it had good actors and not well at all with indifferent ones . . . I am quite sure that with the right people it would 'carry' thoroughly and be a very good introduction to the stage for you.

As a 'curtain raiser' it would almost certainly be flung away . . . What I believe you should aim at is to get it produced first on some special occasion such as does occur – a benefit – special matinée – with another piece by someone of repute etc. – your sole purpose being to have it tried in circumstances in which you *could* have hopes of it being well done. Then the thing would be to try to get Du Maurier first. You should let me write to him about it if you like this idea. Don't be silly about bothering me. It isn't any.

Another notion would be to let me show it to Barker to whom I think it would appeal and he might put it on in a regular bill . . . It makes me feel you have a natural instinct for play-writing, which you might not have despite the *Punch* things, and I wish you would tackle a three-act piece, not because I personally prefer them to one-act, but because it is easier to place them satisfactorily. If you do, please let me see it.

In the meantime Barrie sent the one-act play to Harley Granville Barker. Barker was enthusiastic and accepted it for production, adding 'But the important thing is that you should immediately write me a full-length play.' Milne felt this was the moment he had really been waiting for, ever since he and Ken had written their first play together more than ten years before. He was escaping from the treadmill of weekly articles. He was going to be a dramatist. But that first play was never performed.

'As it turned out,' he wrote in his autobiography, 'I was to escape in other circumstances. War was declared.'

Up till now, we have, on the whole, been able to ignore the outside world. 'History, of course, is always there. Governments rise and fall: famous men live and die: there are earthquakes in Italy, floods in China.' There have been elections, royal deaths and coronations, but characters in novels and real people in biographies live in their own worlds. They may live through all sorts of major events without commenting on them. 'They can live through History up to 1914 . . . and never once will the reader be forced to wonder or the author to have decided' what has been happening about Tariff Reform or Home Rule or who is Prime Minister at any particular moment or whether our hero is worrying about the Armenian Massacres or the Dreyfus Affair.

After 1914, all this was changed. Milne says in his autobiography that he would have liked to ignore the four years he spent in the army. 'I should like to put asterisks here, and then write "It was in 1919 that I found myself once again a civilian." For it makes me almost physically sick to think of that nightmare of mental and moral degradation, the war.' But of course the war cannot be ignored. In 1914, no one (reader, writer, or hero) can ignore history.

Alan Milne overheard hideous talk in the smoking-rooms of golf clubs and recorded it in the issue of *Punch* that came out the day after war was declared. 'What England wants,' someone said, leaning back and puffing at his cigar – he was, of course, himself well past military age – 'What England wants is a war. (Another whisky and soda, waiter.) We're getting flabby. All this pampering of the poor is playing the very deuce with the country. A bit of a scrap with a foreign power would do us all the good in the world.' He disposed of his whisky at a draught. 'We're flabby,' he repeated. 'The lower classes seem to have no discipline nowadays. We want a war to brace us up.'

It is difficult for us to understand, after the killing of one Archduke had led to the deaths 'of ten million men who were not archdukes', just how widely the war was welcomed in 1914. The newspapers carried pictures of grinning young men, rejoicing and waving their hats on their way to the recruiting offices. Asquith, the Prime Minister, wrote to Venetia Stanley: 'The streets are full of cheering crowds,' and the Commons applauded his announcement of the ultimatum, although the Kaiser had already described the treaty respecting Belgian neutrality as a mere scrap of paper. *The Times* reported that, outside Buckingham Palace, 'for more than four hours the singing and cheering of the crowd was maintained without a break.'

'How glorious is the complete unity of the nation,' wrote Daphne's aunt, Anne de Sélincourt, on 19 August. 'So many of the finest types in Britain one feels are *meant* for a crisis like this. Liège will go down in history like the Seven against Thebes or the Pass of Thermopylae, won't it?' Two years later, when Alan Milne was himself on the Somme, she would write sadly from a hospital in France, where she was working for the American Red Cross: 'One really begins to feel that every young creature one has ever heard of is going to be killed.'

'War,' Milne had often said, 'is the most babyish and laughably idiotic thing that this poor world has evolved.' But now that England was actually at war, and there was nothing laughable about it (he could also see clearly, as so few people could at the beginning, that there was nothing glorious about it either), Milne felt he had to do *something*. As soon as war was inevitable, he had written to Edward Marsh, begging him to find him some work in the Admiralty, and on 6 August followed it up.

My letter was seriously meant and I still have a faint hope that you may be able to give me something to do, though I know it sounds absurd... Though I loathe war and the idea of war and think it both wicked and childish, I am *absolutely* in favour of this war. O.S. called it yesterday 'a war against war' and that is what I believe it to be. In anticipation of what the Navy will do I take my hat off to Winston. Good luck to you all at the Admiralty.

Later he could hardly believe he had written such a letter. He would scarcely, at the time, have been so keen to take his hat off to Churchill if he had realized just how eagerly he, with all his war paint on (in Asquith's words), was longing to sink the German battle-cruiser *Goeben*, even before the ultimatum had expired. Seaman's newly minted phrase 'a war against war' was a close relation of the title of an article H. G. Wells was writing the day before: 'The War that will End War', a phrase that would eventually become a sad cliché. Many people were similarly deceived. Milne, unlike some of the deceived, also had some faint hope that England was fighting for a more democratic world, for many things symbolized by the end of the top hat. But the war failed to kill the top hat 'as it failed to do so many of the things which we hoped from it'. Milne hoped the war would make people realize the true futility and lunacy of war, and end the sentimentality about it. Starting by thinking war 'comically unheroic', he would come on the Somme to know it as 'a degradation which would soil the beasts, a lunacy which would shame the madhouse'. It had nothing whatsoever to do with the flashing swords, the whirlwind rush of brave soldiers that had thrilled him as a small boy.

Edward Marsh, apparently, could find no use for A. A. Milne at the Admiralty. But as early as 2 September, Lehmann recorded in his diary that A.A.M. was late for a *Punch* dinner, 'having been drilling with a new public school corps'. The son of another member of the Table, C. L. Graves, had already been reported missing. 'Nothing in men's minds and faces here but the seriousness of the War,' J. M. Barrie wrote after the retreat from Mons. It was obvious it would not be over by Christmas, as so many people had expected.

Milne's third collection of *Punch* pieces, *Once a Week*, was published on 15 October 1914, the first of many of his books that were dedicated to Daphne. The first page read:

TO

MY COLLABORATOR

WHO BUYS THE INK AND PAPER

LAUGHS

AND, IN FACT, DOES ALL THE REALLY DIFFICULT

PART OF THE BUSINESS

THIS BOOK IS GRATEFULLY DEDICATED
IN MEMORY OF A WINTER'S MORNING
IN SWITZERLAND

Barrie thanked Milne for his copy, which, arriving at Long Leave, had already disappeared to Eton with Michael Llewellyn Davies. 'I did contrive to keep it long enough to read it and I found it such a happy and witty book and wise too and good, as if the author had someone of that kind in his home nowadays. For all which I am glad.'

Daphne and Alan Milne would not be together in Embankment Gardens much longer. Everyone was joining up. Aubrey de Sélincourt, one of Daphne's young brothers, who had been at Oxford ('a jumping Blue of Univ.', Milne called him) was already in the North Staffordshire Regiment. George Llewellyn Davies was in France by the end of 1914 and dead within three months. At *Punch*, Owen Seaman wrote to E. V. Knox congratulating him on his commission: 'I'm very glad for your sake (not for my own, except as a matter of *Punch*-family pride).' Seaman himself wrote some stirring verses; one can imagine how Milne felt as he read them:

> England, in this great fight to which you go
>   Because, where Honour calls you, go you must,
> Be glad, whatever comes, at least to know
>   You have your quarrel just . . .
>
> Forth, then, to front that peril of the deep
>   With smiling lips and in your eyes the light,
> Steadfast and confident, of those who keep
>   Their storied scutcheon bright.

It was the sort of language Milne hated, but it was a note *Punch* continued to sound, reaching its peak (or nadir, according to your point of view) with Mrs Robertson Glasgow's verse from 'Dulce et Decorum':

> You snatched the sword, and answered as you went,
>   For fear your eager feet should be outrun,
> And with the flame of your bright youth unspent
>   Went shouting up the pathway to the sun.
> O valiant dead, take comfort where you lie.
>   So sweet to live? Magnificent to die!

One cannot help wondering whether she ever read Wilfred Owen's poem of the same name, written less than two years later.

The atmosphere in London, and in the *Punch* office in particular, was becoming intolerable. *Punch* was full of jokes against the 'shirkers' and Milne would not have been surprised if Seaman (too old to go to war himself) had produced a white feather from his pocket. Milne's Trinity contemporaries, Lytton Strachey and Clive Bell, would be able to declare themselves conscientious objectors, but for Milne this was an impossible solution. Even Strachey, for all his convictions and his lack of fitness, had felt a momentary urge to fight. He had written to his brother on 18 August: 'Yesterday I felt for the first time a desire to go out and fight myself. I can understand some people being overcome by it. At any rate one would not have to think any more.' 'Life in wartime is hell anyway,' A. A. Milne would write, 'And only in uniform can one escape thinking about it.'

R. C. Lehmann's diary records what happened six months later when Milne had eventually brought himself to volunteer.

February 10, 1915. Milne has got a commission in the Warwickshire Regiment. We all drank his health . . .
February 17. Milne has gone to join his battalion of the Warwickshire and is, I think, in the Isle of Wight . . .

Army records confirm that Milne reported for duty that very day in the Special Reserve of Officers of the 4th Battalion.

February 24. Milne being away with his regiment, my old friend Locker has been taken on to do his work temporarily . . .

Algernon Locker had 'in his time edited the *Globe* and the *Morning Post* and some other papers, so may be presumed to be a capable journalist. Milne apparently has been haggling about money terms during absence and is unpopular in the office.' Unlike many officers, Milne had no private income.

March 3. Nobody had heard from Milne, but he is supposed to be at Golden Hill Fort, Freshwater, I.W.

It was a sad end to what had been, as he called it in his dedication to Owen Seaman of *The Sunny Side*, his final collection of *Punch* pieces, 'nine happy years at the *Punch* office'. It was nine years almost to the day since he had heard with amazement, at the age of twenty-four, that he was to be assistant editor of what was still his favourite magazine. He remained a member of the Table; he was on half-pay. How long would it be before he could return to Bouverie Street?

In the barracks at Golden Hill he forgot the grind of the weekly article and the political rows. Even the boring dinners took on a charm they had not had at the time. (Back in London, the dinners were going from bad to worse. Lehmann reported that Charles Graves had said one day that 'He would rather eat cold meat in a urinal than dine with L. Bradbury,' one of the proprietors. 'My sentiments, but we go on all the same.')

The loss of freedom was for Milne the worst thing about being in the Army – that is, before he got to France, where there would be many far worse things. The loss of freedom was 'hell itself to one who had been as spoilt by good fortune as I,' Milne said. Ever since he had left Cambridge he felt he had been his own master, fixing his own hours, under no one's discipline. Now, of course, he expected to be bossed around as a raw recruit, 'rated, abused and sarcasmed as if we had been little careless boys: "Don't look at your feet there; they won't run away." "Stand at ease, 's you were." "Eyes front, 's you were." ' Over and over again.

It had been rather like that, drilling with the Old Boys Corps in London. But now it stood him in good stead. Milne continued to be, as, it seemed, he had always been, extremely fortunate. It had to make things easier that his Adjutant was a nephew of Charles Graves – Charles Massie-Blomfield (a cousin of Robert Graves) – who was well aware of the distinction of his new subaltern. Alan wrote to Ken from Delaware, The Avenue, Totland Bay, Isle of Wight – not far from Golden Hill Fort. Ken's fourth child, Antony, had recently been born (Milne thought it an excellent name); fortunately Ken's government work made *his* enlistment out of the question. He would soon be working for the Ministry of Pensions and his health was already worrying Maud.

Alan's first letter is almost euphoric with relief. 'It's all very interesting and not quite so alarming as I thought.' Because of his experience, he was allowed to show off his drilling straight away.

I then got going in a beautiful clear voice as follows: 'Move to the left in fours, form fours, left, by the left quick march ... At the halt on the left form sections ... by the right quick march ... at the halt on the left form lines, remainder left incline ...' all given with the air of one to whom all this was utter child's play. We progressed at a terrific pace and I ran about and waved my stick and by the time the Adjutant caught us we were nearly off the Island. He said 'Look here this is company drill; you're supposed to be doing platoon drill' and then tried to get his breath again. I said 'There's so little to do in platoon drill, sir.' He said 'Well get them in line of sections in fours at twenty paces interval facing *there*' and he pointed to the right. Laddie, I was like Naaman: it was too easy for me.

There was a lot more description of the drill. It was obviously addictive – the language and the beauty of it, making all those men move in response to his words. The Adjutant told the Senior Major that Milne had 'a most artistic way with him'. The next day there was a route march; there was no one left for him to drill. 'Perhaps I might have got leave to join them but instead I got a rifle and bayonet issued to me, took them down here and spent a morning with the musketry instructions learning all about the insides, how to fix bayonets etc.'

Twenty-five years later he would say:

My knowledge of firearms or (as they are called, I never discovered why) weapons of precision, was not worth passing on. It is true that my men carried rifles, and that I inspected them from time to time, but I never knew what I was looking for. Sometimes at my request a man would open the breech and put a dirty thumb-nail at one end while I squinted down the other, and if I had seen a mouse crawling about inside I should have known that something was wrong. But I was handicapped, as I so often am, by feeling that the man was better informed than I; and that if I had said 'I say, isn't that a lot of rust?' and he had said 'No, sir, blood,' we should have been at an impasse. I never, as they say, fired a shot in anger, and only twelve under the impetus of any other emotion. These all missed the musketry instructor, but hit the Isle of Wight. It was he who was angry.

The reason for this happy state of affairs (for his pacifist conscience, it was essential he should hurt no one), was that 'through a variety of accidents' he had been able to become a signals officer. In early August 1915, he was sent to Southern Command Signalling School at Wyke Regis near Weymouth, for a nine-week course.

Milne wrote to E. V. Lucas on 6 November soon after he returned to the Isle of Wight, regretting that Lucas would not be in London when he would be on leave the following week. 'I had meditated a special descent on the Table.' In Lucas's absence, he did in fact call in, but very briefly. Lehmann wrote in his diary on 10 November: 'Shortly after we began dinner Milne arrived in khaki and stayed a quarter of an hour. He looks very fit.'

In his letter from Sandown Milne had told Lucas:

Just at present I'm not on the Active Service list of the battn. – being registered as 'Indispensable to the Training of the Battalion.' I've just been through the Signal School and am now a Qualified Instructor. It's rather a pleasant job in its way; I'm entirely my own master; order my own parades

– and do things entirely in the way I think best. Does the whole battalion go on a route-march? 2nd Lt Milne does not. Is every blooming subaltern orderly officer (a *rotten* job) in turn? Yes, but 2 Lt Milne escapes – being indispensable' etc . . . (see above) every minute of his time. I tell you – some Signals Officer; you should see me at the blackboard (covered with chalk) giving a lecture on short circuits or the theory of the heliograph.

So I really seem settled here for a bit (we have just moved for good from Golden Hill) and in fact I am taking a furnished house, and Daff is coming down with the servants. If you know of anybody who wants a nice flat in Chelsea send him along. No doubt when we're settled in our house here I shall be sent abroad (the sort of thing that happens here) but it will be as, probably, a Brigade Signal Officer, an interesting job and not as wet as the trenches. I've been lucky you know. Had I not been Signals Officer, I should have gone out in July to the 2nd battalion (I know this for a fact) and the 2nd battn. was wiped out to a man, or rather to an officer in the advance (Sept 25th). 3 of ours killed and I should have been one. Then as you know I tried to get into the Flying Corps – as observing officer in a particular squadron that a man I knew was getting up. I was pilled on my sight. The squadron flew over to France 3 weeks ago and the man who took me up at Brooklands – this friend of mine – was killed in an air-fight last week. Well, I might have been behind him – observing the panorama for the last time . . . Daff and I are pretty thankful one way and another; she in fact is happier than she has been since the war began, which is a blessing.

There was plenty to be thankful about – quite apart from the basic fact of being still alive. Milne had had his first book published in America – a collection of *Punch* pieces had appeared under the title *Happy Days*. The *New York Times Book Review* wrote: 'These light-hearted sketches are more poignant since their author is now in the British trenches.' Thank God there were no trenches on the Isle of Wight. Or thank something. Milne had long ago given up thanking any kind of god and felt keenly the irony 'among all the other ironies of the time, that all the nations are praying to the same God'.

On the Isle of Wight life was pleasant enough. Alan had been missing Daphne painfully, and writing her daily letters. He described them to Ken as a sort of 'hourly diary'. Now they were able to rent 'the prettiest cottage' in Sandown, with the promise of lilac and cherry blossom in the spring, if only they were there that long. Daphne and the Colonel's wife (mother of five children) got together and decided it would be nice if the signals officer, remembering his pre-war trade, spent his evenings writing a play for Daphne and the five children to perform as part of an entertainment for the troops, 'whether the troops liked it or not.' Milne protested he was much too tired in the evenings, whereupon Daphne (whom, after all, Alan had already named as his 'collaborator' in the dedication of *Once a Week*) offered to do all the actual writing. All A. A. Milne had to do was lie in an armchair and tell her what to write. This was easy enough and he would always afterwards look back with pleasure to that winter of 1915: 'I in my chair before the fire, my collaborator, pen in hand, brown head bent over table, writing, waiting, laughing.' The short play was duly performed with Daphne as the Wicked Countess and various children as assorted princes and princesses.

The play has not survived, but it was the germ of what some would call A. A. Milne's first children's book: *Once on a Time*, written in the same way in that Sandown cottage. As well as the evening sessions, there were walks on Sundays along cold cliffs and over springy downs, when 'the characters in the book came with us, listening to us as we settled their fate for the next chapter.' In his preface to the 1925 edition (the year between *When We Were Very Young* and *Winnie-the-Pooh*) Milne wrote:

This book was written in 1915, for the amusement of my wife and myself at a time when life was not very amusing; it was published at the end of 1917; was reviewed, if at all, as one of a parcel, by some brisk uncle from the Tiny Tots Department; and died quietly, without seriously detracting from the interest which was being taken in the World War, then in progress.

No one really knew who it was for. It looked like a children's book, but was full of rather sophisticated jokes. One reader even thought the characters were satires of the Kaiser, Mr Lloyd George and Mr Asquith. Milne asked:

Who are children anyway? A boy of three, a girl of six, a boy of ten, a girl of fourteen – are they all to like the same thing? And is a book 'suitable for a boy of twelve' any more likely to please a boy of twelve than a modern novel is likely to please a man of thirty-seven; even if the novel be described truly as 'suitable for a man of thirty-seven'? I confess that I cannot grapple with these difficult problems.

But I am very sure of this; that no-one can write a book which children will like, unless he write it for himself first . . . Read in it what you like; read it to whomever you like; be of what age you like; it can only fall into one of the two classes. Either you will enjoy it or you won't.

Over the years, a good many readers of assorted ages have enjoyed it, not least for the parts that are undeniably by the same author as the *Pooh* books. 'What *are* you?' the Wicked Countess asks poor Prince Udo, who finds himself, unaccountably, one third rabbit, one third lion and one third woolly lamb. He is obviously really a prince in disguise and the Countess knows well 'how men are always glad to talk about themselves.' There were indeed advantages for Udo in his present predicament. 'As a man he had never been listened to so attentively.' But there is the problem of what this strange animal is going to eat. Like Tigger, he has no idea what he really likes. Prince Udo even says, as Tigger might easily have done if Udo hadn't got there first: 'I don't suppose any of you here have any idea how very prickly thistles are when they are going down.'

The lilac and cherry are in flower. It is now the spring of 1916 and *The House at Pooh Corner* is still a dozen years away. At any moment, having finished *Once on a Time* in his spare hours from instructing soldiers, Milne may be sent to France. There is just time before he goes to write that three-act play J. M. Barrie and Granville Barker have both urged him to try. It has to be a comedy, of course, and on a subject which has nothing whatsoever to do with the war. It is called *Wurzel-Flummery* and the whole play revolves round the unlikely question: Would anyone be willing to assume the name Wurzel-Flummery, in order to receive an inheritance of £50,000?

It is basically an interesting question – what people will do for money – but is it a strong enough subject to sustain three acts? This was the question that would often be asked of the themes of Milne's plays. As soon as he had finished it, Milne sent it to Barrie, who had been saying for several years that he would do all he could to launch Milne as a playwright. Barrie liked the play and sent it to the actor-manager Dennis Eadie, who invited Milne to lunch with him at the Carlton Grill to talk it over.

Milne managed to get a day's leave and went up to London. Eadie seemed really keen on the play and wanted to do it, but there was something not quite right with it. 'If I knew what it was, I would tell you, but I don't . . . Why don't you ask Barrie? Or read it through again yourself? It's so nearly right.' Milne felt sure he could get it right – tighten it up a bit perhaps. He arrived back on the Isle of Wight feeling rather optimistic. Daphne and he had a happy dinner together, 'building the wildest castles in Shaftesbury Avenue'.

Half an hour after they had gone to bed, there was a loud knocking on the front door of the cottage in Sandown. Milne was to report to the Mess. He was for France in forty-eight hours.

France and the First Plays

THERE IS NO question that Alan Milne had been extraordinarily lucky in the Army so far. Not only had he managed to retain an unusual degree of independence (though he had exaggerated a little, perhaps, in that letter to E. V. Lucas), but he had proved himself a competent signals officer, at least in theory, and a good teacher. The man who had joked that he thought light fittings grew on walls was now an expert on laying telephone lines, on signalling lamps, power-buzzers and heliographs – not to mention the cruder devices, Morse code discs and semaphore flags, which were still used in some situations.

Milne had contributed only three pieces to *Punch* since joining the Army and nothing at all of his appeared between 16 June 1915 and 22 November 1916. He was uneasy about the role of humorist in wartime. It was possible, of course, to be funny about ridiculous regulations, Army bureaucracy, not getting promoted or a clever recruiting ploy. Funny things were still going on. On one occasion Milne's Commanding Officer received a communication from the Secretary of State for War telling him he would be held 'personally responsible' if any more men arrived in France without toothbrushes. Such absurdities really did happen, but in fact Milne drew on his experiences of the Western Front very little; disgust, loathing and fear do not often lead to humour. It is hard to joke about a 'nightmare of mental and moral degradation' – to use again that phrase in which Milne summed up the war.

In his history of *Punch*, R. G. G. Price wrote:

Milne did not, as he was accused of doing, treat the Western Front like a house-party. His war-articles have been rather neglected in comparison with his pre-war leisure hour stuff. They had the same versatility and gaiety and they dealt with the only aspects of the subject that could possibly be treated humorously. It is preposterous to suggest that a humorous periodical, providing one of the few alleviations in the middle of blackness, should have produced every number in the style of Remarque or Barbusse.

'*Punch* does us all good out here,' General Julian Byng wrote from the front to his friend, Sir Owen Seaman. Milne's most bitter writing about the war would never appear in *Punch* – not even the poem called 'O.B.E.' which has become his best-known comment. It had to wait for publication until 1921 in his own collection *The Sunny Side*.

O.B.E.

I know a Captain of Industry,
Who made big bombs for the R.F.C.,
And collared a lot of £ s. d. –
And he – thank God! – has the O.B.E.

I know a Lady of Pedigree,
Who asked some soldiers out to tea,
And said 'Dear me!' and 'Yes, I see' –
And she – thank God! – has the O.B.E.

I know a fellow of twenty-three,
Who got a job with a fat M.P. –
(Not caring much for the Infantry.)
And he – thank God! – has the O.B.E.

I had a friend; a friend, and he
Just held the line for you and me,
And kept the Germans from the sea,
And died – without the O.B.E. Thank God!
He died without the O.B.E.

Milne travelled to France in July 1916 with a quiet boy who was joining the same battalion of the 11th Royal Warwickshire Regiment. He was not long out of school and the younger of two sons. His elder brother had been killed a few months earlier. His parents had bought for him (and 'you may laugh or cry as you will', said Milne)

an under-garment of chain mail, such as had been worn in the Middle Ages to guard against unfriendly daggers, and was now sold to over-loving mothers as likely to turn a bayonet-thrust or keep off a stray fragment of shell; as, I suppose, it might have done. He was much embarrassed by this parting gift, and though, true to his promise, he was taking it to France with him, he did not know whether he ought to wear it. I suppose that, being fresh from school, he felt it to be 'unsporting'; something not quite done; perhaps, even, a little cowardly. His young mind was torn between his promise to his mother and his hatred of the unusual. He asked my advice: charmingly, ingenuously, pathetically. I told him to wear it; and to tell his mother that he was wearing it; and to tell her how safe it made him feel, and how certain of coming back to her. I do not know whether he took my advice ... Anyway it didn't matter; for on the evening when we first came within reach of the battle-zone, just as he was settling down to his tea, a crump came over and blew him to pieces ...

Dulce et decorum est pro patria mori.

But just why it was a pleasant death and a fitting death I still do not understand. Nor, it may be, did his father and mother; even though assured by the Colonel that their son had died as gallantly as he had lived, an English gentleman.

One of the reviews of *The Day's Play*, in those far-distant days before the war, had said that: 'Mr Milne carries with him an abiding sense that it is great fun to be alive.' He no longer carried it with him, of course; he had left it behind in England with Daphne. What he carried was an increasing sense that it was a miracle to be still alive.

On 28 July 1916, only a few days after he had joined the regiment, he wrote to Ken, under the address, 'attd. 11th R. War. Regt. BEF'

This battalion was in the thick of it, and is now resting (which means that you do about twice as much as you did at home) but we are going up again in a few days. There is a signalling officer here, curse him, and my Brigade job hangs fire. Result that I am a dashed platoon commander. However the C.O. has spoken to the Brigadier about me ... I expect something will turn up soon and as a p.c. the sooner wounded the sooner back home ... I don't mind telling you I miss Daff dreadfully. And when fat Garvins say [Garvin was editor of the *Observer* and stood for all newspaper editors, comfortable at home], 'However long this war lasts we must clench our teeth and hold on until we gain a complete victory,' I want to slap him. It's easy work clenching teeth in London.

The CO Milne mentioned was Lt.-Col. C. S. Collison. Twenty years later Milne would write his obituary in *The Times* and recall someone immensely charming and civilized, a revelation to a young subaltern who hated the Army and was 'prepared to resent all Regulars'. Writing to Daphne, Milne would soon say, as he rarely said: 'I love him.'

Resting out of the line, life was not so bad, though the sound of guns and aeroplanes overhead all the time made it impossible to pretend they were on manoeuvres. They were camped in an orchard above Bécourt and had all their meals under the sky. Someone had brought peaches from Amiens and someone else had got hold of a gramophone. It was 'a heart-rending business,' Alan told Ken, listening to the tunes he had shared with Daff, lying on his back in the grass after dinner on beautiful summer evenings, 'smoking and listening and thinking of London'. He often imagined death and considered how little he would leave his collaborator. Though the papers in England had been distorting the situation, the officers in France knew how badly the battle was going. It was said that as many as 20,000 Allied soldiers had died on the first day alone (with another 40,000 wounded) and 10,000 more were being killed or wounded every day that passed.

Three days after his letter to Ken the orchard was shelled as the men sat about on the grass cleaning their rifles, shaving, talking. It had seemed so safe and was thought to be out of reach of the German guns, but fifty-one men were killed or wounded, including the chaplain and two newly joined subalterns – one of them the boy in the chainmail underwear. Even after all those deaths and wounds, there was a strange air of unreality. 'After dinner it was customary to mount the opposite rise, where a wonderful view could be had of the line of bursting shells from our own artillery. Intermixed with these, rockets of all colours were continually ascending, some of which broke into great clouds of sparks, like golden rain.' So Colonel Collison wrote in his diary.

When they were back in the line, there was no grass. Even in the summer they were fighting in a field of mud, among smashed and leafless trees. The ground between Bazentin and Mametz 'was ploughed and furrowed by shellfire'; legs and arms stuck out of the mud. It was very hot and the smell was terrible. What had struck Robert Graves in the same place a couple of weeks earlier was 'the number of dead horses and mules lying about'. He had got used to human corpses 'but it seemed wrong for animals to be dragged into the war like this'. There was only one insistent sound competing with the guns, 'the incessant humming of blue bottles . . . preying on the bodies of the dead and hovering above them in black droning swarms. They hung permanently above the makeshift latrines . . . By August all the troops had diarrhoea. The flies carried the pestilence, alighting on the carrion of the bloated dead, breeding on the decaying flesh and hatching fresh generations to prey in their turn on every crumb of food a soldier ate and to cling and crawl round the rims of tin mugs, sticky with the vestiges of a dozen or more brews of strong sweet tea.' All water had to be treated with chlorine and tasted foul. Everyone had to be inoculated against typhoid. If there were any objectors, Milne's Commanding Officer had them remanded for medical examination on the grounds of insanity. But there were those who thought the insanity was in being there in the first place.

Their positions in and about Mametz Wood were heavily shelled. One company lost all four of its platoon commanders within twenty-four hours. Colonel Collison suggested to Milne that he should go into action with the signals officer to add some practical knowledge to all his theory. Milne felt relieved that he had something other to do than try to kill or wait to die. On the afternoon of 11 August, 2nd Lt. Harrison, the signals officer, and three men, with Milne accompanying them, ran out a line to the front trench by a devious route, for it was thought that the existing line would never stand against the opening counter-barrage. Milne wrote: 'On the way we fell into a burst of whizz-bangs, and Harrison was knocked out. We got him back to the first-aid post, I reported to the Colonel, and became signalling officer. At four o'clock next morning we went out again, this time by the ordinary communication trench, such as it was, and laid a line, elaborately laddered according to the text books, and guaranteed to withstand any bombardment.

'H.Q. was in a deep German dug-out, facing, of course, the wrong way. In an adjoining dug-out was the H.Q. of the East Lancashires with whom the attack was being made. In the space between these two underground rooms were my signallers. At eleven o'clock that night the Colonel, the Major, the Adjutant and I sat round a table by candle-light smoking and talking, waiting for our barrage to begin. But the Germans, who knew all about it, began first. And the line went.

'The sergeant-major of the East Lancashires went up the steps with some idea, I suppose, of getting information, and was blown out of existence before he reached the top. My signallers announced this, and added that the line to Brigade was also down. We sat there completely isolated. The depth of the dug-out deadened the noise of the guns, so that a shell-burst was no longer the noise of a giant plumber throwing down his tools, but only a persistent thud, which set the candles dancing and then, as if by an afterthought, blotted them out. From time to time I lit them again, wondering what I should be doing, wondering what signalling officers did on these occasions. Nervously I said to the Colonel, feeling that the isolation was all my fault, "Should I try to get a line out?" and to my intense relief he said, "Don't be a bloody fool."

'It was about two o'clock in the morning that a runner got through. The attack, as was to be expected, was a complete failure . . .

' "Am I to go back, sir?" ' [Milne asked the Colonel.]

' "No." He caught the Major's eye. The Major got up and strapped on his revolver. It was all too clearly the moment for me to strap on mine. Perhaps somebody else would do *Wurzel-Flummery* – afterwards.

' "Use your common sense," said the Colonel. "If it's impossible, come back. I simply cannot lose three signalling officers in a month."

'I promised, but felt quite unable to distinguish between common-sense and cowardice. The whole thing was so damned silly.

'I told my sergeant that we were now going to run out a line, and asked him to pick two men for me. I knew nothing of the section then, save that there was a Lance-Corporal Grainger who shared my passion for Jane Austen, unhelpful knowledge in the circumstances. My sergeant said at once: "I'll come for one, sir," which I thought was sporting of him, although it was obviously wrong for both of us to go. He picked on another man, a company signaller who had joined headquarters for the occasion, and we attached ourselves to the Major. We dashed. The Major went first – he was going to "re-organize the troops"; I went second, God knew why; the sergeant and the signaller came behind me, running out a line neatly and skilfully. No laddering now, no text-book stuff, it was just dropped anywhere. From time to time the Major flung himself down for a breather, and down we flopped and panted, wondering if he would get up again. To our relief each time he was alive, and so were we. We passed one of the signal-stations, no longer a station but a pancake of earth on top of a spread-eagled body; I had left him there that evening, saying. "Well, you'll be comfortable here." More rushes, more breathers, more bodies, we were in the front line. The Major hurried off to collect what men he could, while I joined up the telephone. Hopeless, of course, but we could have done no more. I pressed the buzzer . . .

'I asked to speak to the Colonel. I told him what I knew. I ordered – what were telephones for? – a little counter-bombardment. Then with a sigh of utter content and thankfulness and the joy of living, I turned away from the telephone. And there behind me was Lance-Corporal Grainger.

' "What on earth are *you* doing here?" I said.

'He grinned sheepishly . . .

' "I thought I'd just like to come along, sir."

' "But *why*?"

'He looked still more embarrassed.

' "Well, sir, I thought I'd just like to be sure *you* were all right."
Which is the greatest tribute to Jane Austen that I have ever heard.'

This gives some idea of what Milne's work was. Harrison's life had
been saved by his steel helmet, but he was out of action. Milne wrote
to H. G. Wells: 'I got his job, much the most interesting work in the
infantry, with the great advantage that one is the only officer in the
Battalion who knows anything about it, and is consequently one's
own master – a great thing to a civilian in the Army. I simply can't
tell you how I loathe the Army.'

Milne meant exactly that. He could not write about the filth, the
smells, the lice, the rats, the lack of any privacy, the constant fear.
He could not describe the corpses, including the suicides, and the
men executed for cowardice or desertion – all the things that life in
the Army meant on the Somme in 1916. He could not write now
about the meaningless lunacy of the whole horrible business. That
would come later.

There were some breaks in the horror. There was a horse he could
use. The signals officer's official mount was a bicycle, but it was not
much good in the mud. Milne had never had much to do with horses,
but he liked Toby. 'This is a beastly War,' Milne wrote in his first
Punch piece to appear for many months, but it had its compensations
and one of them was Toby. It was pleasant too, when he was out of
the line again, resting at a place called La Comté, and the telephone
rang in the HQ Mess one night. The Divisional General was on the
phone. The General was an old friend of Owen Seaman's and an
admirer of A.A.M.'s writing in *Punch*. He was asking Colonel
Collison to bring Milne to lunch with him at Divisional Headquarters. The Adjutant, Major Rooke, tried to suggest this was bad
for discipline – a mere subaltern lunching with a general; but he
didn't really mind. When Rooke went on leave in October, he invited
Daphne to lunch. He lived at Colchester, not too far from Burnham-
on-Crouch, where Daphne was keeping her mother company in
Alan's absence. The Major was able to give her a first-hand account
of 'the famous non-stop run with the telephone-line', and mislead-
ingly comforting news of Alan.

At that point they thought they were established at Bully-Grenay for the winter. On 13 October Alan wrote to Ken and Maud (and indeed said it was for Marjorie too, who, now ten, had just written him a 'wonderful' letter): 'My nine cable-lines and exchanges were becoming quite a fascinating game . . . But alas – we're off again.' As he was writing, the gramophone was playing 'The Pink Lady' and the sentimental music, he said, 'makes me almost cry'. For once his heart was unbuttoned:

Oh Maudie . . . When the war is over Daff and I are going to sit hand in hand for the rest of our lives. We shall never go and see anybody, and if anybody comes to see us they will have to shake Daff's right hand and my left. If you want to know what being in love is like come out here.

. . . Daff bet me 10/- when I came out that I'd be home by October 20th – nothing but a nice cushy wound can do it now, so I look like being 10/- up. I have already chosen my present – a case for her letters. At present I carry them in my pocket, and there are enough now to make a bullet think twice.

In his other pocket, Milne carried a toy dog, a mascot, which Daphne had slipped into his bag on his last morning in England, between the revolver and the boracic powder. 'Just to look after you.' He was thus frailly protected; but he had had enough of the Somme. It was not a 'nice cushy wound' but a fever that took Alan Milne back only nineteen days after the date Daphne had bet on. He told in his autobiography how it came about:

'I had my men out on a little hill one morning, and was walking as usual, from station to station to see how the messages were coming through. It was a warm November day, so warm that each station seemed a mile, rather than a few hundred yards, from the next, and I wondered how I could drag my legs there. At lunch in the H.Q. mess I went to sleep; spent the afternoon and evening sleeping in front of the stove; and when I went to bed was given the usual couple of aspirins by the M.O. Next morning my temperature was 103. The M.O. went off to arrange for an ambulance to take me to the clearing station. By the time I was introduced to it again, the thermometer was soaring up to 105. Next day the battalion got the order to move; the attack was to begin. My sergeant came to say good-bye to me. I handed over my maps, commended the section to his care, wished him luck, and went to sleep again. He was lucky. He only lost a leg.

'Ten days later I was at Southampton. Some kind woman offered to write a telegram for me. It was to Daphne, saying that she would find me in hospital at Oxford. I woke up one afternoon and saw her at the end of the bed, crying.'

On 14 November, six days after Milne had been invalided home, the Battle of the Somme itself could be said to have died, as snow began to cover the wasteland. The battle marks a crucial point in the history of the First World War. The army that sustained those horrendous casualties on the first day, back in July, was still largely the volunteer army that answered Kitchener's call – optimistic and hopeful of a decisive victory. By the time Milne arrived, any hope of a German surrender had gone. The battle that had been conceived as the Big Push had turned into a war of attrition – calculated perfectly to confirm Milne's pacificism. Hundreds of thousands died on both sides achieving absolutely nothing. The Allies were still four miles short of Bapaume, which the cavalry had hoped to take in the opening attack. Milne would have called it a farce, had that not been a word he wished to reserve for happier things. 'The whole thing was an absolute muck-up,' said Sgt W. J. Hoyles, who had lost every single man in his section.

'For God's sake don't think I shall swank after this war because I was in it,' Alan wrote to Ken a few days before he was invalided home. 'Possibly when Barry talks about his hair-breadth escapes in Newcastle, I may want to mention Arques, but certainly never to you unless because you want to hear about it. Really, old son, I don't feel any superiority over you; I *do* over people out here in the A.S.C., and (sometimes) over people at home in the Canteen Inspecting Dept., but c'est tout . . . You must have loathed this one as much as I have.'

There would be a certain amount of feeling in Milne's plays about people who had not been through it – the lover in *The Camberley Triangle*, who had been 'engaged on important work for the Government of a confidential nature', the uncle in *The Boy Comes Home*, who felt he had done his bit by providing jam for the troops and had 'suffered from the shortage of potatoes'. In his story 'The Return' Milne showed his contempt for the man who thought life was difficult in London – and of 'profiteering skrimshankers'.

Writing to his brother, Milne was trying to be very honest; he knew he was glad he had been on the Somme, hideous as it had been. It would give him so much more right to speak out against the whole bloody business. He knew what he was talking about. It has been said that A. A. Milne had a quiet war. Certainly he was lucky to spend less than four months in France; but no one who spent any time on the Somme can be said to have had a quiet war. The Somme was only quiet if you were dead. The fact that, as a signals officer, he had not been required to kill, helped to preserve Milne's sanity, but it would be many months before he was well again and he would never forget the sights he had seen.

Alan Milne left the front line on 8 November 1916, invalided home with what was called trench fever. He was fortunate that his temperature was high enough for there to be no question about it. He had the same sort of feeling of 'beautiful irresponsibility' H. G. Wells had had when, as a young man, a haemorrhage had temporarily removed him from life: 'There was nothing more for me to do, nothing I could possible attend to and I didn't care a rap. I had got out of my struggle with honour and no one could ask me to carry on . . . I might write or I might die. It didn't matter.'

Milne had certainly got out of the struggle with honour. Even so, years later, watching the first production of *Journey's End*, one can imagine his feelings when Laurence Olivier as Captain Stanhope sneered at Hibbert as 'another little worm trying to wriggle home'.

'How long's he been out here? Three months, I suppose. Now he's decided he's done his bit. He's decided to go home and spend the rest of the war in comfortable nerve hospitals. – He thinks he's going to wriggle off before the attack . . .' Milne knew himself, of course, to be 'not the stuff of which soldiers are made'. 'I felt quite unable to distinguish between common sense and cowardice,' he had admitted. The sensible thing now (was it also the cowardly thing?) was to make sure he did not return to France.

Milne was in hospital for several weeks, but well enough on 13 December to attend the *Punch* Table dinner. After Christmas he and Daphne went back to his regiment on the Isle of Wight and took another cottage in Sandown. Milne had fortunately proved himself to be an excellent signals instructor; the Army had plenty of use for him at home.

On his thirty-fifth birthday, Milne had the best present he could have had. By chance, it was the day that there arrived from J. M. Barrie a letter saying that the actor-manager, Dion Boucicault, would include *Wurzel-Flummery* in a programme with two Barrie one-act plays, if Milne could reduce it to two acts. 'To cut even a line is painful, but to cut thirty pages of one's first comedy, slaughtering

whole characters on the way, has at least a certain morbid fasci-
nation.' It was not, as we have seen, Milne's first comedy, but it was
the first one with, at long last, a chance of professional production.
Milne did the cutting and the play appeared at the New Theatre in
London with Boucicault himself as the solicitor and Nigel Playfair
as the pompous MP.

Daphne and Alan Milne (he with forty-eight hours' leave) went up
for the first night on Saturday, 7 April 1917. It was the day after the
entry of the United States into the war. In France the Allies were
about to launch their Spring Offensive – with the Canadians' tanks
stuck in the mud and Vimy Ridge waiting to be stormed. The theatres
in darkened London were full of troops on leave. Denis Mackail
called it 'a distinctly appetising night', the Milne play sandwiched
between the Barries. Milne was introduced that night to Irene Vanbrugh, Boucicault's wife, who was in one of the Barrie plays. For
years she had been one of the best-known actresses on the London
stage; Boucicault asked Milne to write a play for her. It was exciting;
Milne felt his career as a playwright had taken off – though Owen
Seaman told the young W. A. Darlington that he thought 'Alan
wasn't quite at home yet in the new medium.' The run was a brief
eight weeks but the reviews were rather good, with words such as
'witty', 'delightful' and 'brilliant' freely used. *The Times* welcomed
'the first acted play of A.A.M. of *Punch*'.

One weak point in the play is that it does not prove its point ... Another
is that Mr Milne stops too long to argue it all out, does not argue nearly
as well as he jests, and does not always fit his argument in with his peculiarly
happy and surprising strokes of wit. Still, the play shows him attempting
'bigger' and deeper work than any that he has done before and may mark
the beginning of a new period in his development.

It did indeed. Every moment now that the Army left him alone,
Milne was writing plays. 'My job was soldiering and my spare time
was my own affair. Other subalterns played bridge and golf; that
was one way of amusing oneself. Another way was – why not? – to
write plays.'

The soldiering involved a move because Milne was put in charge
of a company, one of four in a newly formed signalling school at
Fort Southwick, where all signallers of the Portsmouth Garrison
could be trained together. Milne told an interviewer a few years later:
'We had a cottage at Porchester, two miles away. I got up at 6.45
every morning, staggered up to the fort 400 feet above us, taught

there till 4.30, staggered home, had tea and then sat in the garden and dictated to my wife. That was really rather an effort, as I was ill at the time.'

On 18 June, Milne told Clement Shorter, who was asking for an article for *Sphere*: 'Really I have found the Army very inspiring and I've done much more work in it (literary, I mean) than I ever did in peace-time.' It was partly, of course, because of the end of any normal social life. It was easier to write in Columbia Cottage, Portchester, without the distractions of living in Chelsea. He was trying to write the play Boucicault had asked for – a play with a starring part for Irene Vanbrugh.

But other ideas kept getting in the way. *The Lucky One* had no possible part for Miss Vanbrugh and was indeed never put on in the West End of London, though it had a Theatre Guild production in New York in 1922. The first English performance of this play was in 1925. It was in a large converted chapel in Kingston Square, Hull, Yorkshire. The cast included Colette O'Neil (Miles Malleson's wife, Bertrand Russell's lover) and Roland Culver. 'For 1925, this play's morality was daring.' The probable reason why the play did not find a producer in 1917 was the fact that the plot was so disturbing and unconventional. The girl ends up married to the wrong man, totally upsetting the audience's happy expectations. 'Audiences (and managers) like their whites white and their blacks black,' Milne once wrote to Curtis Brown, 'which is not nearly so much fun for the author.'

Gerald, 'the lucky one', the one who 'has always been so good at everything, 'even as a baby', loses his fiancée, Pamela, to Bob, his elder brother, who has found himself in prison for some dubious dealing in the City. Bob's feelings about Gerald are as Ken's so easily might have been about Alan, if Ken had been a less remarkable person. Bob is the one who has had the hard time. He wins Pamela because, she sees, he will always be in need of her. But one's sympathies end up entirely with Gerald, still outwardly 'the lucky one' but, in fact, unlucky, having lost the one thing that really mattered to him.

Milne wrote a one-act play too: *The Boy Comes Home*. It is a good, thought-provoking piece about a returned soldier, containing one moment of electrifying drama, which never failed to make the audience gasp when it was performed, often by amateurs, over and over again throughout Milne's life. The returned soldier (the boy of the title, who is no longer a boy) points his loaded revolver at his profiteering, bullying uncle. The play started its career the following year as part of a music-hall programme, with Owen Nares as the 'Boy', at the Victoria Theatre; Nares had earlier come to dinner with the Milnes (their first actor guest) and they had 'cut the Boy's hair and trimmed him up a bit'.

Still the play for Irene Vanbrugh was not written and Milne was getting tired. The staggering up the hill to the Fort each early morning, and the long intensive working days, were more than he could manage any longer. He did not want to explain the theory of induced currents ever again. Daphne became very concerned about his health. He was terribly thin. He made much play in a *Punch* piece in July of a doctor, who ran his pencil up and down his patient's ribs, producing 'that pleasing noise which small boys get by dragging a stick along railings'. Milne had never fully recovered from the illness that had sent him home from the Somme. He felt he wanted to go to sleep for a year. It was in this mood that he wrote a poem, which included such immortal longings as these:

> When the War is over and the Kaiser's out of print,
> I'm going to buy some tortoises and watch the beggars sprint;
> When the War is over and the sword at last we sheathe,
> I'm going to keep a jelly-fish and listen to it breathe.
>
> When the War is over and we've done the Belgians proud,
> I'm going to keep a chrysalis and read to it aloud;
> When the War is over and we've finished up the show,
> I'm going to plant a lemon-pip and listen to it grow.

Milne was sent to the military hospital at Cosham and then to the convalescent hospital in Queen Victoria's old home at Osborne on the Isle of Wight for three weeks. Robert Graves was there. He had left the Somme on a stretcher, after being given up for dead, on the very day Milne had arrived in July 1916, a whole year earlier. Graves had been out there again, in the hardest winter for twenty years. He had been invalided home with bronchitis after a night spent looking for horses stolen from his battalion. After a spell in hospital in Oxford, where Milne had been a few months earlier, he had arrived at Osborne at the same time as Milne. They had bedrooms which had once been the night nurseries of Queen Victoria's children. They could take all the Queen's 'favourite walks through the woods and along the quiet seashore'. As the Queen herself had said: 'It is impossible to imagine a prettier spot.' It was the strawberry season.

But Osborne House itself was gloomy and full of people, Robert Graves thought, who should rather have been 'in a special neurasthenic hospital'. Graves found A. A. Milne gloomy too – 'in his least humorous vein' – if not actually neurasthenic. All he wanted to do was rest and read and play the occasional game of golf. He said, 'I know nothing which gives me so complete a feeling of luxurious rest as settling down to a novel in a deck-chair immediately after breakfast, with the knowledge that one is safe from the reproaches of conscience.'

Graves, determined to wake things up, founded the Royal Albert Society, open only to those with some connection with Albert – those who had been born in the province of Alberta in Canada, won the Albert Medal, worked at the Albert Docks, performed in the Royal Albert Hall and so on. It was the very stuff of a pre-war Milne article, but the evidence suggests that Milne did not join.

By the beginning of August, with some further sick leave, Alan was with Daphne at Brooklands, Sarisbury Green, in Hampshire, the house belonging to her father. It was a house where he would often stay when he wanted to relax.

Milne told H. G. Wells that a medical board had 'recommended sedentary work' as he had not been well since his return from France. This was in a letter in September 1917, thanking him for an invitation to visit him and Jane at Easton Glebe. Wells had actually visited the Somme the year before (under a government scheme to dispatch influential writers on brief visits to the front; Barrie had been too) and had come to regret his early and uncritical jingoism. Alan had given *Mr Britling Sees it Through* to Daphne the previous Christmas ('the nine million and oneth copy sold' he joked to Wells – for it was a tremendous bestseller); it had left them 'gaping with admiration' as it traced Wells's own changing attitude to the war.

When Wells sent him *God the Invisible King*, Milne did the sensible thing of thanking him for it the moment it arrived. He hardly thought he would be able to accept Wells's new theology. He did hope to accept the invitation to Easton Glebe, even if he was not yet quite up to what Frank Swinnerton called the 'whirls of unceasing activity' – the charades and tennis and games of every sort, which made up weekends at Easton, and which were just the sort of thing in which the pre-war Milne had taken such joyous part.

Milne had not long been back at Fort Southwick before the regiment was told that it was being transferred to Dover. This was grim news, for Dover was having regular night raids and there was no question of Daphne joining Milne there. If they were to write the long-delayed play for Irene Vanbrugh together (he dictating, she writing it down), there was some urgency.

Milne always boasted afterwards of the speed with which *Belinda* was finally written. The account varied. At the time, he told Ken it was written in seven days. When he wrote his autobiography, more than twenty years later, he was thinking he had started on a Thursday at 5.30, after work, and had finished the following Tuesday evening. The important thing was that by 12 October he was able to write to Ken from Dover:

I've just had a play accepted by Boucicault. Not the one I consulted you about, which still lacks an intelligent manager [*The Lucky One*], but another, very light and ridiculous, written hopefully for Irene Vanbrugh, and now apparently to be played by her . . . Tell Maud to get a dress ready for the first night.

The jolly old regiment has moved to Dover; I hope to move to London, but it hasn't come through yet. Daff tells me that there is a letter for me from the W. O. now on the way from Brooklands to Dover. It started three days ago, so it looks as if the Germans were holding it back. The Hidden Hand again.

                        Much love to you all,
                            Ever,
                            Alan (England's premier playwright)
P.S. Dover is a beastly place.

By November 1917 Milne was writing to Curtis Brown, now his agent, from 25 Sheffield Terrace in Kensington. They had not been able to get their sub-tenants out of the Chelsea flat. Milne's job at the War Office in London had come through and he would be there most of the time until he was demobbed fifteen months later. The suitable 'sedentary work' was writing '(horrible word) propaganda'. Milne wore the green tabs of Intelligence. He had a room to himself and wrote pretty much what he liked. 'If it were not "patriotic" enough, or neglected to point the moral with sufficient hardihood, then the Major supplied the operative words in green pencil.' In September 1918 – when the tide of war had at long last turned – Milne would pay a mysterious two-week visit to France. But, apart from that, he seems to have been in London, working a regular day in his office and writing regularly most evenings at home. It was a habit he had got into.

Arrangements for the production of *Belinda* were causing Milne the sort of worries he would, like all playwrights, experience again and again. Nothing was yet signed. Irene Vanbrugh loved the part. Dion Boucicault wanted to put it on. But his management was committed to a Pinero play and that had priority for the available theatre. Milne wrote to Curtis Brown: 'It is disappointing that *Belinda* should be postponed in this way, but I am very keen that Miss Vanbrugh should play the part, and if we get a definite agreement for production, I think it is worth waiting. But he *must* see you at once, and fix it up.'

Belinda eventually opened at the New Theatre in London on 8 April 1918, with Irene Vanbrugh, indeed, in the title part. John Gielgud saw the production as a boy of fourteen and always remembered the opening scene, where Irene Vanbrugh spent an entire five minutes deciding how to swing herself into a hammock without showing too much leg. 'I can see her now, amid the property hollyhocks and cut-out tree wings.' His cousin Dennis Neilson-Terry was the languid poet in an impeccable grey flannel suit. 'How I longed to possess one like it.'

It was Milne's first real first night – the year before he had shared it with Barrie. He felt he had been waiting for it for a very long time. He watched Irene Vanbrugh with the same unalloyed pleasure as the critics. Miss Vanbrugh, the *Observer* said, 'is the only living actress who could be trusted to handle this delicate stuff aright.' In New York, at the Empire Theatre, Ethel Barrymore tried, a month later – but the play closed after only another month. (There would be a 'radiant and charming revival' in 1922.) One of those in the audience in London was apparently Bernard Shaw. For when Milne met him for the first time in 1923,

Shaw held out his hand and said eagerly, as if he had been brooding about it for five years and was glad to get it off his mind: 'You know, your Belinda was a minx, that's what she was, she was a minx!' Naturally I was surprised that he had seen a play of mine, sorry that it had not been a later and a better one, flattered that he remembered it and identified me as the author, and not at all hurt by his estimate of its heroine. In acknowledgement I said something less than all this (as it might have been 'Oh?').

About three years later I met Shaw again. This time I was the least important guest at a Men Only dinner party given for him by Sir Henry Norman. On my arrival I was presented to him; and he said eagerly, as if he had been brooding about it now for eight years, and was determined to get it off his mind:

'You know your Belinda was a minx, that's what she was, she was a minx!'

... I am not sure that 'minx' is the exact word for her, but if it conveys the sense of an incorrigible, middle-aged 'flirt' (as she would have been named in those days) with all the charm of Irene Vanbrugh ... then it will do. In any case, it doesn't matter what you call her. She was the heroine of a purely artificial comedy whose only purpose was to amuse, and she herself no closer to reality than any character in, say, *The Importance of Being Earnest*. In short, she didn't exist. A minx, was she? Well, what I wanted to say to Shaw ... was 'And how about Candida?' For that did matter. Candida does exist.

There are, one realizes reading this, some interesting parallels between *The Lucky One* and *Candida* – but it is the reference to *The Importance of Being Earnest* that is more important. It was the play, Milne said, that he would most like to have written. His admired Irene Vanbrugh had played Gwendolen in the first production in 1895. W. A. Darlington once said, looking at Milne's later plays: 'In this matter of dialogue, he is eminent enough to be chosen as the champion of the "natural" writers against Oscar Wilde, or whom you will; and he and Wilde have only one quality in common – brilliance.' But certainly, with *Belinda*, naturalness was the last thing Milne was aiming at and he must have been delighted when one review ended perhaps somewhat ambiguously: 'It all reminded us a little of *The Importance of Being Earnest* at its best.' The *Pall Mall Gazette* thought that 'nothing could be wished for apter to the time's need'. It was pure escapism, at a most desperate time.

On the very day in April 1918 that *The Times* carried the headlines 'A Frivolous Play. *Belinda* at the New Theatre', the leading article said: 'Beyond all doubt, this is the sternest and most critical hour of the War.' It was a year since the first night of *Wurzel-Flummery*, a year since Vimy Ridge had been taken and 'Today,' wrote *The Times*, 'most of the strong places won in that first day of success a year ago are again in the possession of the enemy.' The Germans had renewed their offensive in the hope of achieving victory before the arrival of the Americans. In three weeks the Allies lost 400,000 more men. *Belinda* survived London's worst air raid and was taken off after nine weeks. 'It was difficult,' Milne said, 'to regard its ill-fortune as a matter of much importance.'

Milne wrote to Philip Agnew, one of the proprietors of *Punch*: 'I am glad you like *Belinda*. I think our chief pleasure in it has been meeting Irene Vanbrugh, who is as delightful off the stage as on it.'

There are several letters that testify to this developing friendship; in her autobiography Irene Vanbrugh writes of Milne like this:

> He was a fair-haired, gentle, rather shy personality, with a certain detachment of outlook . . . So apparently inconsequent was his dialogue that a little friend of mine said to his mother, 'Does Rene never learn her words or just say what comes into her head?'

Barrie, who was Milne's first sponsor, delighted in this play, but felt that Belinda was a creation who was worthy of a more important setting. I personally felt the airy cobwebs held this butterfly quite firmly enough.

Twenty years later, at her jubilee matinée, celebrating her fifty years on the stage, in the presence of the Queen, one of the items Irene Vanbrugh chose to appear in again was the first act of A. A. Milne's *Belinda*.

Milne's letter to Philip Agnew on 24 June was in answer to one from him, saying that *Punch* had decided to discontinue the allowance (half his assistant editor's salary), which it had been paying to Milne to supplement his Army pay. Milne's reply gives a good idea of his financial situation at the time.

> I cannot complain of your letter, but in justice to myself I think I must disillusion you as to the fortunes made by unsuccessful playwrights.
>
> 'Wurzel-Flummery' and 'Belinda' have finished their run, here and in America; so far as I know, I have nothing more to get out of them. My total receipts from these two plays, averaged over the years you have been making me this allowance, do not even bring that allowance up to my old salary as assistant-editor. My total receipts from *all* sources since I have been in the army (including, of course, your allowance) average out at a good deal less than two-thirds of my income before the war.
>
> I only tell you the truth about my 'affluence' for my own satisfaction, because I should like you to know that it was always my intention, if any play of mine were in the smallest degree a financial success, to suggest that my allowance should be discontinued. Unfortunately the facts did not give me an opportunity of forestalling your suggestion as I had hoped. At the same time I quite appreciate the firm's point of view, and accept its decision in perfectly good part. So let us say no more about it.

In fact, *Belinda* had brought Milne £311 from its English and American productions (that is, about £12,000 or $20,000 in 1990 terms). It was an excellent addition to his income, but hardly enough to make him feel confident about giving up *Punch* altogether when the war finally came to an end. He was taking it for granted that he would return to Bouverie Street, as soon as he was free of the War

Office – at least for a while. And Daphne still imagined him stepping eventually into Sir Owen's shoes.

Milne was working on another full-length play and had already sent the first act of *The Great Broxopp* to Curtis Brown in July 1918, asking for his encouragement. 'Between ourselves, I think a lot of this play. But I am quite happy thinking about it, and I want encouragement to write it.' Curtis Brown did what was required ('You have made me quite keen,' Milne wrote). When it was nearly finished, Milne told Curtis Brown to 'give a hint to the managers to start lining up for the production rights', but the play was not put on until 1921 in New York and 1923 in London. Milne was addicted to writing plays now, but already well aware of the horrors of being a playwright. 'Writing plays is delightful,' he would say, 'Your pleasure in it ends at the moment you write the word CURTAIN.' 'There is no certainty of anything save disillusionment.'

At least he now had enough plays to publish – a far simpler process than getting them put on in the theatre. In September Milne wrote to Frank Swinnerton at Chatto and Windus saying, 'I'm going to bring out a book called *First Plays*, as soon as I have time to put them together. If C. & W. are terrified of missing it, you'd better take your place in the publishers' queue at once.' The book was published by Chatto almost exactly a year later. Swinnerton was already a friend; he now became one of Milne's editors as well.

In 1918 Milne was still contributing intermittently to *Punch*. One of his contributions was a poem called 'The Last Pot', a threnody for marmalade:

> Much have I sacrificed: my happy home,
> My faith in experts' figures, half my money,
> The fortnight that I meant to spend in Rome,
> My weekly effort to be fairly funny;
> But these are trifles, light as air when weighed
> Against this other – Breakfast Marmalade.

The poem brought him marmalade from Scotland, just as Lehmann's piece on John's stamp-collecting had brought the boy stamps from all over the world. Milne's thank-you letter to Mrs Calder is typical of the trouble he would often go to, in these pre-Pooh days, to write warm letters to complete strangers:

To tell the truth, although I pretended to be celebrating the last pot, I hadn't even that much to sing about really. I had had no Marmalade for months and months. It was my swan-song as I was about to expire. Well, you have saved me. I have many happy weeks in front of me, for my wife *doesn't like marmalade*. How little one bothered about that sort of thing in the old happy days when one got engaged. She doesn't like marmalade. Of course she would pretend she didn't anyhow, but she really doesn't. And as she can't help looking as though it were her fault that I can't have just what I like for breakfast, she is as glad about Mrs Calder's marmalade as I am, and we both send you our very grateful thanks. As we raise the toast to our lips tomorrow – my piece well marmaladed, hers merely jammed – we shall say 'Mrs Calder!' and our thoughts will travel to the north.

As the war finally, amazingly, came to an end in November 1918, Milne was still at the War Office and working in his spare time on a new project. Nigel Playfair, with whom Milne had become friendly the year before, was looking for a theatre to take over as manager. (Arnold Bennett had organized a syndicate to back him.) He found the Lyric, Hammersmith, neglected, abandoned, in a backstreet full of rubbish – and brought it back to life, with a series which would include John Drinkwater's *Abraham Lincoln* and an enormously long-running production of *The Beggar's Opera*. Playfair wrote:

Among my earlier visitors at the theatre, called to admire its possibilities, which faithfully, if silently he did, was my friend, A. A. Milne, then himself almost very young . . . He had his name yet to make as a playwright, though I had lately been acting in what I still think was the most delightful of all his works, *Wurzel-Flummery* . . . I suggested that he should write for us a sort of Christmas entertainment, and the project had no terrors for either of us, though it was to be composed, cast, rehearsed and produced within a period of about four weeks

– if it was to open, as it did, on Christmas Eve. There was a feeling of relief and celebration in the air. It was the first peacetime Christmas for five years.

Playfair himself wrote the Prologue to Milne's *Make-Believe*, which consisted of three loosely connected short plays. Playfair discovered at the Margaret Morris Dancing School in Flood Street, Chelsea, two young sisters called Angela and Hermione Baddeley to play Scissors and Paste and open the evening. They were also 'battle-scarred pirates' in the Desert Island scene, which formed the most popular act. Hermione, who was then twelve, remembered how Angela happily covered her face with realistic wounds and scars, but that she herself could not bear to make herself ugly. They were a great success and were encored night after night.

A. A. Milne's own comment, looking objectively at his play when he prepared it for publication in *First Plays* (with a new Prologue of his own), was that, 'The difficulty in the way of writing a children's play is that Barrie was born too soon . . . We who came later have no chance.' *Peter Pan* is certainly a hard five acts to follow, and Milne makes comparisons more likely by not denying himself pirates and a desert island, 'the island we have dreamed of all our lives'. Milne came out of it rather well at the time. 'Children will celebrate this play as the first theatrical event of any real importance since Captain Hook came to add to the sweeter terrors of existence,' one review said. It is 'that rarest of all dramatic treasures, a really original and diverting play for children'. Only Herbert Farjeon saw that it was really a play for grown-ups, not for children, because it makes fun of the things that children take seriously and it takes seriously (if very amusingly) the particular Christmas longing of the childless for children. 'It is alive with fun, fancy and invention,' someone said of *Make-Believe* in 1918. But it has not stood the test of time.

As early as 24 November, E. V. Lucas had written to Charles Turley Smith about Milne's position at *Punch*: 'So far as I can gather there is a little bother about Milne and he may not return. I hope he will.' Milne should perhaps have been warned that all was not well by Philip Agnew's letter in June, withdrawing his half-salary. But it seems he went along to see Owen Seaman early in January 1919 (with six weeks' leave from the War Office, prior to demobilization) and asked for a letter to show the Army authorities; he had been told release would be quicker if he could produce something showing how much he was needed.

The fact was that he wasn't needed. Seaman was embarrassed. It seemed that Algernon Locker, his elderly substitute ('a kindly amiable old boy, who enjoyed producing a stream of little puns over his tea') was excellent in the office, and *Punch* was not very pleased that Milne had spent so much of his spare time writing plays rather than *Punch* articles.

Of course, Sir Owen said, Milne's place was still open to him, if he wanted it. There was much talk everywhere of 'justice for our fighting men'. *Punch* would not want there to be any suggestion that they had not been fair. 'Your place, of course is waiting for you; there is no question about that.' Milne would use that statement and much else from his own experience in a bitter short story called 'The Return', which appeared in the *Fortnightly Review* in 1922. And he would say much later that, though the Government had boasted that it would make a new England 'fit for heroes to live in', the only difference was in the number of its unsold vacuum cleaners.

Writing about his reception at *Punch* in his autobiography in 1939, Milne suggests that the worst thing about it was telling Daphne – but there is no doubt at all that he was very hurt that he was not encouraged to return to the salaried comfortable routines of before the war and choose his own moment, later, to become a freelance again.

Seaman said to Milne that it seemed a pity he should waste his time on the mechanical work of sub-editing when he could write such brilliant plays. 'Of course (I said) I should like to devote myself exclusively to playwriting but after *Punch*'s generosity to me', more than three years on half-salary, 'I could not possibly put the paper to any inconvenience.' Very politely Sir Owen made it clear. They were not expecting him back – not as assistant editor, that was. Of course they hoped Milne would still write an article each week and continue as a member of the Table. Milne said something to the effect that Daphne (after all she could well come into the conversation; she *was* Sir Owen's god-daughter) had always hoped that one day ... 'This took him off his guard, and it was not until the third attempt that he found words which made it seem rather a compliment that, whatever happened, I should never be Editor.' The fact was that to Seaman Milne was, as he had always been, 'an unpatriotic Radical'.

That was really the end of A.A.M. of *Punch*, though he would continue to contribute occasionally – most notably in 1924 when most of the poems in *When We Were Very Young* would appear in *Punch*, before they came out in book form. And again in 1939 and 1940, when he published a long series of poems relating to the war which eventually became the book *Behind the Lines*. Milne said goodbye with mixed feelings, 'grateful for all the fun I had had there, sorry to be done with it, glad to be off on the track of something else, regretting, not regretting, hopeful, fearful – in fact, much as I had already felt when fifteen years earlier I left Cambridge and came to London.' Then he had been on his own. Now he was married. He had to tell Daphne.

She was dressing when he got home from the *Punch* office. They were going out to dinner. They were in the taxi when he told her. She burst into tears and was still crying when he paid off the taxi. 'We walked round the dark and silent square, beneath a rain-laden sky which threatened to fall at any moment, while she tried to get control of herself. I promised her that we shouldn't starve. I promised to make a success of the theatre. It was a little like telling a woman whose loved cottage has been burnt down that you will build a more expensive one in the ruins. It doesn't really comfort her at the time.' He wrote to H. G. Wells: 'I have retired from *Punch* . . . It is rather like ceasing to be a member of the Church of England.'

He was also, that very month, ceasing to be a member of His Majesty's armed forces. He wrote to Frank Swinnerton from a hotel in Tunbridge Wells on 5 February 1919; 'It's snowing hard, the Mess is crowded with officers whom I've never seen before, and I've taken refuge here for dinner. Curse the Army; I've already spent ten weeks in London trying to get out of it, and now here I am.' He was finally released on St Valentine's Day and travelled joyfully home to Embankment Gardens, Chelsea.

Six days later he wrote his formal letter of resignation to Philip Agnew, both from his job and from the Table – the Table because 'apart from the fact that man cannot live on one contribution to *Punch* a week, I have other interests now'. He wrote 'in the friendliest spirit, and without any sort of resentment against the paper which had done so much for me'.

It was not too difficult for Milne to feel friendly, though some hurt would remain. He was almost sure, as he put Agnew's letter in its envelope, that he was already working on the play that would make his fortune.

15, EMBANKMENT GARDENS,

CHELSEA, S.W. 3

20·2·19

TEL. 5636 KENSINGTON.

My dear Phil,

I have been waiting until my demobilization (which took place last week) to write to you about my future relations with Punch, although meanwhile I have had several informal conversations with Owen. I have learnt from him his own feelings on the subject, and perhaps not inaccurately (though, of course, quite unofficially) your feelings. It only remains to tell you mine — with the assurance first that I write in the friendliest spirit, and without any sort of resentment against the paper which

— 9 —

Playwright

IN 1922, THE year A. A. Milne was forty and two years before the first of the famous children's books was published, a caption to his photograph in a London newspaper carried the words: 'Milne came to Fleet Street years ago in search of a fortune. As a dramatist, his income at times ranges from £200 to £500 a week.' This really was a fortune in 1922; it was more in a week than most people earned in a year. That joking boast, 'England's premier playwright', which Alan Milne had used when signing a letter to his brother Ken in 1917, was never exactly justified. But he was certainly one of England's most successful, prolific and best-known playwrights for a brief period, a fact that now seems almost incredible, when so many people who know his name and love his books have no idea that he ever wrote plays. There is a particular irony that the one play of Milne's that is still regularly performed is *Toad of Toad Hall*, his adaptation of another man's book: Kenneth Grahame's *The Wind in the Willows*.

The play that was Milne's first real success was *Mr Pim Passes By*. It had been in his mind during those last weeks in the Army. On the Tuesday night in February 1919 that he had broken the news to Daphne that he was not going back to *Punch*, they had met at that dinner party the actress Lillah McCarthy, whom they had frequently seen on the stage. There were only five people at the dinner table; the actress was sitting next to Milne. Three days later he had a letter from her, saying she was just starting in management, had taken the Kingsway Theatre, and that J. M. Barrie had suggested that A. A. Milne might have a suitable play for her. Would he come to tea the following Tuesday to discuss the possibility?

It was a Friday morning when the letter arrived. Milne sat down after breakfast to think of a play for Lillah McCarthy. By the Tuesday afternoon he had written the first act of a comedy. He went round to see her, full of hope. She was charming. He told her about the play; she asked him to send it to her. They talked; they had tea. Milne said goodbye. Lillah McCarthy murmured how delightful it had been to meet him.

Milne said, 'Well, of course, we did meet last Tuesday.'

She said, 'Oh – did we?' At that moment, seeing her puzzled, disbelieving look, Milne decided that he would never again expect his name or his face to mean anything to anybody. 'It saves a lot of anxiety.' So he said. But he was determined, in fact, to make sure that his name, at least, did mean something to a great many people. His son would confirm how much it mattered to A. A. Milne that people (even visiting journalists) should have read his books, should have some real sense of who he was. ('What did he do? I thought you knew,' Christopher Milne quoted, adding that, 'Those who knew were welcomed into his friendship.')

It was not a simple arrogance. He believed passionately in the value of the artist. In 1919 he wrote in a piece in the *Outlook*, that, during the war, writers such as himself 'asked ourselves gloomily what use we were to the State', as compared with miners, boot-makers, farmers and the like. But now he realized that in peacetime it is the artist who counts; the others are merely the Army Service Corps of civilization. A world without its artists would be 'as futile and meaningless a thing as an army composed entirely of the A.S.C.' We might not be able to live without them. They may try to suggest we are decorative, inessential. But 'they would have no reason for living at all, were it not for us.' They leave nothing behind; we do.

Even so, Milne was under no illusions that even the greatest writers mean much to the world at large. He told a funny story about Mr Thomas Hardy being presented to the Lord Mayor (a member of the Worshipful Company of Linendrapers, perhaps). The City Remembrancer (provided for just such an eventuality) sees the blank look on the Lord Mayor's face and mutters in his ear: '*Tess of the d'Urbervilles*.' The Lord Mayor declares how delighted he is to welcome the author of *Death and the Door-bells* to the City.

And there was a less apocryphal story about an experience of Daphne's, when unusually (for he hated making speeches) Milne had accepted an invitation to speak at a City dinner. The stranger next to Daphne Milne, having consulted her name card and the menu, said: 'I see your husband is talking to us tonight. Let me see, isn't he something to do with the Gas, Light and Coke Company?' Milne's comment on this was a mild: 'That, I think, did me an injustice.'

It was in 1919 that A. A. Milne joined the Garrick Club. He was proposed by E. V. Lucas, seconded by Alfred Sutro, and among the sixteen supporters who signed his application were Hugh Walpole, Somerset Maugham and Nigel Playfair. The club was to give him a great deal of pleasure (a refuge, another home, particularly in the thirties) – pleasure he would reward on his death with a share of the *Pooh* royalties. The Garrick was the appropriate club for a playwright, far more so than his old club, the National Liberal. The Garrick was full of actors. He lunched one day in his 'best blue suit' with the legendary Sir Squire Bancroft, who, half a century before, had, almost single-handed, revived the Victorian theatre and paved the way for Sir Henry Irving. The Garrick was full of writers too. It was there Milne first met Arnold Bennett. 'I liked Bennett. We seemed to get on all right,' Milne wrote to Swinnerton. 'When we couldn't think of anything else to talk about, we mentioned you.' Milne now had a wittier line in such conversations than in the days long before when he and William Archer had mentioned H. G. Wells.

Milne in 1919 was ambitious, and not just to make a lot of money. Towards the end of his life, he summed up his feelings like this:

Of all the foolish things which Dr Johnson said, the most foolish was: 'No man but a blockhead ever wrote, except for money.' What he should have said was that a writer, having written what pleased him, was a blockhead if he did not sell it in the best market. But a writer wants something more than money for his work: he wants permanence ... He yearns for the immortality, even if only in the British Museum, of stiff covers.

Milne made sure that most of his plays were published in an attractive uniform edition from Chatto and Windus, in a stylish brown cloth with a well-designed label on the spine. 'It is very jolly indeed,' he told Frank Swinnerton, when he saw the proofs of *First Plays*. Twenty of Milne's plays survive in this form, and not only in the British Museum. But the true immortality was to come, of course, from the children's books, a fact he would live to realize and regret.

Early in 1919, Lillah McCarthy read the first act of Milne's new play, *Mr Pim Passes By*, and an outline of how the play was to be finished. 'She sent back the script,' Irene Vanbrugh recalled, 'saying she did not care about it, as she felt the fact that Olivia's first husband had been a criminal would militate against any chance of sympathy for the heroine.' We can smile at the crassness of this sort of reaction, but it was an important factor in shaping Milne's career. It seemed to be the story of *The Lucky One* all over again. Milne's favourite of all his plays, at that point, had still not been produced. Was it really possible that the audience could object to *Mr Pim Passes By* because the heroine had *once* been married to someone who had been in prison for fraud? The real problem is the suggestion of bigamy – Mr Pim's twittering revelation that Olivia's husband is still alive. 'Bigamy. It is an ugly word, isn't it?' as Milne says. But the whole point about the new play was that nothing is as it seems in the first act. Milne had learnt a great deal since *The Lucky One*. He used the farcical complications of Mr Pim's interventions to explore the hypocrisy and intolerance of just such attitudes as Lillah McCarthy's. It was extremely clever. But was it going to find a management prepared to risk it? Milne was clearly identifying himself with Olivia, Brian and Dinah (on the side of socialism, progress, orange and black curtains) and opposing the values of George Marden, 'a typical, narrow-minded, honest county gentleman', the archetypal Tory; though of course, as he is married to Olivia and a happy ending is essential, George has a heart of gold under his conventional exterior.

As one critic would put it, for a short time *Mr Pim* looks like an Ibsen tragedy, 'with another Nora finding out her husband in the moment of crisis', but then, he thanked heaven, humour comes to the rescue. Bernard Shaw, Milne thought, was the only playwright at the time who was able to get away with anything really challenging, and even *Heartbreak House* was to have a very mixed reception in 1921. (When *Mr Pim* opened in Chicago in 1927 the *Tribune* would declare it 'a play that is, without endangering Shaw's general reputation, at least five hundred times better than *Heartbreak House*.') A London theatre which had cost only £25 a week to hire before the war, could now cost as much as £500. So few managements were prepared to take any risks. They were looking for glamorous shows, or at least for amusing plays, with satisfactorily happy endings. Most of the critics wanted Milne's plays to be as light as thistledown. Approving comparisons with that flimsy pappus occur with extraordinary frequency in reviews of his plays. Only very occasionally will a critic suggest he would do better if he tried harder for some underlying seriousness, if his jam contained more useful pills. The odd *critic* would suggest that, but neither managements nor audiences wanted A. A. Milne to be serious. If he had 'a secret feeling that he was really intended for a maker of pills', as W. A. Darlington put it, they wanted him to ignore it. 'His jam is a proprietary article, and the best of its own particular kind.'

Most people going to the theatre just after the war did not want *anyone* to be serious. Milne was particularly aware, in the early months of 1919, how audiences were reacting. Finding himself in need of a little regular income after his rejection by *Punch*, he had taken on, as well as another weekly column in the *Sphere*, the job of dramatic critic for the *Outlook* at six guineas a week. There was a lot to be said for 'having your idea given to you, instead of having to search for it'. The proprietor of the *Outlook*, Lord Lee, invited the Milnes to Chequers, which he had not yet given to the nation for the use of its prime ministers. Milne thought Lee a good fellow, though he had not apparently read any of Milne's books – nor had he read *The Wind in the Willows*, always a test of character, as far as Milne was concerned.

Milne was a dramatic critic for just six weeks when he began to realize that his position was impossible. It had been different in the days when he had reviewed plays for *Punch*; then he had not been a playwright. 'If I do it honestly, I make it awkward for myself – and, on the other hand, the Mutual Admiration Society is a thing I loathe,' he wrote to Frank Swinnerton on 4 April 1919, knowing he had already condemned himself for ever in Marie Lohr's eyes by a review of her performance in a play called *Victory*. 'One could not damn a manager's play and then send him a play of one's own; still less could one praise it and then send him a play of one's own; least of all could one tell other dramatists how to write plays when one's own imperfect plays were available for comparison.'

In a few years' time, when Milne found himself conducting a sort of running battle with St John Ervine, the playwright who was dramatic critic of the *Observer*, his own experience stood Milne in good stead – remembering how the red-letter nights were the nights when plays were bad and one could spend a mere hour 'standing on the body of the dramatist', delivering a funeral oration. A good play, on the other hand, might take six hours. 'They do work under extraordinary difficulties,' Milne conceded, recalling a Charles Frohman repertory season, most of which he had watched from a seat behind a pillar.

It was St John Ervine, looking at *The Theatre in My Time* in 1933, who saw the contrast between the demanding theatre before the war and what was happening in those years when Milne was making a name for himself. Ervine looked, for instance, at a 1910 season at the Duke of York's, which included Galsworthy's *Justice*, Shaw's *Misalliance, The Madras House* by Granville Barker and Pinero's *Trelawney of the Wells*, together with a couple of one-act plays by J. M. Barrie and another by George Meredith. Just after the war, Ervine said, it was escapism audiences were after. The theatre was still the most important source of entertainment. 'Moving pictures and wireless sets' had not yet come into their own. There was a passion for distraction.

A million men had been killed in the war and these were, for the most part, the flower of the nation. Millions of people, half educated and nervously agitated, were growing up without discipline or training, to take the place of the dead . . . Jazz bands took the place of musicians, cocktails took the place of decent drinks, and an extraordinary mania for shuffling movement possessed the young, who waddled like demented ducks . . . Haste and noise became the essentials of entertainment.

Cooks began to give place to tin-openers, and orchestras were replaced by canned music. The young leapt into powerful cars and drove at full speed from A to B and back again from B to A, knowing little of A, less of B and nothing at all of the road between.

St John Ervine was not an old man looking at the 1920s with the jaundiced eye of old age. He was a year younger than Milne, in his forties in that decade which *Mr Pim Passes By* would open at the New Theatre in London on 5 January 1920. It was a hard audience to woo. The great successes of the 1920s were *Chu Chin Chow* and *Hassan*, glamorous and specifically exotic musical shows, which fulfilled to perfection people's need for a good night out. In the straight theatre, the playwright's best hope was to make people laugh. He also had to remember all sorts of practical things. Theatres were less well disciplined places than they usually are today. 'If yours is an 8.15 play, you may be sure that the stalls will not fill up till 8.30 and you should therefore let loose the lesser-paid members of the cast in the opening scene.' You should be careful not to waste your jokes 'on the first five pages of dialogue'. There would be a crackle of stiff white shirtfronts, a jingle of beaded evening bags, a shuffle of programmes, as the audience settled themselves into their seats. And at the end of the evening the playwright had to remember that many people, living for instance in Chislehurst, would be catching last trains and missing the final five minutes of every play they ever saw, together, of course, with countless renderings of the National Anthem.

In April 1919, Lillah McCarthy and her manager, A. E. Drinkwater (John Drinkwater's father) had still not finally decided about *Mr Pim*. Milne was trying to get Curtis Brown to encourage them to make up their minds. 'I want her to do it,' Milne wrote. 'She has a nice small theatre, which suits me, and particularly *Pim*.' Even when a management agreed to take a play and had a theatre available for it, there were always problems with the casting. Milne once wanted Gladys Cooper, for instance, but she had 'a charming habit of withdrawing into a nursing home' at the crucial moment.

It was cheering that Godfrey Tearle was appearing in a revival of *The Boy Comes Home* at the Coliseum, but *The Great Broxopp*, as well as *Mr Pim*, was looking for a home and a cast in the spring of 1919. 'I don't see Hawtrey playing a flamboyant, slightly vulgar character. He is so very much the reverse. I am trying to get hold of Ainley; and also reminding Du Maurier of our proposed lunch together to discuss it,' Milne wrote to Curtis Brown. He gave one of his characters in *Broxopp* a different father, in response to an objection from Du Maurier. But still no one seemed to want it. 'My own feeling is that it is really good (if I may say so) and that we simply must get someone to take it . . . I leave it to you to make brilliant suggestions.'

There was a more personal problem. The Milnes were becoming worried at Daphne's failure to conceive. They both wanted children. They had now been married for nearly six years; the war had not kept them apart for any great periods of time. There were consultations with a gynaecologist. In May 1919, Daphne went into a nursing home. 'I fly there in all my spare minutes,' Milne wrote to Swinnerton, adding that he was trying to write a novel called *Nocturne*, but kept putting it aside. The operation Daphne underwent was 'officially' for the removal of her appendix, but it seems likely that something else was done at the same time; perhaps the fallopian tubes were insufflated. Whatever happened, in April 1920 J. M. Barrie would be able to congratulate Milne: 'By far the choicest lines (the best you have ever written) are about your wife and I rejoice with exceeding joy over that news.' Daphne was expecting a child in August.

The nursery was ready. They had moved into 'the prettiest little house in London,' Milne wrote to Frank Swinnerton in August 1919, describing 11 Mallord Street, Chelsea, SW3. It is a short quiet street just a few minutes' walk from the King's Road.

The house is narrow, in a terrace, and had been built not long before the war. It has three storeys and a basement and is much bigger than it looks from outside, having been designed rather cleverly round a well for light. The house was much described in the late 1920s, when hordes of journalists traipsed through it on their way to Christopher Robin's nursery. In 1919 it was decorated very differently, in the 'futurist' style Olivia hankered after in *Mr Pim Passes By* – those black and orange curtains, symbol of everything George Marden feared. 'Originally Mallord Street had been done in colours influenced by the Russian Ballet, black carpets, bright cushions, very impractical as the carpets showed every bit of cigarette ash,' a friend of Daphne's remembered her saying. 'She told me that the thing to be at that time was – different.' The house had to be 'an artistic whole, a showplace'. Milne's nieces remembered that a set of six dining chairs he had had before they married had been firmly banished by Daphne and gratefully received by Ken and Maud.

Some of Milne's own exuberant pleasure in his new house comes across in a piece he published in the *Sphere* on 9 August 1919, very soon after they moved in. It was the first time, he said, that he had had the chance to go upstairs to bed and come downstairs to breakfast for nineteen years – in other words since he had left Streete Court for Cambridge.

Of course I have done these things in other people's houses from time to time, but what we do in other people's houses does not count . . . Now, however, for the first time in nineteen years, I am actually living in a house. I have (imagine my excitement) a staircase of my own.

Flats may be convenient (I thought so myself when I lived in one some days ago), but they have their disadvantages. One of the disadvantages is that you are never in complete possession of the flat. You may think that the drawing-room floor (to take a case) is your very own, but it isn't; you share it with a man below who uses it as a ceiling. If you want to dance a step-dance, you have to consider his plaster. I was always ready enough to accommodate myself in this matter to his prejudices, but I could not put up with his old-fashioned ideas about bathroom ceilings. It is very cramping to one's style in the bath to reflect that the slightest splash may call attention to itself on the ceiling of the gentleman below. This is to share a bathroom with a stranger – an intolerable position for a proud man. To-day I have a bathroom of my own for the first time in my life.

I can see already that living in a house is going to be extraordinarily healthy both for mind and body. At present I go upstairs to my bedroom (and downstairs again) about once in every half-hour; not simply from pride of ownership, to make sure that the bedroom is still there, and that the staircase is continuing to perform its functions, but in order to fetch something, a letter or a key, which as likely as not I have forgotten about again as soon as I have climbed to the top of the house. No such exercise as this was possible in a flat, and even after two or three days I feel the better for it . . .

But the best of a house is that it has an outside personality as well as an inside one. Nobody, not even himself, could admire a man's flat from the street; nobody could look up and say, 'What very delightful people must live behind those third-floor windows.' Here it is different. Any of you may find himself some day in our quiet street, and stop a moment to look at our house; at the blue door with its jolly knocker, at the little trees in their blue tubs standing within a ring of blue posts linked by chains, at the bright-coloured curtains. We have the pleasure of feeling that we are contributing something to London. We are part of a street now, and can take pride in that street. Before, we were only part of a big unmanageable building.

That being 'part of a street' was not quite as community-minded a remark as it suggests, although Milne would become friends with some people who lived near by. Harold Fraser-Simson, the composer, had a house across the street and belonged to the Garrick Club. Denis Mackail and W. A. Darlington and their families lived only a few minutes' walk away. They would all see each other from time to time. Darlington described his first visit:

As I rang the bell of his house in Mallord Street I was attacked by a fit of shyness. I had admired his work so deeply and for so long that I had a sudden absurd feeling that I was a fag in the lower fourth who had been sent for by a member of the upper sixth. This vanished the moment I met him. Milne in the flesh was all I had hoped to find him, warm, friendly and amusing.

Milne had invited Darlington to call. Darlington's review of *Mr Pim Passes By* was written on the night of the confirmation of his appointment as drama critic of the *Daily Telegraph*, a job he was to hold for the rest of his career. The Milnes were not callers. 'We don't call very well,' Milne said, 'My fault, I suppose. I hate knowing people for geographical reasons.' Their neighbours felt the same. When the Milnes were burgled the people next door sent a note of sympathy. Even then they did not speak to each other. 'Suburban chumminess' never appealed to Milne. Already he felt it necessary to protect his privacy. But he was not always consistent. Milne once said to Swinnerton: 'Does any person think so consecutively and business-likely as novelists make them think?' Real people are never as consistent as the characters in fiction. Milne could be said, at some points, to have been someone who kept himself to himself. On other days, in other moods, he would welcome the warm curiosity, the genuine interest of a fellow human being.

The one generalization which always does seem to be true of Milne – unfashionable and indeed repugnant as some people find it – can best be left in Frank Swinnerton's own words, the words of someone who knew him really well. 'He loves goodness . . . He stands for virtue.' He had been brought up to believe that, without virtue, nothing is worth anything. This does not mean, of course, that he always himself did the right thing but rather that he had a strong moral sense. Swinnerton saw this as a problem for Milne professionally. 'He combined with a gift for persiflage the sternness of a Covenanter, which I think restricted the range of his dramatic performance. Any writer of imaginative work who cannot give the Devil his due . . . becomes moral-bound. He dare not let sinners have a flutter. This is as true of Milne as of Eliot.' 'Rectitude is fatal to humour,' Graham Greene would say, hitting Milne when he was already down, in the 1930s. The redeeming fact was that Milne's admiration was for real goodness, not for those Victorian virtues, or indeed 'the prevailing social codes', which so often pass as such. But it would, as we shall see, earn him some dislike. Those who stand for goodness risk being called prudish, priggish and proud. 'I felt uncomfortable in his company,' one of his publishers told me. 'Those who disagree with him complain of his rigidity in argument and severity in outlook,' Swinnerton said, adding, 'That is not my experience. I have always found him overflowing with good spirits.'

The Milnes apparently spent a good deal of time at Brooklands in Sarisbury Green, Daphne's father's house in Hampshire. Quite a number of Milne's surviving letters were written there during weekend visits. But there were tensions in the de Sélincourt family. They were 'not always on speaking terms with each other', as Christopher Milne would record. Someone said that if the de Sélincourts could have a feud they did; one of them had actually disappeared to Paris just because another one had used his shaving soap. Daphne, long afterwards, described her brother Aubrey conventionally as the black sheep of the family. He would no doubt have had other equally dismissive things to say about her. After Gallipoli and service with the RAF in France, he had, according to Daphne anyway, refused to finish his degree at Oxford and made an entirely unsuitable marriage to a woman older than he was, a writer called Irene Rutherford McLeod. Daphne, in particular, took violently against her.

His father put up the money for him to start a school but Aubrey, brilliant as he was as a teacher, seems to have had no head for business and he began to ask Alan for loans. 'The requests got larger and the repayments slower until the latter ceased but the former continued.' There is a glimpse of Alan's feelings on the subject in one of his novels: 'Cousins, brothers-in-law, aunts – God what a crowd. All trying to borrow money or asking him to use his influence.' The relationship between Daphne and Aubrey broke down completely. She would not speak to him again until the day their children married. But she and Alan continued to spend quite a lot of time in the luxury of her father's house – much more, it seems, than they spent with Alan's own parents.

It may, of course, only indicate that when he was with his own parents, Alan was not writing letters. But there is certainly a suggestion that the eldest son, Barry, the solicitor, on his motor bike, sometimes with Ken in the side-car, came more frequently than Alan – and that J. V. Milne and Maria knew their other daughters-in-law, Connie and Maud, far better than they ever knew Alan's wife, whom they still called Dorothy in letters, as she had been first introduced to them. Alan had dedicated his first book of plays 'To my mother', thinking it might be the last book of his she would see published. (It was his seventh book, not counting the American editions.) But Barry had always been closest to her, however much she tried to disguise the fact. As for Alan's own relations with Barry – 'Whoever heard . . . of two frogs assuming a friendliness which they did not feel, simply because they had been eggs in the same spawn. Ridiculous . . .' They were still in touch from time to time in the 1920s but there was little real friendliness; and soon there would be none.

J. V. Milne and his wife were living in the war years and just after in a house called St Andrews at Burgess Hill in Sussex. One of Ken's children remembered: 'To a child from suburbia, St Andrews was heaven.' It was 'a compact Victorian country house, brick, gabled, with a squat tower', standing in its own grounds. There was Pears' soap in the bathroom, a grandfather clock in the hall, stone lions and passion-flowers at the front door. Maria by now was ailing,

1 J. V. Milne with his three sons, Barry, Ken and, seated, A. A. Milne. This is the photo referred to on page 2, probably taken in 1886, the year of *Little Lord Fauntleroy*.

96 Boundary Road
Nov 20 th 1896

My dear Mama
We went to
Hamstid Heft.
yestoday. We had
a scramble. We
had piggy-backs
I want sme tools
like Mama

last of *oooooo o o ooo
oo oo o oooo oo o oooooo oooo*

* You loving

Alan

2 The letter written by Alan two months before his fifth birthday.

3 and 4   The young Alan Milne and his teacher, H. G. Wells. Wells came to Henley
House in January 1889, the month Alan was seven. At that time Wells was 'frail
and Stevensonian'. Mrs Milne was keen he should eat well at her table. The skeleton
was not at Henley House but T. H. Huxley's at the Science Schools in Kensington.

5   Alan as a Westminster schoolboy, with his father.

6 Alan Milne at Seatoller in Cumbria, June 1904, with a group who had been playing hare and hounds. They were mainly Trinity men, including Francis Cornford, Erasmus Darwin, Frank Sidgwick and W. W. Greg. Note the number of pipes.

7　A family group, 1908. Back row, left to right: Maria and J. V. Milne, Maud and Ken with Marjorie. Front row: Connie (Barry's wife) with John, Barry, Alan.

8　Downe House cricket match, 1913. Back row, left to right: George Ll. Davies, T. L. Gilmour, Will Meredith, G. Meredith, jun., Denis Mackail, Harry Graham, Dr Goffe. Middle row: A. A. Milne, Maurice Hewlett, J. M. Barrie, George Morrow, E. V. Lucas, Walter Frith. Front row: Percy Lucas, Audrey Lucas, T. Wrigley, Charles Tennyson, Willie Winter.

9   At Easton Glebe, 1921. Back row, left to right: Harold Laski, St John
Ervine, Daphne Milne, Charlie Chaplin, H. G. Wells, Mrs Laski. Middle row:
Gip Wells, Mrs Byng, Mrs Ervine. Front row: Hugh Cranmer Byng, Frank
Wells, A. A. Milne.

10   P. G. Wodehouse at the wheel of Ian Hay's car, 1928.

11   J. M. Barrie in his favourite fishing hat. He was on a fishing holiday in
Harris when he wrote to thank Milne for *The Holiday Round*.

12   A group at the gate: Mr. A. A. Milne, Mrs Milne, and Irene Vanbrugh.
'Mr A. A. Milne, the "A. A. M." of *Punch*, of which he was at one time
assistant editor, is the author of a number of good stories, as well as a very
successful playwright. His comedy *Mr Pim Passes By* is a delightful piece of
work with subtle touches of humour and occasional sarcasms directed at the
attitude and pose of "the county". It is a worthy medium for Miss Vanbrugh's
art, and Olivia Marden is one of her best roles. Mrs Milne was Miss Dorothy
de Sélincourt before her marriage.' *Sphere*, Summer 1920.

moving only slowly round the house, with a stick, a shawl and a lace cap. She taught her grandchildren a moral verse, as she must have taught her own children, thirty years before.

> For every evil under the sun
> There is a remedy or there is none.
> If there is one, try and find it;
> If there isn't one, never mind it.

'J. V. Milne was more sprightly, a small man (he got smaller with age) with a neat white beard and a panama hat. He wore pince-nez and showed his Scottishness by pronouncing "grass" with a short "a" . . . He would stroll round the garden (hands behind back) with us, telling us useful and funny things.' The garden was full of frogs and apples. The house often resounded to 'Trumpeter, what are you trumpeting now?' on the gramophone and to Harry Lauder singing 'I love a lassie'. Later in 1923, Alan gave his father 'and Barry and Ken, the wireless installation'. 'Tonight,' J. V. Milne would write, 'I am looking forward to hearing, here at home, *The Magic Flute* transmitted from Covent Garden Opera House,' adding with amazed satisfaction, 'There is a programme for every evening.'

The elderly Milnes' great source of pride and pleasure was, of course, A. A. Milne's rise to fame and fortune. Alan had given his father a subscription to the General Press Cutting Association Ltd, as early as 1910, and J. V. stuck the cuttings neatly into a stout black note-book. At the other end, he stuck cuttings (not from an agency) of occasional pieces by Ken, both light verse and funny prose, not easily differentiated from those of his famous younger brother. He had gone to the Ministry of Pensions in 1917, becoming Assistant Secretary three years later. The same year he was awarded the CBE and in the immediate post-war years there were official missions to South Africa, Canada and the United States. He was on the path to a knighthood.

Ken's family lived in Avondale Road in Croydon. Angela's best friend in her class at school was a girl called Peggy Ashcroft, who remembers being immensely impressed by the fame of her friend's uncle, and receiving his collection of essays, *Not That it Matters*, as a present in 1919, the December she was twelve. It was dedicated to 'K.J.M.', her friend's father, 'in memory of the nineties'. A. A. Milne became, she said, 'rather a hero'. She remembered meeting him too, 'slim, with pale hair' in the Croydon house. Going to see *Mr Pim*

Passes By with Ken's family was Peggy Ashcroft's first visit to a London theatre.

Mr Pim Passes By was eventually taken by Dion Boucicault; Olivia was a splendid part for Irene Vanbrugh. In spite of his great admiration for Miss Vanbrugh, Milne had been rather reluctant to let Boucicault have it, after his experiences with *Belinda*. ('I don't like his business methods – bad advertising, no trouble taken about sending it on tour and so on.') *Mr Pim* was a cheap play to produce – 'only one scene, six characters and no change of dress' – but Boucicault was cautious. He *had* said he would not put on another play in London until theatre rents went down. He took *Mr Pim* (for 5 per cent and no advance to the writer), in the first place only for a fortnight at Manchester, but with an option for a further six months. It opened at the Gaiety on 1 December 1919 and its popularity was immediately such that Boucicault engaged the New Theatre for a London opening on 5 January 1920. Milne sat in, as he always did when he had the chance, on some of the rehearsals. The writer's position in the theatre is not an easy one: 'Obviously nobody wanted him. Equally obviously, if he didn't interfere, nobody minded him.' This is Milne's own account of the first night:

I have attended many first nights in the miserable role of author, but never one like that. The house was so delighted to see its loved and lovely Irene back again that in sheer happiness it extended its favour to the play. Calls went on continuously, there were continuous cries for 'Speech!' – the author was pushed on and pushed off; and still Dot and Irene were bowing. As I sat in the wings among the stage-hands wondering if it were true, a very weary voice behind me said: ''Ere go on and give 'em a speech, guv'nor, and let's all get 'ome.'

Leslie Howard, later to be so much loved as a film star, played Brian, the young socialist painter. Dion Boucicault himself, known as Dot, played Mr Pim. During rehearsals he had not been on the stage at all. His understudy spoke the words while he directed from the front. 'It was with amazement on the first night,' Irene Vanbrugh said, 'we saw him stroll on the stage . . . a very clear example of what can be done with a short part, because actually he was not on the stage more than about twenty minutes throughout the play. Yet his personality permeated the whole of the evening.' The former Prime Minister, Herbert Asquith, coming backstage, said to Irene Vanbrugh, 'I trust you will forgive me, Mrs Boucicault, but, charming as you are, it is to Mr Boucicault the success of the play belongs.'

Alan Milne, giving the manuscript (partly in his hand, partly in Daphne's) to Irene Vanbrugh for Christmas 1922, wrote in it: 'Here are the bones to which she gave life.' He would stress his debt to her and her husband by dedicating to them his novel *Mr Pim*.

But, of course, a great deal of the success was thanks to Milne, and most of the critics gave him plenty of credit. The *Daily Express* recorded the cheering and the applause and said 'Mr Milne, the author, toyed with the puppets delightfully . . . The fun may have been as thin as gossamer, but the texture was woven with an inimitable touch.' The *Pall Mall Gazette* called it an 'altogether delicious light comedy' and, after comparing it favourably with *The Importance of Being Earnest*, went on:

Its action is almost defiantly slender, and it breaks the most rigid dramaturgical law by allowing the chief practical mystery to be completely solved at the end of the second act. But since Mr Milne charms us just as much after as before that event, one can only give him the credit for being amongst the high order of dramatic magicians who are above these rule-of-thumb maxims. Indeed it proves how charming the play is that can beguile us with wit and sympathy when even such gossamer plot as there was had been whisked away like a conjuror's handkerchief.

Complimentary adjectives littered the reviews: delicate, delightful, subtle, humorous, tender, intelligent, clever. It was 'a pleasant trifle, playing round the verge of deeper feelings without tumbling into them'. Mr Pim, himself, intrigued everyone and was variously described as Wordsworthian and Dickensian. The *Morning Post*, however, was offended enough, perhaps by 'the occasional sarcasms directed at the attitude and pose of "the county" ' to chide Milne for his treatment of the serious subject of 'Whether a woman is married to the man she lives with.'

Few people, critics or audience, realized just how clever Milne had been. The *Chicago Tribune*, however, would see that 'under the somewhat fantastic and sparkling dialogue runs the threads of a perfectly sane and serious study of marriage'. It was a theme Milne would return to again and again. And *The Times Literary Supplement* would suggest, when *Mr Pim* was published in *Second Plays* the following year, that it was 'one of the best plays in our modern drama. "Slight" as it is supposed to be, you can hear, if you listen, tremendous implications – a whole philosophy of life and love.'

Desmond MacCarthy in the *New Statesman* wrote the most interesting review of all, a long one running to nearly a page and a half, in which he analysed, with typical Bloomsbury sharpness, both what is original and what is commonplace about the play, as Milne draws back from 'the region where ideas, problems and emotions lie'. 'Milne's originality lies in his having chosen an unusual and yet plausible instance of tiny causes producing great results.' Mr Pim is totally convincing, the sort of person who, when a host, might easily inform a Mr Broadwood that his piano was at the door or, when calling on his friend Bryant, ask sympathetically after Mrs May. MacCarthy could see that, much as he himself really despised this sort of theatre, the public would love it. 'I shall not be surprised if next year Mr Milne has three plays running in London and others revolving in the provinces.' Substitute New York for London, add one more for London itself, and this becomes an accurate prediction. Before long there would be productions of Milne plays all over the place in little theatres and community playhouses; in, for instance, the Albright College Chapel in Reading, Pennsylvania, in the Art Institute of Chicago, the Golders Green Hippodrome, the Baltimore Auditorium, the Little Theatre in the Woods and the Birmingham Rep. In the west of England, two boys who would grow up to be Charles Causley, the poet, and J. C. Trewin, the drama critic, would both remember *Mr Pim Passes By* as their first happy experience of the theatre.

It ran in London for 246 performances and opened in New York for another successful run on 28 February 1921. For the rest of Milne's life it would continue to make him money. J. M. Barrie wrote in July that he had just seen the play and delighted in it: 'The freshness and humour and quaintness are all your own and abundantly explain its success . . . You will have a fine time now (till you get tired of it).' He meant being famous. Milne had had a sort of fame for years, of course, as a *Punch* humorist. Now the morning post increased dramatically. He was much in demand. Photographers wrote wanting to photograph him. 'Very handsome, long-headed, keen-faced', as Swinnerton described him, he looks out from dozens of photographs taken in the 1920s. The North Finchley Literary and Debating Society was not alone in being anxious that he should take part in a discussion on the modern theatre. The editor of *Home: An Exclusive Journal for Women* wanted to see where he lived and meet his wife. The secretary of the Incorporated Society of Authors, Playwrights and Composers wanted him to join not just the society but the committee of management, with meetings on the first Monday in each month. (He accepted.) The vicars of several churches wanted signed copies of his latest books for sale in aid of their Restoration Funds. Women (particularly women) wrote for autographs, forgetting to enclose stamped addressed envelopes. Milne pleased the Society of Authors by selling his autograph in return for half-crown contributions to their Pension Fund. He irritated most of his other correspondents by getting Daphne to reply to their letters in her role as his secretary, 'Celia Brice'. It was a task that suited her pregnant state.

Milne himself was writing his novel based on the play. 'I know very little about the writing of novels – or the writing of plays for that matter – but I hope I am learning. And, anyway, it is much more fun trying to do things which you can't quite do than doing them when you can.' The novel, *Mr Pim*, included most of the dialogue from the play, but it was 'a real book', Milne said, 'and not just the dialogue with "he said" or "she said" tacked on.' The idea had not been Milne's own, but it worked extremely well. T. B. Swann, who has written the most substantial critical book on Milne that there is, calls *Mr Pim* 'his finest novel'. It probably is, though that may not be saying a great deal. If, in the theatre, the plot had seemed a little flimsy, reading the novel one sees just how clever it is. By the end, after Mr Pim has finally passed by, everything is the same as it was in the beginning, except that Olivia is not the Olivia of the morning, nor George the George. They have really changed and their marriage will be much stronger and more interesting for the changes.

Milne had already finished another novel, a detective story, *The Red House Mystery*, though it would not be published until 1922, after *Mr Pim*. In February 1920 he wrote to J. B. Pinker: 'Great people the Americans. One harmless native turned up here a few months ago to whom I happened to mention that I was writing a detective story, and since then the news has spread all over the world. The Emperor of China is already saving up for his copy. I hope I shan't disappoint him.' He said, modestly, much later: 'The result would have passed unnoticed in these days when so many good writers are writing so many good detective stories, but in those days there was not so much competition.' It was actually written just before the publication of Agatha Christie's first book *The Mysterious Affair at Styles* (a book which, thirty years later, he would call 'the model detective story') and published a year before Dorothy Sayers's first novel. In an introduction to a later edition of *The Red House Mystery* Milne comments on his agents' lack of enthusiasm for the new project. He was, after all, typecast as a humorist. But it was in Milne's nature, and demonstrated throughout his career, to refuse to be typecast. It was always more interesting to try something new. He once wrote to E. V. Lucas, 'And did you never hear, Mr Lucas C.H., of the Rotation of Crops?' Milne was always eager to move on to something different. 'It has been my good fortune as a writer that what I have wanted to write has for the most part proved to be saleable. It has been my misfortune as a businessman that, when it has proved to be extremely saleable, then I have not wanted to write it any more.' This would be true in turn of humorous essays, detective stories and children's books.

The Red House Mystery has been the most successful of all Milne's books, apart from the four children's books. The trouble with Milne's other novels was that they were neither what Thomas Hardy called 'comfortable, resigned and conforming' as were the most popular novels, nor, by any stretch of the word, literature. A detective story has other criteria and Milne's works brilliantly, within his own rules. He had a passion for the form and so did his father, to whom he dedicated *The Red House Mystery*:

TO

JOHN VINE MILNE

MY DEAR FATHER,

Like all really nice people, you have a weakness for detective stories, and feel that there are not enough of them. So, after all that you have done for me, the least that I can do for you is to write you one. Here it is: with more affection and gratitude than I can well put down here.

A.A.M.

The classic 'Golden Age' detective story (which had been more or less invented by E. C. Bentley, whose *Trent's Last Case* had been written just before the war) was reacting against the thrillers of Rider Haggard, Edgar Wallace, John Buchan – the imperial romancers – the tradition that returned with Ian Fleming, if it had ever really gone away. Thrillers rely on the hunt and the chase. The detective novel is an intellectual game. There seemed to be a great need for new games to play in that period between the wars. (It was the era that invented the crossword puzzle, the scavenger hunt and Monopoly, to name but a few). The body in the library was not yet a cliché. It was long before anyone asked, as Edmund Wilson would, 'Who cares who killed Roger Ackroyd?'

It was – and still is – a reader-writer game, in which the writer plays fair and makes it perfectly possible for the reader to compete with the book's own detective, typically a clever amateur. It is no good, Milne thought, having a detective who relies on microscopes or laboratory analysis. 'What thrill do we get when the blood spot on the missing man's handkerchief proves that he was recently bitten by a camel? Speaking for myself,' Milne wrote, 'none. The thing is much too easy for the author, so much too difficult for his readers.'

The Red House Mystery has had many admirers. Alexander Woolcott ('The man who came to dinner') once called it one of the best three mystery stories of all time. Julian Symons called it 'probably the most entertaining book of its kind written during the twenties; the charm remains potent'. When Raymond Chandler in *The Simple Art of Murder*, while admiring Milne's style, quibbled about the police procedure, he was really missing the point. Detective novels are 'no more to be judged by realistic standards than one would judge Watteau's shepherds and shepherdesses in terms of contemporary sheep-farming' – as Robert Graves once put it. Milne's book had an immediate success, and was eventually translated into many languages including Swedish, Serbo-Croat and Japanese. It was serialized in *Everybody's* between August and December 1921 as *The Red House Murder* and published as a book in London in April 1922 and in America the following July. On 2 July, eighteen-year-old Christopher Isherwood wrote from Repton School to his mother: 'Sykes and I . . . have both been very busy over the weekend, dramatising A. A. Milne's *The Red House Mystery* for the end of term House Supper.' Oddly enough, it was a task Milne never attempted himself.

Something else was taking up Milne's time in the spring of 1920 as the play *Mr Pim Passes By* outran expectations and had to move because of prior bookings, first from the New Theatre to the Garrick and then from the Garrick to the Playhouse. Everyone was becoming interested in the cinema and hoping to get on the bandwagon of the new entertainment industry. A. A. Milne was on the board of Minerva Films, the creation of Adrian Brunel, and spent a good deal of time trying to persuade his friends to take out shares in the new company. Barrie congratulated him on being a director, but told Milne, 'My interests are in a rival firm.' Swinnerton obligingly paid five shillings a share for a hundred shares. H. G. Wells was also 'very sporting' about it. On 25 May 1920 Milne wrote to him, 'We are just going away for three weeks, having left three films behind us.' In fact, at the trade show in October, four films were shown. They were silent two-reelers, written by Milne, directed by Brunel and with casts including both Leslie Howard and C. Aubrey Smith (later so often to be Hollywood's perfect Englishman). After the first four short comedies, which are preserved in the National Film Archive, the company did little more and apparently quietly collapsed. When *Mr Pim Passes By* was filmed the following year, another company was involved. There would be a number of other films, both silent ones and talkies, made from Milne plays, the last one *Michael and Mary* in 1932. Milne would not live to see what Walt Disney did to *Winnie-the-Pooh*, though in fact he might not have objected as much as some people assume. In 1938 he was to write to Kenneth Grahame's widow about *Toad of Toad Hall*: 'I expect you have heard that Disney is interested in it? It is just the thing for him, of course, and he would do it beautifully.'

Eighteen years before, it was early days in the history of the cinema, and Milne gives a vivid picture of how painful it could be and how he never suffered fools gladly:

God how slowly their minds moved! Other people's minds. At a cinema half a dozen sentences were put on the screen, and one had to wait for minutes before the crowd had assimilated them. Minutes! It seemed like hours sometimes. What were their brains doing all that time? They had to say things over and over again to themselves before any meaning emerged. How hellish to be born with a brain like that ! No – how heavenly! Never to have to wait for other people . . . Never to be waiting – waiting – waiting for fools to catch up.

Milne had a sort of arrogance which his family rarely saw. His niece, Angela, remembered Milne telling her 'that he had a superiority complex; not boasting, or confessing, simply stating a fact. I am sure it was true,' she said. 'All Milnes have been brought up to believe that never mind about money . . . it's BRAINS THAT COUNT.' It would be poor Pooh's lack of brain that would cause most of his problems and give Christopher Robin (and the listening child) that delightful feeling of superiority that Milne enjoyed so much of the time, even if, occasionally, it was accompanied by intolerance and impatience. Friends and acquaintances could find this very difficult, though he often managed to cloak it with a becoming self-mocking modesty. With his strong conviction of his own worth, there went a sad inability to accept criticism. W. A. Darlington put it like this:

Alan and I spent most of our time together on various golf-courses, where we had, or soon acquired, a number of mutual friends. It was from these that I learned the disconcerting fact that, devoted to Alan as they were, they all found him on occasion very difficult to deal with. The trouble was, I was told, that he simply could not take any form of adverse criticism. 'Say the wrong thing to him,' I was warned, 'and he freezes stone cold and won't speak to you for the rest of the day.'

It is not an uncommon trait in the creative artist to desire praise and shrink from censure, but Alan evidently had it to an abnormal degree. The violence of his reaction against even a hint of blame had in it something pathological, as if he were short of a skin.

Was it perhaps that he had never needed in that glowing cherished childhood to grow any form of protective coating? One remembers the blow of that first bad Westminster report for the boy who had spent his early years as the Headmaster's beloved Benjamin, the child so lapped in love and admiration that he thought he could do anything. Milne had, indeed, as many writers have, an intense need for praise. He once wrote about 'that sense of inspiration and power that only comes upon me after violent praise'. And, on another occasion, when asked by an interviewer whether Daphne, so often at this period still involved in taking his dictation, ever criticized what he had written at the end of the day, he said, 'No, she just praises . . . Praise is what an author really wants when he is actually writing.' It was, in fact, what he *always* wanted.

This lack of a thick skin could be quite well disguised in the 1920s when everything, or almost everything, was going his way, though Milne would still, from time to time, have cause to explode jokingly to Curtis Brown: 'I swore (once more) never to write another play, and enquired about the price of a ticket to South America.' W. A. Darlington was nervously awaiting the time when Milne 'would write a play that I couldn't praise'. Milne's extreme sensitivity to criticism would make for considerable problems when things began to go really wrong. But that time was still far ahead.

The Arrival of Billy Moon

IN THE SUMMER of 1920 Daphne Milne gave birth to their first and only son in the house in Chelsea. It was not an easy birth. Daphne told a friend long afterwards about it. 'It's difficult to believe,' the friend said to me, 'but until she was actually giving birth, she had no idea of the mechanics of it. It came as a thoroughly traumatizing shock and made her absolutely determined never to repeat the performance.' It is not so difficult to believe. In Milne's novel *Two People*, the wife says her mother had told her absolutely nothing before she was married – nothing about anything. Even Nancy Nicholson, Robert Graves's wife, that thoroughly modern young woman, had had no idea what was going to happen when she gave birth to her first child, the year before. 'It took her years to recover from it,' Graves wrote in *Goodbye to All That*.

It seems likely, from clues in his fiction, that Alan Milne was the traditional anguished husband, pacing up and down through the hours of labour, in a room not far away, pulling on his pipe. 'Because his son had been so long in coming, he had been more than usually frightened,' Milne wrote in a late short story. 'He looked at his son, and felt as other husbands have felt looking at their first-born, "All that for this; so small, so ugly; and yet what a burden to have borne." ' Another of his characters says, 'When my boy was born, we lived in two rooms. Mary was in one; I was in the other.' He *heard* the birth. 'It was not for me to say how many children we should have.' ' "I can't bear to think of your being frightened and ill and so terribly hurt," he cried out, in sudden shame of himself, of his sex, of all that women have suffered from men.' And in his own voice, A. A. Milne said clearly: 'To me, the miracle of Human Birth is more worthy of awe than the miracle of Virgin Birth . . . What a piece of work is a man!'

Christopher Robin Milne was born on 21 August 1920 and so

registered, but he was to be known immediately as Billy and later Moon – from his own pronunciation of Milne. On the 22nd, his father wrote to Frank Swinnerton:

A tremendous event has happened, unrecked of by the minor novelist. THERE IS A JUNIOR MILNE! This is a creation of my wife's (Daff – short for Daphne or, as some say, Daffodil) and before it the trumpery creations of the aforesaid minor novelists pale their ineffectual fires. (Shakespeare, or one of those people.) Locally this creation is known as Billy.

Sir, if you never grovelled before, grovel now in the presence of this miracle. When women can do these things, why do we go on writing, you and I? (You observe that I put us both on one level, but I am in a generous mood this evening.) Why do we continue to call ourselves lords of creation when we so obviously are not? Why – but I must not overtax your brain!

Salute Chatto for me, slap Windus on the back. Tell them to mark August 21st in letters of blood on their calendars. And believe me to be, Sir,

Your mental superior

A. A. Milne

who shines equally as Husband, Father, Citizen and Author.

He wrote rather more soberly a few days later to Biddie Warren, a friend of his parents, in reply to her congratulations: 'Daff and Billy (to be Christopher Robin but called Billy) are both extremely well. He weighed ten pounds or so the Nurse said, but I suspect that Nurses are rather like fishermen, and he has lots of curly brown hair, and not a bad little face for his age. We did rather want a Rosemary, but I expect we shall be just as happy with this gentleman.' J. M. Barrie wrote: 'All my heartiest congratulations to you both, or strictly speaking to the three of you. May Billy be an everlasting joy to you. From what you say I gather he is already a marvel, but I shall decide about this for myself when I see him, which I hope will be soon.'

There has grown up a definite idea, encouraged by Milne's own need to distance himself from his children's books, that A. A. Milne was not particularly interested in children or good with them. He wrote in his autobiography in 1939, at a time when he most wanted to remind his readers that he was a writer, not just a children's writer: 'I am not inordinately fond of or interested in children; their appeal to me is a physical appeal such as the young of other animals make. I have never felt in the least sentimental about them, or no more sentimental than one becomes for a moment over a puppy or a kitten. In as far as I understand their minds the understanding is based on the observation, casual enough and mostly unconscious, which I give to people generally: on memories of my own childhood:

and on the imagination which every writer must bring to the memory and observation.' He had both remembered and observed, he said, 'the uncharming part of a child's nature: the egotism and the heartlessness'.

The idea of the children's writer who does not like children is a paradox that seems to lodge in people's minds — minds that are nowadays often rather suspicious of Lewis Carroll's delight in little girls. Peter Green gave wide circulation to the idea that Milne was uneasy with children in his biography of Kenneth Grahame, though all the evidence is that Milne did not share Grahame's habit of ignoring them. People often say: 'Oh, A. A. Milne? He didn't like children, did he?' It is the thing they think they 'know' about him. Christopher Milne's own memoir of his childhood is presumably largely responsible. He wrote: 'Some people are good with children. Others are not. It is a gift. You either have it or you don't. My father didn't — not with children, that is. Later on it was different, very different. But I am thinking of nursery days.'

It is certainly difficult to dispute the evidence of the child himself. But all the letters of those nursery years suggest that Milne, if not in the simplest sense 'good with children', was always intensely interested in his son and not just far more observant (a natural corollary of the fact of being a writer who had always drawn on the world around him), but much more involved in his son's life than the great majority of fathers of the period.

There is hardly a letter of Milne's surviving from his son's childhood, whether it is to Irene Vanbrugh, Barrie, Swinnerton, Turley or his brother, which does not mention the child, and very often he sent photographs as well. ('Which one is Billy?' asked J. M. Barrie looking at two unidentified babies in October 1921. 'I'll come and find out. Don't tell me.') The reviews of Christopher's autobiography all picked up the same impression as the *Daily Mail*: 'The Christopher Robin of the stories scarcely knew the busy writer who was his father.' That was what Christopher himself thought, looking back fifty years later: 'If I cannot say that I loved my parents, it is only because, in those early days, I just didn't know them well enough.' Christopher may not think he knew his father, but his father certainly knew him. From the very beginning the child dominated the household. Inviting Edward Marsh to lunch to meet him (and 'that great actress Athene Seyler'), Milne names the time as one-thirty. 'It has to be 1.30, because Billy insists on his lunch at 1.' He was then two months old. The following June J. V. Milne wrote to a friend: 'Alan says he spends too much time with Billy, seeing all the work before him.'

We have already seen Milne's particular interest in Ken's daughter, Marjorie, the first child he knew well. And long before Christopher was born, there is plenty of evidence that Milne, unlike Daphne, really knew about babies. There was another child-centred series in *Punch* called 'The Heir', at the time of the birth of Ken's first son, which again shows Milne in his most characteristic attitude to children: fascinated but totally unsentimental.

Dahlia gushes about her infant. He is the living image of his father. 'I looked closely at Archie and then at the baby. "I should always know them apart," I said at last.' Milne shows a confident superiority when Samuel, a godfather, who knows nothing about children, bestows an enormous teddy on his tiny godson, saying 'I've been calling it Duncan on the train, but of course he will want to choose his own name for it.' He expects a ridiculous amount from the child.

'Is he tall for his age?' he asks.

'Samuel, pull yourself together. He isn't tall at all; if he is anything he is long but how long only those can say who have seen him in his bath. You do realize that he is only a month old?'

'My dear old boy, of course . . . I suppose he isn't even toddling?'

'No, no,' Milne says, 'Not actually toddling.'

'We did rather want a Rosemary,' Milne said in that early letter. One of his son's earliest memories would be of a time when he was still small enough to be in a pram. Relaxing outside a grocer's shop in Oakley Street, he heard someone say, 'Oh what a pretty little girl!' Like his father before him, he would have to wait a long time for his first haircut. His long hair reminded his mother of the girl she'd wanted and his father of the boy he himself had been. Christopher Milne would remember: 'I had long hair at a time when boys didn't have long hair . . . I used to wear girlish clothes, too, smocks and things. And in my very earliest dreams I even used to dream I was a girl.' The child's image was 'surely Daff, not Alan', one of his cousins commented. Milne himself, looking at the long-haired child in the pretty clothes, must have remembered his own childish feelings of 'battling against the wrong make-up'. Perhaps he thought if it hadn't done him much harm (and indeed, as he suggested, had made him the sort of person he was, the sort of writer he was) then it would not do Billy much harm either.

Alan had felt himself bold and brave under his girlish disguise. His son, on the other hand, suggests image and reality were more closely related in his case. There was not much battling going on. He was content to be gentle, shy and quiet. W. A. Darlington remembers 'a nice little boy . . . being brought up on rather soft and effeminate lines'. His own daughter, Anne, eight months or so older, a tougher character, became the boy's closest friend. They were 'devoted and almost inseparable – Anne with a slight touch about her of the elder sister.' And Alan and Daphne were equally devoted to Anne: 'Anne was and remained to her death the Rosemary that I wasn't,' Christopher Milne would write.

At least with a boy there is the chance to dream of him playing cricket for England. Years before, Milne had said that 'the important thing in christening a future first-class cricketer is to get the initials right'. Christopher Robin was, in fact, never christened, but his names were undoubtedly something to do with having the right sort of initials. 'What could be better than W. G. as a nickname for Grace? But if W. G.'s initials had been Z. Z. where would you have been?' Years later Milne wrote

When Christopher Robin was born, he had to have a name. We had already decided to call him something else and later on he decided to call himself something still else, so that the two names for which we were now looking were to be no more than an excuse for giving him two initials for use in later life. I had decided on two initials rather than one or none, because I wanted him to play cricket for England, like W. G. Grace and C. B. Fry, and if he was to play as an amateur, two initials would give him a more hopeful appearance on the score-card. A father has to think of these things. So, one of us liking the name Christopher, and the other maintaining that Robin was both pleasing and unusual, we decided that as C. R. Milne he should be encouraged to make his name in the sporting world.

There was no idea yet, of course, that it would be his father who would make his name for him, by using those names which he never used himself and which seemed to have so little to do with him – so that there would come a time when, not C. R. Milne, but Christopher Robin, could be described as one of the 'six most famous children in the world'. Long afterwards the child himself would write of the fairy who must have pronounced over his cradle 'one of those cryptic spells that fairies had always been good at: "And his name shall be famous throughout the world." It was one of those spells that sound like a blessing but turn out to be more like a curse.'

In the meantime his father pondered on the fact that there were still four years to go before Billy could possibly have his first cricket lesson; and got on with his next play. This stage of Milne's life would undoubtedly become tedious to the reader if all sixteen of A. A. Milne's plays, short and long, which were produced in the 1920s, were examined in as much detail as *Mr Pim Passes By*. But there were landmarks and highlights which cannot be ignored. There were recurrent excitements and recurrent disappointments. 'Plays always go well on a first night,' Milne would suggest in his novel *Two People*, 'and then the critics tell you why you didn't really enjoy it as much as you thought you did, and how much nicer it would have been if someone else had written quite a different one.' By the time *Mr Pim Passes By* came off, plans were already well advanced for *The Romantic Age*, which opened on 18 October 1920, two months after Christopher's birth. Only three days later, Milne wrote to Eddie Marsh, thanking him for praising the play: 'Your letter bucked me up enormously, because – only partly due to the strike perhaps – people aren't exactly rushing to the Comedy at present, and we were feeling a little dispirited.' The reviews were mixed, some critics complaining that there could be no one in twentieth-century England quite as romantic as Melisande, with her contempt for bread sauce and the money-market and her yearning for chivalry.

It was certainly not going to repeat the success of *Mr Pim*, but Milne had plenty of other irons in the fire. That winter he felt justified in planning a really splendid holiday in Italy. In February he wrote to Max Beerbohm in Rapallo for advice. They had met through a mutual friend, Edmond Kapp, whose first exhibitions of drawings and caricatures had been shown in London in 1919.

My wife and I, and two friends, are going southward at the end of March for a month or so. You know what happens. You announce at the dinner table that you are going to A, and your neighbour says 'Oh you mustn't go to A in March! Where *you* want to go is B.' So you decide to go to B – until you meet somebody who says that C is the only possible place. We have been travelling in this way for the last two months, and having touched at pretty nearly every resort on the map, have at last come back to our starting-place, Santa Margarita. (Probably I have spelt it wrong, but then, you see, I haven't been there for two months.)

Now I implore you, for the love of Kapp, to help us. So many people say 'Italy is impossible just now', and talk of strikes, absence of food, bad travelling, baggage robbery, and the things that Burns wrote an ode to. Is it so? I don't believe it. Anyhow, I say, not at Santa Margerita. Secondly, is S. M. (I shan't try spelling it again) fairly warm at the end of March and in April? All we want is sun, blue sky, a clean and comfortable hotel and eatable food – and an absence of casinos and smartness. Have we found the place?

Forgive my ignorance, forgive my stupid questions, forgive my bothering you. But I should be really grateful for your help.

Beerbohm wrote back warmly, praising Santa Margherita, suggesting Portofino and inviting all four of them to the Villino Chiaro. Milne replied:

Your invitations are delightful. We accept at once – all of them. Our travelling companions are the Hastings Turners. He writes an occasional not-as-yet-too-good play, and many revues. She was Laura Cowie – played Anne Bullen at His Majesty's, Hermia in Barker's production, and – but all this was a little after your play-going days, I suspect. Anyhow a delightful couple and she has an Italian air (the result of playing in *Romance*) which we hope will pull us through, none of us knowing the language.

Yes, we much prefer being unseasonable. Roughly our idea is to divide our time between lying on our backs amidst purple anemones gazing into an azure sky, and sitting on a golden beach throwing stones idly into an ultramarine sea. I feel sure that your coast can supply all the necessary properties.

The holiday was a great success, 'in spite of the inevitable grandeur' of their expenses, to use a phrase of Swinnerton's. He had thought them 'excessively courageous' to 'dart into the middle of a revolution', good copy perhaps but physically risky. In fact, everything was very quiet, Mussolini was far to the south and Portofino '*the* most lovely place I have ever seen'. Milne never used this or any other of his subsequent mild Continental holidays as material for his writing. The friendship with the Hastings Turners flourished and would last the rest of their lives and into the next generations.

They were able to leave Billy for the month without worrying for they now had the perfect nurse for him – Olive Rand – whom her charge would always call 'Nou', but who would become known to the world as Alice, because of a happy rhyme with Palace. ('They're changing guard at Buckingham Palace/Christopher Robin went down with Alice . . .') 'The English mother is fortunate,' said Daphne Milne in an interview in New York in 1931, forgetting all the English mothers who weren't. 'The English mother is fortunate in being able to place such full confidence in her children's nurse. Often the trusted and beloved "Nanny" remains in the employ of the family for years . . . She is especially trained for her work, which she regards as a real profession, worthy of her pride and deepest interest.'

Olive Rand would remain with the Milnes until Christopher went to boarding school in 1930. She wore a grey uniform with a white cap and starched cuffs indoors and a veil when out in the streets. The two of them lived mainly on the top floor of the house in Mallord Street, in the adjoining day and night nurseries. Christopher said: 'So much were we together that Nanny became almost a part of me . . . Other people hovered round the edges, but they meant little. My total loyalty was to her.' He said his father's picture of her in 'Buckingham Palace' was entirely inaccurate. She was not the sort of person who would brush off a child's question with a meaningless 'Sure to, dear, but it's time for tea'. And writing of 'Disobedience', the James James Morrison Morrison poem, Christopher Milne maintained that, although he could not be sure how he felt about anything at the age of three, 'I can only guess that, though I might not have missed my mother, and would certainly not have missed my father, I would have missed Nanny – most desolately.'

Olive Rand was no ordinary nanny; she had had a far more challenging experience than most. She had been nanny to the Chilean Ambassador's children in London and had travelled widely with them. Indeed they had been stranded in France for a while at the beginning of the war and she had then gone with them to America and Chile. She spoke to the *Sunday Times* about A. A. Milne in 1965, with the air of one who had been asked the questions many times before but was still not tired of the subject: 'He never scorned Christopher Robin's fancies and if the boy wanted his nursery pets to be included in conversations and games, Mr Milne always entered into the spirit of the thing and spoke to the toys as if they were real people.' Olive Rand had a fiancé who worked as a Post Office engineer after his discharge from the Army and who kept hoping Olive would leave Christopher and get married, but she could not bring herself to leave the child until he no longer had need of her.

By the summer of 1921 A. A. Milne had finished two plays, *The Truth about Blayds* and *The Dover Road*, which were to run far longer than *The Romantic Age* and become, like *Mr Pim Passes By*, not only successes in London and New York, but staples of amateur dramatic societies and repertory companies all over the world. The success of his plays in that heyday of amateur dramatics was such that he could tell John Drinkwater in 1924 that he was making £2,000 a year from amateur rights alone. (In present day money perhaps £76,000 or $130,000.) 'He is going ahead at a tremendous rate,' his father reported to Biddie Warren on 6 June. If one wonders what he did with the rather staggering results of his popular success, it is obvious that he realized, like any writer, that it could not last. He lived well – but most of his money he invested against an uncertain future.

On the 26th J. V. Milne wrote again and told his friend that Maud reported Billy to be adorable, which suggests that his grandparents had not been seeing much of him, if indeed they had seen him at all. In June Alan promised to motor down in August, but it was September before they got there, though it was hardly a difficult journey. Billy was thirteen months old. 'So his grandmother saw him to her great happiness.' She was already 'deaf, too blind to read or work, and not able to cross the room without a stick.' She died not long afterwards. 'When she left me, a sword went through my heart and I was broken,' J. V. Milne wrote to Biddie Warren, but he did his best to disguise his feelings from his family and the world. 'I think it is one's duty to bear one's own sorrow privately. So I am as cheerful as possible in company. One lady said this to me the other day: "Mr Milne, you will never grow up." '

He was lonely at Christmas, although he had assured his sons he really preferred to stay at home. 'Of course the boys cannot leave their families on that day. It would have been such a disappointment to their children. So I dined alone . . .' J. V. Milne never criticized his sons overtly and was thrilled when Alan would send a car to take him to the theatre. 'Alan's success is marvellous, but he remains the same dear son. I hope soon to see *The Dover Road* with Maud and Connie. Alan's direction was to take a motor there and back and he will meet us and do the rest.' But there is often a loneliness in his letters. Once, for want of anything better to do, he invited two ladies – total strangers – to tea. They came and eventually departed, thanking him warmly. He never discovered their names. And on another occasion, delighting to hear a friend was going on a motor tour, he could not resist exclaiming: 'Nobody offers to take me!'

It is not unreasonable to imagine that the child's teddy bear (a present from Harrods on his first birthday the month before) made the journey to Burgess Hill too, in September 1921. He was not yet called Winnie-the-Pooh, but he was already a palpable presence in the household as Christopher Robin tried out his first words. He managed an impressive 'Owdyerdo' at eighteen months, when his father said he was 'in tremendous form now, just walking and talking and trying to do both without stopping all day'. His bear was simply Bear or Teddy or more grandly, to his elders, Edward Bear. 'A row of teddy-bears sitting in a toy-shop, all one size, all one price. Yet how different each is from the next. Some look stand-offish, some look loveable. And one in particular, the one over there, has a specially endearing expression. Yes, that's the one we would like, please.' So Christopher Milne in his autobiography, imagining the purchasing of Winnie-the-Pooh. What he does not admit is that the bear we know, the bear who would become familiar to millions from E. H. Shepard's drawings, is not really *his* bear at all, but another bear from an earlier nursery, of quite different shape and already with a pronounced character of his own: Graham Shepard's Growler.

Growler was, according to Shepard, 'a magnificent bear. I have never seen his like.' In 1915, when Shepard had been at home and the family away, he had written to his son, seven-year-old Graham: 'Growler and Puck have been an awful nuisance; they talk and jabber all night.' Puck was a mere 'cork-filled gnome' and not part of our story, but it is obvious that Growler was a real character and would play an important part in the forming of our image of Winnie-the-Pooh.

The Milnes liked to get out of London from time to time, if not often to Burgess Hill. There were occasional weekends at Easton Glebe with H. G. Wells. Once, notably, in September 1921, St John Ervine, Harold Laski and Charlie Chaplin were fellow guests. Chaplin was at the height of his early fame (*The Kid*, his first full-length film, co-starring Jackie Coogan, had just been released) and a crowd from the village lined the hedge at the end of the garden, trying to catch a glimpse of him. Laski apparently looked much more like Chaplin than did Chaplin, as he had the right sort of moustache, so Wells took him for a walk on the lawn and the spectators went away, satisfied. A. A. Milne had not got *that* sort of fame. Chaplin obligingly signed a sheet of Easton Glebe writing paper (his signature complete with his trademarks – hat, eyebrows, moustache, stick, boots) for Milne to send to his niece, Marjorie, aged fifteen, to impress her friends at boarding school.

In the same month, the family paid the first of several visits to a thatched cottage called the Decoy at Poling, near Arundel and Littlehampton in Sussex. It was at the Decoy that Christopher Robin fed the swan on the lake and called *him* Pooh. 'This is a very fine name for a swan, because if you call him and he doesn't come (which is a thing swans are good at), then you can pretend that you were just saying 'Pooh!' to show how little you wanted him.' There were cows who came down to drink at this lake and Milne couldn't help thinking: 'Moo rhymes with Pooh! Surely there is a bit of poetry to be got out of that . . .' And there would eventually be one poem with a swan and another with cows, but with neither a Moo nor a Pooh in either of them, because that is the way it often happens with poems.

In July 1922, they stayed for a month with a Mrs Hobbs in Woolacombe Bay in Devon. This was the place, Christopher says, where he first encountered 'sand-between-the-toes', though, at not yet two, he was still at the age for eating it and really too small for clutching sixpences tight. (A more likely venue for that poem would be Whitesand Bay near Plas Brondanw in Wales, where they were the following summer, when the poem was written.) Swinnerton wrote to Woolacombe: 'If the weather where you are has been anything like the weather I have been having on Arnold Bennett's yacht, I am sorry for you. On the other hand, if it has kept you indoors to write more plays, it has done good work, and in that case only Billy and his mother are to be sympathized with.' Milne replied to 'beloved Swin': 'We've had three fine days and spend most of our time changing our clothes. But we enjoy ourselves and Billy and Daff are blooming. So am I. And also very slack. When I return to London, I shall WORK; a constant stream of GREAT PLAYS and POWERFUL NOVELS will flow from my pen.' Writing to Swinnerton, Milne was always at his most self-mockingly boastful.

There were certainly not many visits to Burgess Hill. One can imagine what a bore Daphne must have thought that expedition, and it was even worse when J. V. Milne moved after his wife's death to suburban Purley. 'It must have been an awful come-down' one of Ken's children commented. It could hardly compete with the de Sélincourt house, Brooklands on the Hamble, with its fine gardens, staff of servants and every sort of luxury. The Milnes would soon be looking for a country place of their own. Kenneth Grahame offered Boham's at Blewbury in Berkshire, which he was leaving in the anguished aftermath of his son's death on the Oxford railway line. But Milne wanted to buy, not rent, and in the meantime the Decoy would do.

Milne had been in contact with Grahame because of Curtis Brown's suggestion that he should dramatize *The Wind in the Willows*. The play was not produced until 1929 – after Milne's own success with his children's books – but it was as early as 1921 that Milne responded to his agent's suggestion. Curtis Brown had been trying to get managements interested in it earlier, but had reactions to the idea very much like that of the publishers themselves when the book was first written. When they finally accepted it, Methuen had not even had enough faith in the book to pay a guaranteed advance. But in spite of the famous *Times Literary Supplement* review ('As a contribution to natural history, the work is negligible') and Arthur Ransome's in the *Bookman* ('If we judge the book by its aim, it is a failure, like a speech to Hottentots made in Chinese'), it is difficult to believe, from the list of editions that followed, that *The Wind in the Willows* was as much in need of Milne's one-man crusade to publicize it as he always suggested. Already in 1921, thirteen years after its first publication, it had gone into eleven editions. Milne was always pressing it on his friends. In 1919 he wrote of *The Wind in the Willows* as 'a book which should be a classic, but is not'.

Usually I speak about it at my first meeting with a stranger. It is my opening remark, just as yours is something futile about the weather. If I don't get it in at the beginning, I squeeze it in at the end. The stranger has got to have it some time. Should I ever find myself in the dock, and one never knows, my answer to the question whether I had anything to say, would be, 'Well, my lord, if I might just recommend a book to the jury before leaving . . .'

and much later, in an introduction to a new edition, Milne added:

One does not argue about *The Wind in the Willows*. The young man gives it to the girl with whom he is in love, and if she does not like it, asks her to return his letters. The older man tries it on his nephew, and alters his will accordingly. The book is a test of character . . . When you sit down to it, don't be so ridiculous as to suppose that you are sitting in judgment on my taste, or on the art of Kenneth Grahame. You are merely sitting in judgment on yourself.

Some people would come to feel the same way about *Winnie-the-Pooh*. There is no doubt at all, though the links are subtle, that *The Wind in the Willows* lies behind *Winnie-the-Pooh* and that, without it, Milne's book might well not have been written. Milne, like Grahame, remembered his childhood as the great, good time. 'The queer thing is,' said Grahame, 'I can remember everything I felt then. The part of my brain I used from four till seven can never have altered.' Coming back to the Thames Valley wakened every recollection for Grahame. Milne had no such clearly defined childhood playground to return to, but it was all there inside his head. E. H. Shepard would report that one of the first questions Milne asked him was indeed whether he had read *The Wind in the Willows*. This was, of course, long before he illustrated it and made the link between Grahame and Milne seem ever closer. 'I realized even then,' Shepard said, 'what a very great influence it had been on him. It all seemed to come from that, and he was quite frank about it. He was an honest bloke; he had an admiration for the book.' No wonder that when Curtis Brown wrote to him with the proposal that he should dramatize it, Milne responded like this on 15 November 1921:

The Wind in the Willows – now you're talking! If Kenneth Grahame is willing, and if you feel pretty sure that you can find the right manager for it (as I think you should be able to), I will do it. And I shall love doing it. In fact, as soon as I got your letter, I began sketching it out, and I think I see how it can be done. I think it should be a children's play, with a little incidental music.

It's no use talking to me about novels now – I'm much too excited about this here play. Boucicault, if he had a regular theatre, would be the man. I'm seeing him tomorrow and will talk to him about it.

As he worked on it he realized what a difficult task he had undertaken. We will look at *Toad of Toad Hall* more closely when, at long last, it comes to be produced. In the meantime there are other plays, adult plays, with titles which may still ring faint bells in some readers' ears (*The Truth about Blayds* and *The Dover Road*) and immediately, only a fortnight after the letter to Curtis Brown, a rare appearance for Alan Milne as an actor.

The occasion was a curious one, though never recorded by Milne himself. It was a revival, seventy years later, of a play by Lord Lytton which had first been performed in Devonshire House in the year of the Great Exhibition by Charles Dickens and a group of his friends, for some charitable scheme. Dickens had directed a cast which included not only Wilkie Collins but Tenniel, Cruikshank and Mark Lemon, the first editor of *Punch*. In 1921 *Not as Bad as We Seem* was directed by Nigel Playfair, still glowing from the success of his

Beggar's Opera at Hammersmith. The object of this star-studded performance in Devonshire House – soon to be demolished – was to raise funds to endow a children's library in the very house in Somers Town, in north London, where Dickens, in his own poor childhood, had once discovered a few old books in a garret. The heterogeneous cast included many names that are still familiar. W. H. Davies played 'a newsman' and 'insisted on arriving by the kitchen door, on the grounds that he was a tramp poet'. 'A watchman' was played by Compton Mackenzie. His sister, Fay Compton, had been wanted for the heroine (the part their grandmother had played in the original production) but she was busy in Barrie's *Quality Street* at the Haymarket; so Tennyson Jesse played the role. Milne himself played 'Sir Thomas Timid, a frequenter of Wills's Coffee House'. Rebecca West, Ian Hay and William Orpen were also involved. Compton Mackenzie wrote:

It was an execrably bad play and most of the performers were as wooden as the play. Indeed the only exception was young Ivor Novello, who played excellently the part once taken by Dickens himself.

When the play was mercifully over, there was a quadrille in which three of Dickens' grandchildren and myself danced. This was led by Neville Lytton and Adeline Genée. Other dancers were Alfred Noyes, Gerald Duckworth and, at the very top of her form, Margot Asquith.

Mrs Asquith, as well as dancing, had been invited to play 'the Silent Woman of Deadman's Lane' – the paradox appealed to everyone, though she herself had apparently said, 'If Nigel Playfair is clever enough to revive *The Beggar's Opera*, he is quite clever enough to write something for me to say.' There was one nasty moment when Mrs Asquith started to show Adeline Genée, the great ballerina, how to dance a quadrille, but fortunately she was distracted by the fact that one of Compton Mackenzie's buttons, at the side of his silk breeches, was undone and she abandoned her demonstration and 'plunged down quickly and buttoned it'.

There was an epilogue written by Alfred Noyes, author of that banal poem about going down to Kew in lilac time ('It isn't far from London') – but then, so John Drinkwater recalled, he had 'had the publishers and editors figuratively waiting on his doorstep'. Twenty years later John Betjeman would bracket him with Milne as two of the 'well-known bad authors' who sat on the Council of the Society of Authors.

John Betjeman, on that occasion, was putting himself on the side of the highbrows. Milne would always have a hard time from them. After Milne's death, Swinnerton would think of his friend as 'buried under the weight of highbrow disapproval'. The young Raymond Mortimer's dismissal of Milne in the *Nation* (to which Milne had often been a contributor) so irritated Hubert Henderson, the editor, that a vehement row broke out between literary editor and editor on a visit to the Keyneses. Leonard Woolf, the literary editor, wrote to Hubert Henderson afterwards: 'I really could not agree to the return of the reviews because I am convinced it would have been most unfair. It would have been to send a first offender to jail for a month on the ground that he was drunk and disorderly, when in fact he had only got a little merry on ginger ale.'

Mortimer had begun the review by musing about the appalling state of the British theatre. It was so bad that some 'sane men are still found to say, and even to believe, that a National Theatre would be beneficial. They have evidently never visited the Comédie-Française.' The real problem, Mortimer reflected, was that the theatre depends upon the general taste of the middle-class public and 'that in England is now just deplorable . . . The people who fill the stalls are the people who read *Punch*. They have never heard of St John Hankin, and they cover with laurels the nice, the unassuming head of Mr Milne.'

Mortimer preferred St John Hankin, whose plays he was also reviewing, but he was not very illuminating in making a distinction between them.

It is difficult to compare Hankin's comedies with Milne's without coming to the conclusion that the quality which gives Hankin's plays their value also makes them unpopular and that it is the absence of this same quality in Mr Milne's plays which makes them both bad art and good business . . . Mr Milne's earlier plays are his best, though in them he was too often occupied with giving popular actresses an opportunity for that desperately anxious exercise of charm that is too often mistaken for acting. His latest play represents a *dégringolade* beyond which it seems impossible to fall.

Raymond Mortimer was an almost lone voice, at this stage. Indeed, it was even said that *Mr Pim Passes By* was 'the most brilliant light comedy since Oscar Wilde', praise that was slightly more convincing than similar remarks, years earlier, about *Belinda*. The other young critic who had just joined Leonard Woolf's team at the *Nation*, and who was also worrying his editor, was George Rylands. Sixty-five years later he would take a different line on A. A. Milne from his friend Mortimer: 'The highbrows scorned his light comedies which acted wonderfully – excellent entertainment,' he said. He and Arthur Marshall would appear together at Cambridge in a production of *The Dover Road*. Marshall was less tolerant: 'I remember that we tended to mock the text a little. There was a terrible speech about being introduced to a chicken ("Her mother was a Wyandotte," or something).' He remembered the exact words after all those years. He also recalled with some nausea the skittish pieces in *Punch*: 'They always seemed to start with "It was all Cynthia's fault" and ended with "As I said, Cynthia was to blame". Sometimes the ladies were called Dahlia.' They were indeed.

Alan Milne would tell his brother Ken that he had become 'sick of and entirely uninterested in politics' since the war. That was certainly true of party politics but he continued to hold his strong pacifist convictions and to follow the international news closely, reading both *The Times* and the more left-wing *Daily News* at this period. As a pacifist who had experienced the Somme, Milne was even more deeply concerned than most that that should indeed have been the war to end all wars. It was bitter to realize already how unlikely that was to be so. In September 1922, Lloyd George nearly brought the country to war with Turkey. It was when, having encouraged the Greeks to invade Turkey (after the nationalist revolt which threatened to upset the allied post-war settlement), Lloyd George saw the Turks rout the Greeks and move right up to the barbed wire of the British positions at Chanak in the Neutral Zone. There was not only a threat to navigation in the Straits but, some said, a debt owed to the British war dead at Gallipoli. This chauvinistic suggestion was ridiculed by A. A. Milne in the *Daily News* on 4 October 1922 in an article which impressed E. M. Forster.

They have almost brought it off, the War to End Peace, for which they have been striving for three years. What an incredible joke! A war 'to defend the freedom of the Straits and the sanctity of our graves in Gallipoli', says *Punch* magnificently. Of course you can think of it like that, and it sounds quite dignified and natural. But you may also think, as I do, of those five or ten or twenty men, our chosen statesmen, sitting round a table; the same old statesmen; each with his war memories thick upon him; each knowing his own utter incompetence to maintain a war or to end a war . . .

Forster, taking up Milne's title, 'Another Little War', wrote five days later:

Sir, – Mr A. A. Milne's brilliant article deserves special thanks for its scathing analysis of 'the sanctity of our graves in Gallipoli'. Our rulers knew that their policy would not be popular, and in the hope of stampeding us into it they permitted this vile appeal – the viler because the sentiment that it tries to pervert is a noble one and purifies the life of a nation when directed rightly. The bodies of the young men who are buried out there have no quarrel with one another now, no part in our quarrels or interest in our patronage, no craving for holocausts of more young men. Anyone who has himself entered, however feebly, into the life of the spirit, can realize this.

It is only the elderly ghouls of Whitehall who exhume the dead for the purpose of party propaganda and employ them as a bait to catch the living.

Forster and Milne never met, but this warm support from the distinguished writer must have returned to Milne's mind two years later when *A Passage to India* was published. It is tempting to imagine that he might have felt he could really have written a POWERFUL NOVEL himself, as he had joked in his letter to Swinnerton, if only his long-ago servant had not concealed the letter which could have led to his own passage to India, if only he had had some wider experiences, if only he had been a different person.

As early as June 1914, Milne had imagined the life of a successful playwright:

The successful playwright is indeed a man to be envied. Leaving aside for the moment the question of super-tax, the prizes which fall to his lot are worth something of an effort. He sees his name (correctly spelt) on 'buses which go to such different spots as Hammersmith and West Norwood, and his name (spelt incorrectly) beneath the photograph of somebody else in 'The Illustrated Butler'. He is a welcome figure at the garden-parties of the elect, who are always ready to encourage him by accepting free seats for his play; actor-managers nod to him; editors allow him to contribute without charge to a symposium on the price of golf balls. In short he becomes a 'prominent figure in London Society' – and, if he is not careful, somebody will say so.

In January 1922, when his father was able to boast, 'Alan has at this moment *five* plays running! Three in America, one in London, one in Liverpool', A. A. Milne himself was certainly not grumbling. There were some disadvantages in being so successful, but his increasingly secure financial situation gave him great pleasure and the reviews of his latest plays left little to be desired. It was the following year that George Jean Nathan decided, damningly, that Milne was the best exemplar of those British playwrights who suffer 'from their heavy effort to be insistently light'. He said that going to a Milne play was like going to a dinner party 'whereat all the exceptionally dull guests have endeavoured to be assiduously amusing'. This would seem to us, today, a reasonable description of *The Dover Road* anyway; a reading of it earned from the contemporary playwright, Michael Frayn, the epithet 'terrible'.

At the time most people apparently enjoyed it: P. G. Wodehouse's admiration for it would often be expressed; he called it his favourite play. 'There were those who said he was the new Barrie, there were those who said he was better.' Selecting it as their Play of the Month in June 1922, *Play Pictorial* actually compared Milne with Congreve and Wycherley. The house on the Dover Road is owned by a mysterious Mr Latimer, who had made it his task in life to inveigle into his parlour couples who are 'in quest of unconventional felicity' on the Continent, and prove to them, before any real damage is done, that the new partner is not really a great improvement on the old. It is actually quite an interesting idea and it must have worked on the stage. J. C. Trewin in his *The Theatre since 1900* remembered it with the most pleasure of all Milne's plays. On the page, in Frayn's words, it can only be described as 'a bad case of moralizing whimsy'. The thing was, of course, that the 1920s middle-class theatre audience (the *Punch* readers Raymond Mortimer so despised) liked moralizing whimsy, particularly when Henry Ainley played Mr Latimer and 'that clever young actress' Athene Seyler was one of the errant women.

The Great Broxopp had opened, at long last, in New York on 15 November 1921 and had been greeted by Alexander Woolcott in the *New York Times* as 'a merry satiric fantasy – a slightly uneven but generally gorgeous comedy, which takes the natural appetite for advertisement as its principal target'. It is interesting that the Broxopp baby, whose life is ruined by being identified with Broxopp's Beans for Babies, entirely pre-dates the appearance of Christopher Robin – for Milne (as we saw) had written the play as long ago as 1918, though he would rewrite the last act ('for the nth time') after the New York production.

The Dover Road and *The Truth about Blayds* both opened before Christmas 1921 – the first at the New Bijou in New York, where it ran for 204 performances, and the second at the Globe in London, where it ran for a decent 124. In January Milne received a cable from New York: DOVER ROAD GREAT SUCCESS ARTIS-TICALLY AND FINANCIALLY STOP SEND BLAYDS. It opened on 14 March.

In England a revival of *Mr Pim Passes By* followed *The Truth about Blayds* at the Globe and capitalized on its success; it was still running when the first English production of *The Dover Road* opened at the Theatre Royal, Haymarket. Irene Vanbrugh and Dion Boucicault were back in their old roles in *Mr Pim*: 'The curtain had not been up for thirty seconds before laughter broke out . . . The piece is, of course, of thistledown lightness, but the characterization is so excellent, the dialogue so witty, that the interest is never allowed to slacken.'

The Truth about Blayds was not thistledown. One American critic said that Milne had laid aside 'the mild satire and the delicate wit that have been his forte and falls to asking social questions and pumping hidden shames with a vengeance.' For the first time perhaps, Milne had 'a big and ingenious theme', Swinnerton suggested. 'The play exposed a poet who had become a G.O.M., by passing off as his own the work of a dead friend.' The dead poet had been extraordinarily prolific, having produced enough unpublished work before his early death to carry Blayds through a lifetime of unmerited glory. Oliver Blayds dies at the end of the first act, having made his confession to his daughter.

The first night on 20 December was glittering. The gossip column in the *Pall Mall Gazette* was not:

Last Night's Play.
Everyone at the Globe Theatre last night was talking about Mr Norman McKinnel's wonderful acting as the ninety-year-old Oliver Blayds in 'The Truth About Blayds', Mr A. A. Milne's latest play. Miss Irene Vanbrugh, as attractive as ever, was simply wonderful, too, and the honours of the evening were equally divided between them. I do wish, though, that people with bad coughs would come well armed with lozenges or else stay at home.

* * *

The Princess Royal, accompanied by Princess Maud, was in a box. Sir James Barrie and Mr Stephen Leacock, Mr Somerset Maugham and Lord Latham were there; so was Lady Kathleen Pilkington, Lady Colefax and the usual regular 'first night' audience.

J. M. Barrie was asked his opinion of the play as he left the theatre. His laconic reply was, 'I should have kept the old man alive.' He had both admired and enjoyed it, but it was impossible for the play not to be something of an anticlimax after the brilliant ending of the first act. One critic actually said that Henry James would have given his little finger to have written that first act. Some critics had their reservations, but in February it seemed settled in for a long run. Milne wrote to Turley: '*Blayds* is a success. I feel rich and lazy.' He had been playing golf with Bernard Darwin, grandson of Charles, golf correspondent of *The Times*, a Cambridge blue, who played for England against America that very year. Golf often seemed to Milne the thing he most wanted to do when he was not writing, playing with Billy or having lunch at the Garrick. 'Mrs Milne encourages me to go to my club every day; she says it brightens me up and that I bring her back plenty of good stories,' he told an interviewer that same month. And of course, if Milne was out to lunch, Daphne herself could have lunch with her own friends; already they tended to have different friends.

The Truth about Blayds was a good play – but could have been an even better one. Swinnerton considered Milne's fault was to show too clearly his disapproval of the family's decision to keep the deception alive. It was his puritanism, his strong sense of right and wrong, betraying his dramatic sense again. Milne thought he had written a play about what happens in a community when its god is discovered to be a false god. So he spent his first act establishing the god and then killed him off, because what interested him was the group's reaction to the fact that he was not a god after all, that he was not even great. But first he had to get his audience to believe in the greatness of Oliver Blayds.

Now nothing is so difficult to put on the stage as a Great Man; and of all great men the most difficult to project across the footlights is the literary genius. For it is obvious that a character in a play can never be wiser or wittier than the author of the play. The author may tell himself that in real life no genius is uniformly wise or witty: that the great writers whom he himself has met have shown nothing of their particular quality in conversation. This may be so. Barrie told me of an occasion when he was present at a gathering of young authors all very busy talking about style. An older man sitting aloof in a corner, but listening intently, was asked to contribute to the discussion. He confessed uncomfortably that he had never thought about the subject: he would rather listen and learn what he could: he really would have nothing to say of any value: they all knew much more than he did. Fearing to be drawn more deeply into the argument, he added that he had to go now, and slipped out. 'Who *was* that?' Barrie was asked. Barrie, who had brought him there, explained that it was Thomas Hardy. But not a Thomas Hardy who could have made the crossing of the footlights. For stage life, as I have said, can never hope to be real life, but only life which seems real in the unreal conditions of the theatre.

The genius, in fact, must carry immediate conviction of his genius to the audience. Taciturnity is not enough. But if the author be not himself a genius, how is he to create one?

J. M. Barrie's remark as he left the theatre was a measure of Milne's success in getting the audience to believe they had indeed seen a great poet. 'I had established the Great Man so firmly that for most of the audience Blayds was now the play.' The audience, as Milne ought to have guessed, was more interested in the man who had been guilty of the fraud, who had passed off another man's poems as his own, than in the effect of the smashing of their idol on the other members of the group. At least the *Daily Graphic*, and it was not alone, felt that Milne had established himself in the front rank of contemporary dramatists – along with Pinero, Galsworthy and Maugham. 'The *Punch* humorist has arrived!' Milne thought that actually he had arrived some time before. It was extraordinary how people still thought of him as a *Punch* writer who had temporarily strayed into the theatre.

Milne continued his spate of productions. In America in 1922 *Blayds* was followed by *Belinda* and *The Romantic Age*, which had both already had London productions and, at last, on 20 November, by *The Lucky One*, which had still not appeared in London. Neither *The Romantic Age* nor *The Lucky One* had much of a run in New York. In London the long list of successes, culminating in 267 performances of *The Dover Road*, was followed by cool reviews for the long-delayed first English performance of *The Great Broxopp*. John Galsworthy, whose long-running *Loyalties*, running in tandem with Barrie's *Shall We Join the Ladies?*, had preceded Milne's play at the St Martin's, wrote to sympathize:

I gather from your letter that you've had one of those douches which are administered to our spines from time to time by those who know how plays should be written by others . . . Don't forget that you've had the full whack of favour which the critics will permit before they turn the wheel.

Milne's run of luck was certainly coming to an end. St John Ervine's joking piece in the *Observer* in the spring of 1922 now had a hollow sound.

Something, preferably of a harsh nature, will have to be done about Mr Milne. He is steadily monopolizing the theatres of the habitable globe for the performances of his plays. In London we discover him at his most ambitious. If we go to India or to Australia, behold he is there, too. Hardly had I put my nose inside the city of Liverpool last week when I encountered him again. He has not yet taken possession of the sixty theatres of New York, but if he continues to occupy them at his present pace, the whole lot will soon be labelled, 'Reserved for Mr Milne!' His rivals will then be obliged to take to drink or go into the Civil Service or abandon themselves to some other form of debauchery. Nothing else will be left to them. It may be said, of course, that they should strive to write as well as he writes, which is as much as to say 'Why doesn't Mr De Valera hold his tongue?' or something equally silly and impossible. No, that sort of advice is of no use to us who, stiff with envy, contemplate the extending range of Mr Milne's work. We shall have to make up some scandalous story about him, say, that he is secretly addicted to mathematics or known to visit the British Museum. If we can only blacken his character in this manner we may be able to shove him off the stage. I shall have to bring this matter up before the next meeting of the Authors' Society.

A year later, in February 1923, Milne told Turley that he had just finished his masterpiece. He called it *Success*, because that was what it was about, but he later wished he hadn't. He remained tremendously confident. Surely now he had got it perfect – an important theme (no less than the old one of how does it profit a man if he gains the whole world and loses his soul), with just the right mixture of political reality, irony, pathos, romance and humour. '*Success* is by far the best thing you have done, and I feel uncommon proud of my Mr Milne,' wrote Barrie after reading the typescript. Ivor Brown, writing in the *Manchester Guardian*, was practically the only critic who agreed with Barrie and Milne himself. He saw it as 'a bitter and moving play' with a large element of social criticism: 'It strips the robes and furred gowns from the backs of authority . . .'

The second act, a dream sequence taking the hero, a cabinet minister, back to his childhood, inevitably suggested Barrie to the critics but 'Barrie cannot be achieved by the mere process of writing an ordinary comedy and interrupting it along toward ten o'clock with a gulpy dream scene,' wrote George Jean Nathan, who preferred the up-and-coming Frederick Lonsdale. The last act owed something to Wilde's *The Ideal Husband*. The mixture was entirely Milne's own but it was not a success. 'Success a failure', the papers said, when it opened on 21 June 1923. 'Success? Not likely!' 'Success – that's all Mr Milne thinks about now.' Milne, reeling from the unexpectedly bad reviews, took particular exception to a suggestion by St John Ervine, whom he felt should have known better, that *Success* was a restatement of Barrie's *What Every Woman Knows*. Milne wrote to him in September 1923:

Why, dear Ervine, are you such an ass? Do all people with titles seem alike to you? Lady Sybil is as unlike Lady Jane as any two women could be; the one, soft, clinging, all for love, utterly ignorant and incapable of politics – the other, hard, efficient, ruthless in her ambitions for her husband, and incapable of love. If Lady Jane is like anybody in any of Barrie's plays (which she is not) she is much more like Maggie.

The obvious truth of it is that *What Every Woman Knows* never ever came into my head; and could never have come into yours, had not it suddenly been revived some months after my play was written, but (unluckily) a week or two before it was performed. In any case, you, as a dramatist yourself, ought to know that plays are not written like this, and it is stupid to spend your time, as a critic, in searching for such origins.

Ervine resented the suggestion he was an ass, and Milne wrote again, showing that whatever Darlington's friends might have said about him being unable to take criticism, he could on occasion behave in a very diplomatic way:

Oh, Ervine!

To be called touchy by you! You can say what you like about me in your various papers, but when I tell you quite good-humouredly that you are an ass to say that *Success* was meant to be a re-statement of *What Every Woman Knows*, you boil over with indignation – and call me damned touchy! Good Lord, if you criticise me, why on earth shouldn't I criticise you? You may point out my faults as a dramatist, but if I say a word against your criticism, I am 'working myself up into quite a state', being 'damned touchy', 'damned offensive', and all the rest of it! Why? . . .

So let me suggest that we lunch together at our temporary club, The Reform, one day this week. I haven't been there yet, but am prepared to brave it with you. Then if I say that you are an ass, you will see that I say it endearingly, whereas if I write it, you read it in terms of knotted brow and clenched teeth. And you can say that I am damned touchy, or damned offensive, or damned anything else you like, and I shall only ask you to pass the salt. I will also tell you the story of my life, if you have the rest of the week free. Any day but Tuesday.

Yours ever – or anyhow for the rest of the week
A. A. Milne

On the same day Milne wrote to Irene Vanbrugh, who was playing in *Mr Pim Passes By* in Australia.

Dearest Irene – the est slipped out off my pen, but I feel like that when I think of you.

The play was a complete failure . . . My head is bloody but unbowed. I am (1) the master of my fate (2) the captain of my soul (3) the husband of the best friend in the world and (4) the father of a Complete Duck. And I would sooner have written *Success* than captured Corfu – as Wolfe said.

Daphne picked up the letter and said, 'You're not to tell her the play was a failure; it isn't true.' So Alan added: 'To be absolutely accurate then: it ran six weeks to little money – partly no doubt because of a coincident heatwave; it infuriated the critics; BUT I have never had a play so praised by other dramatists and by actors and actresses. And it is certainly the best I have written.'

In an amusing, combative introduction to the Chatto and Windus edition of *Success*, it is obvious that the reviews had further confirmed in Milne a total contempt for theatre critics. He would come up with the startling idea – since become familiar – that plays should not be reviewed on the first night, when conditions were entirely abnormal. 'The first night is critical; too critical to receive the brunt of critical judgement.' Milne had already, a few months earlier, suggested what would have been the fate of *Hamlet* if the play had been first performed in 1922 and Shakespeare had had the attention of a twentieth-century theatre critic.

Mr William Shakespeare, whose well-meaning little costume play *Hamlet* was given in London for the first time last week, bears a name that is new to us, although we understand, or at least are so assured by the management, that he has a considerable local reputation in Warwickshire as a sonneteer. Why a writer of graceful little sonnets should have the ambition, still less conceive himself to have the ability, to create a tragic play capable of holding the attention of a London audience for three hours, we are unable to imagine. Merely to kill off seven (or was it eight?) of the leading characters in a play is not to write a tragedy. It is not thus that the great master-dramatists have purged our souls with pity and with terror. Mr Shakespeare, like so many other young writers, mistakes violence for power, and, in his unfortunate lighter moments, buffoonery for humour. The real tragedy of last night was that a writer should so misunderstand and misuse the talent given to him.

For Mr Shakespeare, one cannot deny, has talent. He has a certain pleasing gift of words. Every now and then a neat line catches the ear, as when Polonius (well played by Mr Macready Jones) warns his son that 'borrowing often loses a man his friends,' or when Hamlet himself refers to death as 'a shuffling off of this mortal toil'. But a succession of neat lines does not make a play. We require something more. Our interest must be held throughout: not by such well-worn stage devices as the appearance of a ghostly appar-ition, who strikes terror into the hearts only of his fellow-actors; not by comic clowning business at a grave-side; but by the spiritual development of the characters. Mr Shakespeare's characters are no more than mouth-pieces for his rhythmic musings. We can forgive a Prince of Denmark for soliloquising in blank verse to the extent of fifty lines, recognising this as a legitimate method of giving dignity to a royal pronouncement; but what are we to say of a Captain of Infantry who partly finishes off a broken line with the exact number of syllables necessary to complete the *iambus*? Have such people any semblance to life at all? Indeed, the whole play gives us the impression of having been written to the order of a manager as a means of displaying this or that 'line' which, in the language of the day, he can 'do just now'. Soliloquies (unhampered by the presence of rivals) for the popular star, a mad scene for the leading lady (in white), a ghost for the electrician, a duel for the Academy-trained fencers, a scene in dumb show for the cinema-trained rank-and-file – our author has provided for them all. No doubt there is money in it, and a man must live. But frankly we prefer Mr Shakespeare as a writer of sonnets.

Christopher Milne says that there were really very few things his parents enjoyed doing together. They had been married for ten years and certainly Alan had given up hope that Daphne would become a golfer. She had had lessons but she had never really taken to it. Harvey Nichols and Harrods were the playgrounds she preferred. What she enjoyed most of all was something Alan hated – having the decorators in and changing the appearance of a room. Alan would retreat to his study – a small dark room at the back of the house – and try to ignore the upheaval and the smell of paint. He would make all the right appreciative noises when it was safe to come out again. Daphne spent a great deal of time at her hairdresser's and at Elizabeth Arden being groomed. She was not in the least beautiful but she was beautifully turned out – immaculate and untouchable. People described her as glamorous, sophisticated and elegant. She enjoyed her dressmaker and visiting her milliner; her clothes and hats were very important to her.

She wore a particularly splendid hat to the dress rehearsal of *Success*. One hopes there was no one sitting behind her. Milne told Irene Vanbrugh a story that suggests how different they were. Apparently the dress designer, 'Madame Handeley Seymour' of New Bond Street – who had been responsible for the leading lady's clothes – told Milne that she had never seen a more lovely hat than the one his wife was wearing. Daphne was thrilled. She felt, Milne said, 'as I would feel if Thomas Hardy patted me on the head'. There was very little chance of that happening. Though Hardy lived for another four and a half years, he and Milne never met. Barrie could easily have arranged a meeting, but he must have realized that Hardy would have no interest in Milne, however much interest Milne had in Hardy. 'How I loathe Christopher Robin,' Florence Hardy would one day say, perhaps with a touch of sour grapes as her own children's stories had had so little success.

There had been a long, admiring article in the *Boston Transcript* two years earlier by J. Brooks Atkinson, which urged Milne not to 'stoop to pot-boilers and routine pieces of hack-work. Mr Milne's knowledge of human nature and his bubbling sense of humor qualify him for more note-worthy achievement.' Certainly he didn't want to write pot-boilers and he had no need to. He regretted having signed a contract with Curtis Brown on 15 November 1922 for three novels: the first was supposed to be published in 1923, following *The Red House Mystery*. An American editor had been so impressed by that, that on his next trip to London he made his own contract with Milne, offering him no less than £2,000 for the serial rights of his next mystery story. But there never was another one. And his next novel did not appear until 1931. Perhaps it was his admiration for Jane Austen, for Samuel Butler, for Thomas Hardy, that made the novel so difficult for him. He was not sure he could write the sort of novel he would want to have written.

There would be other plays, but now it seemed time for a change. During the previous winter, Milne had written a poem for Daphne (it was not a children's poem) inspired by a glimpse of Billy, aged two, kneeling by his cot, being taught by his nanny to say the words so many children have been taught to say: 'God bless Mummy, Daddy and Nanny and make me a good boy.' 'Mr Milne crept in and watched for a few moments,' Olive Brockwell (as the nanny became) remembered many years later. 'Then I heard him going away down the stairs chuckling as if he was very pleased about something.' With hindsight she thought A. A. Milne was 'chuckling' because he had come up with a brilliant idea for a poem. 'Such lovely words,' she said. 'And they were true. I did have a dressing gown hanging on the door of the nursery.' But Milne was surely smiling first, of course, because the child looked so sweet and, secondly, because he seemed so perfectly to embody the fact that prayer meant nothing at all to a small boy. Indeed it meant very little to Milne himself. Milne had no time at all for orthodox Christianity.

The sight of a child at prayer 'is one over which thousands have been sentimental,' Milne wrote in his autobiography. 'It is indeed calculated to bring a lump to the throat. But, even so, one must tell the truth about the matter.' And the truth is not only that prayer means nothing to a two-year-old but that, although children do have 'an artless beauty, an innocent grace', along with 'this outstanding physical quality, there is a natural lack of moral quality, which expresses itself, as Nature always insists on expressing herself, in an egotism entirely ruthless.'

The critic Humphrey Carpenter has pointed out that there was really no need for 'Beachcomber' to parody the poem, not long after it first appeared. ('Hush, hush, nobody cares! / Christopher Robin has fallen downstairs.') 'Vespers' itself is intended to be an entirely ironic picture of childhood. It is interesting that in his memoir of his childhood, Christopher Milne himself disputes what he calls his father's 'cynical' attitude. A. A. Milne was obviously putting it forward so strongly to counteract the general idea of 'Vespers' as a sentimental poem about a good little boy saying his prayers. But his son himself felt much closer to Wordsworth's view of childhood than his father's. He remembered 'those first affections, those shadowy recollections' as 'the fountain light of all our day'. Adults, though better at disguising it, are often as heartlessly egotistic as children.

In those days of splendour and glory I certainly felt myself nearer to God – the God that Nanny was telling me about, who lived up in the sky . . . – than I do today. And so, asked to choose between those two views of childhood, I'm bound to say that I'm for Wordsworth. Maybe he is just being sentimental. Maybe the infant William has fooled the middle-aged poet in the same way that the kneeling Christopher Robin fooled so many of his readers. Maybe my cynical father is right. But this is not how I feel about it.

Alan Milne gave the poem 'Vespers' to Daphne as a present. He told her that if she liked to get it published she could keep the money. She sent it to *Vanity Fair* in New York. It appeared in January 1923 and she received $50. Over the years, 'Vespers' proved the most lavish present Milne had ever given his wife. (One remembers that de la Mare is supposed to have sent a son through Eton on the proceeds of 'The Listeners'.) The following winter Milne would be invited to provide one of the tiny books in the library of Lutyens's elaborate Queen's Dolls' House, which was to be shown at the Empire Exhibition at Wembley before finding a permanent home at Windsor. The whole scheme was 'ineradicably silly', Arthur Benson suggested, but it was in the nature of a royal command. It seems only Shaw refused and 'in a very rude manner', according to Princess Marie Louise; Milne dutifully copied out 'Vespers'. At least it was short. For many years afterwards there would be copies of 'Vespers' hanging in nurseries all over the world, with the words at the bottom: 'Reprinted by permission from the Library of the Queen's Dolls'

'House'. Milne was already, though he did not yet know it, on his way to becoming some sort of poet laureate of the nursery.

VESPERS

by A.A.MILNE

with decorations by

E.H.SHEPARD

Little Boy kneels at the foot of the bed,
Droops on the little hands little gold head.
Hush! Hush! Whisper who dares!
Christopher Robin is saying his prayers.

God bless Mummy. I know that's right.
Wasn't it fun in the bath to-night?
The cold's so cold, and the hot's so hot
Oh! God bless Daddy – I quite forgot.

Mine has a hood, and I lie in bed,
And pull the hood right over my head,
And I shut my eyes, and I curl up small,
And nobody knows that I'm there at all.

If I open my fingers a little bit more,
I can see Nanny's dressing-gown on the door.
It's a beautiful blue, but it hasn't a hood.
Oh! God bless Nanny and make her good.

Oh! Thank you, God, for a lovely day.
And what was the other I had to say?
I said "Bless Daddy," so what can it be?
Oh! Now I remember it. God bless Me.

Little Boy kneels at the foot of the bed,
Droops on the little hands little gold head.
Hush! Hush! Whisper who dares!
Christopher Robin is saying his prayers.

This poem is from
"When We Were Very Young" (Nathan)
where it was reprinted by permission
from the Library of
The Queens Dolls' House

241

When We Were Very Young

THERE WAS A house party in North Wales in the summer of 1923. Milne had agreed to share with Nigel Playfair the cost of the lease of a house belonging to Clough Williams-Ellis, who would soon develop Portmeirion near by. It was Plas Brondanw at Llanfrothen near Portmadoc. It is in a peculiarly beautiful part of Britain. The Londoners looked forward to walking up Cnicht and Snowdon, to exploring Harlech Castle and to bathing in Cardigan Bay.

Playfair was feeling rich and generous as a result of *The Beggar's Opera* and issued lots of invitations. Frederic Austin, who had adapted the music for Gay's entertainment, was there, and Grace Lovat Fraser, the wife of the designer, and Joan Pitt-Chapman, aged sixteen, whose father had played Macheath, but had died during the run. There was also a woman called Mrs Malcolm, whose husband had recently been accused of murder and acquitted. There were others, too, coming and going. Richard Hughes and his mother came to supper one evening and found themselves warmly welcomed by Mrs Playfair – 'Oh do come in, Mrs Beard and Mr Beard.' It was the way the family were accustomed to refer to them, for no better reason than that Richard Hughes had a beard at that time. The rest of the evening was a little sticky. Everyone had heard the welcome.

It was a strange house party. All might have been well if the weather had been good and the planned expeditions had been able to take place. But 'it rains all day in Wales', Milne wrote gloomily to Swinnerton. All day and almost every day. Giles Playfair, aged thirteen, took some photographs with his Kodak Brownie on one of the three fine days and glowered at the assembled company. 'I disliked everyone who neglected to take the trouble to interest themselves in me. Very few people did. Certainly the house-party in Wales (the Milnes included) found me a silent, sulky, dull and stupid boy.' His brother Lyon shone in comparison, writing a play about Perkin

Warbeck and reading it aloud one wet afternoon to his audience's amusement. Milne sat down there and then to write a preface.

Nigel Playfair made tremendous efforts to keep everyone's spirits up as wet day followed wet day. He was determined people should enjoy themselves. His son Giles remembered

While he was about, everyone was laughing despite their depression at the persistent climatic gloom. He always came down last to breakfast. Before he arrived no noise emerged from the dining room save the desultory clatter of knife and fork on plate. But his entry was invariably a signal for an outburst of wild merriment which continued unabated until the meal was finished.

He made us all play an absurd game called 'I met a sheep'. The rules of this game were simple. You said to your next-door neighbour 'I met a sheep', who replied, 'What did it do?' You then waved both hands and explained, 'It went, "ba, ba, ba".' The game continued until everyone round the table was intoning, 'ba, ba, ba' and waving both hands. The sight of young and old, diffident and superior, famous and obscure, all indulging in this curious ritual was irresistible.

The game, in fact, did little to dispel Milne's gloom. Moreover there was a depressing butler called Griffiths (who had come with the house), who seemed to have taken a particular dislike to Milne, always serving him last, when the food was lukewarm. And Billy, aged three that month, had been whisked away to the nursery wing with his nanny to join the youngest Playfair, four-year-old Andrew, and was rarely seen. Indeed Joan, the then sixteen-year-old, looking back, could not even remember the infant, absorbed as she was in her grief at the death of her father and trying to concentrate on a black and white check dress she was making – but she did remember Alan and Daphne Milne. In her memory, the holiday seemed a sort of background 'out of which that couple protruded'. She was particularly interested in A. A. Milne because she had had a small part as one of the children in his play *Make-Believe* at Hammersmith, five years earlier. She had never met Daphne before, and now she found them, ten years married, 'honey-mooney, as they were always together and speaking very little to anyone else'. She thought them 'a nice and attractive couple, both tall and he ascetic-looking and serious, not laughy', as one might have expected.

Giles Playfair confirmed her memory, saying, 'They adored each other.' He found Milne himself 'prudish, very, very proper', disliking anything vulgar. 'Oh, yes,' he said, 'my father and he liked each other very much.' But obviously, to the thirteen-year-old, the well-known playwright was not at all as he felt a writer should be. When one lists the things Milne disliked one can easily see how priggish he could have appeared to young Giles Playfair. He disliked not only beer, but gin and whisky too ('Why are you the devil of a fellow if you like drinking whisky, and the devil of a prig if you don't?' as a boy in one of Milne's plays would ask.) He disliked professional football and hated all blood sports ('the taste for killing small animals'). He had no interest in racing and disliked all gambling – the whole business of getting something for nothing, whether the gambling was on sport, on the stock exchange or on a state lottery – the possibility of one was being discussed at this time, as so often. Milne had no time for jazz: he was not particularly interested, in fact, in any kind of music – though he once enjoyed a cello recital, by one of Ackie's daughters, rather more than he expected. Above all, Milne loathed, and made clear that he loathed, all forms of aggression, all unthinking talk of the glories of war. It was rather a rebarbative collection of feelings for a thirteen-year-old to stomach.

Milne became increasingly irritated by the proximity of his fellow guests. 'In a week', he wrote later, 'I was screaming with agora-phobia' – not *claustrophobia*, but the dislike of public places, dislike of the drawing-room. He needed to get away. The post one day brought him, forwarded from Chelsea, the proof of a poem he had written for Rose Fyleman for a new children's magazine she was starting, called *The Merry-Go-Round*. Milne retreated gladly to a summer-house to correct the proof.

Rose Fyleman was the author of numerous books for children, with such titles as *Fairies and Chimneys* and *The Fairy Flute*. Fairies were fashionable in the early 1920s. Children, if not just an attractive form of interior decoration, were seen as imaginative little creatures whose fancies must be allowed to flourish and not be quashed by sceptical adults. There was some feeling that children should be sealed off in pretty nurseries from the painful realities of the outside world and there was a tremendous suspicion of 'progressive' parents who, like some of their Victorian predecessors, but for very different reasons, distrusted fairy tales and those who offered sails to minds that rather required ballast. Compton Mackenzie would satirize parents who surrounded their children with nothing but meccano and clever mechanical toys and who offered them *The Wonder Book of Why and What*, concentrating on pictures of steam engines and aeroplanes, and banning 'stupid stories about fairies, or ghosts, or the heroes of the past'. There was a revulsion from their tendency to explain that the rings in the grass are actually caused by fungi or that Cinderella's glass slipper, through an error in translation, was actually made of fur.

Rose Fyleman was also editing the annual *Joy Street*, which came out this year for the first time, just a month after the first issue of *Merry-Go-Round*. *Joy Street* was promoted as 'a meeting place for literally all the best writing for children', but Rose Fyleman was definitely on the side of the fairies. Her famous, banal 'There are fairies at the bottom of our garden!' was only one of scores of verses she contributed to *Punch* in the 1920s, verses that were certainly not intended to be funny. It was only a year since Conan Doyle in *The Coming of the Fairies* had examined the case of the Cottingley fairies, those much-publicized photographs, which seem such obvious fakes, and yet on which he returned an open verdict.

'It is too late for a modern mother,' Milne wrote in 1925, 'to wonder if her children ought to be brought up with a belief in fairies. Their acceptance of fairies is as natural as their acceptance of the Milkman or the Mayor . . . To say that a child has no need for fairies when there are so many beautiful birds and butterflies in the world, or no need for seven-league boots so long as five and five most wonderfully make ten, is like saying that a man has no need for Switzerland until he has exhausted (as none of us has) England, nor any need for Wordsworth until he has mastered every line of Shakespeare.'

The trouble was that most fairy stories and poems were feeble by any standard. Enid Blyton's second book was published this year. It was called *Real Fairies*, and the *Morning Post* commented 'Children have received a new educational charter restoring their right to believe in fairies.' The *Morning Post* had obviously forgotten the children's answer to Peter Pan's regular question each Christmas, saving the dying Tinkerbell.

In 1924 there was also, nauseatingly, *The 'Normous Saturday Fairy Book*, which included some verses by Marion St John Webb, the author of *The Littlest One*, which had first appeared in 1914 and had sold 50,000 copies by this time. It was a collection of verses told in the first person by a six-year-old boy, complete with lisp and appropriate spelling. Milne had himself, years earlier, poured scorn on the taste for baby-talk, hypocorisma, as it is technically called. 'It is important,' one of the Rabbits had said long ago, 'that even as a child he should always be addressed in rational English and not in that ridiculous baby-talk so common to young mothers', and had then been challenged himself for calling the child 'his nunkey's ickle petsy wetsy lambkin'. There was masses of it in *Punch* – but also some signs of a revulsion against it, as in an A. E. Bestall cartoon in which a nurse says to her charge: 'Look, Dickie, what a dear little bow-wow!' and the child replies coolly: 'Do you mean the Cairn or the Sealyham?' People often found it quite hard *not* to use such talk, to address a tiny child as straightforwardly as someone of their own size. And in rendering children's own speech, many writers (even Wells) apparently did not blush to write 'pritty f'owers' or 'Do it adain, Dadda'. Milne actually used the device sparingly, but would come to regret using it at all, when Dorothy Parker got hold of him.

The poem, whose proof he was correcting in that Welsh summer-house as the rain poured down, was the first he had written deliberately for children, but there were no children in it, no hypocorisma and no fairies. When Rose Fyleman first approached him, he had said no. In 1925, two years later, he said it was on the grounds that he was too busy, but that then he began to wonder what he would have written if he hadn't been too busy. In 1939, in his autobiography, when he was so intent on denying the label of children's writer, he gave a slightly different explanation. He said he told her he didn't write verse for children; 'I didn't and couldn't, it wasn't in my line.' And then, after he had posted his letter turning down the suggestion, he began to wonder what he might have written if he had not refused; and then he *did* write it, and it turned out to be one of the best of all Milne's children's poems – 'The Dormouse and the Doctor'. The misguided doctor in the original illustrations by Harry Rowntree is himself a rather large rodent, in top hat and striped trousers, prescribing milk and massage-of-the-back, and freedom-from-worry and drives-in-a-car, and above all chrysanthemums, quite oblivious of the fact that there is nothing at all wrong with the dormouse, except for a longing

> '. . . to be back in a bed
> Of delphiniums (blue) and geraniums (red).'

There was a lot wrong with poetry for children in 1923, quite apart from the prevalence of fairies. Viscountess Grey of Falloden in her introduction to *A Child's Book of Lyrics*, compiled by Philip Wayne and published by Methuen that year, wrote of the time as being 'this age of psycho-analysis when everyone is becoming aware of the importance of first impressions'. And yet, she went on, 'If I could buy up all the Christmas annuals and school periodicals and magazines that provide verse written specially for children and burn these things publicly in the market-place, I would do it with both hands. The mass of sickly nonsense of this nature that appears today is a great evil. Popular carelessness allows rubbish to be given to children for no better reason than that children are young.' 'They don't get any richness into their words – they don't get any flavour. There's no bite,' as Milne put it in a story about a poet's daughter. (This poet's first poem about his child, had, owing to a misunderstanding, been used to wedge the nursery window, which rattled at night. It was probably the fate the poem deserved.)

When Milne had finished correcting his proof, the work of only a few minutes, and had addressed the envelope to Rose Fyleman, he had to think of an excuse not to return to the house and his fellow guests. Obviously he must write something. One might think of him, standing, looking out of the summer-house window at the relentless Welsh downpour and trying to cheer himself up.

> *Is it raining?* Never – mind –
> Think how much the birdies love it!
> See them in their dozens drawn,
> Dancing, to the croquet lawn –
> Could our little friends have dined
> If there'd been no worms above it?
>
> *Is it murky?* What of that,
> If the owls are fairly perky?
> Just imagine you were one –
> Wouldn't you *detest* the sun? . . .

Milne had written that a couple of years earlier: not as a children's poem, of course, but just for fun, on another wet summer's day. Perhaps writing children's poems wasn't so much out of his line after all. And he certainly wasn't too busy. He sat down and started playing with words. He had a reddish marbled quarto exercise book and a pencil with an eraser on it ('just the thing for poetry'). He felt slightly embarrassed about what he was doing, as so many children's writers have done over the years. Wouldn't it sound much better if he could report progress each evening at dinner on that second detective story everyone was so keen for him to write? (He could not help remembering he had been offered a contract for £2,000 for the serial rights alone.) It was, perhaps, all right to be turning out some children's verses on holiday – but was it really what he wanted his next book to be? Writing for children was not taken very seriously, as Lady Grey had observed. It was something, people thought, that anyone might do in an idle moment. But Milne never underestimated the genre. He remembered *The Wind in the Willows*, the book he had admired for so long, and knew that 'no one can write a book which children will like, unless he writes it for himself first.'

That the book, when written, should satisfy children must be regarded as a happy accident, just as one regards it as a happy accident if a dog or a child loves one; it is a matter of personality, and personality is the last matter about which one can take thought. But whatever fears one has, one need not fear that one is writing too well for a child . . . It is difficult enough to express oneself with all the words in the dictionary at one's disposal. With none but simple words, the difficulty is much greater. We need not spare ourselves.

Not that Milne believed in a strictly limited vocabulary; he wanted his words to have richness, flavour and bite, and he knew the power of the occasional unfamiliar word – just as Beatrix Potter did when she commented in *The Flopsy Bunnies* on the report that the effect of eating too much lettuce is 'soporific'. If one hears a small child refer to someone as 'well-intentioned' ('Ernest was an elephant and very well-intentioned') or to someone else 'wandering vaguely quite of her own accord', one knows one is in the presence of a Milne-listener. But most of the language in A. A. Milne's children's poems is, without being boring to an adult, easily understood by a three-or four-year-old, and that is a remarkable achievement. Milne wanted to make his position quite clear. He said of his first collection: it 'is not the work of a poet becoming playful, nor of a lover of children expressing his love, nor of a prose-writer knocking together a few jingles for the little ones, it is the work of a light-verse writer taking his job seriously, even though he is taking it into the nursery.' Milne's technical skill is admirable. It is his dextrous use of rhythm and rhyme that makes his children's poems lodge in the head, and this was what he most wanted. He said once in a preface addressed to young readers:

Now you know of course that verses have rhymes in them; but even more important than the rhymes is what is called 'rhythm'. It is a difficult-looking word, but what it means is just 'the time that the verse keeps'. Every piece of poetry has a music of its own which it is humming to itself as it goes along, and every line, every word, in it has to keep time to this music. This is what makes it difficult to write poetry; because you can't use any words in any order as long as its sense and grammar, but you have to use particular words in a particular order, so that they keep time to the music, and rhyme when you want them to. If you can find words which keep time to the music, and which are just the words you want to say, then the verses which you write are verses which sing themselves into people's heads, and stay there for ever, so that even when they are alone and unhappy they have this music with them for company.

Milne also made it clear that there were three sources for the poems. 'There are three ways in which a writer knows about people: by remembering, by noticing, and by imagining.' He was remembering his own childhood, the things he and Ken had done, the things he had felt himself. 'As a child I kept a mouse; probably it escaped – they generally do. Christopher Robin has kept almost everything except a mouse. But he did go to Buckingham Palace a good deal (which I didn't) . . . And most children hop . . . and sometimes they sit halfway down the stairs.' He was obviously 'noticing' his small son, never very far from his thoughts. Billy had a new pair of braces and was proud of them. Perhaps they were a present for that third birthday in Wales. Certainly 'Growing Up' was one of the poems that was written in the summer-house and so was 'Happiness', as the small boy splashed through the puddles in his Great Big Waterproof Boots. In that poem Milne called the child John (as he had often called Ken in his writing). Although Christopher Robin comes 'very trippingly off the tongue', as Milne remarked, it certainly didn't work in that poem. In fact, as Milne said, 'Christopher Robin is definitely associated with only three sets of verses'. He is actually named in *four* out of forty-four in that first collection. But even Milne, for all his remembering and observing, could not resist imagining a few fairies, though Twinkletoes (without the illustration) could easily be a butterfly.

Milne had written about a quarter of the book by the time they left Wales. Giles Playfair suggests the Milnes left early.

They decided to cut their holiday short and leave before the proper time. They were at no pains to conceal their pleasure at going and I shall never forget their happiness on the morning of departure.

My father, however, refused to be outdone. He made his family and house-party see the Milnes off. We were instructed to form a circle round their car and sing in lusty voices, 'The Milnes are going, hurray, hurray,' to the tune of 'The Campbells are coming . . .' The Milnes drove away with the song ringing in their ears.

Milne now had to break the news to his agent and publishers that his next book was to be, not the detective story or straight novel they were hoping for, but a collection of children's verse. John Macrae of Dutton's was over in London that autumn. He had published both *The Red House Mystery* and the collection *The Sunny Side* in New York the year before. Milne took him to lunch at the Garrick. There was talk of Milne making his first visit to America in the winter. 'So far it is mostly talk. But I have promised to so often that I must. We feel it would be good for trade.' It would be another eight years before he got there. His American publisher remembered:

During the halting conversation, which is likely to take place between author and publisher, Mr Milne genially informed me that he was about to send me his new manuscript – a volume of poetry for children. We are all aware that probably the most hopeless kind of manuscript a publisher expects to receive from his favourite author is that of poetry for children.

I have no complaint about children's poetry by a genius. However, Milne had not yet demonstrated that he could write poetry. You can imagine my chagrin and disappointment. However, I covered up my feelings and held them in harness until the manuscript arrived.

Milne was aware of Macrae's lack of enthusiasm for the project and he realized himself, as he indicated in a letter to Irene Vanbrugh in late September, what a mixed collection the poems were.

I am writing a book of children's verses. Like Stevenson, only better. No, not a bit like Stevenson really. More like Milne. But they are a curious collection; some *for* children, some *about* children, some by, with or from children.

In this same letter, we get a glimpse of the daily life of father and son. They went for a walk after breakfast every morning in their indoor shoes and without hats ('quite informal, not party at all'). They walked each day as far as the Fulham Road and then home again by a different route. Every day they passed the same middle-aged postman. One day Milne said, 'Say good morning to the postman.' Three-year-old Billy obediently said, 'Good morning.' When the postman took no notice whatsoever, the child sensibly suggested, 'He doesn't know me,' which seemed to his father 'a dignified way of concluding the episode'. Only too soon a great many people *would* know the child and murmurs of 'That's Christopher Robin!' would accompany his walks.

In October E. V. Lucas seems to have been worried that Milne was playing too much golf. He thought Milne would be the better for a little more structure in his life and suggested that he should start writing regular prose again for *Punch*. Milne did not resent Lucas's advice about his 'literary career'. 'I have always been grateful to you for your interest in it', but he rejected the suggestion that he was idle – though he hesitated to mention that, for the moment, he really had no need to work, with money constantly flowing in from performances of the plays all over the place. A production of *The Truth about Blayds* by Liverpool Rep had been a particular success and earned Milne the best review (in the *Manchester Guardian* from C. E. Montague) that he said he had ever had in his life. *Mr Pim Passes By* even ran for three months in Berlin in a German translation and accumulated 'a trifle of two thousand billion marks or so' at that time of runaway inflation in Germany. *Mr Pim* was also put on in Vienna that year. Milne wrote to Lucas:

I think my indolence is more apparent than real; or perhaps I should say that it is real, but I overcome it pretty well. I have written in the last five years: six full-length plays, four short plays, two novels, about a book and a half of essays and sketches, a book of verses, three short stories and various oddments: in addition, of course, to the more mechanical labour of seeing 9 books through the press, and rehearsing seven full-length plays, which is not too bad.

Quite frankly I could not bear to write regularly for *Punch* again. I'm sorry, but there it is. It would make me miserable. And I suspect that what you really want is that 'Billy Book' you have been urging me to write; and you feel that, if I began a few chapters for *Punch*, I should be more likely to pull it off. Fear not. I will do it yet. I like writing; the sort of writing which doesn't come into plays; and I will do that book, or some other book, directly, which will make you say 'I always *said* he could write.'

I will send you 20 or 30 of the poems next week, if you would like to see them – officially as Methuen's friend, or unofficially as mine. A mixed lot. So mixed that I think (hooray!) that they will require a prose introduction.

The poems duly arrived in Lucas's office at Methuen. E. V. Lucas was extremely influential at both Methuen and *Punch* at this time. He was just about to become chairman of Methuen and he had been Owen Seaman's deputy at *Punch* from the days when Milne had first worked there. Although in his memoir *Reading, Writing and Remembering* Lucas praises both Milne and 'his collaborator with the pencil, Ernest Shepard', he does not himself claim responsibility for that remarkable partnership, which was to seem as apt and inevitable as Gilbert and Sullivan. But there seems no question that it was his idea.

As soon as Lucas saw the children's poems, he realized that they would make a splendid book when there were enough of them, and that, in the meantime, some of them should appear in *Punch*. It was obviously important to find the right illustrator. 'Vespers' had not been illustrated when it first appeared and Harry Rowntree, who drew the pictures for 'The Dormouse and the Doctor', was extremely good at animals (he spent days at the London Zoo), but not so much at home in the nursery. Lucas was sitting next to Shepard at the *Punch* Table when he suggested (so Shepard remembered) doing some drawings and seeing what Milne thought of them.

Milne knew Shepard's work well, though Shepard had not actually joined the Table until 1921, after Milne had left *Punch*. Before the war, when Shepard was contributing his first cartoons, Milne had actually said more than once to the art editor, F. H. Townsend, 'What on earth do you see in this man? He's perfectly hopeless.' And Townsend had replied complacently, 'You wait.' Shepard had always had difficulty with the jokes.

The Shepard who illustrated Milne's first collection of children's poems, and who would go on to illustrate the other children's books, was the one for whom Milne had waited. As men, they had very little in common and were never friends – in spite of some odd links. For instance, there was the fact that they had lived as small children only a few streets apart, and Shepard had actually been at the same kindergarten in Upper Baker Street as Milne's friend, Nigel Playfair. Later his sister Ethel had been bridesmaid at the wedding of John Vine Milne's most famous ex-pupil, Alfred Harmsworth. Harmsworth, who had showered pennies on small Alan Milne, had taught young Ernest Shepard how to bowl overarm. That was not much of a basis for friendship, and they were of very different temperament. Milne found Shepard's attitude to the war particularly hard to take. 'For him,' Rawle Knox would write, ' "The Great War" was a natural extension of his life, practically all activity interested him and this was more exciting than most . . . He had always been fascinated with guns.' Shepard ended up 'a pillar of Sussex society', as Milne would never be. Shepard thought him 'a rather cagey man, Milne. It was difficult to get beyond the façade, as it were.'

There were plenty of other candidates for the job. Looking at *Punch* for the year before the book came out, one sees E. H. Shepard's drawings of children as no better and sometimes rather worse than those of several other artists. The choice might easily have fallen on A. E. Bestall (who would become less famous for another bear, Rupert, when he took over Mary Tourtel's creation) or D. L. Ghilchik or G. L. Stampa. But Shepard turned out to be perfect in most people's eyes, though R. G. G. Price would speak of his bourgeois 'prettification' and Geoffrey Grigson (notoriously hard to please) of his 'splendid insipidity'. Milne himself was delighted from the moment he saw the first drawings Shepard did – the ones for 'Puppy and I', the poem that recalls that long-ago Gordon Setter, Brownie, who appeared out of nowhere just as the puppy does in the poem. The child and the puppy demonstrate admirably Shepard's particular pleasure in what Penelope Fitzgerald has called 'the characteristic movement of the design from right to left'. It was the feeling of life, 'the tension of suspended movement', in Shepard's drawings that made him so outstanding when he was doing his best work.

One critic would say that Shepard's illustrations belong to the verses 'as intimately as the echo does to the voice'. Certainly the extraordinary success Milne would enjoy owed a good deal to Shepard, but any suggestion that it was because of Shepard can be easily dismissed when one looks at the long-forgotten books of children's verse Shepard would also illustrate delightfully in the next few years, such as Georgette Agnew's *Let's Pretend* and Jan Struther's *Sycamore Square*. A lot of people would try to jump on the merry-go-round. One can't help wondering what Milne felt as he read E. V. Lucas's own contribution *Playtime and Company* (published a year after Milne's first poems), complete with Shepard's Pooh-like bear on a bed, a Christopher Robin look-alike and even a poem about rice pudding, with these strange lines addressed to the reluctant nursery eater:

> . . . When you next the pudding view,
> Suppress the customary 'Pooh!'
> And imitate the mild Hindu.

Milne with Bestall or Ghilchik might easily have had the same impact as Milne and Shepard. Shepard without Milne nearly always sank without trace, unless he were illustrating, as he would, books that were already established, such as (to Milne's great pleasure) new editions of *The Wind in the Willows* and *Bevis*.

Milne came to acknowledge fully how much he owed to Shepard, but, at the end of 1923, he was worrying mainly about a title for the series of poems that were to appear in *Punch*. He wrote to Owen Seaman: 'They want a general title and I can think of none better than *When We Were Very Young*, but I am ready to be persuaded if you, or anybody, can suggest something. *Children Calling* was my only other idea, but Uncle 2LO has made that vulgar.' Seaman was obviously not quite happy about *When We Were Very Young* because Milne, a few days later, sent a list of further suggestions:

Alternative titles:
A Nursery Window Box
From a Nursery Window (or Through the NW)
Pinafore Days
Swings and Roundabouts (probably been used before)
Buttercups and Daisies
I think the first of these is the best, but I am not sure that it is better than *WWWVY*.
My brain has given out, and I can think of no more.

It was Milne's own idea that the series should start off with three short poems, and they duly appeared, under the title *When We Were Very Young*, in *Punch* on 9 January 1924. They did not look very impressive. Unillustrated, they were rather squashed up together. First, 'Brownie', the one about the creature behind the curtain; then 'In the Fashion', the poem about tails; and finally 'Before Tea', where Emmeline has not been seen for more than a week, having gone off in a huff when someone told her her hands weren't clean. A week later 'Puppy and I' appeared as a full-page spread with E. H. Shepard's drawings, much larger than they would be in the book, surrounding the five stanzas. Milne would at one stage identify it as his own favourite of all the poems.

The other poems that would appear in this way were 'The King's Breakfast', 'Teddy Bear', 'Nursery Chairs', 'Lines and Squares' (including two pictures – one of a replete bear who has just finished tucking into a passer-by – which would not get into the book), 'Market Square' and 'Little Bo-Peep and Little Boy Blue'. There were others that appeared unillustrated – and then the whole series of twenty-five ended with another four full pages: 'The Three Foxes', 'Jonathan Jo', 'Missing' and 'Happiness' – the last again with extra pictures: John putting his boots on. Four more would appear in the American children's magazine *St Nicholas* during the summer and autumn. These were illustrated by Reginald Birch, who had become famous nearly forty years earlier for his drawings for a book which had made publishing history: *Little Lord Fauntleroy*. Before we look at the similar extravagant reactions to the publication of *When We Were Very Young* the following winter, we should see what else had been affecting Milne in 1924.

The health of Ken, his brother, had been causing worry for some time. Ken's doctor had diagnosed tuberculosis (usually then called consumption), and in the spring of 1924 it was decided that he must resign from the Ministry of Pensions and leave Croydon for the country. At that time, when there were no effective drugs to fight the disease, there was great belief in the restorative power of fresh country air. Milne was in the middle of rehearsals of his new play *To Have the Honour* (written some time earlier) when he heard the news from his father that Ken was having to leave the Civil Service. He wrote immediately to propose they have lunch at the National Liberal Club, which he still used from time to time when he did not want to be sociable. He suggested that they should discuss ways and means. There would obviously be problems, with Ken's pension – only a third of his salary – entirely inadequate to support his four 'good and clever' children, all still in full-time education. Tony, the youngest, was only nine and just about to join Tim at Streete Court, his grandfather's old school. Eventually they would both go on to Westminster. The girls were at the Godolphin School in Salisbury. In 1922, when Ken had been in Pretoria on his government mission, J. V. Milne had sent one of his friends a family photograph and commented affectionately: 'Look at happy Maud – always the same.' Things would no longer be the same; Alan Milne would be a necessary tower of strength to Maud for the rest of his life. In 1924 he wrote to his brother:

As a throw-out I suggest that you let me pay £100 a year each for the education of your children; i.e. £400 a year now, £300 when Margery is settled, and so on. But more important than this is yourself. You'll *have* to write now, and really to stick at it, whatever the disappointments. As a start, I think I could get O.S. to let you try your hand at reviewing books for *Punch*. Turley made over £200 last year from this. If you got on all right at this, then I think there might be other openings. The Editor of the *Nation* is rather well-disposed towards me at the moment, but I fancy that we should have to be able to quote *Punch* to him first. Of course one feels that 'any fool can review a book', which may or may not be true, but the mere feeling creates an enormous amount of competition – which is why I am butting in. For God's sake don't think I mean by all this: 'You've jolly well got to set to, and earn some money' – You know I don't; but I do mean, old boy, that you're only 43, and that it's no good regretting the brilliant service career which has been denied you, when there's another sort of career still open and waiting for you. There are dozens of good novels and plays waiting to be written, and hundreds of articles; but a little regular reviewing would be a great help meanwhile, not only financially, but artistically. And you know that if I can help in any way, I will. My love to dear Maud. In a sneaking sort of way I envy you both going to live in the country!

Yours ever affectionately,
Alan

By the summer, Ken and Maud were settled at Shepton Mallet in Somerset. 'He is very brave about it all,' his father commented, describing how Ken sleeps 'out of doors in one of those revolving shelters and at 7.30 Maud comes in her dressing-gown with their early tea,' across the damp grass. There had been some talk that J. V. Milne might join them in Somerset – he would miss them sorely in south London – but 'Maud will have all her work looking after Ken.' There was no suggestion that Daphne would tolerate her father-in-law. He spent the two and a half weeks of his housekeeper's annual holiday alone in the Red Lion at Handcross in Sussex. His neighbours in Purley were doing their best. He imagined them saying, 'We must see what we can do for this lonely man.'

From now on, until Ken's death, there are regular letters from Alan, seeking to cheer and entertain his brother in his rural isolation, so that we know far more than we would otherwise have done, if Ken had remained in London, about Alan's activities during the years of publication of the four children's books. Several times Milne invited Ken to visit them in the country. Whether he went or not we do not know. Christopher could not remember meeting his uncle. Occasionally Alan would go down to Somerset (never with Daphne), occasionally at the beginning Ken would come to London (sometimes with Maud); sometimes there would be telephone calls ('Maud's voice on the telephone did me a lot of good, and made me feel much nearer to you both'); sometimes Alan would meet the children off trains. But for the most part there were just the letters, often long.

Alan treads a delicate tightrope, knowing how interested his brother is in what is going on, wanting him to know how much money is coming in, so that he can realize how easily Alan can afford to help him (this year Tony had considerable medical expenses, which

256

Alan cheerfully paid, when the boy's appendix flared up) – but not wanting to seem to boast or to make it difficult for Ken to accept. It is always harder to receive than to give, as Christopher Milne too would find. ('I am bad at receiving, bad at having to be grateful.') It seemed particularly hard for Ken that the bitter end of his own career should have come just before the time of Alan's greatest triumphs.

But in April 1924 Milne was having a terrible time with Gerald Du Maurier during rehearsals at Wyndham's of *To Have the Honour*, struggling to get him to produce it 'in the proper fantastic-comedy spirit'. How Du Maurier must have loathed the interfering author. Milne was relieved to get down to the rented cottage at Poling in May. At least the reviews were reasonable. It was, *The Times* decided, 'Mr Milne at his lightest. The fun is in the details and you don't trouble yourself over much about the story.' The first act kept the house 'in a perpetual ripple of laughter, you hardly knew over what. Let us say over Mr Milne's pleasantness, and the pleasantness of everybody concerned . . . They are all "nice" people, who say witty or frankly natural things. It is the tone of Mr Milne's work that chiefly pleases . . . In fine, an agreeable evening.' Du Maurier himself took the part of the imposter Prince, and, when he found they were playing to full houses, decided after all that 'it's a hell of a good play'. It would have its 150th performance in September.

But, as usual, there were people longing for Milne to do something bigger. The *Illustrated London News* critic begged him to 'drop his masquerade and forget to be polite'. It was all very well for him to poke gentle fun at the British love of rank and titles, but, the critic suggested, he should 'use his splendid gifts in serious satire, to be less gracious and more in earnest, for we have sore need of his talents.'

On the same page as the review of 'The New Milne Comedy' the magazine carried a picture of 'The First Labour Premier and his daughter as guests of the King and Queen at Windsor'. Milne started at about this time a habit he would continue for the rest of his life of writing letters to *The Times*. A few months earlier the General Election had ended in a stalemate – the Tories with 258, Labour with 191 and the Liberals with 159. When the final outcome was still in the balance, Lord Hawke, well known as a cricketer (captain of Yorkshire for many years) had written to *The Times* appealing to the Tories and the Liberals to form a coalition to keep Ramsay

MacDonald out. Milne could not resist drawing Hawke's attention to an interesting precedent.

Lord Hawke, horrified at the political prospect, makes a despairing appeal 'from a sportsman's point of view' to Messrs Baldwin and Asquith. From the same point of view, I make an appeal to him. I remind him, in short, that not only was Australia ruled by Labour for many years without detriment to the Empire, but that it was actually under a Labour government that she won the last Test Matches, and under a Coalition Government that we lost them. I would ask him, therefore, to consider, before he commits himself to a new coalition, whether the prospects for 1924–1925 are really as desperate as he imagines.

This rather teasing letter is indexed solemnly by *The Times* as 'on possible Labour ministry'; and the possibility, as we know, became an actuality. Ramsay MacDonald, with the support of the Liberals (determined to keep the Tories out of office) formed the first Labour government. There was a generally jumpy attitude to the new government. Milne must have smiled wryly at one particular cartoon in *Punch*, where a golfer groans 'I'm dead tired tonight' and his wife tries to cheer him up with 'Never mind, dear, perhaps the Labour government will abolish golf.'

Late in the year, just at the time of the publication of *When We Were Very Young*, Milne was enraged by a letter from the Bishop of Gloucester in *The Times*, written on board the Cunard liner RMS *Berengaria*, complaining because he could no longer afford to keep three gardeners. No wonder, he said, that there is so much unemployment when everyone is pricing themselves out of the market. The Bishop also bewailed the way the lower classes wasted their money. Milne adopted a highly satirical tone in his reply:

It is refreshing to find that the higher clergy are as human as ourselves, and one sympathizes with the Bishop of Gloucester's feeling that if his income tax were lower, and if he could employ three gardeners for the price of two . . . not only would he himself be happier, but that a reflected glow of happiness would probably spread itself over the rest of the community. We have all felt like this from time to time; we have felt, as does the Bishop, that less taxes for us and harder work, longer hours and lower wages for others, is the only rational solution of the country's difficulties. For some cold-blooded economist to argue with his lordship on these matters would be neither profitable nor kind.

But upon one point in his letter I ask for further enlightenment. He writes of the wealth which, by the lower classes, is squandered on 'the pictures' and charabancs as 'economically an unprofitable employment of labour'. From one of our spiritual instructors this is a little surprising. What does he hold to be the reason of our existence – the provision for each other of bread and boots, or the development of our souls? Agriculture, he insists, is a 'profitable' employment of labour, presumably because the product of it is not 'wasted' – it helps to keep us alive? But why are we keeping alive? Apparently in order to make boots and build houses for each other – good, profitable employment. Profitable employment in short, is employment which benefits the body; unprofitable employment, squandered money, is that which is devoted to the soul. Strange teaching for a Bishop! The pictures and charabancs, poetry and painting, the view from Richmond Hill, and the silence of a Cathedral, a concert and a day in April, these things, like education, were admirable when the country was wealthy; but now, with the wages of gardeners what they are, money spent on them is money wasted. Is this indeed what the Bishop wishes us to believe? and are there never moments when he understands that 'pictures and charabancs' are not merely profitable, but the only profitable things in life? I seem to remember a text . . .

'Man does not live by bread alone.' It was the same argument Milne had used years before to justify the life of the writer, the artist. But did he ever have a sneaking feeling that plays like *The Dover Road* and *To Have the Honour* (good entertainment, certainly; enjoyable, apparently) were not exactly developing anyone's soul? Did he read *The Waste Land*, which had just been published, and admire it? Probably not. But he went to see Sybil Thorndike in *Saint Joan* that year and perhaps felt a pang of envy. He certainly admired Shaw. In a letter to *The Times* Milne would say:

Let us curse the present state of the theatre (or whatever we call the managers who refuse our plays) as heartily as we like, but don't let us wash our hands of it with a superior air, and then look around for sympathy. That was not how *Saint Joan* came into the lives of the half-crown public.

At Poling that summer (just about the worst summer on record; it was even wetter than Wales the year before) Milne wrote yet another light comedy: *Ariadne*. He described it in a letter to Ken: 'It is about a solicitor'; he knew about solicitors. He was still seeing something of his eldest brother Barry. J. M. Barrie was always saying how one should write about things one knows. Milne repeated his story about the man who wrote a play about three doctors. He obviously didn't know anything about doctors. 'What do you do?' Barrie asked the man, 'I'm a reciter,' the man said. 'Well, write a play about three reciters then,' Barrie said briskly.

It's 'rather low life, I fear, for the Haymarket', Milne went on to Ken, 'but very funny: and there are two glorious bounders in it.'

When he was writing it, it seemed rather satisfactory. But when it was eventually produced in the spring of 1925, with Fay Compton as Ariadne – a couple of months after its production in New York – it didn't last long. The Haymarket director managed to avoid any suggestion of low life and Milne got blamed for that and for much else. James Agate wrote: 'Mr Milne's characters are like caged dormice, putting from time to time a passionless paw into the outer world and drawing it back again . . . Provincial solicitors do not have drawing-rooms of the dreamy and creamy exquisiteness of the one in Ariadne's house at Melchester. (Where have I heard that name before?) As usual, Mr Milne lacks the courage of his first act. What we want to see is how Ariadne will behave at the clandestine lunch. What we get is the reason why it did not take place.'

The *Theatre World* critic sighed: 'To see Milne in revolt against that English middle-class family life in which he has his whole soul, strength and being (as a dramatist) is no less of a shock than it would be to see Lord Banbury turn Communist.' Apparently the last thing anyone wanted was for Milne 'to take a leaf out of the "Self and Sex" books of Maugham, Lonsdale, Coward and Co.' The *Times* review was awful too. It talked of 'extremely unpleasant people' (critics usually complained that Milne's characters were too nice) and 'the fact that one couldn't anyway believe in them for a moment'. 'Nobody, of course, meant what they said, or what they did, or very nearly did.'

Reading *The Times*, Milne swore once more never to write another play, but his brother, Barry, telephoned to say the *Express* was very good (it was typical of Barry to read the *Express*) and so were the *Telegraph* and the *Morning Post*. Milne told Ken that 'our staff, the faithful Penn and Gertrude' – who had been with them since their marriage – 'adored it'. But after Milne's death, his old friend, W. A. Darlington, would speak of the 'unintentional obscenity' of the businessman, Ariadne's admirer. The actor who played the part seemed to have as little knowledge as the author of the kind of character intended. 'The result was like hearing a nice-mannered child break out into Billingsgate.' When *Ariadne* came off, Milne said, as he would often until people started forgetting that he had ever been one, 'Thank God I'm not only a dramatist – a horrible profession.'

At Poling, between the acts and showers, Milne took photographs, and sent them to Ken. The captions included:

'1) Child in pursuit of elusive cabbage-white. Nurse saying "He'll never catch it"; Mother saying, "Surely those are the Parkinson-Smiths over there."

'2) Child examining captured butterfly. Observe the latter's antennae.' Milne sent that snapshot to Irene Vanbrugh, as well, boasting about the antennae and about the beauty of the child. It would seem to be the photograph so familiar from the cover of the Penguin edition of Christopher Milne's own memoirs, but it is impossible to see the antennae. Milne wrote to Irene:

I bore all the Garrick with it and it is, by general consent, *the* most perfect photograph ever taken. You might think I was become rather an expert with the camera but I have to confess, Madam, that these things are largely a matter of luck.

'3) Child preparing Father's bran-mash for breakfast.' In the absence of this actual photograph, we cannot be sure that this was really what the child was doing, mixing some ancestor of muesli, but it's a nice thought.

There were more than cabbage whites at Poling. Alan wrote about butterflies to Ken, remembering the far-off golden summer of 1892, when Ken had had *British Butterflies* as a birthday present. There were plenty of Red Admirals and Peacocks in Sussex in 1924, 'but the Painted Lady seems to have died out since our day and we've only had one Brimstone.'

The best thing in the summer of 1924 was that, after considerable search, the Milnes found the country cottage they had been looking for. Irene Vanbrugh was in New Zealand when Milne wrote to tell her about it. ('New Zealand is the one country in the world I envy you.' He would say something similar in a reply to a fan letter years later, 'I always suspect the others of being full of the worst kind of insect, Kangaroos that kick you, and other unpleasant beasts.') 'We get possession (delightful word) in October', but it was 'more or less derelict before we came'. There was so much to be done it would be well into the spring of 1925 before they would be able to use it. Milne called it a cottage, but it was actually an old farmhouse – sixteenth-century perhaps, parts of it even older. It was known as Cotchford Farm and was near Hartfield in Sussex, half-way between

Tunbridge Wells and East Grinstead, on the borders of Ashdown Forest.

This is the Forest where, not long afterwards, Winnie-the-Pooh would take up residence 'under the name of Sanders' and E. H. Shepard, drawing the actual places, would add a new landscape to the imaginations of readers all over the world who had never set foot in the forest. Shepard's impression of Cotchford Farm itself is in the background of 'Buttercup Days' in *Now We Are Six*, with Christopher and Anne Darlington, to whom the book is dedicated, in the foreground.

In October Alan sent Ken a photograph of it, with a detailed description of the alterations. They were building on a servants' hall adjoining the kitchen with, over it, 'a dressing-room for me next to Daff's bed-room'. They were converting attic rooms into servants' bedrooms and making 'a sort of ping-pong playroom for him and us'. The chief sitting room was a splendid room. Milne called it 'the most lovely room in the whole world', with a huge fireplace in the middle of it and french windows out on to a lawn – then overgrown – running down to a stream. They were converting a barn into a garage with a flat over it. Alan was taking his father down to see it the following week, but, for the most part, it felt, as the builders worked on it, tantalizingly out of reach. The Milnes were merely poring over seed catalogues and dreaming of a time when there would be a resident gardener with a wife who, in their happy imaginations, would have a delicious meal waiting for them on Friday evenings, when they arrived for the weekend.

When We Were Very Young was published in London on 6 November 1924 and in New York on 20 November. Methuen placed an order with the printers, Jarrold of Norwich, on 17 September for a special edition of 110 large copies on handmade paper and for 5,140 regular trade copies. On 18 November they ordered the printed endpapers (with nine of Shepard's small boys – called variously Percy, John and Christopher Robin – and one little girl, Emmeline) and these were first used in the second impression, which followed hot on the heels of the first, as that sold out on publication day. Milne had a royalty, of course, but Shepard had apparently accepted a lump sum of £50 for the illustrations, on top of what he had had from *Punch*. 'The next day Methuen decided to give me a cheque for £100 as a bonus,' Shepard remembered. They could well afford to do so. By the end of the year, less than eight weeks after publication, Methuen already had 43,843 copies in print. And John Macrae of Dutton's, who had published a fortnight later, was able to cable Milne for Christmas, saying he had already sold 10,000 in America. 'Not so bad,' Milne commented. He already had some confidence in the extraordinary potential of this slim children's book.

The cream paper jacket (which carried four more small boys, Little Bo Peep and the bear we now think of as Pooh) made much of the fact that this was a novelty from an already distinguished author.

> Here is a departure from this popular
> author and dramatist's usual lines. He
> has always amused and delighted
> grown-up readers and playgoers; in
> this gay and frolicsome book he will
> enchant the nursery too. Mr Shepard's
> drawings are in keeping with Mr
> Milne's irresistible fun and fancy.

Milne had first dedicated the book simply

TO THE LITTLE BOY
who calls himself
BILLY MOON

but the final version (perhaps encouraged by Daphne) identified the child clearly not only as Milne's own son, but as the character in some of the poems. It reads:

TO
CHRISTOPHER ROBIN MILNE
OR AS HE PREFERS TO CALL HIMSELF
BILLY MOON
THIS BOOK
WHICH OWES SO MUCH TO HIM
IS NOW
HUMBLY OFFERED

Many adults undoubtedly bought the book for their own pleasure, but the papers invariably reviewed it as a children's book as the publishers intended. Most of them gave it a good deal of space, though the *Star* gave it only two lines 'between the *Chatterbox* Annual and the *Girls of St Monica's*' and the *Morning Post* headed its review 'Jingles for the Nursery' and continued in that vein 'to our utter disgust', Milne said. John Drinkwater's review in the *Sunday Times* was one of the most interesting. He told Milne beforehand that it would sell 'thousands of copies' – but 'whether of his books or mine' Milne wasn't sure before he read it.

Drinkwater made a strong distinction between 'the inventive fun' of the rhymes written 'for a young fellow called Christopher Robin' and the stuff which seems to have strayed in from any book of bad poetry for children 'into an extremely good one'. Drinkwater particularly disliked 'Twinkletoes' which 'had reduced even Mr Shepard to a level of ordinary fairy inanity'. Dismissing such poems as 'Water Lilies' and 'Spring Morning' and 'There's a cavern in the mountain where the old men meet' (all the ones that nobody remembers), Drinkwater spoke out for the arrival of 'a new prophet', someone fit to be mentioned in the same breath as Lewis Carroll.

Mr Milne's deftness is not to be questioned, but the fortunate thing is that it is, apart from the few lapses, always at work, as Lewis Carroll's was, on a sound common sense foundation . . . Mr Milne treats his small companion as a sensible being who, indeed, wants to make up things, as is proper, but wants to make them up about real life and not about fairy doodleum. These two go about in the gayest and most whimsical of tempers, but the things that engage their attention are the soldiers at Buckingham Palace, the three little foxes who didn't wear stockings and didn't wear sockses, the gardener, the king who asked for no more than a little butter for the royal slice of bread . . . It is all great larks, but I wonder whether the Sterner Critics will realize that it also is a very wholesome contribution to serious literature.

Milne would fortunately not live long enough to read the sternest critic of all, Geoffrey Grigson, fulminating about the book even while realizing that 'few other poems have sold so enormously', not since Byron and Tennyson, anyway. Grigson would see Betjeman's debt to Milne. 'How is it that no one is asked, in Advanced Level English or even in the Tripos to estimate the influence' of Milne on 'Miss Joan Hunter-Dunn', for instance. But Grigson thought Milne's poems smug poems, poems for Us, marking us off from Other People – from titled people as well as the plebs, he observes, remembering Bad Sir Brian Botany, who has to be cured of his arrogant ways and become one of Us as B. Botany Esquire. The children in the poems, he says, live in the right London squares and, if male,

are earmarked for the better schools, then the better colleges, high on the river (*mens mediocris in corpore sano*), at one of the 'two' universities; and that male and female they come of families comfortable, secure, self-certain, somewhat above the middle of the middle class.

Are the poems for other children of such homes? No, rather than yes. Children, in my experience, of every generation since and including the

Twenties, have found the poems nauseating, and fascinating. In fact, they were poems by a parent for other parents, and for vice-parental nannies – for parents with a war to forget, a social (and literary) revolution to ignore, a childhood to recover. *When We – We – Were Very Young* the book is named, after all, indicating its aim; which, like the aim of all natural best-sellers, was not entirely explicit, one may assume, in the author's consciousness.

Here mamas of the middle way, and fathers, and nannies, those distorting reflectors of the parental ethos, could be sure of finding Innocence Up to Date. Little Lord Fauntleroy – here he was, stripped of frills and velvet (as we can tell by the splendid insipidity of the accompanying drawings) for modern, sensible clothes; heir, after all, to no peerage, but still the Eternal Child. No hint in these poems of children nasty, brutish and short, as *Struwelpeter* or Hilaire Belloc made them . . .

Are there ever tantrums, as these nice children say 'cos', and 'most', and 'nuffin', and 'purfickly', and 'woffelly', in their nice accent?

> *What* is the matter with Mary Jane?
> She's perfectly well, and she hasn't a pain.

If there were tantrums, it is rice pudding again; but not the child psyche, not infant sexuality, not Freud, who had now entered the pure English world.

The innocence of *When We Were Very Young* – of course it chimes with the last tinkle of a romantic innocence which by the Twenties had devolved to whimsy. Christopher Robin comes trailing the tattiest of wisps of a glory soiled by expectation and acceptance. The clouds have gone grey. The Child, in spite of Westminster and Trinity, is all too much at last the Father of the Man. And whenever the Child's impresario allowed an entr'acte, it came in parallel modes of the expected and decayed – daffodowndillies and the last fairies (inherited from the more fanciful – and sinister – inventor of Peter Pan), Twinkletoes upon the apple leaves, the Lake King's daughter on the water-lilies, cave ancients tapping at golden slippers for dainty feet, bluebells, and blackbirds' yellow bills . . .

These poems for people towards the top with children beneath the age of literary consent have the qualities of rhythm, shape, economy, and games with words – good qualities, after all. Would it be too ponderous to say as well that they were poems for a class of middle to top people who had lost their intellectual and cultural nerve, who expected of right things which they had not earned, and who had scarcely looked a fact in the eye for fifty years? It might be too ponderous. But it would be true.

There is some common ground between the two poet critics, writing exactly fifty years apart. They dislike the same poems; they admire Milne's deftness, his technical skill. The difference is mainly that Drinkwater was writing at a time which took the class background completely for granted, and indeed when the word 'whimsical' could be used without pejorative undertones. Grigson, though born into such a world, was unable to enjoy the verse for the sociology. He is nauseated, in fact, as many have been, not by the rhymes themselves, but by the whole paraphernalia of nannies and afternoon walks and clean hands for nursery tea. 'It's that bloody nanny,' Roald Dahl said to me, admiring Milne enormously and regretting how his books have dated. In fact, the nanny (or 'Nurse') appears in only five of the forty-five poems in *When We Were Very Young* and in another four in the second collection *Now We Are Six* – and, of course, not at all in the Pooh books.

Compton Mackenzie, writing in 1933, also saw the first book, above all, as a social document.

When We Were Very Young marks an epoch as positively as any children's book has ever marked one. It is not extravagant to surmise that a distant posterity may find in that volume of children's verse a key with which to unlock the present more easily than with any contemporary novel, poem or play.

Yet if one reads the poems objectively, ignoring the charming period illustrations (many of which, surprisingly, have *not* dated all that much – look at the boy putting on his raincoat) the main impression is of a number of entirely natural children, egotistical, highly imaginative, slightly rebellious, as children still are. Certainly, as we saw in the first chapters of this book, Milne's own memories of childhood, which play such an important part in the poems, have little to do with nannies and nurseries, and a great deal to do with adventuring, without adults, with freedom and growing independence. The children in the poems are always wanting to break free from the constraints that are constantly being imposed on all children, from whatever social background. ('Don't do that!' 'Come here.') Milne's children want to get 'up the hills to roll and play', to watch the rabbits on the common, to ignore the boring injunctions to 'Take care, dear' and 'Hold my hand.' They want to go down to the wood where the bluebells grow or to travel to South America or to sail through Eastern seas.

It is not a bland world. The menaces and uncertainties of real life are there all right, but perfectly adjusted to a small child's understanding. There are the bears waiting to eat the sillies who tread on the lines of the street. There are the Brownies hovering behind the curtain. There is the constant worry of pet mice, and mothers, going missing – a fear, common in children, that the beloved animal may escape, that the person who goes out of the door may never come back. Bruno Bettelheim considers that the listening child can only enjoy the warning and has to repress the great anxiety that he will be permanently deserted. But the child in the poems is protected by his own egotism, is perfectly in control. Life goes on. ('If people go down to the end of the town, well, what can *anyone* do?') He would never be such an idiot as to tread on the lines; the bears are certainly not going to get him. There is a pleasureable thrill of danger, but ultimately a reinforced security.

The child answers politely all the endless grown-up questions (seething quietly inside) and thinks if only he were King of France he would not brush his hair for aunts. Indeed, if he were King of Greece, he would go so far as to push things off the mantelpiece. This seems to be a reasonable indication of three-year-old rebellion. The poems, in fact (and this is why they have lasted so long), are a true expression of the child psyche, as recognized by the child himself and as observed by his elders. They work both for children and for adults who can see through the class trappings to what is actually there. It helps too when one knows, as Grigson did not, that Milne did not come from a moneyed, smug background, or expect things which he had never earned. In fact, he was constantly worried by the established social order and the priorities of many of his readers, who were indeed very often just the sort of people both he and Grigson disliked and who took Milne's verses to their hearts.

'It is all most odd,' Milne reported to Ken. 'Yellow-faced Anglo-Indian colonels, with no livers and a general feeling that somebody ought to be shot down dammit sir, tell me with tears in their eyes how important it is to avoid the lines of the street and thus escape bears. And they light a long cheroot and tell anybody who is interested that they have knickers and a pair of braces.' And 'Pinero, of all people, patted me on the shoulder yesterday and told me what a wonderful book I had given the world. I don't suppose he has seen or read a play of mine in his life.'

It *was* all most odd. At Methuen there was a packers' strike and someone from the production department later remembered how he and every available person had volunteered to try to keep up with the demand as booksellers' orders for thousands of copies poured into the office every day. In America, the bookshops were taken totally by surprise by the demand. The initial advance orders taken had been for 385 copies. The critics were not particularly enthusiastic, but there are times, John Macrae of Dutton's would say, when 'the American public makes up its own mind'. By 1927, when *Now We Are Six* came out, they had sold 260,000 copies of *When We Were Very Young*. The demand owed a lot in the initial stages to the extraordinary enthusiasm of Macrae's son, who was then sales manager and sent copies of the book to anyone he thought would talk about it.

The letters of appreciation came pouring in – the first ones as a result of all the sales manager's free copies – from thirty-eight state governors, six members of the Cabinet, three Justices of the Supreme Court, eleven Rear Admirals, twelve Major Generals and everyone from Hendrik van Loon to Fred Astaire. One letter, headed F. Ziegfield, New Amsterdam Theatre, New York, was from Lupino Lane and read like this:

I have to do an extra tumble tonight in the 'Follies', slide down a flight of steps or jump through an extra trapdoor. Why, you ask? Oh, simply to express my exuberance over the fun I got in reading A. A. Milne's *When We Were Very Young*.

Even President Coolidge was delighted, or so his secretary said.

Kermit and Theodore Roosevelt (sons of the former President) called in on Milne in London on their way to shoot tigers in Indo-Turkestan, 'a curious and delightful couple', Milne told Ken, 'all agog to have their copies of *When We Were Very Young* signed. Kermit has got a first edition (English) and Theodore was almost in tears because he only had an American first edition.' They were very proud (not realizing how little it would impress Milne) that a newspaper had published a verse about their projected hunting trip:

> Kermit, Theodore
> Roosevelt, Roosevelt,
> Said to themselves, said they,
> There isn't a beast
> In Turkestan
> That we aren't prepared to slay.

Everyone was quoting the poems and parodying them. A university wife in Kansas wrote to say 'No dinner with guests is complete without "Sir Brian Botany" or "James, James" or "Mr Teddy Bear". (You'd be surprised at the number of faculty people trying to reduce.)' Children at table no longer asked for butter but for 'some butter for the Royal slice of bread'. If anything was big, it was always 'enormouse'. And whenever something was lost, the cry would go up, 'Has anyone seen my mouse?'

A woman in Nashville, Tennessee was typical of many who said that the poems appealed to all ages – her four-year-old 'found and recognized himself in almost every poem', but her eleven-year-old also loved 'The King's Breakfast', 'Bad Sir Brian Botany' and 'Three Foxes'. The most bizarre report was from the Hon. Edwin Samuel, who said he had read some Milne verses at a Jaffa Chamber of Commerce lunch. 'All those busy Arab merchants took the afternoon off for endless repeats of "Christopher Robin goes hoppity, hoppity, hop".' Everyone was hopping. A New York woman reported, 'We all had to hop. We kept it up until I was overcome by exhaustion and avoirdupois. Then just the children hopped.' They wanted to know about Christopher Robin. Does he really hop *all* the time?

An uncomfortable spotlight was already beginning to shine on the small boy himself. 'Grown-up readers as well as his contemporaries will thank him for helping to inspire the gay verses,' said someone on the *Sunday Herald Post*. The accompanying photograph of Milne showing a book to his curly-haired child, with a rather cool Daphne looking on, is captioned 'A. A. Milne, his wife and little daughter'.

The book was the subject of a leader in the *New York Herald Tribune*, in March, which quoted Coventry Patmore's 'The Toys' and said that 'pathos digs perhaps the most treacherous of pitfalls' when one is writing about children. 'Our own emotions get between us and the child's. It takes genius to identify itself with a child's blithe inconsequence . . . Lewis Carroll had the gift. Stevenson had it . . . Kipling when he wrote the *Just-So Stories*. There are unmistakable signs of it in Mr A. A. Milne, the English playwright.' The paper suggested that anyone who didn't appreciate the book was a 'biffalo-buffalo-bison, who deserves to find treacle in his sockses'.

Milne wrote to Lucas on 3 April saying 'It's in its 23rd edition in America! But of course not such big editions as you have been printing.' Sales escalated throughout the year, reaching a tremendous high with the run-up to Christmas 1925. 'Everybody's Talking about this Book', above a photo of Christopher Robin, was a headline in the *New York Telegraph* for November 1925, and in the following January the *Retail Bookseller* said that the record of *When We Were Very Young* 'is practically without parallel *for any book* in the last ten years'. It was generally agreed to be a book to put alongside

Stevenson's *Child's Garden*, and A. A. Milne himself to be as 'quotable, contagious and personal an institution as Lewis Carroll'.

Milne pondered on the whole extraordinary business. Before he had heard the mounting chorus of adulation, he had been a little irritated by Drinkwater's review which had 'a delightful air about it of how *dare* this fellow try to write poetry without a proper licence?' But could he now call himself a poet? If he found being a dramatist so horrible, what sort of writer did he want to be? A time would come when Auden would make a slightly ambiguous reference in his 'Letter to Lord Byron':

> Light verse, poor girl, is under a sad weather;
>   Except by Milne and persons of that kind
> She's treated as *démodé* altogether.
>   It's strange and very unjust to my mind . . .

Kingsley Amis in the introduction to his *New Oxford Book of Light Verse* noted Auden's 'good word' for A. A. Milne and quoted at length, and with tremendous approval, Milne's account of light verse in the course of an essay on C. S. Calverley, his old hero. Part of it echoes neatly Milne's account, in his autobiography, of writing for children, already quoted.

[It] is not the relaxation of a major poet in the intervals of writing an epic; it is not the kindly contribution of a minor poet to a little girl's album; it is not Cowper amusing (and how easily) Lady Austin, nor Southey splashing about, to his own great content, in the waters of Lodore. It is a precise art . . . Light verse is not the output of poets at play, but of light-verse writers . . . at the hardest and most severely technical work known to authorship . . .

From time to time anthologies of light verse are produced. The trouble with most of the anthologists is that, even if they have an understanding of their subject, secretly they are still a little ashamed of it.

The same can be said of many writers for children. When the two come together, light verse written for children, there are some complex feelings going on, even as the writer looks at his extremely satisfactory bank balance.

Milne had done so much for Methuen's bank balance that in April 1925 they published a small collection of his adult light verse, *For the Luncheon Interval*, in card covers at one shilling and sixpence. It went into a second edition within the year, but no one regarded it as anything but a poor relation of the children's poems. Neither Auden nor Amis, when they came to make their light-verse anthologies, could find a single specimen of Milne to earn a place, though, curiously enough, Grigson did include 'Lines written by a Bear of Very Little Brain' in his *Faber Book of Nonsense Verse*. Stephen Potter in his exploration of the *British Sense of Humour* in 1954 suggested that there had been a revulsion against Milne by his generation, almost *because* he seemed then, in the early 1920s, 'so deliciously funny', with the funniness 'toppling over into sweetness and niceness'. The second half of the twentieth century prefers its humour blacker, less nice.

Milne would go on speaking out for comedy to be taken as seriously as tragedy, for light verse to be taken as seriously as serious verse. After all, 'in modern light verse the author does all the hard work, and in modern serious verse he leaves it all to the reader . . .' But he would gradually have to accept that it was only as a writer for children that anyone would take him seriously. In a poem in *For The Luncheon Interval* addressed to his nephew Jock, Barry's elder boy, and written long ago, in 1909, Milne had brooded on

> . . . we, who bear your name;
> Content (well, almost) with the good old game
> Of moderate Fortune unrelieved by Fame.

He had now won, in no small measure, both Fame and Fortune. Whether they would make him content was another matter.

Drinkwater sent him his review copy to be autographed and Milne amused himself by parodying 'Happiness' in the front of it:

> John has a
> Great Big
> Actor-proof
> Play on,
> John has a
> Great Big
> Mayfair flat . . . etc. etc.

He gave him a bit of 'The Christening' too:

> I sometimes call him Terrible John
> 'Cos his plays go on –
> And on . . .
> And on.

It served him right for being so rude about 'Twinkletoes'.

Four days after the Drinkwater review, another book was published: *Fourteen Songs* – verses from *When We Were Very Young*, set to music by Harold Fraser-Simson, Milne's neighbour in Chelsea. When the poems were coming out in *Punch*, Milne had been approached by all sorts of composers wanting to set them to music. At one stage it seemed as if Frederic Austin, who had been on the wet Welsh holiday, would do them, and Walford Davies was also keen. But Milne decided on Fraser-Simson, then immensely well known for his record-breaking musical *The Maid of the Mountains*. (A selection from that had been played at the New Theatre before the first act of *Mr Pim Passes By*, back in 1920.) One reason, apparently, was that Billy was extremely fond of the Fraser-Simson's liver and white spaniel, Henry Woggins; they often met on their daily walks. It was the beginning of a long collaboration – in the end there were sixty-seven songs. 'The music is exactly right,' Milne wrote to Curtis Brown. Not that he knew much about music.

The story behind the dedication of *Fourteen Songs* is worth telling:

It was dedicated (by the composer of course)

By special permission of
H.R.H. Princess Mary
Viscountess Lascelles
to
Hon. George Lascelles
Hon. Gerald Lascelles

This was really Methuen's idea (E. V. Lucas being thick with Royalty just now), but there is a limit to the number of Lascelles possible in a dedication, and I suggested – if they had to be dragged in –

By permission of H.R.H. . . .
to
The Autocrats of her Nursery

– which has been allowed. But I really don't know why we drag in Princess Mary at all. A much more popular dedication would be:

By permission of
'Mr A'
to his illegitimate children
in every clime

This was in a letter to Ken. 'Mr A' was a source of constant interest and speculation at the time. He was, in fact, Sir Hari Singh, whose financial dealings and involvement with a Mrs Robinson were making headlines in the papers. A few days later Milne wrote: 'The bother is that it's no good telling you now who "Mr A" is, but of course I knew weeks ago . . . God how I see life . . . Mrs Robinson has refused an offer to appear on the films, but will merely write her life for the papers instead. I want to stand on tip-toe and scream.'

The Lascelles dedication of the extremely successful book of songs – and a further dedication in the second book of songs to the Princess Elizabeth (the present Queen) – added to the feeling that Milne was somehow the Top Children's poet, and added to the hostile reaction that was beginning to be felt in some quarters. (Stephen Spender, for instance, whose parents had apparently been keen on keeping him from children who were rough, would later speak of the 'pure horror' of Christopher Robin). Most people probably thought the dedication wholly appropriate and Milne kept his own feelings about royalty to himself most of the time. But on one occasion he could not help speaking out. He was dining at a private house and one of the other guests was Princess Marie Louise, granddaughter of Queen Victoria. It was she who had organized the Queen's Dolls' House not long before and she was graciously interested in A. A. Milne, whose tiny leather-bound 'Vespers' was in that exclusive library. 'I talked to her for about an hour after dinner, said "Ma'am" as little as possible, put my foot in it once or twice probably, withdrew it with a loud sucking noise and continued cheerfully.' The princess was foolish enough to lament to him 'the objection to work shown by the lower classes'. Milne swallowed and murmured that, indeed, 'every one of my friends would rather win £50,000 in a sweepstake than by working for it.' It was the best he could do on the spur of the moment. Her Royal Highness could perhaps hardly believe that the man she was talking to, whom, of course, she had supposed to be a gentleman, was identifying himself and his friends with 'the lower classes'. Milne reported to Ken, 'She didn't say anything, but a faint twinge of pain seemed to pass across her face, as if the first violinist were playing out of tune. Very sad.'

Milne could also speak out clearly on the golf course. One of his opponents, making the usual assumption that Milne would be a right-thinking supporter of the right, was grumbling about the government. 'What we need is a Mussolini,' he declared, and was somewhat discomfited when Milne replied coldly, 'Oh, do you like murderers?'

Milne also showed where he stood, 'on the side of the people against privilege', in a review in the *Nation* of a collection of the cartoons of the left-wing David Low, which had a text by Rebecca

West, writing under the name of Lynx. When he wrote, Milne did not know the identity of Lynx and assumed her to be a man:

Perhaps I am prejudiced for Lynx's way of thought happens to be similar to mine . . . One follows behind Low with a fearful joy, knowing that the next top hat is for it, yet wondering just how; but one precedes 'Lynx' confidently after a little, saying over one's shoulder, 'Come on, there's a man in white spats over here, absolutely made for you . . .' To Low's pencil Birkenhead and Thomas are equally comic, Bennett and Belloc equally worthy of deflation; but 'Lynx' separates the sheep from the goats and, if for the most part, his pens bear the labels which I had long given them in my own mind, I at least have no cause to complain.

Milne even began to think that he was Lynx himself, so closely did he identify with this writer 'from the *New Statesman* school'. In his review he does not mention the description of his own plays, which cannot have been at all to his taste and makes his praise of the book all the more generous and interesting. After praising his children's books, Rebecca West went on to say:

And when he turns to what is professedly his adult work he really does not move out of the nursery. What gives his plays their curious sense of eeriness which exists however matter-of-fact the content may be, and their unaccountably touching quality, is our feeling that somehow the limitations of age have been transcended and we are watching the British child, its fair hair beautifully brushed, its eyes clear, its skin rosy, well trained, sweet-natured, very truthful and knowing no fear at all save that there may perhaps be some form of existence which is not the nursery and will not be kind however good one is, looking at life.

And in the meantime the yellow-faced Colonels and shingled hostesses clamoured to clasp him by the hand and gush over his book, misled, as Grigson would be years later, by the superficial trappings, into thinking that Milne was a contented, smug and fully paid-up member of the Establishment.

The Beginnings of Pooh

IN THE MIDST of the acclamation for *When We Were Very Young*, and over the triumphant years to come, Alan Milne had to face over and over again Ken's sadly contrasting situation. Ken was following Alan's advice. Saving his strength in Somerset, he was trying to write. But he was intensely aware of how much he walked in his younger brother's shadow. Writing about his dog, Pete, for *Punch*, he could not help remembering Alan's pieces on Chum, years earlier. Alan tried to reassure him, before he had seen the article: 'I am sure it derives from Pete and not from me.' When it was published on 10 December 1924 (as the third impression of Alan's book had already been ordered) he wrote to Ken:

Dear boy,

100000000000000 congratulations on *Pete*. It is admirable. Is it cheek if I say that I never suspected you of it? It is so damnably unforced; so leisurely; so mature; so – everything that it ought to be. The ghost of Chum salutes you: I strongly suspect him of saying sadly 'Yes, that's how my man ought to have done it.'

Give Maud my congratulation. I hope she is proud of you. In point of style it is miles ahead of the ordinary *Punch* article. Buy another piece of blotting paper, and stick to it. And I should be inclined to say 'Stick to *Punch*'. If you write about your left boot like that Seaman couldn't refuse it.

Your very happy
A.A.M.

Ken would also, thanks to Alan, eventually do some regular reading for Methuen, though they were not encouraging at first. Alan tried to cheer him. 'There are so many available for this sort of work that other things than ability must count: proximity, for instance. Or some other case, even harder than yours, may have turned up.' At last, they did take Ken on and Alan was able to pass on an appreciative report from E. V. Lucas: 'You can tell your brother we regard him as a very valuable ally. He is so quick and decisive.'

In January 1925, Milne wrote to Maud with news of 'a new consumption cure' in Denmark. It was undoubtedly 'genuine: hall-marked by the *Lancet* and the *B.M.J.*'. He urged her to persuade Ken to try it, or at least to send the preliminary reports and X-rays, which would allow the Danish doctor to decide whether to take the case on for the eight-week cure, or not. Alan offered not only to cover all the expenses involved, but even to put up with the certainty of sea-sickness on the North Sea in winter and to cross with him. But he was determined not to badger Ken about his health or, 'so far as I can help it, have him badgered'. He just needed Maud to know how much he wanted (and *how* much he wanted he seemed hardly to be able to bring himself to say) Ken to take every chance there was of a cure. He said to Maud that he realized Ken might feel, 'Leave me alone – I'm sick of doctors': and that was presumably how Ken did feel, for he never went to Denmark.

Milne did not know quite what to do with himself in these early days of 1925 as the sales of *When We Were Very Young* continued to mount. He tried a novel, wrote the first chapter in the hope that the other chapters would write themselves, but 'some of these novels don't seem to try', he told Swinnerton. There were lots of invitations. Sometimes he was forced to meet people he found even more rebarbative than the Princess Marie Louise. He loathed Michael Arlen. 'He is in our eighth hell,' he told Ken. 'Above or below Gilbert Frankau?' He couldn't decide.

There were lots of letters to write. Daphne seemed to be losing the interest she had had in being Alan's secretary. There usually seemed to be other things she would rather be doing. Alan himself had always been bad about clearing his desk. In March Chatto and Windus sent him an agreement for the publication of *Four Plays*. When the manuscript arrived in December, Swinnerton had to beg for the counterpart agreement. 'Its twin, resting here, is becoming blurred with grief and yellow with age.' Milne liked getting letters. He told one fan: 'Letters like yours are the best part of the game'; but it wasn't, of course, quite the same when they had to be answered.

Probably the fan letter that moved him most was from Rudyard Kipling. He replied, 'If you can remember what you once said to Tennyson, you will know what your letter makes me want to say to you. I am proud that you like the verses.' Kipling had said to Tennyson: 'When a private is praised by his General he does not presume to thank him, but fights the better afterwards.' Only to Kipling himself would Milne have repeated such an analogy.

He was watching a certain amount of sport – rugger at Twickenham, the Boat Race – and playing a great deal of golf. His handicap was 'now officially 9, fortunately for our domestic happiness'. As long as Alan's handicap was in double figures, 'Daff hardly dared to mention it in polite society'. Daphne's feelings really did matter to Alan – on all things, great and small. She was very powerful. In this same letter, Milne joked, referring to himself and the four-year-old Billy, 'We men are in a minority.' Daff and he were laughing together over P. G. Wodehouse's lament in *John o'London's Weekly* over the decline of the old English sport of hawking. It was all golf nowadays.

> Golf and the world golfs with you;
> Hawk and you hawk alone.

Alan Milne boasted to Ken (who was still able to play a gentle game himself) of going round Addington in 84, including an 8 at the last, where he lost a ball. Bogey was 77. 'I did 10 holes running in 2 under bogey!' At the new Royal Wimbledon course he did the first hole, 445 yards, with a 3 and 'just missed a 3 at the next, 455. That's the sort of man I am.' He went round Walton Heath in a satisfactory 85, though it was

about the most difficult course in London, with heather a foot high on each side of a narrow fairway, and a perpetual wind. I play a terrible lot of golf now – always twice and often 3 times a week, and it's really time I settled down to work again. But I don't know what. There is a perpetual murmur of 'Detective Story' going on in everybody's brain but mine: Daff's, Curtis Brown's, Methuen's, Dutton's (my American publisher), Hearst's (who want the serial rights), Mr A's (probably) and the Lord Mayor's.

Ken sat at home in Somerset listening to an actress called Rita Ricardo reading 'The Three Little Foxes', 'The Dormouse and the Doctor' and 'The Christening' over 2LO, on the 'wireless installation' that Alan had given him. And he read Alan's long letters. Alan told him Billy was learning to count. When his father, hearing '1 – 2 – 3', asked him how far he could go, he said with surprise, 'Up to the end.' It was an answer that appealed to the latent mathematician in Milne. The boy was also learning to read and write.

He autographed a copy of his book for somebody yesterday. Entirely by himself – except that he had to be told what letter came next . . . The silly woman had written asking for his 'mark' – for a X – Bah! We Moons are a cut above that at 4¼.

Milne discussed the child's feelings about the book in a letter to Lady Desborough, whom he had met a few times and who had written him a fan letter:

At the moment (4¼) Christopher Robin is a man of action rather than a man of letters, and I doubt if the book makes the appeal to him which it does to more studious natures . . . But he quotes from it sometimes; and, indeed, just to hear him call it 'My book' is happiness enough.

'Just now he has the Meccano craze (and so have I as far as I am allowed),' Milne wrote to Ken. The boy also had a passion for drawing and painting. In February of 1925 he produced his master-piece, which he told his father was 'St. George and the Dragon'. Milne wrote, 'It is of the Impressionist School. Daff and I were admiring it publicly and privately indulging in a little discussion as to some of the details. Billy meanwhile was finishing his lunch at the other end of the table, and, having finished it, said his grace to himself. This was it: "Thank God for my good lunch – and let those people understand the dragon." How well I know his feeling!'

Milne was not yet wary of allowing the child to become involved in the public reaction to the book. There was some discussion over whether to take him to the private view of an exhibition of Shepard's illustrations to *When We Were Very Young*, but that was probably because he might not enjoy the occasion. At this stage Milne's son had barely heard the words 'Christopher Robin' and most of the boys in Shepard's illustrations were certainly not him. Their hair was much shorter for one thing, though you couldn't always see it because of the hats. It was because of the dedication that it was *his* book; it was written for him. He *was* there, of course, in 'Hoppity', in 'Buckingham Palace', in 'Vespers' and in 'Sand-between-the-toes', and he felt he was there in some of the others. But he was not, like Tootles in *Peter Pan*, dazzled by being in a story. It all seemed perfectly natural. Daphne suggested it seemed no more extraordinary than it did to other children to find their pictures in the family photograph album. None of Milne's stories of Billy at this time suggest the shy creature of Christopher Milne's memories. It is impossible not to think that he was *made* shy, and his natural confidence eroded, by the attention he received in the following years. If

Christopher Robin had played a minor part in *When We Were Very Young*, in the next book he would take a starring role.

The child's passion for St George and the Dragon determined one of his fifth birthday presents that summer: a shining suit of armour. It is interesting that Christopher Milne's own story in *The Enchanted Places*, written nearly fifty years later, tallies exactly with the story Milne told at the time in a letter to Ken, a letter which Christopher never saw. Did he really remember so accurately or was it, more likely, a story his father often repeated?

As you know, he is very keen on dressing up, particularly as St. George v. Dragon. I was trying to teach him to catch last weekend, and he wasn't very good at it. I said, 'You *must* learn to catch, or you will never be any good at cricket. And you know when you're nine or ten, you'll think of nothing *but* cricket.' And he opened his eyes very wide and said 'Nothing but cricket? Not *armour*?' A dreary prospect opening up before him.

The catching practice was going on at Cotchford, the farmhouse in Sussex, where the Milnes would now spend most weekends, as well as the Easter and summer holidays. Nanny would, of course, always go down with them. She would come in useful for fielding when it came to cricket, but it is remarkable how seldom Milne mentions her in his letters. She came between him and his son – there was no doubt about that – and he was jealous. Christopher Milne would say that jealousy was his father's besetting sin. 'Jealous by nature – as I was too – more than anything he hated rivalry.' And Nanny – not Daphne – was his true rival for the love he longed for from his son.

Milne bumped his head happily on the low beams as he learned to live in the old house. He had a small, rather dark study with a window looking out across the front courtyard to the kitchen wing. Daphne had lavished a good deal of attention on the rest of the house, getting it just the way she wanted it, but it was in the garden that she really came into her own. There was something, it seemed, that she had always been wanting to do and that was to make a garden. She had a full-time gardener to help, but it was *her* garden and the picture we have of her in the country is very different from the image of her in London, with her hats and hairdressers and leisurely luncheons. 'She responded to the beauty, the peace and the solitude' that the country offered. 'She found this in the garden and she found it too in the countryside beyond. Solitude. She was happiest alone . . .' But their son would see Milne as 'a Londoner, a real

Londoner with a deep love of London in his bones. For him the country had always been, not where you lived, but where you went. Where you went on holiday. Where you went to do something – to ride a bicycle, to climb a hill, to look for birds' nests, to play golf. Like a dog, he couldn't just be in the country, sitting or strolling aimlessly.' So Christopher would say, but once, in a novel, Milne himself would write that the good thing about the country is that you *can* do nothing there, because that means 'doing everything: thinking, seeing, listening, feeling, living.' But it was true enough that, like a dog, he was never happier than when chasing a ball. He needed someone to play with and Daphne hated all games.

So there was tiny Christopher Robin, still called Billy, being trained to throw and catch, an ancillary of his father. And there was Daphne, absorbed in planting and planning her garden. Their pleasure in their first 'picnic weekend' was rather spoilt when they returned to find there had been burglars in Mallord Street. Alan wrote to Ken:

Fortunately they were only out for the jewellery, and ignored all the silver spoons and forks. Still more luckily they searched every drawer in the house for Daff's jewel-case, and the actual case (which they probably thought was a tea-caddy) looked on and laughed at them. All they got was
    Two silver boxes
    Ciro-pearl necklace (which I hope they thought was genuine)
    Jade and diamond brooch
    Ear-rings
    My gold wrist watch
    My gold 'albert' (which I haven't worn since 1914)
and

    Two pairs of cami-knickers and two chemises of Daff's! (You ought to have heard me describing the cami-knickers to two stolid policemen.) About £70 worth. Insured, of course. The visitors came in politely by the front door which they burst open with a jemmy. They did no damage whatever inside, owing to the lucky fact that not a single drawer, cupboard or desk is ever locked in this house. But bills, letters and clothes were scattered all over the rooms. Holmes (or Gillingham) would undoubtedly have said that they were really searching for the secret will or the compromising photograph.

Gillingham was Milne's own amateur detective in *The Red House Mystery*.

I have been interviewed by detectives, insurance people, bloodhounds and what else, and have reconstructed the scene of the crime a dozen times. There is no doubt we shall get our money back all right which reminds me – what do you think of the Miss Tebbs? I gather that Barry doesn't; he was very sinister about them the other day. Father threatens to bring them down to Cotchford for the day.

The two Miss Tebbs, Evangeline and Julia, kind neighbours of John Vine Milne, were obviously thought by his eldest son to have designs on him. 'Father mentioned the matrimonial hopes of his friends in a letter to me too, but I didn't feel he meant it seriously,' Alan wrote in a later letter to Ken. 'Obviously we should have no right to object; equally obviously we should strongly.' It is not quite clear what Alan was worrying about; Barry was worrying, not about his father's happiness, but about his money.

The bulbs Daphne had planted on day trips from Chelsea with sandwiches and a thermos flask, when they had first got possession in the autumn, were coming into flower – hundreds of Darwin tulips that May. Just as Daphne's role in Milne's writing was simply admiration and praise, so was Milne's role, officially, in relation to Daphne's garden. He admired very much what she and the gardener were doing, but perversely took even more pleasure in the self-sown things, the flowers that sprang up of their own accord – eschscholtzia, coreopsis, sidalcea and aubretia. 'A cynic might say that my love is no more than delight in an unearned, unexpected bonus. This is entirely to misjudge me. It comes from a feeling that ... this unclaimed, unworked-for bounty is in some mysterious way the product of my own idleness.' He did pull up an occasional weed, priding himself on the length of its root, and he wondered at the miracles of nature. 'That a nasturtium seed should take any further interest in life is the most optimistic thing that happens in the world.'

The garden was Daphne's kingdom and Milne never considered himself more than an under-gardener. In 1929 he would inscribe *The Secret* 'For Daffodil Milne' with 'the homage of the under-gardener'. But already in the summer of 1926 he would write, 'I am getting wildly keen on the garden, and slightly less unintelligent about it.' His own territory was the putting lawn and he was allowed to worry about the water. Water is always a worry as well as a pleasure. Its habits are quite unpredictable. There was a sort of ditch at the bottom of the garden, which tended to dry up in the summer. Later Milne would discover a spring and form a pond, which caused endless problems. It was perhaps something to do with chalybeate, the iron in the soil, or perhaps it was oil. Milne lived long enough to worry about the first explorations in the area by Sir Henri Deterding of the Royal Dutch Petroleum Company.

Across the ditch there was a meadow and beyond the meadow the river, a tributary of the Medway. They called it a river, though it was really only a stream, to distinguish it from the stream which was really a sort of ditch. The river was deep in a channel lined with alders. 'It was just the right width: too wide to jump, but where a kindly tree reached out a branch to another kindly tree on the opposite shore, it was possible to swing yourself over. It was just the right depth: too deep to paddle across but often shallow enough to paddle in and in places deep enough to swim.' It is of course the river, only Milne calls it a stream, in which Roo will squeak 'Look at me swimming!' and be rescued with the North Pole. Upstream, a short walk south-west of Cotchford, was the bridge, the scene of games of what would be called Poohsticks, and beyond the bridge was the forest.

'It is difficult to be sure which came first,' Christopher would write. Did they play the game Poohsticks before the story or only afterwards? It's such a natural sort of game, throwing sticks into a river and watching them come out on the other side of the bridge, seeing which one had won, that no one really needed to invent it. Probably there were already people playing it all over the world. But there would soon be many more.

And what was Winnie-the-Pooh, the teddy bear himself, doing all this time? He was certainly travelling the hour and a quarter each way, down with the others from Mallord Street to Cotchford and back in the new car driven by Burnside, the chauffeur. (Milne himself would drive, but on the whole he preferred to be driven. He drove 'terribly slowly and terribly badly', one of his nieces said, and he would later claim to be 'the only man in Sussex for whom cars did not start'.) And sometime about now – it is difficult to fix the exact moment – the bear acquired his highly individual name. He had already acquired a voice – 'Pooh's gruff voice as inspired by Moon', as Milne described it to Ken in 1928 when Billy had become Moon. Ten years or so later Milne said it was Daphne who had given the animals their voices. It was probably a bit of both. 'He and his mother gave them life,' Milne said. The child and his toy bear 'indulged in lengthy conversations', according to Daphne, 'Christopher interpolating fierce growls for the bear, feeling thoroughly convinced about it'. There was also some suggestion that the child would say things in a gruff Pooh voice which he knew would hardly be acceptable if he said them in his own.

The teddy bear himself played a very small part in the first book. Apart from his leading role in 'Teddy Bear', he makes only two very minor appearances in the illustrations. He had certainly not yet come into his own. If in physical form he was based on Graham Shepard's bear, in habits and domicile Teddy Bear (or more formally Mr Edward Bear) was certainly the Milne bear.

> He gets what exercise he can
> By falling off the ottoman,
> But generally seems to lack
> The energy to clamber back.

The ottoman was in Billy Moon's nursery on the top floor at Mallord Street, and the toys slept in there at night. The bear was the absolute favourite, the child's inseparable companion. Eeyore was already around (a present for Christmas 1921); he was a donkey with a drooping neck which naturally gave him a gloomy disposition. (Soon there would be a real donkey called Jessica in the thistly field beyond the Cotchford garden where later, after the animal's death, they planted a wood.) There was Piglet too, a present from a neighbour in Chelsea.

There have been many explanations of Winnie-the-Pooh's name, so many that it is a wonder Milne did not make a story out of them, in the manner of the *Just-So Stories*. There is no question that the Winnie part came from an American Black Bear called Winnie, who was one of the most popular animals in the London Zoo at this period. (If you go to the Zoo now you can see a sculpture of a bear cub, which celebrates the link between them.) The real bear had crossed the Atlantic as the mascot of a Canadian regiment, the Princess Pat's, and had been left on Mappin Terrace in the safekeeping of the Royal Zoological Society in 1914, when the regiment went to France. She lived there until her death in 1934.

Christopher Milne certainly met this bear on more than one occasion. There are various accounts of how he reacted. His father, as reported by Enid Blyton, would say 'the bear hugged Christopher Robin and they had a glorious time together, rolling about and pulling ears and all sorts of things.' It sounds rather hazardous. E. V. Lucas was a member of the Society and knew many of the keepers. Through him it was possible to open doors and gates not normally opened to the general public. Laurence Irving, Henry's grandson, told a story – which had wide circulation in a letter to *The Times* in 1981 – of a visit to Winnie, when he invited the children of two of his Garrick friends, A. A. Milne and John Hastings Turner, to join his daughter Pamela on her fifth birthday. Mrs Irving's version was that Pamela, who had a keen sense of smell, had exclaimed 'Oh Pooh!' on meeting the docile beast; Daphne certainly told the story that Christopher had said the same, but with pleasure rather than distaste, having decided he liked the bear after some natural initial trepidation on meeting the huge if friendly beast. ('The girls held their ground, Billy wavered, retreated a step or two, then overcame his awe.') However, the date of the expedition, so firmly fixed by Irving on his daughter's fifth birthday, makes it impossible that saying 'Pooh!' to Winnie the bear at the Zoo can have had anything to do with the naming of Christopher Robin's teddy. Pamela was five on 22 March 1926, certainly seven months before the book was published, but three months after the first Pooh story had appeared in print.

Irving, writing to the paper so long afterwards, might well have confused the birthday. But the expedition cannot have taken place in March 1925, because it is also linked firmly with *Vaudeville Vanities*, a revue in which all three men – Irving, Milne and Hastings Turner – were involved. Irving had designed the sets for a rendering of 'The King's Breakfast', set to music by Fraser-Simson. It was an item which caused problems, as the producer felt sure that the Lord Chamberlain would object to the life-size cow's pale terracotta udders. Milne and Irving were both on the side of the udders – 'the source of the butter on which the plot depended'. *Vaudeville Vanities* opened late in 1926, after the publication of *Winnie-the-Pooh*. Indeed, if the visit to Winnie took place, as Irving says, 'during the long run of the revue,' it must have been to celebrate Pamela's sixth birthday, in March 1927.

If I seem to have laboured this point it is because Irving's story has been much repeated. 'How did Winnie-the-Pooh get his name?' is a common question; it is such an odd name. Christopher Milne says 'I gave it to him' but nearly always uses just 'Pooh' and it is that part of the name that causes most problems. I have heard children, sadly, refuse to take the book off the library shelf 'because of its silly name'. A child psychotherapist was much taken with the fact that it was a *swan* that was first called 'Pooh' – a swan, in its pure whiteness, being the antithesis of the current association, in nursery language, with faeces. This association – supposedly from the exclamation at anything smelly or disgusting – did not come into the language until the 1930s (according to Eric Partridge) and whether it has anything to do with Pooh Bear it is impossible to say. There is nothing smelly or disgusting about Pooh.

Really it seems best to leave most of the explanation to A. A. Milne himself. He says that when they said goodbye to the swan at Arundel, 'we took the name with us, as we didn't think the swan would want it any more'. And when Edward Bear wanted 'an exciting name all to himself, Christopher Robin said at once, without stopping to think, that he was Winnie-the-Pooh. And he was.' Milne could not remember whether Winnie at the zoo was called after Pooh or Pooh after Winnie, but we know that that large American bear was Winnie long before Christopher was born. Then there is the complication of the bear's sex and of the mysterious 'the' in the middle of the name. Milne again:

When I first heard his name, I said, just as you are going to say,
  'But I thought he was a boy?'
  'So did I,' said Christopher Robin.
  'Then you can't call him Winnie?'
  'I don't.'
  'But you said – '
  'He's Winnie-ther-Pooh. Don't you know what '*ther*' means?'
'Ah yes, now I do,' I said quickly; and I hope you do too, because it is all the explanation you are going to get.

It only remains to remember that Pooh had such stiff arms, 'from holding on to the string of the balloon all that time that they stayed up straight in the air for more than a week, and whenever a fly came and settled on his nose he had to blow it off. And I think – but I am not sure – that *that* is why he was always called Pooh.' Well, it's possible.

And as for it not being possible for a male creature to be called Winnie, it is just worth wondering whether Pooh helped Churchill's nickname during the war and reinforced his tubby reassuring image when Britain stood alone.

In the Spring of 1925 Winnie-the-Pooh was still a toy bear and not a book. He was not even in a story. But after the success of the poems, everyone forgot about the detective story and started pressing

Milne to produce another children's book. *When We Were Very Young* was already firmly established as 'the greatest children's book since *Alice*'. Indeed its rare status had been acclaimed immediately on publication: 'It is a book that all children will adore. It is a book that mothers and nurses will laugh and cry over. It is a – classic!'

Carl Pforzheimer, an extremely rich book collector, began as early as 1925 to build up the collection of manuscripts, typescripts and Shepard pencil sketches which would eventually, after his death, sell at Sotheby's in London in 1986 for £120,000 ($180,000). Milne obviously thought at this stage that his success might not last and he should cash in on it while he had the chance. Later he regretted very much that he had let the material go; he would be more careful in future.

Milne had always prided himself on his financial astuteness, but he made another mistake in 1925. An American publisher, David McKay Co. of Philadelphia, wanted him to write some stories to go with some paintings by an artist called H. Willebeek Le Mair. On 29 March Milne wrote to Curtis Brown, 'At present I am still wrestling with the McKay pictures. As soon as any sort of book begins to heave in sight, of course I will let you know.' As he was merely adding some words to a set of existing pictures, he foolishly agreed to a lump payment with no royalty. The *Bookman* said, 'If you like Mr Milne's verses, you will like his stories . . . They all come from the same mint.' But posterity (and Milne himself) distinguished the wheat from the chaff. A recent critic said *A Gallery of Children* 'intrudes like a pale white slug between two butterflies' – but it sold on the strength of Milne's name. He wrote to Turley Smith in November: 'For God's sake don't buy it. I sold the thing outright to an American publisher – in a moment of madness – for £200. He has already sold 50,000 copies at 3½ dollars. Take 10% on that and you perceive that I have thrown away thousands.' He told Ken that 'MacKay had the nerve to write and say that he looked forward to doing another book with me – verses with Shepard illustrations he airily suggested – on which he would "be willing to pay a royalty". I told him to go to San Francisco and chew gum.'

Milne *was* working on more verses. He wrote to Curtis Brown in April 1925: 'Yes, I am prepared to do a dozen more verses of the *When We Were Very Young* kind for serial use in the next year if you can make a deal with the Hearst people.' Harper's offered 'up to £100 for 12 verses' but Milne argued for fifteen guineas each, and got that. He had actually had twenty guineas at Easter for a poem in the *Star*, 'and America is supposed to pay so much better than England.' He wrote to Ken:

Cassells are paying 200 guineas for the English rights of the twelve, provided that they average 30 lines each.

> 'The King asked –
> The Queen and – '

Now you see the point of putting it out like this.

He was encouraging Curtis Brown to insist on 25 per cent 'all through' when it came to his next children's book. What this would be he was still not at all sure. Certainly he wanted to work with Shepard again, and indeed he had written to him early in 1925 to ask him if he would be interested in illustrating a new edition of *Once on a Time*, which had made so little impact when it was first published during the war.

My dear Shepard,
    Did you ever read a book of mine called 'Once on a Time'? No. However, I forgive you, as nobody else has. It was published – Hodder & Stoughton – in 1917, and died at birth. But until W.W.W.V.Y. I always thought it my best book.
    And now, spurred on by our joint success, H. & S. want to bring out a new edition, illustrated by you. It is a long fairy story, and cries aloud for my one and only collaborator. Will you do it? H. M. Brock did it last time – 4 full pages, bad; and 20 chapter headings, not bad. If you would do it, it really might have a very big sale next Christmas. Hodder & Stoughton are writing to you. Methuens were very keen to get it away from them and publish it (with your illustrations, of course), but H. & S. weren't having any.
    I should like you to do it in the verse manner – with decorations all over the place – but I don't know what the publishers' idea is. Anyhow, it is a book on which I have always been very keen, and which I have always felt has never had a chance, so you can understand how keen I am that you should do it. It is full of Kings & Princesses and dragons & other strange animals – and, in fact, shouts for you. So come.

But Shepard was presumably too busy. Everyone was wanting him to do things. Milne hoped he might illustrate a gift edition of his old children's play *Make-Believe* for Chatto and Windus (cashing in on his new fame as a children's writer), but he did not do that either. In 1925 Hodder and Stoughton brought out another edition of *Once on a Time* with delightful illustrations by Charles Robinson, Heath Robinson's elder brother, most famous for his illustrations of *The Secret Garden* by Frances Hodgson Burnett. When he was very young, he had decorated the first edition of Stevenson's *A Child's Garden of Verses* and it seems quite natural that someone would think of him now in connection with Milne, but in fact the Robinson illustrations for *Once on a Time* had appeared in America three years earlier. In spite of Milne's efforts, for he was immensely fond of it, no one ever took a great deal of notice of it.

'Kings and Princesses and dragons and other strange things' seemed to be much in Milne's mind these days. He had written a fairy story called 'The Green Door' earlier in the year when he was asked for something for a Christmas issue of the *Ladies' Home Journal*. The theme of the story kept returning to his mind.

It seemed that there was very much more in the idea than I had, as yet, got out of it. For a little while I played with the thought of turning it into a modern comedy, but the difficulties were too many. Moreover I had already used much the same theme – the Indestructibility of Legend – in an earlier modern play, *The Truth about Blayds*. So reluctantly I kept to the medieval setting, realizing that, by doing this, I was in danger of being called 'whimsical' by the American critics for the thousandth time.

That was written with hindsight. The play was *The Ivory Door*. It would not be produced in New York until 1927 and not in London until 1929, but at the time he was extremely confident. Once again, he thought, as he had with *The Lucky One* and with *Success*, that he had written his best play yet. After *Ariadne* he had vowed, as so often, never to go through the whole dreadful process again. But when it came to the point he could not resist it. The theatre had him in thrall. As usual, it was to Swinnerton that he wrote his most exuberantly optimistic letter: 'You may like to know, as the eventual publisher of it, that I have just finished the world's greatest play, somewhat in the Shakespearean style' – by which he meant it was 'a costume play of twenty characters and lots of scenes'. To Turley he wrote: 'I don't suppose anybody will do it.'

It was finished by December and he tried to forget about it (as we shall) for the next two years. These were two years in which – for the first time for many years – there were no Milne plays on in London or New York. But the book which was to make far more impact than any play and even than the children's poems, was – though it seemed impossible at the time – not far off. Christopher's bedtime stories consisted largely of the stuff of fairy tales – dragons and knights, giants and princesses and so on. Milne knew, as most parents do, that it is no good making things too exciting at bedtime.

In fact, the more boring the story is, the more quickly the child goes to sleep. Nameless knights and indistinguishable princesses did the usual sort of things – 'a completely contemptible mix-up' Milne called it. But occasionally there was one story that was a little different. It was a story about the child's bear and a balloon and some bees. And the bear, as we have seen, had recently acquired his very unusual name – Winnie-the-Pooh, that good name for a bear who had to blow flies off the end of his nose because his arms were too stiff to be useful.

Milne was much in the public eye at the end of 1925, as a result of the continually bestselling, continually reprinting *When We Were Very Young*. There was a large supplement to the Christmas *Bookman* – eight pages entirely devoted to Milne's life, his family and his work, with lots of compliments and lots of photographs. The writer concluded: 'If you look back at his early sketches, and over the lengthening line of his plays, you will feel that from the first to the latest, they are linked up and related to each other by a charm of personality which gives colour to them all ... The dominant note in everything he has written, for mature people or little folk, is a joy in all life and a spirit of youth that never survives in the foolish.' There was a photograph of Milne offering a toy penguin to a dubious three-year-old with the teddy bear standing on the sidelines; there was one by Marcus Adams of a rather cool five-year-old, 'Christopher Robin Milne, to whom *When We Were Very Young* is dedicated'; one of Shepard's illustration to 'Little Bo-Peep and the Little Boy Blue' 'from the original drawing which now hangs in the nursery of Christopher Robin' – and an extremely striking portrait of 'Mrs Milne' in profile, by E. O. Hoppé.

Milne wrote to Ken on the day that Daphne had been to the studio. She had been there with him once or twice before, and on her return said:

D.   I didn't know he was so French. He used not to be.
Me. Well, of course he has got an accent on the 'e'.
D.   Yes – well, it was very acute this morning.

Daphne was actually revelling in all the fuss. She wrote at the end of one of Alan's letters to Irene Vanbrugh: 'We are all very well and happy and pleased with each other and everything else!' Alan wrote to Ken:

There is a new paper (for 'Mothers') coming out next month with a special feature, 'Nurseries of the Highly Nourished' or some such title – anyway, Billy leads the way in the first number. He and his nursery were photographed all ways up, and Daff was interviewed, and explained how important it was to combine firmness with kindness, and I said nothing, and – well, get it. I wish I could remember the title for you.

Milne could not get away from his fame – and he did not really want to – even when that month he had to do four days' jury service. ('I 'ate the Law' was his only comment on the case.) The day before he had signed five hundred copies of *A Gallery of Children* – a limited edition in England. He was glad to have the hundred guineas for the signing, not because he needed it, but because it was certainly rankling that he had been so stupid in accepting the lump-sum payment from the American publisher. The day after the case he had to sign a hundred copies of a special edition of *The King's Breakfast*, and when the jury retired to consider its verdict a fellow jurywoman produced *Not That It Matters* – a collection of his essays that had just gone into a 'new popular edition' – and she asked him to sign that.

A few days later Christopher – still Billy – and Daphne were involved in a theatrical occasion. Milne wrote to Ken on 11 December:

Billy is being a Holy Innocent (with 20 other children and Gladys Cooper) at a matinée on Tuesday. At a sort of committee meeting, attended by parents of Innocents (Holy) to consider costumes, Daff said 'Oh, *no*!' in a loud voice from the back of the room when somebody suggested dark-grey flannelette (or whatever it was) – whereupon she was immediately elected Managing Director or Wardrobe Mistress of the whole scene. The result is that every ten minutes the telephone bell rings, and some anxious if aristocratic mother is heard imploring Mrs Milne to let her little darling wear blue. Two of them have already been here – '*any* time Mrs Milne would see me,' they say humbly to me – and throw themselves at Daff's feet. Even a father – the Colonel of the Grenadier Guards, no less – took up an insignificant position in the drawing-room, while Daff issued orders. What snobs parents are about their children!

As all the preparations for the matinée went ahead, Milne was racking his brains to think of a children's story for the Christmas number of the *Evening News*. Daphne, preoccupied with the Holy Innocents, assured him it was easy and that all he had to do was to write down 'any one of those bedtime stories'. Milne assured her it was not easy and that they weren't really stories at all – all that stuff about 'dragons and giants and magic rings'.

'Wasn't even *one* of them any good?' she pleaded. And then Milne remembered 'that there was just one which was a real story, about his bear'. He sat down and started writing:

This is Big Bear, coming downstairs now, bump-bump on the back of his head, behind Christopher Robin. It is, as far as he knows, the only way of coming downstairs, but sometimes he feels that there really is another way, if only he could stop bumping for a moment and think of it. And then he feels that perhaps there isn't. Anyhow, here he is at the bottom, and ready to be introduced to you. Winnie-the-pooh.

That was the first time he had written the words Winnie-the-pooh. (The 'p' is definitely small in the manuscript.) He went on writing until he got to the point where Christopher Robin asks, 'Is that the end of the story?'

'That's the end of the story.'
Christopher Robin gave a deep sigh, picked his bear up by the leg and walked off to the door, trailing Winnie-the-pooh behind him. At the door he turned and said,
  'Coming to see me have my bath?'
  'I might,' I said.
  'I didn't hurt him when I shot him, did I?'
  'Not a bit.'
He nodded and went out . . . and in a moment I heard Winnie-the-pooh – bump, bump, bump – going up the stairs behind him.

It was indeed a real story, with a beginning, a middle and an end. In the book, after Christopher asks, 'Is that the end of the story?' Milne says, 'That's the end of that one. There are others.' In December 1925 there weren't, but the first story 'became Chap I. The rest inevitably followed.'

Explaining all this he would say that he never wrote anything 'without thought of publication'. After all, he was a professional writer. He would also say that he was lazy, and needed 'somebody or something to set me off'. If Milne had not had such a keen sense of what would make a publishable story, it is easy to imagine (so great was his fame the *Evening News* would have printed anything) that the next children's book after *When We Were Very Young* might have been about yet more knights and 'dragons and giants and magic rings', rather than the entirely original adventures of one boy's bear. On Thursday 24 December 1925 the main news headline in the *Evening News*, stretching right across the front page of the paper, read A CHILDREN'S STORY BY A. A. MILNE and under,

in only slightly smaller letters, the two words CHRISTOPHER
ROBIN. And then:

Page 7 To-night – Tomorrow
Night's Broadcast
A new story for children
'Winnie-the-Pooh' about
Christopher Robin and his Teddy
Bear, written by Mr A. A. Milne
specially for the 'Evening News'
appears tonight on Page Seven.
It will be broadcast from all
stations by Mr Donald Calthrop,
as part of the Christmas Day
wireless programme, at 7.45 p.m.
tomorrow.

The headline was above and in far larger print than GREAT STORM
SWEEPS OVER DERBYSHIRE (White Christmas over two thirds of
Britain), LORD COBHAM'S MANSION ON FIRE, and WHITES'
DANGER IN TIENTSIN. On page 7 there was another enormous
banner headline right across the page, simply

WINNIE-THE-POOH.

The illustrations were not by Shepard, who had presumably been
too busy. He *had* managed to do a rather splendid version of Milne's
poem 'Binker', with a girl in the main role, which appeared the same
month in *Pears' Annual*. The *Evening News* illustrations for the story
were by J. H. Dowd. Winnie-the-Pooh, not yet looking quite himself,
had started his public life. He was on his way to becoming 'the most
famous and loved bear in literature'.

Winnie-the-Pooh

IN JANUARY 1926, Milne wrote to Ken with a long list of 'things which ought to be done'. They included:

1) A book of verses (about 15 done to date) to appear in 1927 or 1928, but they have to be done fairly soon, so as to be illustrated and then serialized (horrid word) in America. [This would be *Now We Are Six.*]

2) A book – at Daff's and Billy's special request – of Winnie-the-pooh. 2 done. The *Evening News* one, and one for *Eve* in February.

3) A book of short stories I want to get out some time. There are about 6 available and I want to do some others – am, in fact, in the middle of one now – grown-up ones, of course. [This would be *The Secret and other stories*, but it contained only four stories and appeared in 1929, in a limited edition only.]

4) Playfair thinks I'm doing a pantomime for the Lyric, Hammersmith next Christmas, but I think I'm not.

5) I *am* doing an introduction for a collected edition of *Saki* [*The Chronicles of Clovis*, 1928].

6) Proofs of *Four Plays* to correct.

It was not actually a very substantial or demanding list, at least not for someone with Milne's fluent pen. The manuscript of *Winnie-the-Pooh* does not really show how few changes he made because it was his practice to make a pencil draft, which was thrown away, before the surviving ink manuscript, but there is no doubt that he did write quickly and fluently, that the stories came easily. Eeyore, Piglet and, of course, Pooh, the toys already in the nursery, were at the heart of the book. He had invented Owl and Rabbit, and then he and Daphne had returned to the toy department at Harrods on a deliberate mission to acquire a new character or two. Kanga and Roo had looked the most promising candidates and duly inspired the seventh story. By March *Winnie-the-Pooh* was largely written.

None of the stories in *The Secret* were written after the date of the list. The proofs of *Four Plays* were swiftly returned, in time for

Chatto and Windus to publish on 15 April. There was no hurry about the Saki introduction or the further children's poems, and he remained reluctant to write anything for Playfair.

So it is no wonder that he had plenty of time to involve himself in the whole business of the illustration, design, layout, production and finances of *Winnie-the-Pooh*. 'Milne's instructions were detailed, far more so than any Kipper had received from other authors,' said Rawle Knox. 'Kipper' was Shepard's nickname, but Milne never used it. They were still not at all close. 'I always had to start again at the beginning with Milne every time I met him, I think he retired into himself – very often and for long periods,' Shepard said much later, but the letters suggest Milne was not at all withdrawn at this point. He often pressed Shepard for meetings.

Shepard had always worked from models – 'The idea of working without models never occurred to him.' Milne knew this and was anxious, in March 1926, that the artist should come to Mallord Street and meet the toys. 'I think you must come here on Thursday, if only to get Pooh's and Piglet's likeness.' But he wanted Piglet small 'as you will see when you read the sixth story' – that is the one where Piglet is too small to reach the knocker. In the original sketch, in the *Royal Magazine*, Piglet is shown in mid-air, jumping up and down. For the book, Shepard provided a convenient flowerpot. In fact it was even more important that Piglet should be small for the seventh story – the rather disquieting story where Kanga and Roo are not welcomed to the Forest, and Piglet impersonates the kidnapped joey and jumps into Kanga's pocket in his place. 'It is hard to be brave when you're only a Very Small Animal,' says Piglet, and Rabbit responds, 'It is because you are a very small animal that you will be Useful in the adventure before us.'

The trouble was that, in 'real life', Christopher Robin's original Piglet was almost as big as Pooh; he came up to his shoulder anyway. Not at all the right shape or size for that adventure. As for Pooh, Milne wrote (sending four of the stories 'so that you can get an idea of them at once'): 'I want you to see Billy's Bear. He has such a nice expression.' But Shepard had been drawing teddy bears for years, based on his son Graham's Growler, that magnificent bear, and he was really not inclined to change now. Growler was there already, anyway, in *When We Were Very Young*, not only as himself in 'Teddy Bear', but clearly identified as Christopher Robin's own bear, on his bed in the last picture in the book.

Shepard would even go so far as to say (after Milne's death and, indeed, after the death of his own son) that he used Graham as the model for the child: 'Christopher Robin's legs were too skinny. So I decided to draw my own son, Graham, who was a sturdy little boy. Otherwise I was a stickler for accuracy. All the illustrations of Christopher Robin and Pooh and Piglet and the other animals were drawn exactly where Milne had visualized them – usually in Ashdown Forest.' It was a natural enough claim for Shepard to make in his extreme old age. But Graham was eighteen at the time of *Winnie-the-Pooh*, and indeed anyone who has seen the juxtaposition in Christopher Milne's own memoirs of the 'butterfly photo' and one of Shepard's drawings would find it difficult to give much credence to Shepard's claim. Christopher's real legs look quite as sturdy as in the drawings, and Christopher himself would say, 'It is true that he used his imagination when he drew the animals but me he drew from life. I did indeed look just like that.' The clothes, the hairstyle – that was just how they were, his mother's ideas carried out by Nanny, who made the smocks and shorts and cut (rather rarely) his hair.

John Macrae of Dutton's, Milne's American publisher, claimed to have been in the room, presumably in March 1926, when the partnership was in action.

During the process of bringing *Winnie-the-Pooh* into existence, I happened to be present at one of the meetings of Milne and Shepard – Milne sitting on the sofa reading the story, Christopher Robin sitting on the floor playing with the characters, which are now famous in *Winnie-the-Pooh*, and, by his side, on the floor, sat E. H. Shepard making sketches for the illustrations which finally went into the book . . . Christopher Robin, the true inspiration of these four books to both the author and the artist, was entirely unconscious of his part in the drama.

This sounds a little too neat, a little too good to be true, but it is accurate enough to what we know (Shepard did sketch the animals in pencil from what Milne called 'the living model') and was written only nine years after the event.

Milne's own view of his American publisher was rather more astringent. 'He is an old man with a beard, and he calls me "Sir" all the time. Not "Yes, *sir*" *à la Americaine*, but "Yessir", like a Boy Scout. Very trying. He is always bowing to me, and telling me how I go straight to the hearts of the people.' After all, there had never been anything quite like *When We Were Very Young*. 'I also go straight to the heart of his banker, I should imagine,' Milne wrote to Ken.

In the spring of 1926 Shepard was having to work against the clock, as the *Royal Magazine* had taken six of the stories, needed to go to press, according to Milne, 'months in advance' and was naturally anxious all the stories would appear before the book was published in October. At one stage, Miss Pearn, in the magazine department at Curtis Brown, wrote to Milne 'Will you be so kind as to pass this SOS on to Mr Shepard' and three days later wrote to Shepard to say, 'Mr Milne has asked us to communicate direct with you in future in connection with the Winnie-the-Pooh drawings.' In April Shepard was in Rapallo and the *Royal Magazine* was getting a bit nervous about timing. 'I am relieved to hear that you are now at work,' Miss Pearn wrote.

Milne seemed to be acting as a financial middleman, as well as being closely concerned in the content of the illustrations. 'They were going to pay you £12.10 a story' (that was for one large and four to six small drawings). 'I have told C.B. to try and raise them, as I didn't think you would be satisfied with this; but in a way it is all extra, and I hope we shall get much more from America. The trouble is there is so little time.'

Dutton's were very anxious to get the original two – Bees and Rabbit – out as soon as possible for their salesmen to take round to the bookshops. Frederick Muller at Methuen agreed to get those two stories (which had already appeared in the *Evening News* and *Eve*) 'set up in galley proof ... then we had all three better meet and try to arrange the make-up of it' – that is Muller, Milne, Shepard. At the *Royal Magazine* they were making up the pages for their first story, actually the fourth in the book, called at that stage: 'Winnie-the-Pooh finds a Tail'. In the magazine it was squashed into only four and a half pages, with Shepard providing thirteen pictures altogether, including nine of Eeyore in various odd positions – rather than the six or seven Milne had suggested would be called for. In the book itself, 'In which Eeyore loses a tail and Pooh finds one' takes up twelve pages. On 24 March Daphne was able to write to Shepard (as A. A. Milne *pp* D. M. – having abandoned a fictitious 'Celia Brice', at least as far as Shepard was concerned) to tell him that 'the *Royal* has gone up to 15 guineas'.

It was Milne's idea that Shepard should have a share of his royalties this time, recognizing his permanent share in the books. It was extremely unusual for an illustrator at this period. The agreed proportion seems to have been Milne's own suggestion. The contracts remained primarily between Milne and the publishers, with subsidiary agreements made between Milne and Shepard. The contract for *Winnie-the-Pooh*, signed on 15 March 1926, said 'that the publishers agree to publish the said work with illustrations by E. H. Shepard, to be provided by the author without cost to the publishers'. The contract for *When We Were Very Young* (10 April 1924) had said the publishers agreed the book should be 'suitably illustrated at their own expense'. The two further children's books would follow the pattern for *Pooh* – and when the rights to reproduce Shepard's drawings as toys, wallpaper and so on were granted in both England and America, again it was 'by agreement with the author'. The characters, both Christopher Robin and the toys themselves, adapted by Shepard from the reality, and Owl and Rabbit imagined by Shepard from Milne's invention, were never, in any sense, Shepard's property.

Milne wrote to Shepard:

Brown has drawn up the agreements with Dutton and Methuen for *Winnie-the-Pooh*. In them you get £200 on account from M. and £100 from D. (less commission) – i.e. you get £270 anyway, if not a single copy is sold. Which is better than *When We Were Very Young*, for, I should imagine, fewer drawings. As regards royalties Dutton and Methuen were prepared to pay 20% and 25% (i.e. 4% and 5% for you) but protested that it wouldn't leave them much margin for advertisement. So now D. pays 15% to 5000, and then 20%, and Methuen pays 20% to 10,000, 22½% to 15,000 and then 25%. If it is the success we hope and expect it to be, we ought to do at least 50,000 in England and 100,000 in America – in fact there is really no limit to what we might do, and the sales will go on for a long time.

A little later, when presumably the advance had been increased, Milne wrote to Ken:

Shepard and I are having a joint agreement, dividing in the proportion of 80 to 20. Actually he did all the WWWVY illustrations for £200, and as on this book we are getting £1000 in advance from England and £1000 from America, he gets £400 straight off. And, of course, should eventually get much more. But when I told Daff of the suggested division, 80% to me, 20% to him, she said, 'I am sure you make it sound all right to him, but it will want a lot of explaining to *Mrs* Shepard.'

The two women had met when the whole Shepard family went down to Cotchford for the day to give the artist a chance to sketch and explore the actual setting of the book, 'all the spots where the things happened'. If Milne seemed reticent and rather stiff in Mallord Street, it was not so in Sussex that spring. 'He was a different man,' Shepard remembered many years later. 'He was quite different, going over the ground and showing me the places.' Milne had, in fact, had only just a year to get to know Ashdown Forest, but he already loved it, and as he wrote the stories, though the landscape is hardly mentioned, they are set firmly in a real place under a real sky.

Another good writer, Barbara Willard, who lives on the edge of the Forest and has used the place in her own books, said to me that the Pooh books, 'could just as well have been set on Hampstead Heath', but the stories have a much more rural feeling than that suggests and the illustrations are still recognizably of the Sussex background Milne showed to Shepard more than sixty years ago. The October 1987 hurricane did terrible damage in the Forest and devastated the wood the Milnes planted in the field along the lane from their house – but Gills Lap is still recognizable as 'the enchanted place on the very top of the Forest' though many of the pines have lost their tops and there is now some undergrowth and not quite so much of the 'close-set grass, quiet and smooth and green', where you can sit down carelessly like Pooh.

Milne and Shepard walked up to Gills Lap across open country that is more heathland than forest, over dry golden grass, between bent dead bracken (with no sign yet of the new season's growth), tangled gorse and heather. They saw, as Pooh and Christopher Robin did, 'the whole world spread out until it reached the sky'. Now, in a secluded spot, a 'warm and sunny spot', if it's that sort of day, you can find, if you look hard enough, a memorial to the two men, writer and artist.

On that spring day they walked down the hill to the river in the valley and saw under the trees in Posingford Wood clumps of yellow primroses, sheets of white anemones ('like driven snow against the trees'), patches of bluebells and the buds of marsh marigolds just beginning to show a little gold. They crossed the wooden bridge and returned along the lane in time for tea. Mary, Shepard's daughter, would remember Christopher Robin's delight when Graham her big brother (soon to go up to Oxford), played with the child in the stream, 'with an old log floating there that became a battleship, an alligator . . .' She thought Christopher Robin reacted as one who had never known 'anyone older than himself actually *playing* games with him'. In fact, the only child spent a good deal of time playing what he called 'dog games' with his father – running after balls, hitting balls, catching balls – but there were also messier, less structured games: scooping mud and scum and weed from the stream, looking for lost golf balls, and landing instead grass snakes and nobbly newts. He had a number of companions nearer his own age too – Anne Darlington, when she was visiting, as she did very often; Brenda Tasker, the gardener's daughter, who would remember building huts out of bracken, playing cricket and riding Jessica, the donkey; and Hannah, who lived only half a mile away, and was good at climbing trees. It was in the apple orchard up the lane – full of excellent trees for climbing – that Roo was lost and never found again. Olive Brockwell remembered the heartache of that search all her life.

Part of the strength and charm of the stories comes from the juxtaposition of toy animal and forest. Milne writes something simple, such as Pooh was 'walking through the forest one day, humming proudly to himself', and Shepard shows a jaunty toy bear walking through real Ashdown Forest over real rough grass with real trees in the background; or Milne writes: 'One fine winter's day when Piglet was brushing away the snow in front of his house', and Shepard shows a diminutive toy piglet making a tiny path with a tiny broom away from the trunk of a fine beech tree. Trees dominate the books. Rabbit lives in a burrow, which has some relationship to Badger's house in the middle of the Wild Wood (but there are no stoats and weasels, no cudgels or pistols in Milne's forest); nearly everyone else lives in trees, including Christopher Robin himself.

It had all started in a tree in the garden at Cotchford – an ancient walnut tree (now long gone). 'The tree was hollow inside and a great gash in its trunk had opened up to make a door.' It was the perfect tree-house for a five-year-old. 'There was plenty of room for a boy and his bear.' They could sit on the soft crumbly floor and see, high above them, 'a green and blue ceiling of leaves and sky'. And even if Nanny could hear him if he called, it was a sort of independence and he was getting more adventurous every day. Christopher would recall: 'So if anyone wonders why in the stories so much time seems to be spent in trees or up trees, the answer is that this, in real life, was how it was.' Milne wrote in 1927, just after Christopher's seventh birthday: 'At the moment he is mad on tree-climbing, which he really does rather well and pluckily, even after doing the last eight feet (downwards) on his head the other day.' This is the sort of boy behind the stories, not the long-ago kneeling child with the little gold head.

There have been critics who have found Christopher Robin, even in the *Pooh* books, a stumbling block to their full enjoyment. 'Was there ever a more insufferable child than Christopher Robin?' wrote the critic Chris Powling on the sixtieth birthday of the book. Like Geoffrey Grigson on the poems, again he seems to let sociology and class-consciousness get in the way.

Every inch of him exudes smugness – from the top of that curious, bobbed haircut to the tip of those tiny-tot sandals (and the smock and shorts in between are just as irritating). Okay, so we shouldn't take him at face value. Maybe there *is* deep irony in this twentieth-century version of the Victorian Beautiful Child. In Christopher Robin's case, however, we must certainly heed the wise advice of Oscar Wilde that it's only a superficial person who does *not* judge by appearances. With Milne's prose [his 'sheer literary craftsmanship'] reinforced by E. H. Shepard's superb line-drawings, Christopher Robin must surely be what he seems. And what he seems is a serious affront to anyone who believes children are simply people who haven't lived very long.

Powling, in fact, comes round to knowing that the stories can survive even the 'insufferable' too-perfect child:

The permanence of the Pooh books has nothing whatever to do with their psychological depth or the sharpness of their social comment or their status as morality. These don't matter a jot. What's important, through and through, is their success as storytelling. And this is a triumph. It survives shifts in fashion. It survives Christopher Robin. It even survives that odd tone-of-voice which, for all Milne's simple language, never quite settles for a child audience. The world Pooh creates is completely unique and utterly self-sustaining. Yes, it is a world that's very like ours . . . but much, much more like itself.

That phrase 'the world Pooh creates' seems at first like a slip. Didn't he really mean to say 'the world Milne creates' or 'the world of Pooh . . .'? In fact, it gives us the clue why Christopher Robin is the way he is – too perfect, flawless, *not* falling out of trees. It is because he is seen in relation to Pooh and the other animals. Pooh and Piglet are the children and the boy himself takes on the role of the adult. The listening or reading child identifies with the superior strength and power he sometimes resents in the adults around him, however much he loves his parents. Christopher Robin is always resourceful and competent; he is the child as hero. In 'the world Pooh creates' it is Christopher Robin who reads sustaining books at moments of crisis, who comes to the rescue, who will make sure that no harm comes to the kidnapped Roo (whatever befell him in real life) and protects the animals from the teeth of fierce things. ('If Christopher Robin is coming, I don't mind anything.') He dries Eeyore's tail after its immersion in the river (having nailed it on on a previous occasion) and does all the comforting and useful things that parents do. The boy is brave and godlike to the toys, just as the loving parent is to a small child. It is absolutely beside the point to criticize him for being too good to be true.

Just occasionally, as any adult does too, Christopher Robin reveals his frailty, his feet of clay, and this surely adds to his appeal. He has forgotten what the North Pole looks like. ('I did know once . . .') It is Pooh who is childlike, egotistical, hungry, alternately boastful and self-deprecating, occasionally managing to be brave and unselfish, accepting things without really understanding them, as children so often have to accept ununderstandable explanations. The listening or reading child recognizes himself in Pooh and recognizes himself as he longs to be, as he thinks he *will* be, in Christopher Robin. He recognizes and enjoys the wit and tenderness of the books.

But after *The Pooh Perplex*, Frederick Crews' 1963 parody of a student casebook, one cannot attempt the most rudimentary criticism without seeming to be joking. After 'The Hierarchy of Heroism in *Winnie-the-Pooh*' and 'A la recherche du Pooh perdu' (*Weltschmerz*, alienation and the rest) one's pen freezes in one's hand. Perhaps, with all that chasing after honey, the books explore the universality of the sexual urge or the bestiality of the free market? Perhaps the great Heffalump expedition really is a paradigm of colonialism? Eeyore is certainly the archetypal outsider, if not the spokesman for the disillusioned post-war generation of the 1920s. 'There is something a little frightening about *The Pooh Perplex*', as Benedict Nightingale wrote in a review. You begin to wonder if those invented critics may not have something after all, underneath their ludicrous jargon.

As Alison Lurie put it, Crews managed 'to stifle almost all critical comment on *Winnie-the-Pooh* for a decade'. She felt she was, in 1972, merely following up one of the suggestions made by 'Smedley Force', a prominent member of the Modern Language Association of America, who was struck by 'the paucity of biographical connections between *Winnie-the-Pooh* and the lives of A. A. Milne, "Christopher Robin", and the historical personages who probably lie behind the fictional portraits of "Pooh", "Piglet", "Kanga" *et alia*.' Lurie makes the suggestion that Pooh's relation to Piglet is much like that of Milne's older brother, Ken, to Milne himself. She sees something of J. V. Milne in Owl and something of Milne's mother Maria in, not Kanga, but Rabbit. She points out, as many others have done, that we all know people like Tigger, like Eeyore, like Kanga. Humphrey Carpenter suggests, 'Don't we, indeed, recognize them in ourselves?' He saw that Milne makes it possible for a child 'to carry into adult life a perception of human character acquired from his readings' of the Pooh books. If Milne sets out to depict only a very small fraction of human behaviour, 'he manages to do so completely within a child's understanding; the Pooh books can be taken in fully by all but the smallest children.' And yet the adult reading aloud is not bored. It is an extraordinary achievement.

Richard Adams has suggested that Eeyore is 'the first portrait in English literature of a type of neurotic we all know only too well' – though he may owe a little to Dickens's poor Mrs Gummidge in *David Copperfield*, 'the lone lorn creetur', who did not appear to be able to cheer up, drowned in self-pity as she was. 'My trouble has made me contrary,' she said, and Eeyore's troubles make him contrary too, but Milne makes self-pity far funnier and more lovable. Eeyore has moments of happiness which save him from being a caricature – for instance, when his tail is restored and when he puts his burst birthday balloon into his useful pot. Adams says it was from the Pooh books that he learnt for *Watership Down* (one of the few comparable best sellers, at least in the initial years) 'the vital importance, as protagonists, of a group of clearly portrayed, contrasting but reciprocal characters', though he does not claim that his rabbits come anywhere near Pooh and his friends.

There have been many different reasons given for the enduring appeal of the books. It has been suggested it is because they are stories of 'universal perplexity', that we are all bears of very little brain trying as Pooh does to bluff our way through life. 'Hardly anybody knows if those are these or these are those.' And as Pooh can be a brave and clever bear, we feel we could be too, if only life would give us the chance. If the critic John Rowe Townsend, realizing 'how very good they are', considers the stories 'as totally without hidden significance as anything ever written', another critic, Peter Hunt, responds by saying that they are 'still the complex work of a complex man, and they include a fascinating series of subtexts that can tell us a lot about the relationships of child, adult, story and book.' It is 'sophisticated writing, the pace, the timing, and the narrative stance all contributing to the comic effect'.

Alison Lurie suggests it is because Milne 'created out of a few acres of Sussex countryside, a world that has the qualities both of the Golden Age of history and legend, and the lost paradise of childhood – two eras which, according to psychologists, are often one in the unconscious mind'. The small adventures are concerned entirely with the things children are most interested in – friends, food, birthdays, tree-houses and expeditions, jokes and songs. They are concerned, as children are, with courage that comes and goes. There is no economic necessity or competition. The dangers are all natural ones – bees, heffalumps (possibly), bad weather – and what is celebrated is community, the spirit of co-operation and kindness, most clearly seen in *Winnie-the-Pooh* when Christopher Robin and Pooh rescue Piglet when he is entirely surrounded by water.

Humphrey Carpenter has pointed out that Milne's humour is that of a mathematician. 'Each humorous situation in the Pooh books is reached by the logical pursuit of an idea to the point of absurdity.' Milne's pleasure is in playing with words. Carpenter suggests he 'handles words in the kind of detached manner in which a mathematician deals with figures' but, in fact, there is plenty of emotion in the Forest. If Christopher Robin is godlike, he is certainly the god of love. The feminist critic, Carol Stanger, sees that the stories appeal because 'they respect what is traditionally given low status in patriarchal society, nurturing and emotion'. They reflect a pre-sexual, pre-literate world that is kinder and more attractive than the world as it is; and even critics who say – like Roger Sale and Margery Fisher – that they can no longer enjoy the stories as much as they did as children, or as much as college students often do today, none the less find themselves still moved by the thought of their own vanished Pooh-reading childhoods.

In July, three months before the book was published, someone was already after the manuscript. Milne wrote to E. V. Lucas: 'If I give a price now, I say £350. If the book is a complete failure, this may be reduced to 2/9; on the other hand, it may go up to £500 ... I wouldn't give £350 for anybody's manuscript ... But I don't want to make the mistake I made with the verse.' In fact, he never did sell the manuscripts of *Winnie-the-Pooh* or its sequel, and in his will instructed his trustees, after the death of his wife, to offer the two

manuscripts to the library of Trinity College, Cambridge as a gift.
And that is where they are now.

Winnie-the-Pooh was dedicated to Daphne in one of those almost
embarrassingly open gestures which seem so strange from a man
whose son would say 'My father's heart remained buttoned up all
through his life'.

TO HER

HAND IN HAND WE COME
CHRISTOPHER ROBIN AND I
TO LAY THIS BOOK IN YOUR LAP.
SAY YOU'RE SURPRISED?
SAY YOU LIKE IT?
SAY IT'S JUST WHAT YOU WANTED?
BECAUSE IT'S YOURS
BECAUSE WE LOVE YOU.

Here it seems that Alan Milne is wearing his heart on his sleeve – a
necessary gesture, perhaps, when the child's mother has been so
totally excluded from both the books for children. Nanny was in the
first, *When We Were Very Young*, over and over again, and so was
Milne himself – Shepard actually drew him (with cap and pipe) in
'Sand-between-the-toes'. All Daphne got was 'God bless Mummy'
and a possible (undesirable) association with the disappearing mother
of James James Morrison Morrison. Long afterwards, Ronald Bryden
in the *Spectator* looked at the poems and decided that whether the
mother's absences 'betoken drink, drugs, insanity or infidelity, the
child has obviously been driven by some emotional deprivation into
a life of lonely fantasy, inventing a series of imaginary playmates':
Binker, mice, beetles, even raindrops – quite apart from the toys
themselves. The mother has surely failed in her role. Now in *Pooh* the
conversations between the boy and his father make the framework of
the book, and there is no room at all for the mother.

A copy of the book would later carry Milne's inscription:

When I am gone
Let Shepard decorate my tomb
And put (if there is room)
Two pictures on the stone:
Piglet, from page a hundred and eleven
And Pooh and Piglet walking (157) . . .
And Peter, thinking that they are my own,
Will welcome me to heaven.

That is Piglet 'blowing happily at a dandelion and wondering whether it would be this year, next year, some time or never', whatever 'it' was; and Pooh and Piglet (Pooh clasping his special pencil case, so like Christopher Robin's real one) walking thoughtfully home together in the golden evening, at the very end of the book.

In the spring of 1926 the *Evening News* had carried an article by Milne, lamenting the attitude to writers of the British Broadcasting Company, formed three and a half years before. Milne wrote to Ken, sending him his play *The Ivory Door* to read:

I also send the *Evening News:* sorry you don't read it, nor live in London where the whole metropolis is placarded on these occasions with my name, practically life-size. On second thoughts, I think perhaps you're lucky . . . I called it 'Authors and the B.B.C. by an author' and asked for 10 guineas, to which they said promptly '15, if you sign it'. Did I hesitate? Not for a moment.

It seems worth giving most of the article here for, if the BBC has, in over sixty years, improved its attitude and payments, the general feeling about writers seems to have stayed much the same.

Complaint was made in *The Evening News* a few days ago that the programmes of the B.B.C. were of a much lower standard on the literary side than on the musical side. I should like to suggest, from the author's point of view, some reasons why this is so.

Authors have never been taken very seriously by their fellow-men. 'A singer is a singer,' the attitude seems to be, 'a painter is a painter, and a sculptor sculpts; but, dash it all, a writer only writes, which is a thing we all do every day of our lives, and the only difference between ourselves and Thomas Hardy is that Hardy doesn't do anything else, whereas we are busy men with a job of real work to do.' And since writing is, in a sense, the hobby, or at least the spare-time occupation of the whole world, it has become natural for the layman to regard the professional author as also engaged merely upon a hobby, the results of which, in accordance with the well-known vanity of the hobbyist, are free for the inspection of anyone kindly enough to take an interest in them.

For instance, you who read this would not think of asking a wine merchant, whose nephew had been at the same school as your son, for a free dozen of champagne on the strength of that slight connection; but you would not hesitate to ask an author, similarly connected, for a free article for some ephemeral publication in which you were interested, or for permission to perform his play without the usual payment of royalty. Indeed, you would feel that you would be paying him the same sort of compliment that I should be paying you if, dining, at your house, I asked to see the fretwork soap-dish in your bathroom. 'Oh, are you really interested?' you would say. 'Fancy your having heard about it! How awfully nice of you!' But this is not what the author says.

Now the B.B.C. exploits to its highest power this attitude of kindly condescension to the author. To the B.B.C. all authors are the same author. There is a 'regular fee' for the author, whoever he is; the fee is what advertisers call 'nominal'; and with any luck the B.B.C. can avoid paying even this ridiculous amount by an ingenious scheme of its own. It says to the author, 'If we pay you a fee, we won't mention your name or your works or your publishers or anything about you, but if you will let us do it for nothing we will announce to our thousand million book-buying listeners where your work is to be bought. And if you don't like it, you can leave it, because there are plenty of other authors about; and, if it came to the worst, we could write the things ourselves quite easily.'

Now imagine if other concerns behaved like this. Suppose, for instance, that Mr John Galsworthy wrote an article in *The Evening News*. Would *The Evening News* (with certainly as many readers as, on any one night, the B.B.C. has listeners) say to Mr Galsworthy: 'Well, if we give your name and tell our readers who you are, of course you can't expect to be paid'? Would the Editor ask Thomas Hardy for a free poem on the ground that it was a good advertisement for him? Does a Theatre Manager tell a young dramatist that he mustn't expect a royalty on his first play, as it will undoubtedly help to sell his second? Of course not.

But the B.B.C. is obsessed by the thought of advertisement. Publicity might never have been heard of until the B.B.C. was born. After all, if the B.B.C. says to the author, 'I shan't pay you, because I'm helping your books to sell,' why on earth shouldn't the publisher also say to the author, 'And *I* shan't pay you, because I'm helping you to get taken up by the B.B.C.'? Why should the Broadcasting Company be the one, and the only one, not to pay?

I suggest, then, that the reason why the literary standard of the B.B.C. is low is simply that the Company has made no effort to attract authors, and is entirely out of touch and sympathy with authors. Let me give an example or two from my own experience.

(1) I was offered two guineas to read one act of one of my own plays. Whether this was an attractive proposition for listeners-in is not for me to say, but how could anyone think that it was an attractive proposition for the author? Let anybody consider what, in the way of preparation and performance, the author would have to go through, and ask himself if the offer was likely to be accepted.

(2) On a very special 'Gala Night' I was asked to read something of my own during the Children's Hour. I was offered five guineas, and it was explained to me apologetically that the Children's Hour had to be run cheaply. (As if that was any reason why I should help the B.B.C. to run it cheaply!) I replied that I didn't want to read my work aloud. An Editor, a Manager, a Publisher, would then automatically have said, 'Would you do it for *ten* guineas?' or 'What *would* you do it for?' – or something of

that sort. The B.B.C. voice at the other end of the telephone said in heart-rending accents, 'Not even for the sake of the Little Ones?'

(3) I was asked, in common with, I think, every known dramatist from the highest downwards, if I would write an original one-act play for the Company. I said that, apart from anything else, it would be impossible for the B.B.C. to pay a fee at all comparable with the royalties one might expect from a stage-play, and that, in this case, such a fee would be necessary, seeing that there were no subsidiary stage-rights to be got from a play specially written for listeners only. I was told proudly in reply that, indeed and on the contrary whatever, they were prepared to pay as much as fifty pounds! Now what on earth do they think Shaw has made from 'How He Lied to Her Husband', or Barrie from 'The Twelve Pound Look', or, for that matter, Gertrude Jennings from 'Five Birds in a Cage'? Fifty pounds!

(4) And finally a letter from America; for indeed the Broadcasting Manner knows no frontiers. But in this case there is a difference. An author, to the American B.C., is, at any rate, an individual. In a letter to my agent the A.B.C. says lyrical things about me, such as the B.B.C. never felt about any author. *Why* can't they broadcast my plays – those lovely, adorable things? What can they do to persuade me? Are tears, prayers, quotations from Ella Wheeler Wilcox, letters of introduction from the President, alike useless? 'What is the next step we can take? What is there I should do?' It is a cry from the heart.

And then, suddenly an inspiration occurs to him. Can it be? Absurd! Still – you never know. Just worth trying, perhaps. So he tries.

'Is it a question of royalty? *You have but to say the word if that is what is holding him back.*'

Yes, it was. Fancy! An author wanting money, just as if he were a real worker! What on earth does the fellow do for it?

Milne was much in demand. A film producer telephoned to ask if he could come and film the author at work: 'Entering the Library after Kissing Wife Farewell – Deep in Thought – Interrupted by Prattling Child – Takes Child on Knee and Pats Head of Same – Sudden Inspiration – Throws Child Away and Seizes Pen – Writes – Fade Out.' Milne said he did not think it was much of an idea, whereupon the producer, almost like the BBC, brought up the educational effect, if not on the Little Ones, then certainly on the Lower Classes. ('Like you and Maud,' Milne said, describing the conversation to Ken.) The producer then brought out his most compelling argument: 'In fact, Mr Milne, I assure you that I would sooner – you will hardly credit this but it is true – I would sooner film a really great artistic genius than an Earl.' To clinch the matter he then added that he had already got Gilbert Frankau. And Milne rang off.

Milne also refused the blandishments of an envoy of Pears' Soap. They had had a tremendous success years earlier when they had bought Sir John Millais' Academy painting *Bubbles* and, inserting a cake of soap into it, had created the most widely known advertisement in the world. Now they wanted Milne to follow his contribution to the previous year's *Christmas Annual* with a story actually tailor-made to their product. They had dined and wined him in a private room in the Ritz with the other distinguished contributors to the *Annual* (E. V. Lucas and Heath Robinson among them). Might not this have softened him up for what they really wanted – a children's story about soap bubbles? Clara Hawkins, who had edited the *Annual*, recorded her visit to Mallord Street, which she apparently thought to be a great deal older than it really was.

A. A. Milne lives in Chelsea, and there I went upon appointment. The houses of Chelsea are old and gracious of manner; with the classic red brick and white paint austerity of their Georgian origin relieved by brilliant doors of primary reds or blues or yellows – the happy inspiration of their present day bohemian owners. Mr Milne's doorway was a brilliant blue. There was a little stoop in front of it where I stood for one moment to catch my breath. I rang. A maid admitted me and led me into a grey, orange-curtained little room that was austere and cold. I was glad I had an appointment. This little room had an atmosphere forbidding to autograph hunters or timid maiden writers seeking comfort.

At last the maid returned and led me down a little hallway to a room at the end, the door of which she opened, at the same time announcing 'Miss Hawkins'. Inside the room there was a bluish haze of nice-smelling pipe smoke, and inside the smoke there was a lean, pleasant young man. He got up lazily as if he were a little tired after a long tramp on the moors. That was my impression of him – tweeds, dogs, gorse, and a pipe. As a matter of fact I don't believe he is especially any of these things; I just thought of them as he stood up to shake my hand . . . [Later he said] 'Are you interested in houses?'

I answered, 'I have been envying you this one ever since you have been talking to me.'

He looked pleased and said, 'It really is a nice one isn't it? Would you like to see it? It's rather a hobby of my wife's and mine.'

I followed him up the stairs, little winding stairs that led a charming way up to the second floor. He opened a door and out came a shower of golden light. We entered the drawing-room. It was a perfect little room, with Georgian panels and original cornices and a fireplace in the manner of William Kent. The whole of it had been painted a brilliant glowing yellow, with the mouldings picked out in gold. On the walls, in the centre of each panel, there were pictures that were great blobs of red and yellow and orange done in the modern manner and extraordinarily effective. The room was a burning sun in the middle of grey and sober London! Milne looked at me and I nodded my head.

'You like it?' he said. 'Now come and see my wife's room.'

Down a narrow passage we went, through a door, and again gold flooded out upon us. Only gold this time with a glowing rose-colour mellowing it. There was a great Italian four-poster, painted Italian chairs. It was a curious combination of modernity and ancient grace, very well done.

'My wife rather goes in for this sort of thing,' he said. We returned to his study.

'You're an American,' he said. 'Of course you must be, else you wouldn't have been so interested in my house.' And then abruptly he turned to me:

'You want me to write about soap bubbles, do you, as an advertisement?'

'For children, Mr Milne,' I said pleadingly.

But Milne was not to be persuaded – 'not even for the sake of the Little Ones'. No money was mentioned, and Miss Hawkins had to be content with the promise of another contribution to *Pears' Annual*. She left 'glowing because he was so nice. I had absolutely forgotten that he hadn't done a thing I'd asked him to do.'

Milne was also approached by the makers of Wolsey children's underwear. 'The story would of course be left entirely to Mr Milne, subject only to there being included in it some, so to speak, fatherly remarks upon the warmth and wisdom of children being under-clothed in wool.' But Milne was no more inclined to promote underwear than soap.

Christopher Robin had made a fleeting appearance during Miss Hawkins's visit – sucking his thumb and sitting on the stairs. Miss Hawkins had seen him as the three-year-old she had wanted to see, but in fact he was a schoolboy now. He had started at Miss Walters' School in Tite Street, in Chelsea. He went with Anne Darlington and the daughters of another neighbour, who had also become a friend – Denis Mackail, grandson of Burne-Jones, brother of Angela Thirkell, whose mother's first cousins included Stanley Baldwin and Rudyard Kipling. Milne had written to him after *Greenery Street* – they had met long ago at that Downe House cricket match – and found him decidedly interesting as a person, with his 'special fits of depression', his 'special brand of nightmares' and his occasional 'flickers of sunshine', as he tried to support with his pen an extravagant household in another Chelsea house. They had a lot of friends in common – J. M. Barrie (Mackail would write his first biography), P. G. Wodehouse, 'Ian Hay', the Darlingtons. The new friendship survived a disastrous first lunch party. Mackail wrote:

It was as near a complete failure as anything could well be. I was desperately shy, but so was my host. Moreover the Milnes had a refectory table in those days, which when four people are seated at it means that two are much too close together, while the other two are much too far apart. Yet though I should like to blame the table entirely, I know that I was dull and tongue-tied and that Alan . . . must bitterly have regretted ever having posted his letter.

Later they would laugh at that first occasion as they dined with each other over and over again. (There was one particularly memorable evening in November 1927 when a taxi went through a wall on the other side of the road and no one heard it because they were all listening to Barrie – 'There was always considerable anxiety before-hand as to whether he were going to lift the whole party to glorious heights or plunge it into silence and gloom.') Milnes and Mackails went to theatres together ('Every outing concluded by our being deposited, in their bright blue car, at our own front door'), visited each other's country cottages in the summers and each other's children's parties at Christmas. Mary was a year older than Christopher Robin and Anne was two years younger than both Christopher and Anne Darlington. The Milne children's party was always an outing to the theatre, combined with some sort of splendid meal. Milne and Wodehouse together put Mackail up for the Garrick and, though Wodehouse resigned almost immediately afterwards ('I loathe clubs . . . I hated the Garrick more than any of them'), Mackail would often go in Milne's car for lunch in Garrick Street.

Milne described the Tite Street school in a letter to Ken in June 1926:

Billy loves his school, though I never quite know what he is doing. He brings home weird works of art from time to time, hand-painted pottery and what not, which has to be disposed of by Daff. They also teach him to catch. (This is really rather a good school.) Yesterday he bounced the ball on the ground and caught it with the right hand 20 times running, thus earning a penny from his gratified papa. He says he's done 10 times with the left hand, but not visibly.

The boy was also giving some thought to the future. One afternoon when Daphne and Nanny were both out, father and son had some serious talk on their own. 'Do parents and children understand each other better than they did?' an interviewer would ask A. A. Milne, who replied: 'I think they try more and they certainly should . . . But there is still a kind of shyness between the child and the parent.' On this occasion Milne told his son that when he was about ten he would go to a boarding school. The boy said, a little wistfully, 'Do

I ever come back to you after that?' They talked about careers too, and after the boy had rejected various suggestions the idea of elephant hunting came up. 'As long as I wasn't eaten,' he said, and then, after a moment's thought, 'Or trodden on.' ('I can't bear to think of him being trodden on by an elephant,' Milne wrote to Ken.) When he was grown up, Christopher said that he had never told anybody that it was an elephant, a real live elephant, that he had most wanted. What he had at Cotchford (on a count in 1927, when he was seven) were 'two bantams, two rabbits, several kittens, six snails, a lot of caterpillars and a horrible collection of beetles'.

Milne also reported a walk when he was beginning to get irritated because his son was continually lagging behind.

Me: Come on, Moon.
Moon: I'm just looking at something, Blue. [That was what Christopher normally called his father, as did many other people.]
Me (rather impatiently): Oh, do come on!
Moon (running up, terribly respectfully): Yes, father. Yes, father. Yes, father!
Which makes all parental sternness simply impossible.

Milne once said that he thought it impossible for anyone with a sense of humour to be a good father. 'The necessary assumption of authority and wisdom seems so ridiculous.' 'It is the old conflict of duty and affection, and correction is still a difficulty . . . Over and over again you hear the threat "If you do that again I'll punish you . . ." and, if he does it again, how can we help admiring his pluck, seeing how small he is and how big we are.'

Christopher, when adult, would have some interesting things to say about this; he thought that his father 'had inherited some of his own father's gifts as a teacher', but that he could never have been one himself. 'He could radiate enthusiasm, but he could never impose discipline.' His 'relationships were always between equals, however old or young, distinguished or undistinguished the other person'. Christopher remembered how, at about this time, his father had chided him gently for sitting at the lunch table, between mouthfuls, with his hands on the table, knife and fork pointing upwards. 'You oughtn't really to sit like that,' he said. 'Why not?' the boy asked, surprised.

'Well . . .' He hunted around for a reason he could give. Because it's con-sidered bad manners. Because you mustn't? Because . . .
'Well', he said, looking in the direction that my fork was pointing, 'sup-

pose somebody suddenly fell through the ceiling. They might land on your fork and that would be very painful.'

When the young Enid Blyton came to interview Milne for *Teacher's World* that October, just before the publication of *Pooh*, they naturally spoke of teachers and schools. Milne talked sympathetically of teachers who 'spend their days struggling in the poorer districts with terribly large classes'. And he couldn't resist showing off Christopher Robin's prowess with problems – exactly the same sort of problems John Vine Milne had set him nearly forty years before. 'He likes problems . . . there are 500 cows in a field. They go out of a gate at the rate of two a minute. How many are left after two and a half hours?' Miss Blyton did not reveal whether the six-year-old answered that one promptly, but she did say: 'Christopher Robin finds no difficulty with problems of this sort.' A similar problem would crop up two years later in the 'Contradiction' to *The House at Pooh Corner*.

The young mathematician that day seemed to be not quite sure whether he was a dragon or a knight. He stared at Enid Blyton fiercely and blew tremendously hard. He had paper tied round his legs and she asked why. 'So's dragons won't bite me.'

He carried an enormous Teddy Bear, which he informed me was Pooh. He stood there in his little brown overall, with his great shock of corn-coloured hair, and looked about the room seeking for what he might devour. His bright eyes fell upon his father's fountain-pen and he immediately took it up and pulled it into as many pieces as possible.

This sounds destructive, but fountain pens did come apart in a rather satisfactory way and undoubtedly Christopher would have been able to put it together again, its flabby rubber tube tucked neatly away, without disgorging any ink. Christopher was already very good with his hands and would be indignant about his father's poem 'The Engineer', in *Now We Are Six*, which seems to have him saying:

> 'It's a good sort of brake
> But it hasn't worked yet.'

'If I'd had a train (and I didn't have a train) any brake that I'd wanted to make for it – any simple thing like a brake – WOULD HAVE WORKED.'

There were numerous interviews in these years. There were numerous descriptions of the house in Mallord Street ('a rhapsody in azure and primrose' – carpets 'a heavenly blue', walls yellow) and of

Milne's booklined study – 'a neat and cosy room', looking out on 'a tiny townish garden'. Christopher would remember the smells of fuchsia and geraniums in Chelsea. There were numerous questions about how Milne liked being famous ('Well, if I am famous, then, yes, I do like it'), numerous tributes to his good looks ('his fine spare features, tanned and healthy-looking'), to his laughter, his diffidence and modesty, to his own charm, his charming wife and even more charming child.

The child was not asked at the time but he would say, much later, that 'I also quite liked being Christopher Robin and being famous. There were indeed times . . . when it was exciting and made me feel grand and important.' It was only later that he grew out of his part and came to resent the books so fiercely, to resent the fact that it seemed, almost, as if the father had got to where he was by climbing upon the child's own puny shoulders.

The child's grandfather said that winter: 'Alan's boy (6½), Christopher Robin, or, as he calls himself, Billy Moon, is quite unspoilt. He complains that his school is "easier than ever", but Alan thinks he learns quite enough. He makes up for it by learning chess and whist at home!' His cousin, Tony, just twelve, had been telling his grandfather that he was sure he could get a Westminster scholarship 'and is not going to be behind his father or his uncle or his brother'. When Tony's brother, Tim, had got the top scholarship to Westminster in 1925, Milne wrote to Ken: 'I only hope Billy will be as clever, but I doubt it,' and a little later added, 'I suspect him of striking out an entirely new line of his own, like Archery and Spanish. But as long as I love him as I do now, I don't mind.'

There were a lot of hard acts for Billy Moon, alias Christopher Robin, to follow, but so far he seemed to be bearing up well. He was showing little sign of strain though he was already famous, even before *Winnie-the-Pooh* brought him further into prominence. A piece in an American magazine *Town and Country* in May 1926, itself raving about Milne's 'adorable nonsense' and coining the word 'Milnenomaniacs' for his fans, carried the following caption under his photograph:

A. A. Milne. English playwright. Children's poet laureate by divine right of whimsy. His plays have been successfully produced in New York. *And* he is the father of Christopher Robin.

Milne seemed to see no need to protect the child from all the publicity. Daphne positively encouraged the press. There is no evidence for Christopher's adult suggestion: 'I imagine that the door was guarded with extra vigilance.' Milne would say later that all the talk about Christopher Robin seemed to have nothing to do with the real child, Billy Moon. But the photographs were, of course, of the real child, whatever he was called. Milne was always allowing photographs to be taken of the two of them together. There is the famous image by Howard Coster, now in the National Portrait Gallery – Christopher Milne would say of that photograph that his father never held him like that. There are lots of other studies in less or more awkward poses. And plenty of the boy alone. Milne seemed totally confident, at least on the surface, that Christopher Robin would be able to cope when he got to prep school:

Years ago, school was a world of blips and buffetings, and a boy might have had a hard time, perhaps, if he had been a nursery celebrity, but conditions today are vastly different . . . I am not uneasy. A delicate or lonely boy used to have a terrible time, but those days are gone, thank goodness!

How could he have felt so sure?

In New York that spring there had been a ripple of sensation when Milton, Balch and Company published a rather clever parody of Milne and Shepard entitled *When We Were Rather Older*, focusing attention on a generation of 'modern' young things with cocktails and Charlestons and fast cars. There was some talk of a libel suit, but in fact the book (which went into a second edition immediately) did nothing but good to the original. Milne's verse was so obviously much more skilled than that of Fairfax Downey. But the book is now a collector's item itself with its own sociological interest and period charm.

> James James
> Morrison's Mother's
> Had her hair shingled off.
> She's late
> Home for her dinner
> Being out shooting golf.
> Jim says
> Somebody told her
> That was the modern view,
> And since it's the rage not to be your age,
>   well, what can any son do?

Milne wrote to Ken in 1926 not only of Christopher and all the interest as the Pooh stories began to appear regularly month by month in both England and America, but also of politics, of cricket and golf and of servant problems. It was the year of the General Strike, but nothing survives to tell us what Milne thought about that. The 'politics' at one point related to personalities. Apparently Milne had sneered at Lord Bridgeman, First Lord of the Admiralty, and Ken had admonished him. In his reply to the admonition, Milne referred to an Academy painter, another old Etonian, John Collier, whose portraiture was described as achieving 'a sober veracity slightly reminiscent of Frank Holl', now hardly himself a name to conjure with. The passage seems worth quoting at length because it shows so clearly Milne's attitude to the Establishment, his inability to suffer fools gladly, which was always so characteristic of him. It also suggests Milne had a rather less conventional attitude to the avant-garde in art than some might suppose.

Talking of Bridgeman:
Suppose Roger Fry (say) were to be talking of the more advanced continental painters, and were to end up: 'Meanwhile for England the shining genius of a Collier is enough' – and suppose you were to say 'Why sneer at Collier? His artistic genius is his own affair. It may not be great, but it is adequate for the work he does, work done competently and honourably' – what could Fry answer? I suppose something like this.
'I am not "sneering" at Collier particularly; or, if I am, only in as much as he pretends to be something he isn't – that is, in as much as he gives himself the airs of a great painter. What I am really "sneering" at is the artistic perception which looks for nothing higher than a Collier, which is satisfied with a representative Academy full of Colliers, which tolerates the bestowal of rewards on the Colliers and the Colliers only.'
Bridgeman (from his looks, and from all I have heard of him from those who know him) is an utterly uninspired, unimaginative, rather bewildered mediocre little man, such as you could find in thousands all over England. If you say that such a man is entirely competent to fill the post of First Lord, I have no doubt you are right. But one is allowed to ask oneself: 'In that case: (1) Ought such a man to get the £5000 a year and the honours and glory that, for some obscure reason, we have been in the habit of giving our First Lords? – and (2) Ought we to be satisfied with our methods of government, if government means nothing more than a Bridgeman rather red in the face saying "Yes. Yes" and signing something?'
Hence these sneers. The truth is that since the war I have been utterly sick of, and utterly uninterested in, politics. Perhaps the fact that I played round Ashdown Forest behind Joynson-Hicks at Easter has intensified my contempt for statesmen. My God, the profound mediocrities that emerge.

He went to see the MCC play the Australians and was pleased when the England team for the first test match turned out to be almost exactly the one he had predicted to Ken ('Larwood for Allen is the only difference.' He had wanted Larwood 'and he may go in yet'.) The brothers were jubilant in August when in the last match of the series a tremendous partnership between Hobbs and Sutcliffe meant the Ashes would return to England after fourteen years. 'It was a triumph for the selectors,' the papers wrote, and Milne almost felt he had been one of them.

When the family returned to London at the end of August they found that their new cook ('our Penn has left us', he had told Ken a little earlier) had been entertaining a young gentleman from Jermyn Street.

They had been living happily, honeymooning so to speak, at 13 Mallord Street, kindly borrowed from Mr and Mrs A. A. Milne. We knew nothing of this until Monday morning when we came down to breakfast and found that the cook (who had welcomed us home beamingly the afternoon before) had vanished in the night. Thereafter we heard all and more than all we wanted to. The charwoman, who comes once a week, told Daff that our house had been turned into a 'bad-ouse'; in fact from all we heard Daff and I might have been arrested for keeping one.

They returned hastily to Cotchford. Christopher did not go back to school until half-way through September. After some initial problems, they were now being very well looked after at Cotchford by a reliable couple. The handsome gardener, George Tasker (someone said he looked like a Spanish sea captain), would stay with them for the rest of his life and put up, apparently quite willingly, with Daphne's imperious ways. She was immensely pleased with the prizes they won at local horticultural shows and would introduce Tasker to visitors as her 'head gardener'. (He had a nephew who helped.) Though the Taskers lived in a cottage at the top of the drive, Tasker's daughter Brenda would remember that the only time Mrs Milne ever came there was just after the gardener's death. She came with a friend for support and Brenda could not decide 'if she was a very shy person or a complete snob, who was quite unaware of any other person around'. She had certainly been irritated many years earlier when she had to find a new cook at Cotchford because Mrs Tasker was expecting her second child, Peter.

Winnie-the-Pooh was published on 14 October 1926 in London and on the 21st in New York. There was one annoying misprint. Somehow Milne had left 'his' instead of 'her' for Kanga at the end of Chapter VII, having started off interestingly thinking the kangaroo a father, in spite of the pouch. (He originally wrote, 'An animal who carries his child about with him in his pocket . . .' The male pronouns are crossed out heavily in the manuscript; somehow the final 'his' in the chapter slipped through and survives in the first edition). And some officious copy-editor had corrected Piglet's spoonerism 'spleak painly' in the same chapter: it was years before that was noticed and put right. But, in general, Milne was extremely pleased. The balance between type and illustrations was so much more satisfactory than it had been in the cluttered pages of newspapers and magazines, where the stories had made their first appearances.

The reactions to those first appearances, and the initial orders for the book, had prepared Milne for the fact that he was about to repeat the success of *When We Were Very Young* – but the reviewers could hardly believe it. The *New York Herald Tribune* said, 'As you read the conviction grows on you that Mr Milne has done it again. There are not so very many books that, sitting reading all alone, you find yourself laughing aloud over. This is one of them. Here is nonsense in the best tradition . . . with the high seriousness about it that children and other wise people love.'

Vogue thought it was 'not quite as nice as *When We Were Very Young*, but still it has tremendous charm and is great fun to read aloud'; a St Louis paper also couldn't convince itself that the new book was quite as clever as the first one. But the great majority of the reviewers raved about it. 'Almost never has there been so much funniness in a book.' 'Mr Milne has repeated the rare coup. Once more he has written the perfect book for children.' 'It is even better than *When We Were Very Young*, which is saying much,' said the *Saturday Review*, and a week later May Lamberton Becker wrote in the same place: 'When the real Christopher Robin is a little old man, children will find him waiting for them. It is the child's book of the season that seems certain to stay.'

And, like the first book, it was apparently not only the child's book but the adult's book as well. It seemed Milne's books always had the double ability to open up the future for the child looking forward (filling in obscure pieces of the puzzling jigsaw that is life), and the lost past for the adult looking back. My own copy of the first edition of *Winnie-the-Pooh* was given by my father to my mother long before they had any children. 'Adults loved him first,' Elliott Graham of Dutton's told me, extravagantly. 'Every intellectual knew the books by heart. It was easily a year and a half before any children saw the books.' Earlier in the year, the *Churchman* had congratulated adults on the way they had taken the poems to their hearts. 'This book appeared in childless New York apartments, in Pullman smokers and in doctors' offices – an innocent best-seller. Mr Milne's success seems to indicate that Americans are as yet neither completely commercialized nor completely sophisticated.'

The phenomenal success of both *When We Were Very Young* and *Winnie-the-Pooh* was seen as a tribute to the mental health of thousands of Americans. One hundred and fifty thousand copies of *Winnie-the-Pooh* were sold in the United States before the end of the year. Three weeks later, Milne would say: 'In America, by the way, they seem at least twice as keen as they were on WWWVY' – so it seemed, though sales of the poems would keep slightly ahead of *Pooh* for many years. That was also true in England where the reviews were similarly enthusiastic. 'Another book full of delight for all children under seventy,' the *Nation* said rather strangely. (Why exclude all those over seventy?) In spite of the fact 'that it has not the advantage of demanding that it be learned by heart', it is likely 'to gain quite as many firm and unshakable admirers'. Milne would soon report that Christopher Robin himself 'knows *Winnie-the-Pooh* absolutely by heart', and there would be many like him.

Methuen had had such confidence that the first English printing was seven times the size of that of *When We Were Very Young*. In the shops on the day of publication were 32,000 copies bound in dark green cloth. Another 3,000 were bound in red, blue or green leather and there were other limited editions, specifically aimed at book collectors. For *Now We Are Six*, the following year, the first printing would be 50,000 and for *The House at Pooh Corner* 75,000. Within a remarkably short time the worldwide sales of Milne's four children's books, in a multitude of languages, would be counted in millions.

— 14 —

The End of a Chapter

NOT LONG AFTER *Winnie-the-Pooh* was published, the Milnes were at Cotchford for the weekend and had one of Piglet's floods on the Saturday night. They were not entirely surrounded by water (Cotchford Farm is built on the side of the valley) but the water came up to the wall at the edge of the terrace 'and from there was one large sheet of water as far as you could see in the moonlight. Unfortunately Billy was asleep, which was very unfair.' Milne resisted the temptation, writing to Ken, to quote himself: 'It wasn't much good having anything exciting like floods, if you couldn't share them with somebody.' After all, Daphne was there, gazing out at the water too; and if she was not quite as excited as the boy would have been, that was only to be expected.

He went on:

Moon tells me that *Pooh* is 'what I call a good sort of book', which has encouraged me greatly. He is terribly sweet just now – and so is Daff – and so am I – and I have just finished with the dentist for another 9 months or so, and am feeling rather bucked.

There was none of that terrible uncertainty about what he was going to do next. Half of the poems for *Now We Are Six* were already written and the ending of *Winnie-the-Pooh* deliberately paved the way for a sequel:

'And what did happen?' asked Christopher Robin . . .
'I don't know.'
'Could you think, and tell me and Pooh some time?'
'If you wanted it very much.'
'Pooh does,' said Christopher Robin.

Indeed the *Evening News* Christmas edition again carried a new Pooh story, just as it had the year before. Milne had every reason to feel pleased with himself, but he could hardly believe his luck would last. He was finding the financial side of things difficult to manage. 'I feel I must save quickly, and I never know how much. It's so easy for a writer to drop out and be forgotten. I have just been helping Edwin Pugh,' he told Ken, 'who is starving and has had *one* article accepted in the last 18 months.' The lack of security never interfered with his generosity.

One indication of Milne's unusual reputation at this period was that he was invited to join the Athenaeum 'under the provisions of Rule II'. Most men put their names on a waiting list and waited, hoping to get there in the end. To be invited was a considerable honour and a rare one; certainly not one to be refused. Rule II required that the Members elected should be 'persons of distinguished eminence in Science, Literature, or the Arts or for Public Services' and that at the relevant meeting 'nine at least of the Committee be actually present, and the whole of those present *unanimous* in their Election'. Milne was rather pleased about it. He thought when he first lunched there that the denizens were more human than he expected. The *Chicago Daily Tribune*, giving the story of Milne's election, called it 'one of the most awesome and one of the most legendary places on earth'.

Writing to Swinnerton on 9 March 1928 he said: 'I feel poetical for some reason. Possibly the result of joining the Athenaeum. But I'm afraid I must chat to Sticko – I mean stick to Chatto.' Swinnerton had left the firm, after eighteen years reading for them, and was trying to persuade Milne to take his plays away. But Milne would not be persuaded. Harold Raymond, at Chatto, if not as entertaining an editor as Swinnerton, seemed keen and conscientious. Profits and sales were tiny compared with the children's books, but at least the plays were kept in print in attractive editions, which was the most important thing.

One source of income – from his manuscripts – Milne was not at all keen to exploit. When Carl Pforzheimer approached him for the manuscript of *The Ivory Door*, Daphne wrote

My husband has found the MS of *The Ivory Door* and suggests that I ask 1000 dollars for it. He doesn't suppose that it is worth this or any other particular sum, but if it hasn't got any considerable value for anybody else, he would sooner keep it – partly from sentiment, because it is his favourite play, and partly because manuscripts sometimes get more valuable later on. Of course he will quite understand if you don't want to pay this for it – in fact he says that in your place he certainly wouldn't.

But Pforzheimer was not to be put off. He asked for a 'special foreword' for his wife and, when that arrived, dispatched $1,000.

Milne was extremely famous, but there were still some people who had never heard of him. One night the telephone rang and Daphne said to the stranger at the other end of the line that Mr Milne was out.

Stranger (after apologies) What I wanted to ask Mr Milne was, Has he any relations living in Weybridge?
Daff I don't think so. I've never heard of any.
S. Oh! (*With an apologetic laugh*) You see, we're having a Treasure Hunt in Weybridge, and one of the clues was something to do with A. A. Milne, so I looked him up in the Telephone Book to see his Weybridge address, and found that he lived in Chelsea, so I wondered if any of his family–
D. But surely it referred to one of his books?
S. His what?
D. Books!
S. I'm sorry –
D. Books!
S. (*bewildered*) Oh!
D. You knew he was the well-known author –
S. The what?
D. AUTHOR!
S. Oh! . . . Oh, well, you see, I'm afraid that's not much in my line, all that sort of thing. Thanks so much. Sorry to have troubled you for nothing. Good-bye.
  (*Exit to resume hunt – but I doubt if he was successful.*)

The Milne phone number was obviously not ex-directory and there would sometimes be calls from strangers with hard-luck stories. There would also be begging letters, among the piles of praise and requests for articles, appearances, autographs. It was now that Milne began to develop the habit Christopher Milne describes of doing nothing about some things – which, as Owl said wisely, was sometimes the best thing. But Milne had plenty of charitable impulses: he gave generously both to the Royal Literary Fund and the Society of Authors Pension Fund. He would often write something for good causes. In a sense it was guilt money. He would say how easy it was to give money, how difficult to *do* anything for those worse off than ourselves. At least writing fund-raising letters was more worthwhile than just writing cheques. He raised funds for the Children's Country Holiday Fund, writing regular annual letters about the scheme in *The Times*. In one he said, 'Ladies may regret their last hat, and a man the new brassie which has not added twenty yards to his drive.

The only money which we are never sorry to have spent is the money which we have given away.'

Milne supported Toc H. In one appeal he wrote for Tubby Clayton he expressed again his feeling that no one should congratulate themselves as having earned their good fortune, no one can claim to be a self-made man. 'Idiots we are, if we can look at ourselves, however high our achievements, however great our success, with anything but humility and thankfulness. Our achievements, our possessions, are *not* of our own making; they were given to us. There is only one honest answer to that hackneyed question of the interviewer: "To what do you attribute your success?" And the answer is "Luck!" ' He appealed to people to say thank you for their good fortune by helping others who had been less lucky.

On another occasion he wrote an extremely successful appeal letter on behalf of a hospital, signing thousands of letters and writing hundreds of thank yous. It began like this.

I expect you know the story of the man who took his friend to the bar, and said, with a large and generous air, 'Now then, what would you like?' – to which the friend replied that he thought he would like a pint of champagne. 'Oh!' said his host, 'Well, try thinking of something nearer threepence.' What the Hampstead General Hospital would like is £10,000, and it would be a simplification of its finances if you were charming enough to send them a cheque for that amount in the enclosed envelope; but if you would prefer to think of something nearer threepence I shall understand. Not near enough to give you the bother of buying stamps or postal orders; something in guineas, I suggest, which will give you no more trouble than the opening of your cheque-book. But just as you like, so long as you help us.

Milne drew the line at appearing at the Savoy luncheon or the Mayfair Hotel dinner, in connection with the appeal. He rarely appeared in public. 'I may be unique in not wanting to say anything aloud at any time,' he once said, and on another occasion: 'I dislike public appearances, always avoid them, and am, in fact, not very good at them.' ' "Some can and some can't, that's how it is", as Christopher Robin's friend, Pooh, used to say,' Milne quoted, at a time when he was still quoting Pooh. (There would be times when the very name would make him shudder.)

With the extraordinary success of the children's books, Milne altered his life in no way at all. He had completed the purchase of Cotchford Farm almost at the very moment that *When We Were Very Young* was published. He had no wish for any larger or grander home either in London or the country. Both houses were comfortably equipped and furnished and staffed. He ran a good enough car (later there would be another, which stayed permanently at Cotchford) and employed a chauffeur. Milne said he had inherited from his father a love not of money but of not having to worry about it, of being extravagant in a thoroughly sensible way. 'We set our standards within our income and then enjoyed them carelessly . . . I shouldn't be happy if I couldn't be reckless about golf-balls, taxis, the best seats at cricket grounds and theatres, shirts and pullovers, tips, subscriptions, books and wine-lists.' He liked buying expensive lingerie for Daphne at Christmas, going to Harvey Nichols, consulting the assistants and choosing with enormous care – 'soft, pretty crêpe-de-chiney, lacey things. What fun!' He enjoyed these minor extravagances. (Daphne would enjoy more major extravagances of her own.) He made sure he was always salting enough away not only for the future of his own family, but for Ken's as well.

Milne never gambled, but he would put up money for something he thought worth doing. For instance, in the summer of 1928 his friend P. G. Wodehouse was looking for an extra backer for Ian Hay's dramatization of his novel *A Damsel in Distress*. Wodehouse wrote: 'The management, Ian and I are each putting up £500. We needed another £500 to make up the necessary £2000 and A. A. Milne gallantly stepped forward and said he would like to come in. I don't think we shall lose our money as Ian has done an awfully good job.' It indeed proved a safe investment.

Milne had taken on the responsibility for Ken's family with a real joy that he was able to do it. 'CVSD' (*Ça va sans dire*) he would say to Ken, over and over again, when some question of education or medical expenses came up. They were such a rewarding family. 'I love you all,' he ended one letter to Ken and obviously meant it. At the end of another letter he wrote 'You must be very proud of your family. So am I – I mean of yours, but also of mine. He is a darling. Much too good for me. So is Daff.' (Viola Tree had just described him in the *Woman's Pictorial* as 'a natural bachelor'. 'For a natural bachelor I have done well,' he wrote. Certainly a great deal better than Kenneth Grahame, that other 'natural bachelor'.)

It was fortunate for both families that he had done so well financially. But he never let his riches go to his head. He remained sensible about money. Christopher Milne would say, 'There was something not quite nice about being rich.' A. A. Milne could hardly believe that he was or that, if he really was, that he would remain so. He always had the feeling at the back of his mind that in some mysterious way it would suddenly stop, that no one would buy his books or produce his plays and he would have to live on his savings. One of Ken's children remembered that he always read bills carefully before paying them and was often appalled by high prices (a relic surely of the time when he first came to London). He would be amazed at the cost of Christopher's school clothes or of a particular restaurant ('Gosh, this costs more than the Mirabelle!') and his niece once caught him out in an extraordinary small economy, 're-using last year's diary, altering the days'. Perhaps it was really just that he had kept forgetting to buy a new one until the point when there were none left in the shops. He sometimes failed to realize just how short of money Ken's daughters were when they were first working in London. He would ask them to dinner at Mallord Street before the theatre, forgetting how the cost of the taxi, which they would need to take because of their theatre-going clothes and the time factor, meant that they would have to cut down on their lunches for a week.

J. V. Milne took a particular pleasure in his son's new kind of success. It was as if he had been waiting all the time for the children's books. He relished every sales figure, every sign of their widespread fame (Pooh prints being given away with *Home Chat*, 'Vespers' being sung on the wireless). Alan wrote to Ken: 'Father seems so terribly happy and excited that he makes me feel ashamed of not having made him happy before.'

Christopher Robin had other things on his mind besides Pooh, now that he was six and a half. His world was expanding. Someone had given him a map of Africa, which hung on the wall of his bedroom and fed his imagination. One day he would travel far further than A. A. Milne ever had. Books fed his mind too. 'Moon is devoted to the *Children's Encyclopædia*, which I gave him at Christmas, and brings a volume down to breakfast whenever he comes. Flags, beetles and the inside of engines seem to be his favourite reading.' Years before, Milne had surprised a nursery of Ken's children similarly absorbed. He had gone up expecting to have to impersonate a bear but had found there was no demand for bears. 'Each child lay on its front, engrossed in a volume of the *Children's Encyclopædia*. Nobody looked up as I came in. Greatly relieved, I also took a volume of the great work and lay down on my front.' He considered many of the answers were aimed more at him than at the children.

Take a question like 'Why does a stone sink?' No child wants to know why a stone sinks; it knows the answer already – 'What else could it do?' Even Sir Isaac Newton was grown up before he asked why an apple fell, and there had been men in the world fifty thousand years before that, none of whom bothered his head about gravity.

Christopher was particularly concerned about his wildlife, and not just beetles. He went off to stay with the Darlingtons on one occasion taking the volume containing CATERPILLARS with him, much to his father's dismay when he wanted to check on a curious caterpillar he had found in Christopher's absence. Was it a Death's Head Hawk Moth? It was certainly bigger than a Poplar Hawk. He wrote to Ken that it 'Looked exactly like a small snake in marking and colouring . . . and the *Enc. Britt.* isn't very forthcoming on the subject.'

Now We Are Six was slowly taking shape. Milne wrote to Shepard after a day at Methuen. 'Muller and I got to work on the book today, and I saw the new drawings. At present we have pasted up 14, taking 42 pages.' Milne told Shepard how much space he was reckoning 'for some of the poems which you have still to do'. He planned, for instance, that 'Forgiven', the one about Alexander Beetle, should take up three pages, giving Shepard the chance to draw the disappearing beetle over and over again as he runs away and disappears off the page. But it didn't work out quite right. It should have been a right hand page. As it is, poor Alexander Beetle looks as if he has been cut in two.

Milne was slightly worried about the length of the new book. In the end it turned out to be a couple of pages longer than *When We Were Very Young*, though there were nine poems fewer. Shepard was already working on the second collection of *Pooh* stories. Milne had bought another new character and looked forward to seeing him for the first time: 'I'm longing to see the "Tigger" illustrations', he wrote. Shepard had introduced the toys into the illustrations for *Now We Are Six* far more than Milne had into the poems themselves. Pooh goes nearly everywhere that Christopher Robin goes, of course, as Milne suggests in 'Us Two':

> Wherever I am, there's always Pooh,
> There's always Pooh and Me.
> Whatever I do, he wants to do,
> 'Where are you going today?' says Pooh:
> 'Well, that's very odd 'cos I was too.

Let's go together,' says Pooh, says he.
'Let's go together,' says Pooh.

He goes along, just as he always did, with Anne and Christopher on their morning walk. But Eeyore and Piglet and Kanga and Roo are there from time to time too. They wait on the platform in 'The Engineer'. They had become such public figures they could hardly be left out entirely. Methuen's advance publicity would say the new book was 'better' than *When We Were Very Young*. 'This is doubtful,' Milne said – but he thought it 'pretty much as good as'. Certainly it contained a number of poems – 'King John's Christmas', 'Sneezles', 'The Old Sailor' and 'In the Dark', for instance – as memorable as anything in the earlier book.

With four of the *House at Pooh Corner* stories under his belt, Milne was spending August at Cotchford working on a play – 'a Detective Play which is fun to do'. Plays were always fun to do. The awful part came afterwards. Negotiations for *The Ivory Door* were still going on. That was the 'Shakespearean' one – the costume play with masses of characters. There was the possibility it might be done that autumn in both New York and London. In the event it opened in New York in October – but it was not until April 1929, after the detective play, that it came on in London. 'I have given up bothering about it,' Milne told Ken, but it was still very close to his heart. A headline in a Canadian paper the year before (of a review of his Chatto volume *Four Plays*) read

A. A. MILNE'S STAR IS NOW IN
ASCENDANT AS PLAYWRIGHT

It was hardly a snappy headline and he knew, in any case, it was not true. Already too many people were thinking of him primarily as a children's writer. A review of the same book in *Granta* began:

I think Mr Milne, at some time in his career, must have whispered to himself, ever so gently, 'One day, I shall write a great play'; and I'm also certain that after completing this volume, he whispered, even more gently, 'I shall never write a great play.'

The volume included *Success*, one of the plays for which Milne had had such particularly high hopes. The *Granta* reviewer liked it too. 'In parts there is a vigour and a strength, which in spite of all the doubts, leave a hope; and I have hoped for and enjoyed Mr Milne for so long that I can't give up the habit. Perhaps, after all, he hasn't whispered that second sentence.' I think, in fact, that he had. There is no way, really, that a 'detective play' can be a 'great play'. He would write half a dozen more plays. He would never write a great play.

The Fourth Wall, which would be produced in New York as *The Perfect Alibi*, was certainly an ingenious play – 'an exceedingly interesting one from a technical point of view. In the first act it shows us a murder. We see the crime committed and who has done it. In the second and third acts we watch the other characters trying to unravel the mystery. Such a scheme is, of course, the very opposite of what generally happens in "detective plays" . . . Courage and originality of treatment are things to be thankful for, and for their sakes I rank *The Fourth Wall* as far above any other "detective play" I have seen,' one reviewer would say. The bus-boards would read 'the best murder in London' in a season when nearly every first act contained a corpse. At the Royal Court there was an even more ingenious play that didn't: *The Adding Machine* by Elmer Rice. Rice would later be a name to worry about.

But in the summer of 1927 Milne was really not worrying about anything as he sat in a deck chair on the lawn at Cotchford writing to Ken:

We are terribly happy here. I could go on and on doing nothing but watch Daff weed, and she could go on and on weeding. Really the garden is lovely now, and I wish you and Maud could see it. We have just been ordering our next year's improvements. I shall leave something beautiful behind anyway. Moon had a tent, two bantams and a rope-ladder among his birthday presents. The lady bantam laid her first egg yesterday, and he has just eaten it. He knows the name of *every* flower in the garden; and when the expert horticulturist points to a small green, as yet unflowering, bush, and says 'What's that? I don't think I know that?' Moon pipes up, 'Zauschneria – or Californian fuchsia'. And he not only knows but can spell Eschscholtzia, which nobody else can do.

Now We Are Six was published on 13 October in both England and America. Christopher Robin's copy was inscribed

> For my Moon
> From his Blue
> Now I am 45

Milne wrote to tell Ken in November: 'The reviews have been poor in England but much better in America. If I were a critic I should loathe A. A. Milne. How could one help wanting to say that he was falling off, or taking success too easily or whatnot? However this is the end of the verses; and then, after one more *Pooh* book, I must think of something else. In fact, it's time I tried a novel.' The reviews were mixed, with plenty of critics in both countries enjoying the new book. In England the *Spectator* said: 'The severest criticism that can possibly be made . . . is that it does not quite reach the extraordinarily high standard he has set himself.' In America the *New York Times* said that it might not be 'as fresh as *When We Were Very Young* but it comes close'.

In fact, it did not matter very much what the reviews said. The new book sold immediately and enormously on the strength of the earlier book of poems. By Christmas in England, J. V. Milne was able to write to his friend, Miss Pinnington: 'The success of Alan's books is remarkable.' He set out these English sales figures:

Now We Are Six 94,000
Winnie-the-Pooh 80,000
When We Were Very Young 169,000

So the new book, not much more than two months after publication, had already overtaken the best-selling *Winnie-the-Pooh*, published a year earlier.

At Christmas Milne looked back on the year. Things were good. '*The Ivory Door* goes on well in New York, playing to bigger houses each week, and should be in for a good run. But it had to fight its way against the seas of Sex and Crime which pour down Broadway at the moment, and nearly got swamped. Talking of Crime, the Haymarket has just taken my detective play.' It would open on 29 February 1928 – the day after a revival of *Mr Pim Passes By* at the St Martin's, with Marie Tempest in Irene Vanbrugh's old part. 'Having had no play in London for three years', Milne rather wished *The Ivory Door* was coming on first, but *The Fourth Wall* would be far more successful than *The Ivory Door*.

Life was a little overshadowed in December 1927 because 'our beloved Moon has chicken-pox' – not too badly, but 'he was to have sung various solos and duets at his school breaking-up and now he won't. We were looking forward to it more eagerly than to any first night of mine. He sings jolly well.'

He did indeed, well enough only a little later to make a recording of four of the poems Fraser-Simson had set to music.

When the idea first came up, the following argument took place, or so Milne would lead Ken to believe.

Me: (when it was first suggested) Bah!

Daff: It will be a Wonderful Thing to Have!

Me: Who *is* Moon? . . . I'm the only important person in this house. Christopher Robin doesn't exist. He is a pigment-figment of the imagination. Why should a small unimportant boy –

Daff: It would be a Wonderful Thing to Have – Afterwards.

Me: After what?

Daff: I mean –

Me: Now if they'd asked Me –

Daff: I thought you said they did?

Me: Oh! I didn't know I'd told you that.

Daff: I wish *you* would! It would be a Wonderful Thing to Have – Afterwards.

Me: After what?

Daff: I mean –

Me: I think the Whole thing is Perfectly Disgusting; I'll have Nothing to do with it. You can do what you like about it. I wash my hands of it. (Exit to bathroom.) So Daff went to the Gramophone Co., they all fell on her neck –

and the record was the result. Whether the whole idea was Daphne's own, as this suggests, we don't know for certain.

One of Christopher's cousins remembered the record well and thought it 'the unacceptable face of Poohdom'. That was not so much 'the sound of the record as the idea'. As for the record itself, 'it was the voice of a small boy who was obviously musical – dead in tune and sweet of tone – and who was obviously giving the performance all he'd got. (Perhaps this added to my feeling that the poor child was being exploited.) There were four songs – Vespers, Buckingham Palace, Fishing and the one about the train brake that didn't work.'

There were preliminary rehearsals in the first-floor drawing-room at Mallord Street (the room with the golden walls), a final practice in the Fraser-Simsons' house round the corner (with some coaching from Cicely Fraser-Simson, to whom *The Hums of Pooh* would be dedicated in 1929) – and then to the HMV studio. In fact, there must have been two records, for the one that Christopher remembered included 'The Friend'. He had to put on a Poohish voice when he sang: 'Well, *I* say sixpence, but I don't suppose I'm right.' Rather a difficult thing to do.

It was 'Vespers', however, that returned to haunt him years later when boys in the next study at Stowe would play it over and over again, remorselessly. It was 'intensely painful' for the singer. 'Eventually the joke, if not the record, wore out, they handed it to me' (the record not the joke) 'and I took it and broke it into a hundred fragments and scattered them over a distant field.' Years later, his cousin Angela allowed her children to hang the record on a tree, a string through the hole in the middle, and to throw things at it. One wonders how many copies remain in attics along with Ernest Lush singing 'O for the wings of a dove' and Harry Lauder's 'I love a lassie'.

Christopher had another important part in the spring of 1928. Milne wrote to Ken:

Daff is terribly busy, and so am I up to a point, in arranging this *Pooh* party. Beginning with no more than a kindly interest in the proceedings, and a gracious permission to certain performers to sing certain songs, we have got more and more dragged into it, until now we provide the whole programme, company, organisation and everything else. Moon makes three appearances – besides acting as host and shaking hands with the 350 odd guests! (We have told him to ooze away at about the 50th.) He sings *The Friend* with Pooh by his side – delightfully and really funnily. He recites with another small boy (W. G. Stevens' son) *Us Two*, and he plays in *Eeyore's Birthday* the part which is *Owl's* in the book, but has been made *Christopher Robin's* in the play. He loves it, is quite unshy, and speaks beautifully. *Piglet* is played by a darling little fat girl, Veronica, aged 4, with a very deep voice which comes out loudly and suddenly on all the unimport- ant words – 'Many happy returns OF the day' – 'Perhaps EEYORE doesn't like BALLOONS so very VERY much' – it's frightfully funny, and she looks superb. *Eeyore* is Anne Hastings Turner – terribly bad, but from sheer vanity may pull it off on the afternoon – and *Pooh* is the Stevens boy, also quite unshy and intelligent, but unfortunately with rather a niminy-piminy voice, quite unlike Pooh's gruff voice as inspired by Moon. Anne Darlington, alas, wasn't allowed to appear, as she gets too excited and upsets herself. Dress rehearsal this afternoon. We burst two balloons at every rehearsal, which seems rather a pity.

And in July 1929 there would be a pageant in Ashdown Forest twice a day for four days. The Mackails would go down with the Milnes ('the sun nearly roasted us to death,' Mackail foolishly com- plained) to see Christopher Robin (afternoons only) playing himself and the children of Park House School playing 'Winnie-the-Pooh and the other toys'. It would be the finale of the Pageant – which included practically every historical character you could think of: Earl Godwin, Queen Elizabeth, Nell Gwynn, Cromwell, Lady Hamilton, Wellington . . . And then, at the end, there was 'Ashdown Forest today where a boy and his bear will always be playing'. Christopher enjoyed it: 'Exciting without being frightening. For there was nothing to be nervous about, nothing to go wrong. It was not like acting in a play or making a gramophone record when your voice might go funny.' There was nothing to go wrong. But for Milne himself by July 1929 everything had gone wrong.

We have leapt ahead, following the boy in his starring roles, enjoying for the last time his part as Christopher Robin. Now we must go back and look further at the children's books – *Now We Are Six* and *The House at Pooh Corner* – which were keeping them all so firmly in the public eye, on both sides of the Atlantic.

In America 90,000 copies of *Now We Are Six* had already been ordered on publication day in October 1927. The *Retail Bookseller* said it was 'another unquestionable bullseye'. It was top of the general best seller list during its first month on sale. 'For the third time A. A. Milne has demonstrated that a book for children can outsell all other books in the country.'

One strong voice stood out against the general murmur of pleasure. Dorothy Parker, disguised as 'Constant Reader', mounted her first attack. In the *New Yorker* on 12 November 1927 she had great fun with two new children's books – *Now We Are Six* and Christopher Morley's *I Know a Secret*, which the publishers had claimed to be fit to stand in the company of *Alice*, *Peter Pan* and *When We Were Very Young*. Miss Parker said she found it difficult not to confuse Christopher Morley with Christopher Robin. Indeed she found that 'during those fretful hours when I am tossing and turning at my typewriter, during the mellow evenings, during the dim, drowsy watches of the night, my mind goes crooning:

> Christopher Morley goes hippety, hoppety
> Hippety, hippety, hop.
> Whenever I ask him politely to stop it, he
> Says he can't possibly stop . . .

The thing is too much for me. I am about to give it all up. I cannot get those two quaint kiddies straightened out.' But Miss Parker doesn't give up. She goes on and on and on, just like the tail of Christopher Robin's dormouse. She says if anyone had addressed her, as Morley does, as 'dear my urchin', when she was a little one, she would have doubled her dimpled fist 'and socked him one right on the button', and we can well believe it. Morley's book 'set new standards of whimsy, plumbed new depths of quaintness'. Unlike

Now We Are Six, it has sunk without trace and was hardly worth Miss Parker wasting her typewriter ribbon.

When she finally leaves Morley and gets to Milne, it goes like this:

While we are on the subject of whimsies, how about taking up Mr A. A. Milne? There is a strong feeling, I know, that to speak against Mr Milne puts one immediately in the ranks of those who set fire to orphanages, strike crippled newsboys, and lure little curly-heads off into corners to explain to them that Santa Claus is only Daddy making a fool of himself. But I too have a very strong feeling about the Whimsicality of Milne. I'm feeling it right this minute. It's in my stomach.

Time was when A. A. Milne was my only hero. Weekly I pounced on *Punch* for the bits signed 'A. A. M.' I kept 'Once a Week' and 'Half Hours' [she means 'Happy Days' presumably] practically under my pillow. I read 'The Red House Mystery' threadbare. I thought 'The Truth About Blayds' a fine and merciless and honest play. But when Mr Milne went quaint, all was over. Now he leads his life and I lead mine.

'Now We Are Six', the successor to 'When We Were Very Young', is Mr Milne gone completely Winnie-the-Pooh. Not since Fay Bainter played 'East is West' have I seen such sedulous cuteness. I give you, for example, the postscript to the preface: 'Pooh wants us to say that he thought it was a different book; and he hopes you won't mind, but he walked through it one day, looking for his friend Piglet, and sat down on some of the pages by mistake.' That one sentence may well make Christopher Morley stamp on his pen in despair. A. A. Milne still remains the Master.

Of Milne's recent verse, I speak in a minority amounting to solitude. I think it is affected, commonplace, bad. I did so, too, say bad. And now I must stop, to get ready for being ridden out of town on a rail.

CONSTANT READER

Anne Darlington could be numbered among those unspeakable characters who reveal the awful fact that Father Christmas does not exist; Christopher Milne can still point out the exact place where one morning on the way to the kindergarten in Tite Street with their nannies, Anne made her revelation. *Now We Are Six* is dedicated to Anne:

TO

ANNE DARLINGTON

NOW SHE IS SEVEN

AND

BECAUSE SHE IS

SO

SPESHAL

That spelling of 'special' has made other gorges rise besides Miss

13 and 14 Christopher Robin as seen by E. H. Shepard in the last chapter of *The House at Pooh Corner*, and as photographed by his father at Poling in 1924. Milne provided the caption: 'Child examining captured butterfly'. It is the picture he described, when sending it to Irene Vanbrugh, as 'by general consent, the most perfect photograph ever taken,' but added, 'These things are largely a matter of luck.'

15 A. A. Milne, Winnie-the-Pooh and Christopher by Howard Coster, 1926. This is in the National Portrait Gallery and is the best known of all the photographs of Milne. Christopher himself thinks the pose unnatural.

16 The Toys, now in the New York Public Library: Eeyore, Pooh, Kanga, a later incarnation of Piglet, and Tigger.

17 Daphne Milne photographed by E. O. Hoppé. This appeared in a special
A. A. Milne supplement to *The Bookman*, Christmas 1925.

18 A photograph of A. A. Milne which appeared in the American papers in
1921 at the time of the 'brilliant' Theatre Guild production of *Mr Pim Passes By*.

19 Christopher with his nanny, Olive Rand, Pooh and the original large Piglet.

20 Christopher and Anne Darlington on their way to school in Tite Street, Chelsea.

21   Christopher by Marcus Adams in March 1928. He remembers the
photographer 'looking a little like Einstein . . . He may have been technically
brilliant. He may have had the right society connections. As far as I was
concerned, he was gentle and kind and any expertise was well hidden behind
the manner of a pleasant bumbling, rather foolish old man.'

of course as soon as Kanga unbuttoned her pocket, she saw what had happened. Just for a moment she thought she was frightened, and then she knew she wasn't; for she felt quite sure that Christopher Robin would never let any harm happen to Roo. So she said to herself, "If they are having a joke with me, I will have a joke with them."

"Now then, Roo, dear," she said, as she took Piglet out of her pocket. "Bed-time!"

"Aha!" said Piglet, as well as he could after his Terrifying Journey. But it wasn't a very good "Aha!" and Kanga didn't seem to understand what it meant.

"Bath first," said Kanga in a cheerful voice.

"Aha!" said Piglet again, looking round anxiously for the others. But the others weren't there. Rabbit was playing with Baby Roo in his own house, and feeling more fond of him every minute, and Pooh, who had decided to be a Kanga, was still at the sandy place on the top of the Forest, practising jumps.

"I am not at all sure," said Kanga in a thoughtful voice, "that it wouldn't be a good idea to have a cold bath this evening. Would you like that, Roo, dear?"

Piglet, who had never been really fond of baths, shuddered a long indignant shudder, and said in as brave a voice as he could:

"Kanga, I see that the time has come to speak plainly."

"Funny little Roo," said Kanga, as she got the bath-water ready.

22 A page of the manuscript of *Winnie-the-Pooh*, with Milne's spoonerism near the bottom.

23 and 24   Poohsticks Bridge as seen by E. H. Shepard and in May 1989.

25 Leonora Corbett, the actress Milne loved, with Pauline Vilda, Harold Warrender and Maurice Evans in Milne's play *Other People's Lives* at Wyndham's in 1933.

26 Cotchford Farm, showing the front door. The river is over to the right, beyond the 'wing', containing on the ground floor the large sitting-room with French doors to the garden, and above it Milne's own room 'small and dark, with a window that looked over the courtyard'. Christopher's bedroom was next to it, a larger room with two windows.

27   Christopher and Milne at Osmington Mills, Dorset, in 1934.

28   At a different rented house in Osmington in August 1937. Back row: Milne and Maud. Middle row: Jack Lovelock, the New Zealand Olympic runner, and Angela Milne. Front row: Anne Darlington and Christopher.

29   Daphne and Alan Milne in the sitting-room at Cotchford, 1950.

Parker's. Somehow it seems all right when Christopher Robin can't spell and leaves his famous note:

GON OUT
BACKSON
BISY
BACKSON

When Milne himself pretends he can't spell, there is a good deal of revulsion from even his most dedicated admirers. But his inscription in Anne Darlington's own copy of the book is beautifully turned and shows clearly his special devotion to the child:

This book of songs
  Dear Anne, belongs to you.
It carries much
  Of love and such from Blue.
And for the rest
  It says as best it can
'Be never far
  From Moon, my darling Anne.'

Her father, W. A. Darlington, would remember the children playing on the nursery floor in Mallord Street with Daphne who 'helped to bring the toy animals to life and give them their character'. He said that Alan Milne 'never joined in their games but watched them with delight'. Christopher's nanny, as we saw, remembered Milne himself entering into the games; he 'spoke to the toys as if they were real people.' Both could be right. Other days, other moods. Christopher would remember that he and his mother and the toys played together, 'and gradually more life, more character flowed into them, until they reached a point at which my father could take over. Then, as the first stories were written, the cycle was repeated. The Pooh in my arms, the Pooh sitting opposite me at the breakfast table was a Pooh who had climbed trees in search of honey, who had got stuck in a rabbit hole . . .'

Certainly from Milne's letters one would imagine that all the ideas for the stories came entirely from Milne's head (together with Owl and Rabbit) and that it was only the toy animals themselves which came from the nursery – their characters and voices certainly owing a good deal to Christopher himself and Daphne. Daphne was undoubtedly obsessed by the pretence that Pooh and the others were alive. There is a rather rebarbative glimpse of her in a gushing article by the American May Lamberton Becker, who had first met the

Milnes a few years earlier and had sent Christopher a marvellous Indian head-dress as a present. Daphne's ecstatic thanks perhaps gives a flavour of her talk: 'Christopher Robin was simply too enchanted . . . It was really lovely of you to remember him and he does thank you ever so much . . . I do wish you could see him going out in it, he does look such a duck.' Gushing seemed to be the flavour of the time . . . In 1928 Miss Becker came more as a friend than a reporter. When she arrived, Christopher was attacking his father with boxing gloves.

A long nursery with walls the colour of sunshine; an eminent author crouched in the window-seat, clutching to his breast a fat yellow sofa-cushion; facing him at a convenient distance for attack, a little boy in boxing-gloves, his golden hair tossed back from the brightest and brownest eyes in London, his feet tapping back and forth in the proper professional preparations.

The real Christopher Robin still looks like Mr Shepard's pictures; that is, in moments of comparative repose, and when completing a particularly good tea at the round table in the yellow nursery. But only a cinema, an earnest one up to its business, could deal with Christopher Robin's boxing. It is the real thing and no mistake. Besides his school, he now goes to a famous gymnasium – oh yes, he's still a little boy, but when you say he is, you should stress the second word instead of the first.

As I watched the pillow take punishment, a small, gruff voice – the voice Pooh uses when Mrs Milne is in the room – cried 'Here! hold me up! I mustn't miss this!' and a brown bear came tumbling over my shoulder down into my lap. I had him right-side up directly; I kept my cheek on his good comfortable head for the rest of the bout. I was thinking of the American children whose eyes would shine when I told them, 'It was just this way that I held Pooh in my arms so he could watch Christopher Robin boxing.'

Pooh has been told that there will be no more books about him after this one that is just coming, *The House at Pooh Corner*. I do not know if he has quite taken it in; ideas come rather slowly to Pooh, and he makes no special effort to assimilate unpleasant ideas. What! retire from literature just when one has performed the unprecedented feat of changing the name of a household institution on the other side of the earth? for this is what happened when almost over night all the Teddy-bears of America became Pooh-bears in the vocabulary of childhood.

. . . It seems there are to be positively no more Christopher Robin books. Mr Milne says so, and he ought to know. 'No more Christopher Robin books!' said Mrs Milne. 'Look, Pooh's crying!' And indeed the brown bear in her arms had his paws over his face. But between them his candid eyes looked out confidently. Pooh knows that his place in literature is safe.

Claude Luke, another visitor that year, gave readers in *John o'London's* a further view of the happy family in the sunny house in Chelsea which somehow, mysteriously, seemed full of the 'breath of morning, morning in a very young world'. After some lamenting over 'the tragic ephemerality of such splendid childhood', Luke yet managed to convey a very realistic small boy and his nursery – the animals ('not the original Piglet which, alas, had been chewed by a dog' and replaced by one of more suitable size), the books, including *Dr Dolittle*, the walls hung with Shepard drawings, a coloured Spy sketch of his father, that pictorial map of Africa, that Indian head-dress. When Luke asked him the obvious question about whether he liked his father's books, instead of doubling up his dimpled fist as the young Dorothy Parker would have done, Christopher Robin just 'gazed at me for a moment, amazed at the immense foolishness of humans and then turned to his nurse with the expressive remark, '*Do* I, Nanny?' as though to say, 'Throw out this absurd man!'

When Nanny had gone downstairs to see about lunch, Christopher favoured Mr Luke with a glimpse of a row of bottles in a secret corner:

'They're my poisons!' he whispered, in a voice that would have thrilled Edgar Wallace. I read the labels inscribed in a childish scrawl. One was 'Salerd dressing for letters'; another 'Cind of frute salerd – it is good to drink'; and a third 'Loshun for the mouth'. He opened one for me to smell.

'I can't face that one', he admitted, wryly, and confessed that it was composed of ipecacuanha wine, flour paste, and ink! We agreed it had a deadly odour.

It was all getting a bit much. The time had obviously come to call a halt, to bring the whole business to an end. Milne would try, but as May Lambert Becker had said, 'Pooh's place in literature was safe', and that meant that Christopher Robin would never go away either. Somehow the real boy, whose name had been taken, would have to continue to live with him, would have, eventually, to come to terms with him.

The House at Pooh Corner was published in both New York and London in October 1928. On the British jacket the totals of the sales were now

> *When We Were Very Young* 179th thousand
> *Winnie-the-Pooh* 96th thousand
> *Now We Are Six* 109th thousand

In America they were correspondingly larger. The reviews in both countries were almost unanimously enthusiastic. Everyone had been told it was the last book and again and again reviewers lamented the fact. *Punch* said: 'The last book is as good as the first. It is too bad that Christopher Robin has to grow up.' The *Saturday Review:* 'The stories have lost none of their charm. It is a shame to see them end.' Even *The Times Literary Supplement*, although it congratulated Milne on deciding to avoid 'the temptation to repeat his successful formula mechanically', said: 'It is sad to see the stories end.' Only Dorothy Parker, the Constant Reader, returning to her attack of the previous year, poured scorn on Pooh's hum, the one about 'The more it snows, tiddely-pom'. It was an easy target.

It 'seemed to him a Good Hum, such as is Hummed Hopefully to Others.' In fact, so Good a Hum did it seem that he and Piglet started right out through the snow to Hum It Hopefully to Eeyore. Oh, darn – there I've gone and given away the plot. Oh, I could bite my tongue out.

As they are trotting along against the flakes, Piglet begins to weaken a bit.

' "Pooh," he said at last and a little timidly, because he didn't want Pooh to think he was Giving In, "I was just wondering. How would it be if we went home now and *practised* your song, and then sang it to Eeyore tomorrow – or – the next day, when we happen to see him."

' "That's a very good idea, Piglet," said Pooh. "We'll practise it now as we go along. But it's no good going home to practise it, because it's a special Outdoor Song which Has To Be Sung In The Snow."

' "Are you sure?" asked Piglet anxiously.

' "Well, you'll see, Piglet, when you listen. Because this is how it begins. *The more it snows, tiddely-pom –*"

' "Tiddely what?" said Piglet.' (He took, as you might say, the very words out of your correspondent's mouth.)

' "Pom," said Pooh. "I put that in to make it more hummy." ' '

And it is that word 'hummy', my darlings, that marks the first place in *The House at Pooh Corner* at which Tonstant Weader fwowed up.

Milne hated it, of course. He had resisted the temptation to reply the year before and now he would wait more than ten years. In his autobiography he wrote:

The books were written for children. When, for instance, Dorothy Parker, as 'Constant Reader' in *The New Yorker*, delights the sophisticated by announcing that at page 5 of *The House of Pooh Corner* 'Tonstant Weader fwowed up' (sic, if I may), she leaves the book, oddly enough, much where it was. However greatly indebted to Mrs Parker, no Alderney, at the approach of the milkmaid, thinks 'I hope this lot will turn out to be gin', no writer of children's books says gaily to his publisher, 'Don't bother about the children, Mrs Parker will love it.'

Milne had made the decision to stop long before Mrs Parker. She simply added to his satisfaction in his own decision, so clearly included in the book itself. At the end of *The House at Pooh Corner*, shades of the prison-house are beginning to close around Christopher Robin; it is all coming to an end. School and growing up are claiming the boy as they claim every child. Things would never be the same again.

That Christmas, Christopher had his first pair of football boots and wore them in the house, 'so as to get used to them'. In January 1929, just three months after the book was published, he started at prep school, at Gibbs' in Sloane Square, in a bright red blazer, with a bright red cap on his newly trimmed hair. Nanny took him in the number 11 bus along the King's Road. Milne wrote to Ken:

Moon is in the thick of school life. Daff thinks he's aged ten years. I don't think it's quite as bad as this, and anyway, if he's 12 one moment, he's 2 the next. Also instead of saying 'No, Blosh' (corruption of 'Blue') when I tell him to do anything, he now says 'Yes, sir' and does it. But somehow I fancy that the novelty of this will wear off. He is very happy, and began Latin and French on the same day, and is now grappling (a little prematurely, I think) with the domestic life of the four Georges.

It was time to leave the Forest. As Christopher Robin said to Pooh:

'I'm not going to do Nothing any more,'
'Never again?'
'Well, not so much. They don't let you.'

This is not sentimental. It is an occasion for real feeling and, if we cannot accept it, it is our fault, not Milne's. It is only in the memory that 'a little boy and his Bear will always be playing', as the final often-quoted words of the last children's book have it.

To stop while the going was good, that was the point; and, if possible, to protect his son from any further glare of publicity. In 1929 Milne wrote at length, and cogently, about the reasons behind his decision. He had been amazed at the way readers, back in 1924, had singled out the child.

You can imagine my amazement and disgust, then, when I discovered that in a night, so to speak, I had been pushed into a back place, and that the hero of *When We Were Very Young* was not, as I had modestly expected, the author, but a curiously named child of whom, at this time, I had scarcely heard. It was this Christopher Robin who kept mice, walked on the lines and not in the squares, and wondered what to do on a spring morning; it was this Christopher Robin, not I, whom Americans were clamouring to see; and in fact (to make due acknowledgement at last), it was this Christopher Robin, not I, not the publishers, who was selling the book in such large and ridiculous quantities.

Now who was this Christopher Robin – the hero now, since it was so accepted, of *When We Were Very Young*; soon to be the hero of *Winnie-the-Pooh* and two other books? To me he was, and remained, the child of my imagination. When I thought of him, I thought of him in the Forest, living in his tree as no child really lives; not in the nursery, where a differently named child (so far as we in this house are concerned) was playing with his animals. For this reason I have not felt self-conscious when writing about him, nor apologetic at the thought of exposing my own family to the public gaze. The 'animals', Pooh and Piglet, Eeyore, Kanga, and the rest, are in a different case. I have not 'created' them. He and his mother gave them life, and I have just 'put them into a book'. You can see them now in the nursery, as Ernest Shepard saw them before he drew them. Between us, it may be, we have given them shape, but you have only to look at them to see, as I saw at once, that Pooh is a Bear of Very Little Brain, Tigger Bouncy, Eeyore Melancholy and so on. I have exploited them for my own profit, as I feel I have not exploited the legal Christopher Robin. All I have got from Christopher Robin is a name which he never uses, an introduction to his friends . . . and a gleam which I have tried to follow.

However, the distinction, if clear to me, is not so clear to others; and to them, anyhow, perhaps to me also, the dividing line between the imaginary and the legal Christopher Robin becomes fainter with each book. This, then, brings me (at last) to one of the reasons why these verses and stories have come to an end. I feel that the legal Christopher Robin has already had more publicity than I want for him. Moreover, since he is growing up, he will soon feel that he has had more publicity than he wants for himself. We all, young and old, hope to make some sort of a name, but we want to make it in our own chosen way, and, if possible, by our own exertions. To be the hero of the '3 not out' in that heroic finish between Oxford and Cambridge (Under Ten), to be undisputed Fluff Weight Champion (four stone six) of the Lower School, even to be the only boy of his age who can do Long Division: any of these is worth much more than all your vicarious literary reputations. Lawrence hid himself in the Air Force under the name of Shaw to avoid being introduced for the rest of his life as 'Lawrence of Arabia'. I do not want C. R. Milne ever to wish that his names were Charles Robert.

The comparison between Lawrence of Arabia and Christopher Robin, which at first seems rather ridiculous, has real reverberations. Robert Graves once wrote of Lawrence, 'He both despised and loved the legend that surrounded him', and this was also true of Christopher Milne at different stages of his life. The great difference, of course, was that Lawrence's legend was based on his own achievements, Christopher Robin's on nothing he had done himself – and his mixed feelings would eventually transfer from the legend to his father, the author of it.

Milne had another reason to stop writing for children. A writer has to believe that his latest book is his best.

Can I go on writing these books, and persuade myself that each is better than the one before? I don't see how it is possible. Darwin, or somebody, compared the world of knowledge to a circle of light. The bigger the circumference of light, the bigger the surrounding border of darkness waiting to be lit up. A child's world of the imagination is not like that. As children we have explored it from end to end, and the map of it lies buried somewhere in our hearts, drawn in symbols whose meaning we have forgotten. A gleam from outside may light it up for us, so that for a moment it becomes clear again, and in that precious moment we can make a copy of it for others. But when the light has gone, to go on making fair copies of that copy – is it worth it?

For writing, let us confess it unashamed, is fun. There are those who will tell you that it is an inspiration, they sing but as the linnet sings; there are others, in revolt against such priggishness, who will tell you that it is simply a business like any other. Others, again, will assure you (heroically) that it is an agony, and they would sooner break stones – as well they might. But though there is something of inspiration in it, something of business, something, at times, of agony, yet, in the main, writing is just thrill; the thrill of exploring. The more difficult the country, the more untraversed by the writer, the greater (to me, anyhow) the thrill.

Well, I have had my thrill out of children's books, and know that I shall never recapture it. At least, not until I am a grandfather.

A. A. Milne never did know himself to be a grandfather. His only grandchild, Clare, was born, severely disabled, a few months after his death.

Milne called that essay 'The End of a Chapter', as he came to the end of the five years or so in which he had been involved in writing the four children's books for which he will always be remembered. There was another much longer chapter – indeed one should rather call it a book – that was also coming to an end. Just after *The House at Pooh Corner* was published his brother Ken became seriously ill. He had been ill with tuberculosis for years, but he had learned to live with it, to move around, to live a quiet but almost normal life. Now he had to take to his bed.

At first his brother was not really alarmed. Ken had been in bed before. There was no reason to suppose he would not recover from this setback. Ken was having the best medical advice and treatment his brother could procure for him. '*The Perfect Alibi* (anglice *The Fourth Wall*) has made a small sensation in New York, so don't be afraid of having another specialist if you want one,' Milne wrote. Milne himself was rather ill in December 1928 and joked to Ken in a pencil-written letter from his own bed. He told him he was 'a homeopathist'.

At least my doctress is so I suppose I am. I am suffering from a Bronk and a Honk and a Husk and a Wheeze and a General Reluctance to Get Up and am having the homeopathic treatment for all that.

> 'Flashed o'er the wire the electric message came –
> He is not better, he is much the same,'

As the candidate for the Newdigate said on the historic occasion of the Prince of Wales' typhoid. I think this staying in bed grows on one.

Here is my day (a sample):

8.30 am	Moon and Nan come in, bringing me an early cup of tea, letters and *The Times*.
9 am	Daff brings me *her* letters and the *Daily News*.
9.30 am	Gertrude brings me breakfast.
10 am	Nan brings me evening paper.
10.30 am	Burnside brings me detective story.
11 am	Dr Blackie brings me thermometer.
12	Mrs Gulliver brings me egg beaten up in lemon.
1 pm	Moon brings me bunch of violets.
1.30	Daff brings me lunch.

And at half-hour intervals somebody rings up and Daff says she's very sorry but whatever Mr Milne may have promised he can't do it *now* because he's *ill*. Which is a great comfort.

One cannot really imagine that this letter, obviously meant to cheer and amuse, actually comforted Ken in Somerset, really ill and worrying about the strain his illness put on Maud, without such a crowd to minister to his needs.

A few days later Alan was well enough to go to Twickenham for the Rugger Match. He was also able to see his son as Sir Andrew Aguecheek in *Twelfth Night:* 'It's a rotten part. For pages at a time he says nothing but "Ay, 'tis so" and, after an enormous wait, "And me too." But he did make an effort to keep the thing going, and other people say he was very good. I suppose my standards of acting are too high.' He also told Ken of a visit from their father's friend, Miss Shreeve ('I always call him Daddy') who had decided she was going to write fairy stories. The question was 'What ought she to do with them first?' Milne said 'Write them' and she said 'Yes, but after that?' The obvious answer, Milne thought was 'Burn them', but she went on, 'Should I send them to Sir Max Pemberton' – the advertisements for his London School of Journalism were in every newspaper – 'or would it be better to send them to Sir James Barrie?' They compromised on Ken's daughter, Marjorie, so Alan told him to warn her. He went on to warn Ken of a possible visit from their brother.

You are threatened with a visit from Barry, but I can't believe you really want to see him. If you do, you must terribly want to see me – unless you've been lying for the last 47 years. And I can't believe that anybody who is ill can want to see me. So what's the answer? I shall send you a copy of *The Ivory Door* (American edition) *instead*.

The Fourth Wall is a great go in New York. But I get terrible set-backs to make up. A Scarborough school-master wrote to ask if they could do a scene from *Pooh* without paying a fee. Daff wrote back certainly as long as it was a private performance etc, etc. Now he writes: 'I wrote to *you* last Sunday, and received a reply from 'Celia Brice'. I was not asking her but you. As you write (if you have written it) in this discourteous way, the dramatization of that, or of any other scene in any of your works can go to blazes, and you with it. Yours faithfully.' So I have nothing to hope from Scarborough.

Life was not always plain sailing, even for the rich and healthy. 'The Fiat broke down next to the Nurse Cavell statue and had to be towed home. I haven't heard yet when if ever I shall see it again.' Milne ended his letter. 'Get well, please. Ever your very very affectionate, Alan.' In the months to come, he would say that over and over again: 'Get well, please.'

Writing to Miss Pinnington from Purley on Christmas Eve, J. V. Milne commented on the dreadful weather and told her Alan had 'called here on Friday and we had a good time together'. Barry and Connie had been in with Christmas greetings that evening. He was keeping fairly well himself – he was now eighty-two. 'I get colds, of course, but so does my doctor.' As for Kenneth, there was encouraging news. Marjorie had just written: 'Daddy had a fairly good night, and today had a little chicken for lunch, which is a great event. He thoroughly enjoyed it too.' 'Go on getting better, please,' Milne begged. Even at this difficult time, Maud organized a special pencil with his name on it for Christopher's Christmas present. Alan sent them not a cheque but a large bank note, hoping that would make it more likely that they would spend it on something nice but 'entirely unnecessary'. 'A happy Christmas to you with your family,' Alan wrote to Ken, not allowing himself to realize it would be the last time he could send such a greeting. 'I hope that you will all have a happier New Year.'

Daphne and Alan Milne went to Grindelwald for skiing in February 1929; Ken and Alan had been there together in 1907, soon after Alan had joined *Punch*. Ken was much in his mind. He recalled an enormous walk they had done together. He showed it to everyone on the map and 'nobody believes it'. His last visit to Switzerland had been in 1913 – when he and Daphne had become engaged. He thought of that time too.

Sixteen years ago, I just went down moderate slopes, falling at the bottom and Daff didn't go down, collapsing at the top. But there appears to be a lot more in it than that. Everybody here is terribly keen and many of them terribly good. Some of the things they do are beautiful to watch, and I feel, as I feel about anything I can't do, that I would sooner do this one thing than everything which I can do. (Which isn't much.) In fact I feel like Wolfe.

He told Ken about a *Boy's Own Paper* lunch he had been to just before going to Switzerland.

The Editor in replying to Baldwin's toast told us of some of the questions boys ask him; and said that one boy – about 10 by his writing – asked for the price of an expedition to the North *or* South Pole, 'for one man and his dog'. I gave one great 'O-oh!' when I heard this, and unaccountably found a tear trickling down my nose.

He knew Ken would understand why he was so moved. He was weeping for the boys that he and Ken had been. He was weeping for lost childhood and for all the expeditions and adventures that they had had together, the two boys and their dog, that long-ago mongrel Brownie. He was also weeping, perhaps, for the fact that life, rewarding and comfortable as it was, had not given him the challenges that he had imagined as a child, that the only snow he knew was the snow of safe comfortable Switzerland, not of the North Pole.

Milne wrote to his father early in April 1929, thanking him for 'two dear letters'. 'I am so glad I have made you happy.' He was feeling rather happy himself when he wrote. He was full of hope for *The Ivory Door*, which was at last about to open at the Haymarket. It was still doing very well in New York; surely *this* was the best play he had ever written? And just the day before there had been an article in the *Evening News* 'by the Professor of English Literature at London University. In which, after discussing all kinds of modern writers, he says that of books and authors whose work will be alive 100 years hence the two certainties are "Conrad and A. A. Milne's *House at Pooh Corner*". Nunc dimittis. I am content,' Milne said. After sixty years, we can see that Charles Sisson, the first Lord Northcliffe Professor of Modern English Literature, had considerable percipience. Milne was happy about it then; later he would think that that was *not* how he wanted to be remembered.

And even then he was not really happy. He could not be in that spring of 1929. There was the constant worry about Ken. Alan tried hard not to fear the worst. He told his father in that same letter:

Tomorrow – in answer to your call – I am going down to Ken for the weekend. Back on Sunday night. Sometimes I feel that Barry is something of an alarmist, and I will try to find out the truth for myself. It is possible that it may not be as bad as he thinks; but possible that Ken wants to see me (among other reasons) to be reassured that I will look after Maud and the children. As goes without saying.

The truth was as bad as it could possibly be. Ken died the following month, on 21 May 1929 at his home, Chanters House, at Pilton near Shepton Mallet in Somerset, at the age of forty-eight. Mr Punch recorded the death with deep regret; he had been 'for several years a valued contributor to his pages'. *The Times* recalled his distinguished career in the civil service and his 'attractive personality'. His father wrote to Miss Pinnington: 'I think you have heard that I have lost my dear son, a young man of great promise.'

Ken's funeral was in the church of St Peter and St John the Baptist at Wivelsfield in Sussex, near Burgess Hill, where his parents had lived until the time of his mother's death. There had been a plan that he should be buried beside his mother – but in the event there was a muddle (Barry's fault, Ken's children said) and he wasn't. Alan was not at the funeral service. He could not bear to sit there in the church. But he could not bear to stay away either. Ken's children remembered seeing him in the churchyard alone among the graves, in his blue suit.

The year before, A. A. Milne had published a small pamphlet outlining his religious beliefs in a series called 'Affirmations: God in the Modern World'. His own contribution was called *The Ascent of Man*. I have in front of me, as I write, the copy Alan sent to Ken, wanting his approval, delighted when it came (for all of it apart from an 'unapproved tenth'). The inscription reads simply 'For K. J. M. from his always affectionate A. A. M.'. I think it is possible that, as he stood in that country graveyard on that late May day, he thought of some of the words he had written and Ken had read:

It is in the presence of Beauty that we feel ourselves to be in the presence of God . . . I cannot say what my God is, for it seems to me that one's God cannot be reduced to thought. I can say more easily what he is not. He is not the God which Man has made in his own puny image. To conceive the Creator and Inspirer of the universe as anything less tremendous, less terrible, less beautiful, less life-giving than the Sun, is, to me, ridiculous. All life came from the Sun, scientists tell us; all life is sustained by the Sun. I do not think of him as the Sun, for my mind is not large enough to conceive him at all; but when I think of the might and the majesty and the dominion of the Sun, and then turn my thoughts upon myself, I feel that I am in less danger of losing my sense of proportion than are those who think of him in human terms . . . Life and Death are matters beyond man's understanding . . . The Common Plan, whatever it may be, is something of which he is only a little part, something which must still go on. 'Let not my will, but thy will, be done.' It is an expression of humility and of belief in the Ultimate Purpose. How can such an expression not bring comfort, whether it be said aloud, or to one's soul; to this God, or to that? . . .

Will Man, then, be immortal? But what does one mean by immortal? Is Shakespeare dead? If he is not, then none of us need die. We brought nothing with us into this world, we take nothing out; but what shall we leave behind? All of ourselves. For there is nothing that we do or say but makes its ripple in the everlasting sea. We die, but the world goes on; and for those who come after us Life is different from what it would have been had we never lived . . .

Life in this world can flow on continuously, for ever; and when we die, we become part of its stream, and are at last immortal.

There was another death the following month, that of Milne's old theatre director and friend, Dion Boucicault. The words Milne wrote to comfort his 'dearest, dearest Irene' can stand for the comfort he needed himself at this bleak time.

If I could say anything to comfort you, how quickly I would say it. Yet perhaps it may be of some help to you to feel that your friends are all round you, and that you have only to put out your hand for a moment for some one of them to press it, and say 'Be brave, dear, he was so proud of you, let him be proud now.' So, please, I am just one of those friends near you, indistinguishable from the rest, intruding himself on your grief only to assure you of his love, and wanting no acknowledgement of it but the sight of your courage.

— 15 —

Toad of Toad Hall and America

MILNE NEVER WROTE of the death of his brother; he barely mentions it in his autobiography except, in a sense, in the dedication:

1880–1929
TO THE MEMORY OF
KENNETH JOHN MILNE
WHO
BORE THE WORST OF ME
AND
MADE THE BEST OF ME

It would seem that life continued superficially much as before. But, as Milne once said of one of his characters, 'He didn't much let you know what was going on inside him.' His most vivid link with his childhood had gone. Memory, that wellspring of his best writing for children, was now painful.

There was one great consolation. His relationship with his son was becoming even closer. Christopher was off to boarding school, his nanny, Olive Rand, left the household, and there was no one to come between father and son in the holidays. Milne furnished her cottage, which she called Vespers, as a present for her long-delayed wedding. It was too late now for her to have children of her own. Her garden was full of stone children, one like the stone figure of Christopher Robin, which still remains in the garden at Cotchford. Talking to a reporter towards the end of his life, her husband said, as he had often said before, 'Ours are naughty children; they never come in at night.'

For Milne, Christopher could be, as he grew up, in some ways a substitute for Ken. The letters to Ken in Somerset (once Alan had written, 'This is the world's longest letter, except one or two of St Paul's') became letters to Christopher at school. In the holidays they did things together more and more, if not, understandably, in the totally equal relationship that Milne always found easiest. From now on – for the next ten years, anyway – Christopher seems to have been his father's closest friend. There were other friends – Denis Mackail and Bill Darlington particularly – and Milne retained a devoted affection for Darlington's daughter, Anne. There remained a certain amount of contact with Wodehouse, Barrie, Wells, Swinnerton, E. V. Lucas. There were plenty of acquaintances at the Garrick Club and on golf courses. There was the occasional dinner party or cocktail party with neighbours. But his wife had been the centre of his life, his chosen friend, for sixteen years and all the slim evidence suggests that in the 1930s his marriage changed.

Milne had been feeling low in the spring of 1929, even when he was still trying to persuade himself that Ken would not die. He would later sum up what had happened in a letter to Charles Turley Smith: 'We had a sickener last year with a play we were terrifically keen about which ran a fortnight.' It was the play he had jokingly called to Swinnerton, when he had just finished it in 1925, 'the world's greatest play, somewhat in the Shakespearean style'. *The Ivory Door*, after a shaky start, had had a tremendous success in America eighteen months before, running for no fewer than 310 performances, even more than his earlier successes, *Mr Pim Passes By* and *The Dover Road*, had run in England. Milne was full of optimism when *The Ivory Door* opened at the Haymarket Theatre in London on 17 April. But it was withdrawn on 4 May, after only twenty performances, less than three weeks before Ken's death.

Milne had been in Switzerland when it was first in rehearsal. Curtis Brown had written, breaking the news to him that Watson the manager had had the idea of inserting a song for the Princess Lilia, because the actress happened to have a charming voice. Milne was horrified and sent a telegram followed by this letter:

In case my telegram was not clear enough, I repeat emphatically that Angela Baddeley is *not* to sing a song. If she really wants to sing, she should go into Grand Opera. If any of the other members of the cast can conjure, juggle, ventriloquize, or stand on their hands, they also are not to stop the play in order to do their favourite trick. Only a complete idiot would think that a song, in the middle of a play, would save a bad play or help a good one. On the contrary, those who like hearing Miss Baddeley sing would be annoyed that she didn't go on singing for the whole of the rest of the play, and those who came to the theatre to see a play would be annoyed to have the play interrupted for an entirely undramatic reason.

You can also tell the manager that if he introduces performing seals in Act III, I shall sue him without hesitation.

Milne was taking the play seriously; he thought it was the best play he had ever written. How often had he thought that. As soon as he got back from Grindelwald, he spent a good deal of time at the rehearsals. His note on the first night to Francis Lister, who played the lead, King Perivale, thanked him not only for what he knew would be a 'beautiful performance' but also 'for being so understanding and forgiving at rehearsals'. He thought the play deserved to be taken seriously by his critics and he had been foolish enough to say so in his preface to the Chatto and Windus edition, which had already appeared by the time the production opened in London.

Milne had been called 'whimsical' as early as 1910 when the *Scotsman* talked about 'the whimsical sketches . . . which make up this merry collection'. Again there was no derogatory connotation in 1912 when another collection had been reviewed in the *Morning Post:* 'Excellent comedy may be based on the most trivial incidents when these are presented in the light of whimsical comment.' In fact, Milne had often been praised for being whimsical, for instance by St John Adcock, who called *Mr Pim Passes By*, in the *Theatre Guild Quarterly*, 'that exquisitely whimsical, quaintly emotional comedy' and again in the *Graphic* where someone remarked: 'He has the good fortune to be gifted with an insistently whimsical humour that is distinctively his own.' If whimsy is simply a freakish and capricious humour, then certainly it is possible to be whimsical in many ways: 'to delight and titillate; to annoy and even nauseate'.

By 1928 Milne had become entirely nauseated by the word, even when it was used by a friendly pen. 'In a world gone serious and cynical, few people have the inclination, let alone the talent, to be whimsical.' He feared the world did not want whimsies and he knew he was irrevocably labelled as whimsical. In *The Ivory Door* preface he wrote:

It is always a convenience to have a writer labelled and card-indexed; so that, with the knowledge in front of you that the author is a Realist, you can pull open the appropriate drawer and waste no time in searching for such words as 'meticulous', 'sordid' or 'precision'. The next author is Whimsical, and the 'W' drawer tells you at once that his plays are *soufflés;* 'delicate', if you wish to be polite, 'thin', if you don't; 'charming' or 'nauseating', as you happen to feel; 'tricksy' and what not; but, in any case 'too finely spun out to be a full evening's entertainment'. For these are things you say of 'a whimsical play' . . . but what 'whimsical' means, I, of all people, have the least idea.

And, I suppose, I have the least chance of finding out. For I have the Whimsical label so firmly round my own neck that I can neither escape from it nor focus it. It seems to me now that if I write anything less realistic, less straightforward than 'The cat sat on the mat', I am 'indulging in a whimsy'. Indeed if I did say that the cat sat on the mat (as well it might), I should be accused of being whimsical about cats; not a real cat, but just a little make-believe pussy, such as the author of *Winnie-the-Pooh* invents so charmingly for our delectation.

Here, then, is a whimsical play – or so I was assured by the American critics when Mr Charles Hopkins gave it its first production. There is a Child in the Prologue; talk of a Magic Door and a Beautiful Princess . . . Criticism could safely write itself. Even though the Door turns out not to be magic, the Princess not beautiful; even though the child is obtruded on you for little longer than the child in *Macbeth;* yet the name of the author tells you all that you want to know about the thing. Why should you trouble to read it?

However I hope that you will. For I think (if an author may make these confessions) that it is the best play which I have written; even if it reminds me, not in the least of my favourite *Pooh*, but very much of an earlier play, not noticeably whimsical, *The Truth About Blayds.*

It was foolish of Milne to say that he thought it his best play. It asks for contradiction, even if J. M. Barrie had agreed with him – 'Far and away the best thing you have ever done for the stage; I am filled with admiration and pride.' It was foolish of Milne to grumble about the American critics. Most of them had enjoyed the play and so had the audiences. In England the preface was like a red flag to a train. The critics brought the play to a halt, alerted and alarmed. 'If Mr Milne thinks that this play is the best he has written,' one said, 'it only goes to show that playwrights are not always their own best critics.'

The clown wants to play the villain, the hero wants to play the fool, and so the world wags. A. A. Milne is peevish because the critics will not regard him as a heavy-weight. What does the man want? He has written one of the best and most popular modern comedies; he has written one of the best and most popular children's books of all time; he has written some delightful essays. Is he annoyed because he did not write Shakespeare and Johnson's Dictionary? Surely he cannot be jealous of people like Granville Barker, who is praised by the critics for plays which the public will not look at. Mr Milne anticipates trouble by roasting his critics in his preface. He forbids them to call the play 'whimsical' or 'tricksy' or 'make-believe', and as no other adjectives describe it so well, it seems superfluous to describe it at all.

The *Evening Standard* took the same line. Is he grateful to the public for hailing him as a genius as a writer of children's verse? Not a bit of it. 'For his highest ambition is to be recognized as a serious dramatist and the public refuse to be much impressed by his plays.' This was not quite true. The public had often been impressed but did not get much chance to be in this case. As Milne said: '*The Ivory Door* is damned and slammed not by the public' but by the critics. In *The Times* Charles Morgan ignored the preface and saw that Milne did indeed have a serious theme, and he had a style – but it was not a style that matched the theme:

Connoisseurs of style may be pleased to speculate on the use that other dramatists might have made of Mr Milne's theme, nor would such a speculation, if pursued in the right spirit and humour, be critically barren. The theme is, briefly, this: that legend has so great an influence on men's minds that they will reject all proofs in contradiction of it and deny the evidence of their own eyes rather than forsake it. Is there not here a great mocking tragedy of the stature of *Peer Gynt* or a drama of a tormented spirit that might have matched *The Master Builder*? Is there not a hint in it of a savage attack on sacred prejudices that might have tempted Mr Shaw? Or might not some poet, leading us through the follies and sufferings and disillusionments of legend-worship until we were all complacently patting our rationalism on the back, have swerved suddenly to reveal the truth that dwells in the heart of all great lies – that truth which all the supreme legends have borrowed from the hosts that have had faith in them? Mr Milne has used none of these methods, for he has a method of his own, the charm and the limitations of which are, by consideration of other possible treatments of his theme, made apparent.

Mr Milne has a style, and for this we are profoundly grateful. It gives distinction to all his work, and there is no mistaking his hand. It is a style which requires that tragedy be not harsh, that mockery be not cruel, that sacred prejudices, if attacked, be attacked not with savagery but with the good humour of a schoolboy who sticks a pin not too deeply into his neighbour. But it is a style which, having these limitations, has also the merits of them – a gentle playfulness, a discreet humour, a smoothness of texture never broken by the extravagances of passion.

Milne wrote to E. V. Lucas from Cotchford where he was working on his introduction to *Those Were The Days*, his collected writing from *Punch*, which would be published later in the year:

Please go and see, or read, the play – I would send you a copy if I had one here – and tell me that it's not bad. I thrive on your praise for there is none that I value more. The critics damned it as if it were worse than the worst film you have seen (one can't go lower than that) and Daff and I have been feeling terribly sunk, because we loved it childishly. So I cannot tell you how touched we were by your note, and how charming of you we thought it was.

In fact, several of the critics had showed considerable perception. The *Yorkshire Weekly Post* saw the problem exactly when reviewing the book: 'If this theme is not cynical, I don't know what is. Yet it is told so lightly, with such charm, that I shall not be at all surprised if, on its production, it is described as a delicately sentimental piece of fantasy.' There were other problems too, defined by the *Sunday Sun* ('It lacks sex-appeal') and the *Sketch*: 'In its quiet way it asks the audience to think and that is of course a thing that no author should do and that no management, which did not want to risk ruin, should permit . . . Nobody says anything amusingly indecent.' The *Era* took up Milne's challenge without blushing, 'It is certainly Whimsical with a capital W', and the *Evening Telegraph* got things completely wrong by calling it 'but another excursion into the whimsical fairyland that has proved so remunerative to him'. *The Times Literary Supplement*, reviewing the published play, even went so far as to write of 'a whimsically bitter preface'.

On 23 April, Milne wrote an extremely long letter from Cotchford to St John Ervine, whose review of *The Ivory Door* in the *Observer* had been a great comfort. 'Until we read it, we were not sure whether I had committed a murder, assaulted school-children or betrayed my country; but at least we felt that we were safer down here, away from the chorus of hate which I seemed to have aroused.' In fact, Milne seems to have overreacted because he already knew the play had been killed. None of the London critics had gone as far as the *New Yorker*, which called it 'A lethal combination of whimsy and lethargy'. But in New York the play had run and run.

In London Milne knew already, six days after it had opened, that it wouldn't run. He spelt out the situation in a later letter to Ervine.

1) It is indisputable that however greatly your 900 audience likes a play, if your 50 critics damn it, the play is dead.
2) Francis Lister, who was playing in the succeeding play, was given his new part on the evening after *The Ivory Door* was produced, and the photographic call for the following day was cancelled. That is to say, as soon as he had read the notices, Watson knew (as I did) that the play was killed.
3) Obviously it would have saved Watson money if he had submitted the play (with names of producer and cast) to the 20 leading critics before production and only produced it if they approved of it . . . I should have assented . . . I don't like seeing managers losing money. I don't like seeing

actors and actresses losing their jobs. I don't like going through all the trouble and anxiety of rehearsals for nothing at all.

Milne knew that Ervine objected strongly to an arbitrarily appointed censor, the Lord Chamberlain. How much more so do playwrights object to arbitrarily appointed critics:

You have probably said often enough '*Why* Lord Cromer?' I say '*Why* Agate?' '*Why* Swaffer?' Even '*Why* Ervine?' '*Why* should we have to pass this barrage before we get to the public at all?'

Someone had reported to Milne hearing Swaffer say, 'Milne always bores me'. Milne resented the fact that he took his prejudice with him to the theatre. Nothing that applies to criticism generally applies to criticism of the theatre.

Gerald Gould dislikes my new book. Do I mind? Not a bit. The book is still there. The public still has every chance of reading it. If it hesitates to risk its money, it can get it from the library for nothing. Why *should* this one man Gould like my book? Why should any one man? But I have every hope that some few people will, and there the book is, waiting for them until they are ready to read it.

Wilenski damns a picture as insincere tripe. Nobody automatically comes round to the artist's studio and slashes the picture into ribbons. The picture remains – until the artist himself wants to destroy it . . .

BUT if Agate tells 100,000 readers in the *Sunday Times*, and 1,000,000 listeners-in, and God knows how many more thousands who read him under some *nom-de-guerre*, that he heartily dislikes a play, that play suffers a wound which may be mortal. We can't say six months later, 'Well there it is, if anybody wants to see it.'

In other words dramatic criticism has an entirely different *effect* from that of any other sort of criticism.

Moreover it has an entirely different *value*.

A picture or a book is meant for an individual, and, when judged by a critic, is judged by an individual. A play is meant for a *crowd*, and, being judged by a critic, is judged by an individual who deliberately holds himself aloof from the crowd. Moreover, it is meant for a crowd in a certain state of sophistication and it is judged by a critic in a more advanced state of sophistication. (A conjuror tries to mystify and amuse a public of laymen, not a public of conjurors.)

Milne ended the discussion by asserting, as he had felt for years, that 'first night criticism (as now practised) is aesthetically, ridiculous and theatrically, disastrous.' It was a theme Milne often returned to: 'I don't think anyone knows (except actors and author) the extraordinary differences between rehearsals and the first night. And again the vast abyss between the first night – when the play is coming to life by what means none of us is altogether sure – and all the other nights of its short or long existence . . . The first night is critical; too critical to receive the brunt of critical judgment.' Now, of course, it is quite common for a play *not* to be reviewed on its first night. Milne would certainly have approved. In all his disputes with the critics he was entirely concerned about the future of the theatre, of the straight play as opposed to the musicals and revues which tended to flourish anyway. Before the first war costs had been so much lower; there had been no government tax. Managers had been able to afford to keep a play running long enough for the public to express their own opinion.

In 1929 Milne told Ervine:

It is not so bad for me. I have already had a good deal, both artistically and financially, out of the American run. Moreover the play is in print, nothing can destroy that. If I feel now that I never want another play of mine to be fouled by Swaffers and their like, well I may get over it; and even if I don't, neither the theatre nor I will suffer greatly by it. We can do without each other.

But, in fact, it seemed that Milne could *not* do without the theatre. 'Every dramatist,' he said, 'who has written a dozen plays has taken a dozen oaths that he will never write another play.' But there he was, in that summer after Ken's death, working away on another play. It was to be his last real success: *Michael and Mary*.

Soon after the funeral Milne went down to Somerset to talk things over with Ken's widow, Maud, and her daughters Marjorie and Angela. The boys were now both at Westminster. Maud was hoping to find some sort of job, 'preferably some such thing as keeping house for masters at a school or looking after a few extra boys who have to be boarded out. She is writing to one or two people in this connection, and later will let me know how much she thinks she will want.' Milne had been fond of Maud for twenty-five years. Now he very much admired the way she was coping. 'She is full of fight,' he told his father. 'She has no sort of intention of sitting down and doing nothing.' She did get some kind of job, attached to a boys' preparatory school in Enfield Chase, but it did not last long. By 1931 she was living with the girls in Gledhow Gardens off the Brompton Road, not very far from Mallord Street. Milne would call in and have lunch or tea with her. Friends of Angela's – after Marjorie's marriage – would remember meeting Milne in St Leonard's Terrace, where they lived later in the 1930s. There was still not much love lost between Maud and Daphne. Maud would see Daphne sometimes 'swanning along the King's Road, dressed in her outrageously noticeable way, – theatrical rather than fashionable' – and would come home and describe her to her daughter 'with what you might call just a touch of malice'. Very occasionally, hardly ever, they would meet socially.

Milne settled £10,000 on Maud (today it would be worth perhaps £300,000 or $500,000): a very large sum, enough for her to pay for the boys to finish at Westminster and go on to university (there were costs obviously even with their scholarships), enough for her to live comfortably for the rest of her life on the interest. Two of Milne's closest relationships during the last part of his life were with his two sisters-in-law, Maud and Connie. It is clear from his plays that Milne was unusually interested in women – again and again it is the women who have the best lines, who come out of it best. For Maud and Connie, his devotion was to them as women, women to whom he could be openly devoted without any suggestion of scandal – but his generosity in both cases was because of his brothers. He had sympathy and admiration for both women, surviving so admirably the blows that life had brought them through their marriages to his brothers – the one widowed early after years of having to cope with poverty and illness, the other suffering the infidelities and financial problems involved in remaining married to Barry. He could love them without guilt, without complications.

In the same letter in which Milne wrote to his father about Maud's plans he also discussed the changes his father planned to make in his will, following Ken's death. J. V. Milne was now eighty-four and there was obviously some urgency to get it settled.

About the will. If it would make you feel more comfortable to write on a sheet of notepaper 'I leave everything of which I died possessed to A. A. M., knowing that he will carry out my intentions as expressed in my previous will,' then in the event of your sudden death, all would be well. (Of course it would have to be witnessed by two people.)

Milne recommended his father should use a solicitor who had been at school with him and with Ken, a man called Gwatkin, a close friend of Ken's. 'He is in McKenna's (brother of Reginald's), a very well-known firm of solicitors.' Without actually saying so, Milne shows quite clearly that he felt it wise to keep the making of the will away from his solicitor brother, Barry. The McKenna will, dated 20 December 1929, shows that Barry was in debt to his father ('I release and forgive my said son David Barrett Milne ... any sum or sums of money now due ... and I direct my executors to pay out of my general personal estate any death duties which may be payable by reason of the release of such debt.'). It also makes provision to give to his son Alan Alexander Milne 'for reasons of which he is aware' 'free of duty War Loan to the nominal value of £5,000', 'such War Loan representing part of the moneys my said son has given to me during my lifetime'. After bequests of £1,000 to Barry and £1,000 to Maud and £100 each to his housekeeper and to his grandchildren (apart from Christopher – who obviously had no need of anything), he left the residue of his estate 'in trust for my two granddaughters, Lilian Marjorie Milne and Angela Mary Milne.' J. V. Milne's reasoning presumably was that Ken's two brilliant sons would be able to fend for themselves but that the girls, who had not a penny in the world beyond their own small earnings, would need some inheritance. It would be up to Barry, so it seems he felt, to provide for *his* two sons. But Barry had no intention that this will should be his father's final testament, as we shall see.

Milne was at Cotchford not just to get away from the critics. He found more and more that there was where he could best work. Ideas did not come quite as easily as they once had. 'I dread this interval between one idea and another,' he said in 1931. 'My trouble now is not too many ideas, but an almost total absence of them.' They certainly did not come, however much he would pretend they might, at Lord's or on a golf course. They came when he was sitting at his desk. The attraction of playwriting was that it was 'an exciting sort of game in which one has to defeat the apathy, the preconceptions and the defective memory of one's antagonist. The idea for *Michael and Mary* came with the thought that it would be dramatic, wouldn't it, if a man died in one's sitting-room and the police, naturally, wanted to know all about him, and the one thing which couldn't be given away was the reason why he had come to the house?' The husband and wife – Michael and Mary – are desperately trying to make up a convincing story as the minutes tick by and the police are about to arrive. There could be nothing whimsical about that.

The reason for the arrival of the man is blackmail. He has just come back to England and has seen a photo in the paper of Mary, wife of the well-known writer, Michael Rowe, and he recognizes Mary as his own wife, whom he had deserted fourteen years earlier and from whom he had never been divorced. Mary is apparently a bigamist and surely that might put her errant husband in the way of a thousand pounds.

Such is the melodramatic plot – but the play is not a melodrama. It is a study of marriage. Marriage was much on Milne's mind in the summer of 1929. In June Christopher, aged nearly nine, had been a page, one of ten attendants, at the marriage of Daphne's niece, Barbara de Sélincourt. She was married at St Margaret's, Westminster, sixteen years after Daphne and Alan had themselves been married there. Three weeks earlier Alan had written to his father, 'We have been, and are, terribly happy together. She is a perpetual joy to me and I think I am to her.' It was as if he were trying to reassure his aged father, after Ken's death, that some happiness survives, that some things endure. But he was never *sure*. 'I think I am to her.' It was not Daphne's habit to let him be sure. She was always a little aloof, a little unobtainable. In the next ten years they would lead increasingly separate lives.

In *Michael and Mary* Milne explored what marriage really means by looking closely both at the reasons why Michael and Mary married illegally and why, after the death of Mary's first husband on their sitting-room floor, they did not think it necessary to go through another marriage ceremony, even though they had a son. The themes had been explored lightly in *Mr Pim Passes By*, but in that play it had all been hypothetical. In the later play, there is real danger. Milne had never believed that marriages are only made by the law or even by God. What matters is the binding pledge. Real morality has nothing to do with either the law or religion, but everything to do with human relationships. The most important moment in the play is in the last act where the son is challenged to accept and forgive his parents his own illegitimacy. Milne makes the young man cross the room and take the joined hands of his parents and kiss them.

Some of the critics, Milne said in the preface to the play when it was published, found this kiss hard to take. (*The Times* critic for one had hardly been able to believe his eyes.) Milne could see that the son

does a terrible thing for an English audience to witness: he kisses his father's hand. When Romeo and Juliet kiss on the English stage, you will generally hear a nervous giggle from some girl in the gallery; so that one cannot complain if, on this occasion, a nervous giggle is heard from one or two gentlemen in the stalls . . . David kisses 'the joined hands of Michael and Mary', so that Michael's hand only gets, so to speak, half a kiss; but . . . 'I mean to say, dammit, a fella, public school and all that, kissing half the hand of another fella, I mean to say half-kissing the hand of a fella, I mean dammit' . . . No, I shall not apologize. I shall just congratulate the many who have stood it so well.

It certainly caused a stir, that scene. One critic complimented young Frank Lawton, 'who is, one imagines, the only actor who could possibly kiss his father's hand on the English stage and make the gesture entirely devoid of awkwardness.' And yet this was at a time when, as Michael put it, 'almost nothing you want to do is wrong', at least to the young. Michael himself was brought up at a time 'when one still felt that right was right and wrong was wrong, but one didn't quite know which was which.'

Michael is Milne's age exactly – twenty-three in 1905 at the beginning of the play. Like him, he is a young writer starting out on his career. Like him, he has a son. In the last act when the son, David, has gone off with his own wife, Michael says to Mary, 'I suppose you do know, Mary, that, much as I love him, I love your little finger – your funny little finger, more than all of David.' And in Daphne's own copy of the book, Milne wrote:

> For my darling
> from her Blue
> 'I suppose you do know –'

Milne wanted that to be true. Daphne herself believed, and would tell any interviewer, that marriages only work if partners put each other before their children and if wives devote themselves entirely to their husbands. 'I think modern women are falling down dreadfully in their real careers, the careers of being wives. I'm sure it sounds old-fashioned, but I think the disruption of marriage is nearly always in the woman's hands. A successful wife just simply cannot be egotistical, and modern women are cultivating their egos too strongly. I honestly think the only really successful marriage, disregarding the few exceptions that prove the rule, is that in which the wife is interested only in her husband and his career – I mean in which that career dominates her whole life, and is the thing she really lives for.' That particular interview went on to describe how Mrs Milne acts as her husband's secretary, answering letters from all over the world, 'takes care of the numerous visitors, many of them tourists from other lands, who want to see Christopher Robin's nursery' and 'arranges the sort of quiet social life which Mr Milne likes.' Daphne at forty-two is described as 'a very youthful, cheerful and friendly person, with dark curly bob, dark eyes and a vivacious manner'.

In the 1920s, with Milne at the height of his career, it was easy for Daphne to let it 'dominate her whole life'. Her enthusiasm for the Pooh books remained extravagant – and that itself became a cause of difference between husband and wife when, in the 1930s, as his career declined, Milne sometimes wished he had never written them. Milne did not have, as Daphne observed, 'the disagreeable temperament so usually associated with famous men, and, in fact, has a most even and genial disposition. He makes life very interesting and amusing for us. He doesn't save up his best thoughts for strangers.' Under his quiet exterior, Milne had not just a genial disposition but a romantic and passionate one.

He had had the highest and most romantic expectations of marriage and this would in itself cause problems. He had never accepted the view that was becoming common (and which one of his characters had expressed in *Ariadne*) that 'love and marriage are two different things.' In *Michael and Mary* he seemed on the defensive over his view of their long-lasting married love and said in the preface, 'In those distant days' – looking back twenty-five years to the time when he himself was young – 'it was not uncommon to meet men and women who believed in marriage': that is, not marriage as a social convenience but marriage as a marvellous partnership. In *The Ivory Door* he had put it like this: 'In all your acts, in every hope and every fear, when you soar to the skies and when you fall to the earth – always – you are holding the other person's hand.' That was what he wanted, that was his impossible dream. In 1929 he still hung on to his ideal; he still thought (in spite of the separate bedrooms) that he and Daphne had something together that was precious and remarkable.

When he finished *Michael and Mary* that summer he started almost straight away on a novel, *Two People*, and that, more than anything else he wrote, suggests how things would move in the years ahead as Milne's career deteriorated and no longer dominated Daphne's whole life as she had said it must if they were to be happy. She also began to find that 'the quiet social life' Milne liked was not enough to satisfy her. She looked around for other worlds to conquer, other men to admire her.

There would come a time, soon, when, to use Milne's own phrase, both would be 'marginally in love with other people'. But they kept the marriage intact. Marriage was always what really mattered. 'Free love and free verse – they're a damn sight easier. I like difficult things.' 'The secret of a loving marriage is to have a partner to whom you don't have to explain things,' Milne would say, adding, 'I didn't say a happy marriage. I said a loving marriage.' They would always have a loving marriage, though they would often in these years find their happiness with other people. Milne had always recognized the total equality of the sexes and had expressed it clearly years before in *Mr Pim Passes By:* 'I shall try to remember that marriage is a partnership, in which the man is not inevitably the senior partner.' As for fidelity, 'I bring to my wife no less than I receive from her; I expect from her no more than I can keep for her. In this matter, I recognize no shadow of a difference between the two sexes.'

Milne wrote an essay on 'Love and Marriage' in this year, 1929, which appeared in *By Way of Introduction*, together with a number of introductions he had written to books and a good deal of assorted journalism. He looked at the changing relationships within marriage – as women started questioning their traditional roles. 'Man is suddenly in the horrible position of realizing that "a happy marriage" in some ridiculous way has got to mean happiness for the woman also. Is it any wonder that there is this rush of unhappy marriages? What would happen to all the happy shooting-parties each autumn if they had suddenly to include happiness for a vocal pheasant?' Women had kept their secrets to themselves 'just as the fox keeps his secret to himself, and enables us to assure him that he enjoys being hunted.' Now women were speaking out against their servitude, against the prospect of endless child-bearing.

In one of his early plays, Milne had written: 'Just think of the average marriage. It makes one shudder.' And now it seemed that he himself must begin to settle for something much less than his ideal. If the most important thing in marriage was 'knowing that the other person will never lie to you', then he had to remember not to ask the questions that might give answers that he did not want to hear.

In *Two People*, Sylvia – the writer's wife – is too much of a dumb blonde, too beautiful, too stupid, to be identified with Daphne. Daphne disliked her intensely. 'You know that woman in *Two People*, Sylvia, sort of gave me a pain', an American interviewer reported her saying, though the form of words seems unconvincing. 'I suppose all men have an idea like that hidden away somewhere in their minds – some absurd woman who never becomes human at all, who is perpetually mysterious, the perfect housekeeper, quite dumb yet forever beautiful, so beautiful that it doesn't matter if she is dumb, always admiring and loving, who never gets in the way, never bothers them, always agrees, and who has some fount of feminine wisdom nevertheless, and runs the whole household with some hidden magic . . .' Certainly it was very important to Milne that no one should identify Sylvia with Daphne, for *Two People* is a portrait of a man who adores his wife for no good reason, who loves her passionately, physically, though his mind tells him she is not worthy of his love. Sylvia has so little interest in her husband's work that she has not even realized he is writing a novel and reacts with an inadequate 'Fancy!' when told. Daphne – though less involved than she had been – would still read Milne's work as he wrote it, and praise it: 'Praise is what an author really wants when he's actually writing.' Sylvia was certainly not Daphne. But there is, I have been assured, a great deal of autobiography in *Two People* and there are certainly scenes, amid a good deal of sentimentality, which ring so true that one finds oneself assuming they were based on real life, as so much of Milne's writing had always been.

In *Two People*, Wellard's novel is an unexpected bestseller and about to be produced as a play. He and his wife take a house in town as a result, abandoning their quiet life and delightful house and garden (closely resembling Cotchford) for the more dubious joys of the theatre and of society. It is a different world where 'wives and husbands were so seldom mentioned', where they led separate lives. Wellard does not find it easy:

I am being damnably jealous for no reason at all. Why can't she go her way, I mine? And then we meet in the evening, . . . at night . . . and are one again. I have my secret thoughts – why should not she? It's this damnable possessive instinct which men have. I want to be free, but I want her not to be. And yet I am less free than she is, for I have that faint uneasy feeling of disloyalty to her when I am with another woman. Does she have that feeling? Of course not.

Wellard agonizes about breaking the news to his wife about having tea with the actress Coral Bell, only to find, when he does finally tell her, that she knows about it already and attaches no importance to it whatsoever. Then there is the night when he comes back at half past eleven from an unexpected theatre party. He had telephoned, but he is wracked with guilt at the thought of Sylvia having had a lonely, boring evening on her own. He is full of apologies as he lets himself into the house – only to find it empty. Afer his call, she had gone off at the last moment to a first night with the profligate Lord Ormsby, not leaving a note, thinking she'll be back first. Milne convincingly conveys Wellard's changing mood as he waits up, not knowing where she is, until her radiant return an hour later. He says all the wrong things. They quarrel and go to bed in their separate bedrooms. Wellard lies awake, hoping Sylvia will come to him and apologize.

He went over in his mind all the other quarrels which they had had. Not quarrels, disagreements. Never like this. Never before had they carried a disagreement over into the next day. A quarrel, an apology, friends again, lovers again. That was the way when, as Coral Bell put it, you were still on the higher plane, still in love. Once safely on the lower plane, your quarrels need not be made up. You were cross, you went to bed, you woke up uncross, and all went on as comfortably as before. But when you were still in love, everything mattered so terribly, for each could still hurt the other with a word, with a look, and every wound, left untended, slowly festered.

He pictured her in the next room, awake, miserable, wondering if he would come to her, wondering if she should, after all, go to him. Suddenly he felt that it would be a very shameful thing if she came in now to say that she was sorry, when the fault was his. No, he would go to her, lying there awake, miserable, and ask her forgiveness. Somehow they must be friends again tonight.

He went to her, gladly, eagerly. Eagerly he opened her door and called 'Sylvia!' He turned up the light by her bed, eagerly. There she lay . . . deeply, beautifully, utterly, asleep.

So it all meant nothing to her! He went back to his room resentfully, slammed the door and lay awake for another hour. Then he too went to sleep.

'The really difficult thing', Coral Bell had said, 'is knowing when and how to fall *out* of love.'

'Oh, come! There *are* people who stay in love with each other all their lives.'

'Of course, and we all hope that's what our own marriage is going to be like. And it's because people will go on hoping when there's obviously no hope that there are so many failures. You see, if you're in love, every little difference has to be made up before you're happy again; if you're "out of" love you can quarrel as often as you like and still keep happy and friendly.'

'On a lower plane.'

'Yes. But it's in the descent from the higher plane to the lower that most marriages crash. If only they can get safely on to the lower plane, they're all right.'

Milne would give a vivid impression of the lower plane in his 1938 play *Gentleman Unknown*, where one woman reflects to another on her marriage: 'The first six years were the worst . . . We're perfectly happy now.' 'Which means that you have separate bedrooms and smack each other on the back.'

Smacking each other on the back was not quite the Milnes' style, but certainly at some point in these years their marriage slipped from the higher to the lower plane and survived without crashing.

In *Two People* Wellard was spending a great deal of time in the theatre, as Milne had so often done himself. He was watching rehearsals of the dramatization of his novel.

'Going to the theatre, darling?' Sylvia asked at breakfast. Silly question. She knew quite well he was going. She only said it to make it look as if he were wasting his time going to the theatre; to let him know that she knew quite well how unnecessary this theatre-going was; to make him feel awkward if he spoke to another woman there. What was the answer? He thought: If one hated one's wife, one would say, 'Well, naturally', in the coldest voice possible. If one loved one's wife, one would say eagerly, 'Yes, if you'll come with me. Do!'

'Going to the theatre, darling?'

'Well, naturally,' he said in the coldest voice possible.

Milne was himself spending a great deal of time in the theatre in the winter of 1930. After many years of waiting, *Toad of Toad Hall* – his 'loving and efficient and amusing' adaptation of *The Wind in the Willows* – was at last being rehearsed for its first London production. The play, which he had written as long ago as 1921, had actually been published and had had a first production at the Liverpool Playhouse the year before. It was, as the *New York Herald Tribune* put it, 'a serious challenge to the producer', which was presumably why it had taken so long to find one. But after its London success it immediately established itself as a regular Christmas treat for children, until a time when it could be called, almost as much as the *Pooh* books, 'one of the very few classics for children'. In fact, it is the only Milne play that is still regularly produced. Much as he admired Grahame, much as he loved *The Wind in the Willows* and thought he had done a reasonable job in bringing it to the theatre, its success above his own adult plays would inevitably cause Milne some very mixed feelings. Was he really to survive only as a writer for children? It is interesting to speculate that if Milne had been approached in 1929, not in 1921, by Curtis Brown, he would almost certainly have refused the commission. The last thing he wanted was further identification as a children's writer.

It is easier in England to make a reputation than to lose one. I wrote four 'Children's books', containing altogether, I suppose, 70,000 words – the number of words in the average-length novel. Having said good-bye to all that in 70,000 words, knowing that as far as I was concerned the mode was outmoded, I gave up writing children's books. I wanted to escape from them as I had once wanted to escape from *Punch;* as I have always wanted to escape. In vain.

There was no escaping the children's books. The four went on selling vast numbers each year and they were joined by the first of the spin-offs – *Tales of Pooh* (selections of the stories), *The Hums of Pooh* (yet another song book), *The Christopher Robin Birthday Book* (Milne took a considerable interest in that: 'The quotations should hope to apply to the person who writes in it rather than to the day . . .'), the Very Young Calendar, the Pooh Calendar – and so on, not to mention Pooh birthday cards and Christmas cards and games and toys and china. In the early 1930s Pooh had already become an industry.

And now here was Milne unexpectedly finding himself identified with another childish creature, Toad, as the author of 'one of the best holiday entertainments imaginable'. Everyone seemed sure, as indeed it proved, that the play would 'join the strange company of plays, of which *Peter Pan* is the chief, that appear year after year at Christmas'. The *News Chronicle* said that 'the court scene, which is entirely his own work, is as funny as anything in *Alice in Wonderland*. That may seem too high praise to give to any living author, but I give it all the same.'

The play has had its critics (notably Peter Green, Grahame's biographer, who thought it 'mawkish') but at the time most people seemed to agree with Charles Morgan, who said in *The Times* that it was 'an extremely adroit adaptation of a difficult original'. The difficulty was that Kenneth Grahame 'did not greatly trouble to keep all his scenes on the same scale.' 'It was as if a rabbit were to be your guest at dinner on Monday evening and to become by Tuesday morning a miniature beast, scuttling over the toe of your boot . . . On the stage uniformity of scale must be preserved and Mr Milne's first task was, by judicious selection of his scenes, to preserve it. Set Mr Milne free in a world of fantasy and he is at ease; it is only when he fantasticates our own world, without always being aware of his departure from reality, that he sets our teeth on edge.'

Milne chose his 'scenes', not just because of the problems of scale, but because he knew there were parts of the book that simply could not be transplanted to the stage. 'It seemed clear to me,' he wrote, 'that Rat and Toad, Mole and Badger could only face the footlights with hope of success if they were content to amuse their audiences. There are both beauty and comedy in the book, but the beauty must be left to blossom there, for I, anyhow, shall not attempt to transplant it.' *The Wind in the Willows* had become 'a romp instead of a pastoral', as one critic put it, but it is a very enjoyable romp. It is only odd that Milne makes it Marigold's dream when he would criticize Carroll for the unnecessary dream framework of *Alice:* 'Who is ever interested in somebody else's dream . . . It was no dream, no story for children. It happened. He was there himself.'

In the *Daily Telegraph* Milne's friend, W. A. Darlington, saw that one reason for the success of *Toad of Toad Hall* is that 'the Wild Wood of Mr Grahame's book is quite evidently only a mile or two away from the Forest in which dwell Mr Milne's own creations, Winnie-the-Pooh and the rest . . . It is this sense of being at home in Mr Grahame's domain, of being able to walk about in it without watching his step and to talk in it without having to keep a guard on his tongue that has enabled Mr Milne to make such a delightful play . . .'

Milne said that constant attendance at rehearsals made him so familiar with the spoken dialogue that he became more and more uncertain as to which lines were taken direct from the book, which lines were adapted and which lines were entirely his own invention. Milne recalled Kenneth Grahame's own visit to the play:

When he and Mrs Grahame first came to see the play, they were charming enough to ask me to share their box. I was terrified, for had I been the writer of the book, and he the dramatist, I should have resented every altered word of mine and every interpolated word of his.

He was not like that. He sat there, an old man now, as eager as any child in the audience, and on the occasions (fortunately not too rare) when he could recognize his own words, his eye caught his wife's, and they smiled at each other, and seemed to be saying: 'I wrote that' – 'Yes, dear, *you* wrote that', and they nodded happily at each other, and turned their eyes again to the stage. It was almost as if he were thanking me in his royally courteous manner for letting him into the play at all, whereas, of course, it was his play entirely, and all I had hoped to do was not to spoil it. For, when characters have been created as solidly as those of Rat and Mole, Toad and Badger, they speak ever after in their own voices, and the dramatist has merely to listen and record.

It had not been so simple. But Milne showed in a practical way how much he considered the play remained Grahame's work, by taking a much smaller share of any possible film rights than Curtis Brown had suggested.

That had been back in 1921; ten years later Milne was very exercised over the subject of film rights. He published a spirited article on the subject in the autumn 1931 issue of the *Author*, urging his fellow writers not to be browbeaten into giving theatre managers a share of the subsidiary rights of the plays they put on. This was not long after the release by RKO of Basil Dean's version of Milne's detective play. It had a confusing array of titles, but in America both play and film were called *The Perfect Alibi*. All the exteriors were filmed at Easton Lodge, the home of H. G. Wells's neighbour, Lady Warwick. Filming ended with a splendid fête with balloon flights, floodlit dancing, blue cocktails and Gerald Du Maurier bobbing up and down on a floating stage – but nothing would reconcile Milne to the film industry. He wrote in the *Author:*

In America where it is now taken for granted that the manager has fifty per cent of the film rights, the theatrical manager is rapidly being driven out by the Film Magnate, who takes theatres and puts on plays, simply in order to have a cheap and constant supply of film material . . . My normal practice is to say that I am offering a play to what I assume to be a Theatre Manager. The questions as to whether I want it made into a film, and whether I want it, if made into a film, made in America, and how I shall spend the money, are of academic interest only. The Manager's usual practice is to say that in that case he can't take the play, and I say 'Right', and try to forget about it altogether – which is not really difficult, as one is then writing something else. A month later the Manager says that on second thoughts he will let me keep the film-rights if I give him half the amateur rights, and I say that if he doesn't like the play he should send it back to my agent. Later still he says that he doesn't really want the film or the amateur rights, but what he simply *must* have is the publishing rights . . . And so on and so on. In the end he realizes that I am offering him a licence to perform a play professionally in America for a number of years, and with any luck he signs the agreement.

Milne showed himself to be astute and adamant. His stand was one reason why so many of his plays at this period had to wait years for production. With the money from the children's books, he could afford to stick to his principles. Many writers could not afford to, but Milne was not alone in his deep suspicion of the cinema and the effect it would have on the theatre. A columnist in *Play Pictorial*, as the 'talkies' became established, commented on the general alarm in the theatre. 'A horde of mice suddenly introduced in the midst of a mothers' meeting could not produce more squeals of terror', he said unimaginatively, and was foolish enough to believe that the cinema would 'take neither a prominent nor a permanent part in the art life of a nation . . . when the craze of novelty disappears.'

'Talking picture rights' to *The Dover Road*, which had earlier been made as a silent film, were bought by the Paramount Studios for $10,000. It was filmed under the title *Where Sinners Meet*, with Diana Wynyard and Clive Brook. Now *Michael and Mary*, directed by Victor Saville for the Gainsborough Studios, was certainly Milne's most successful film and would be highly praised in the *Picturegoer Weekly* in America. Far from being simply a 'photographed stage play' as Elmer Rice's *Street Scene* was (reviewed on the same page), it included such delights as the celebrations of the Relief of Mafeking (which had happened five years before the play started) and glimpses of the old Cheshire Cheese where 'one could almost sniff the beefsteak, kidney, oyster and lark pudding, not overlooking Dr Johnson's seat at the end of the narrow table'. It was suggested more scenes like this should be included in British films – 'for even though they may not enhance the value of the picture in some sections of America, in others it will count in the film's favour and in the British colonies it means a great deal.' (Similar tactics are frequently used nowadays by television directors hoping to sell abroad.) In a letter to St John Ervine at this time Milne listed the cinema among his dislikes. But lots of people were loving it. Even the columnist in the *Hollywood Spectator* found himself 'crying softly' as the final scene of *Michael and Mary* faded from the screen.

One result of the success of *Toad of Toad Hall* was an eventual letter from Arthur Ransome asking Milne to dramatize *Missee Lee*. Milne's reply explained why he would find this impossible:

A play has to be in one key throughout . . . *Missee Lee* is a story of real adventure among fantastic pirates whom the real adventurers never take seriously. One can read about this knowing all the time that it is only a story, yet carried away alternately by the adventure and the fantasy. But seeing the children in flesh and blood on the stage, hearing them talk like real children, we can't help wondering what we are supposed to do about it. Are we to tremble for their danger? Are we eager for them to escape? But escape from what – Death, or Latin? This uncertainty makes things difficult for the audience; and 'stage craft' = 'making things easy for the audience'.

In *Peter Pan* children and pirates are alike fantastic; the note is struck at the rise of the curtain by Nana; but here the conflict is between real children and cardboard pirates. Moreover children, however delightful to read about, can never carry a play: this must be done by the grown-ups: but in Chinese and pidgin English, what chance have they? What makes *Robinson Crusoe* such an absorbing book is Defoe's absorption in the practical details of how things work. This is, if I may say so, your shining quality and, I suspect, the quality which attracts your readers. But it is not a dramatic quality.

Milne was no longer on the committee of the Society of Authors at this stage, but he kept an alert eye on everything that concerned the professional writer. In the winter of 1929–30, H. G. Wells was involved in a dispute with the Society, which had taken up the case of another member whom he had commissioned to work with him on a project that he had then abandoned. Wells sent Milne – along with other members of the Society – a booklet he had had privately printed, *The Problem of the Troublesome Collaborator*, and invited Milne to comment to the Society. Milne told Wells the booklet had given him 'at least one sleepless night', but he felt better after sending the committee a five-page letter:

Two members of the Society have opposing stories to tell, and you take it on yourselves to say that the distinguished one, the member of your Council, is the liar. Is it a tragedy or a screaming farce? As either it is so unnatural as to be intolerable . . . The one principle by which an artist lives is the principle that he will not write what he feels he cannot write . . . Your committee is now fighting for the principle that if an author has contracted to produce a word in collaboration *sine die* he must (on discovering that the work is beyond him) either sacrifice his artistic scruple and produce it, or sacrifice his moral scruples and let the work hang over indefinitely; but that if he does the morally and artistically honourable things and withdraws at once from the collaboration, then the Committee of the Society which he adorns and supports shall lead out the whole pack of authors to harry him . . .

I feel strongly on the subject. I can hardly suppose, after your utter disregard for one whom many would consider your most distinguished member, that you will have much regard for a member so much less distinguished . . .

At least he had done his best and, sending a copy to Wells, he had shown his old teacher again how much he respected him. It was a small return for all the support he had had in his own early years as a writer, but it was something.

On 2 January 1931 the Milnes' usual Christmas holiday treat took the form of a visit to *Toad of Toad Hall* with tea on the stage afterwards. Denis Mackail recorded the occasion in his diary, remarking that he himself had never been behind the scenes at a theatre until he was fifteen or sixteen – 'but Mary and Anne had greater advantages'. Christopher spent a great deal of time in his Christmas holidays being coached at cricket. Milne thought he was 'terribly good' – telling Charles Turley Smith that the boy 'really looks like a cricketer'. But he had to admit that at Gibbs' he had got no further than twelfth man in the second eleven. 'He is always the youngest boy in any form he has been in and generally top, so I think he is scholarship form. Forgive a proud parent; he is a duck; and on a baby billiard table we have, he made a break of 23 the other day. At the moment, however, he is maddest about Meccano and Riding.' By the time of the *Toad of Toad Hall* treat he had had two terms at Boxgrove near Guildford, where the headmaster was a man called Caldwell who had been up at Cambridge with Milne and Captain of Golf.

Milne told Turley how much he had enjoyed his new schoolboy story *The Left Hander*. 'You still do this sort of book better than anybody.' He went on:

And yet, as a father, I read with mixed feelings. For why? Well – on the very first day of the summer holidays, I took Moon to the Oval, where Woolley made a century before lunch. After lunch it rained. We sat in the pavilion, and I wondered if it was worth waiting, but Moon didn't like to give up hope of more cricket. I said 'Well, what can we do?' and he said 'Let's do Algebra', which we did on the backs of old envelopes. On the first day of these present holidays, he was given a diary (sent as an advertisement by some school outfitters) which contained long lists of Latin, French and Greek verbs. Immediately I had to teach him the Greek alphabet, which he now knows by heart (and has passed on to the cook). Well now, Turley, I hope I'm not a prig, but there seems to me no reason why this passion for knowledge, which all the *very* young have, should not persist a little longer; and as a prig or a parent (I don't know which) I get saddened by the gay assumptions in so many school books that his brain is the last thing which any boy might use.

Small and unnecessary sermon by Milne. Sorry. I wish you could see Moon's off-drive. Is there any chance of your being in London for a day or two? It is on view daily at Faulkner's school.

Milne put forward the same view, priggish or not, in one of his rare public speeches. He remembered:

I was a guest at a dinner of Preparatory Schoolmasters. They all, so it seemed, made speeches; two Public School Headmasters made speeches; and the burden of all their speeches was the obstructiveness of the Parent to their beneficent labours. I had disclaimed any desire to make a speech, but by this time I wanted to. That very evening, offered the alternatives of a proposition of Euclid's or a chapter of *Treasure Island* as a bedtime story, my own boy had chosen Euclid: it was 'so much more fun'. All children, I said (perhaps rashly), are like that. There is nothing that they are not eager to learn. 'And then we send them to your schools, and in two years, three years, four years, you have killed all their enthusiasm. At fifteen their only eagerness is to escape learning anything. No wonder you don't want to meet us.' It was not a popular speech . . . But afterwards a Headmaster came up to me and said: 'It was absolutely true what you were saying, but why is it? What do we do? I've often wondered.'

Just at this time when Daphne was saying how important it was to put partner before child, Milne was enjoying his son's company more and more. After the long years in which Christopher and his nanny 'had not been out of each other's sight for more than a few hours at a time – apart from her fortnight's holiday every September – Milne was enjoying having the boy to himself. Now, in the holidays, father and son would sit side by side on the sofa at Cotchford solving simultaneous equations. The son wrote:

He was lucky. We were together until I was eighteen, very, very close. He knew he was lucky, that he had got perhaps more than he deserved, and he was very grateful. And once, a little shyly, he thanked me . . .

Father and son. What sort of relationship is it? Does the father look down to the son, the son look up to the father? Or does the father get on to his hands and knees so that they are both on the same level? Sometimes the one, sometimes the other; but in our case neither would do. We had to be on the same level, but we both had to be standing, for my father couldn't bend, couldn't pretend to be what he wasn't. We could do algebra together, and Euclid, and look for birds' nests, and catch things in the stream, and play cricket in the meadow. We could putt on the lawn and throw tennis balls at each other. We could do those things as equals. But what about those other moments, which adults pass in casual chit-chat, which husband and wife can so happily share in complete silence, content to be in each other's company? Meal times. Car journeys. After dinner in front of the fire. Conversation with a small child is difficult. Perhaps instead one might learn the morse code. My father had learnt it during the war when he was battalion signals officer. So now he taught me and with hand squeezes we were able to pass messages to each other as Burnside drove us down to Cotchford. Then at lunch time mightn't I feel a bit left out if he and my mother discussed dull, grown-up things? So 'How about a game?' he would say, and we would play clumps, or go through the alphabet to see how many flowers we could name beginning with each letter in turn. And finally, after dinner, almost a ritual, there was *The Times* crossword, with my mother (to give her a slight advantage) reading out the clues and my father trying not to be too quick with the answers.

My father had a passion for crosswords. We shared *The Times:* this was the rule. It was fairly easy. It took about half an hour, and though he would get most of the answers (including all the quotations), my mother and I would be able to manage a few contributions. On Sunday we took the *Observer* and so on Sunday evening we did the 'Everyman' crossword. This left my father to wrestle single-handed with his favourite Torquemada ...

Solving crosswords is immensely satisfying. In a way it is the same sort of satisfaction you get from solving mathematical problems. Pencil, paper and brains: that's what you need.

Pencil, paper and brains. Sometimes it seemed that life would be much easier if that was all one had, if one could ignore the heart. Christopher, looking objectively at his parents in these years, summed up the great gulf between them in the difference in their eating habits:

Knives and forks being tools, it is perhaps not surprising that my mother handled hers with great dexterity, my father with his usual clumsiness. (It was generally agreed within the family that my father couldn't eat a pear without getting his elbows wet, and that after a honey sandwich he had to have a bath.) ... There was something cat-like about the way my mother ate. Just as a cat will lick at a saucer on and on until not even the ghost of a smell remains, so would my mother scrape at her plate, not greedily, just methodically, until it was spotless. My father, on the other hand, mushed his food up and then left all the bits he didn't like – the gristly bits, the stringy bits, the skinny bits – round the edge. And because they were so different, each found the other's habits mildly irritating. 'I wonder why you always have to mash up your strawberries in that rather repellent way.'

Christopher and his father went to Purley to visit J. V. Milne just before the boy went back to school in January 1931. J. V. Milne was eighty-five and 'growing older every day', as he told Miss Pinnington. 'Christopher is a clever boy all round – in school work and in games – and the darling of his father!' At Boxgrove he had begun his 'love-hate relationship' with his fictional namesake. 'I began to dislike him, and I found myself disliking him more and more the older I got. Was my father aware of this? I don't know.' Certainly Milne made no attempt to keep him out of the papers. There is a photo of the ten-year-old boy on a pony called Cracker with a long article on Milne published the day before the visit to Purley.

It is interesting that all the interviewer's emphasis is on *When We Were Very Young*, which is seen as Milne's assurance of immortality. One can imagine how Milne's heart must have sunk as he read the charming description of his charming self looking 'so youthful that it is difficult to believe that he was born in 1882'. 'There is one word which it is impossible to resist using of him, though it has been taboo even in newspaper offices for a long time, and that is the word "whimsical". The final touch to his personality is just that.'

Milne was working on *Two People* at this time, rather sporadically (he had begun it eighteen months before), and spoke of the pleasure of not having to worry whether he was boring somebody in the stalls – 'Writing a play, you have to consider the audience. Writing a novel, you only consider yourself.' When asked what he considered his best work he said: '*The House at Pooh Corner* and *Michael and Mary*, I think. But probably most people would say *When We Were Very Young* and *The Truth About Blayds*.'

Milne had almost given up journalism. He had stopped writing short stories. He had apparently given up writing verse, or at least publishing it, if one excepts a frivolous contribution to a debate (with one Denis Browne, among others) in *The Times*, on the subject of the horrors of the second verse of the National Anthem. Milne suggested (having worked himself into the mood of 'robust patriotism' demanded by a Mr McClure Smith):

> O Lord our God, arise,
> Guard our securities,
> Don't let them fall.
> Scatter all party hacks
> (Save those my party backs)
> And make the income tax
> Optional.

The last word, sung 'Op-shee-un-all' would be very effective. Mr Denis Browne could repeat this 'unashamedly and from the heart' after paying his first instalment.

In 1931 Alan and Daphne Milne at last paid their visit to America. It was Milne's only visit, but Daphne would return again and again until war made it impossible. They arrived on the *Aquitania* on 27 October. Milne felt immediately cheered because the customs officer recognized his name and said he knew his books: 'Can you imagine an English customs man who had read the works of an American author? Why, most of them do not read books by Englishmen,' Milne said later to a reporter. It was fine that the customs officer should know about Christopher Robin and Winnie-the-Pooh. It was not so good when it turned out that that was what everyone else was interested in, too.

Milne was overwhelmed with hundreds of questions from dozens of interviewers. He told everyone that he was determined to establish two records for a visiting English writer – he was not going to lecture or make any public speeches – and he was not going to write anything about the United States. Surprisingly, he succeeded in sticking to his pledges. Some of the journalists found him rather difficult: 'Mr Milne shrank into himself as soon as each question was answered, usually in the briefest possible manner.' This was at the very first interview, even before he had set foot in Manhattan. 'Sunk in a deep chair in the library of the *Aquitania* and pulling on a pipe, Mr Milne submitted with some trepidation to his first experience of an American interview. He carefully avoided passing judgment on American institutions, habits or writers, and said that "pleasure" was the word he had filled in on the admittance form. It was his only quest in coming to America, he volunteered.'

This was not quite true. They were in New York 'partly to see about the opening of Mr Milne's new play *They Don't Mean Any Harm*' (which would be called *Other People's Lives* in England), and partly to stimulate interest in his new novel, *Two People*. As Milne had said years before of an American visit: 'We feel it would be good for trade.' The children's books were, of course, in no need of any boost. The papers repeated over and over again the extraordinary fact that their total sales had now already reached a million copies. In that first interview: 'Mr Milne laughingly confessed to twinges of professional jealousy over being known solely as the father of Christopher Robin . . . I always like my last book best but I find it's impossible to get away from the Christopher Robin atmosphere. When my new novel *Two People* was reviewed in London, all of the critics harped on the same string.'

Milne's visit to New York, with all the attendant publicity, undoubtedly helped to put *Two People* on the American bestseller list, though perhaps most people who bought it were interested mainly in seeing what Christopher Robin's father was up to now. One strange result of this was a parody of William Faulkner under the title 'Popeye the Pooh' in *Vanity Fair*, celebrating the simultaneous appearance in the bestseller list of *Sanctuary*, so grim, so pessimistic, with 'such strenuously optimistic novels' as J. B. Priestley's *The Good Companions*, Warwick Deeping's *Ten Commandments* and A. A. Milne's *Two People*.

A small dog was worrying a long limp object on the lawn. 'It looks like Eeyore', Milne said. The puppy shook the object back and forth, wagging his stubby tail. Popeye shot him. 'He gets into everything', Popeye said. He leaned over and picked up . . . the limp human arm . . . which the dog had been worrying. 'Jim's', he said, and tossed it carelessly into the bushes . . . 'The more it snows (Tiddley pom) the more it goes (Tiddley pom) on snowing', Milne said happily, spreading several slices of bread and butter with the contents of a jar marked 'Strawberry Jam'.

While Milne was in America, a review of *Two People* appeared in *Time*, under the title 'If you are very young', grumbling about 'bathetic Barriesqueness' and about Sylvia as the Perfect Woman 'whom every adolescent knows but of whom not many would speak, at least in broad daylight.' At almost the same moment, P. G. Wodehouse was writing from Hollywood to his friend William Townend: 'Have you read A. A. Milne's serial *Two People* in the *Daily Mail*? It's colossal. The sort of book I shall buy and re-read every six months or so. What a genius he is at drawing character. Did you ever see his *The Dover Road*? My favourite play.' Wodehouse's high opinion of *Two People* survived the passing of the years and the eventual rupture of their friendship. More than twenty years later, he wrote to Denis Mackail: 'Any news of A. A. M.? You know he did write some damn good stuff. I can re-read a thing like *Two People* over and over again and never get tired of it.'

Wodehouse seemed to be the only person in America who did not think of Milne primarily as a children's writer. This was particularly odd and irritating for Milne at this point, when he was trying to re-establish his adult reputation and when, only the year before, *Michael and Mary* had completed a satisfactorily long run of 246 performances in New York, followed by a tour of the principal cities and numerous productions by stock companies all over the United States. It had been 'the last season's matchless and distinctive success', in spite of some very mixed reviews. George Jean Nathan, in an extraordinary attack, had dubbed Milne 'the Chelsea Pollyanna'. 'I am told that, in his personal being, this Milne is an entirely normal fellow who eats meat, shaves and cusses at a tight cork, just like any of us, but the moment he gets out his writing tools something very peculiar happens to him . . . He can't check himself from going pansy with a vengeance.' It was obviously that kiss that had riled him. Several reviews had included the dread word 'whimsical', fulfilling his prophecy in the published preface. Really he had hoped, with *Michael and Mary*, to get away from it. But apparently he could not. 'For the most part engrossing and delightful, although perhaps overly whimsical for a play built on ideas', said *Theatre*; and Joseph Wood Krutch in the *Nation* regretted that 'one short dramatic scene in this sentimental comedy-drama is surrounded with padding which may be judged whimsical or infantile.'

The headline in the *New York Herald Tribune* on Milne's arrival in New York read:

A. A. MILNE HERE
LOATHING NAME
OF 'WHIMSICAL'
Author of *Winnie-the-Pooh*
Hates Whisky, Fears Interviewers,
will not lecture
—
Never in America Before
—
Christopher Robin, Now 11,
Remained Home at School.

Even if Charles Hopkins, its producer, had thought *Michael and Mary* 'a play of rare beauty and extraordinary charm' and many thousands of people had enjoyed it in the theatre, the newspapers had decided that Milne's plays were not what people were interested in.

'Christopher Robin was our chief concern,' Fanny Butcher wrote in the *Chicago Tribune*, going on to suggest to Milne that: 'There's your next novel. The story of Christopher Robin at the age of twenty-two, when he reaps the harvest of his childhood.'

'If I make a success of Christopher Robin as a person I will consider it my greatest creative work,' Milne said to her. The headline of an interview in the *New York Times Magazine* was MILNE'S HARDEST JOB IS BEING A FATHER. 'It is difficult to guide a boy, to direct him in certain channels and at the same time to make him retain the feeling that you are his companion and that there is no separation caused by the gulf of years.' It was what he most longed for, an equal companionship with his son. He obliged reporters by showing his photographs of Christopher, the long-ago one with the butterfly, and a more recent one of him with his cricket bat, 'looking very grown-up and very competent'. He was apparently so remarkable a cricketer 'that authorities on the subject proclaim him the future defender of England'. And he had produced a prose piece called 'The Inexperienced Husband', written in the first person, a strange achievement for a boy of eleven.

Daphne was being asked about Christopher Robin too. If he had once wanted to stay six for ever and ever, he was now finding it just as much fun being eleven. He was that sort of boy. 'Pooh sheds a tear occasionally when he remembers that he and Christopher Robin were exactly the same size on that day, ten years ago now, when the friendly bear joined the Milne family.' But Pooh could hardly blame Christopher Robin for growing up. It was just one of those things a boy had to do and a bear didn't. 'Yet he is younger, I find', his mother said, 'than most American children of his age. English children seem to belong longer to the nursery than their American cousins. They are less sophisticated, quite babyish really in comparison . . . Inhabiting a little world all their own, it is not surprising that English children stay very simple and young. Over here life seems to throw American children into closer contact with the older members of the family . . .'

The Milnes were staying at the Lombardy Hotel on East Fifty-Sixth Street. One interviewer said: 'He loves the streets of New York already and you can't keep him in.' Milne kept taking brisk walks, as one way to escape the telephone calls and the queues of journalists. New York was, Daphne insisted, 'much more beautiful, much more interesting and much more delightful' than they had expected. She longed to go to a speakeasy; but Milne said he was 'extraordinarily uninterested' in the liquor question.

Milne played golf on Long Island and in Westchester. They were both enjoying going to the theatre nearly every night. Milne was struck by how much more integral a part of American life at this time the theatre was. American audiences seemed interested in it for its own sake. 'At the average lunch or dinner party, the theatre is the principal topic of conversation.' In England, on the other hand, most people saw it only as a place for celebrating special occasions.

Milne and Daphne together visited Ned Sheldon (a friend of their friend Denis Mackail), whose play *Romance* had once had a long run on the English stage. Sheldon was a stirring example of the victory of courage over disaster. By this time he was both blind and paralysed. Mackail would report that the Milnes had visited him in some trepidation and had then been overwhelmed by Sheldon's exemplary sweetness. Mackail said, 'His visitors come away and say "I can't believe in God now'', or "Now I believe in God". But both statements mean exactly the same thing – that all their previous notions about everything have received a pretty severe jolt.' *Parents' Magazine* gave a tea party for A. A. Milne at which the editor, Alice Dalgleish, said 'his poetry showed a true understanding of children and had brought America and England closer together'.

John Macrae of Dutton's gave a much larger tea party at the Waldorf Astoria. 'They invited everybody – literary, dramatic and dilettante. The guests came in droves and each had his blunderbuss loaded with a question which he let fly the moment he held Mr Milne's right hand . . . Meeting people in droves is not Mr Milne's long suit.' It was said there were 400 people in the room. Among the guests were Mrs Franklin D. Roosevelt, the British Consul-General, Walter Lippman, Norman Thomas, Fannie Hurst and Christopher Morley – the one with whom Dorothy Parker had pretended to confuse Christopher Robin in her devastating review of *Now We Are Six*. Morley's copy of *Two People* bears the inscription:

> – a ridiculously inadequate
> acknowledgement of himself, his books and
> his kindness to his friend, A. A. Milne.
> New York. Dec. 4. 1931.

A lot of people were being very kind. A letter from Milne to May Lamberton Becker suggests that Daphne was not always very efficient in dealing with the numerous invitations, that she was not a very good secretary. (Indeed her letters over the years, on Milne's behalf, suggest that too. They were nearly always undated, and part of that Yorkshire headmaster's dissatisfaction with his letter from 'Celia Brice' was perhaps because of Daphne's scrawling unattractive handwriting.) Milne hoped Miss Becker was feeling well and friendly because 'The fact is that Daphne, with my watchful eye off her, has muddled it again.' She had agreed to a lunch on a date when they would not actually be in New York. 'We go to Philadelphia on Monday and then to Toronto for a day or two.' Milne ended the letter: 'Do forgive us, and realize how difficult it is for us to keep our heads in this avalanche of hospitality which has descended on us.'

Among the people who entertained them was Elmer Rice, the

playwright, whom they had met in London the year before when he had been in England for the production of *Street Scene*, which had won the Pulitzer Prize in the States. Milne admired both Rice's politics and his plays – particularly the stagecraft of *The Adding Machine*, which he had mentioned in the same sentence as *Hamlet* in his preface to *Michael and Mary*. New York in 1931 was not, of course, all tea parties at the Waldorf Astoria. Two years after the Wall Street crash, it was difficult to ignore the effects of the depression. There were soup kitchens, bread lines, people sleeping out in the parks, even in the November chill. Elmer Rice (born Reizenstein), for all his enormous success in the theatre, was someone who had a concern for social justice which Milne found very sympathetic. Red-haired and tall, Rice came from a poor Jewish background – as a boy he had shared his grandfather's bedroom. Shaw had turned him into a socialist and a playwright. His first two plays had been on feminist themes. The second, *The Seventh Commandment*, was an attack on 'the social code that condemns in a woman what it condones in a man.' His third play, *On Trial*, written when he was still only twenty-one, had been an extraordinary success, bringing him eventually $100,000, an apartment on Claremont Avenue and a collection of marvellous paintings: Picasso, Braque, Dufy, Rouault, Léger, Modigliani, Derain. He remained a socialist and a pacifist and an ardent advocate of women's rights, active in the American Civil Liberties Union, the National Council on Freedom from Censorship and the Dramatists' Guild. For all his awareness of social realities, he retained (as he put it in his autobiography) 'a kind of romantic idealism' and a feeling that 'life is potentially good, that people are potentially trustworthy'. Elmer Rice and Alan Milne had a good deal in common, but it was Daphne, rather than Alan, who responded most completely to Rice's charm. She had other American friends as well, but it was Rice principally who drew her back to New York again and again in the following years. She would see him in London too.

Milne himself had become acquainted, not long before he and Daphne went to America, with a young actress called Leonora Corbett, who had played Delia, Belinda's daughter, in a revival of Milne's play, *Belinda* at the Embassy Theatre in Swiss Cottage. He would get to know her better when (perhaps at his suggestion) she played Lola Waite in his new play *Other People's Lives* in November 1932 at the Arts Theatre in London.

In many ways this play – the one known as *They Don't Mean Any Harm* in New York – is the most interesting of all Milne's plays. It is full of tragic implications and even 'Ibsenish irony', but it is also one of the most deeply flawed. The *Saturday Review* called it 'a savage attack on the new generation' and said that 'a nearly great play is disappointing'. 'Christopher Robin having been packed off to boarding school, Mr Milne has revived his Myras and Archies' – those long-ago Rabbits from *Punch* – 'They are, however, of a more modern and less agreeable vintage.' The 'new generation' consists of two young couples, the Waites and the Bellamys, of a kind still familiar to us from Noël Coward comedies. 'The world and all that happens in the world is an opportunity for them to exhibit the agility of their minds . . . their deadly heartlessness. The first act contains some of the neatest verbal nonsense that has come to the stage for several years.' The Waites and the Bellamys decide to amuse themselves by interfering in the lives of the sad people in the flat below, the Tillings, father, mother, daughter. But Milne's problem is that, unlike Coward, he loathes his bright young things too much, the Tillings are not fragile but merely pathetic, and 'the evil of heartless charity is not proved by accidental misfortune attending its results.' The play goes to pieces after a strong first act. One or two of the critics thought that the unhappy ending suggested that Milne had at last achieved adult status, but the general opinion was more with the *Theatre Arts Monthly*, which decided that 'Milne continues his sentimental decline'.

They Don't Mean Any Harm was a disaster in New York. It ran for only fifteen performances and was the last of Milne's plays to be produced on Broadway. Curtis Brown said that 'Charles Hopkins, who had constituted himself purveyor-in-chief of Milne plays in America, came a cropper with the cruel little comedy and lost faith in his idol.' His cable address was Chopkins. When the news arrived Milne was working on the novel that would be called *Four Days' Wonder*. He wrote to his agent:

Entirely blasted by the shattering disruption of the Chopkins legend, I sat down before the one written chapter of my novel and reflected gloomily that two years would elapse before I rose like a Phoenix from the dust, and faced the world again with a smile, and wreathed vine-leaves in my hair. And, metaphorically speaking, I hurled the novel in the W. P. B. and said,

'No, I'm damned if I sit down under a failure like that. I will write another and, if not a better play, at least a happier one'. Well, the whole point of this letter is that I have written two acts of it, and am on my way through the third. It is the lightest *Belinda* – *Hay Fever* – *Importance of Being Earnest* thing, and if it isn't funny, I will eat Chopkins's Stetson.

It was *not* funny, whatever it was. Or, if it was funny, nobody seems to have thought so; nobody wanted to produce it. Reviews of a revival of *The Truth about Blayds* that April brought back 'memories of days when A. A. Milne was a rather exciting figure in the theatre'. In the *New York Times*, Brooks Atkinson suggested that 'by indulging himself in whimsy, Mr Milne has thrown away a strong career.' A more recent critic has said, 'Milne blamed Pooh for overshadowing his later plays. But Pooh was blameless. Throughout the 1930s, Milne produced nothing to overshadow.'

There is no doubt that Milne's career as a successful playwright came to an end at this point. But he could hardly accept the fact. He gave a good impression of being still optimistic and buoyant. He wrote two plays just at this time. One was probably *H for Helena: a Midsummer Night's Folly*, which survives only in manuscript. The other was certainly *Sarah Simple*, in which Leonora Corbett would eventually star in London, but not for five years. He wrote in the Easter holidays of 1932 to his father – his last surviving letter to him:

I have just finished the pencil-draft of my second play since the end of February – and am now writing it out properly in ink. I feel very play-ful just now; but I wish one could get plays produced as one gets novels published – automatically, as soon as the thing is finished. To find in the same person the actor or manager you want and the actor or manager who wants *you* is always a difficulty.

Moon rides every morning very happily, and amuses himself (and us) in a hundred other ways for the rest of the day. He has grown physically *and* mentally a lot this term, but hasn't grown away from us, and all the things he loves here, in the least. His bowling has improved a lot, I'm glad to say, and his throwing, and he ought to be certain of getting in the XI this term. He is now 12th in the school (in work) and will be 5th (at least) in September.

I don't want to interfere, but I should suggest that if you are altering your will for Connie's sake, you should leave the money definitely to *her*, not to Barry.

I expect Maud has told you all about the wedding. Marjorie looked very well and happy. I have just had a postcard from Venice saying that marriage has surpassed all her expectations and the sun is shining and everything is delightful. I wish the sun would shine here.

Milne's suspicions over his brother Barry and the will were well founded but, as he said, it was difficult for him to interfere. He had no idea of the changes Barry was persuading his dying father to make. Marjorie was sad that her grandfather was not well enough to attend her wedding in the Henry VII Chapel in Westminster Abbey to T. M. Murray-Rust, a master at Westminster School, where she had for some time been secretary to the Bursar. Milne stood in for Ken and gave her away, the girl he had so often written about in *Punch* twenty years before.

That was on 8 April. On 18 April John Vine Milne signed a new will, completely different from the one he had drawn up three years before, with Alan's guidance, after Ken's death. In that, as we saw, Milne was to have had returned to him the £5,000 he had given his father to provide extra income in his lifetime and the residue of the estate was to go to Ken's daughters, Marjorie and Angela.

The solicitors involved in drawing up the new will were 'My Son, David Barrett Milne and my Grandson John Barrett Milne of 30, Theobalds Road in the County of London', who were also to be Executors and Trustees. Some of the legacies from the previous will survived – Tim was still to get his grandfather's gold watch and chain and Tony 'the clock in the Sitting Room and the framed photograph of Ditchling Pond', Alan was still to get 'the walking stick given to me by my wife' and Daphne 'the framed photograph of Christopher Robin Milne, and the Venetian Glass on the mantelpiece in the Sitting Room'. But the basic provisions of the will were totally changed. There was no mention of returning to Alan his £5,000 and Angela received only the sum of £100. Marjorie, who had been extremely close to her grandfather and in constant contact with him, received nothing at all. The residue of the estate, 'all the real and personal property except property otherwise disposed of by this will', 'I devise and bequeath unto my said son David Barrett Milne for his own use and benefit absolutely.' If John Vine Milne's wish, as Alan's letter suggested, had been to safeguard Connie's future, he had failed absolutely.

The wicked Barry had achieved his own aim. He did not manage to prevent Maud seeing her dying father-in-law. John Vine Milne said to her – so she told her daughters – 'I am sorry about the will.' Apparently Barry had persuaded his father that Marjorie's new husband, the Westminster schoolmaster, was rich, rich enough to take care of Angela too, if necessary. (Why then, J. V. Milne might have asked, were they living in a small cottage in Gilwell Lane, London E4?)

The will could have been contested, but Alan could not bear the idea. He simply determined to have nothing whatsoever to do with his brother from now on. He felt very strongly that his nieces had been cheated of their inheritance by an unscrupulous uncle. He had never much cared for this brother and now it would be best to put him right out of his life. Six years later he wrote to H. G. Wells at a time when Barry's son John (the Jock he had once commemorated in verse, as a very little boy) was trying to get out of his father's office. 'He hates it like hell and is trying to escape into something, as he thinks, more respectable, like publishing.' (He would eventually become unquestionably respectable as an Anglican clergyman.) Wells, of course, remembered Barry – and Ken – from his days at Henley House. Milne wrote:

In confidence I may say that (for what I think are very good reasons) I have not been on speaking terms with Barry for some years, and see nothing of his family: it is Ken's family which command my interest and cheque book.

Alan Milne never spoke to Barry again, not even when Barry was dying of cancer of the throat and wrote to suggest a reconciliation.

In *Michael and Mary*, Michael had said to his father words which Alan might well have said to his: 'I do honour you, father. There's something about sheer goodness that always gets me . . . Sometimes you irritate me intensely and yet I believe I love you.' He and Ken had often joked about their father's monologues, his 'talks about things'. But they had always loved him and now Alan thought only of how much he owed him. He was glad he had given him so much reason to be proud of him, so much opportunity to boast to his friends. For years there had been guilt, as well as love, as he thought of his father eating his lonely meals in Purley. And now, on 11 June 1932, he was dead and Barry was beyond the pale. All the family had gone; all the links with his childhood were severed. And somehow his own life, too, seemed to be slipping away. He was fifty. All his adult life, he had been looking forward to the next book, the next play, full of optimism and enthusiasm. It had always seemed that he was still making his reputation. But now he had to accept that he had made it, and it was not the one that he had wanted.

— 16 —

The Thirties

MILNE PUBLISHED SIX books in the next five years. One was the novel *Four Days' Wonder* (1933), four were single plays or collections of plays, all except one of which he had already written. There was only one book, *Peace with Honour*, which would make any difference to his reputation. Milne had begun thinking about it soon after Ken's death. It is his most serious book; he himself thought it his most important book. He wrote to John Macrae at Dutton's: 'You have always told me that personally you thought more of *Winnie-the-Pooh* than of any book I have ever written. Please let me tell you that I think more of *Peace with Honour* than of any book that I have ever written.' Macrae would eventually go so far as to say: 'I believe that *Peace with Honour* will have the greatest influence of any book in modern times.' It is a passionate plea for peace, for the renunciation of war.

Milne had called himself a pacifist since 1910 and his experiences on the Somme had inevitably reinforced his conviction that war was an appalling way to settle international disputes. He found the book difficult to write. He told John Drinkwater how hard it was to get along without dialogue – having 'to do all the work myself, and not leave it to the characters'. In a preface dated August 1934, Milne wrote: 'I have been trying to write it, and, in a sense, trying not to write it for the last five years ... I have actually written it in the twelve months between July 1933 and July 1934.'

A letter to Harold Raymond of Chatto and Windus, in August 1933, apologizing for not having prepared his play *Other People's Lives* for publication, shows how he was feeling as he started work on *Peace with Honour*. The play had just come off in London and he said: 'I felt sick of the whole thing and not at all in the mood to grapple with it for the press; in fact, I felt that I never wanted to see the dashed play again.' He ended the letter:

Curse the theatre.
Curse all plays.
No matter – avanti.

It was much pleasanter acting as 'private chauffeur (unpaid) to my boy, who has been playing cricket matches all over Sussex'. It was also pleasanter (as he told Marjorie) sitting in a deck-chair in his beautiful garden at Cotchford, doing nothing very much at all. At this period he was always telling people how lazy he was ('I'm a born slacker really'). But he had a puritanical streak which actually made it difficult for him to enjoy the garden or the golf unless he had some work in progress. There were other things, too, interfering with his enjoyment of the garden that summer. There were too many horseflies about for his comfort: 'They definitely like me – even if the critics don't.'

An article the following summer in *Punch* suggests what was going on in those last two summer holidays before Christopher went on to Stowe. Christopher makes a lightly disguised appearance as John (the name Alan had always used for Ken in his writing), a prep-schoolboy who is a good cricketer and has 'a pleasant touch on the ukulele' (the instrument Christopher played, much to the disgust of the music master when he arrived at Stowe), but is definitely not an organizer. He dives neatly and sings in the choir, but he is not good on the telephone and his father is co-opted to help in organizing a holiday cricket match.

This article – the first Milne had had in *Punch* for many years – was published under the name of C. P. Brice. Milne sent a manuscript of it to Marjorie in the same letter that he congratulated her husband on becoming a housemaster at Westminster. They would from that September be living in Westminster School and Milne – but not Daphne – would see much more of them.

I am terribly glad and do congratulate you. Isn't it rather grand to miss out H.B.B. and Ashburnham like this?

Moon came back last Thursday, and we had two heavenly days at Lords. Walters and Wyatt – 160 in 80 minutes – you never saw such batting! We hugged each other in ecstasy at Walters: the most lovely bat in the world. (Moon is now practising Walters' shots).

Will you be an angel or get Angela to be one? Egged on by the family I have written the enclosed (obviously from life) and am sending it to *Punch* anonymously. Could you – would you – type it for me? My handwriting might be recognised. It's not to be A. A. M. in any case, and I thought it would be fun to see if *Punch* encourages the unknown beginner, and Daff thought it would be fun to send it in as from 'C. Brice' and pinch the money. And her writing is not quite manly enough.

Punch did not encourage the unknown beginner, or perhaps just did not think much of the piece. Milne's experiment had the same result that Doris Lessing's rather grander one did many years later. Without the well-known name attached to it, the article was returned by the editor. Milne was annoyed and, perhaps foolishly, returned it to *Punch*, saying, as his niece Angela put it, ' "What the hell?" So they accepted it. He can't have been very happy about this episode.' But he continued to read *Punch* and five years later he would write regularly for it again.

As for Westminster – he was dining there with Marjorie and her husband one night when they told him the boys were rehearsing *Wurzel-Flummery*, the play that had begun his career in the theatre nearly twenty years before. He went round to see the rehearsal. The young director was Michael Flanders. Milne found himself extraordinarily moved as the boys, watching, laughed in all the right places and the ones on the stage enjoyed themselves with his words. He came back – again alone – to see one of the actual performances, as one of an appreciative audience of parents and sisters. The play survived, whatever had happened to his reputation.

Daphne was in New York on her seventh or eighth visit when that play was put on. As early as March 1932 – only a couple of months after they had both returned from New York – Milne, signing a Dutton contract for *The Christopher Robin Verses* (the two books in one volume), had asked that Curtis Brown's New York office should retain $750 of the advance 'for the use of Mrs Milne' when she next returned to America. For all her talk of the dangers of wives, of 'modern women, cultivating their egos too strongly', Daphne Milne was, with her husband's agreement, pursuing some sort of life of her own. The *New York Post* quoted her explanation:

Auburn-haired Mrs A. A. Milne, wife of the novelist and playwright, arrived on the *Aquitania* today for what she called 'my annual vacation from my husband'. Smiling she told ship news reporters: 'Sometimes I act as his secretary and do all sorts of tasks for him – so he thinks I ought to have a rest from him once a year. I'll stay a month, go to the theatres – and see his producers! Still working for him, you see.'

In fact, Daphne Milne regularly took an apartment at the Lombardy on East Fifty-Sixth Street for more than a month, and the real explanation was that New York offered her the sort of romance and social life she had always enjoyed and which she no longer shared with her husband. 'She got a bit bored with him,' someone said who knew her well. 'Women need someone else – she used to say – to take them out to lunch and spoil them.' There is very little evidence of her relationship with Elmer Rice, that brilliant and controversial playwright who had so attracted her on their first meeting, beyond the fact that they were close friends. It is difficult to understand what Rice – an imaginative realist – can have seen in someone who looked at life so indefatigably through rose-coloured spectacles. But there is no denying Daphne's wit and charm. The actress Fabia Drake described her extraordinary gaiety, her brightness and warmth, which attracted many people. A passage from Rice's own autobiography, referring specifically to this time, is worth quoting:

Since I had not found within my marriage the satisfactions I sought, I had either to forgo them, terminate my marriage or seek to supply its deficiencies elsewhere. The third course seemed the best . . . I had no moral compulsion to monogamy. It is my belief that man is not by nature a monogamous animal . . . In general, statutes making adultery a crime are seldom enforced; the Scriptural injunction is perhaps the least heeded of all the Decalogue's negations.

To me sexual fidelity seemed a personal, pragmatic matter, like a belief in God or in life after death. Its validity depended upon whether or not it worked for you. I think that when a man and woman find complete emotional satisfaction in each other fidelity becomes a matter of course. That was certainly true of my second marriage. But on that basis the first would never have survived.

It did survive for another twenty years, during which I always had outside attachments. I did not flaunt these relationships, nor did I discuss them with my wife; but I was not furtive about them either. Indeed she was often inclined to suspect intimacy where none existed. The fact that she did not seek a divorce is evidence, I think, that for her too the maintenance of a home and the pleasures of family life outweighed other considerations. Of course I conceded to her the same freedom I demanded for myself; nor did I protest when she availed herself of it. Fortunately for myself and for others, my many grave faults do not include possessiveness and sexual jealousy. I have been hurt and angered by spiritual betrayal, but physical infidelity has never disturbed me. Since I am no Casanova, eager to parade his conquests, I shall have little more to say on this subject. In fact my love relationships were not 'conquests' at all. I did not go about seeking adventures; but neither did I reject opportunities when they offered themselves. I never made advances unless I had reason to believe they would be welcome; if I found I was mistaken, I desisted. Some of these relationships were transitory, the spontaneous expression of mutual attraction. Others, deeply charged with emotion, went on for years. None, however casual, was sordid, tawdry or mercenary. Some of my partners were married, others not; almost without exception they were women of superior intelligence, talent, sensitivity and character. Over the years these attachments were a source of stimulation and contributed immeasurably to my understanding of myself and other people.

Daphne Milne was certainly one of these attachments – and their relationship went on for several years. She told one of Milne's nieces how much it hurt when Rice was no longer interested in her. Fabia Drake said that, after Milne's death, 'I think Daphne regretted having followed his own path of infidelity.' The family thought it was she who had taken the path first. Daphne told a young friend, towards the end of her life, that she always wished she had really said sorry to her husband for those absences. Milne seemed to accept the situation and was open with his friends when she was away, at a time when it was extremely rare for wives to take such holidays from their husbands.

A rhymed letter to John Drinkwater (living in 'Mortimer my favourite Crescent' – Milne's childhood street in north London) refused an invitation for a Sunday visit, on the grounds he would be at Cotchford:

> I'd love to come and see you one day
> But cannot ever manage Sunday.
> In Sussex, that enchanted spot,
> I have a little weekend-cot
> Intended, as one might deduce,
> For Saturday-to-Monday use.

The letter ended:

> P.S. Perhaps I ought to say
> My wife is in the U.S.A.
> If not, she also would be sending
> Her thanks, apologies, and ending
> My letter this November P.M.
> 'Yours jointly A. A. M. and D. M.'

They were certainly leading rather separate lives; Milne, for his part, was spending more and more time with the young actress, Leonora Corbett, but this letter to Drinkwater suggests how much Milne still wanted to present a united front to the world. There must have been gossip. Milne once, in a play, challenged the ridiculous assumption that any man and woman seen having luncheon together were lovers. 'In these days?'

Milne often had lunch with Leonora Corbett at the Ivy or the Mirabelle and there were theatre people who assumed they were lovers. 'The Leonora Corbett affair was well known', Fabia Drake said. Leonora's first appearance at the Arts Theatre in Milne's play *Other People's Lives* coincided exactly with Daphne's first lone visit to New York in October 1932. As Lola Waite, the moving spirit behind the bright young things' intervention in the lives of their pathetic neighbours, the actress got one or two rather mixed notices. ('Leonora Corbett behaved in her usual cool and detached manner, which occasionally was marred by awkward movements.') Milne found it a curious experience, hearing her say his lines. 'You did rather get me tonight,' his *alter ego* says in *Two People*. 'I do like intelligence in a woman, provided she's got a certain amount of looks. Of course I know that the things that you said tonight weren't your own . . . indeed they were mine. But you do say things like that pretty often.' His niece, Angela, said Leonora Corbett spoke Milne's language, was as quick-witted and amusing as he was.

It was generally agreed that Leonora was unusually attractive. Griffith Jones, the actor, described her as 'enchanting, witty, elegant, sexy' and quoted her as saying, 'No-one can accuse me of having got here by my acting.' He remembered a cousin of hers ('the daughter of a rural dean, if you please') saying, 'Leonora *is* naughty and can be dangerous, but she has a heart.' Godfrey Kenton also remembered her as 'witty and intelligent': he recalled talk at one point that she was having an affair with A. R. Whatmore, who had directed her as Delia Tremayne in the revival of Milne's *Belinda* at the Embassy Theatre, would direct her again and again in the 1930s and act with her too.

Milne had a low opinion of Whatmore's acting. 'He played Tremayne at the Embassy and was very bad,' he wrote to Irene Vanbrugh, when there was some question of him playing the same part in the celebration of Miss Vanbrugh's jubilee on the stage in 1938. 'Leonora Corbett longed to play Delia when she heard about the matinée, but realized that she was probably too old.' By then she was thirty and had starred in Milne's *Sarah Simple*. By then, too, it seems almost certain (the description, according to Ken's children, fits so well) she had become the Leonora of Louis MacNeice's memory in *The Strings are False* – the actress who ended a 'make-believe' relationship by throwing a tea-table at him. It was Leonora who gave rise to MacNeice's remarks on the sexual state of England at this time:

I see England in the Thirties as a chaos of unhappy or dreary marriages, banal or agonised affairs. The pattern of every night shot through with the pounding and jingling of bedsteads, but somewhere in the hearts of the couples on the beds is a reedy little voice of enquiry: Is this enough? or Is it what I really want? or Can this possibly go on? . . . Freud having taught my generation that sex repression is immoral, fornication had become a virtue. It remained to discover that neither fornication nor chastity is an end in itself.

Milne of course belonged to an earlier pre-Freudian generation and had no illusions of that sort. If he once said: 'Don't miss any happiness that is going or you'll find it gone', he also said that happiness, when we are adult, is always 'tainted with the knowledge that it will not last, and the fear that one will have to pay for it.'

It is just as difficult to reconstruct Milne's relationship with Leonora Corbett as it is Daphne Milne's involvement with Elmer Rice in the same years. Letters have been destroyed and no one now living seems to have known quite what was going on, though Fabia Drake thinks 'Daphne knew of his infidelities and they hurt her.' It was certainly an acknowledged and open friendship. When Milne and Denis Mackail gave a mixed lunch party at the Garrick in 1936, in a 'mysterious apartment' reserved for such a purpose, the guests who ate the salmon, lamb and *soufflé surprise* included, as well as their wives, Peter and Margaret Llewellyn Davies (he one of J. M. Barrie's boys), Harry Graham (he of the *Ruthless Rhymes for Heartless Homes*), the playwright Roland Pertwee – and Leonora Corbett.

Ken's grown-up children met Leonora on a number of occasions and thought of her as 'a counter-blast to Daphne's activities in New York'. Angela saw Leonora as 'one of Nature's tie-straighteners', remembering her straightening 'Alan's tie or his collar or something' with a rather proprietorial air. There is no doubt that they were close friends over a number of years. He did not see her again after 1941, when she went to New York, played Elvira in Noël Coward's *Blithe Spirit*, and never returned to England.

All we can be sure of was that at the time both relationships were important, but that the marriage survived. Sometimes people discard each other because there has been too much expectation, too much hope, too much tenderness. But it is really the expectation, the hope, that should be discarded. The Milnes settled for things as they were and retained a good deal of tenderness and affection. It was not the marriage Alan Milne had dreamed of. It was not the sort of marriage his parents had had, those warm Victorians in their double bed – 'sweethearts to the very end' as their friend Biddie Warren had said. But it was still a great deal better than the average marriage, the sort that 'makes me shudder'. If they led separate lives a lot of the time, they were usually glad to see each other when they came together again. Daphne still laughed at Milne's jokes. They were both devoted to Cotchford and the garden. They were both devoted to Christopher, even if Daphne was glad enough to have him safely away at boarding school for weeks at a time – and rarely went near the school. Milne would turn up alone for prize-givings and cricket matches, both at Boxgrove and later at Stowe.

Milne generally preferred lunching or dining out with just one person, male or female. In the holidays his son was his favourite companion – but in the holidays they were usually at Cotchford and of course it was in London that the eating out went on. Christopher did remember dining in style at the Ivy in the winter holidays, and more importantly those occasional happy lunches at the ABC in the King's Road – Christopher and Alan 'and the ghost of Ken'. Milne often entertained his niece, Angela, when she was on the *Evening News* and later when she was writing regularly for *Punch*. She enjoyed it, thinking of him as 'a radiant being', even during the years when he was having so little new success as a writer. She accepted that 'you had to talk about what he wanted to hear'. They would go to 'the Mirabelle, the Coq d'or, the Berkeley and Luigi's in St James's, where you got wonderful haddock omelets à la Arnold Bennett', she remembered.

Milne also liked entertaining close friends, such as the Mackails, with dinner and a visit to the theatre. They saw all Noël Coward's plays together. He was not at all good at parties these days – going to very few and, when he did, taking very little trouble to please. Christopher would say his father's silences resulted from fear of being thought either a bore or a show-off. Other people would have different explanations. H. F. Ellis, who joined *Punch* in 1931, remembered his only meeting with A. A. Milne.

I met him once at a cocktail affair at the home of Lawrence Bradbury, then a sort of sleeping partner in the proprietorial firm of Bradbury and Agnew.

I was then a very new addition to the editorial staff and was greatly thrilled when somebody said 'That's Alan Milne over there', because in my school-days he and Knox and Herbert had formed a kind of Pantheon of humorous writers in my mind. Milne's characters, Myra and Thomas and Simpson, all those Rabbits, had seemed to a teenager just the sort of attractive people one would like to meet. And to meet their creator, well!

What hilarious witticism would greet me, when I was introduced? Was it even possible that the great man would say he had enjoyed my last week's article? What he actually said was 'Have you managed to get hold of a drink? I haven't.' That was the sum total of our conversation. Ichabod.

Milne's novel *Four Days' Wonder* was published in October 1933 and was dedicated to E. V. Lucas, the chairman of Methuen, who had recently been made a Companion of Honour for his services to literature.

TO
E. V. LUCAS
WHOSE COMPANY
NOW OFFICIALLY AN HONOUR
HAS ALWAYS BEEN A DELIGHT

In spite of the dedication, Milne did not feel that Methuen had done all they might have done for the book. His grumbling letter is worth reading as it suggests how little his publishers wanted to promote Milne as a writer for adults.

I know that Publishers get as annoyed by the importunities of Authors as Schoolmasters by the importunities of Parents. And probably rightly. But I also know that there has never been a less importunate author (or, for that matter, parent) than myself. So now I shall indulge myself and ask: Cannot you make a bit of a fuss of *Four Days' Wonder* in the way that every other publisher does for his best-selling author? In *The Observer* last Sunday, there were great thick slabs of space taken for practically every book published at the same time as mine – half a column for *Trumpeter, Sound!* – and not even the usual inch in a long list of other books (which is Methuens idea of letting themselves go) for *F.D.W.*

Why cannot Methuens occasionally have picturesque, eye-catching adver-tisements of *single books*, as *every* other publisher does? What is there about Methuen advertisements (when there) which makes their books seem so damn dull? Now I entreat you to spread yourselves on an advertisement of *F.D.W. by itself* with some or all of the enclosed extracts from the reviews. Some of the papers may not amount to much, but the total effect of 'just-what-is-it-exactly?' is considerable, and would send anybody to the library or the bookshop. I hate pushing myself on you like this, but I really think the firm owes me something, and to be perfectly candid, my dear E.V., I cannot feel that it has done anything for me yet.

Lucas was obviously influenced by this letter, for a few days later Milne wrote: 'The advertisement was much appreciated in the Forest country. Many thanks.' The allusion to the Forest country suggests that when he was on Ashdown golf course, in the club house, or at some local gathering, it was clear that his neighbours knew he had a new book out. Whether that meant they would *buy* it was, of course, another matter. His Sussex neighbours were not great book buyers. Once, when Angela was staying at Cotchford, Milne said he would show her a colonel and they drove over to see one, as visitors to East Africa might be driven out to see a giraffe. In *Two People* Milne has a passage perhaps based on his neighbours' reactions to his publishing a book. This occasion is a tennis party:

'Fella in the Sixtieth out in India wrote a book', said Colonel Rudge suddenly.
    'Oh?' said Reginald.
    'Fact', said the Colonel. 'Fella in the Sixtieth.'
    Reginald waited for the rest of the story, but it seemed that that was all. The Colonel was simply noting the coincidence of somebody over here writing a book and somebody in India also writing a book.

Most of the neighbours were *interested* in the book. When the writer on one occasion is told by his wife how one of her friends has 'heard such a lot of your book and is *so* interested', he asks as carelessly as he can, 'Has she read it?'

'No, darling, you see they've given up their library subscription, it lapsed or something, she did explain to me, and so – But she's going to, as soon as ever she can get hold of a copy.'
    'She can buy it', said Reginald, annoyed with the woman.
    'I must tell her. I don't think she thought of that . . .'

It *was* annoying – people had never found any difficulty about buying the children's books. That was different. One had to give children presents, of course, and it was important for them to learn to read and to have something to practise their reading on. The sales of the children's books never slackened. There were always new children being born and becoming old enough for the books. And it was not only in England and America. Already in the 1930s the Pooh books had been translated into a number of different languages and many more would follow after the war. At home the characters became more and more familiar. This year (1933) Milne's account sheets from Curtis Brown included proceeds from 'hygienic plush toys, jig-saw puzzles, modelling sets and cardboard games'.

The adult books – and *Four Days' Wonder* in particular – were a different matter, even when Methuen were able to quote from *The Times Literary Supplement*: 'An entirely delightful and brilliant novel . . . Elegant and gay – it is all capital fun.' Over fifty years later the judgement seems unlikely. The heroine, Jenny, is far too silly for the reader to feel sympathetic or even entertained as she rushes off to avoid being accused of her aunt's death. The aunt's death turns out to be accidental – a point apparently missed completely by John Macrae at Dutton's in New York. Milne grumbled to Lucas: 'I hear that Macrae has entirely ruined the book by publishing it as my "latest mystery story" with a corpse on the cover. Hell. Why don't people learn to read?' The reviewer in the English *Spectator* said that Milne 'has stated definitely, since publication, that it is not a detective story. One suspected that. I had even suspected it of being a nursery satire on detective fiction.'

At dinner at the Mackails', Milne inscribed P. G. Wodehouse's copy of the book with the following verse:

> As welcome as the dews that wake
>   Each morn the drooping salpiglossis,
> As soothing as a pound of steak
>   On battered eye or bruised proboscis,
> As warm as in a shower of sleet
>   The comfort of a 'lifted' brolly
> So – to the undersigned – so sweet
>   Your liking for his Four Days' folly.

Wodehouse was not, in fact, alone with *The Times Literary Supplement* in liking it. It sold rather well for an adult novel (poorly only in comparison with Milne's children's books). It had sold 8,000 by the end of 1933 and was eventually translated into French, Hungarian and German. Just before it came out, Harold Raymond at Chatto, not knowing of its existence, was urging Milne to 'turn from the boards' and write 'what the world is waiting for, and that is a humorous novel. That particular field is a gaping void . . . I would give much to laugh again as I used to laugh with your Rabbits, which I can still quote in chunks.' But after *Four Days' Wonder* it would be thirteen years before, in 1946, Milne would publish his next and final novel.

One person who certainly did not share Wodehouse's and Raymond's appreciation of Milne's humour was Graham Greene, who had just published *Stamboul Train*, the book that first gave some indication of the novelist he was to become, and who was then reviewing fiction for the *Spectator*.

In his piece on 17 November 1933 Greene was looking at a novel called *Mediterranean Blues* by a now long-forgotten Yvonne Cloud. He thought, this young reviewer, that he had better start out by defining his own sense of humour:

In recommending a novel as funny, one is haunted by a number of long faces registering disapproval or a complete inability to see the joke. The reviewer, to avoid disappointing those whose taste in humour is not his own, should perhaps try to explain once and for all what he considers funny and why. On what general law is the taste formed of those who, like himself, find the novels, poems or articles of Mr A. A. Milne, of Mr J. B. Morton, of Mr A. P. Herbert, of Mr Denis Mackail, or of almost any of the contributors to *Punch* peculiarly dismal, while they enjoy the works of Mr Peter Arno, of the authors of *Is Sex Necessary?* and of Miss Yvonne Cloud?

There is one obvious difference between these two groups: Mr Milne's group is on the side of the big battalions. A French psychologist has said that laughter is 'l'expression de l'individualité', but these writers are the cheer-leaders in a great community laugh. In the *Daily Express* Beachcomber bludgeons the small minority which does not share the popular taste in art; at Hammersmith Mr Herbert produces his refined musical entertainments for the great *Punch* public. All these writers have the same attitude to themselves. It is obvious in their work that they have clean minds, a refinement of the popular taste of their time, and that they believe (how they believe it!) that they are right.

Their rectitude is fatal to their humour, for if to be right means anything in their case at all, it means the acceptance of the prevailing social codes, from which it should be the function of humour temporarily to release us. But Miss Yvonne Cloud is not concerned about being right. She is funny because she shocks; that is to say, she gives a sense of sudden release from the sexual taboo. She expresses, to quote Dugas again, 'la réaction de l'individu contre l'ordre des choses établies qui l'écrase'. It is the only form of humour which does not date; it is the humour of *Twelfth Night*, of *The Country Wife*, of *South Wind*; it is not the humour of the right-thinking, eminently sane man, Burnand, who was the Victorian counterpart of Mr Milne. And nowadays does anybody read Burnand? The inferior humorist flatters his public; he laughs with them at what they do not understand, thus easing their self-distrust, but the material for this kind of humour changes with every generation. The material of the good humorist does not change. Miss Yvonne Cloud's novel seems today very very funny. It is more than likely, if time does not pick holes in the technical qualities, that it will still seem funny in twenty years, for her material will not have altered.

Milne naturally hated being called 'peculiarly dismal', perhaps particularly in comparison with Yvonne Cloud. He replied at length and as, in the course of his letter to the editor of the *Spectator*, he says a good many revealing things about the nature of his own attitude to humour and in particular of his revulsion at being labelled so wrongly as one who accepts 'the prevailing social codes', it seems worth giving his letter and Greene's reply in full. It is all very curious, as Greene says.

HUMOUR AND MR GREENE

Sir, – I have been reading an article in your paper on Fiction by Mr Graham Greene. Mr Greene's sense of humour is his own. Nobody is going to quarrel with him about it, least of all the author who does not amuse him. But when he sets out to 'explain once and for all what he considers funny and why', he simply cannot be allowed to get away with it. For at any moment he may try to explain something else. It becomes a public duty, therefore, to which I sacrifice myself not unwillingly, 'once and for all' to expose his methods.

Mr Greene dislikes four writers – Mackail, Herbert, Morton and Milne – who have nothing in common but the fact that he dislikes them. Having called them 'Mr Milne's group', he is then in a position to identify them all with *Punch*. Milne himself resigned from *Punch* fifteen years ago; about the time when Mr Churchill, that ardent Liberal, resigned from the Liberal Party. Mackail has never written for *Punch*. Morton not only has never written for *Punch*, but is definitely (and, I fancy, vociferously) antagonistic to it. This leaves only Herbert, the one *Punch* survivor; a writer whose contributions to *Punch* are quite notably out of alignment with the rest of the paper. No matter to Mr Greene. All his fierce reaction against *Punch* (which in some odd way he seems to hold responsible for his sex-repressions) can now be transferred to the Milne Group. The Wicked Four are 'on the side of the big battalions'; they accept 'the prevailing social codes from which it should be the function of humour temporarily to release us'; they are 'the cheer-leaders in a great community laugh'.

So far, so good. He has said it, and now he looks about for evidence. He drops Mackail at once, fearing perhaps, that the tactless reader may already be saying: 'If this is true of Mackail, why not of Wodehouse?' and not quite knowing what to do about that now fashionable author. So, putting Milne on one side for the moment, he proves his case against the other two, thus: 'In the *Daily Express* Beachcomber bludgeons the small minority which does not share the popular taste in art; at Hammersmith Mr Herbert produces his refined musical entertainments for the great *Punch* public.'

Isn't it wonderful? Week after week in the *Daily Express* Beachcomber ridicules such *choses établies* as Cricket and Our Public Schools; week after week at Hammersmith Herbert mocked at Fox-hunting and Racing. With his genius for special pleading Mr Greene ignores all this. He instances (as if it were all Morton ever wrote about) Beachcomber's occasional mockery of minor poets, and evades the subject of Herbert's refined musical entertainments by misidentifying, either wilfully or in sheer ignorance, the *Punch* public with the public of the Lyric, Hammersmith. Just as he would assume a Queen's Hall audience to be all members of the M.C.C. if it suited his argument.

And so to Milne: 'Miss Yvonne Cloud is not concerned about being right. She is funny because she shocks; that is to say, she gives a sense of sudden release from the sexual taboo. She expresses, to quote Dugas again, "la réaction de l'individu contre l'ordre des choses établies qui l'écrase." It is the only form of humour which does not date; it is the humour of *Twelfth Night* . . . it is not the humour of that right-thinking, eminently sane man, Burnand, who was the Victorian counterpart of Mr Milne. And nowadays does anybody read Burnand?'

Burnand! Again that odd obsession about *Punch*. Burnand's crowded life (as Mr Greene characteristically is unaware, or, being aware, characteristically hopes that his readers won't remember) included not only the editorship of *Punch* and thirteen children, but the adaptation of over a hundred French farces for the English stage, some of which must certainly have shocked the strait and tight-laced Victorian. If he had really wanted a Victorian example of cleanliness, right-thinking and inability to shock, he had a don and a deacon to his hand – Lewis Carroll, an exact contemporary of Burnand's. 'And nowadays does anybody read Lewis Carroll?'

So with *Twelfth Night*. Does its humour date less than that of *A Midsummer Night's Dream*? Yet apart from the fact that the presence of a character called Bottom may give Mr Greene a sense of sudden release from his sexual taboo, is there anything in *A Midsummer Night's Dream* to 'shock' anybody?

All through Mr Greene's article one gets this sense of special pleading and superficial thinking. He never seems to follow his thoughts to any length. If the only stable humour were the humour which shocks, then the capacity of receiving shock would have to be stable; which notoriously it isn't. If there is a *chose établie* in the world, it is the Great Sex Joke, wherefore a humorist's reaction to the extraordinary oppression (and depression) of the Great Sex Joke is the only true humour. If Beachcomber is no humorist in leading a community cheer against Ezra Pound, he would be a true humorist in joining in a select jeer against Ella Wheeler Wilcox. But, in Mr Greene's opinion, Pound (not Wilcox) will be the *chose établie* for posterity so that Morton's only hope of seeming a humorist for posterity is to have reacted against Pound. In other words, he is in the same case as the author of *The Frogs*, which survives because Aristophanes thought that Euripides would not survive, and he did . . . And so on, full circle . . .

Years ago, before he had heard of Dugas or Mr Greene, one of the Milne Group wrote as follows: 'No doubt it is easy to make fun of the dispossessed, but the laughter which follows is a little uneasy . . . The victim of our laughter must be able to afford it, so that we can comfort ourselves with the thought that, if we have the laugh, he, anyhow, still has the cigar. He must be a privileged person; established.'

This seems to be what Mr Greene had vaguely in his mind. It applies, as it was meant to apply, to one particular form of humour. It has nothing to do with the pleasure to be got from *Jeeves, The Hunting of the Snark* and Lamb's letters. Nor does it attempt to explain, as Dugas and Mr Greene so delightfully explain, the difference in survival-value between Jane Austen's humour and the humour of Mr Douglas Byng. – I am, Sir, &c., A. A. Milne. 13 Mallord Street, S.W.3.

[Mr Greene writes: 'Mr Milne is characteristically unaware (or, being aware, characteristically hopes that his readers won't remember) that I never claimed a sexual origin for all humour which I personally enjoyed. Actually, of course, I could hardly have found a writer who more satisfactorily fulfilled the definition I quoted than Lewis Carroll. How can an individual react more strongly against the established order than by writing nonsense? As for *Twelfth Night*, its humour, the product of a definite attitude to Puritanism, does seem to me to date far less than the rather haphazard lovers in *A Midsummer Night's Dream*. I don't know what Burnand's sentimental comedies have got to do with the matter (except that they strengthen my comment that he was the Victorian counterpart of Mr Milne), and as for his thirteen children, what is Mr Milne getting at? Does Mr Milne seriously mean to prove from them Burnand's freedom from sexual repression? This is all very curious, as curious as his superficial views on what is meant by *l'ordre des choses établies qui l'écrase*. It is difficult to see how the individual suffers from fox-hunting or racing or cricket. Really, Mr Milne might as well have evidenced Christopher Robin – or even *Punch*, about which he feels so strongly that he is guilty of another misrepresentation, for I certainly have never identified Mr Milne or anyone else with that organ. I gave a list of a number of humorists who seemed to me to have this in common (and Mr Milne's letter at least bears out my last phrase): 'It is obvious in their work that they have clean minds, a refinement of the popular taste of their time, and that they believe (how they believe it!) that they are right.' – Ed. *The Spectator*.]

Reporting the controversy on the other side of the Atlantic, the *Living Age* suggested that: 'Mr Milne is never quite so dull as when he tries to defend his rights as a humorist.' Whether this thrust went home is doubtful but, in any case, Milne had no intention of playing his part as a humorist, any more than as a children's writer, in the winter of 1933–4. As we saw at the beginning of this chapter, he was at long last actually writing the book he had had in mind for many years. It was a time when it was particularly difficult to be funny and much more appropriate to be serious.

Appalled by the black-shirted rally in Birmingham in January 1934 when ten thousand people heard Sir Oswald Mosley ask Britain to return a Fascist majority, Milne did try one piece of light verse, but it was hardly a laughing matter. He saw a bored generation of young men turning to war games to alleviate their boredom:

I taught the dog to beg,
I played picquet with Mabel,
I fixed the wonky leg
Of Elsie's kitchen-table,
I studied *Golf by Vardon*,
I took the dog a walk
Twice round our little garden.

O, Life was a bore
As we said before,
So we joined the Shirts and we played at War.

And now at last our life
Is like a tree that's fruited.
Each night we tell the wife
How often we're saluted.
So fervent is the hail
    Our Leader gets on Sunday,
He simply cannot fail
    To lead us somewhere one day.

Where Hitler was leading their counterparts in Germany was of such grave concern that it was difficult to raise a smile. Hitler had by now taken Germany out of the League of Nations but Milne had not yet entirely lost faith in the League. He still felt strongly that if only the forces for peace could unite, there remained a chance to overcome fascism without another war. Unfortunately the opponents of the League were not always as fatuous as the fifth Earl of Desart. Milne had written to Wells as long ago as 1919:

Did you see a wonderful letter from Lord Desart in the *Morning Post* which began: 'Will some believer in the League of Nations explain how he reconciles it with Joel XIII, Daniel VI, VII, Hosea XIX etc etc . . . *Are these prophecies worth the paper they are written on or are they not?*' I always thought Joel wrote on bricks. But I think it is a delightful question to ask, and I hoped you would answer it.

Milne felt enormous sympathy with the young men who had caused a different kind of public concern the year before when they had voted at the Oxford Union 'That this House will in no circumstances fight for its King and Country'. He stayed out of the controversy until the point when 'Mr J. A. Spender loosed off his cannon'. Mr Spender 'seemed typical of that Elder Statesmanship which, left to itself, will never abolish war'. Milne wrote in the *News Chronicle*:

If I swear that I won't hit Mr Spender unless he hits me first, and if he swears that he won't hit me unless I hit him first, then my announcement that I won't hit him *in any circumstances* is not more than an expression of my belief that he is not a perjurer. In just the same way the Oxford motion expresses, not merely the determination not to fight an aggressive war, but the confidence that the youth of other nations is equally determined . . .

Fortunately, however, the supporters of the motion meant to vote for more than that. They were putting on record (I think and hope) two convictions:

1. It is impossible to ensure Peace so long as a distinction is drawn between aggressive and defensive war.

In his heart Mr Spender knows this just as well as I do. He knows that never in history has a war been fought without each side claiming that the other was the aggressor. Indeed, one might almost say that no country had ever fought anything but a defensive war. Not only that, but no country has ever fired the first shot. In thick letters adjoining Mr Spender's own column appear the inevitable words: 'The Japanese assert that the Chinese opened the fighting.' Delightful, isn't it? One knew they would. By tomorrow the Chinese will assert that the Japanese opened the fighting. Fortunately both sides are pledged to fight for King and Country when attacked, so the war can go on comfortably . . .

But there is another reason why Peace can recognize no distinction between attack and defence. It is that you cannot have defence without armaments, and that armaments, as Mr Spender knows, are the deadly enemy of Peace. To readers of the *News Chronicle* this is such a truism that one apologizes for mentioning it. But until I read Mr Spender's article I should have apologized for defending the Oxford motion in the pages of the *News Chronicle*.

2. The one thing which has kept War alive, now that its hideous wickedness and waste has been revealed, is sentimentality.

For England that sentimentality is epitomized in the words 'King and Country'. You can take – no, let me say that in 1914 you could take any decent, chivalrous, clean-living, God-fearing young man, whisper the words 'King and Country' in his ear, and send him off in an aeroplane to disembowel women and children, and he would go cheerfully, with the knowledge that he carried with him on his errand the love of his own women and the prayers of his Church.

In 1899 you could whisper 'King and Country' in the ears of honourable, fair-minded, intelligent men, and set them waving their hats and screaming for a war as undefensive and unadmirable as the Boer War. There is no infamy for which the words 'King and Country' do not provide adequate cover. 'My country, right or wrong!' How tragically easy war becomes waged in these mists of sentimentality.

So I rejoice that two hundred and fifty young men have had the courage to say boldly that War is a Crime, that it is a Crime which must be renounced without condition, and that it is not less a crime because 'King and Country' demand it. Strange as it may seem to certain people, one can say it and yet love one's country and honour one's King.

And if anyone doubts the urgent need of saying it let him study the response which the 'loyal' and the 'patriotic' have made: the white feathers, the shriek of 'Cowards!' There you have the hysterical war-mind, ready to talk good, comfortable, patriotic, conditional peace until the next Armageddon.

In commenting on the 'Peace' chapter in Drinkwater's new book in 1932, Milne had said: 'I am convinced that every such sort of writing helps to kill the war spirit; and the fact that you have anticipated so many of the brilliant things I was about to remark myself will not deter me from saying them again, less brilliantly.' The trouble was that there was very little chance for anyone to say anything original against war. It had all been said before, if sometimes much less fluently and charmingly than Milne would say it in *Peace with Honour*. Thanking Lord Ponsonby for a copy of his *Disarmament*, Milne said, 'I feel both ashamed and proud; ashamed that I had not read it before, and proud that, starting to think out war all over again, I have used so exactly your arguments and reached so finally your conclusions . . . Between us we *must* be right.'

The failure of the 1932 General Disarmament Conference in Geneva and the overt militarism, already in 1934, of Japan, Italy and Germany, had changed the general attitude to pacifism, which had flourished in the 1920s when the vast majority of people in Britain had agreed that some other way than war, than the bloody battlefields of Flanders, must be found to settle international disputes. Already in 1934 a further war had begun to seem inevitable as chilling reports came in from Nazi Germany of Hitler's appalling policies.

With hindsight, Milne seems to have been naïve, idealistic and unrealistically hopeful that still it was not too late to save another generation of young men going through what he had gone through on the Somme. He was not so naïve and unrealistic as to believe he could achieve his aim, which was no less than to change millions of men's minds, to create a climate in the world where it would be impossible for the leaders of nations (the men who made the terrible decisions and nearly always themselves escaped death) to ignore the voice of the people against war. 'If everybody reads the book (which is unlikely), then the thing is done. There is an end of war.'

When he was working on the book, longing for it to make an impact, Milne wrote to E. V. Lucas wondering whether Methuen were the right firm to publish *Peace with Honour*. It needed a publisher who would push it to the utmost limit, not just for the sake of the sales but for its creed.

That is why I lean to some more 'advanced' firm like Gollancz – I mean advanced politically. Methuens may be too respectable. You aren't, thank Heaven, but Rieu is, and he will definitely hate the book, and be very cold and tight-mouthed about. You will like it, I think.

Macrae will do it in America. He is just the man for it and will send a copy to every Senator and every clergyman in the country, and let himself go over it. (You realize, of course, that my anxiety for enormous sales is the anxiety of a Pacifist rather than of a tax-payer . . .)

Milne answered a questionnaire in the *Bookman* in May 1934, which tried to discover how a great many writers responded to the political situation. The first question was heavily loaded: 'Can you, as an individual, declare the state of things today, even in our own country, is in their totality humanly tolerable?' A number of writers with their heads in the sand, including Clifford Bax, Hugh Walpole and R. H. Mottram, thought that things were better than at any time in the past. Milne thought they were absolutely unacceptable. All his answers show that his mind was 'intolerably preoccupied' with what was going on in the world – and that it was only by writing about it that he could cope with the pressure. To the question 'How would you briefly define the relevance of your art to these existing conditions?' Milne answered: 'All art is witness to the sanctity of the individual and never was such witness wanted as it is today.'

On the domestic front there were some things to be happy about in that summer of 1934 – as Milne told Charles Turley Smith:

Moon left his prep school (Boxgrove) in July, being then top of the school, leader of the choir, captain of cricket and in the football XI . . . He got the second scholarship to Harrow in March, and I refused it, hating Harrow and always intending him for Stowe. Norwood was very sticky about it and wouldn't let him try for a Stowe schol. (some new 'Headmaster's Rule') but Roxburgh sent him the papers unofficially and of course he got it easily.

In one of Milne's stories there is a reference to a school which put boys in for scholarships not to the schools the parents wanted but to the schools which would bring greater glory to the prep school itself.

Milne was still happily unaware how much his son would soon resent his fame. The boy did not blame his father at this stage, but 'Christopher Robin', as he himself put it, 'was beginning to be what he was later to become, a sore place that looked as if it would never heal up.' *Parents' Magazine* in America had recently named him as one of the most famous children in the world – along with Yehudi

Menuhin, Crown Prince Michael of Roumania, Princess Elizabeth of England and Jackie Coogan, the child filmstar. At this stage the boy was still an uncomplicated delight to his father, as he would so often boast to his friend, Turley.

When *Peace with Honour* was published in September 1934, Milne sent Turley a copy, urging him to read it aloud to all his General friends: 'It may do them good.' Later he asked Lucas to send the King a copy too: 'He won't read it. But it may do the Dean of Windsor a bit of good.' He longed for his book to wake people up, to make them think as he did. The reaction to the book was so enthusiastic that Milne said that he was feeling 'more hopeful at the moment than I have ever felt before.' The *New York Times* reported that *Peace with Honour* was in greater demand at the London book-stores than any other publication in the non-fiction class except H. G. Wells's autobiography. By the end of the year – only three months after publication – it had already sold 12,000 copies. There remained a tremendous popular longing for pacifism, whatever was going on on the Continent. But Milne knew that everything depended on the European leaders. 'I suppose one must assume that Great Statesmen are real people; and go on talking, and writing, in the hope that somehow, sometime, one will make contact.' If the statesmen of Europe really wanted to resolve things without force then they should be prepared to take an oath renouncing war, in the knowledge that they would themselves be hanged were it to break out – a fanciful notion that, like a good deal else in the book, bore little relation to any possible reality. Who would do the hanging?

The professional response to the book was mixed. *The Times* was enthusiastic, carrying the headlines:

THE CASE AGAINST WAR
MR MILNE'S BRILLIANT ATTACK

'Mr Milne's tremendous earnestness has not weakened the happiness of his literary touch.' It considered the book 'a very serious and able challenge to conventional thought' but suggested 'that if Mr Milne will turn to the first book of Thucydides, it may become clearer to him that issues can arise which will simply not submit themselves to arbitral decision, even by the most impartial minds, and that those who hold that war cannot be renounced unless it can be prevented have something of a philosophy to back their view.' In the *National Review* Hugh Kingsmill wrote: 'The aim of this book is to convince mankind that war is both wicked and silly. Where Tolstoi, a wrathful prophet, failed it is unlikely that Mr Milne, an irritable publicist, will succeed.' But Milne said he was discussing *modern* war – an evil, that is, which neither Thucydides nor Tolstoy had known, an evil in which they could have hardly believed. There have always been those who say 'What can any one man do?' in any struggle between civilization and barbarity. 'The moralist would answer that at least a man cannot do less than he can. A writer can write, even if he cannot write as well as Tolstoi; even if he is only a professional humorist or an irritable publicist . . .'

Basil Liddell Hart reviewed the book in the *Daily Telegraph* and that distinguished military historian entirely agreed with Milne that 'a more irrational way of settling a question than by force is rationally inconceivable'. He saw that it is the irrational, the lunatic, the animal in man that is the relevant factor.

I can never understand why the trite question: 'Would you stand by while an enemy raped your mother or sister?' is so popular with those who disbelieve in pacifism. A far more pertinent question would be: 'Can you hope to reason with a mad dog?'

Liddell Hart also disputed Milne's assertion that it was '*absolutely certain* that another European war would mean the complete collapse of civilization'. And time has of course proved Milne entirely wrong about that, though he was right, to within a few months, about the date of that new war, which he knew would happen – without a miracle.

Captain Liddell Hart was interested in Milne's mind and in his arguments. After a considerable correspondence, he wrote: 'With much that you add I am in agreement but there are certain aspects which I feel might both help to clear our own minds if we were to thrash out points in discussion, so I suggest that, if you have time, we might lunch together one day. Would you care to suggest a date and lunch with me at the Athenaeum?'

There were a lot of people who wanted to hear Milne talk on the subject. He wrote to E. V. Lucas:

I ought to have thanked you before for the Arch B's letter, remarkably friendly considering this and that.

O Lord, what have I let myself in for? . . . Shall I ever be able to write a novel again? I wish I were Gilbert Frankau or Hugh or somebody who really *wanted* to

1) Make a Lecture Tour of Europe.

2) Occupy the pulpit of Crouch End Congregational Church on Sunday next.

3) Address the boys at the Holt School, Gresham or the Gresham School, Holt, I forget which.

4) Give a running commentary (with occasional close up) for a League of Nations Union film for the young.

5–23. Take 19 chairs in different parts of England on Armistice Day.

24. Debate at the B.B.C.

And damn it, I *am* doing the last. Not for Reith's bright eyes, or my own, or yours (though it will be dashed good advertisement) but entirely because I have a sick, uneasy feeling that it is my DUTY (Duty).

Really, there is only one word in the English language which is essential to the conduct of life and that is 'No!' And to say it a mere 23 times out of 24 isn't anything like enough.

Ever
A.A.M.

(Anonymous author of 'The Private Life of the Water-Beetle')

Gresham's School, Holt might not mean much to him but, in fact, one of the things that pleased him most about the reception of the book was being invited to speak 'about Peace and War' at three schools, Stowe, Uppingham and Marlborough. 'A few years ago one couldn't have come within a mile of a public school with a book like this in one's pocket without police protection', he wrote to Turley. 'Moon tells me that "hundreds" of boys at Stowe have read it.' Presumably the boy was glad it was taking their minds off Christopher Robin.

Milne did not accept any of the invitations to speak. ('Unfortunately this is a thing which I don't do.') He really did hate public speaking, even for a cause that he cared about so passionately. There is a note in Methuen's files: 'Milne refuses to speak at the *Sunday Times* exhibition or elsewhere.' Milne mentioned the schools' invitations over and over again in his letters. Obviously things *were* changing. 'Twenty years ago it wouldn't have been possible without the protection of half a dozen policemen and an emergency Union Jack.' 'A few years ago one would have wanted a false beard . . . Even schoolmasters are becoming human.'

Milne received several hundred letters after the publication of *Peace with Honour* – many from people who agreed entirely with his thesis and were grateful. One of the most unexpected was from Queen Marie of Roumania, writing from Bucharest:

This letter will probably astonish you – I know nothing about you, not even if you are old or young, but I had to write and tell you that I wholeheartedly agree with nearly all you say . . . I am but a retired queen who has to sit still and contemplate with horror the blind rush towards destruction, which seems to have taken possession of great and small . . . Here in my faraway corner, I spend hours pondering over what could and should be done, deploring that the strength is not given to me to stand up and cry Stop! before it is too late; like the prophets of old I would cry out the truth, and try to tear the bandage from their eyes, force our leaders to work for peace instead of war, for mutual understanding instead of daily adding to the increasing distrust and paralysing fear of each other . . .

Many other letters were from people who called themselves 'pacifists' but wrote from their own particular angle. There were 'letters from Communists who insist that we can never get peace until capitalism is abolished, from Social Creditors who proclaim that Social Credit is the only way to peace, from Oxford Groupers who maintain that peace cannot come save through the change of heart which Dr Buchman assures his followers. At any moment,' Milne felt, 'I may get a letter from a Flat Earther warning me that only in a completely flat world can we hope to escape from war.' To all of them Milne reiterated that 'war is, in almost all cases, neither a cure nor a prevention of the disease which it seems to treat, but merely a postponement of it.'

There were others affected by the book who did not write to Milne, but whose lives were changed by it. One such was David Spreckley, at the time in India in the army.

I was a very young Second Lieutenant in a posh cavalry regiment (1st The Royal Dragoons, if you must know) stationed in Meerut. I was very lucky since a series of unconnected and fortuitous happenings had already started my tiny cloistered mind thinking for itself. The Establishment, the British Raj, the Church of England – were they, after all, such a good thing? Why should I, a spotty (probably) boy of twenty have twenty-three Indian servants? Yes, twenty-three – one of whose sole function was the emptying of my 'thunder box' (earth closet). One day I walked into the library of the Officers' Club and picked up – unbelievably – *Peace with Honour*. Don't ask me how it got there. I read it, then read it straight through again. It was, so far as my memory goes, very simple stuff – just right for my mind at the time – and it did the trick. The fragile glass ball which had cocooned me was shattered. Six months later – to the great relief of my fellow officers – I resigned my commission. I wanted more time to think so I rode round England on a horse for three months, then signed Dick Sheppard's pledge and joined the staff of the Peace Pledge Union.

Milne was not himself a member of the Peace Pledge Union ('in spite of Dick Sheppard's appeals. I don't like pledging myself to *anything*') but *Peace with Honour* was one of only three books named as recommended reading in the list of hints that the Union sent out to members to help them to be more effective in presenting the case for pacifism ('Keep your humour', 'Be courteous in debate', etc.). Milne went on putting his own energies into support for the League of Nations Union, which he still believed to be the best agency for promoting peace. His emphasis was always on the international approach, on freeing England from its attachment to its colonies, to its obsession with its status as a Great Power.

When the patriot cries that England's prestige is in danger, he means that England's reputation as a Great Power is in danger; by which he means only this: that England's reputation for war-capacity is in danger.

Milne could see that to the rest of the world 'the British Empire is not a guarantee of peace but a guarantee of trouble.'

Is it not understandable that the sacro-sanctity of the Empire, and of every line, visible or invisible, connecting up the Empire, does not seem to the foreigner to be the clue to the world's happiness . . . It would be an advantage if just occasionally we could discard that hypocrisy which, to the foreigner, is so infuriatingly characteristic of England. We announce complacently that we have done all we can for peace: we offered to disarm; we set the example . . . and so on. Just so might the great landowner offer to reduce the number of his man-traps if the starving villagers threw away their guns and stopped poaching the preserves which he had appropriated from the common land. Of course we want peace. What dictator, once in power, what tyrant, what plutocrat ever wanted civil war?

He considered that the real reputation of England would not be endangered if she lost her status as a Great Power. (The real reputation of England certainly had something to do with the fact that it had given birth to Shakespeare, to Jane Austen and Thomas Hardy.) It was a deeply unpopular view at the time.

In 1935 Milne wrote a widely circulated pamphlet for the League of Nations under the title *Five Minutes of Your Time*, working on the obvious assumption that nobody in England really wanted war, but that hardly anyone was doing anything to prevent one. The pamphlet takes the form of a dialogue between the author and someone he is trying to persuade to join the Union.

Now for the first time in the history of the world we are trying a new international law, a new way of thought. And your reason for turning it down is that it hasn't been immediately successful! Why, you might as well have turned down steam engines because Stephenson's first train ran into a cow.

I suppose it's because I'm British, and don't like the idea of getting mixed up with other nations . . .

You can't help being mixed up with other nations in these days. Any part of Europe is nearer to England today than London was to Liverpool in 1800 . . . The world *is* a League of Nations whether you like it or not.

Earlier the same year, a few months after the publication of *Peace with Honour*, Milne came up against his most formidable opponent, T. S. Eliot, whose *Murder in the Cathedral* had its first performance a few months later. Milne had been well aware of Eliot's poetry for years. His own taste in poetry, as we have seen, lay in metre, rhyme, strict and demanding techniques. But in a piece of light verse he wrote in the 1930s it would seem he was certainly putting himself on the same side as Eliot in some wider context than technician. It is a song 'sung by the Carruthers Brothers: all Colonels' and it is titled 'Carruthers, is it cricket?' Milne without question is on the side of soft collars, pacifists ('At Eton they've the nephew of a Pacifist in Pop!') and birth control – all deeply controversial issues at the time – and he always had it in for colonels. The last verse goes like this:

Carr. ma.: I was staying down at Ascot and I came across a book –
The other two (surprised): Carruthers, is it cricket? Play the game!
Carr. ma.: Well I wasn't feeling sleepy, so I thought I'd take a look –
The other two (reproachfully): Carruthers, was it cricket? Play the game!
Carr. ma.: Well, we all know Rudyard Kipling, there's a man who is a
                                                                    man.
    I've recited Fuzzy-Wuzzy till the perspiration ran –
    But this blighted feller's verses – why they didn't even scan.
All: T. S. Eliot, is it cricket? Play the game!

In 'Notes on the Way' in *Time and Tide* on 12 January 1935, Eliot took Milne to task for being 'so devoured by the thought that War is Bad, that he cannot see that a great many other things are bad too' and, indeed, worse. The distance between Eliot's and Milne's social attitudes is illustrated by the way Eliot challenges Milne on a small remark that Milne had made very much in passing. 'It is true that we should all like to abolish the tip, the gratuity, the pourboire', Milne had said. 'I question this assertion', Eliot says and goes on about it, suggesting we may grumble if 'a now almost mythical American Tourist gets more attention than we do through the size of his tips'; but for all that, he says, 'I like giving tips', at least 'in the present state of society'. Eliot criticized Milne for not saying anything about the need for a change in society when, in fact, such change is implicit in almost everything Milne says.

Eliot goes on, 'I am not reviewing Milne's book, but only taking it as an instance of what seems to me a frequent type of confused and insufficient thinking about war. And it is appropriate I should consider Mr Milne rather than any of the more professional writers about war, such as Sir Norman Angell', naming the very man who twenty-five years before had converted Milne to pacifism, 'because I take him to be a simple man of letters like myself, with a sense of public responsibility. I share his feelings about militaristic utterances by foreign statesman.' What he did not share was his total condemnation of war. Milne might think that any kind of peace was preferable to the hell of the Somme. Eliot said you cannot condemn war in the abstract unless you assert

a) that there is no higher value than Peace.
b) that there is *nothing* worth fighting for; and
c) that a war in which one side is right and the other wrong is inconceivable.

Eliot was very unfair to Milne, quoting him out of context and making him sound much more naïve and idealistic than he in fact was. But, of course, Eliot was right, as history proved and as Milne himself would come to realize. There are things worse than war. There are things worth fighting for. There are wars in which one side is mostly right and the other mostly wrong. But in 1935 many people thought the only way to avoid another disastrous war was not to admit this, that by admitting it they would make war more likely. Eliot finished: 'The difference here is between those who believe in original sin and those who do not. War is in itself a bad thing, we all agree. But what, as things are, is Peace? Or as things may be?'

It was a deeply provocative ending. Lady Rhondda, the editor of *Time and Tide* wrote on 7 February:

I am not going to pretend that I am on Mr T. S. Eliot's side in respect of the hornets' nest he has brought about his ears by his article on Mr Milne's *Peace with Honour*. Mr Eliot has not convinced me. I still believe that the elimination of war and the fear of war is the task laid upon our generation.

The correspondence columns buzzed for weeks with responses to the article. Milne's own letter appeared on 19 January:

I should not have considered it possible that anybody could read my book and suppose that I regarded Peace as beautiful in itself, or the social system as perfection. But, no doubt, if I denounced the slums, Mr Eliot would tell us that writers of my type suffered from the prejudice that house-room was a beautiful thing in itself; and would assure us that the only mansion worth having was a mansion in the skies.

For his rule of life seems to be that nothing is worth doing unless you can convince yourself that there is nothing better worth doing, and as you can never do this you had better do nothing. He says:

'I do not see how you can condemn war in the abstract unless you assert a) that there is no higher value than Peace; b) that there is *nothing* worth fighting for; and c) that a war in which one side is right and the other is wrong is inconceivable. I am prepared to admit that any number of particular wars have been unjustifiable by either side, but not to admit the fore-going assumptions.'

I should have supposed that 'you could a) condemn adultery without asserting that there is no higher value than not living in adultery; b) believe that there are things worth fighting for, and worth dying for, but not worth bombing babies for; and c) condemn duelling in the abstract without asserting that a duel in which one side is right and the other wrong is inconceivable. Mr Eliot, however, will not admit any of these assumptions. And thinking like this in his third column, stating that for these reasons he cannot condemn war in the abstract, he arrives in his fourth column at the remarkable conclusion: 'War is in itself a bad thing, we all agree.' A bad thing, but he cannot condemn it – nor help us to make an end of it.

So we must go on by ourselves, hoping not to distract Mr Eliot's attention 'from the matters that are more urgent'. It was an awareness of these matters which made me assume in my book that I felt more passionately about war than the Pope or the Archbishop of Canterbury. Mr Eliot, standing, I suppose, somewhere between these two prelates, rebukes me for my assumption. If his Notes on the Way are an indication of the passionate feeling about war in which Popes and Archbishops indulge, it is difficult to believe that his rebuke was justified.

Few people indeed seemed to consider there was any justice in Eliot's rebuke. Rebecca West was the most passionate supporter of Milne's case, joining in the controversy over and over again. Eliot's article, she considered, not only demonstrated 'the peculiar brand of pretentiousness with which Mr Eliot has defaced contemporary thought', but 'a tissue of confusions', libelling Milne's thinking. She took Eliot to task for scorning Milne for holding a 'prejudice' that Peace is, in itself, a beautiful thing. 'It is not, it appears, because of poverty . . . On this I can possibly speak with more authority than Mr Eliot. I passed during my childhood through a period of bitter poverty; and I know that my lot would have been infinitely worse had my family not only been ill-clad and monotonously fed but had bombs dropped on it and the intellectual life that sustained it paralysed by conditions of warfare.'

Virginia Woolf, waiting at this moment for a letter from Rebecca West, thanking her for praising *The Harsh Voice*, reflected on her 'queer illbred mind, with all the qualities I lack and fear'. This was on the very day that she recorded a visit from 'Tom Eliot'. 'We – L. rather – argued about the T. and T. correspondence. Highly philosophical: on war: suddenly T. spoke with a genuine cry of feeling. About immortality: what it meant to him – I think it was that: anyhow he revealed his passion as he seldom does. A religious soul: an unhappy man.' It was that that had really offended Eliot about *Peace with Honour*. It was Milne's attitude to death – his belief that death was final. Eliot said: 'If I thought that death was final, it would seem to me a far less serious matter than it does . . . And life would seem to me much less important than it does. I only mention this point to suggest that pacifism like that of Mr Milne is not a very *Christian* pacifism' – which was the last thing that Milne himself would have suggested it was.

For all Eliot's gibes, full of that 'animating animus' Christopher Ricks finds characteristic of Eliot, Milne certainly had the weight of public opinion on his side. Eliot might think that 'Mr Milne continues to involve himself, like a cat in fly-paper, in comparisons or analogies which he cannot control.' Eliot might jeer ('not knowing that Mr Milne had begun thinking about war, I did not know that he had finished'), but there was no question that a great many people were very well aware that Milne was thinking about war and liked what he was thinking. His opponent's formidable qualities, and the fact that Eliot would be eventually proved right, did not prevent Milne emerging from the encounter with a good deal of credit.

A few months before the *Time and Tide* correspondence, Gilbert Murray, Regius Professor of Greek at Oxford, had written to Milne to congratulate him on a letter in *The Times* about the Peace Ballot the League of Nations had organized, to discover the level of support in England for the League. 'Dawson has put up a high tariff wall against any letters defending the Ballot, but by sheer charm of style you have got over it', Murray wrote.

Milne had written about all the letters against the Ballot:

Lord Rennell is afraid that . . . nobody will know whether he is saying that, on the whole, peace is nicer than war, or whether he is insisting on complete and immediate unilateral disarmament. Lord Darling, on the other hand,

fearing that nothing which he can say will do more than convey the idea
that he prefers Hatfield to Hell, throws his ballot paper into the rubbish
basket, where it is joined by the ballot-paper of Sir Austen Chamberlain
(who thinks it silly to ask the first question when the answer is so obviously
'Yes') and by that of Lord Beaverbrook (who thinks it silly to ask the first
question when the answer is so obviously 'No') . . .

No doubt most of us prefer peace to war; Hatfield to Hell. But we do
not get to Hatfield by sitting down at Hendon and waiting for Hatfield to
arrive. The great men who have been writing to you all talk of 'wanting
peace' as if this were all that is to be said for it. What remains to be said
is how much (if anything) a man, or a country, is prepared to sacrifice for
it. I suggest to the ordinary man that he begins by sacrificing a little of his
time in answering the questions 'Yes' 'No' or 'see below' and amplifying
his answers. After all, what else can he do?

Milne's last question must surely have made most ordinary men
reading the letter mainly reflect that there really *was* very little they
could do. The ballot obtained eleven million signatures in support
of the League of Nations but it was not very long before Milne
himself realized how little it would be able to do to stop the rise of
fascism.

Gilbert Murray said that he 'loved' Milne's book, but the following
year he went on to suggest that Milne had left out of account the
actions of lunatics.

I have just been looking up a passage in Hitler's *Mein Kampf* where he
explains that the annihilation (Vernichtung) of France is only one necessary
step in the realization of Germany's proper position. The others, if I understand his rather obscure style, are the removal of all racially impure persons
(Slavs, Latins, etc.) from Europe, so as to leave it in the possession of two
hundred and fifty million Germans.

Few people could imagine the degree of Hitler's ambition and lunacy.
Milne certain could not. 'As for the insatiable ambitions', he wrote
to Professor Murray, 'Has anyone tried satisfying them? "A thousand
pounds?" "Ha! Thou hast touched me nearly!" How many insatiable
ambitions could be satisfied for a tenth of the cost of the last war . . .
But, of course, lunatics *are* the difficulty.'

It would be several years before Milne, and many like him, would
realize that an England safe for democracy was not an England
without weapons to use as a last resort against the dictator and the
maniac. In the summer of 1935 Lady Rhondda invited Milne himself
to contribute 'Notes on the Way' to *Time and Tide*, as one of a
distinguished list at that period which included not only Eliot but

Aldous Huxley, Bernard Shaw, André Maurois and E. M. Forster, and, indeed, no names that are not still familiar fifty-five years later. Milne started by picking up Mussolini's recent words to his army, as they prepared for the invasion of Abyssinia: 'Men, remember that black troops have always been defeated by Italians'. To say that, 'as the climax of a heroic speech', Milne suggested, 'is to make an exposure of the person at the same time funny, pathetic and shameful; in which attributes it is completely in keeping with the war that inspired it.'

In the same column, Milne defined his political position:

I happened to say casually the other day that I was a Liberal. Naturally I was challenged to explain what I meant by 'a Liberal'. The only definition I could give was 'One who hates Fascism and Communism equally'. The important word is 'equally'. I know Conservatives who hate both, and Socialists who hate both, but I also know under which, if they had to choose, they would choose to live. To the good Liberal (if that is what I am) there is no choice possible, for they are the same thing: the negation of everything which makes life worth living.

Milne also had some passing remarks about log-rolling, about the incestuous nature of English literary life, reviewers reviewing their best friends' books and the like. He realized it was nothing new: 'Let X = Stevenson, Y = Gosse' and we know we have seen it all before. More worrying is a new tendency for books to be sold as commodities, with 'the methods of the business world rather than of the book world'. 'The books of a little firm, with little money to spend on advertising, are not like the books of any other firm, whether big or little. They have a personality of their own, which should be given a chance of survival.'

There were more important worries as 1935 progressed. In August Mussolini declared that the Abyssinian dispute could only be decided by force. On 6 September *The Times* published a letter from Milne which shows that he had himself at last lost faith in the League of Nations. He wrote in despair:

The League of Nations represents man's first fumbling approach to national decency . . . designed to include extra-European nations, solely in order to include America, which refused to join it . . . Its covenant demands from its members a pledge to abstain from war, to which is added a pledge to make war on any nation which breaks its pledge; to which is added an assurance that, if one nation breaks this second pledge, the other nations are allowed to break it too: that is to say, the covenant assumes dishonourable conduct to be possible and bases its remedy on the assumption that further dishonourable conduct is impossible. In short, the League of Nations is a paradoxical, misshapen absurdity, such as might be expected from a businessman who had always despised the arts and was now busy designing the Taj Mahal.

The League enshrines a noble idea [but] . . . a league which openly rests its policy on force is a league which discounts honour in advance. Let the present League go, and let the nations begin again. Since all pacts and conventions to which Italy has put her name are now proved worthless, let them be cancelled by mutual consents, and let it be recognized in future that a word of honour is worth exactly nothing if you do not trust to it. Let the new League . . . start its career by making a new Treaty of Geneva, whose astonishing feature will be that nations which have sacrificed so much in the cause of war shall prove willing to sacrifice something in the cause of peace.

For the truth is that the League of Nations and the millions who support the League of Nations are facing separate problems. The inarticulate, peace-loving millions (to whom, after all, belongs the world) are passionately seeking a new way to peace: the League of Nations is asking itself how, on the old system of large armed forces and an exclusively national outlook, it can avoid war.

Milne found it very hard that Professor Murray's response to that, in a further letter to *The Times*, was: 'Then Mr Milne – I hate differing from Mr Milne – actually says we are to scrap the League and make another, a "League of contented nations". This strikes me as "very, very young".' Poor Milne. Could he really not get away from the children's books, even in the middle of a serious political discussion?

They continued to sell, the sales actually increasing with each year that passed. In America in 1935 John Macrae of Dutton's, bringing out a cheap one-dollar edition, which he felt sure would spread their fame still further, said: 'I believe Milne's four books are better known throughout the breadth and length of this land than any children's book in modern times.' Milne tried to keep his distance from writing for children in general, but he had made one exception the year before, when he introduced the first English translation of Jean de Brunhoff's *The Story of Babar*. He had come across the French version at a friend's house two years earlier. 'Since then I have been insisting that my publishers should take out naturalization papers for them . . .' We can easily see why the Babar books appealed to Milne with their gentle satire of French bourgeois and colonial life, their confident mixture of reality and fantasy. If you did not respond, Milne suggested, you deserved 'to wear gloves and be kept off wet grass for the rest of your life.'

By 1936 Milne was still writing the occasional letter to *The Times* and identifying himself as 'an ordinary idealistic Englishman', as if he still had some ideals intact, but he was becoming entirely disillusioned with politics. Soon after German troops re-entered the demilitarized zone of the Rhineland, he wrote briefly to Charles Turley Smith in Cornwall about the international situation, before going on to the much pleasanter subject of his son.

The world is foul. I hate the insular egotism of France, I loathe the German government, I detest Musso, I abominate Communism, I – but why go on? At times I wish I were a Norwegian.

Moon, the Stoic, is in grand form. He got his certificate (if that conveys anything to you) last summer at the age of 14. He also got his Junior Colts. He is now in the Upper School, specializing in Maths. He only just missed playing for his house at fives; he should get his Colts colours next term, and play for the school the year after. If only he would grow a bit. He was in terrific form at the nets in the Christmas holidays, and Sandham and Strudwick both think he's IT. He does *The Times* cross-word every day at school (though not always successfully); and (this is a *non-sequitur*) is the most completely modest, unspoilt, enthusiastic happy darling in the world. In short, I adore him. At this very moment he is in for a House Golf Competition!

Milne told Turley he had been spending most of his writing time ('It was nearly a year's job – six months reading and thinking, six months writing') on a dramatization of his 'favourite book' – *Pride and Prejudice*. Milne describes in his preface to *Miss Elizabeth Bennett* how he had started out thinking he would write about Jane Austen herself, and how unfortunate in the end it proved that he had decided on *Pride and Prejudice*.

The characters began to assemble on the stage. Mr and Mrs Austen, Cassandra, the cheery brothers, Uncle Leigh; and at her table in a modest corner, busy, over the chatter, at what the family would call 'Jane's writing', Miss Austen herself. Soon she will have to say something. What sort of a young woman is she? What will she say? And as soon as she had said it, I knew that it was just Miss Elizabeth Bennett speaking.

So the play, then, must be about Elizabeth Bennett. It must in fact be a dramatization of *Pride and Prejudice*. Was this possible? I read the book again. I read all the other books again. I went back to *Pride and Prejudice*. Quite impossible, I decided at last, but considerable fun to try. I tried . . . Six months later it was finished; and on the day upon which it was finished I read that a dramatized version of *Pride and Prejudice* was about to be produced on the New York stage . . . There was still England. Should one hurry to get the play on with any cast that was available, or should one wait for the ideal Elizabeth, now unavailable? In the end the risk was taken;

arrangements were made for the early autumn; the Elizabeth I had always wanted began to let her hair grow; the management, the theatre, the producer, all were there . . . and at that moment the American version arrived in London.

The 'American version' was *Pride and Prejudice* by Helen Jerome. As the *New Statesman* reviewer of Milne's text would say: 'This dramatization is vastly more scholarly than the version now visible at the St James's Theatre. Even Mr Milne trips up occasionally. But these are tiny blemishes compared with the enormities of the American version.' Only his friend, Edward Marsh, spotted one blemish. Milne commented: 'Yes, Norris must have come from *Mansfield Park*. God knows how. I have been going hot and cold ever since. I knew I should make some fantastic mistake somewhere, and this is it.'

For all its faults, Helen Jerome's version had got in first and had enough of Jane Austen in it to run for some time. There was no room for two such inevitably similar plays in the West End. *Miss Elizabeth Bennett* was extremely well received as a text and had a successful run at the Liverpool Playhouse. Milne went up for the first night on 3 September 1936 and actually made a brief and modest speech, 'in the absence of Miss Austen'. It would be another eighteen months before the play would be seen in London and then only for a short run at the People's Palace.

St John Ervine, praising the play in the *Observer* in August 1936 after he had read it, said that 'Mr Milne, for the first time in his life, I suppose, has been unlucky.' This is an interesting comment. He *had* suffered setbacks, he had experienced pain and loss, but perhaps this was indeed the first time he had actually been 'unlucky' – that chance had dealt him a blow. He obviously still gave the impression, as he had often done in the past, that he was a natural winner, that most things he touched turned to gold, that the gods were on his side.

This was no longer the case. There were two more plays, both performed in London and New York. Both were failures. In *Sarah Simple* Milne turned his back entirely on any serious theme. In the world as it was he felt he could offer nothing but diversion, an evening's enjoyment. The play was produced in London on 4 May 1937 at the Garrick and in America at the Provincetown Playhouse – but not until November 1940, when one critic would reflect that the man who twenty years ago wrote such excellent plays as *Mr Pim*

Passes By, The Truth About Blayds and *The Dover Road* 'now writes with about as much maturity as Christopher Robin'. 'The play gives to sex the carnal quality of a game of drop-the-handkerchief.' The London production was just before the Coronation of George VI, in a country not only appalled by the international news but still reeling from the abdication of Edward VIII.

The *New York Times* carried the following report from Charles Morgan:

On the stage, after the first performance of his new piece, *Sarah Simple*, Mr A. A. Milne made a little speech. 'We wanted', he said, 'to make you laugh. You have laughed. There is nothing more to say except, "Thank you".' It is a speech which might well serve as an epitaph on the English theatre as an imaginative and intellectual force. But Mr Milne knows on which side his bread is buttered.

Almost every theatre has been hard hit by the approach of the coronation; a heavy mortality may be expected before the traffic begins to move again and the mob ceases to wander about the streets, gaping at itself; but it is reported that *French Without Tears* and *George and Margaret* are running to full houses. Why? Because it is not their purpose to make you feel, see, wonder, imagine or understand. Because they are in no sense a criticism of life. Because they require no effort of their audience, neither thought nor any response to communicated suffering or joy, because they have neither unity or tension, but obtain their effect by a rapid fire of trivial (and clever) wisecracks.

Their purpose is 'to make you laugh', and that is what the English theatre has come to. Look down the current list of plays. There is no tragedy among them; there is no serious romance; there is not one piece whose object is to move its audience, even in the sense in which audiences were moved by such a piece as *The Barretts of Wimpole Street*. But Mr Milne's play will succeed because its purpose is to have a giggle in every line and, in its own meaningless kind, it is, from the polite English point of view, highly competent.

It is all about a man (Mr Whatmore) whose young wife (Miss Leonora Corbett) ran away from him a few years ago. Proceedings for divorce were muddled and they are still married to each other. The girl returns to find him weakly philandering with an arch clergyman's widow and pretends that she is willing now to be divorced by him. A co-respondent will be needed with whom she can pretend unfaithfulness. As no one else is available, the husband puts on a large false mustache and pretends to be some strange man whom the girl receives by night at the local inn.

Of course, they are reconciled, the clergyman's widow is routed and everything ends happily. The scene in the inn is, in the tradition of soup and false mustaches, extremely successful, and is written not badly but with a special neatness of humour that gives it an impress of style. The rest of the play has the kind of polite, meaningless banter which Mr Milne writes better than most men. In brief he has, as he said in his speech, done what he set out to do. Moreover, plays of this kind have a legitimate place in the theatre. The peril – and the boredom – lies in the everlasting repetition of them. If only we might be allowed to think or feel!

The Times review in London contained this memorable sentence: 'When there is nothing whatever to say, no one knows better than Mr Milne how to say it', and *Drama* agreed that the play was an agreeable example of Milne's 'Art of making something out of nothing'. J. C. Trewin remembered seeing it and reflecting that by then 'Milne was quite out of fashion. It was the essence of the old *Punch* transferred to the stage.'

Eighteen months later, in November 1938, Milne's last full-length play *Gentleman Unknown* had its first night at the St James's Theatre. Daphne was in New York, as she had so regularly been at that time of the year. Christopher, released from Stowe, his cousin Angela and Anne Darlington shared Milne's box. Angela remembered:

Alas, though it was politely received, it was not a success. The man in the opposite box (a beetle-browed playwright-cum-physician) got up and left in the interval. I sat and suffered, really suffered, in silence; I can only imagine how A. A. M. felt.

The Times suggested that the play improved in the second act but that was too late for the beetle-browed fellow playwright and too late, too, it seems for Milne himself. He would never subject himself to such an experience again.

Milne's mind in the 1930s was more on the real world than on the world of the theatre. *Peace with Honour*, now in a cheap edition, continued to sell in vast quantities; but the outbreak of civil war in Spain, the Stalin show trials, Mussolini's victorious speeches from the balcony of the Palazzo Venezia in Rome – all made Milne realize how puny his efforts had been, that there was nothing now the pen could do and that his writing was hardly of more significance than his luncheons at the Ivy or the Mirabelle.

In the four summers from 1934 to 1937 Alan Milne and Christopher joined Ken's widow, Maud, and her family in a series of holidays on the Dorset coast. Daphne joined them once – at Ringstead in 1935 – but it was not her scene; she preferred Capri or Taormina. She and Alan had a number of spring holidays on the Mediterranean.

Christopher would later describe the significance of the Dorset holidays. Of his father, he said:

He, I now suspect, saw me as a sort of twin brother, perhaps a sort of reincarnation of Ken . . . He needed me to escape from being fifty. It was a private dream of his but he did once share it. I say once but I really mean in one place. The place was Dorset. Quite naturally, quite unselfconsciously, we skipped, back through the years to our schooldays. I would put our age at around twelve. Five twelve-year-olds playing happily together. I don't for a moment think that this was done deliberately in order to level out our assorted ages. Nor do I think that it was my father who led us back. I think it just happened because we were all Milnes and this is a thing Milnes can do. We do it without effort and we do it for our own private delight . . . For us, to whom our childhood has meant so much, the journey back is short, the coming and going easy.

Maud, dearly loved as she was by them all, was not a Milne and was not one of the five 'twelve-year-olds'. 'Maud presided. She was mother of us all, a regal figure moving quietly in the background . . . Maud, aged about fifty, remained fifty. The rest of us became children': Alan, Christopher (still known as Moon) and three of Ken's children, now young adults: Angela, Tim, Tony. Marjorie and her husband, the Westminster housemaster, now had a small daughter of their own and their visits did not coincide with Alan's. There were occasional additions to the group in different years – once Jack Lovelock, the New Zealand Olympic runner, then Angela's boyfriend, twice Anne Darlington, now a beautiful adolescent and still a close friend of both Christopher and his father.

Alan paid for everything, of course, but left all the practical arrangements to Maud. He and Christopher went down by car. It was, it always seemed to Angela, a miracle that he could drive. She remembered a blue Vauxhall ('the Sunbeam was always driven by Burnside', the chauffeur), and her uncle arriving 'in a pale blue bow tie, making his eyes very blue, and I think a grey suit. It could hardly have been pale blue, yet that is how I think of it.'

On holiday he wore longish shorts, as people did, a hat to keep off the sun which occasionally shone, a short-sleeved shirt and a sleeveless pullover. And as always, he smoked a pipe. The first year – and in 1936 and 1937 – they were at Osmington. The old coastguard's cottage had a flat roof for sunbathing and a flagstaff in the garden, up which they ran a striped bath-towel each morning and struck it at sundown.

They would trail happily down to the shingly beach each day – over a stile, across a field, over another stile, along the cliff top and down the cliff:

In 1934 we had this piece of shingle all to ourselves (necessary solitude) with no sand and the sea quite good for bathing in, sloping down, no traps, not much tide. We took one or two bags down with us and an awful lot of things:

towels
bathing-suits (This was the days before they had to be called swimsuits
whether you could swim or not.)
oranges
suckers (sweets)
Times (for crosswords)
pencil
other books no doubt
ball
ginger nuts

We changed without huts or shelter, therefore covered ourselves with towels with the maximum of inconvenience. We sat on towels, I think, no lilos or cushions, and spent much time Looking for Pebbles, not that there weren't plenty but we looked for special kinds, having competitions and shows with different classes e.g. leg of mutton or joint of beef class, there being stones that look like cuts of meat. We threw pebbles at A. A. M.'s hat on a stick. Also ducks and drakes.

Back at the cottage they sat on the roof and played a game Milne himself made up of guessing who would come up over the hill from the sea, what sort of person it would be. There was always the possibility it might be the dreaded Mitler, a villain compounded from the Nazi dictator and the despotic landlord of the local pub, the Picnic Inn, now much smartened up but in those days a humble hostelry where you could buy cheap lobsters. They were there at Osmington when Hindenburg died and Hitler announced he was to be known as Fuehrer and Reich Chancellor and Supreme Commander of the Armed Forces, exacting an oath of unconditional obedience not to Germany but to himself personally. 'It was a proud day for Mitler,' the Milnes said uneasily.

On wet days there were endless paper games, including Picture Consequences and 'the Story Game when you wrote a bit of a story and folded it over and handed it on'. Angela remembered princes, swords, dragons and so on getting into nearly everything Milne wrote. 'He drew quite well in a maddish way and we probably played the Picture game the most. The room was always full of long bits of paper. I think we tended not to throw them away so they silted up and up.' A previous tenant at Ringstead had left behind a Norwegian magazine and they tackled the crossword, knowing no Norwegian.

One year there was a boat, which they rowed very gently parallel with the shore. Two years there were tennis courts at different houses in Osmington. One year there was a parrot, who never spoke when anyone was in the room, but started up the moment the room was empty, imitating not only all the foolish 'Pretty Pollys', but also the cat and the nagging wife of the Mayor who owned him. There was a putting green in the last year's garden, which made Milne feel particularly at home. Christopher was used to the routine. Angela and Tony remember getting 'a bit fed up the way we had to do it every day and go on until we had finished.'

Back in London, with Christopher returned to Stowe, Milne collaborated with Ken's children, as he had collaborated years before with Ken, on a special Milne song. They called themselves the Owls. Only four lines survive:

> Look for the rainbow in the sky!
> Look for the kidney in the pie!
> Look for the ointment round the fly!
> Rally, Owls! Rally!

It was a suitably optimistic message for the Milnes. Alan Milne had always been an optimist. But there seemed few reasons for optimism as the 1930s progressed. At the height of the Munich crisis, the Mackails drove up to Chelsea from their country place to collect a few valuables, including all the material Denis Mackail had gathered for his biography of J. M. Barrie. By chance they met Alan Milne, 'and all had a gloomy lunch together in Sloane Square'. They could not bear to talk about the future. More and more, Milne found himself looking back rather than forward. He was thinking about writing his autobiography.

Hitler's War

MILNE WROTE TO H. G. Wells in March 1938: 'I am writing my autobiography and enjoying it as certainly nobody else will: which I take to be the main object of writing.' For one who usually wrote so clearly this is rather an obscure sentence. He cannot surely have meant that the whole point of writing is to enjoy yourself more than your readers will – but he was certainly emphasizing that the writer's enjoyment is paramount and that if writing is to do with communication, that is subsidiary. He had always maintained that that was the problem of writing for the theatre, that you had to keep worrying about holding your audience's attention, about getting it across. That was a more fundamental problem than the tedious business of casting, of finding available theatres and so on. But, in a book, the writer could relax, thinking of no one but himself and trusting that, if he enjoyed himself, everyone else would too.

'In this book,' he wrote in the introduction, 'as in everything which I have written, I have humoured the author. Whatever happens to the public, the author is not going to be bored. I have enjoyed looking back on the past, and if others now find enjoyment in looking over my shoulder, I am as glad as my publishers will be.' The English edition had the title *It's Too Late Now*, which the Americans did not like. It was to be serialized by the *Atlantic Monthly* under the title *What Luck!* and Dutton's edition was simply *Autobiography*, but Milne, while admitting that it was open to misinterpretation ('It does not mean that if I had my life again I should be an engineer or a clergyman or a stockbroker or a better man, and that unfortunately it is too late now to be any of these things'), argued that *It's Too Late Now* perfectly expressed the theory he had subscribed to all his life that 'heredity and environment make the child, and the child makes the man, and the man makes the writer; so that it is too late now' – and it had always been too late for A. A. Milne to be any other sort of writer or any other sort of man.

When I am told, as I so often am, that it is time I 'came to grips with real life' – preferably in a brothel or a public bar, where life is notoriously more real than elsewhere, minds more complex, more imaginative, more articulate, souls nearer the stars – I realized sadly that, even if I made the excursion, I should bring back nothing but the same self to which objection had already been taken.

The 'sadly' was not quite honest. If he was not quite complacent, yet he certainly accepted entirely in himself that slight prudishness which had saved his ears at Westminster from the dirtiest jokes, which young Giles Playfair had detected on the holiday in Wales, and which the actress Fabia Drake, at just this time, would notice as an attractive characteristic when he took her to dinner at the Savoy. ('I was prudish myself,' she said.) If his imagination was out of step with the times – and so Denis Mackail would see it, turning aside from his own 'clean bright fiction' to concentrate on his J. M. Barrie biography – then Milne would rather think it the fault of the times. If readers these days thought 'drink and fornication' more real than golf and gardening, well, that was up to them. Milne was still wincing at a ridiculous passage in the *Times* review of his most recent play *Gentleman Unknown* suggesting that it had little to offer 'except to those who find golf and generals intrinsically entertaining'.

As Milne wrote his own life, it seemed as clean and bright as a Mackail novel when he looked back on it, not allowing himself to explore any of the darker episodes – Ken's death, Barry's deviousness, Daphne's separate pleasures. Most of his emotional energy went into the early chapters. He himself said that it was always the first part of any biography he read that interested him most. 'What accident, what environment, what determination placed them where they are?' He could not bring himself to say that he was most interested in childhood – that would have been playing into the hands of those who were eager to label him finally as a children's writer, a label he relished less and less as the years went by. But he devoted more than half of his autobiography to his own beginnings – child, schoolboy, undergraduate – and only a handful of pages to the four famous children's books, though he must have guessed that that was the section a great many people would read with particular interest.

Milne ended that section reflecting how, in England, the writer, like the cobbler, is expected to stick to his last.

As a discerning critic pointed out: the hero of my latest play, God help it, was 'just Christopher Robin grown up'. So that even when I stop writing about children, I still insist on writing about people who were children once. What an obsession with me children are become!

The real Christopher Robin – still Moon to his father – was now himself almost grown up. He was nineteen in the summer of 1939 when, with the book finished and in production, father and son took a holiday on the edge of Dartmoor, at the Bullaven Farm Hotel near Ivybridge in South Devon. Christopher had left Stowe School with a major scholarship – a more impressive award than his father had won forty years earlier – to his father's old college at Cambridge. Milne told H. G. Wells that the boy was even to have his father's old rooms in Whewell's Court. Christopher had shown no signs yet of resenting his place in his father's shadow. For ten years he had been very close indeed to his father, 'adoring him, admiring him, accepting his ideas'. He had shown no signs of any normal adolescent rebellion. What he did show was the signs of nervous tension, of an increasing shyness, the outward expression, presumably, of a subconscious worry that he could never fulfil his father's deepest ambitions for him, that he could never be the sort of debonair young man the world expected that charming, competent child, Christopher Robin, to become – if, indeed, they imagined him growing up at all. The schoolboy Christopher Milne both trembled and stammered. He remembered the stammering like this:

Around the age of eight – and not altogether surprisingly – my voice had begun to get itself knotted up. By the age of twelve, though I was fluent on occasions, there were other occasions when the words got themselves sadly jammed. By the age of sixteen the jamming had got worse and my shyness wasn't helping things. Grandfather Milne could at least say 'Good morning'; I would have stuck at the 'G', and, aware of an unsurmountable 'G' approaching me down the road, I would have hurried up a side street to avoid it. What does a parent do in such circumstances? Does he (for example) say 'If you want it you must go and buy it yourself'? Or does he say 'All right, let's go and buy it together'? Rightly or wrongly, it was the latter that my father did, and I blessed him for it and loved him all the more.

The boy remained anxious in all he did to please his father. He hated to disappoint his expectations. There had been some disappointment already. The first time Milne went to see his son play in a school match, he was out for a duck, not scoring a single run.

My father had always hoped that one day I would be a great cricketer, captaining the Stowe Eleven perhaps, or even playing for Cambridge. But at Stowe the tender plant that had been so devotedly nourished hour after hour at wickets during the holidays drooped and faded: I got no further than the Third Eleven.

Milne gave up mentioning the boy's cricket in his letters. In any case, Charles Turley Smith, the friend who had been the chief recipient of his boasting confidences, died the following year. Twelve years later – when everything had gone wrong in that father–son relationship – Milne would deny all the undoubted keenness and talent Moon had had as a small boy. In a letter to his great-niece, Alison, Marjorie's daughter, Ken's granddaughter, Milne was commenting on the fact that he had heard that the schoolgirl Alison had been bowled out by Moon:

I have played with him in a net for hours and weeks and years, and I doubt if he bowled a ball inside the net more than three times, and then only by hitting one of the posts first and bouncing inside. So he must have improved a good deal – or perhaps he was bowling underhand.

> As the whole of a boot to a button
>   As a plank to the nail which you've hammered in,
> So is Compton inversely to Hutton,
> And Moon, most inversely to Ramadhin.

What Milne thought of Denis Compton, compared with Len Hutton, is defined tersely in another verse:

> Denis
> Should stick to tennis,
> And leave cricket to men
> (Like Len).

That much was part of a running battle between Alison – a Compton supporter – and her great-uncle.

In 1939, on holiday in Devon, Milne and his son were still extremely close and would remain so throughout the war, though for several years separated by many hundreds of miles. Much of Milne's writing energy would go into letters to his son – first to Cambridge, then to army camps at Newark, at Barton Stacey in Hampshire, to Aldershot, to Sible Hedingham in Essex – and then to destinations all over the Middle East, North Africa and Italy as the young man travelled here and there with the fortunes of war. It was the war that would eventually allow him to make the necessary escape from his father, to be himself, to put his childhood finally behind him. Those five years, he would say, 'provided me with a foundation stone, strong and lasting, on which to build my adult life.'

Milne's autobiography was published in both England and America in September 1939. This was just three weeks after father and son, sitting side by side on the sofa at Cotchford, had heard on the wireless the declaration 'in the doleful voice of Neville Chamberlain' that Britain was now at war with Germany. It was a difficult time for a book to appear. People's minds were naturally on other things. Through Curtis Brown, Methuen asked Milne if he would accept an advance on publication of just £375 ('That represents the full royalty on the first edition of three thousand copies') rather than the £1,000 that had been agreed. Milne's acceptance was considered 'a most generous gesture at such a difficult time as this'. Methuen were being very cautious about sales, but they would not be steamrollered into what they thought of as an unfair agreement when Foyles Book Club wanted to make Milne's autobiography their choice. The Club would have printed 180,000 copies, but they would not pay more than 10½d a copy for flat sheets. Methuen had originally wanted 1s 1d, came down to 11d and refused to go any lower. So the deal did not come off.

As it was, the book did surprisingly well. It was widely reviewed and well reviewed, and the sales were very good for such a book, at such a time – though the West End that Christmas was 'a very great disappointment'. C. W. Chamberlain at Methuen had written on 13 October:

Yes, I do agree that the notices for *It's Too Late Now* have been wonderfully good, and there is an excellent one by Robert Lynd in today's *News Chronicle* . . . I feel pretty certain that we shall soon have to reprint . . .

The Times Literary Supplement in London suggested that 'the autobiography of this independent and unrepentant writer is further testimony to his originality.' The *New York Herald Tribune*, reeling a little from 'the happy life of a happy author' ('Some of Mr Milne's new readers will repair to the fresh atmosphere of the cellar with a copy of Faulkner or *Tobacco Road*'), yet found 'much of it downright witty, deeply felt, admirably written, and studded with excellent portraits'. In the same paper, a few days earlier, Lewis Gannett had regretted Milne's 'silly bitterness' in his response to Dorothy Parker:

'I'd like to meet an author some day who really didn't care what critics said' – a rather unrealistic wish. Gannett was perhaps a little prejudiced by memories of reading *When We Were Very Young* to his five-year-old, Michael, 'some fifty times that winter' of 1924, 'after which I could recite them with my eyes shut'. Gannett realized – like many reviewers – just how little Milne had actually revealed about his 'essential self'.

The *New York Post* suggested that 'like his own Mr Pim, he passes by at the very moment one would like to have him sit down and talk'. In the *New Statesman* in London Cyril Connolly found himself getting angry at the 'well-written book' because of its lack of intimacy, its 'gentlemanly good taste which veils both a shrewd eye on the main chance and perhaps a fear of life'. 'He reminds me of Noël Coward, a pre-war Noël Coward springing from the same unexpectedly lower middle-class stock, but moving with pre-war acceleration into a smooth heaven of light verse, cricketing weekends, good society, whimsical taste and money, money, money. How fond A. A. Milne is of it! Cheques and success in all around he sees . . .' One detects a faint taste of sour grapes in this, Connolly being so conspicuously, at this point, short of both cheques and success. He regrets that there is 'never an unkind word for anyone' and wonders 'what Christopher Robin himself is like now, and what he would make of it'. Christopher was presumably pleased at his own extremely brief appearance in the book and grateful that nothing further was being added to the legend – beyond the revelation that he might easily have been called Rosemary, and the confident assertion that all the publicity 'which came to be attached to "Christopher Robin" never seemed to affect us personally'.

As for the absence of 'unkind words', regretted by Connolly, Charles Graves (his old colleague from *Punch*) took strong exception to Milne's description of Owen Seaman, calling it 'a mean, ungenerous and untruthful record', in a letter to Seaman's nephew. There is certainly nothing bland about Milne's autobiography, whatever Connolly suggested and however much Milne leaves out his own most intimate experiences.

Anthony Powell in the *Spectator*, after paying tribute to Milne's 'directness and modesty', was the only critic who picked out Milne's own 'psycho-analytical' assessment of the sources of his art, already quoted in Chapter 1 of this book: 'I should ascribe everything that he has done and failed to do, his personality as revealed in his books and hidden in himself, to the consciousness implanted in him as a child that he was battling against the wrong make-up.' That was the 'make-up' of Little Lord Fauntleroy, and his sweet appearance as the headmaster's Benjamin, the third brother of the fairy stories. But had he always been battling against it – or had he often accepted it? Certainly, except in his political writing, his campaigning for peace, he had never tried to shock, as the angelic choirboy does when he swears and betrays his appearance. If he had never been the conventional Englishman that his pipe-smoking, golf-playing appearance suggested, he had rarely strayed very far from the fold, and now, as Britain declared war on Germany, he came back into it. Surely, this time, this really would be the war to end war. After everything he had written against war in the preceding years, it was important now to show exactly where he stood. In his autobiography he had written so recently: 'It seems impossible to me now that any sensitive man could live through another war. If not required to die in other ways, he would waste away of soul-sickness.'

Now he saw that the only way to save his soul from sickness was to face up to things. In his autobiography, he had begun to write like an old man: 'Waves, like everything else, are not what they were . . .' Now he took up his pen again with new vigour. He wrote to the Ministry of Information offering his services. They would make occasional use of him, and he would find other platforms too.

If physically he retreated to his study and garden in Sussex, as he was allowed to do at his age (though he was still not sixty until 1942), mentally he was as involved in the war as anyone. He once wrote:

It is not easy for a writer to convince himself that the little he can do is all he can do. He has not devoted himself to his profession for so many years, nor esteemed it so highly, that he can now lay it on one side.

At least he could help to make sure that people realized Hitler, Goering and Mussolini were 'blood-stained criminals', though for years many, who should have known better, had been treating them as if they were politicians and ignoring 'the filthy sadism of their concentration camps.'

At this stage, Milne would not let himself believe that the war would last long enough for Christopher to take part. Sending a copy of his autobiography to H. G. Wells ('It isn't as good as yours, but the early chapters may interest you'), he told him Christopher was at Cambridge: 'He has a year before – but it may be over then. It must be.'

Milne had a letter in *The Times* on 4 September 1939 under the general heading 'Why Britain Goes to War'. He looked back on the outbreak of the last war and went on:

May I, then, urge the necessity of making it clear at once, not only that we differentiate now between the Nazi government and the German people, but that through all the horrors and the heat of war we shall continue so to differentiate ... An honourable peace will be negotiated gladly at any moment with an elected assembly representative of the German people. As the first point in our peace terms let us proclaim unequivocally that a totalitarian state ... can have no place in a civilized world. Our leaders have been accustomed to say ... that a nation's form of government is its own concern. It is not; it is the very great concern of its neighbours ... We are fighting not to make the world safe for democracy but because we are convinced that only by democracy can the world be saved, only under democracy can the world live at peace.

It was a useful distinction and one Milne would use again in another letter, two years later, to *The Times* – which published no fewer than fifteen of his letters in these war years. He would always emphasize that it was not just our own democracy we were fighting for but the future peace of the world, and the restoration to Europe of civilization and humanity. He could not get out of his mind the chilling statement Joseph Kennedy had made on his resignation as US Ambassador in London:

My plan is to devote my efforts to what seems to me the greatest cause in the world today and means, if successful, the preservation of the American form of democracy. That cause is to help the President keep the United States out of the war.

Milne wrote:

It seems strange to me that in two years of exhortation the moral argument has never been emphasized as the principal argument – and to a pacifist the only argument – for American entry into the war. Continuously America has been urged to take part in a war of self-interest: never has she been summoned to take part in a crusade. Just for a moment, then, on this second anniversary of a fight for Humanity against Bestiality, I ask Americans ... to try to visualize what has been happening to Poland for the last two years; to let their minds dwell, if only for a moment, on such a fantasy of horror, such a nightmare of cruelty, as the world has never known. What are they going to do about it? [Are they] content that this horror should spread over the world – so long as it stops short of America? ...

Since when have American lives had this special value to Heaven? Would an American mother have her son watch a baby drown while he wonders what its nationality is? . . . What a travesty of American manhood! How has a great and proud country been allowed to proclaim herself so falsely?

Milne appealed to America's chivalry, not on Britain's behalf but 'on behalf of those countries whose sufferings have been so much greater'. He was rebuked by an American living in London for asking for a unique standard of conduct from America. All nations are governed by self-interest, he said, and suggested that the only way to bring America in was to convince her that her 'vital national interests are involved'. (That life went on in Britain in some ways much as before is suggested by a letter from Sydney Cockerell in the same issue recalling that William Morris never wore a necktie for the last quarter of his life.)

It is interesting that in this 1941 letter to *The Times* Milne deliberately refers to himself as a pacifist. It was a description and a position he would have to defend over and over again. He maintained he could still claim to be one because he believed so passionately that war should never be used as an instrument of policy. He spelt out his position clearly in an introductory note to his own *War Aims Unlimited* in May 1941: 'For a Pacifist the only legitimate war-aim is complete military victory and the only legitimate peace-aim the abolition of war.' The existence of fascism anywhere would always be a threat to world peace. Was not Mussolini on record as saying that 'Fascism does not believe in the possibility or utility of perpetual peace'? Milne quoted that on numerous occasions to prove how useless it would be to negotiate with any fascist leader. But his position laid him open to a good deal of criticism.

In the autumn of 1942 Liddell Hart, the military historian, would actually write to Milne and suggest he re-read his own book *Peace with Honour* – on the day that Milne had chided Aneurin Bevan in the *News Chronicle* for giving comfort to the enemy by belittling Churchill. Milne rhymed:

> Goebbels, though not religious, must thank heaven
> For dropping in his lap Aneurin Bevan.

Liddell Hart wrote to Milne from the Athenaeum where they had lunched together eight years before:

There is no more grievous casualty of war than a fallen angel; the devil, though not religious, must thank Heaven when one drops in his lap – a greater windfall then ever falls to Goebbels. The best way to avert such a triumph for humanity's arch-enemy is to hold fast to the spirit that inspired the author of *Peace with Honour* – that is why I hope you may renew your acquaintance with him.

Milne was undoubtedly hurt by the letter. He had not imagined the full horror of Nazism when he wrote the book. How could Liddell Hart say that he had betrayed his cause. 'An angelic protest against Field Sports in England' would hardly be justified 'if vultures and tigers were suddenly found in every village'. Things had changed since he was writing in 1933.

In a column in *Time and Tide* he described the sort of letters that arrived daily in his morning post. On one day there were four letters from strangers who had read his book. He defined their attitudes:

1) Surely you believe that we are right to take part in this war?
2) Is it not the duty of Pacifists to concern themselves, not with this war but only with the peace that shall follow it?
3) You do still believe, don't you, that *all* war is wicked and that we are right to resist this one, and insist on an immediate peace.
4) I hear that you support this war. You are a traitor.

It was in answering one of the last sort that Milne wrote the following letter, which puts well his general attitude and shows again how, in spite of his support for the war against Hitler, he still considered himself a pacifist. Although Christopher would stress in his autobiography how rarely his father answered letters about the Pooh books, with *Peace with Honour* it was different. 'Every writer has a moral responsibility for what he writes,' Milne said. He knew that his book had turned people into pacifists. Now he had to follow his arguments through.

I am afraid I am not with you; for I believe that war is a lesser evil than Hitlerism. I believe that Hitlerism must be killed before War can be killed. I think that it is more important to abolish War than to avoid or stop one war. I am a practical pacifist. In 1933 when I began *Peace with Honour* my only (infinitesimal) hope of ending war was to publish my views and hope that they would have time to spread before war broke out. They did not. One must try again. But since Hitler's victory will not abolish war; and since Peace now (which is the recognition of Hitlerism) will not abolish war; one must hope to be alive to try again after England's victory – and in the meantime to do all that one can to bring that about.

He wrote in *Time and Tide* (and he had thought along similar lines in 1914):

To say, when one's country is at war, 'I refuse to take any part in war' is as meaningless as to say, when one's house is on fire, 'I refuse to take any part in this fire.' The fire is there, the war is there, and since one is there oneself, one is part of it. The only escape is suicide. If one remains alive, one must adapt oneself to the circumstances in some other way than by proclaiming that one doesn't approve of arson.

Milne's main public statements about the war were in two pamphlets, *War Aims Unlimited* and *War with Honour*. He suggested that because the last war had not proved the war to end all wars, there was no reason to suppose that this one could not be. Does an expedition attempting Everest turn back dispiritedly when it remembers that the last attempt failed? Did George Stephenson, finding his first steam engine did not work, decide to collect butterflies instead? *War Aims Unlimited* ended: ' "Whatsoever things are true, whatsoever things are honest . . . Think on these things" – for the enemy whom we are fighting would destroy them all.'

Milne also wrote later, at the request of the Ministry of Information, a pamphlet to be read by British troops going into Europe. It took him five weeks and he was paid twenty-five guineas. 'I didn't expect to be paid at all . . . I was proud indeed that at my age my services could be of use in wartime.' He set out clearly for the forces the reasons for fighting the war, in this order.

1) To deliver the victims of oppression
2) To save our own country from the fate of the oppressed
3) To ensure that no country shall ever again have reason to fear the oppressor.

These are the things for which we are fighting. If they are not worth fighting for, then nothing is worth fighting for.

He suggested to the reading troops just what oppression meant: 'Those who escape the slave-market and the brothel, the firing-squad and the concentration camp, are slowly starving . . . In all records of barbaric invasion, in all the tales of man's inhumanity to man, in all the blood-stained, tear-blotted pages of fiction or history, there has been nothing to equal the profundity of suffering which Hitler has brought upon occupied Europe.'

He also outlined his hope for a Britain after the war. After the last one the few surviving 'heroes' found themselves 'living in an England which only differed from the old one in the number of its surplus vacuum-cleaners. These were in good supply and the heroes were allowed to peddle them from one unsympathetic house to the next . . .' Milne likened England to a beautiful house crammed to the ceilings with furniture and books, some valuable, some rubbish, all of it in hopeless confusion, crowded in anywhere without taste or method. You feel vaguely that you might do something about it some day, but it will be a tiring job [and you have, or think you have, a weak heart.] You wake up one night to find the house on fire. Frantically you throw out of the windows or drag out of the doors as much of its contents as you can. You save most of them, and in saving them make two discoveries: Your possessions have been brought into the light, and you know now exactly what things of value you have and what of rubbish; moreover you realize that exertion is not so fatal as you had supposed. If the fire brigade can conquer the flames, your house, when restored, will be as beautiful as ever outside; but now, for the first time you will exert yourself to see that the inside is in keeping with it.

But post-war Britain could not yet be our main concern, he thought. Delivering Europe from the Devil will not be the end of it. Our responsibility – with America – will be the feeding and clothing and housing of Europe, the conquest of disease in Europe, 'the recovery of the deported, the search for the missing, the identification of the murdered'. Now the British, who have never quite regarded themselves as part of Europe, will be going into every corner of it, and the Europeans 'will be seeing for the first time, not the few moneyed travellers and careless holidaymakers, but the real British people . . . By you they will know the Britain of the years to come: a Britain not entirely devoted to her own interests; a chivalrous Britain; a Britain who has made mistakes in the past but who has redeemed them and will continue to redeem them.' It was stirring stuff, well suited to the mood of the time.

After the war, Milne told the *Evening News* that, while it had been going on, 'apart from political articles he had had little appetite for writing'. C. W. Chamberlain at Methuen would, from time to time, inquire about the progress of a novel he was supposed to be writing ('I should much like to learn of the further career of Chloe'). It would be 1946 before it was eventually published. But in the early months of the war Milne had found great solace in practising his long-neglected talent for light verse in a series of poems which appeared in *Punch*. His 'High Purpose' and 'The Third String' in the issue of 4 October 1939 seem to have been the first poems Milne had had in *Punch* for over twenty years (since the one he had written at the time of his demob in February 1919), and the first poems he had published anywhere for ten years. There were thirty-six in *Punch* altogether, continuing until 5 June 1940, and they were published, together with a handful more, as *Behind the Lines* later the same year.

It had been Milne's idea to add some prose comments. He wrote to Chamberlain at Methuen:

By the time they come out, they will be neither urgently topical, nor 'untopical'. But what they *will* be is a record of the first 8 months of the war, and, so to speak, historical. It has suddenly come into my mind that it would be 'fun', useful, interesting, attractive, to add a prose postscript to each poem. In some cases it might be no more than an explanation of some reference whose point would now be forgotten, or a reminder of the occasion which prompted the verses; in others I might elaborate the theme, defend my attitude, or embroider with anecdote ('in Mr Milne's inimitable style', thank you.)

This would bring the book more into the 'war-diary' class; which is the one sort of book which can never be out-of-date: the more 'out of date', in fact, the more interesting. See what I mean? . . .

Tell me if you like the idea. I think it gives the book an attraction which verses (alone) lack for many people.

Milne sent it off to his typist on 4 July 1940. 'The book as completed is GOOD', he told Chamberlain. It is certainly of some biographical interest, though the tone is uncertain and, for some of its subjects, light verse seems remarkably inappropriate, as Milne realized himself. He wished that the Russian invasion of Finland had moved him 'to something more worthy than these trivial lines'. At the time of the Nazi-Soviet pact one might have smiled wryly at

> S is for Stalin. The news has come through
> That they've made him an Aryan under Rule II

or

> So all is well, and Stalin's right
> And will be right until he's dead,
> And black is obviously white
> If each alternately is red:
> A helpful creed, whose only hitch
> Is knowing when the one is which.

The blackout was an obvious subject, and the lost drawing pins which were supposed to hold it in place.

> Each night the same old argument begins.
> We reach the same old impasse every night:
> We can't turn on the light without the pins,
> We cannot find the pins without the light.

431

But what of *Mein Kampf*? All Milne's feelings go, not into the verses, but into the prose note and its comment on Rauschning's book *Hitler Speaks*. 'I do not see how anybody who has read *Hitler Speaks* can have any illusion as to the fate of humanity if Hitler conquers . . . This is not a war between nations, but a war between Good and Evil.'

Milne had no time for empty patriotism (or indeed nationalism of any sort), or mindless devotion to duty and optimism. A marching song he heard with the refrain: 'We'll grin, grin, grin till we win, win, win' made him feel so ill that he went off and wrote his own ironical:

> I march along and march along and ask myself each day:
> If I should go and lose the war, then what will Mother say?

In *War with Honour* – in a series which included pamphlets by Forster, Ronald Knox and Harold Laski – he said, 'If anyone reads *Peace with Honour* now, he must read it with that one word HITLER scrawled across every page. One man's fanaticism has cancelled rational argument.' Milne argued that it was the very ardour of his pacifism which inspired his passion now for military victory. In *War with Honour* he addressed himself specifically to pacifists and wrote as one who considered himself still a pacifist. He remained someone who wished to destroy the conventional belief that war was an honourable way of settling international disputes. He also wished 'to destroy the conventional definitions of "national honour" and "national prestige": the conventional acceptance of war by the Churches: the conventional glorification of war by the poets.' He wished his readers to think about modern war and to see it for what it was. He did not want to ally himself with those who thought war would persist until capitalism was abolished or until sin had been abolished or until the international monetary system was changed. He saw that the renunciation of war can only be effectively preached between wars; just as (he supposed, admitting he had never really gone into the matter) the cause of temperance can only be effectively preached between drinks. Modern war is 'something as far removed from the Napoleonic Wars as they were from a boxing match'. There was no hope for a victory for the cause of pacifism except through democracy. There was no hope for democracy except through the defeat of fascism.

Milne was in the front line of the arguments. A pamphlet published by the Ministry of Information containing statements from Milne, Dr C. E. M. Joad, Bertrand Russell and Maude Royden under the title 'It's different now', suggested that pacifists should join in the war effort. The Peace Pledge Union retaliated with 'It's still the same', in which the Bishop of Birmingham, Sir Arthur Eddington, Dame Sybil Thorndike and Lord Ponsonby explained why they had not 'abandoned their faith'. The Union was particularly incensed by Milne's poem in *Punch* – and later in *Behind the Lines* – called 'The Objector' which included the words:

> Your Conscience thinks the war should cease
> But finds no fault with German peace,
> Accepting with a careless nod
> The kingdom of its anti-God.
> It minds not who seduces whom
> If, safe within its narrow room,
> It still can hug itself and say
> 'We took no part in war today';
> It will not mind who lost, who won,
> So long as *you* have fired no gun.

Denis Hayes in his *Challenge of Conscience*, reprinting the poem, accused Milne of 'unworthily misrepresenting in the first few months of the war the very views which six short years before had made *Peace with Honour* one of the finest expositions of the pacifist case.' The curious thing was that most of the conscientious objectors who wrote to Milne in answer to these lines insisted they did not 'condemn the unconscientious fighter', and, indeed, hoped that Britain would win the war. Milne commented bitterly that the conscientious objector is in the position of the man who says to his family, 'Although we are in danger of starvation, my conscience does not allow me to steal. But I do not reproach you for stealing, since your conscience does allow you to. So I hope you will be thoroughly successful in your efforts tonight, and then we can all have a good meal.' And then Milne, the non-Christian, used a telling variation of the old 'Would you stand by while someone was raping your sister?' He wrote: 'I think that there is a difference between refusing to "use the sword" to defend oneself and refusing to use it to defend the innocent and helpless. I cannot believe that, if Christ in His journeys had come across a sadist torturing a child, He would have been content to preach a parable. The Conscientious Objector does believe this.' For all his constant need to disassociate himself from children, it is noticeable how often in his writing on war Milne thinks of the children of Europe, of Hitler's corruption of the souls of hundreds of thousands of children, of children frightened, hungry, orphaned, wounded, dead.

War Aims Unlimited was specifically an attack on the People's Convention which had 'designed its programme to attract all those who have grievances well or ill-founded against the Churchill government.' Milne's distrust of the People's Convention was shared by the BBC, which had announced it would not employ actors, singers or musicians who supported it – but reconsidered, so great was the public outcry. Milne could not help reflecting that, dangerous as censorship must always be, if the Communists or Fascists were in power, liberals would not be talking on the BBC; they would be liquidated. Democracy needed some protection from those who would undermine it.

Milne tore apart, in particular, the peace proposals of D. N. Pritt, one of the Communist group, saying he was playing into Hitler's hands and despising his defence of the Russian attack on Finland. 'Why was it utterly right for Russia to drop bombs on a friendly country to obtain the bases *she* wanted? Because everybody knows that everything is all quite different if Russia is doing it.' The Communists, he considered, would 'accept that the moon was made of green cheese if Stalin said it was or that it would be if it were to the advantage of Communism that it should be, or if the inferior quality of the cheese could be attributed to Capitalism.' Milne had no illusions at all about Stalin. As he had said many times, the true liberal abhors any sort of totalitarian state – communist as much as fascist.

Milne's opinion of women at this point (and one must presume it was mainly based on his daily contact – or lack of real contact – with Daphne) comes out vividly in his scornful description of a typical Communist:

He has a woman's capacity of ignoring all inconvenient facts, of assuming a special dispensation from the laws of logic, of demanding as by right the best of both worlds, and of doing all this with a naïve unawareness that anyone is noticing it, or if noticing it, can be so unreasonable as to object.

In the same pamphlet there is a glancing reference to the 'spiritual comfort' that women seem to find from 'looking in at a well-dressed shop window . . . and then going inside'. These frivolous, well-dressed women make a further appearance in an interesting context when Milne, deploring the fact that in England there does sometimes seem to be one law for the poor and one for the rich, contrasts the woman who steals bread for her children and ends up in prison, while the 'rich woman, who tries to collect a vanity case without paying for it, is certified by a Harley Street specialist as suffering from a nervous breakdown (due to the fact that she got up at eleven that morning instead of twelve) and is committed (poor soul) to the care of friends, who drop in at cocktail-time to say what a perfect pet the magistrate was . . .'

There is another possible clue to Milne's uneasiness with his wife and the sort of woman she had become in his expressed distaste for cosmetics and the hard, bright, scarlet-lipped faces of the 1930s and 1940s. 'The modern world,' he regretted in his autobiography, 'has accepted the convention that obviously painted lips and obviously gummed-on eye lashes are beautiful . . . I found myself saying the other day that the extravagances of this cosmetic age proved finally that women adorned themselves for women only, not for men; in proof of which I assured my company that without exception every man I knew preferred a clean face to a painted one.' He could not imagine how blood-red fingernails could be thought beautiful or how middle-aged women could spend 'so many hours every week in the retention of beauty'. But it was Daphne's make-up, her immaculate, inappropriate grooming, that so many people in Hartfield, the Sussex village, remembered about Mrs Milne.

Peter Tasker, the gardener's son, thought she 'loved the limelight and drawing attention to herself' with her expensive, urban clothes, her 'dyed hair and bright-red lipstick'. But a close friend considered she did not care what people thought. She was just herself and dressed to please herself and had no feelings of guilt about her extravagance. She was generous to her friends, loving their gratitude, enjoying their enjoyment, but not to the poor apparently. She did not allow herself to think of the woman stealing bread for her hungry children. Such things, she felt, were best not thought about. 'She would pay a thousand pounds for a dress,' one friend said, speaking of a time after the war but surely exaggerating. Another described her as 'like someone out of a Barbara Cartland novel, though she would never have read Barbara Cartland'. It was the same woman who reflected that Daphne Milne would never talk about anything unpleasant; 'she would talk about the autumn fashions but not about internment in Ireland.' She encouraged her friends to talk about their problems, their relationships. She rarely talked about her own.

Milne's own preoccupations during the war were almost entirely political. If, as Christopher would say, his mother had never shared with his father those things that were closest to his heart, now that Milne's writing was entirely war-orientated there was very little that they did share. And yet their lives were inevitably closer than they had been during the 1930s, now that they spent so much time, together and alone, in the country. There were the cats – there was nearly always one or other around for that sort of glancing friendly attention that so often fills in an otherwise empty moment – and there was the garden, the subject of endless talk and pleasure. The quiet days were punctuated by those red-letter days when the postman brought something from Christopher.

The Milnes had left London permanently in 1940, lending their Chelsea house to friends. (They would not sell it until after the war.) At Cotchford the government soon requisitioned one of their fields. The one where Jessica, the donkey, had once grazed was now planted in silver birch. But there was a piece of wasteland 'for which we had never found a use'. And now, in place of thistles, bracken and cowslips, it would grow something more nourishing. With the war everything – trivial and important – changed, for one reason or none.

Milne had arranged to play golf one Friday and, just as he was starting off, the telephone rang and someone told him that Germany had invaded Holland and Belgium. 'So I played . . . and have not played since. I thought of nine good reasons why I should go on playing, and none why I shouldn't. But I couldn't.' It did not seem appropriate. Golf had been one of his greatest pleasures for years. He and Christopher had played regularly together on the course at Holtye – 'with' rather than 'against', Christopher said, on most mornings during his spring and summer holidays from school. Afterwards they refreshed themselves with ginger beer at the nearby pub before driving home for lunch. They would always drive home the same way along a lane that went off somewhere near the second green. For that was the way Daphne would walk when sometimes she came to meet them. Milne would think of those mornings as part of a lost Eden.

In 1940 Cotchford embraced its evacuees, one family after another. Milne persisted in calling them refugees, rather than the official term,

and admitted to liking the two school-age children of an Army
barber, who was said to have cut the hair of Lord Gort. He should
have been proud of his children, Milne said. 'They couldn't have
been nicer.' Brenda Tasker, the gardener's daughter, had now grown
up and gone off to join the WAAF. As a child, she said, she had
felt Milne had been quite fond of her. She had always tried to
remember to play quietly so as not to disturb his writing. Peter,
Brenda's younger brother, was still around. In the house Mrs Wilson
remained in charge, housekeeper as well as cook. Her daughter, Pat,
who had been employed as a maid, had also gone off into the
WAAF, leaving her small son with his grandmother. Milne would
describe a time when, with Mrs Wilson ill, the eight-year-old boy
was their only help in the house. 'Daff and I are both getting terribly
thin,' Milne wrote to Marjorie. He had not been well himself. He
felt it was something to do with the lack of vitamins; perhaps it was
age. He was now sixty. 'I still get massaged once a week and like it.
I'm sure it's good for me.'

After the evacuees had returned to London, when nothing seemed
to be happening, Milne wrote some verses reflecting on how well
they compared with other guests.

> Shall we have no one (oh, the peace and quiet!)
> No one who grumbles, no one hard to please,
> Nobody wasteful, fussy, on a diet . . .
> Shall we (in short) get back our refugees?

But it was pleasanter on the whole not to have anyone; they very
rarely had anyone to stay. Angela, Ken's daughter, remembers one
happy visit:

I have a sweet, totally trivial memory of leaning out of my bedroom window
and A. A. M. balancing a letter from my boyfriend on a rake and steering
it up to me. Another of a sunny morning when I was being the helpful guest
and clearing weeds from the stream, while A. A. M. sat behind in his
deckchair, pipe in mouth, felt hat tipped over eyes, doing *The Times* crossword. At the end of the day we would sit by the drawing-room windows,
drinking gin and orange from Italianate glasses.

Angela also remembers her uncle sending her one Christmas early in
the war, when she was working as a landgirl in Dorset ('living in
quiet desperation, eating turnips and freezing in bed'), 'an immense
box of Charbonnel et Walker's super chocs and 100 Balkan
Sobranies'.

In 1940 – before the blitz began in September – Milne went

regularly up to town once a week to lunch at the Garrick, have his hair cut, see his publishers or do other things that needed to be done. Daphne would go up too, but on a different day and do whatever she wanted to do. With Mrs Wilson well, she remained free of domestic responsibilities and, indeed, of any other responsibilities, apparently not enrolling in the Red Cross or the WVS, as most other women did. The garden flourished.

At times Cotchford seemed more dangerous than Chelsea. After Dunkirk, in June 1940, the fear of invasion was vivid and Cotchford was right in the path of any invading army advancing on London. Christopher, having decided he was not going back to Cambridge, as he was entitled to do, waited for his call-up papers at home and joined the local Defence Volunteers with his father. They would soon be renamed the Home Guard. The Milnes buried their ordnance survey maps and in the fields picked nettles, which were supposed to provide a palatable substitute for spinach. Milne regretted the shortage of butter; he had always liked more than a little bit of butter on his bread. As enemy bombers approached London, they flew directly over Cotchford; on several occasions returning planes released bombs very near to the house. 'The Luftwaffe never ceases to watch over us, day and night', Milne wrote to Ken's son, Tony, in October 1940, congratulating him on a promotion and a move. 'I understood that you were being trained to sip absinthe and overhear German spies talking confidently to each other in French as soon as they knew you were listening. But now what? I suppose you have had to rub up your Arabic.'

Behind the Lines was published in the same month, under extreme difficulties. It was one of the worst periods of the war. At times the whole of London seemed to be in flames; in the previous month seven thousand people were killed in London and many thousands more injured or made homeless. Methuen's Essex Street offices, not far from the Strand, were affected by bombing in the very week of publication. C. W. Chamberlain told Milne about it: 'A huge bomb had fallen at the back of the Temple and we had not a pane of glass throughout the rear of our building. All the furniture in Lucas's old room was lying about battered and broken and the whole place was in a deplorable state. For two whole days we had no water and we are still without gas.' As for the stock of Milne's book, it 'is at present hung up on the railway, I don't know where, but directly it reaches us your copies will be dispatched.' They had optimistically printed 7,500 copies, but with compulsory early-closing hours for the shops and numerous other problems, 'I cannot say the sale at present is satisfactory,' Chamberlain added at the end of November.

The book was dedicated:

> To my affinity:
> C. R. Milne: Mathematical scholar of Trinity:
> And: By the time this appears:
> With any luck Private in the Royal Engineers.

It was not only through luck but Milne's own negotiations that eventually Christopher did indeed become a Private in the Royal Engineers.

How did one become a Sapper? That was the question. And you may well think it was not one worth bothering an Under Secretary of State about. Indeed, you might well think that a greater problem might have been how to *avoid* becoming a Sapper. However, this was what I had set my heart on, and we just didn't know whether we could trust the War Office not to post me instead to an Infantry Battalion. In any case there was little enough else that a middle-aged author could do to help win the war, so my father probably welcomed this opportunity to exert himself on behalf of his son.

I can't remember now what was the outcome of his letter. But I do recollect another string he pulled producing a reply from an Engineer Colonel in which he said how much easier it would all have been if I were skilled in some suitable trade. Was I by any chance an amateur bricklayer? And then it was that we suddenly saw that my one great qualification was not mathematics but carpentry. 'So if the Engineers need a keen carpenter', wrote my father, 'he's your man'. 'And', he added to me, 'while waiting to see where that gets us, you must jolly well make yourself as expert as you possibly can, so that when Lord Gort wants a bridge over the Rhine, Milne is the Sapper he sends for. I wonder if there is a helpful book we could get . . .' And, going once more to the top, he wrote to Christina Foyle, the bookseller, to find out.

It was *Modern Practical Carpentry* by George Ellis, and the whole world of Victorian carpentry with its special language, its coffer dams and caissons, its bullnoses and birdsmouths, its spandrels and dovetails, that eventually allowed him to pass his trade test. But only after a nightmare of a failed medical, when the boy had trembled with nervous excitement (as he had trembled in innumerable cricket matches) and inadvertently deceived the doctors into thinking there might be something seriously wrong with him. Christopher wrote:

What does a father do when he learns that his son is not fit for military service? Does he heave a sigh of relief? Maybe mine did, but it would have been a sigh quickly stifled by an understanding of how I felt about it, and by the thought that here was yet another opportunity for him to do something to help.

Milne went to the top again. He wrote a letter to Lord Horder, then probably the most influential doctor in the country – and the Army agreed to have another look. In February 1941 Sapper C. R. Milne joined the second training battalion of the Royal Engineers. It was not until July 1942 that he was commissioned, and eventually, after seven days embarkation leave with his parents at Cotchford, he sailed for the Middle East. Thanking Chamberlain at Methuen for some books, Alan Milne wrote on 2 September: 'The Libya one, which I enjoyed enormously, has been sent on to C. R. M. who (alas!) is now at sea on his way to that neighbourhood. He got it just before he sailed.' In fact it would take him nearly eight months to reach Libya, via Bombay, Basra and a long wet stay at Kirkuk in northern Iraq.

At Christmas 1942, Milne wrote to Marjorie, who was deep in the problems involved in looking after evacuated Westminster schoolboys:

On Monday we had an airgraph from Moon dated Nov 17th, saying that he had still had no letters. On Tuesday Mrs Wilson had an airgraph dated December 2nd, thanking her for the socks she had sent him for his birthday. So thank Heaven *something* has arrived from England; but why no airgraph for *me* thanking me for my 92 letters? Sickening. Perhaps the censor is getting busy with it again, Milne being now a suspected name. His last airgraph said that it rained every day and they were all up to the neck in mud, 'but I am well and happy, so what more can one want?' Remember this, Mrs M-R, when you are next up to the neck in somebody else's mumps.

Milne told Elspeth Grahame that his son was 'a very good and very regular letter-writer luckily, for we miss him terribly, and live from one letter to the next.' A sense of the importance of those letters comes across vividly in a story called 'Tristram' which Milne wrote after the war and published in 1948. It starts with the father reading his son's letters in the summer-house at the end of the garden. In the story the man's son, the young soldier, is killed. Christopher was not killed, but by 1948 he was beginning to go out of his father's life, and the story suggests that Milne must sometimes have wondered how he would have felt if his son had indeed died and had left untarnished, unspoilt, the memory of that close father/son relationship, exemplified in that long series of loving letters.

Milne used to quote from his son's letters in his own letters to his friends and family. In the spring of 1943 Christopher was watching a film at a mobile cinema in Tunisia, with a full moon rising behind the screen, and was remembering that the last film he had seen was in Tahag, 'the one before that in Kirkuk; the one before that (the only other open-air one) in Baghdad on my way up from Zubair; before that two in Bombay and one in Cape Town.' Milne commented to Marjorie: 'And *you* just go from the Regal in Hereford to the Plaza in Gloucester! (And I don't even do that.)' His son went on, 'When you next find me I may be in Berlin – or coming across the lawn from the garden-house.' It would be another three years before Christopher Milne would return to Cotchford, a very different young man from the one who had sailed for Iraq.

In the August of 1941 Denis Mackail had been woken by his wife, who, unable to sleep herself, had been twiddling with the knobs of their wireless set and had heard 'the mild familiar tones' of their friend, P. G. Wodehouse. They listened together. Mackail said, 'Plum's voice – doubly removed for it was a record that was being played over – was addressing us from Germany, where he had recently emerged from forty-nine weeks of internment. I was much moved, but I can't say that I was indignant. He was being funny; I thought he was being remarkably courageous; he seemed to be making a quiet and almost casual plea against intolerance.'

This was the sort of reaction that Wodehouse had, in his innocence, expected when he gave his five broadcasts specifically (he thought) to his readers in America, then still not involved in the war.

My reason for broadcasting was a simple one. In the course of my period of internment I received hundreds of letters of sympathy from American readers of my books who are strangers to me, and I was naturally anxious to let them know how I had got on . . .

Of course, I ought to have had the sense to see that it was a loony thing to do to use the German radio for even the most harmless stuff, but I didn't. I suppose prison life saps the intellect.

Wodehouse had also written an article for the *Saturday Evening Post* and it seemed to him that he was doing, in his own words, 'something mildly courageous and praiseworthy in showing that it was possible, even though in prison-camp, to keep one's end up and not belly-ache.' Auberon Waugh, long afterwards, described the broadcasts as having 'about as much political content of any sort as the average Donald Duck or Tom and Jerry cartoon'. There was nothing in them, certainly, that was either specifically pro-Nazi or anti-British. Perhaps if Milne had heard one of the broadcasts himself he might have reacted as Mackail did to this ill-judged activity of their mutual friend. As it was, Milne was appalled and joined in the correspondence in the *Daily Telegraph* with a vehemence and an inaccuracy which sometimes seem, absurdly, to have made him come out of the whole business with rather less credit than Wodehouse himself. As George Orwell put it so cogently: 'In the desperate circumstances of the time, it was excusable to be angry at what Wodehouse did.'

Milne certainly agreed with Duff Cooper that it was particularly dangerous at this point in the war for America, still neutral, to be 'told by a famous and respected figure that he was living very comfortably in Germany and that the Germans were very nice chaps who looked after him admirably', though, at the same time, Milne agreed with Wodehouse that it was possible to distinguish between individual Germans and the foul policies of the Nazis. Wodehouse apparently knew nothing of their actual excesses and crimes, of concentration camp atrocities.

P. G. Wodehouse and A. A. Milne had a great deal in common. Milne's nephew, Tony, put it like this:

They were born within three months of one another in respectable middle-class families (though Plum's had some blue blood in it) and went to public schools, where they were both goodish games players – cricket and football.

Both knew at an early age that writing was the only thing they wanted to do. Alan refused to take a job; Plum agreed with great reluctance and left as soon as his writing income exceeded his salary (after two years). Both aimed at the light and 'funny' market, with Alan going for sketches and Plum for stories.

Both joined a club – the same one. Plum hated it and resigned; Alan, though not a truly clubbable man, left a large sum of money to it.

Both loved the theatre and wrote for it enthusiastically, while caring little for the cinema, though both made some money out of it.

They wanted the same kind of life-style, that is a place to write undisturbed, but both married women who wanted more of a social life than that . . .

Both made a lot of money but seemed not to care, except in so far as it was a badge of success. Neither had expensive tastes – the wives made up for that.

Both loved to play golf. Alan watched cricket; Plum's interest was mainly in schoolboy games, but he followed Tests in the newspapers.

Neither could take foreigners seriously. They both . . . avoided trying to speak languages.

Both were single-child parents, Plum a stepfather only. He adored his stepdaughter, and Alan was somewhat over-protective towards his only son. The conclusion is perhaps that they reflected their period and class.

They had always admired each other's work. They had always got on well, though it is doubtful if they had ever had a serious conversation with each other – apart from the one about Milne's backing of the stage version of *A Damsel in Distress*. The great difference between them, which was illustrated so violently in 1941, was that A. A. Milne took an intelligent and passionate interest in international affairs and P. G. Wodehouse did not. Milne was incensed by what he saw (with very little knowledge of the circumstances and facts) as Wodehouse's betrayal of his country.

Milne, like so many people, drew his entire knowledge of the broadcasts from ugly propaganda in the papers and later, after his letter, from a broadcast on the BBC by William Connor of the *Daily Mirror* (under the name 'Cassandra') in a slot after the nine o'clock news sponsored by the Ministry of Information. It was this sponsorship that earned Duff Cooper, then Minister, similar rebukes to those given to A. A. Milne by Wodehouse supporters. Auberon Waugh wrote of Duff Cooper:

For some reason best known to himself, he forced the BBC, against its will, to broadcast a vicious and disgusting attack on Wodehouse, accusing him of treason and selling out to the enemy. Within days all the literary creeps in the country from A. A. Milne upwards, had written to the *Daily Telegraph* to demonstrate their own super-patriotism and jealousy of a man whose shoes they were not fit to clean.

Milne's letter, following one from another mutual friend, Ian Hay, in similar terms, appeared on 3 July 1941. The Cassandra broadcast was not made until 15 July. The whole affair seems to have roused an unusual collection of extreme feelings and inaccuracies, but has been so well documented both in Frances Donaldson's biography of Wodehouse and – at length – in Iain Sproat's account *Wodehouse at War* that it seems unnecessary to try and summarize the rights and wrongs of the case here.

Milne wrote:

The news that P. G. Wodehouse had been released from his concentration camp delighted his friends; the news that he had settled down comfortably at the Adlon made them anxious; the news that he was to give weekly broadcasts (but not about politics, because he had 'never taken any interest in politics') left them in no doubt as to what had happened to him. He had 'escaped' again.

I remember that he told me once he wished he had a son; and he added characteristically (and quite sincerely): 'But he would have to be born at the age of fifteen, when he was just getting into his House eleven.' You see the advantage of that. Bringing up a son throws a considerable responsibility on a man. But by the time the boy is fifteen one has shifted the responsibility on the housemaster, without forfeiting any reflected glory that may be about.

This, I felt, had always been Wodehouse's attitude to life. He has encouraged in himself a natural lack of interest in 'politics' – 'politics' being all the things which the grown-ups talk about at dinner when one is hiding under the table. Things, for instance, like the last war, which found and kept him in America; and post-war taxes, which chased him backwards and forwards across the Atlantic until he finally found sanctuary in France.

An ill-chosen sanctuary it must have seemed last June, when politics came surging across the Somme.

Irresponsibility in what the papers call 'a licensed humorist' can be carried too far; naïveté can be carried too far. Wodehouse has been given a good deal of licence in the past, but I fancy that now his licence will be withdrawn.

Before this happens I beg him to surrender it of his own free will; to realise that though a genius may grant himself an enviable position above the battle where civic and social responsibilities are concerned, there are times when every man has to come down into the arena, pledge himself to the cause in which he believes, and suffer for it.

Denis Mackail, reading this, wrote with some violence to Wodehouse's stepdaughter, Leonora Cazalet, who replied: 'It really is horrid about Plummie, and of course not for me to use obscene language about Mr Milne, but I can't help being pleased when other people do it.' She herself felt 'a bit like a mother with an idiot child that she anyway loves better than all the rest.'

Compton Mackenzie, reading Milne's letter, immediately wrote to the editor of the *Daily Telegraph*:

There is a curious infelicity in Mr A. A. Milne's sneer at Mr P. G. Wodehouse for shirking the responsibility of fatherhood. Such a rebuke would have come more decorously from a father who has abstained from the profitable exhibitionism in which the creator of Christopher Robin has indulged.

I gather that Mr. Wodehouse is in disgrace for telling the American public over the radio about his comfortable existence at the Hotel Adlon. Not being convinced that I am morally entitled to throw stones at a fellow author, and retaining as I do an old-fashioned prejudice against condemning a man unheard, I do not propose to inflict my opinion upon the public, beyond affirming that at the moment I feel more disgusted by Mr Milne's morality than by Mr Wodehouse's irresponsibility.

The editor 'for reasons of space' said he was unable to print the letter. Milne had been particularly foolish to bring up the question of Wodehouse's non-existent son. And indeed his memory had played tricks on him. Wodehouse had never made that remark Milne thought he remembered from a conversation. Milne had read it in *Psmith in the City*. When Richard Usborne, long afterwards, pointed this out to Wodehouse, the writer replied: 'You have cleared up a mystery that has been puzzling me for years. The thing he quoted me as saying . . . seemed familiar, but I was certain I had never said it to him . . . Odd chap, Milne. There was a curious jealous streak in him which doesn't come out in his writing. I love his writing but never liked him much.' Christopher Milne has acknowledged that jealous streak in his father's nature and in his own, and rejoiced that it was not in Ken's. 'How fortunate . . . that if one of them had to suffer from jealousy it was Alan (who didn't need to), not Ken.' But here perhaps, in relation to Wodehouse, he did need to. How much he would have preferred to have had, before 1941, Wodehouse's reputation, rather than his own. How much he would have liked to have been thought of as a successful humorist, not as a writer of children's books, and books so peculiarly vulnerable to attack and parody.

Writing about the Wodehouse affair, Tony Milne has commented:

Our hero doesn't come too well out of this. Just as it is now obvious in retrospect that P. G. W. should never have done the broadcasts, so it is obvious that Alan should never have gone as far as he did, accusing his friend of refusing the responsibilities of fatherhood. Some of his fellow writers – Compton Mackenzie for one – expressed their disgust at this betrayal of a friend at a time when silence was called for if support was impossible.

One can say in explanation that 1941 was a bad time for Alan. He had become obsessed with the war and was in no mood to wait for the evidence before shouting 'Traitor!' The charge of political naïvety could be made against Wodehouse, but it did not become AAM to make it, the same AAM who in the thirties had taken a pacifist stand which – as he later acknowledged – could only have served Hitler's purposes.

Alan could have saved something from the wreck if he had dissociated himself from the disgraceful attack on Wodehouse broadcast by William Connor at Duff Cooper's instigation (backed by Churchill). But he did not. I hate to think that he may actually have liked it.

Small wonder that PGW looked for discreditable signs in Alan of professional jealousy to explain his conduct, and that he took some mild revenge on Alan thereafter in his writings. I wonder though whether he was being quite truthful when he said he 'never liked him much', while still appreciating his work.

Tony Milne's supposition that Wodehouse's remark about never much liking Alan Milne involved a rewriting of history is perhaps supported by Malcolm Muggeridge, who, as a major in the Intelligence Corps in Paris, was in some sense in charge of the Wodehouses in 1944. Wodehouse had been largely out of touch with what had been going on in England for the previous four years, though he was well aware of the general response to his broadcasts. Muggeridge reported their first conversation like this:

Were things still ticking along? Did clubs go on? And the *Times Literary Supplement*? And A. A. Milne? And *Punch*? Wodehouse wanted to know what books had been published and how they were selling; what plays had been put on, and how long they had run; who was still alive and who was dead.

At any rate if Wodehouse did not like Milne, he was always very much interested in him. In 1945, when he knew about Milne's letter, he wrote to Denis Mackail:

I don't know if it is a proof of my saint-like nature, but I find that my personal animosity against a writer never affects my opinion of what he writes. Nobody could be more anxious than myself, for instance, that Alan Alexander Milne should trip over a loose boot-lace and break his bloody neck, yet I re-read his early stuff at regular intervals with all the old enjoyment and still maintain that in *The Dover Road* he produced about the best comedy in English.

Wodehouse remained convinced that his own offence was nothing more than 'a technical one, which had been misrepresented in England and America, and which would be forgiven, not merely by people who knew and understood him, but by the public at large, if it could be explained.' His 'mild revenge' on A. A. Milne took two forms. In 1946 he was in France working on a novel which would eventually be published in 1949 as *The Mating Season*. He wrote to Bill Townend:

I'm haunted with an awful feeling that it is going to fall flat. The set-up is that Bertie has got to recite A. A. Milne's 'Christopher Robin' poems at a village concert, and I shall have to try to make the village concert a big scene. And at the moment I can't see how I am going to make it funny.

Make it funny he did by getting round the problem and not facing that part of the concert itself. Even Milne must have allowed himself a wry smile – for he had always loved Wodehouse's style – when he read his description of Madeline Bassett as a hypothetically typical reader of the Milne children's books:

Though externally, as you say, a pippin, she is the sloppiest, mushiest, sentimentalist young Gawd-help-us who ever thought the stars were God's daisy chain and that every time a fairy hiccoughs a wee baby is born. She is squashy and soupy. Her favourite reading is Christopher Robin and Winnie the Pooh. I can perhaps best sum it up by saying that she is the ideal mate for Gussie Fink-Nottle.

'It is un-nerving,' Bertie Wooster observes, 'to know that in a couple of days you will be up on a platform in a village hall telling an audience, probably well provided with vegetables, that Christopher Robin goes hoppity-hoppity-hop.' Indeed, 'a fellow who comes on a platform and starts reciting about Christopher Robin going hoppity-hoppity-hop (or alternatively saying his prayers) does not do so from sheer wantonness but because he is a helpless victim of circumstances beyond his control . . . While an audience at a village concert justifiably resents having Christopher Robin poems recited at it, its resentment becomes heightened if the reciter merely stands there opening and shutting his mouth in silence like a goldfish.' 'Except for remembering in a broad, general way that he went hoppity-hoppity hop,' Bertie Wooster was a spent force as regards Christopher Robin. He dimly remembered there was 'a poem in the book about Christopher Robin having ten little toes', but that was about all. What actually happened at the concert is anyone's guess for it happens offstage, and has more to do with Esmond Haddock than Bertie Wooster. It is all part of one of Wodehouse's elaborate plots and it need not concern us here. It is of passing interest that Gussie Fink-Nottle, at one point, gives his name to the police as none other than Alfred Duff Cooper. No one could say that Wodehouse did not have a sense of humour.

The second act of mild revenge was a short story, published in *Nothing Serious* a year after *The Mating Season*. It was called 'Rodney has a Relapse' and concerns one Rodney Spelvin who 'had once been a poet and a very virulent one, too; the sort of man who would produce a slim volume of verse bound in squashy mauve leather at the drop of the hat, mostly on the subject of sunsets and pixies'. It seemed that Spelvin had been saved from himself by marriage, by taking up golf – and by turning from poetry to the writing of mystery thrillers. But all is lost when a son is born. His brother-in-law, William, is worried:

'Do you know where Rodney is at this moment? Up in the nursery, bending over his son Timothy's cot, gathering material for a poem about the unfortunate little rat when asleep. Some boloney, no doubt, about how he hugs his teddy bear and dreams of angels. Yes, that is what he is doing, writing poetry about Timothy. Horrible whimsical stuff that . . . Well, when I tell you that he refers to him throughout as "Timothy Bobbin", you will appreciate what we are up against.'

I am not a weak man, but I confess that I shuddered.

'Timothy Bobbin?'

'Timothy by golly Bobbin. No less.'

I shuddered again. This was worse than I had feared. And yet, when you examined it, how inevitable it was. The poetry virus always seeks out the weak spot. Rodney Spelvin was a devoted father. It had long been his practice to converse with his offspring in baby talk, though hitherto always in prose. It was only to be expected that when he found verse welling up in him, the object on which he would decant it would be his unfortunate son.

'What it comes to,' said William, 'is that he is wantonly laying up a lifetime of shame and misery for the wretched little moppet. In the years to come, when he is playing in the National Amateur, the papers will print photographs of him with captions underneath explaining that he is the Timothy Bobbin of the well-known poems – '

Wodehouse gives examples of the hapless Rodney's poems, including

> Timothy Bobbin has ten little toes.
> He takes them out walking wherever he goes.
> And if Timothy gets a cold in the head,
> His ten little toes stay with him in bed.

William saw me wince, and asked if that was the toes one. I said it was and hurried on to the [next] . . .

It ran:

> Timothy
>   Bobbin
>   Goes
>   Hoppity
>   Hoppity
>   Hoppity
>   Hoppity
>   Hop.

With this Rodney appeared to have been dissatisfied, for beneath it he had written the word

Reminiscent

as though he feared that he might have been forestalled by some other poet, and there was a suggestion in the margin that instead of going Hoppity-hoppity-hop his hero might go Boppity-boppity-bop. The alternative seemed to me equally melancholy, and it was with a grave face that I handed the papers back to William.

'Bad', I said gravely.

The situation is saved only when the wretched infant interrupts an important golf match with his idiotic queries, culminating (after some talk about beetles) with 'Daddee, are daisies little bits of stars that have been chipped off by the angels?' This is too much for Rodney Spelvin. Golf and common sense win the day.

Timothy Bobbin had been preceded in fiction eighteen years earlier by another nauseating child, Anthony Martin, who made a memorable appearance in Richmal Crompton's *William the Pirate*.

Crompton's biographer, Mary Cadogan, suggested that in the course of her long saga, Richmal Crompton had 'several side-swipes at Milne's besmocked and whimsical embodiment of childish charm', though she is said to have loved *Now We Are Six* 'because one of the poems in it had a metre taken from Horace'. Anthony Martin's mother writes 'literary stories and poems' about him that 'really cultured people buy'. Anthony boasts to William about his fame.

'Nearly half a million copies have been sold, and they've been translated into fourteen different languages. I've had my photograph in literally hundreds of papers. *Good* papers, I mean. Not rubbish. . . There were several Anthony Martin parties in London last year. *Hundreds* of children came. Just to see me.'

Though Christopher would never have spoken like that, the account of what happened is so accurate that it is hardly funny. William is unimpressed. In fact, he maintains he's never heard of the child, who responds:

'Good heavens! I shouldn't have thought there was *anyone* . . . I simply can't make out how you've never come across those books. They're *everywhere* . . .' It was clear that he felt a true missionary zeal to convert them to his cult.

But of course William is more than a match for Anthony Martin and the reader discovers the true character of the child behind such poems as 'Homework': 'Anthony Martin is doing his sums'.

Both Richmal Crompton and P. G. Wodehouse were acknowledging how, over a period of more than twenty years, Milne's children's books had remained so much part of the English tradition that you could use them, taking it for granted that everyone (apart from William) had heard of them. Fifty years after their publication a critic would claim that such things as the Expotition to the North Pole, the problem of what Tiggers like to eat and the game of Poohsticks are lodged permanently 'in what could almost be called the folk-memories of the 20th century.' Just before the war, Frank Swinnerton, who had known Milne for so long, had looked at his reputation in his book *The Georgian Literary Scene*. 'The name of Christopher Robin Milne,' he wrote, 'has long been as familiar to thousands of readers as that of Peter Pan.' Swinnerton saw that Milne had made three reputations in a quarter of a century – as humorist, playwright and children's writer – 'unless we call them four on account of *The Red House Mystery*; and as many reputations, of course, to be assailed by all who find the combination of lightness of heart with love of virtue to be an anachronism in the modern sceptic world.'

Milne is so far out of the literary fashion that he failed to detest his parents. His parents had previously failed to ill-treat and misunderstand him. He failed to detest his school and his schoolfellows. He failed to have furtive adolescent sexual misadventures which left him with burning hatred of all females and an illicit love for some fellow-male. He married early, and his marriage failed to be a failure. He had one son, who failed to disappoint or to hate him. And his life has failed to be disagreeable in every particular, perhaps because he has failed to be as unpleasant as possible to every person he met . . .

In appearance Milne is extremely, extraordinarily fair. He is of the middle height – perhaps a little above it – and to this day is as slim as he was when he first came down from Cambridge. His eyes are very blue, his face is thin but not pale, and I think it would be impossible to see him without realizing at once that he has an active and quickly – smoothly – working mind. There are authors who look stupid and angry; nobody could miss the intelligence of Milne's expression, and the ready but not especially effulgent kindness of his agreeable smile. An observer who knew nothing of his books and plays would probably discover that the face was notably keen and handsome, free from any sign of malice or cruelty, but lacking in what I may call the lines of boisterousness. He would not at first, I think, find it easy to understand what Milne said, owing to the inaudibility and little slurring quickness of his speech. He would notice that, like Barrie, Milne is devoted to the game of cricket. What else he would notice I do not know.

Milne dresses with marked taste and care (I mean no more than that); and he walks at considerable speed without looking very much at those who pass him. I do not think he is at all interested in the casual. Certainly he is not interested in manufacturing conversation with strangers. An American visitor to England was once left sitting with Milne on a log while the rest of a cordial house-party went for a longish walk. Upon their return, the walkers found Milne and the American still sitting on the log, perfectly content, and still in the attitudes in which they had been last seen; and the

American joined his hostess for the short journey back to the house. As they strolled, he said thoughtfully; 'You English are a wonderful people. You convey so much. And yet you don't say a word.'

Unlike the man whose mind is unoccupied, then, Milne does not tirelessly volunteer conversation. Nor, however, does he repress it in others, as do the haughty; a fact from which I draw an inference concerning Milne the writer as well as Milne the man. The inference is that while plentifully blessed (as Barrie had been) with fancy, and even more plentifully blessed than Barrie with verbal adroitness (as witness his versification), he does not command that gift of the great romancers and novelists, a profuse fecundity of invention. Although by no means unappreciative of these traits in other men, he is deficient in vulgarity, in energy, in largeness of thought, and in exuberance of action.

Swinnerton saw that it was by his plays that Milne had made his most ambitious claim to attention and considered that the plays, over and over again (particularly the most serious of them), 'suffer from a kind of punitive zeal against wrongdoing. Milne has such a contempt for backsliders and materialists and sycophants that he cannot withhold a moral foreclosure which affects the structure of his play.' For all that, Swinnerton found much to admire and, in particular, considered *Success* 'deserved quite another fate than failure'.

But Milne's reputation as a playwright now depended mainly on the selection that had extremely wide circulation during the war in the Penguin *Four Plays*, and contained some of his lightest plays: *To Have the Honour, Belinda*, and *The Dover Road* as well as *Mr Pim Passes By*, which remained many people's favourite. Milne's work as a humorist was also kept in front of the public during the war in *The Pocket Milne*, which Dutton's issued in America in December 1941 and Methuen in England not long afterwards. In his introduction, dated Christmas 1940, Milne reflected on how difficult he had found it, when he started writing for the theatre, to shake off his *Punch* persona. 'For years afterwards he was always in the picture; posing at one time as a model to which I was failing to live up, at another as an artist's proof that nothing which I was saying ought to be taken seriously. In fact, he became, as one's past is apt to become, both a rival and a millstone . . . This little book contains the best of what my rival was writing thirty years ago.' *Those were the Days* was also kept in print as far as possible – C. W. Chamberlain told Milne in April 1943 that he was expecting 2,500 copies 'but these I must ration to the end of the year'.

As for the children's books, they continued to sell so well that

Methuen had considerable difficulty in getting enough paper to keep them in print. Methuen's files are full of carbons of letters to Milne commenting on the fact that the four books have been out of stock 'for a good many weeks', but that they hoped to print 25,000 of each soon. In November 1941 Chamberlain wrote: 'With your famous "four" we are rationed to under five hundred of each per week, and even then the binder sometimes lets us down. Had we been able to get a thousand per week of each, we could easily have sold them.' It was in 1941 that for the first time the sales of *Winnie-the-Pooh* for the six-month period were almost exactly the same as for *When We Were Very Young*, with *The House at Pooh Corner* not far behind, third, and *Now We Are Six* a poor fourth – though even that sold 8,554, several thousands more than in the corresponding period of the previous year. They were actually increasing in popularity, not just holding their own. 'I only hope we shall be able to keep sufficient stock to meet the demand over Xmas, but the problem of production gets greater and greater.' There were similar increases in sales abroad. In neutral Sweden sales soared during the war, until in 1946 *Winnie-the-Pooh* was selling nearly 5,000 copies a year.

In 1943 the decision was made to have 4,000 copies of each title printed in Australia 'to help meet in a small way the demand for Australasia . . . We can get the books produced in Melbourne and offered to the public at precisely the same price as when we ship our own stock out there.'

The autobiography went into a new and cheaper edition in 1943, and there was also an edition of 3,000 of *The Red House Mystery*. Milne might well have felt that his name was as well known as it had ever been, but he told a story against himself at this time.

One day during the war, having to be in London for various reasons, I went into a large store to buy a sponge. We pumped our own water at that time, so we could not complain of its quality, but it was death to sponges. All the springs in these parts have iron in them, and the iron enters into the soul of the sponge, making the yellow, as Macbeth was saying, one red; after which the whole thing disintegrates.

The price of a sponge has always come as something of a shock to me. Sponges don't look expensive, as does a charmingly coloured piece of soap embossed *Rêve d'Amour*. They have a ragged uncared for appearance, as if their owner had never taken any pride in them. One feels that one should get for one's money something more regular in shape, with fewer holes in it. It is true that sponges live at the bottom of the sea, which makes the overhead considerable, but there seems to be no lack of them . . .

I chose a large healthy specimen, once, no doubt, the pride of the reef. Its price was wired on to it; otherwise I should have supposed the figure to be a rough valuation of the department, or possibly the whole store . . . I gave the assistant my name and address.

The girl's face lit up. This does happen sometimes, and on the rare occasions when it does, my face lights up too. It was pleasant to think that she had read my books, or (more probably) knew somebody who had. We smiled at each other in a friendly way, and she said that I must be feeling proud of myself. I gave a modest imitation of a man who prefers to have it said rather than to say it.

'Taking a holiday now?' she asked.

This puzzled me a little. One need not take a long holiday in order to buy a sponge; and, of course, if one had known the price, one would have known that one couldn't afford to. There was no reason why I shouldn't have left my heroine in my hero's arms, rushed to London, bought sponge, and dashed back in time to hear her say 'Oh, darling, I never dreamed it would be like this.' However, I gave her another smile, and went to another department to buy a pair of slippers.

It was to a man this time that I gave my name and address. His face also lit up; so, of course, did mine. Never before had I been such a public character. He said 'Well, you've been doing a fine bit of work.' Had I known him better, I should have asked him to which manifesto or pamphlet he was referring, for one likes to be told these things. As it was, I said with a shrug 'Oh well, we must all do what we can.'

He agreed.

'Got it all in?' he went on.

This baffled me. It seemed to be, but could hardly be, a low reference to the nominal fee which I accept sometimes for these things. But before I could answer, he added and put the afternoon at last in its true perspective:

'We owe a lot to you farmers.'

After all these years of authorship it is disheartening to find that it is not one's name but one's address which raises admiration in the breasts of strangers. Yet if one is to be mistaken for what one is not, I would as soon be thought a farmer as anything.

. . . Indeed, I have sometimes played with the idea of making this place a farm again, but the amount of writing which it would involve has stayed me. I do enough writing anyway.

When the army had wanted to requisition his field he had found the paperwork so appalling (the sixty questions about its history, its rotation of crops for the last six years, its value as ploughland, the average profit expected over the next six years, its outgoings on 'artificial manures' and so on) that in the end Milne had handed it over as a gift rather than fill in the forms.

The sponge story first appeared in the *New York Times* in a piece Milne wrote on life in war-time England – his evacuees, the sporadic bombing, the Home Guard, the limitations of dried egg and the prevalence of pilchards. Food parcels arrived regularly from kind American readers.

As for the fame of his name, of course he hoped 'A. A. Milne' would mean something to people, and preferably not the children's books. There was one occasion when he was introduced to the cricket writer, the Hon. Robert Lyttelton, at a test match by a woman who could think of no better way of doing it than by calling Milne 'Christopher Robin's father'. To Milne's pleasure (or so he said in a note to Lyttelton's obituary in *The Times*) Lyttelton replied, 'One of the Middlesex Robins?'

In February 1943, in one of his frequent letters to *The Times*, Milne commented on the Casablanca meeting between Churchill and Roosevelt. Like many others, he said he 'could have wished that Casablanca had produced, not only final plans for the defeat of the Axis, but some statement to the enemy of what that defeat would mean.' He then set out his own detailed, six-point statement with clauses which he felt, if broadcast to Germany and Italy by the Allies, could actually hasten the end of the war. Milne's statement ended:

The peace dictated by the Allies will make any subsequent war of revenge by the Axis utterly and finally impossible. Apart from this, its main purpose will be to give the German and Italian people an equal opportunity with the rest of the world to enjoy the Four Freedoms: freedom from want, freedom from fear, freedom of religion, freedom of expression. The complete victory of the Allies can be delayed but cannot now be prevented. In the light of the allied intentions here set out it is for every German and every Italian to wonder whether any advantage to himself or his country will be gained by delay.

Francis Meynell was one of many who supported Milne's proposal for 'potent propaganda [which would] show both our might and our mercy and will do much to split the people from the party in a Germany and Italy where growing depression must mean growing disillusionment.'

This was just the time when Christopher, now a subaltern in the Royal Engineers, was about to begin the long trek from Iraq towards the Axis surrender in Tunisia. At one of his wayside halts in Transjordan that spring he picked 'a tiny anemone, the brightest crimson, like a drop of blood' which weeks later, dried, paler, reached his father at Cotchford in one of those longed for letters. Christopher's letters were full of optimism as he moved in an immense caravan south and then west across that extraordinary landscape – thousands of men, hundreds of lorries, guns, bridging equipment, moving in the right direction. 'In my letters I could write about my home-coming, as certain now that I would one day see Cotchford again as I had before been certain that I would not.' Near Benghazi, 'next to the corpse of a German tank, I found a lark's nest bubbling over with young life. War and peace, side by side, the one however devastating never able to obliterate the other.'

Milne followed Christopher's progress as best he could, and with tremendous anxiety once he got into Italy – particularly when he knew him to be 'in the Salerno inferno', when the Germans were putting up stiff resistance, immediately after the Italian surrender. More than once, Milne quoted Christopher's letters in his own letters to *The Times* – but without naming his informant. He felt closely in touch with what was going on, with the only things that really mattered in those years. Milne was proud to quote a letter written 'from the Anzio beach-head' in which, as a Sapper, Christopher had said:

Of all unjust things I think the most unjust is that the infantryman should be the lowest paid soldier in the British Army. His is by far the hardest job, and it is a job that is utterly different from his civil occupation. It doesn't seem fair that the mechanic who tinkered with tappets before the war, and who is now in Naples still happily tinkering with tappets, should be earning more than the farm labourer who is living in a hole somewhere near Cassino.

In July 1944 Milne was in correspondence with Elspeth Grahame over her book *First Whispers of The Wind in the Willows*, which he reviewed in the *Sunday Times*, one of the very few book reviews he wrote during the war. He told Mrs Grahame of Christopher's movements:

For the last two years he has been abroad. First to Irak: then three thousand miles across deserts to join the 8th Army at Enfidaville: then with the 5th Army for the first landing at Salerno: then Anzio: and then, after seven months continuous fighting in Italy, back to the Middle East: preparatory, I suppose, to some new landing somewhere. When last heard from he was bathing in the Sea of Galilee.

It was not long after Christopher's visit to the Holy Land that his father sent him two books: Renan's *The Life of Jesus* and *The*

Martyrdom of Man by Winwood Reade. It was the latter that meant so much to Milne himself. More than any other book, it explored his own belief that God had not created Man in His own image, but rather that it had been the other way round: Man had created God.

Christopher was in Italy again by the time that he read it, lying in a tent 'somewhere on the narrow strip of sand that divides Lake Comacchio from the Adriatic'. Winwood Reade's arguments convinced and satisfied the son, just as they had, many years before, convinced and satisfied the father. It was a further cement, Christopher saw, binding them together in greater sympathy and understanding. For twenty-four years Milne had allowed 'the Church a free hand to use all its influence and persuasiveness (though never its force and that was why I had not been christened)', Christopher now realized. Milne had never, until the young man himself responded to Winwood Reade, made clear his own beliefs, but apparently he had always hoped that one day Christopher would come to share them. To be fair, he had packed Renan in the same parcel. But it was Reade who won the contest, resolved all the doubts, answered all the questions and brought a further dimension to that father/son relationship.

This reticence over his own beliefs was typical of Milne. He loved reticence, which others might call taciturnity. And he always found writing easier than talking. If Christopher commented, a little sadly perhaps, on the fact that his father's heart 'remained buttoned up all through his life', there was something in both of them that despised loquacity and openness, that admired, in particular, those who were modest.

Milne had a favourite story of an elderly woman and her husband who found themselves at a village fête in England where the main attraction was an Indian snake-charmer. 'It so happened that at the moment when all the snakes had come out of their box to gather round the snake-charmer and sway to his pipings, he was overcome by illness, dropped his pipe and fell back unconscious.' It was then that the elderly wife, whom we shall call Mary, came into her own. She picked up the pipe and at the very moment that panic was beginning to spread among the spectators, as the masterless snakes started looking for amusement in the crowd, she sat cross-legged on the ground and began to play. The snakes heard the music and hurried back entranced. One by one she picked them up and returned them safely to their box.

'Why, Mary darling,' her husband said, 'we have known each other for more than fifty years, and you never told me you could charm snakes!'

And Mary said, 'You never asked me, John.'

In a further letter to Elspeth Grahame early in August 1944, when she had written a charming letter to him about his review of her book, Milne wrote:

Of course I send your blacksmith my autograph – hoping that he will have heard of me. As for C.R.'s that must wait until he makes a real claim on his own merits to a place in anybody's collection. It is on these lines that I have tried to bring him up: I think successfully. At any rate he was, and is, the most modest, unassuming boy I have ever known. He has now gone back to Italy; and on the whole we are glad. He has been out of the war for four months, and his division was bound to go back into it soon, somewhere; and Italy takes him farther from – what every parent and wife dreads – the Far East. His division, by the way, is the 56th, and it has seen almost as much of the world as the Sea Rat.

Christopher Milne had been in Italy for only a couple of months on this second spell of service as a platoon commander with the Sappers, when, on 7 October, the telegram Milne had been dreading was delivered at Cotchford Farm. The War Office gave the bare announcement that Christopher had been 'wounded', 'leaving it to the imagination', as Milne said, 'to work on any horrible picture that rose to the mind'. Three days later a further telegram gave details: The officer had suffered a 'penetrating shell wound in the right upper occipital region' and was 'seriously ill'. The telegram had omitted the word 'small' which had been on the card attached to Christopher at the Advance Dressing Station on the Lombardy Plain. It seemed to confirm their worst fears. The young man had been wounded in the head and was seriously ill. A day later an air letter was received from the matron of the general hospital to which he had been taken, saying no more than that he had been 'seriously wounded'.

As Milne wrote to Chamberlain at Methuen

We have had the hell of an anxious time, the news being conveyed by the W.O. in the most frightening way possible . . . I was unable to think of much else for some days.

In fact the wound had not been very serious. Christopher had had an extremely lucky escape. He had been operated on under a local anaesthetic for the removal of pieces of broken bone from his head on the day of his admission. 'Surprisingly,' Christopher wrote of the operation, on the fifth day after he had been wounded, 'I rather enjoyed it. It was something entirely new, an experience and most interesting.' Reporting Moon's words to Chamberlain, Milne added, with something like awe, 'He has inherited a lot from me – but NOT THAT.' He was prouder of his son than ever.

Christopher could have written earlier, if he had known how worried his parents were; he had imagined he was giving them the first news of his wound as he assured them there was nothing to worry about and that he would be quite fit again in about six weeks.

Milne's relief at Christopher's letter was mingled with the fear as he recovered that he would 'be back in the battle again in a few weeks'. The father was still extremely shaken by the shock of the two telegrams when he wrote, without naming Christopher, to *The Times* on 26 October a letter which was published two days later under the headline 'Casualty Notifications'. If it is necessary, as it apparently is, to classify all head wounds as 'serious', then it is all the more necessary that 'the Matron should fill in the picture . . . and that her letter should be delayed until she has seen [the casualty] for herself and given him an opportunity, if he can avail himself of it, of sending a message home. I should like to add that the patient had nothing but gratitude for the kindness and sympathy shown him at the hospital. If a little imaginative sympathy were also shown for the next-of-kin it would save much unnecessary suffering.'

There would be no further occasion for similar suffering. Christopher was not wounded again. But there would be other suffering to come, for which Milne was hardly prepared. In Trieste, where Christopher was stationed in his last months in the Army, he fell in love for the first time and it was this girl, Hedda – part Austrian, part Italian – who taught him a great deal and 'helped to loosen the bond that tied' him to his father. If Milne had said, as he often had, that it was his greatest wish that Christopher should grow away from him, stand on his own two feet and make his own name for himself, when the son at last started out on that path, the father found it very hard.

But in the meantime there was rejoicing with the end of the war and the prospect of the boy's coming home to Cotchford – and a final year at Cambridge. Milne was in a mood to see good in even the greatest horror of the war, the atomic bomb. Once he had said, 'Armaments are the deadly enemy of Peace.' Was this new horror really different? On 14 August 1945, the day that Japan surrendered to the Allies, a letter from A. A. Milne appeared in *The Times*.

Sir,—The object of war is to impose the national will upon another nation by the destruction of so much of its resources, human and material, that it cannot resist. Opinion has varied from time to time whether nations have a moral right to do this : (*a*) in aggression on another country ; (*b*) to stop such aggression. The general opinion in England to-day is that (*a*) is a crime against God and humanity, and that (*b*) is a moral duty ; a few people, however, condemn both (*a*) and (*b*), with a kindly recommendation to mercy in the case of (*b*).

It is absurd to suppose that an (*a*) nation, which looks forward cheerfully to killing a million innocent people for the sake of some material end, is going to exhibit a nice humanity about its methods of murder ; and it is insulting to suppose that a (*b*) nation, which has reluctantly accepted an arbitrament repulsive to it, because it believes that there are higher values at stake than human lives, will risk the cause and deny its belief by making an exception in the case of the enemy's lives. If war is to be abolished, it will not be abolished by pretending that one method of killing is pleasing to God, and another displeasing ; by accepting gratefully 200 raids with ordinary bombs which kill 1,000 " civilians " apiece, and exhibiting sanctimonious horror at one raid with an atomic bomb which kills the same number of " civilians " and spares 20,000 airmen's lives. Every distinction between weapons of war as legitimate and illegitimate, as acceptable by or repugnant to humanity, is one more acknowledgment that war itself is acceptable and legitimate ; so long as it is conducted, not in the latest fashion, but in the latest fashion but one.

War will cease when statesmen are intelligent enough to realize, what the man in the street has known for a long time, that it is a wicked game and a fool's game. The atomic bomb brings this moment nearer ; not because it adds to the wickedness of war, for nothing could do that, but because it makes plain, even to the sub-human intelligence, the folly of it.

Yours, &c.,
A. A. MILNE.
Cotchford Farm, Hartfield, Sussex.

— 18 —

The Last Years

IN THE GENERAL Election of July 1945, A. A. Milne voted Conservative for the first time in his life. This was at a time when many electors were voting Labour for the first time and bringing in a Labour government with a large majority, pledged to exactly those social reforms Milne had seen should be the main concern of post-war Britain – setting the inside of the house to rights. Milne still longed for social reform, but he feared the Labour Party's sympathy for Moscow and dreaded that its plans for nationalization and public ownership would pave the way for some sort of communism. He particularly resented a tendency of the time (particularly on the part of the Dean of Canterbury) to call communism 'socialism', seeing this as an attempt 'to cover up the essential tyranny of communism'. As for the Liberals, not only did they have little chance of making much impression on the general situation, they too seemed affected by the general tolerance for the totalitarians in Moscow.

Milne scribbled a verse and titled it: 'Passed to the *News Chronicle* for Confirmation'.

> Our Lib (or Rad)
> Has always had
> A 'right'ness which has kept him from
> Our Lab (or Soc)
> Who, like a rock,
> Stands firmly to the right of Com.
> But, viewing Europe, Lib takes up his station
> At foot of Com, in humble adoration.

Milne had originally written 'admiration' at the end of the line, but crossed it out and substituted the stronger word. He found it sickening.

Indeed, he found the whole situation deeply depressing. It seemed the seeds of a new war were already being sown as Stalin at Potsdam brushed aside the call for free elections in Eastern Europe and the Iron Curtain began to fall even before the end of the war in the Pacific. On the same page as the verse above, Milne wrote:

> I doubt if we have ever had
> A world so sad and mad and bad,
> And, being part of it, I see
> That part of it is due to me.

In two letters to *The Times*, one in October 1947 and another four years later, Milne suggested just how hard it had been for him to vote for a Conservative in July 1945, to overcome his own entrenched revulsion for the Tory party, symbolized in his mind by a vivid memory of the 'profound mediocrity', Joynson-Hicks, on a golf course more than twenty years before.

As late as the spring of 1945 Milne had described himself as 'one of the three Liberals left in the country'. He still considered himself a Liberal but it was beginning to lose the capital L.

Liberals have much to remember and much to forgive. I doubt if there has ever been a more contemptible exhibition of bad manners, bad sportsmanship and selfish stupidity than was given by the self-styled Gentlemanly Party during those years of Liberal ascendancy. Mr Churchill would probably agree. Many Liberals are still living in those far-off days. In the manner of Dr Johnson, they say to every Conservative candidate, 'Sir, I perceive you are a vile Tory'; when they see a Tory they 'see a rascal'. Even if they had to choose between a Conservative and a Communist, they would choose the Communist, fooling themselves, as they have fooled themselves over every Communist-inspired party abroad, into the belief that the farther you move to the 'left', the less like a reactionary Tory you become. Many years ago I defined a true Liberal (meaning myself, of course) as one who hated Fascism and Communism equally. How many true Liberals are to be found now in the Liberal Party? Very few.

So, Sir, there is neither need for, nor use in, these constant petitions of the Conservative Party that the Liberal Party should unite with it to defeat Socialism. Any deposit-forfeiting Liberal candidate will only draw the votes of the Bourbons still living in the glorious days of 1906, all of whom would elect one hundred Socialists to Parliament rather than one vile Tory. Instead it should be the Conservative aim to select candidates with a truly liberal outlook so as to attract those true Liberals who recognize that the left-ward limits of Liberalism have now been passed, and that every further step is downhill. Liberalism, one hopes and believes, will never die. But to confine it to an official party of twelve and to complain bitterly that a repentant Conservative Party is 'stealing' its policy, seems a curious way of keeping Liberalism alive.

Four years later, Milne made even more clear his reasons for voting Conservative. They had little to do with policies within Britain, though he would, at one point, lament that the post-war Labour government's guiding principle at home seemed to be 'If everybody can't have it, then nobody shall . . .' As always, it was the international situation and the prospects for peace that most concerned Milne. His letter to *The Times* was headed 'Buttresses of Peace'.

It is now clear that the chief argument of the Socialists at the coming election will be that peace is more likely if the pacific Mr Attlee, rather than the bellicose Mr Churchill, is at the head of the Government. If this is true, it is curious that we were involved in the 1914–18 war under the placid leadership of Mr Asquith, and marched into the 1939–45 war beneath the tranquil umbrella of Mr Chamberlain. This may be a coincidence; but there would certainly seem to be an advantage to an aggressive nation in the knowledge that its possible enemies are so amiably led.

For myself I do not think that peace depends on the alleged love of peace of this or that Prime Minister; but it does depend on their respective policies. The two main buttresses of the peaceful world which we all want to build are a united Western Europe and an unbreakable friendship between England and America. Electors should consider whether Mr Attlee or Mr Churchill is likely to be, and has so far shown himself to be, the more devoted architect.

There was much to make Milne gloomy in 1945, but there was also much to be glad about. On 'Victory Day' he made a presentation, accompanied by a note: 'To dear Mrs Wilson, a little token of our Gratitude for all she has done for us during the war: not forgetting the delightful time she has had with the Engine. From A. A. Milne.' The Engine was a temperamental generator, which produced electricity when suitably fed. It was something of a triumph that they still had (and would have for the rest of Milne's life) the same cook-housekeeper and gardener that they had had before the war. Mrs Wilson was a force to be reckoned with. She would grumble about Daphne, but the situation at Cotchford suited her very well. Someone said she ruled the Milnes with a rod of iron, and Christopher would remember how important it was never to upset her; it took seven years to persuade her to give them coffee after dinner, and then it was undrinkable. George Tasker, in the garden, had remained a treasure, devoted, in war or peace, to the dahlia and the chrysanthemum, but capable too of supplementing their dreary diet with all sorts of vegetable joys.

It was a tremendous relief for them all that there were no more flying bombs, though Milne thought the house never really 'pulled itself together' after the two that had come so near. There were new cracks and new draughts. It was a relief that there was no more need for the blackout and that the Home Guard had been dissolved. What had got Milne down about the Home Guard had been the perpetual struggle on early winter mornings to start his 1935 car. (He put his name down after the war for a new one – but in 1952 it had still not been delivered.)

Above all, there was a joyful surge of tremendous relief that Hitler was dead:

> 'The Beast is dead!' a million voices shout.
> 'Where is that bottle? Bring that bottle out!'

And then there was Christopher's safe return to look forward to – though he would not be demobilized until August 1946, over a year after the end of the war in Europe.

A detailed picture of A. A. Milne in the early summer of 1945 comes from an unexpected source, the autobiography of Nancy Spain, who was then a young writer, just out of the WRNS. Indeed, she was still *in* the WRNS, and travelling round England recruiting for them, when she wrote on her knee, on interminable train journeys, the book *Thankyou, Nelson*, that was the cause of her meeting with Milne. She was not yet the bold, indiscreet, privacy-invading *Daily Express* journalist from whom Evelyn Waugh would reap his tax-free damages of £5,000, in two separate actions.

Leonard Russell of the *Sunday Times* sent Milne the book to review, without asking him first. Daphne later reported to Nancy Spain what had happened when Milne opened the parcel. He was livid, she said, and threw the book across the room. 'A — war book, by a — girl,' she said he said. The expletives were deleted by Miss Spain. It is the only record there is of Milne losing his temper and the cause seems trivial. Daphne quietly retrieved the book, read it herself and found she could not put it down. She persuaded Milne to read it, though 'it's all about nothing'.

Milne's review appeared in the *Sunday Times* under the title: 'A Wren's Eye View of the Proper Navy' and made Nancy Spain's name. 'That review of A. A. Milne's sold out the whole of the first edition and the whole of the second. Indeed,' she wrote, 'I knew the book must be a success when the Chief Officer Administration at WRNS headquarters said, "The book was disappointing after the review".'

Nancy Spain wrote to thank Milne for his review and, perhaps surprisingly, he invited her to lunch at Cotchford. He wrote:

You will have to work up an enthusiasm for gardens first. Nothing annoys my wife (and me too) so much as seeing a visitor step heavily back on to a clump of aubretia behind her, ignore the tulips in front of her, and ask if we have been to many theatres lately.

Nancy Spain was not quite sure what aubretia was, but she bravely took a slow green train from Victoria and arrived in time for lunch. Years later she remembered every detail of that delicious meal: 'Hot boiled salmon, peas, new potatoes, asparagus, strawberries and cream. A real cricketer's, schoolboy's or schoolgirl's lunch. There is no better lunch in the world.'

It was a glorious summer's day and the Milnes were perfectly right about their garden. All the flowers had come triumphantly into bloom at the same instant: and there was an enormous pink tree like a feather duster over the front door. It looked as though it had been worked in cross-stitch on a tea-cosy until you came closer and saw that the whole thing was real. A. A. Milne and his wife were adorable too.

She called him Blue and certainly he had the bluest eyes I have ever seen in a human being. Matching up to them were his blazer, that summer sky, his socks, his handkerchief and quite large patches of the garden. And everywhere there were relics of Winnie-the-Pooh. Daphne Milne told me that there was a first edition of *The House at Pooh Corner* under the sundial and we drank sherry poured out of a large blown glass orange reproduction of Piglet. The sherry came out of its mouth.

After lunch A. A. Milne took me to the bottom of the garden and sat, hunched up slightly on a wooden seat, biting on a pipe and gazing gravely out over a stretch of very lush landscape indeed. At the bottom of a plashy-looking meadow a string of cows meandered slowly by. I asked if they were his cows. (After all, the house was called Cotchford Farm.) No, they weren't, but practically everything else in sight was . . .

A. A. Milne was a first-class companion. He talked a lot about the importance of light verse and what an excellent thing it was for discipline to drop into it from time to time. 'Light verse writing makyth a very exact man.' He said that the important thing in writing was to keep 'oneself' out of the way of the reader. 'Otherwise the perspiration shows'. And he said that the telephone was a monstrous intrusion on privacy. At the time I was more than a little shocked by this, but now that my telephone rings frequently I know what he meant. C. S. Calverley was the chap to imitate, he said. Calverley, who wrote *Fly Leaves* and *Verses* and *Translations*.

> 'Butter and eggs
> And a pound of cheese

> The dog said nothing
> But scratched for fleas,'

he said, ruminatively. And I, poor uneducated dolt, thought he had taken leave of his senses. Thank goodness I had the instinct to keep my mouth shut, and the sense to ask him for the titles of the books. When I got back to London I even went gravely to the British Museum and read them. He went on mildly talking, this enchanting blue-eyed man, all that precious summer's afternoon, distilling the wisdom of years into a casual conversation.

'Any creative writer's criticism of another is no more than a statement of the obvious truth that he would have written the book differently himself,' he told me. 'All writers write to please themselves,' he said. 'No sensible author wants anything but praise.'

That Piglet-shaped sherry decanter is rather an unpleasant surprise, but Nancy Spain can hardly have made it up. It was presumably a sample of a product – perhaps a prototype – appreciated by Daphne and tolerated by Milne. The Pooh books were doing better than ever, but Milne still had very mixed feelings about them and their effect on his general reputation. In August 1946, he wrote to St John Ervine: 'Whenever a critic begins his notice with a reference to *Winnie-the-Pooh*, I know that, not only will he be insulting, but that he decided to be so before he read the book. Which saves him the trouble of reading it.' Ervine had written to say how much he liked Milne's new novel *Chloe Marr* and to commiserate over a review by Peter Quennell. 'Bless you,' Milne said, 'Yours is the letter of a real friend – and (may I add immodestly?) an obviously super-intelligent critic.'

Milne had started *Chloe Marr* at least five years earlier. Chamberlain of Methuen had inquired tenderly after her on several occasions during the war. When the book appeared in 1946, it was his first novel for thirteen years, and it would be his last. It was a considerable success. It sold 16,412 copies in its first six months in Britain alone, and there were plenty of favourable reviews. In America, Dutton's did a first printing of 30,000 copies and had an $8,000 advertising and promotion campaign. 'The Old Enchanter has done it again,' one of the American papers said. There were comparisons with *Zuleika Dobson* (Chloe Marr was similarly elusive and devastatingly attractive), but a general feeling that Milne had produced something rather original, certainly something quite different from anything he had written before.

The novel explored a theme which had often occurred in Milne's plays and naturally preoccupies a biographer. Twenty years earlier, Milne had made one of his characters ask: 'How does one know anything about anybody?' No one really knows anyone else; everyone is different to different people. Chloe Marr is seen entirely from outside, through the eyes of a series of devoted admirers, and if in the end, on her death in a plane crash, she 'still remains something of a mystery', we should not be surprised, for nobody knows the truth about anyone else. The idea of looking at Chloe only from outside, of deliberately ignoring what was going on in her mind, had come to Milne when he realized how vivid Mr Micawber is, and how much less vivid David Copperfield, though we see Micawber only from outside and Dickens gives us 'every thought in David's mind'.

The Times Literary Supplement decided that Mr Milne had 'gone modern'. The reviewer was more interested in 'the grief and happiness, hopes and fears of the ordinary people' who were attracted to Chloe, than in Chloe herself, but the *Sunday Times* suggested it was 'high entertainment with an almost constant sparkle'. The dread word 'whimsical' surfaced from time to time but mostly the reviewers wrote of charm and wit and scintillating dialogue. One reviewer even went so far as to say: 'Milne has never done a better piece of work than this.' But few discussed the serious underlying theme or drew attention to the fact that Chloe's repeated 'I *wish* I loved you' was not just part of the comedy but a cry from the heart, from someone incapable of love.

In the same letter in which he had thanked St John Ervine for his super-intelligent words about *Chloe Marr*, Milne reported briefly on Christopher's return home. There is no trace yet of the disappointment Milne would feel after all the longing for a reunion, all the loving anxiety and devoted letter writing. Milne was writing to Ervine on 4 August 1946, the anniversary, as he said, of the beginning of the war to make the world safe for democracy.

Our boy is with us, and gets demobilized next week; after which he goes back to Cambridge for a year, chiefly to give the world a little time in which to cool. Having been at Trieste for the last year, he takes a very gloomy view of Stalin and Tito. So do I; and of most other people.

But the garden is looking so lovely that even the sight of Molotov framed in the roses wouldn't spoil it altogether.

The *Evening News* interviewed Milne at the time of the publication of *Chloe Marr* and was interested in Christopher's future.

Lieut. Christopher Robin Milne, whose fortunes have kept pace with the generation that fought this war, is soon to be demobilised after five years with the Royal Engineers . . . He is now recovered from the wound he got in the fighting in Italy . . .

'No, I don't know what he will take up yet', said Mr Milne, just like hundreds of fathers. 'He may write, but it is a difficult time for young writers. Look at the size of your paper.'

Milne was remembering (and would recall this in an article in the *Spectator* introducing its new Undergraduate Page) the time when he had started as a young journalist himself. In those days 'there were eight evening papers in London all of which printed articles from the unknown freelance. Forty-eight chances each week of a guinea', to say nothing of 'the obese morning papers'. Now 'the outlook for the young is become bleak indeed'.

The outlook in general for young Christopher Milne, twenty-six in the summer of his demobilization, seemed rather bleak. His father wrote to Frank Swinnerton that October: 'He thinks of being a publisher. Any suggestions?' Swinnerton invited Milne to lunch early in December. Milne's reply shows that he was certainly not a recluse, though he was turning down many invitations, including one to appear as a birthday guest on the wireless programme 'Monday Night at Eight'. ('I can't think of anything more terrible.') What was of more importance on Tuesdays than the Wednesday meeting of the Royal Literary Fund is not at all clear.

I'm afraid I shan't be coming up for the Literary Fund meeting on Wednesday, so cannot accept your kind invite. I go up on Tuesday every week anyway – of necessity – and on this particular week I am 'judging' at an RADA show at the Lyric on Thursday. To make the stop-at-every-station journey to London and back three days running (or, rather, stopping) is too much for me. It can't be done, alas; but thank you so much for suggesting it.

Tuesdays had regularly been his day for 'going to London to see how it is getting on', for the haircuts and the lunches at the Garrick. It is in this post-war period that Rupert Hart-Davis remembers him there as someone 'gloomy and aloof', which fits in with the sad suggestion in his letter to St John Ervine that he took a gloomy view not only of Stalin and Tito but of 'most other people'. The young Nancy Spain had penetrated his reserve and found him 'a darling man . . . in the golden light of that magic afternoon in the sun'. Nellie Maugham, the wife of the former Lord Chancellor and sister-in-law of Somerset, could always, he said, lift his spirits with an 'irresistible saga of nonsense'. She 'was a tonic for any depression'. But Basil Boothroyd thought of him as 'an austere and somewhat tetchy figure, in contrast with his "charming" literary style' and to most people at this period he seemed cool, if not cold, silent and increasingly bitter.

The bitterness came largely from the realization that he was losing Christopher. In *Chloe Marr* he had written of a boy who had been killed by a car when a child. His father, years later, reflected like this:

Jonathan, if he had lived, would have been grown up by this time; any expressions of love between them would have been bad form, even if there was love left to express. They would meet rarely, write as little as possible. He would dislike his daughter-in-law, or she him. Father and Son would differ in politics, in tastes, in creed. There were so many barriers to unity.

And yet, he wrote, 'You love your children; you will never stop loving them. That's the only love which never changes, never dies.'

Milne had written the script for his own particular version of *Father and Son*. He saw, before it happened, what lay in store. He had said to an interviewer in 1931: 'If I make a success of Christopher Robin as a person I will consider it my greatest creative work', and he *had* made a success of him, in so far as any father can 'make' a son. The son was highly intelligent, modest, thoughtful, caring and competent. He loved making things; he loved literature and music and the natural world. But it was only by getting away from his father and his celebrated childhood that he could be the person he really was. If Christopher was to flourish as himself, his relationship with his father had to be sacrificed.

Christopher has told the story himself of the difficult time when, after his final eight months at Cambridge (and his Third in English Literature), he tried job after job, at first not realizing how foolish it was for him to tread in his father's footsteps, like King Wenceslas's page. He tried being a writer, writing light articles, as his father had done forty years earlier. He nearly always got them back. He tried the Central Office of Information – the civilian heir of the Ministry for which his father had written during the war. And then – on a different tack – he tried being a trainee furniture buyer for the John Lewis Partnership, failed to buy a business suit and got the sack. The very qualities his father had praised ('He is the most modest, unassuming boy I have ever known') made it difficult for Christopher to sell himself.

I was the wrong person in the wrong place with qualifications nobody wanted . . . Other fathers were reaching down helping hands to their sons. But what was mine doing? What, to be fair, could mine do? He had made his own way by his own efforts and he had left behind him no path that could be followed. But were they entirely his own efforts? Hadn't I come into it somewhere? In pessimistic moments, when I was trudging London in search of an employer wanting to make use of such talents as I could offer, it seemed to me, almost, that my father had got to where he was by climbing upon my infant shoulders, that he had filched from me my good name and left me with nothing but the empty fame of being his son.

It was in 1947, Christopher considered, that the cement binding father and son began to crumble. They did not talk about it.

Neither of us knew what the other thought. We could only guess. Did he guess right? Did he sympathize? Was he resentful? Did he have any feelings of guilt? Well, he had his own battles to fight, and, curiously, they were not dissimilar from mine. If I was jealous of him, he was no less jealous of himself. If I wanted to escape from Christopher Robin, so too did he . . .

After the war he turned to short stories. He had always written what he wanted to write. His luck was that this was also what the public wanted to read. Now his luck was deserting him. People didn't want books of short stories. Nor did they want long philosophical poems. Nor even collections of random reflections. He at the top of the hill, I at the bottom: we each had our sorrows, our moments of disillusion. We were both of us unwanted.

In 1948, when Christopher came down for a week's holiday, the situation at Cotchford was extremely difficult. Christopher had ended his engagement to the girl in Trieste – that relationship which had helped him so much to grow up, to become himself. He was living alone in a flat in London and his de Sélincourt grandfather's second wife, Nancy, had thought it sad that he should not know his cousin, Lesley, who was also working in London. Their step-grandmother put them in touch with each other. Lesley was the daughter of Daphne's brother, Aubrey, that same brother she had not talked to for twenty-five years or so, since the row over the borrowed money that had never been returned.

In the years between, Aubrey had proved how wrong his father had been to oppose his marriage. One of Aubrey's devoted pupils at the school where he was now teaching at Shanklin on the Isle of Wight said he had not only transformed her life by his readings from Shakespeare and *Moby Dick*, but that he and Irene had shown her that 'it was possible for middle-aged married people still to be in love with each other'.

Christopher Milne and Lesley de Sélincourt met on 5 February

1948. On Wednesday, 31 March, Milne wrote one of his regular letters to Maud, Ken's widow, to tell her he had had some Turkish Delight from her son, Tim, now working for the Foreign Office in Ismailia. Milne called it 'Is-mile-a' and his son immediately informed him it was 'Isma-eela'. Milne went on:

This is about the limit of Moon's conversation just now. He is (apparently) in love again, and 'thinking of 'er' all the time. We see little of him save at meals, and get nothing from him then except an affirmative, negative or non-committal grunt (it is difficult to distinguish between them) in answer to a direct question. He came down on Saturday night and goes back on Saturday morning; I had no idea before that there were so many meals in a week. Daff is in London today, so I have had to do all the work myself. Luckily she will be back to dinner; she is more dauntless than I am, and got a couple of forced laughs out of him the other day. All very trying, but I suppose it will pass.

It is the sort of thing many parents go through with adolescent children. Adolescence is the time for contempt. Christopher had never been contemptuous as a boy, and now he was twenty-seven and, having found Lesley, almost ready to make a complete break. It would be another twenty-five years – many years after his father's death – before he would finally come to terms with his father and what they had done to each other. 'Children drift away from their parents as they grow up, and it is right that they should,' he wrote in his second book of memoirs. 'I had been very close to mine, especially to my father, for rather longer than is usual, and so the drifting when it came was perhaps a little further than is usual.'

The only consolation for Milne was that Christopher's alienation seemed to bring husband and wife closer together. Even before their son's return to Cotchford, there had been a resumed tenderness, a greater closeness, than there had been since the 1920s. There are attractive glimpses of Daphne in Milne's last contribution to *Punch*, a soft, sweet farewell to her dog, a young golden cocker spaniel killed by a car on the Maresfield road in the winter of 1946.

> She was yours to guard and love . . .
> While she's weeding, there you sit,
> In your mouth, a garden glove
> 'Just in case she's needing it.'
>
> But the tilted head proclaims
> With a plea you cannot miss:
> '*When* you think it's time for games
> Here's a glove, we'll play with this.'

> Racing with her round the fields,
> Watching as she does her hair –
> Morn to night the moment yields
> Something which the two can share . . .

The dog was buried under the silver birches in the wood the Milnes themselves had planted between the house and the Maresfield road. Years later, after Alan's death, Daphne would give instructions that a sculpture of Christopher's head should be buried under those same trees where she would never see it again.

Christopher's 'drifting away', the rift between son and parents, was exacerbated by the fact that it was Lesley de Sélincourt whom he loved and married. 'He would dislike his daughter-in-law', Milne had written prophetically in *Chloe Marr*. He could not help comparing Lesley with Anne Darlington. He could not help hating the fact that she was Aubrey's daughter. He could not help fearing the fact that Christopher and Lesley were first cousins. A friend thought that Daphne, while sharing all of those feelings of Alan's, also bitterly resented the fact that Lesley, far from being enchanted by Pooh, seemed to despise him and add to Christopher's resentment of what the books had done to him. Daphne and Lesley had nothing whatsoever in common; it was difficult to believe they were closely related. There was an instinctive antipathy.

Christopher Milne and Lesley de Sélincourt were married on Saturday, 24 July 1948, at Holy Trinity, Brompton. The wedding was not until four o'clock. To fill in the time, Christopher and his best man, his cousin Tony, went into Hyde Park to watch small prep-school boys playing cricket. *The Times* recorded:

The bride, who was given away by her father, wore a crinoline gown of white net and taffeta, and was attended by two child bridesmaids, Anne-Marie de Sélincourt and Alison Murray-Rust. Mr Antony Milne was best man.

What *The Times* did not record, of course, was that first meeting in more than twenty-five years between the parents of the bride and the parents of the groom, between the estranged brother and sister, Aubrey and Daphne. There were apparently brave public smiles from everyone. Someone remembered somebody saying, 'Oh darlings! How lovely to see you.' At least it *was* a wedding, not a funeral, but the Montagues and Capulets were somewhere in the background. There was no doubt that the marriage would not 'bury their parents' strife', and that Christopher was joining Lesley in the opposing camp.

The atmosphere of that strange and awkward occasion was eased by the young bridesmaids, so unaware of the adult tensions, so happy in their pink and white candy-striped dresses. Anne-Marie was eleven and Alison thirteen, but the younger girl, Nancy's daughter, was Daphne's half-sister and so two generations 'older' than Alison, Ken's granddaughter. The reception was held at Brown's Hotel, Milne's favourite London hotel. He used it quite often for entertaining, now that they no longer had the Chelsea house.

The short stories mentioned by Christopher in that summary of his father's writing after the war were mostly competent and entertaining, and sometimes rather more than that. One of the funniest and most attractive is 'The Rise and Fall of Mortimer Scrivens', told in the form of a series of letters, and a splendid warning to anyone who borrows books and fails to return them. There are some good murder stories and another which is not a murder story at all, but the story of a man who has once killed but lives to earn the Hardyan epitaph: 'He was a good man and did good things.' This story, like a number of others, is written in a female voice.

Milne was creating these stories on the backs of the monthly accounts from the agent who looked after his amateur rights. 'As I have written thirty plays, long or short, there are usually plenty of these. The resulting manuscript is so crossed out, rubbed out, interlined and generally messed up, as to be indecipherable by anybody else, and sometimes by me. I write it all out again in ink (this is rather a bore) and send it away to be typed. This gives me ten days before it comes back; during which I can tell myself that I am still in the middle of that particular story, and may do nothing with an easy conscience.' He actually found doing nothing extremely difficult in winter, though easy enough in the summer with cricket and the garden.

The stories appeared first in all sorts of places – in Leonard Russell's *Saturday Book*, in *Good Housekeeping*, in *Modern Woman*, *Collier's*, *Cosmopolitan* and the *Ellery Queen Mystery Magazine*. Some of them appeared for the first time in his two collections: *Birthday Party* (1948) and *A Table Near the Band* (1950). As Christopher suggests, they did not do well. Dutton's certainly did not expect them to. They printed only 4,000 of *Birthday Party* and, after the initial sales which earned the tiny advance, there were apparently no sales at all in the following six months.

My own copy of *A Table Near the Band*, shows that Milne was still in touch with his sister-in-law, Connie, at this stage. Indeed he tells Maud in one letter, a few years later, that he hears a lot from her, that one of her sons is an 'angel' and the other as 'dishonest as his darling Papa'. In his will he left her £1,000 without comment. *A Table Near the Band* is inscribed simply 'For Connie with love from Alan. November 2nd, 1950.' For Anne Darlington he inscribed the book: 'But for whom the first story would never have been written, and the Milnes would have missed a lot of happiness and laughter – with more than twenty-five years love from Blue.' It was a Christmas present in 1950. Peter Ryde, who married Anne Darlington, remembers the first time the Milnes came to dinner with them, how Anne rushed around polishing everything possible and served oysters and smoked salmon, and how Alan Milne, though charming and pleasant and obviously devoted to Anne, made very little effort to be entertaining and sat almost as if 'barricaded' within himself.

Tony Milne's copy of *Birthday Party* has the only sad inscription I have seen in any of Milne's books. It reads:

> Tony, make room for your Uncle –
> somewhere between
> 'Leprechauns by One of Them'
> and
> – 'What I saw in New South Wales'
> – on the shelf that nobody reads –
> A. A. Milne

It was no consolation that the children's books were still being read.

Milne's reputation as an adult writer was certainly in serious decline in America. That same year Elliott Macrae of Dutton's reported that a large-scale plan to promote Milne's adult books had been a complete failure. Originally they planned to print 600,000 copies of his various titles, but cut it in half at the last moment and, even then, found themselves eventually 'stuck with two hundred and twenty thousand assorted titles.' They remaindered them at below cost.

In England a number of the plays continued to be in the staple menu of many repertory companies. For instance, in 1948 thirteen different Milne plays were produced. *The Dover Road* was performed twelve times around the country and *Mr Pim Passes By* sixteen times. There were American productions too, and both *Mr Pim* and *To Meet the Prince* appeared on Kraft Television Theatre.

But, as usual, by far the largest proportion of Milne's income came from the children's books, their translations and their subsidiary rights. In 1947 alone Milne himself earned over $2,000 from the American sale of toys, games and records. The children's books, as they had always done, gave Milne the freedom to write whatever he wanted to write, not worrying about markets, but he realized more and more how much of his pleasure in writing depended on the praise that followed. 'No sensible author wants anything but praise', he had said to Nancy Spain, and when praise was hard to come by, sales slow, fan letters related, not to the latest book, but only to the children's books, the writing itself began to lose its savour. And life itself seemed pointless; for what was life but writing?

'To a writer one day is very much like another day. He gets up, he eats, he writes, he eats, he thinks, he potters, he eats, he writes, he eats, he reads, he goes to bed.' The writing and going to bed were now apparently happening in the same room. He had abandoned the study on the ground floor – as small and dark as the one in Chelsea – and now wrote in his bedroom on the first floor with windows on two sides, looking over the garden. A women's magazine in 1950 photographed his 'unpretentious desk' and yellow-flowered chintz curtains and the cheap bright Indian rug on the floor. One day he finished a story up there as the cat Cleopatra produced a litter downstairs. 'Hers a greater achievement,' he considered. 'What is one short story to four delightful kittens?'

In 1947 the toys themselves – Pooh, Piglet, Tigger, Kanga and Eeyore – made a triumphant tour of America. Elliot Macrae had visited Cotchford and seen the toys looking rather neglected and fed up with life; he asked if he might borrow them. They crossed the Atlantic with a 'birth certificate' in Milne's own handwriting, giving their histories. On arrival in New York they were immediately insured for $50,000, a vast sum of money more than forty years ago. They then travelled around America for many years, visiting libraries and department stores and occasionally coming to rest in Dutton's offices in New York. There were inevitably stories of Pooh fans travelling hundreds of miles through snow drifts to catch a glimpse of the beloved bear. Elliot Graham, publicity director at Dutton's, recalled that

Everywhere Pooh went we had a guest book for people to sign. We sent the books to Milne so he could see their comments, like 'We love Pooh' and 'I travelled two hundred miles just to see Pooh'. He seemed to enjoy those and decided Dutton should keep the animals. We like to say that Pooh became an American citizen.

Christopher was asked, years later, if he resented the toys' emigration, and he said that they were only toys, 'old and battered and lifeless', and that they should not be compared with 'the real animals who lived in the forest' and obviously live on, not only in the books but also in the heads of all the millions of readers who have loved them. Christopher added: 'I like to have around me the things I like today, not the things I once liked many years ago.'

Handing them over to Dutton's, Milne apparently insisted that the toys should never be cleaned but should look as if a child had just finished playing with them. 'No explanation is needed for the world-weariness of Pooh and Eeyore,' he wrote. 'Time's hand has been upon them since 1921. That was a long time ago.'

Milne's own world-weariness was made explicit in some verses he sent to his great-niece at Godolphin School in Salisbury. She was always begging him for poetry and he was always grumbling about it, but obviously enjoyed meeting her requests.

> I'm weary of this world of strife.
>   I'd like to have a stab
> At living the untroubled life
>   Of (say) a hermit crab . . .
>
> No word of bombs, of A or H,
>   Has ever crossed his lips.
> None talks to him of Shin or Strach.
>   He's deaf to news of Cripps.
>
> His pools are not the football pools,
>   Nor sea the B.B.C.
> No letters come from dolphin schools
>   Demanding poetry.
>
> What if imagination lends
>   Enchantment to the view?
> *Entomostraca!* (George to friends)
>   I would that I were you!

They had a love of cricket in common, Alison and A. A. Milne, and he would often comment to her on matches he had seen. His visits to cricket matches were not always unmixed pleasure:

I am now in a position to state we shall not beat the West Indians. I was at Lords on Tuesday and Wednesday. Unfortunately I sat in front of two people yesterday one of whom was explaining the game of cricket very carefully to the other, a Dutchman, who had only seen ice hockey up to then. Fresh explanations were called for after each ball; and there was one awful moment when the Dutchman said 'Is it not like baseball?' and his friend then began to explain baseball too . . .

He was an obliging great-uncle; on one occasion he sent a page of twelve autographs for her schoolfriends (with 'cut along the dotted lines'). Many years before, when her mother, Marjorie, was at the same school, he had sent her Charlie Chaplin's autograph. Now it was his own that was in demand by girls brought up on the Pooh books. His letters ran on in rhyme. On one occasion, when the Murray-Rusts were living in Yorkshire (Marjorie's husband was now an Inspector of Schools), he chided Alison for travelling north without exploring the delights of her new county:

I don't know why a girl should go to visit Skye and see Glencoe; ignoring Leeds – without compare for one who needs a change of air. Young girls, they say, are never dull who holiday in happy Hull; and dark Glencoe's delights must yield first place to those of Huddersfield.

Milne's most sustained versifying in these last years went into what Christopher would call 'the long philosophical poem'. Methuen called it 'a short poem of a thousand lines': *The Norman Church*. Methuen published a small edition at five shillings each; it was the sort of book which publishers accept 'only out of deference to a writer who has supplied them through many years with better, more marketable books in other fields.' It was never published in America. It was Milne's most serious attempt since *The Ascent of Man*, twenty years earlier, to examine his own religious beliefs, the belief he had shared with Christopher during the war when he had sent him Winwood Reade's *The Martyrdom of Man*. In his introduction, Milne showed himself prepared to be attacked as a heretic and blasphemer, but few seemed to care enough to attack him. If Milne saw himself as a mid-twentieth-century iconoclast, in fact, as someone pointed out, he was raising and answering 'no questions that would have surprised Tennyson'. He reiterated a belief he had expressed before, that the two testaments of the Bible were in such violent opposition that it was ridiculous for them to be both part of the same religion. He made a clear distinction between 'the objective GOD, of whom we can only say with certainty that HE is the Creative Spirit or First Cause, and the subjective man-imagined God' in his various contradictory incarnations – the Pope's God, Mohammed's God, St

Paul's God and so on – a God set up by man. He naturally wanted
nothing to do with a God that decreed that

> babies dying unbaptized
> Were damned in Hell. Was God surprised
> To hear that this was what Himself had authorized?

If the book made little impression on the world at large, in Hartfield, in their own village, some people felt confirmed in their opinion
that the Milnes were atheists and sinners. Someone told me that
Daphne was generous with the flowers from her garden 'as long as
they weren't going to the church'. There were churchgoers in Hartfield who resented Milne's own superior attitude. How did *he* know
what was going on in other people's heads during the sermon?

> The choir-boys shuffle in their seats;
> A housewife mentally completes
> Tomorrow's washing list; her lord
> Adds up the hymns upon the board.
> The Squire, as far as one can see,
> Is interested in a bee;
> A widow, reverently prim,
> Is wondering how best to slim –
> And all the maidens listen rapt, and 'think of him'.

The first section of the long poem works well enough but the style
(in the 'jingling verses') is not really suitable for much of the material.
John Betjeman would manage it better and from a more sympathetic
angle. Yet *The Norman Church* is another reminder that A. A. Milne
was more than a humorist, a writer of stage comedies and the creator
of four of the most popular children's books ever written.

In 1951 Christopher and Lesley Milne left London to start a bookshop in Dartmouth, in Devon. The emotional distance between
parents and son was now confirmed by a geographical distance.
Dartmouth is two hundred miles from Hartfield. Christopher remembered his mother's reaction:

'I would have thought,' said my mother, who always hit the nail on the
head no matter whose fingers were in the way, 'I would have thought that
this was the one thing you would have absolutely hated. I thought you
didn't like "business". You certainly didn't get on at John Lewis. And you're
going to have to meet Pooh fans all the time. Really it does seem a very
odd decision.' She was quite right, of course.

But she was also quite wrong, and any reader who wants to know what happened to Christopher and Lesley Milne in Dartmouth should read his book *The Path Through the Trees*.

In January 1952 A. A. Milne was seventy. 'What are birthdays?' Eeyore had asked long before. 'Here today and gone tomorrow.' But this one seemed more important than most, though he did not feel old. He remembered that extraordinary anticipation he had had of old age when he was a small boy having his hair brushed in the photographer's studio. 'One day I shall be old and it won't matter how long she took over my hair, because I shall be old, and it will all be over.' Inside himself, he felt much as he had felt on that summer day so long before. He did not feel seventy. 'It is indeed an extraordinary age to be: an age at which, without conscious effort, one should be clothed with dignity and authority; and here am I, invested with neither.' A great deal of time had certainly passed. He could surprise people by telling them he had been at Gladstone's funeral in Westminster Abbey and had walked out behind Sir Henry Irving. The reason why a writer does not easily acquire the dignity and authority of old age is that he is never in a position of dignity or authority. 'However long a writer has been in the business, he is still without authority for anybody but himself. All he knows is how to write in his own way.'

He wrote to his great-niece, Alison, now in her last year at school:

I had a very nice birthday. My American publishers sent me twelve bottles of whisky. Can you believe it? Compare this with the picture postcard which my English publishers didn't send me, and where are you? And a neighbour, whom we have only met once or twice and who had seen a paragraph in the *Evening News* congratulating me on being ninety, came round with a large pot of daffodils. As Wordsworth said

> And then my heart with pleasure fills
> And dances with the daffodils,
>   Becoming pardonably frisky
>   When filled as well with all this whisky.

Milne had never liked whisky; in 1931 a headline in the *New York Herald Tribune* had actually proclaimed the fact. Perhaps his tastes had changed, or perhaps it was just the thought that counted. The arrival of the crate had been a pleasant interruption in a quiet life. He told Alison, finishing his letter to her, that Daphne had been busy all day making curtains. 'I shall now go down and say helpfully, "Getting on?" In this way I encourage her to stick to it.'

Milne published his last book, *Year In, Year Out*, in 1952. This was the book Christopher would call 'a collection of random reflections'. In England it came out in June and was generally well reviewed. Virginia Graham in the *Spectator* called his style 'immaculate and sweet, but not excessively sentimental'. *The Times Literary Supplement* said: 'The book demonstrates Milne's erudition, wit and liberalism.' That must have pleased him. The reviewer in *The Times* commented on the fact that Milne called himself 'damnably uncivic' and 'an unworthy vice-president of the local horticultural society'.

Yet he can sometimes be an alarmingly good citizen, as when he writes to the paper on such tremendous topics as income tax or the atomic bomb.

In fact he can write delightfully, amusingly, ironically, and now and again almost ferociously on all manner of subjects. [He provides] a dish of fine, confused eating, offering a wide choice for the reader's money.

That August he wrote a letter to a young journalist in Cornwall who had written in appreciation of the new book. Its survival is the most convincing evidence that Milne had at last, near the end of his life, revived his feeling for Pooh.

I can't remember a letter which has given me as much pleasure as yours. As your own fan-mail increases (as I am sure it will, for it is obvious that you can write), you will find that intelligent praise is the one stimulant which a writer needs. You will also find that, however proud he may be of earlier work, it is praise of his latest book which he appreciates most. So thank you for what you say of *Year In, Year Out*; as you can imagine, I enjoyed writing it – which is the only way I know of firing enjoyment in others. But you are right about *Pooh*. There was an intermediate period when any reference to him was infuriating; but now such a 'nice comfortable feeling' envelops him that I can almost regard him impersonally as the creation of one of my own favourite authors.

When *Year In, Year Out* was published in America later in the year, the reviews were also enthusiastic. The *New York Times* said: 'Milne discusses a hundred or so everyday subjects, but is delightfully surprising, witty and graceful.' To celebrate the American publication, the *New York Herald Tribune* published a photograph of A. A. Milne at Cotchford and asked him to write something about his life to go with it. He chose to write a brief autobiography in verse, which ended with the following lines:

> If a writer, why not write
> On whatever comes in sight?
> So – the Children's Books: a short
> Intermezzo of a sort;
> When I wrote them, little thinking

All my years of pen-and-inking
Would be almost lost among
Those four trifles for the young.

Though a writer must confess his
Works aren't all of them successes,
Though his sermons fail to please,
Though his humour no one sees,
Yet he cannot help delighting
In the pleasure of the writing
In a farmhouse old by centuries
This so happy an adventure is
Coming (so I must suppose,
Now I'm 70) to a close.
Take it all, year in, year out,
I've enjoyed it, not a doubt.

Three days later on 15 October Daphne Milne wrote to Maud in what looks like tear-stained red ink:

Share most terrible news. My darling Alan is very very seriously ill and was taken last night to East Grinstead Hospital in an ambulance. He had a stroke.

I have just come back from the Hospital and he is expected to live two or three days perhaps.

It was so frightfully sudden. I still find it impossible to believe.

My love to you,
Daff.

In fact, Milne lived for another three years and three months, but he remained an invalid. At the beginning, *The Times* reported almost daily on his condition. He was still critically ill on 21 October. The next day he was said to be 'very dangerously ill'. On the 27th he was moved from East Grinstead to the Middlesex Hospital in London. He was still 'seriously ill' on 5 November when a news item in *The Times* recorded the fact that his books had been withdrawn from libraries in Hungary and banned, along with the work of Conan Doyle, Rider Haggard and Daphne Du Maurier. By 19 November, over a month after the stroke, his condition showed some improvement.

In late December, it was felt worth risking an operation on his brain at the Middlesex Hospital. It was supposed to be a 'kill or cure' operation, but it left him worse than he had been before and partly paralysed. For three years, he could move only in a wheelchair, but he could still speak and write to a certain extent. On 27 January, he was moved to a nursing home in Tunbridge Wells, not far from

Cotchford. The operation, Christopher said, made his father a different person. There was a distressing change in his character, everyone said. There was something coarse, vulgar, irritable and perverse, which had not been there before. 'If it is sad to go too soon, it is worse to stay too long.' Christopher saw his father only twice during those more than three years of illness. He recalls an occasion when his own bitterness 'overflowed more publicly than it should have done'.

In November 1952, when Milne was still in the Middlesex Hospital, Christopher rashly agreed to talk to a *Sunday Dispatch* reporter. An article appeared as if he had written it himself. 'Ever since I was quite a small boy, I have hated being Christopher Robin . . . [My father] had as little to do with children as possible. I was his only child and I lived upstairs in the nursery. I saw very little of him . . . It was my mother who used to come and play in the nursery with me and tell him about the things I thought and did. It was she who provided most of the material for my father's books.' As for bedtime stories, he recalled: 'I had one instalment every evening, but I never remember Winnie-the-Pooh being brought into them.'

If Christopher's memories were not very accurate, they did not sound in fact particularly bitter and were certainly not hostile. He recalled his father teaching him cricket and algebra. He said:

I was always very grateful to him for being so good at admiring anything I did make – however hideous it might be. He once put up an almost useless bright blue wall-bracket in his bedroom just because I had made it. He was a good father to me although it wasn't until I was twelve that we really came to know each other well . . . Instead of writing poems about me, he started writing amusing letters to me. He taught me to play golf – that was rather more successful than cricket . . . Today he is very ill in hospital and I am grown up. I shall never get over my dislike of being the "real live Christopher Robin". But now when I sell one of my father's books in the bookshop I own, I can't help feeling a little proud of him.

Daphne tried to keep the article from Milne, who was now back home at Cotchford with day and night nurses. But the 'well-meaning proverbial friend' (who could probably see nothing hurtful in it) 'told all and caused Blue to change his will', according to another friend. Whether this was really so, I have no idea. Christopher's inheritance remained substantial. What is certain is that Milne himself hated the article. He mentioned it to Maud in a letter more than two years later, in the summer of 1955, written in an unrecognizable handwriting and perhaps his last letter.

> Did you read Moon's article on me in the *Sunday Dispatch*, when I was supposed to be dying? You'd have been disgusted. Oh well, I lost him years ago, but I still have Daff. Thank God, though I give her a rotten time, I'm afraid. But from 11.30–1.30 we are out in the garden together, doing the *Times* Xword at lunch-time – the high spot of my day. My hand and eyes are getting tired – so I must stop.

He was giving everyone rather a rotten time. He was not a good patient. In the same letter he thanked Maud and her family for 'about 150 letters, for which I am very grateful and for your patience'.

> Of course life with me goes on much the same since the departure of the famous Monty (I must have told you about him as I had him for ten months – real name Worthington, and the son of a Colonel . . .) – one impossibly foul or incompetent nurse after another; until a month ago when we got an absolute toot called Campbell, very Scottish, says 'Wee Willie' all day long. I told him that if he said it more than twenty-five times a day, I'd brain him. He just laughs. All the others would have given twenty-four hours' notice on the spot. I can say what I like to him and he knows I'm not serious. Wonderful in a Scotsman. But a funny story or a limerick leaves him absolutely blank.

J. G. Campbell, male nurse, of Rose's Hotel, Banff, witnessed Milne's will together with Joan M. Fuller, physiotherapist, of Wadhurst in Sussex. Joan Fuller, now Scoones, has vivid memories of this last period of Milne's life. She was, of course, interested to find she was to give regular physiotherapy – three or even four times a week – to the author of the *Pooh* books, but she came to dislike her visits to the house. He had 'lovely blue eyes' but he was very sour and sad and bitter, she thought – and 'bored to tears'. She was summoned so often – even on Bank Holidays, she said – because she was a diversion in the awful emptiness of his days. She rarely saw Daphne, whom Campbell, the male nurse, had christened 'the bloody Duchess'. Daphne 'couldn't handle illness', Joan Scoones thought, but Milne never said a word against her, though he criticized every-thing and everyone else. 'I still have Daff. Thank God,' he had said to Maud and it was his constant thought. 'How beautiful she is,' he would say to the physiotherapist, with tears in his eyes. He gave the young woman a copy of the American edition of *Year In, Year Out* for Christmas 1953 inscribed

> 'Gratefully and in the hope of improving her mind'.

A present the following year, of a first edition of *The Pocket Milne*, was more elaborately inscribed:

> For
> Joan Fuller
> (aged 23)
> First prize for
> Punctuality
> Neatness
> Physiotherapy
> and
> Imperviousness to Insults
> From
> A. A. Milne
> Christmas Term, 1954.

He very rarely mentioned Christopher, but once, Joan remembered, on a Good Friday, he said: 'We have *all* given our only sons.' Yet there was, he was quite sure, to be no everlasting life.

In February 1954 *The Times* reported that an ambulance had taken Mr A. A. Milne to Brown's Hotel. 'Mr Milne in 1952 underwent a severe operation on the brain; he has since been partly paralysed and unable to walk. This year he wished to repeat for his friends the party he used to give annually. Mr Milne received the guests in a chair and was later driven back to his home at Hartfield, Sussex.' It was a sad occasion, with everyone talking brightly and feeling sorry for him, and rather embarrassed. 'Not my A. A. M. any more', his niece, Angela, remembered. He had put on a good deal of weight and was almost unrecognizable. It was the last time she saw him.

Daphne did not want visitors at Cotchford. 'We are not a normal household', she told Marjorie, discouraging her from going to see her uncle. Three weeks after the party, Milne was seriously ill again. He had pneumonia and was taken to the Lonsdale Nursing Home in Tunbridge Wells once more. Still he did not die. In April he was back at Cotchford.

That month P. G. Wodehouse wrote a sympathetic letter from his home on Long Island to a man called Alastair Wallace. He had long forgotten how much he had once wanted Milne 'to break his bloody neck'.

Poor Milne. I was shocked to hear of his illness. I'm afraid there seems very little chance of him getting any better. It is ghastly to think of anyone who wrote such gay stuff ending his life like this. He has always been about my favourite author. I have all his books and re-read them regularly . . .

Milne was not going to get any better but still could not die. Late in April he was well enough to write his last letter to *The Times*, contributing to a long correspondence on the vexed question of subsidiary rights in books. He had been concerned about the subject for at least twenty-five years.

The president of the Booksellers Association ought to know better than to trot out yet once again the ineffably silly argument that 'nine out of 10 authors would not stand the slightest chance of having their books filmed, dramatized, broadcast etc., unless they had first been published'; and, that therefore the publisher is entitled to a share in the loot. It would be just as sensible to say that their books would not even have been read by a publisher if they had not been typed and that therefore the typist was entitled to a share in the author's royalties . . . All sorts of odd honours come the way of the successful author. He is knighted (if he likes that sort of thing), invited to country houses, asked to make speeches, give away prizes etc. Does he always take his publisher with him, saying to the Lord Chamberlain, his hostess or the headmaster of his country school, 'I hope you don't mind me bringing old Prendergast along. You see, he's my publisher, and but for him you would never have heard of me.'

One last remark: Mr Page seems to have overlooked the fact that it is nearly always the successful books that get etcetered, and that if they are successful the publishers have made their profit – probably more than the author. And I might add that no publisher has yet shown the slightest sign of being an experienced literary, dramatic and film agent.

Milne had lost none of his skill in polemic, but he had lost his taste for life. The last eighteen months were dreary and empty. There is nothing to record. At Christmas 1955 there was a fine new production of *Toad of Toad Hall* with Leo McKern as Toad, William Squire as Rat and Brewster Mason as Badger, but without Richard Goolden, who had made the part of Mole so much his own. Milne was too ill to take any interest in it, and soon after the turn of the year he slipped into unconsciousness. On 31 January 1956 – she always remembered the date because it was her brother Tony's birthday – Marjorie heard of her uncle's death on the eight o'clock news on the BBC; soon after Daphne telephoned. The cause of death on the certificate was given as 'Cerebro vascular degeneration, Brain abscess and Pneumonia'. He was seventy-four.

There was a Memorial Service for A. A. Milne on 10 February at All Hallows-by-the-Tower in London. Nicholas Hannen, who had appeared in *The Dover Road* forty-four years before, read 'Let us now praise famous men', and Kenneth Bird (Fougasse of *Punch*) read the passage from St Mark: 'Suffer the little children to come unto me, and forbid them not; for of such is the kingdom of God.' Norman Shelley sang Pooh's song, 'How sweet to be a Cloud', and recited 'Vespers' to an organ accompaniment. Christopher's wife Lesley did not come up for the service; she had the excuse that she was six months pregnant. Christopher himself dismayed his mother by turning up in an elderly overcoat. He never saw her again, although Daphne lived for another fifteen years.

Daphne wrote to Maud afterwards:

It was rather shattering that my so-called steadying 'dope' seemed to loose its effect at the critical moment when I needed it most! and I was completely overcome at the end of the service (and with no opportunity of even powdering my nose before meeting people! ...)

I, too, felt the service was perfect and just what Blue would have liked.

Angela was less sure, especially about the Norman Shelley contributions. What Christopher felt, as he listened to 'Vespers', can hardly be imagined.

The obituaries made much of the end of *The House at Pooh Corner*. The worldwide sales of the children's books at this point were put somewhere around seven million. 'In the closing words of his last children's book,' *Time* said, 'A. A. Milne unintentionally summed up his own claim to immortality. "Wherever they go", he said of Pooh and Christopher Robin, "and whatever happens to them on the way, in that enchanted place on the top of the Forest a little boy and his Bear will always be playing".' His plays for adults would not survive. (On the page in *Punch* on which his obituary appeared one of the current recommended plays was *Waiting for Godot*.) His books for adults – both prose and poetry – were nearly all out of print. But each year, in a multitude of languages, the children's books sold in ever-increasing quantities. In 1960 a Latin version, *Winnie ille Pu*, sold 100,000 copies in record time and became the first book in a foreign language ever to be an American bestseller. In 1973 *Pooh* was at last translated into Greek, bringing the total number of translations to twenty-five different languages, including Chinese, Japanese, Russian, Croatian, Serbian, Latvian, Icelandic and Esperanto.

The Walt Disney film versions – the first in 1966 – loathed as they were by E. H. Shepard's admirers, and by many admirers of Milne too, increased awareness of the characters and apparently did nothing to diminish sales of the real thing. 'That's not true,' one small girl said indignantly, watching a video. 'What do you mean?' her mother asked. '*I know* what happened. We read it. The book's true,' the child responded and most people agreed with her.

Milne's animals have become part of the English language. It is taken for granted that people know what is meant by 'a particularly Eeyore-like tone' or 'behaving exactly like Tigger'. An editorial in an American newspaper even once went so far as to say that 'few people in responsible positions in society today have got to eminence without the influence of Pooh'.

All over the world, A. A. Milne's children's books are loved and cherished by children and parents together, and by a good many adults who are not parents. There are no better stories for sharing. There are no better stories for reading aloud and for finding one's way back to that childhood world where it is possible to do Nothing, or at least nothing that has anything to do with anything.

In 1926, just after *Winnie-the-Pooh* was published, A. A. Milne had written in the *Nation*: 'I suppose that every one of us hopes secretly for immortality; to leave, I mean, a name behind him which will live for ever in this world, whatever he may be doing, himself, in the next.' When he died, thirty years later, there was already no doubt at all that A. A. Milne had achieved – though not in the way he had wished – that certain immortality.

A. A. Milne: A Selected Bibliography

A full critical bibliography by Tori Haring-Smith was published in 1982 by Garland Publishing Inc. of New York and runs to 344 pages (including the index). The reader is also referred to *A. A. Milne: A Handlist of his Writings for Children* by Brian Sibley (Henry Pootle Press, 1976, 200 copies only) and to John R. Payne, 'Four Children's Books by A. A. Milne', *Studies in Bibliography* (Virginia) vol. 23, 1970.

Lovers in London, London, Alston Rivers, 1905.

The Day's Play, sketches and verse from *Punch*, London, Methuen, 1910; New York, Dutton, 1925

The Holiday Round, sketches from *Punch*, London, Methuen, 1912; New York, Dutton, 1925

Once a Week, sketches from *Punch*, London, Methuen, 1914; New York, Dutton, 1925

Happy Days, sketches from *Punch*, New York, George H. Doran, 1915

Once on a Time, a story, illustrated by H. M. Brock, New York, London and Toronto, Hodder & Stoughton, 1917. (1922/1925 editions illustrated by Charles Robinson.)

Not That It Matters, essays, London, Methuen, 1919; New York, Dutton, 1920

First Plays (Wurzel-Flummery; The Lucky One; The Boy Comes Home; Belinda; The Red Feathers), London, Chatto & Windus, 1919; New York, Knopf, 1919

If I May, essays, London, Methuen, 1920; New York, Dutton, 1921

Second Plays (Make-Believe; Mr Pim Passes By; The Camberley Triangle; The Romantic Age; The Stepmother), London, Chatto & Windus, 1921; New York, Knopf, 1922

Mr Pim, a novel, London, Hodder & Stoughton, 1921; New York, George H. Doran, 1922

The Sunny Side, sketches and verse, London, Methuen, 1921; New York, Dutton, 1922

The Red House Mystery, a detective story, London, Methuen, 1922; New York, Dutton, 1922

Three Plays (The Dover Road; The Truth about Blayds; The Great Broxopp), New York, Putnam, 1922; London, Chatto & Windus, 1923

Success, a play, London, Chatto & Windus, 1923; New York, French, 1924

The Man in the Bowler Hat, a play, London and New York, French, 1923

When We Were Very Young, poems for children, illustrated by E. H. Shepard, London, Methuen, 1924; New York, Dutton, 1924

A Gallery of Children, stories for children, illustrated by H. Willebeek Le Mair, London, Stanley Paul, 1925; Philadelphia, David McKay, 1925. (1939 edition illustrated by A. H. Watson.)

For the Luncheon Interval: Cricket and Other Verses, London, Methuen, 1925; New York, Dutton, 1925

Four Plays (To Have the Honour or *Meet the Prince; Ariadne; Portrait of a Gentleman in Slippers; Success)*, London, Chatto & Windus, 1926

Miss Marlow at Play, a play, London and New York, French, 1926

Winnie-the-Pooh, a story for children, illustrated by E. H. Shepard, London, Methuen, 1926; New York, Dutton, 1926

Now We Are Six, poems for children, illustrated by E. H. Shepard, London, Methuen, 1927; New York, Dutton, 1927

The Ivory Door, a play, London, Chatto & Windus, 1929; New York, Putnam, 1928

The House at Pooh Corner, a story for children, illustrated by E. H. Shepard, London, Methuen, 1928; New York, Dutton, 1928

The Ascent of Man, an essay, London, Ernest Benn, 1928; New York, Dutton, 1928

By Way of Introduction, essays, prefaces, reviews, London, Methuen, 1929; New York, Dutton, 1929

The Secret and other stories, limited edition, London, Methuen, with New York, Fountain Press, 1929

Those Were the Days, collected writing for *Punch*, London, Methuen, 1929; New York, Dutton, 1929

Toad of Toad Hall, a children's play from *The Wind in the Willows*, London, Methuen, 1929; New York, Scribners, 1929

The Fourth Wall or *The Perfect Alibi*, a play, London and New York, French, 1929

Michael and Mary, a play, London, Chatto & Windus, 1930; London and New York, French, 1930

When I Was Very Young, autobiographical sketch, illustrated by E. H. Shepard, limited edition, London, Methuen, with New York, Fountain Press, 1930

Two People, a novel, London, Methuen, 1931; New York, Dutton, 1931

Four Plays (Michael and Mary; Meet the Prince or *To Have the Honour; The Fourth Wall* or *The Perfect Alibi; Portrait of a Gentleman in Slippers)*, New York, Putnam, 1932

Four Days' Wonder, a novel, London, Methuen, 1933; New York, Dutton, 1933

Peace with Honour, a denunciation of war, London, Methuen, 1934; New York, Dutton, 1934

More Plays (The Ivory Door; The Fourth Wall; Other People's Lives), London, Chatto & Windus, 1935

Miss Elizabeth Bennett, a play, London, Chatto & Windus, 1936

Four Plays (*To Have the Honour; Belinda; The Dover Road; Mr Pim Passes By*), London, Penguin, 1939

It's Too Late Now or *Autobiography* (US title), London, Methuen, 1939; New York; Dutton, 1939

Behind the Lines; verse, London, Methuen, 1940; New York, Dutton, 1940

War with Honour, pamphlet, London, Macmillan, 1940; New York, Macmillan (in *England Speaks*), 1941

War Aims Unlimited, pamphlet, London, Methuen, 1941

The Pocket Milne, New York, Dutton, 1941; London, Methuen, 1942

The Ugly Duckling, a short play, London, French, 1941

Chloe Marr, a novel, London, Methuen, 1946; New York, Dutton, 1946

Going Abroad, a pamphlet, London, Council for Education in World Citizenship, 1947

Birthday Party and other stories, New York, Dutton, 1948; London, Methuen, 1949

Books for Children, a pamphlet (prefatory essay), London, Cambridge University Press (for National Book League), 1948

The Norman Church, a long poem, London, Methuen, 1948

A Table Near the Band, short stories, London, Methuen, 1950; New York, Dutton, 1950

Before the Flood, a short play, London and New York, French, 1951

Year In, Year Out, essays, London, Methuen, 1952; New York, Dutton, 1952

Prince Rabbit and the Princess Who Could Not Laugh, two stories for children, illustrated by Mary Shepard, London, Edmund Ward, 1966; New York, Dutton, 1966

Acknowledgements and Sources

I have indicated several debts in the introduction to this book, but must now reiterate them and add many others. My initial thanks go to Craig Raine and the editorial staff at Faber and Faber who opened up the whole question of a Milne biography. The enthusiasm of my Faber editor, Robert McCrum, has been stimulating and sustaining. I am also grateful for the interest of Sam Vaughan, my editor at Random House, who also encouraged me through the years of research, with his letters and practical help.

As I suggest in my introduction, I would not have written the book without the agreement of Christopher Milne. I am aware of the mixed feelings he must have about the whole project. I hope he will feel his tolerance and trust to have been rewarded by the chance to learn a good deal that is new to him about his father's career. I am grateful for his permission to quote, not only from his father, but from his own books, which were an essential source for me and which I recommend for further reading to anyone who has not yet read them, especially *The Enchanted Places* and *The Path Through the Trees*. He also lent me a particularly useful packet of letters from his grandfather to two old friends (sent to him by one of those old friends after the publication of *The Enchanted Places*) and a packet of letters from Barrie, Galsworthy and the Queen of Roumania – all apparently that have survived in the family of letters to A. A. Milne.

Christopher Milne's attitude of quiet acceptance and non-interference has been extremely helpful and I am also grateful for his answers to my factual questions; but, of course, I needed to fill in many gaps by talking to the rest of the family. I was very lucky to have such sympathetic, intelligent, warm and patient help from all four of the children of A. A. Milne's brother Ken. I have named Marjorie Murray-Rust and Angela Killey in my introduction. Marjorie's delightful hospitality over several years and her excellent power of recall made all the difference to me. As we got to know each other, she enriched not only my book about her uncle but also my own life, and I have enormously appreciated the confidence she has shown in lending her own beloved photographs and books and allowing me to photocopy letters. Angela not only answered many questions and talked to me at length, but also wrote down a great many vivid memories for me. A. K. Milne (Tony) was extremely helpful too, especially in connection with P. G. Wodehouse. I have quoted from them both and have been particularly grateful for those words on the page, as my previous experience as a biographer makes me far more at home with written words than with taped interviews. My book obviously owes a great deal to the fact that not only A. A. Milne but also the next generation all write so well. It saddens me that Tony died in November 1989; I am grateful to his wife, Barbara, for pressing me to send him a typescript, so that I have his approval of the book and know of the pleasure it gave him.

I. I. Milne (Tim), though less involved, has also been friendly and helpful. Other friends and relations of A. A. Milne to whom I have reason to be grateful are included in the list that follows, which also includes friends of my own and strangers who responded to my appeals for help. Each one of them has contributed something invaluable.

John Adlard (and his book on Owen Seaman), Oliver Airedale, Peggy Ashcroft, Eileen Atkins, Gillian Avery, Ann Baer, Bruce Banister (Brown's Hotel), Felix Barker, Andrew Birkin, Carmen Blacker, Basil Boothroyd, Caroline Bott, Muriel Bradshaw, Anne Brackenbury, Gyles Brandreth, Alison Brierly (AAM's great-niece, for permission to quote from letters to her), Mary Briscoe, Peter Buitenhuis, John Byron, Charles Causley, Barbara Christopher, Edward Cazalet, Sybil and Raymond Clement Brown (niece and nephew of Seaman), Jeny Curnow, Colin Davis, Peter Dickinson, Frances Donaldson, Fabia Drake, Maureen Duffy (for help with the Methuen archives), Christopher Edwards (Pickering and Chatto Ltd), Alistair Elliot, H. F. Ellis, Gervase Farjeon, Michèle Field, Margery Fisher, Penelope Fitzgerald, Margaret Forster, Gill Frayn, Michael Frayn, Roy Fuller, Georgina Gallaway, Bennitt Gardiner, Gerald Gliddon, Rachel Gould, Richard Perceval Graves, Jane Grigson, John Gross, Valerie Grove, Gina Hall (granddaughter of Laura Cowie and John Hastings Turner), Rosemary and Tim Hammond, Jan and Richard Hanna, Rupert Hart-Davis, Anne Harvey, Michael Hearn, William Hetherington (Peace Pledge Union), Rosemary Hill, Marni Hodgkin, David Holmes, Mollie Hope, Richard Hough, Nancy Hunter-Gray (step-grandmother of both Lesley and Christopher Milne), Tateo Imamura, John Irving (Laurence Irving's son), Faith Jaques, Harriet and Alistair Johns (Cotchford), Griffith Jones, Kate and P. J. Kavanagh, Mary Keys, Godfrey Kenton, Miles Kington, Rawle Knox, Hide Ishiguro, the late John Lehmann, Rosamond Lehmann, Janet Lowe, Dr T. T. Liu, Penelope Lively, Brenda McCallum (née Tasker), Jean and James McGibbon, Roger MacDonald (BBC), Robert J. Mack, the late Arthur Marshall, John Milne, Lesley Milne, Betty and John Milner (Hartfield), Christina Morris, Elaine Moss, Malcolm Muggeridge, Reiko Naito, Eric Norris, John Julius Norwich, Mary Oliphant (Denis Mackail's daughter), Iona Opie, Charles Osborne, Lissa Paul, Margaret Payne, Muriel Pearson-Gee, Tatyana and Rodney Peppé, Catherine Peters, Giles Playfair, Anne Powell (Palladour Books), Anthony Powell, Chris Powling, Peter Quennell, R. G. G. Price, Moyra Rank, Alexis Rassine, Milt Reisman (Victoria Bookshop, NY), John Rhodes (Hartfield), Robert Rice (Elmer Rice's son), J. J. Rigden (Books), Pauline Rumbold (Hermione Baddeley's daughter), Peter Ryde (Anne Darlington's widower), George Rylands, Joan

Scoones, Athene Seyler, Michael Shaw and Elizabeth Stevens (Curtis Brown), Gladys Shemilt, Dave Singleton (Holtye Golf Club), Norman and Sylvia Sherry, Julian Slade, David Spreckley, Hilary Spurling, Stephen Spender, Frederic Spotts, Esmé Squarey, David Stewart, Anthony Storr, Adrian Sutton, Peter Tasker, David Tennant, Richard Usborne, Ellen and Arthur Wagner, Joan Wainwright, Peter Wait, Ian Wallace, Rachel Whear (Low), Penny Whiting, Richard Wildman, Barbara Willard, B. A. Young.

I owe a great debt to Tori Haring-Smith, now associate professor at Brown University on Rhode Island, whose substantial bibliography of A. A. Milne was published in 1982 by Garland. Her work made my task lighter and shorter than it would otherwise have been and I am extremely grateful to her.

I must also thank two Milne collectors, Brian Sibley and Stephen Barkway, who shared with me most generously some rare material in their possession. Gordon Robinson, then of Loughborough University, passed on to me his researches into the nineteenth-century private schools and gave me knowledge of J. V. Milne which would otherwise have been very difficult to acquire. J. C. Trewin went to tremendous trouble in various ways, particularly in tracing for me actors who had appeared in Milne plays and who had known Leonora Corbett.

I must also thank, as I did for their similar work on *Edmund Gosse*, my excellent typist and her husband, Hilary and Dick Tulloch. Now equipped with a word processor but living in Oxfordshire, Hilary's diligence and professionalism were admirable and Dick provided his own enthusiasm and expertise, as audience and consultant. My daughter Alice also gave some useful secretarial assistance, and I was particularly lucky in my copy-editor, Gillian Bate.

The main source of A. A. Milne material outside the family is the Harry Ransom Humanities Research Center of the University of Texas at Austin. I am particularly grateful to Cathy Henderson and the rest of the staff there for making it possible for me to get through the vast amount of material (letters, manuscripts, cuttings and books) in the time I was able to spend in Austin. The security at the library is rigorous (one must leave even one's purse outside) but, once within, the conditions for working are ideal. The other library to which I owe a great deal is (as usual) the London Library. Douglas Matthews and his staff have been unfailingly helpful and encouraging.

I must also single out the library of Trinity College, Cambridge, and thank specifically both David McKitterick and Diana Chardin. And I spent a particularly happy week at the Osborne (and Lillian H. Smith) Collection in Toronto, surrounded by piles of children's books of the 1920s, and I am grateful to Margaret Maloney and her staff there.

I must also thank the librarians, keepers, directors and archivists of the following institutions and firms: Arkansas University Library, Fayetteville (Norma Ortiz); Army Records Centre, Ministry of Defence; the Athenaeum Club; the Beefsteak Club; Bethnal Green Museum of Childhood; City of Birmingham Public Library; University of Birmingham Library; Bodleian

Library (Clive Hurst); the British Film Institute; the British Library in Bloomsbury and Colindale; Chatto and Windus Ltd; Cheltenham College; Reed Collection, Dunedin Public Library, New Zealand (Paul Sorrell); E. P. Dutton Ltd (Elliot Graham and Bill Whitehead); Samuel French Ltd (Amanda Smith); Garrick Club (Kay Hutchings); Houghton Library, Harvard; University of Illinois at Urbana-Champaign; Imperial War Museum (Christopher Dowling); University of Iowa (Robert A. McCown); Kensington and Chelsea Libraries (P. K. Pratt); the Lilly Library, Indiana University, Bloomington; Liddell Hart Centre for Military Archives, King's College, London; Brotherton Collection, University of Leeds (C. D. W. Sheppard); Location Register of British MSS (David Sutton); Local History Library, Margate; Merton College, Oxford; Methuen Ltd (Joy Backhouse, Gillian Wijngaard, Joan Holah); National Portrait Gallery; Berg Collection, New York Public Library; Norwich Central Library; Nuffield College, Oxford; Library of Performing Arts, Lincoln Center, NY; Pierpont Morgan Library; the trustees of the Pooh Properties; *Punch* (Amanda Doran); Reading University (Michael Bott); University of Rochester (Mary M. Hutt); Royal Literary Fund (Fiona M. Clark); Society of Authors (Diana Shine); Sotheby's Department of Printed Books and MSS; University of Southern Mississippi; University of Surrey; University of Sussex; Temple University, Philadelphia; Theatre Museum, London (Alexander Schouvaloff); Victoria and Albert Museum Library and Department of Ceramics; University of Victoria, B. C., Canada; Walt Disney Archives, Burbank, Ca.; Westminster School (John Field); Beinecke Library, Yale (Annette Dixon).

I was lucky to have two extremely careful and critical readers of the typescript, apart from those professionally involved: Michael Millgate and Anthony Thwaite. I thank them both warmly. That the text benefited from their detailed comments and questions is obvious, but any faults that remain are of course my own. Anthony's help was practical as well; I am grateful that for seven months, when I was actually writing, I rarely needed to think about shopping or cooking. He also tolerated my working absences at Hawthornden Castle (where I was able to work on my papers without any interruptions, thanks to the generosity of Drue Heinz), in New York, Toronto, Texas, Sussex and Dorset, over a period of four years. As I have said on earlier occasions, I could not have written the book without his loving support.

Finally, I must thank the Author's Foundation (Trustees: Antonia Fraser and Michael Holroyd) which gave me a grant to help with my research expenses. I hope to return it for the benefit of other writers if this book is a success.

Abbreviations used in Notes and Index

All books and play titles unless otherwise stated are by Milne and can be checked in the Bibliography.

AAM	A. A. Milne
Autob	*Autobiography* – published in US as that and in UK as *It's Too Late Now*
Berg	The Berg Collection, New York Public Library
Bodleian	Bodleian Library, Oxford
BTL	*Behind the Lines*
BWI	*By Way of Introduction*
C & W	Chatto and Windus archives, Reading University, UK
CB	Curtis Brown, Milne's main literary agent
CR	Christopher Robin
CRM	Christopher Milne
CTS	Charles Turley Smith
CU	Cambridge University
DM	Daphne (Dorothy) Milne
DNB	*Dictionary of National Biography*
DP	*The Day's Play*
DT	*Daily Telegraph* (London)
Dutton	E. P. Dutton of New York, Milne's main US publisher
EHS	Ernest H. Shepard
EM	Edward Marsh
EN	*Evening News* (London)
EP	*The Enchanted Places* by Christopher Milne (1974)
ES	*Evening Standard* (London)
EVL	E. V. Lucas
FP	*First Plays*
FS	Frank Swinnerton
FTLI	*From the Luncheon Interval*
HGW	H. G. Wells
HH	Henley House School
HHSM	*Henley House School Magazine*
HPC	*The House at Pooh Corner*
H Punch	*The History of Punch* by R. G. G. Price (1951)

HR	*The Holiday Round*
IIM	*If I May*
Illinois	Library of University of Illinois at Urbana-Champaign
Iowa	Library of University of Iowa, Iowa City
JMB	J. M. Barrie
JVM	John Vine Milne
King's	Library, Liddell Hart Centre for Military Archives, King's College, London
KJM	Kenneth John Milne
K. Fam.	Kenneth Milne's family (Marjorie Murray-Rust or A. K. Milne)
Leeds	The Brotherton Collection, University of Leeds, UK
L in L	*Lovers in London*
MM-R	Marjorie Murray-Rust
NBL	*Books for Children* National Book League Readers' Guide
NWA6	*Now We Are Six*
NY	New York
OPL	*Other People's Lives*
OS	Owen Seaman
OW	*Once a Week*
Path	*The Path Through the Trees* by Christopher Milne (1979)
PGW	P. G. Wodehouse
RA	*The Romantic Age*
RCL	R. C. Lehmann
SP	*Second Plays*
SS	*The Sunny Side*
ST	*Sunday Times* (London)
Swann	*A. A. Milne* by Thomas Burnett Swann, Twayne's English Authors Series, NY (1971)
Temple	Library, Temple University, Philadelphia, Pennsylvania
Texas	Harry Ransom Humanities Research Center, University of Texas at Austin
TLS	*The Times Literary Supplement* (London)
TNB	*A Table Near the Band*
TWTD	*Those Were the Days*
UK	United Kingdom of Great Britain & Northern Ireland
US	United States of America
V & A	Victoria and Albert Museum Library, London
WAD	W. A. Darlington
WIWVY	*When I Was Very Young*
WP	*Winnie-the-Pooh*
WWWVY	*When We Were Very Young*
WS	Westminster School
Year In	*Year In, Year Out*

Notes

To leave room for some additional material which has not fitted into the narrative, and to avoid tedious repetition, I am going to make some general remarks which will account for some apparent gaps under page references. As I did in *Edmund Gosse*, I am following John Gross's suggestion (much as it annoys some people) that every quotation does not need a reference 'as if it were applying for a job'. The notes would take up an even more inordinate amount of space if I gave the source of every glancing remark. I will set out my principal sources here.

Quotations from AAM himself come from *Autob*, and from CRM from *EP*, unless otherwise stated. I have not always pinned down the exact whereabouts of quotations from AAM's *Punch* essays and plays, partly because so many different editions are in circulation. I have also not always specified the exact dates of the many reviews quoted. My main sources for reviews have been JVM's cuttings book (K. Fam.), the collections at Texas and in the C & W archives at Reading. Sometimes these reviews are undated and even unidentified. Other reviews I was led to by the Garland bibliography.

The main sources for letters from AAM are as follows, in alphabetical order of recipient: Beerbohm at Merton; Curtis Brown, copies at Columbia and Texas; Drinkwater at Yale; Elspeth Grahame at Bodleian; E. V. Lucas at Texas or Iowa; Edward Marsh at Berg; K. J. Milne at Texas; Pinker at Berg; Shorter at Berg or Leeds; Charles Turley Smith at Cheltenham College; Swinnerton at Arkansas or Reading; Irene Vanbrugh at Harvard; H. G. Wells at Illinois.

Letters from J. M. Barrie belong to CRM (four of these in *Letters*, edited Viola Meynell, 1942), Irene Vanbrugh's own comments are all from *To Tell My Story* (1948). JVM's letters to Biddie Warren and Eleanor Pinnington belong to CRM. Swinnerton's letters to AAM are from copies at Reading.

In the first two chapters, a great deal comes from *Autob* (checked wherever possible against other evidence) and *HHSM* (K. Fam.). Background information about Henley House, JVM and the education of the time from Gordon Robinson's notes for his MA thesis (University of London, 1966) and his monograph *Private Schools and Public Policy* (Loughborough University, 1971).

497

Chapter 1 'I can do it.'

page

1 'What *is* Learning? A thing *Rabbit* knows!' *HPC*, ch. v.
'Makers of Men' *ES*, 6 Jan. 1928, p. 14.

2 'the third son' 'the third and youngest son is always the nicest of
the family. And the tallest and the bravest and the most handsome.'
RA, Act II, *SP*. See also *OW* 'The King's Sons', *HR*, 'A Matter-of-
Fact Tale', etc.
Little Lord Fauntleroy by Frances Hodgson Burnett was published in
1886. Cedric Errol was the eponymous hero. Stark Young reviewing
AAM's *The Truth about Blayds* in the *New Republic* (12 April 1922)
uses the Fauntleroy image as criticism of the attitude of Blayds's
daughter: 'How full of ringlet curls it is, of sashes and silly affectation!'

3 *Drawn from Memory* (1957) the Penguin edition (1975) had a
photograph on the cover of EHS as a child, together with drawings
from the Pooh books and Grahame's Rat.

4 'at the Kilburn end' *Year In*, June.
Annie Besant (1847–1933) had been on trial for 'obscenity' in 1877,
and was legally separated from her husband. She organized the match-
makers' strike of 1888.

5 The inscription on the house in Clifton Hill reads: 'W. Frith
1819–1909 Painter lived and died here.'
Jamaican connections AAM's brother Barry got his name, Barrett,
from the maiden name of JVM's mother, Harriet, daughter of George
Barrett of Jamaica (1781–1838) and apparently kin of the Barretts of
Wimpole Street.
HGW on Harmsworth *Experiment in Autobiography* (1934).

6 'three of his brothers' Harold, Leicester and Hildebrand were all
honoured. Harold became Lord Rothermere.
'He killed the penny dreadful' quoted in R. Pound and G. Harmsworth, *Northcliffe* (1959).
'the counties and chief towns' and 'Book-bags must be hung' etc.
M. V. Hughes, *A London Girl of the 1880s* (1978).
'an enlightened man' HGW, *Experiment in Autobiography*.
'my only regret' *ES*, 6 Jan. 1928.

7 Kanga's medicine *WP*, ch. VII and *HPC*, ch. II.
'She treasured everything' JVM to Biddie Warren, 16 Dec. 1921
(CRM).

8 E. V. Knox had obviously seen the marriage certificate when writing
AAM's entry in *DNB* as he did not repeat AAM's own error.
'born in Scotland' AAM has often been claimed as a Scottish writer
on the strength of his name but he frequently disclaimed any Scottishness. In *L in L* his *alter ego*: 'I did not wish her to feel her Scotch
inferiority. Nor could I bring myself to say 'scon'; my English blood
boiled at the idea.' See also my p. 84 from *Autob*.

9   'the only letter' (K. Fam.).

10   'sweethearts' . . . 'In my wife'   JVM, 21 July 1924 to Biddie Warren (CRM).
    Owl   WP, ch. IV, HPC, ch. V.

12   'There is a legend'   Year In, March.
    Eclipse story   Year In, March.

14   Infant letters are at Texas.
    Comments on the first letter are in Year In, July.

15   Childhood reading from NBL, Autob, and IIM, 'The Robinson Tradition'. For AAM on Alice see Year In, Jan.

17   fantasy from Autob and MS of WIWVY (Texas).
    Beauty and the Beast   IIM, 'Children's Plays'.

18   Crystal Palace   FTLI. The Palace was created for the Great Exhibition of 1851, and later moved to Sydenham in South London.

19   HHSM, April 1886 'In May he takes the Head Mastership'; Christmas 1893 'has succeeded to the direction of University School.'

Chapter 2   His Father's Pupil

20   end of term concert   'The Conversazione', HHSM, March 1889.

21   Harmsworth's verse, 'Kept In'   HHSM, August 1882.
    HGW, Experiment in Autobiography.

24   ES, 6 Jan. 1928.
    'When you wake up'   WP, ch. X.

25   'some school characters'   HHSM, Easter 1892.
    'One of the advantages'   Year In, July.

26   football match report   HHSM, Christmas 1891.

27   Ashdown Forest walk   HHSM, Easter 1891.

28   'goody-goody' story   WIWVY (Texas) and Autob.
    JVM   ES, 6 Jan. 1928.

30   'You know, I often tell myself'   quoted in EP, ch. 20.
    Interview in US   NY Times, 1 Nov. 1931.
    'The Milnes were proud of the fact'   EP, ch. 20.

31   'the keenest sympathy'   EP, ch. 20.
    'all the "right" labels'   CRM, The Hollow on the Hill (1982), ch. 1.
    V. Woolf, letter to Clive Bell, 21 Feb. 1931.
    'arch-snob'   L. Woolf in Sowing (1960) 'I used to tell Virginia that she was mentally, morally and physically a snob and she was inclined to agree.'

32   HGW, Experiment in Autobiography and Joan and Peter and HHSM. HGW sent AAM J and P in 1918. Letters from AAM to HGW commenting on it are at Illinois.

34   Geoffrey West in his 1930 biography of HGW said there still existed a photograph of 'boys and staff with Mr Milne in the centre of the group, Wells frail and Stevensonian on one side and just behind and

above him with long fair Fauntleroy ringlets the future author of *The Dover Road* and *WWWVY*.' Where is it now?
JVM, *ES*, 6 Jan. 1928.
AAM 1890 letter, Texas; 1902 letter, Illinois.

35 JVM reference for HGW quoted in *The Time Traveller* (1973) by Norman and Jeanne Mackenzie.

36 JVM's activities from Gordon Robinson, op. cit.

37 AAM's taste for hare and hounds apparently continued. A hotel visitors' book in Seatoller, Borrowdale, records his presence there in June 1904 when he acted as a hare for a group of Cambridge and Oxford men. See illustration.

38 South Kensington Museum visit   *HHSM*, August 1889.
'Robinson, Crusoe and Cleaver' Robinson and Cleaver was a flourishing department store. It outlived AAM.
dissecting toad   *NTIM*, 'Natural Science' and *Autob.*

39 Ernest Garrett   *HHSM*, May 1890 and Easter 1891.

41 skimmity rides   *The Mayor of Casterbridge* (1886) is set in the 1840s. Hardy called it a Wessex custom, but it was apparently known all over the country.
childhood reading   *Books for Children*, NBL (1948). Elaine Moss has an interesting essay on AAM's introduction in *Signal* 44 (May 1984).
Bruno Bettelheim, *The Uses of Enchantment* (1976).

42 Sendak's distinguished picture book (1967).
AAM, 1892 letter, K. Fam.

45 JVM editorial on Harmsworth   *HHSM*, May 1890.
'What is being successful?'   *HHSM*, Dec. 1887.

Chapter 3   Westminster

Sources mainly Westminster School archives and *Autob.*

47 'scholarships are only gained'   *HHSM*, August 1892.
Miss Brodie   Muriel Spark, *The Prime of Miss Jean Brodie* (1961).
letter to *Elizabethan*   Nov. 1895.
'If only I had been taught'   *IIM*, 'Some Old Companions'.

48 'young Batsford'   B. T. Batsford of the firm of that name.
'had both done very well'   *HHSM*, Aug. 1892.
Information about Barry from his son, Revd. John Milne. His headmaster in Derbyshire was the brother of Jim Johnston, a teacher at HH who married the boys' governess.

49 Stowe   CRM has a few references to Stowe in *EP* but has never written about it at length.
'Westminster Papers, 1893' (with I. I. Milne's 1925 papers added) are labelled 'Kenneth John Milne Scholarship Jan. 1893 12¼, Alan Alexander Milne Scholarship July 1893 11½.'

Greek rare   General report from W. G. Rutherford to the Governing
Body of Westminster School, Sept. 1899, WS.

51   'It cost a lot of money'   ES, 6 Jan. 1928.
'taking on Streete Court'   HHS was handed over at the end of 1893
to Revd. G. F. Watson, BA.

52   EM and Rutherford from Christopher Hassall's *Edward Marsh*
(1959). There is very little record of AAM's friendships. AAM's
letters to EM are available because EM preserved his letters and they
are now in Berg. In one letter to EM in 1912 AAM writes of a man
called Thorp who is 'one of my best friends'. This must be J. P. Thorp
who started life as a Jesuit and later became a *Punch* contributor and
a student of typography. As with most of AAM's friends, it is impossible to write of their relationship as no letters have come to light.

53   Thieving Lane and Black Dog Alley, mentioned in the *Elizabethan*,
Jan. 1898, do not appear on Bacon's map of London of the period.
Presumably they were very narrow and insignificant.

54   'unreasonable parents'   *The Month*, Feb. 1892. JVM's presidential
address to the Private Schools' Association.
'butter' in *DP*, 'bachelor days'; 'bounced out of bed', *WWWVY*,
'The King's Breakfast'.

55   'Corporal punishment'   JVM *HHSM*, March 1889; HGW, *Experiment in Autobiography*.

56   *History of Westminster*, Reg Airy (1902).

57   'slow white petals'   *WWWVY*, 'The Wrong House'.
Streete Court bird's-nesting   *Autob* and 'Thy Tablets Memory', MS,
Texas.

58   'drugged by nostalgia'   Maurice Wiggin, review of *EP*, *ST* 24 Nov.
1974. (*SOED* calls 'nostalgia' 'severe home sickness'.)
Osbert Sitwell   *Who's Who* entry.
'sliding down banisters'   the way AAM uses the phrase in 'The
King's Breakfast' suggests how much it seemed the right thing to do
when in high spirits.
'divergent'   see Liam Hudson, *Contrary Imaginations: A Psychological Study of the English Schoolboy* (1971). Dr Hudson defines the
diverger (more likely to make jokes than convergers) as moving 'naturally towards the human aspects of his culture – literature, politics
– and shuns the technical and practical; and seems less prone than
the converger to accept beliefs on trust, or to think in conventional
terms.' This fits in well with AAM. The only thing that doesn't is
that the diverger 'seems actively to enjoy the expression of his personal
feelings.' With AAM, this was never so.

59   *The Lucky One*, Act I.
'A recent study'   Liam Hudson, see above.

60   'meticulous accounts'   *Autob* and *DP*, 'Letters to Charles' I.

61   Report of Exam Board   24 August 1896.
Edgar Hackforth   *Who's Who*, 1933.
'counting the words'   *IIM*, 'Some Old Companions'.

editorials on slackness over games   *Elizabethan*, Dec. 1893, March 1895.

62   'one of the fastest'   third in the Open 100 yards; of his cup for Long Jump, he wrote in *Punch* long after: 'It is my only cup and I am proud of it.'

63   KJM's articles not signed until 23 May 1899.
cricket   *Year In*, May; *DP* 'Small Games'.

64   letter to Alison (Murray-Rust) Brierley, 1951, in her possession.
'the greatest to love'   *Nation*, 27 July 1929, review of Neville Cardus etc., reprinted in *BWI*.
'any other inactivity'   *Year In*, May.
'seven more months'   letter to EVL, 18 Sept. 1934, Texas.
John Drinkwater   *Discovery*, (1932).

66   Latin prose   *IIM*, 'The Mathematical Mind'.
report WS   Captain: A. S. Gaye (1881–1960); Monitors: A. A. Milne, F. J. Joseph and W. R. Le G. Jacob.

67   'dormitory in chaos'   *Elizabethan*, 1895.
'Thirty Bob a Week'   John Davidson in *Ballads and Songs* (1894).
rules for the Latin play   WS.

68   electric light   *Elizabethan*, Feb. 1899.
review of *Adelphi*   *Elizabethan*, Dec. 1899. Ten years later AAM and A. S. Gaye wrote the Epilogue to the *Adelphi* production of that year.

70   C. S. Calverley (1831–84)   *BWI*, 'Introducing *Granta*', and in *The 'Granta' and its Contributors 1889–1914* (1924); *Year In*, Dec.
AKM   AAM kept a proprietorial relationship with those initials; when, later, KJM's son, Antony Kenneth Milne, wanted to use them in print, AAM suggested he should reverse his initials.
'You ask for a poem'   AAM published in *Autob* (1939) but by 1952 (*Year In*, Oct.) he was disliking his own Juvenilia. Looking at it he thought that if he made a success after that, 'anybody can do it'.

72   birthday   *Year In*, Jan.
Granta   I like to think that this may have been the special May Week 1900 number, edited by Oliver Locker-Lampson.
F. Anstey   actually Thomas Anstey Guthrie. The F was originally a compositor's error for T – but Guthrie adopted it as a pseudonym.

73   Gaye to AAM on *Granta*   AAM, telling the story in an interview in *NY Tribune* in 1921: 'I apologize for it but it really did happen.' In *Granta*, 1 May 1919, he had told the anecdote and said it was 'a horrible story', but it didn't matter 'as I shall never be eminent enough for people to bring it up against me.'
'succeeded in winning'   AAM was second of the three Westminster exhibitioners and known as a subsizar. The first won a Senior Samwaies for two years; AAM's £23 seems to have been for only one year.
Debating Society, Gaye's report, etc.   WS.

75   Frank Swinnerton in *Figures in the Foreground* (1963).

Chapter 4 Cambridge

Sources mainly Trinity College archives, *Granta*, *Autob* and K. Fam.

76 AAM's Little-go results are in *Cambridge University Reporter*, 13
    Oct. 1900: 3rd class in Part I (Classics) and 1st class in Part II (Maths).
    guidebook A. Hamilton Thompson, *Cambridge and its Colleges*
    (1898).

77 Strachey on Sydney-Turner, quoted by Michael Holroyd in his *Lytton
    Strachey: The Unknown Years* (1967).
    Leonard Woolf's comments all from his autobiographical volume
    Sowing (1960).
    When asked in 1983 by Stephen Barkway of any possible connection
    between Milne and Bloomsbury (prompted by the thought that AAM
    was born in the same year as Virginia Woolf), CRM said he thought
    his father would have recoiled from such 'intellectuals' and that
    'doubtless they would have despised him for his lack of seriousness.'
    Letter to me from SB.
    Russell Gaye, double First and Fellow of Trinity, committed suicide
    in college, 11 April 1909 (*Times*, 13 & 15 April).

78 *The Way of all Flesh* 'the best novel' In 1919 (*NTIM*) AAM called
    it the second best 'so that, if you remind me of *Tom Jones* or *The
    Mayor of Casterbridge* . . . I can say that, of course, that one is the
    best.' In a letter to Sassoon in 1916 Robert Graves wrote, 'The two
    gods of the younger generation are Samuel Butler and Edward Carp-
    enter, but chiefly the former . . . Rupert loves Samuel, Eddie tells me',
    referring to Brooke and Marsh.
    EHS, autob. *Drawn from Life* (1961).

80 'We reached Stavanger,' 'Matilda,' *BTL*.

81 Clarissa canoeing *Granta*, 4 June 1902. I cannot help thinking of
    an editorial that appeared to my amazement in *Isis* (the Oxford equi-
    valent of *Granta*) in the summer term of 1953. It recorded in a style
    rather similar to AAM's, fifty-one years later, a punting expedition
    on the Cherwell. The girl was called by her real name, my name. So
    perhaps there was a real Clarissa.
    'eight daughters' 'They were all good-looking, but Maud, Ken told
    me, was the classical beauty of them all.' Angela Killey talking to me,
    March 1988.
    Bookworms and Beauty 26.111.01 (*sic*), K. Fam.

82 L. Woolf, *Sowing*.

83 'Writing in 1924' in the introduction to *The 'Granta' and its Con-
    tributors*.
    'cagey' EHS on AM in *ST*, 2 Nov. 1969.
    'aloof' Rupert Hart-Davis to me, 1986.
    JVM *HHSM*.

84 maths books *IIM*, 'Some Old Companions.'

85 'two pipes' *Autob* suggests it was early on but in *DP* ('Letters to

Charles' IV) he says he bought his first tobacco pouch in Ambleside in the summer of 1902: 'I smoked my first pipe from it.'

'£1,000, in instalments' In 1927, JVM would say in passing in a letter to *The Times* about so-called 'unearned income': 'I have worked long and very hard for this income. I denied myself many pleasures, such as travel, that I might give my sons their chance in life and myself a refuge when past work . . .'

86 Montagu from *DNB*.
'the most brilliant man' AAM letter to EM, 14 April 1954, in Hassall *EM*.
Montagu in *The 'Granta' and its Contributors*.

87 'the air of one who would be' But Desmond MacCarthy said he longed to tell him he was not 'another Dizzy'.

88 'wasn't in frivolity' The evidence of JVM's cuttings book (K. Fam.) is that Ken went on writing light verse and prose on his own throughout his life.
The X Society met on Saturday evenings. In his memoir of Lytton Strachey in *Old Friends* (1956) Clive Bell says some of them went on to read *Comus* or *Bartholomew Fair* after the X Society – at the Midnight. Sydney-Turner was 'the best reader of the company'. They were all indefatigable readers aloud.

89 *She Stoops to Conquer* In fact, the Shakespeare Society rules laid down that 'not more than one play by any other author to be read in each term'.

90 'passionately intellectual' Holroyd decided she was 'no intellectual'.
Alfred Austin (1835–1913). He was then Poet Laureate.

91 'six periodicals' *Granta* said four, but someone from Oxford wrote in and said six.
'Anna Wickham' was born Edith Alice Mary Harper, but her father called her Anne; from *The Writings of Anna Wickham: Free Woman and Poet*, ed. R. D. Smith (1984).

93 'Jeremy and the Jelly-fish' both do in fact appear in later instalments.
'Why do you always talk' *Granta*, 18 Jan. 1902.

94 Lehmann's diary RCL.

95 'refer only glancingly' 'in the war, and afterwards, he worked himself to his death' (*Autob*).

96 first editorial *Granta*, 18 Jan. 1902.
The River War an historical account of the reconquest of the Sudan, ed. F. Rhodes, 2 vols. 1899, 1 vol. 1902.
General Tucker Sir Charles Tucker, 1838–1935, commanded the 7th Division under Lord Roberts in South Africa – 'Tales about him are legion', *DNB*.
'one of his friends' Nancy Hunter-Gray, Feb. 1985.

97 'wabe' and 'outgrabe' from Carroll's 'Jabberwocky'.
AAM did invent words in the *Pooh* books, but it was not a characteristic of his early humour. In 1927 a reviewer comparing AAM with

Carroll said: 'Like LC, he has a gift for coining words.' 'Heffalumps' and 'woozles' have become part of the language.

'When I was the usual' *Granta*, 1 Feb. 1902.

'Love among the bricks' AKM, *Granta*, 22 Jan. 1902.

98 'Brown was a tutor' *Granta*, 31 May 1902.

'zenith of his cricketing career' *Year In*, May.

'the bad form to be serious' AKM letter to *Granta*, 22 Nov. 1902. AAM to HGW Illinois.

99 'He was a *Granta* man' and 'Golden Memories' in *Granta*, 11 June 1910, reprinted in *The 'Granta' and its Contributors*.

'lived the kind of life' L. Woolf, *Sowing*.

100 'Crème Brûlée' see also *EP*, ch 17.

Chapter 5   Freelance

Sources mainly *Autob*, K. Fam, RCL and letters to HGW at Illinois.

101 Streete Court School   Scobell Chittenden had already by this time joined JVM as 'joint principal'. After JVM's retirement, it would be run by Chittenden and William Longrigg and eventually by G. P. Hoare. The school was evacuated in 1940 and apparently never returned to Westgate. The house still exists, divided into flats. A 1939 guide to 'Education facilities in Thanet' says the school stood in thirteen acres and that the main building was part of a manor house, 'dating to Doomsday Book' (*sic*). Anthony Whittome of Century Hutchinson reports that when he was an unhappy boy there in the 1930s much was made of the Milne connection, though the school had obviously changed in character.

102 'to keep me ... for two years' with hindsight, AAM would say he had 'money to keep me for a year' (interview in the *Bookman*, Feb. 1922).

103 Max on Burnand from *Max* by David Cecil (1964), p. 20.

Burnand at *Punch* H *Punch*, p. 178

'a fan letter' reply to Derek Parker, 3 Aug. 1952, Yale.

India and Kipling In 1919 (6 Sept., *Sphere*; *IIM*, 'Round the World and Back') AAM would write: 'There are several places to which I should be glad to accompany him, but India is not one of them. Kipling ruined India for me ... I picture India as full of intriguing, snobbish Anglo-Indians.'

105 ' "Beatrice" of his sketches' see TWTD, 'Taking Stock', 'A Summer Cold', etc. Beatrice is a bracing sort of sister-in-law. ('When I am not feeling well, I go to Beatrice for sympathy and advice. Anyhow I get the advice.')

'always an autobiographical writer' DT, 4 Jan. 1971.

'*When a Man's Single*' JMB to HGW, 9 Nov. 1897 (*Letters of JMB*, ed. Viola Meynell, 1942): 'I am proud to know that *When a Man's Single* woke you up.'

John Gross in *The Rise and Fall of the Man of Letters* (1969). Some indication of the numerous outlets for a young journalist is supplied by JVM's cuttings book, which contains no fewer than forty-five reviews from different papers and periodicals of AAM's first collection of *Punch* pieces in 1910.

109 William Archer (1856–1924); his humour, *DNB*.

112 'when the war ends' AAM must be referring to the Russo-Japanese war, much in people's minds, though hardly likely to be having an effect on AAM's chances of employment.
'two cheap and dirty rooms' AAM in interview, *NY Tribune*, 22 May 1921.

113 *L in L* Texas has a letter from this time (undated but from 8 Wellington Square) which suggests AAM had approached Grant Richards trying to place *L in L* with him.
Pinker 'unobtrusive, etc.' from Edel, *Henry James: the Treacherous Years* (1969); AAM to Pinker, Berg.

114 Darlington testifies to the fact that when he was at Cambridge (*c.* 1912) 'Milne's name was one to conjure with.' 'All the *Punch* aspirants of my time were under the influence of Milne's faculty for light, gay and apparently effortless dialogue.' *I Do What I Like* (1947).
E. V. Lucas in *Reading, Writing and Remembering* (1932).

115 John Penquarto in 'Men of Letters' in *SS* and *TWTD*.
letters to inquirers both at Texas.
'recent American critic' T. B. Swann, *A. A. Milne* (1971).

116 *Alice SBF Alice Sit-By-the-Fire* by J. M. Barrie.
James Welch was an actor (1865–1917) who does not appear to have had any plays of his own – or with Wells – on the stage.

117 'I decided to shoot a rabbit.' AAM first used this incident in *HR* ('The House-Warming'). 'A very lucky escape for you,' said Archie, 'I once knew a man who was gored to death by an angry rabbit.'

118 Golding Bright Reginald Golding Bright, theatrical agent, also acted for Hardy.
'editor of *Punch*' OS's salary was £1,300. St Loe Strachey wrote to him from the *Spectator* that what we want as editor of *Punch* is a man who is 'a scholar and a gentleman'. 15 Feb. 1906. (Collection Sybil Clement Brown.)

Chapter 6 *Punch*

Sources mainly *Autob*, RCL's diary, John Lehmann's *The Whispering Gallery* (1955) and *H Punch*.

122 'messing about in boats' *Wind in the Willows*, ch. I.
RCL *Granta* was founded in 1889 by RCL, Murray Guthrie and Lionel Holland. RCL co-edited it from Michaelmas 1889 to Lent 1895.
Roosevelt ref. (1897 letter) from *The Whispering Gallery*, p. 33.

123 'when John was grown up' in *The Whispering Gallery*, p. 148.
Chum in *Punch*, 22 Oct. 1913, 21 Jan. 1914 (*HR*). Chum's acquisition by the Lehmanns seems to have been at the time of JVM's
move to Burgess Hill in 1914, but 'he and Duke insisted on fighting'
(RCL's diary Feb. 1914) and Chum was passed on to the Goldie
family.
Rosamond Lehmann on AAM in conversation with me, 1988.

124 Pen Browning's 'terrible' picture had been bought by RCL's father
for the enormous sum of 150 guineas in 1876, to please his friend,
the artist's father (*The Whispering Gallery*).
'Writers in early *Punch*' from the *Nottingham Express*, quoted in
C. L. Graves, MS history of *Punch*, Folder VI, *Punch* library.

125 Penelope Fitzgerald in *The Knox Brothers* (1977).
OS material from *Owen Seaman* by John Adlard (1977), and *H
Punch*. Others have identified Merton Densher as Edith Wharton's
lover, Morton Fullerton.

126 OS as Eeyore William Amos, *The Originals: Who's Really Who in
Fiction* (1985). *H Punch* talks of OS's 'false delicacy' but Adlard says
he was just worried about his readers. Adlard quotes Lord Montagu's
agent, Capt. H. E. R. Widnell, as also saying that OS 'would take
offence with great ease when no kind of offence was intended'.
Versions of the octopus story are in both Adlard and *H Punch* (oral
tradition).

127 'book reviews' As *H Punch* stresses, it is 'absolutely unhistorical' at
any period 'to criticize *Punch* for not devoting all its space to close
analysis of work that was still not making its way beyond a coterie.
There is no point in comparing *Punch*'s book reviews with those in
the *TLS* or *Spectator*. It is to *Punch*'s credit that it did not just use
bad books as a valuable source of humour . . .'

128 Churchill's three shillings letter to EM (David Holmes, Philadelphia).

129 'For a child of ten' RCL's diary.
'Bachelor Days' *DP* and *TWTD*.

131 'typical Milne' Swann says 'his style has been called "feathery", but
it accumulates feathers until they become as ponderous as an over-
stuffed mattress.'
E. V. Lucas *The Old Contemporaries* (1935).
'For what seemed weeks' 'The Sidesman', *DP* and *TWTD*.
'Reverie' *DP* and *TWTD*.

132 The Margery stories were collected in *DP, HR* and *TWTD*.
'a real knowledge' see especially 'A Twice-Told Tale' and 'The Literary Art'.
reply to a fan letter to Margaret Baird, Iowa. See note to p. 144.

133 Letter to JVM K. Fam.

134 NLC National Liberal Club.
H. W. Nevinson left-wing journalist; foreign correspondent for

Manchester Guardian, Daily News, Daily Herald, etc.; wounded in Dardanelles, 1915; on staff of *Nation*.

135   'Society'   There is, of course, more than one definition of Society. The *Yorkshire Post*, reviewing *HR* in 1912, said: 'He is in his happiest vein when dealing with Society folk', refers to his 'subtle sarcasm' and goes on to discuss his portraits of 'the Solicitor, the Civil Servant and the Actor', not perhaps what most of us think of as 'Society folk'.

  letter to EM, Berg   Christopher Hassall says in his *EM* that AAM was one of the people whose books EM 'diabolized' (criticized in detail in MS or proof). I should like evidence of this.

  CTS   EVL called him 'the best letter-writer in Europe'; unfortunately no letters from CTS to AAM seem to have survived. AAM's to CTS were deposited at Cheltenham College by Eleanor Adlard, to whom CTS left all his papers.

136   E. V. Lucas   There was a streak of coarseness in him which he never showed to AAM. EHS would call him 'lecherous old Lucas' and remember him retelling whispered stories he had heard from his manicurist. As a writer, EHS described EVL as 'a bedroom author', meaning that any of his works might safely be put by the bedside of a very young girl or a very old lady.' Denis MacKail would talk of EVL's 'charm and cosy brilliance.' Both descriptions could apply to AAM. A. C. Benson in his diary called EVL 'a bluff, good-natured common sort of man', which could not apply to AAM.

  Audrey Lucas   *E. V. Lucas, a portrait* (1939).

  'with one exception'   Maurice Hewlett, rather surprisingly.

137   'After his death'   *Times* obituary of EVL, 30 June 1938.

  Allahakbarries – a combination of JMB's name and an exclamation 'God help us!' – apparently suggested by one of the original eleven 'Joseph Thomson of Masailand.' Sometime members included Conan Doyle, A. E. W. Mason and PGW. See Denis Mackail, *Story of JMB* (1941).

  'a letter from Kipling'   AAM actually waited fourteen years for such a letter. Kipling wrote in 1924 after *WWWVY* (see p. 276).

138   MS JMB   letters from CRM, printed in Meynell (ed.), *The Letters of JMB*.

  Llewellyn Davies boys   Barrie's five 'adopted' sons.

139   'one of those glorious deep blue days'   'The First Game', *SS, TWTD, FTLI.*

  EM and AAM on Albert Hall Ball from Hassall, *EM.*

  John Julius Norwich in conversation with me, 1987.

  'I am going as Joseph'   'Dressing up', *DP, TWTD.*

140   'Forty years later'   *Year In*, July.

143   Rabbits in *Punch* 16 June 1909   *DP, HR, TWTD.*

  'Strachey . . . hoaxed'   Adrian Stephen, *The Dreadnought Hoax* (1936).

144   N. F. Simpson (b. 1919); his plays include *A Resounding Tinkle* (1958) and *One Way Pendulum* (1959).

Letter (14 Oct. 1914) to Margaret Baird, sister of Dorothea Baird, actress and daughter-in-law of Sir Henry Irving. (Iowa).

145 'Can we be friends?' *RA* (*SP*) Act III.
Morning Post, 30 Sept. 1912.
Meredith reference from *H Punch*.

146 'I think war' *Peace with Honour*.

147 'The only gun' EHS illustration in gilt on cover of first edition and in ch. I.

148 Hugh de Sélincourt: from A. Calder Marshall's *Havelock Ellis* (1959) and Phyllis Grosskurth's biography (1980). In 1912, Daphne's uncle had published *A Daughter of Morning*, which Ellis described as 'First Lessons in Immorality or a Child's Guide to Vice'. In the 1920s the Hugh de Sélincourt household in Sussex included his wife's lover, Harold Child, who wrote 'flattering reviews' of de Sélincourt's books in *The Times*. Ellis's book *Kanga Creek*, written many years earlier, was published in 1922 as a result of de Sélincourt's 'ecstatic reaction'.
'orange trousers' I am not at all convinced by these in Switzerland in 1913. In *Autob* AAM may be confusing them with the trousers he described to Ken (letter at Texas) before a Swiss skiing trip in Feb. 1929: 'Two days ago she bought a pair of trousers such as the best skiers wear nowadays. I am hoping for a private view tomorrow.' In *The Long Weekend* (1940) Robert Graves and Alan Hodge write about beach pyjamas in 1928 as 'the first publicly accepted form of sports trousers for women.'

149 'There are engagements' 'Thomas, and a Turn', *OW, TWTD*.
AAM to EM, David Holmes (Philadelphia). Marsh, the good friend, would himself live and die 'as chaste as the day he was born', according to his biographer.
JMB to CTS, *Letters of JMB*, ed. Viola Meynell.
Ken's and Maud's reactions their daughter, Angela Killey, writing for me.

150 'other people did things' 'Getting Things Done', *Sphere*, 9 Aug. 1919; 'We neither of us know how to get things done', *IIM*.

152 Maria's letter K. Fam.
'I am very fond of Browning' JVM to E. Pinnington, 21 Feb. 1922 (CRM).
Letter to me from the present Lord Airedale.

Chapter 7 Marriage and War

153 Aunt Bessie's letter from Barbara Christopher (her daughter).
'Beloved Chelsea!' Prelude to *TWTD*

154 'light fittings' 'Furnishing', *OW, TWTD*.
gardener's insurance Peter Tasker, his son, talking to me, 1987.
'early play' *The Lucky One*, Act I.

'Milne is at Mullion' RCL diary, 22 July 1914; *Punch* piece on this 12 Aug. 1914.

155 'A Trunk Call' *OW, TWTD*.
'A friend recalled' Tatyana Peppé writing to me, 1988.

156 'bright glitter' *Eng. Review*, Jan. 1924, review of *Success*.
'a good listener' Epilogue to *The Lyric Theatre, Hammersmith* by Nigel Playfair (1925).
'a friend recalled' Tatyana Peppé.
'part in the conversation' Angela Killey suggests that pleasure in each other's conversation continued. 'With Alan you had to be quick on the uptake even to hear what he was saying, let alone appreciate it. Daff was good at that – she herself could be quite funny too. The two of them together with their in-jokes and allusive talk could make a third party feel an outsider.' She was thinking particularly of the 1940s. 'Nothing breaks up the home so quickly as silent meals.' AAM in *RA*.

157 'closest to his heart' CRM, *Path*, Epilogue.
'one of Alan's nieces' Marjorie Murray-Rust.
'She was anti-sex' Esmé Squarey.
Married Love: A New Contribution to the Solution of Sex Difficulties (1918).
'the doom of Holy Matrimony' *The Norman Church*.
Letters to Shorter, Leeds.

158 'Serbs, Bulgars and Sanjaks' intellectuals fleeing the Balkan wars.
'a bank manager' undated to EVL, Texas.
'high spirits' *Glasgow Herald*, 20 Oct. 1910.
'whimsical' *Scotsman*, 6 Oct. 1910.
Edward Shanks *Saturday Review*, 19 Oct. 1929.
'A widow' in review of AAM, *Journal of Education*, July 1912.

159 *Punch* dinners RCL's diary and *Autob.*

160 Anmer Hall born Alderson Horne (1863–1953), actor and manager, educated Westminster, member of Garrick.
'a depraved proceeding' Introduction to *FP*.
'a very good little play' Called *Make-Believe*, a title he would use again later, I have found no trace of it.

161 'History, of course, is always there' adapted from *Year In*, Sept.
'hideous talk' *Punch*, 5 Aug. 1914.

162 'the killing of one Archduke.' *Peace with Honour.*
Asquith to V. Stanley, 3 Aug. 1914 *Letters* (1982).
Anne de Sélincourt letter to Mrs James Pitman in *Anne Douglas Sedgwick: A Portrait in Letters* (1936).
'War is the most babyish' 'The Record Lie', *IIM*.
AAM to EM 6 Aug. 1914, Berg.

163 H. G. Wells's article was collected in a shilling pamphlet published in September under the same title. 'Every sword that is drawn against Germany now is a sword drawn for peace,' Wells wrote.
'top hat' AAM, 'Wedding Bells', *IIM*. Wells also used the top hat

as a symbol of submission to social convention and class distinction. AAM's top hat ended up painted green for CRM as a Kate Greenaway Jack with Jill, first prize at a fancy-dress party.

'the flashing swords' see p. 20 of this book.

JMB letter to AAM 15 Nov. 1914.

164 'a jumping Blue' AAM to M. Baird, Iowa.

OS 'Pro Patria' *Punch*, 12 Aug. 1914.

'Dulce et Decorum' *Punch*, 26 Jan. 1916; in *Poems from Punch* (1922).

165 Pressure to join up By the end of March 1915, the Parliamentary Recruiting Committee had already issued twenty million leaflets and two million posters (in 200 different designs).

L. Strachey to James Strachey Holroyd, *Lytton Strachey*.

'Life in wartime' *Peace with Honour* and in 'Rosemary for Remembrance' (MS Texas) written on 'the 15th commemoration of Armistice Day'.

Golden Hill Fort, now open to the public, is a 'hexagonal, defensible, two-storey barrack', originally designed in 1863. It is built round a yard, which is used as a drill ground. During the first war, the recruits were in a hutted camp round the Victorian fort. Over 30,000 men were trained there. (Solent Papers No. 2, 'The Needles Defences', Anthony Cantwell and Peter Sprack, 1986).

166 Army language from RCL's diary.

AM to KJM Texas.

167 'My knowledge of fire-arms' *BTL* after 'Old Soldier'.

AAM to EVL Iowa.

168 'servants' It seems the Milnes had a 'cook-general' as well as Daphne's maid Gertrude.

'took me up at Brooklands' the racing circuit and airfield near Weybridge, Surrey.

officers killed one was Charles Massie-Blomfield, nephew of C. L. Graves, cousin of Robert, the adjutant mentioned in *Autob*.

'pilled' Partridge's *Dictionary of Slang and Unconventional English* gives a 1908 usage of 'pill' meaning to fail a candidate in an examination.

Happy Days reviewed 24 Oct. 1915.

'whether the troops' In an interview in *NY Tribune*, 22 May 1921, AAM says 'it was received favorably by the men (which, of course, was almost a matter of discipline)'.

169 *Once on a Time* In the first edn., AAM says it is a book for adults: 'It is a fairy story for grown-ups because I have tried to give some character to the people who wander through its pages. Children prefer incident to character; if character is to be drawn, it must be done broadly in tar or whitewash.' By the time he wrote the *Pooh* books, he realized it was possible to be a little more subtle. A version of Prince Udo originally appeared in 'A Matter of Fact Fairy Tale' (*HR* and frequently reprinted). It was in *NY Herald Tribune*, 1 Aug. 1926,

under the title 'A Fairy Story which Breaks all Rules' – a title which could equally well apply to *Once on a Time*. On 5 July 1920 AAM wrote to A. P. Watt: 'I am continually meeting people who tell me they have read all my books and who have never heard of that one.' It was not published in US until 1922. AAM regretted this in a 1921 interview 'because it is the book of which I am most proud'. Swann considers it deserves the status of 'a recognized classic in juvenile literature'. He compares it with *The Sword in the Stone* and *Peter Pan*. The book is dedicated 'To the Officers & Men of the 4th Royal Warwickshire Regiment (among whom it was written) in affection for their good fellowship'.

Chapter 8   France and the First Plays

All letters to KJM at Texas. General background from Graves's *Goodbye to All That* (1929), Colonel C. S. Collison's diary *With the Eleventh Royal Warwicks in France* (1928), *Autob*, *First Day on the Somme* by Martin Middlebrook (1971) and *Somme* by Lyn Macdonald (1983).

172 'Remarque or Barbusse' writers: *All Quiet on the Western Front* (1929) and *Le Feu* (1916)
O.B.E.   Order of the British Empire.
'an under-garment of chain-mail' *Peace with Honour*.

173 *DP* review   *Glasgow Herald*, 20 Oct. 1910.

174 'the incessant humming' from Lyn Macdonald's *Somme*.

175 This long passage from *Autob* is slightly adapted – but using only AAM's own words.
The official history, *The Story of the Royal Warwickshire Regiment* by C. Lethbridge Kingsford (1921), makes little reference to the 11th battalion, but one reference is to the attack which involved AAM's telephone run. 'The 11th Royal Warwickshire took part in an attack towards Martinpuich on August 12, when they were held up within twenty yards of their objective, and forced to retire with the loss of 2 officers and 150 men.'

177 executions   in *Goodbye to All That* Graves says 'executions were frequent in France' and gives evidence for the statement.
'a horse he could use' 'Toby', *Punch*, 22 Nov. 1916.
'The General' Count Gleichen, son of Admiral Prince Victor of Hohenlohe-Langenburg and an English mother. On 26 June 1917, with the order that German titles should be dropped, he became known as Lord Edward Gleichen. After the war he was a neighbour of AAM's in Sussex and they exchanged books: *London's Open-Air Statuary* for *Winnie-the-Pooh*.

178 'a toy dog' the mascot was called Common in *Punch* and *SS*. When Daphne mentioned it in an interview in the *Sunday Express* (26 June

1966) it had become Carmen, presumably Robert Pitman's fault rather than Daphne's.

179 'the volunteer army' Compulsory enlistment had only come in in March 1916. Kitchener died in June 1916. Total casualties (killed and wounded) on the Somme were estimated at over 1,300,000, including 150,000 British dead.

Sgt. Hoyles quoted in *Somme* by Lyn Macdonald.

'a quiet war' e.g. by H. Colin Davis and Antony Miall in a Radio 4 programme (1975) *Whisper Who Dares*: 'not very arduous military service'. Swann: 'a singularly uneventful life.' (Preface).

180 HGW *Experiment in Autobiography.*

Olivier played Stanhope in the Stage Society production in Dec. 1928. AAM probably saw this but just possibly a later production at the Savoy with Colin Clive. R. C. Sherriff admired AAM: 'I am quite sure that all his work will live. Those of his plays which have been broadcast of recent times are as fresh as when they were written.' Letter to Maud, 20 Oct. 1956, K. Fam.

'not the stuff' *Ascent of Man*

'to cut even a line' Introd. *FP*. AAM eventually reduced the play to one act, as some critics had urged. It is published in that form in *FP*. The JMB one-act plays with which it was originally performed were *The Old Lady Shows her Medals* and the first act of *The Adored One* under the title *Seven Women*.

181 Denis Mackail, *Story of JMB* (1941).

OS to WAD in *I Do What I Like* (1947).

Times, 9 April 1917.

'My job was soldiering' Introd. to *FP*.

'told an interviewer' Louis T. McQuilland, *Bookman*, Feb. 1922.

182 *The Lucky One* Hull production – letter to me from Bennitt Gardiner; Golding Bright showed the play to both Eadie and Du Maurier, AAM told CB, July 1918, Texas. It was not performed in London until 11 May 1928 at the Arts Theatre, under the title *Let's All Talk about Gerald*. It ran for forty performances at the Garrick, NY from 20 Nov. 1922, a Theatre Guild production. The *Spectator* reviewing *FP* (11 Oct. 1919) says *The Lucky One* 'cuts deeper than mere enjoyment'.

'blacks black' AAM to CB, 3 Sept. 1918, Columbia & Texas.

183 *The Boy* at Victoria Theatre, London, 9 Sept. 1918, for a week (£20 to AAM).

'When the war is over' 'From a Full Heart', *Punch*, 2 May 1917, *SS, TWTD*.

Victoria quoted in *A Guide to Osborne House* by John Charlton (1960).

184 Graves in *Goodbye to All That*.

Wells's visit to Somme Graves's comment on talking to HGW afterwards is rather disturbing: 'He seemed unaware that I and the friend who was with me had also seen the sights.' (*Goodbye to All That*).

FS at Easton Glebe   *Autobiography* (1937).

185   In *Autob*   AAM says he had a telegram from Boucicault a week
after finishing *Belinda* and in the *Bookman* (Feb. 1922) he says it was
'invented, written, typed, accepted' within a fortnight.

Sheffield Terrace   the Milnes were back in Embankment Gardens by
the end of May 1918.

'propaganda'   AAM's work remains mysterious. He is not mentioned in *The Great War of Words* by Peter Buitenhuis (1989). AAM
talks of his visit to France ('winning the war') in a letter to HGW,
29 Sept. 1918, Illinois.

186   John Gielgud, *An Actor and his Time* (1979).

'radiant revival'   *NY Times*, 30 July 1922; the Empire production
was by Charles Frohman Inc. (Frohman himself had been drowned in
the *Lusitania*).

AAM on Shaw   *Year In*, July.

Sir Henry Norman (1858–1939) MP, Chairman of the Imperial Wireless Telegraphy Committee, 1920.

187   In the *Springfield Republican* (9 Sept. 1920) *Belinda* is compared with
both Shaw's *Candida* and Barrie's *Rosalind*.

'WAD once said'   *Through the Fourth Wall* (1922).

188   Irene Vanbrugh   *To Tell My Story* (1948). In a letter to IV, 3 May
1918 (Harvard), AAM promises at her request to write her a mono-
logue. The MS of this (mostly in Daphne's hand) is at the U of
Rochester, NY. It is called *Charing Cross to Gloucester Road*. I have
no record of its performance.

Letter to Agnew, 24 June 1918   *Punch* archives.

Letter to CB   Texas.

on play writing   introd. to *FP* and interview in *Book Window*, 1928.
FP, C & W, 11 Sept. 1919; Knopf also 1919. FS organized US
publication. 'Do you really know a man called Knopf? What a delightful name.' AAM to FS, Arkansas.

'intermittently to *Punch*'   9 pieces (8 prose, 1 poem) in 1918.

Letter to Mrs Calder   Caroline Gallaway.

190   'Lyric, Hammersmith'   from AAM's epilogue to *Story of the Lyric,
Hammersmith* by Nigel Playfair (1925) also in *BWI*. See also Hermione Baddeley's *The Unsinkable HB* (1984).

190   Margaret Morris was the dancer, choreographer and designer John
Galsworthy loved. See *JG* by Catherine Dupré (1976).

'French composer'   Georges Dorlay.

FP contained *Wurzel-Flummery, The Lucky One, The Boy Comes
Home, Belinda, The Red Feathers*. Three had already been produced.
Of the others, *The Lucky One* had to wait until NY, 1922; *The Red
Feathers*, 'an operetta' with music apparently by Walford Davies, was
'recently successfully produced at the Everyman', according to the
Era, 10 Aug. 1921. Rosemary Hill has a letter from AAM to Marcus
Dods (8 Jan. 1920): 'Of course I should like Dr Davies to write the
music ... I am sure the result would be delightful.'

191 Herbert Farjeon *Daily Herald*, 29 June 1921.

In the *New Statesman*, 17 Jan. 1920, Desmond MacCarthy wrote of *Make-Believe*: 'It was imitative. Sir James Barrie sowed the seed of the flowers ... from Peter Pan's nursery garden.' But seventy years after he had seen the play as an eight-year-old, Giles Playfair could remember the song the woodcutter sang and see him swinging his axe as the curtain went up on Act I (conversation with me).

EVL to CTS Cheltenham.

Algernon Locker *H Punch*; EVL had introduced him to *Punch* (*Reading, Writing and Remembering*) – 'my first journalistic befriender.'

'The Return' is in *The Secret and other Stories* (1929).

192 'unsold vacuum cleaners' MS (1942), Texas.

Leaving *Punch* In interviews AAM would always make it sound as if it were entirely his own decision not to return to *Punch*, e.g. *NY Tribune*, 22 May 1921: 'When the War was over, I decided not to go back to the assistant editorship of *Punch*, with its regular weekly article but keep myself free to write what and where and when I liked.' AAM's letter to Agnew (20 Feb. 1919) shows he could have insisted on resuming his job, but that it would have been difficult and embarrassing for him to do so – and that it had been made clear to him he would never be editor. But after this, according to the Prelude of *TWTD*, AAM did 'at times avail myself of the privilege, still generously offered to me, of dining at the *Punch* Table.' He often suggested, e.g. to H. J. Massingham 30 Dec. 1919 (Texas), he gave up *Punch* because reviewers never bothered to read his collections any more. 'I *detest* the "in his well-known delightful vein" sort of criticism.'

'grateful for all the fun' Prelude, *TWTD*.

193 demob AAM wrote of it in *Punch*, 29 Jan. 1919. He celebrated his release on St Valentine's Day, though a letter to Shorter (Berg) on that day says: 'I became a civilian yesterday for which I thank whatever gods there be.'

Letter to Swinnerton Arkansas.

Letter to Agnew *Punch* archives

Chapter 9 Playwright

See beginning of Notes for locations of most letters, e.g. Barrie, Wells, Swinnerton, Curtis Brown. Irene Vanbrugh in *To Tell My Story*.

194 'photograph in newspaper' *Daily Graphic*, 20 Nov. 1922. It shows AAM on his knees looking rather uncomfortable, giving a ride to an apprehensive two-year-old CRM.

'his income' this at a time when unemployment benefit was less than

£1 a week (18/-) for men. Unemployment stood at over a million, including 368,000 ex-servicemen.

195 CRM in *EP* and in speech at Ashdown Forest memorial ceremony in 1979.
Outlook, 11 Oct. 1919.
Hardy story   *IIM*, 'The Lord Mayor'.

196 'Gas Light and Coke Co.'   *Year In*, Jan; also in letter to *The Times*.
'of all the foolish things'   *Year In*, Jan.
'uniform edition'   FS to AAM: 'a neat plain decent and quasi-attractive cloth and a label as little repellent as possible, the top of the book painted in the same colour as the cloth, and the dust-cover as nearly uniform in tone as possible. This notion may all strike you as intolerably dull or precious.' (August 1919, C & W). As the chosen colour was a greyish-brown, the books *are* a little dull, but elegant.
FP is the only one of AAM's books, apart from the children's books, to be included in the Oxford *Annals of Eng. Lit.* 1475–1950 (1961).

197 Shaw challenging   *BWI*, 'A Note on Stagecraft'.
Chicago Tribune   14 Dec. 1927.

198 WAD 'His jam'   *DT*, 23 June 1921 and in *Through the Fourth Wall*.
'standing on the body'   Introduction to *Three Plays*.

199 'If yours is an 8.15 play'   'The Complete Dramatist', *SS* and *TWTD*.
audience description from 'Melodrama' in *IIM*.

201 Mallord Street   The house first appears in the rate books and in Kelly's *Street Directory* of Chelsea in 1916. The architect and builder are not identified in an article in *Studio* (Oct. 1922) which comments favourably on the development of which Mallord Street was a part. The street would be renumbered in 1925, 11 becoming 13.
'a friend of Daphne's'   Tatyana Peppé.
Sphere piece in *NTIM*.

202 WAD's first visit   'Moon's Toys', *Blackwood's Magazine*, April 1979.
Not knowing neighbours   *Year In*, June.
'suburban chumminess'   *Other People's Lives*.

203 FS on AAM's goodness   in his *Autobiography* (1937).
'brought up to believe'   *HHSM*, JVM's editorial, Christmas 1891: 'Oh the immovable rock is the word VIRTUE. This is the foundation of all.'
'He combined'   FS in *Figures in the Foreground* (1963)
Graham Greene see p. 392 of this book.
'I felt uncomfortable'   Peter Wait of Methuen, letter to me.

204 Irene Rutherford McLeod published a number of collections of poems and novels between 1915 and 1923. She was only three years older than Aubrey.
'one of his novels'   *Four Days' Wonder*.
'two frogs'   from the same book.
'One of Ken's children'   Angela Killey, writing for me.

205 Cuttings Agency   later Woolgar & Roberts of Fleet St.
Dame Peggy Ashcroft (b. 1907), actress, talking to me.

206 AAM on Boucicault, 2 Feb. 1919, to CB.   Texas & Columbia.
'Obviously nobody wanted him'   *Two People*.
The Times said of the first night: 'The audience, after having the
curtain raised again and again, would not depart until they had been
allowed a sight of the author.'

207 *Daily Express*, 6 Jan. 1920; *Pall Mall Gazette*, 6 June 1920.
America was always particularly fond of *Mr Pim Passes By*. It
appeared in numerous collections, e.g. *Modern Plays* (1932), *Theatre
Guild Anthology* (1936), *Sixteen Famous British Plays* (1942). Its
most recent revival in London seems to have been at the Hampstead
Theatre over twenty years ago.
MacCarthy in *New Statesman*, 17 Jan. 1920.

208 Causley and Trewin in letters to me.
'Very handsome, long-headed'   FS in *Autobiography* (1937).
Results of fame   This passage is a mixture of AAM's own experience
and that of his *alter ego*, Wellard, in *Two People*.
Society of Authors archive at BL records unanimous support for
AAM's co-option to the Committee, 3 March 1920.

209 AAM had a form printed to send to inquirers after autographs,
soliciting half-crowns for the Society; some forms have survived.
'I know very little'   *NY Tribune*, 22 May 1921; novel finished
summer 1921.
'a real book'   letter to FS, Jan. 1921, Arkansas.
The idea for the novel was A. P. Watt's.
Letter to Pinker   25 Feb. 1920, Texas.
Affair at Styles   Books and Writers, *Spectator*, 30 June 1950.

210 Letter to EVL   3 Oct. 1933, Texas.
Hardy quotation   letter to L. Alma-Tadema, 21 Jan. 1896 (*Collected
Letters of Thomas Hardy*, vol. 7, 1988).
The Red House Mystery had 22 printings between 1922 and 1965. It
has rarely been out of print.

211 *Watteau's Shepherds: The Detective Novel in Britain 1914–1940*
(1979) by Le Roy Panek (Bowling Green UP) has a chapter on AAM.
Julian Symons, *Bloody Murder: From the Detective Story to the Crime
Novel: A History* (1972).
Robert Graves and Alan Hodge, *The Long Weekend* (1940).
Isherwood   unpublished letter, whereabouts now unknown.
Film information from Rachel Low, *History of the British Film
1918–1929* (1971). In a letter to me she said she thought AAM wrote
only the stories and Brunel the scripts: 'I saw them many years ago
and, as far as I can remember, they are mildly facetious, and it is hard
to believe they were the great success Brunel claims' (21 May 1988).

212 Letter to Elspeth Grahame   Bodleian.
'God, how slowly'   MS fragment at Texas.
Angela Killey writing for me.

213 WAD Moon's Toys, *Blackwood's*, April 1979.
'that sense of inspiration' 'The Little More', *BWI*.
'asked by an interviewer' *Everyman*, 15 Jan. 1931.

Chapter 10   The Arrival of Billy Moon

214 'told a friend' Tatyana Peppé.
'her first child' Jenny, born Twelfth Night, 1919. The Milnes made
sure their child himself knew the facts of life early. AAM to Ken,
April 1926: 'Our cat is (obviously) having kittens, so Daff told Billy
all about it – and him – and herself, and he was so sweet and calm
and pleasantly interested about it all, and thought, as I do, that it was
much more lovely than a gooseberry bush (of which we have several).'
'a late short story' 'Birthday Party', first published as 'Something
Sacred' in *Good Housekeeping*, June 1948. Renamed as title story of
collection.
'Another of his characters' Michael in the play *Michael and Mary*.
'in his own voice' *Ascent of Man*.

215 'not particularly interested in children' see also Isobel Quigly's *TLS*
(21 June 1985) review of Humphrey Carpenter's *Secret Gardens*. He
had said: 'At first his presence in the house seems to have made little
difference to Milne's life.' The evidence suggests the reverse to me.

216 Malcolm Muggeridge in *The Green Stick* (1972) suggested AAM was
'not at all a child-like man' as Grahame was, but really liked children
and 'so wrote about them as it were from without as an adult', which
is one reason why adults like *WP* so much. He felt children's liking
of it is often 'to ingratiate themselves with adults'.

217 'The Heir' *Punch*, 31 July–4 Sept. 1912, *OW, TWTD*.
'Ken's first son' Ian Innes (Tim) Milne born 16 June 1912.
'One of his cousins' Tony Milne to me.

218 'a nice little boy' etc. 'Moon's Toys', *Blackwood's*, April 1979.
'christening a future first-class cricketer' 'He Chooses a Name',
OW, TWTD.
'When CR was born' 'The End of a Chapter', *BWI*.
'most famous children' See bottom of p. 399.

220 Laura Cowie was Hermia in Granville Barker's *Midsummer Night's
Dream*, Apollo, May 1914, Anne Boleyn in *King Henry VIII*, Lyric,
July 1916 and Margharita Cavallini in *Romance*, Queen's, Sept. 1916.
John Hastings Turner, fellow playwright, golfer and member of the
Garrick. He and AAM first met in 1918 when they were involved in
Hullo America! at the Victoria Palace.
DM interview *Parents'* (US), April 1932.

221 Olive Rand Brockwell *ST*, 8 Aug. 1965 and *Washington Post*, 26
Sept. 1965.

222 'a present from Harrods' Pooh's birthday. The accepted wisdom –
from AAM's 'birth certificate' when the toys went to America in
1947 – has always been that CR received Pooh on his first birthday

in Aug. 1921. Pooh's birthday is mentioned only once in AAM's letters: to KJM 10 Dec. 1928: 'It's Pooh's birthday next week and Moon has bought him a violin, so I suppose that's what Pooh most wants.' This would suggest Pooh might have been a Christmas present to CR, but perhaps it was simply that they felt Pooh had already 'lived' some months since manufacture and could hardly be considered a new-born bear when CR acquired him. Pooh's age is given clearly as a year younger than CR's at the end of *HPC*.

223   Growler met his end in Canada, savaged by a dog. By then he was at least twenty-five. He had gone there with Minette, Graham Shepard's daughter, and her mother. Soon after, Graham himself died when his corvette, *Polyanthus*, sank while on Atlantic convoy duties. Graham had been a close friend, at school and afterwards, of Louis MacNeice, who recalled him saying that not only was Growler W the P but that he, Graham, was behind the illustrations of CR. (Information from *The Work of E. H. Shepard*, Rawle Knox, 1979, and from Jon Stallworthy, MacNeice's biographer.)

Chaplin story from *HGW: a pictorial biography*, Frank Wells (1970)
Chaplin signature   K. Fam.

224   'This is a very fine name'   Introd. to *WWWVY*.
'one of Ken's children'   Angela Killey.
Boham's and Alastair Grahame's death   *Kenneth Grahame* by Peter Green (1959).

255   *TLS* review, 22 Oct. 1908.
'Usually I speak about it'   'A Household Book', *Outlook*, 26 April 1919, *NTIM*, reprinted (with variations) as introduction to *Wind in the Willows*, NY Limited Editions Club, 1940, Heritage Press edition 1944, Methuen edition 1951.

226   'what a very great influence'   EHS interview, *ST*, Nov. 1969.
AAM to CB in *Contacts* by Spencer Curtis Brown (1935).
Dickens's scheme in aid of the Guild of Literature and Art, a sort of provident society for writers which would help those who through ill health or age were uninsurable. It bore some of the characteristics of the Royal Literary Fund, one of AAM's favourite charities, to which, in his will, he left a share of the *Pooh* royalties. The Fund regularly receives over £100,000 a year from this source.

227   The 1921 production is described by Alfred Noyes in *Two Worlds for Memory* (1953) and Compton Mackenzie in *Octave Five* of *My Life and Times* (1966).
Betjeman in a letter to Lord Esher at the beginning of the war, quoted by his son in an article in the *TLS*, 21 Jan. 1987.

228   'buried under the weight'   FS in *Figures in the Foreground*.
'Raymond Mortimer's dismissal'   *Nation*, 25 August, 1923.
L. Woolf to H. Henderson, 26 Sept. 1923, Nuffield College, Oxford.

229   George Rylands   letter to me, 4 March 1987.
Arthur Marshall   letter to me 14 March 1987. The ADC production was in 1932.

Forster reference from P. N. Furbank, *E. M. Forster*, vol. 2 (1978).

230 'The successful playwright' 'The Complete Dramatist', *Punch*, 17 June 1914, *SS*, *TWTD*.
Nathan *The World in Falseface* (1923).

231 Michael Frayn letter to me, 23 Jan. 1989.
PGW to W. Townend 14 Sept. 1931 (*Performing Flea*, 1953).
Cable quoted by JVM to Biddie Warren 29 Jan. 1922 (CRM).

232 'One American critic' *Life, Letters and the Arts*, March 1922.
JMB comment on *The Truth about Blayds* FS, *Figures in the Foreground*.
'one critic said that Henry James' Louis T. McQuilland, *Bookman*, Feb. 1922, who also reported 'Mrs Milne encourages me . . .'

233 'his first act' George Lyttelton in a letter to Rupert Hart-Davis (vol. 6) 3–4 May 1961, remembered the 'admirable' act after forty years, but oddly thought it was the second.

234 'the front rank of dramatists' AAM's reputation has not survived. He is not even mentioned in such standard reference books as the Macmillan Press *Twentieth Century Drama* or in *The Oxford Companion to the Theatre*.
Galsworthy letter 10 March 1923 (CRM).
'Ervine's *Observer* piece' quoted in *Life and Letters* (US), March 1922.

235 Brown *Manchester Guardian*, 8 Oct. 1923.
Nathan *Materia Critica* (1924).
'the papers said' AAM said the papers said these things (see preface to *Success*) but WAD tried to check (*DT*, 4 Oct. 1923) and said he could find no such cheap jibes.

236 Letter to Ervine Texas.
Letter to Vanbrugh Harvard.

237 'review' of *Hamlet* Introd. to *Three Plays* (1922).

238 Florence Hardy letter to Pinero 12 Dec. 1939, U of Rochester.

239 *Boston Transcript* 14 Sept. 1921.
'An American editor' with Hearst Newspapers.
Olive Brockwell *ST*, 8 Aug. 1965 and *Washington Post*, 26 Sept. 1965.

240 Humphrey Carpenter, *Secret Gardens* (1985). The parody by Beachcomber, J. B. Morton, has often been reprinted, see, e.g., *Imitations of Immortality*, ed. E. O. Parrott (1986).
A. C. Benson in his diary, quoted by David Newsome in *On the Edge of Paradise* (1980).
Princess Marie Louise in *Memories of Six Reigns* (1956).

Chapter 11   *When We Were Very Young*

242 *The Beggar's Opera* ran at Hammersmith for 2½ years, then toured. Austin 'reharmonized and reorchestrated' the music and it was 'particularly notable'. (Grove).

Richard Hughes (1900–76), author of *A High Wind in Jamaica* (1929). He had already published a book of poems while still at Oxford, and had a play performed at the Royal Court. Nigel Playfair produced his radio play *Danger* (the first original play to be broadcast) the following year.

Details of the house party from Giles Playfair, talking to me in 1987, from his book *My Father's Son* (1937) and from a letter from Joan (Pitt-Chapman) Wainright from Portugal, 10 June 1987.

244 'Why are you the devil' David in *Michael and Mary*.

'one of Ackie's daughters' two concerts by Gena Milne were reported by *The Times* in Oct. and Nov. 1925.

'Fairies were fashionable' see 'The Quest for Fairyland' by Gillian Avery, *Quarterly Journal of the Library of Congress*, Fall 1981.

Compton Mackenzie, *The Enchanted Island* (1933).

245 *Joy Street* AAM's 'Prince Rabbit' first appeared in No. 2 *Joy Street* (1924), along with Belloc, Edith Sitwell, Walter de la Mare, etc. 'The Princess Who Could Not Laugh' appeared in No. 3 *Joy Street* (1925). *Merry-Go-Round* sold for 1/- at a time when most children's papers were 2d. It had an initial print run of 10,000. First issue November 1923, published by Blackwells, like *Joy Street*.

'It is too late' AAM, Introd. to *The Science of Fairy Tales* by E. S. Hartland. See *BWI*.

246 'one of the Rabbits' in 'He sleeps' from 'The Heir', *OW*, *TWTD*.

A. E. Bestall cartoon 17 Dec. 1924.

'even Wells' hypocorisma in *Joan and Peter*.

'In 1925' to Carl Pforzheimer, 2 April 1925.

247 'a poet's daughter 'Miss Waterlow in Bed' in *A Gallery of Children*.

'Is it raining' 'A Song for the Summer', *SS*, *TWTD*.

248 'That the book, when written' *Spectator*, 4 Dec. 1926, *BWI*.

'Now you know of course' 'The Author to His Reader', MS, Texas.

Intros. to *The Christopher Robin Story Book* (selections from all four books) and *Very Young Verses* (both 1929).

249 'As a child I kept a mouse' 'End of a Chapter', *BWI*.

three or four 'Christopher' is in 'Sand-between-the-Toes' and CR in 'Buckingham Palace', 'Hoppity' and 'Vespers'.

'a quarter of the book' AAM remembered in 1939 that he had written eleven poems in Wales. Other evidence suggests thirteen. The poems are numbered in the order they were written in the Pforzheimer TS sold at Sotheby's, July 1986.

Giles Playfair *My Father's Son*.

250 'His American publisher' John Macrae, 22 Sept. 1935. Dutton's press release at the time of the first cheap editions of the children's book. In *Autob* AAM says: 'In the ten years before it [*WWWVY*] went into a cheap edition half a million copies were sold'.

251 AAM to EVL Sybil Clement Brown, Seaman collection.

252 'You wait,' story AAM tells this himself: 'Introducing Shepard', Preface to *Fun and Fancy* (1927), *BWI*.

'a pillar of Sussex society'   Rawle Knox (ed.), *The Work of EHS*.
'a rather cagey man'   *ST* interview with EHS, Nov. 1969.

253   R. G. G. Price   *H Punch*.
Geoffrey Grigson (1905–85)   *The Contrary View* (1974).
Penelope Fitzgerald in *The Work of EHS*, ed. Rawle Knox.
'as intimately as the echo'   *Bookman*, Dec. 1925. Bevis Hillier in *The Work of EHS* (ed. Rawle Knox): 'Only a few artists have been able to petrify movement so as to convey a still continuing force'. EHS always 'drew the classical line'. He was eventually retired from *Punch* in 1952 by Malcolm Muggeridge, when most other artists were using distortion and stylization. EHS would come to regret his close identification with AAM's books. He once called Pooh 'that silly bear'.

254   AAM to Seaman   Sybil Clement Brown, Seaman collection.
'the series of poems'   'Market Square' was not in the original collection, but was written later while the poems were appearing in *Punch*, to replace one he rejected. 'As this was sent direct to *Punch*, the MS of it presumably joined the other wastepaper of the office. I have copied it out here. I have also had to copy out two others, "Rice Pudding" and "The Alchemist". Why the pencilled MSS of these should have disappeared I cannot say, but if they have gone anywhere it is into my own wastepaper basket.' AAM statement for Pforzheimer (2 April 1925) sold with MSS at Sotheby's, July 1986.

256   'settled at Shepton Mallet'   They rented Norris House in July 1924 and moved in the summer of 1927 to quieter Chanters, in Pilton 3 miles away.

257   'I am bad at receiving'   CRM, *Path*, Epilogue.
Illustrated London News, 3 May 1924.

258   *Times* letter, 9 Jan. 1924.
Times letter, 1 Nov. 1924.

260   James Agate   21 April 1925, reprinted in *Contemporary Theatre 1925* (1926).
'*Theatre World*' Critic   May 1925, WAD, *Six Thousand and One Nights* (1960).
'a horrible profession'   AAM to KJM, 23 April 1925, Texas.

261   'an old farmhouse'   In an interview in *Everyman*, Jan. 1931, AAM: 'part of it is fourteenth century.' No one was really at all sure.

262   'under the name of Sanders'   'The Sanders referred to was Frank Sanders, who had a printing works in the Snow Hill area of London.' This firm apparently printed some of AAM's work. (All four children's books are printed by Jarrold of Norwich). Information from Douglas Sanders, Frank's nephew, 1989. Frank Sanders was certainly a friend of EHS, but I can find no AAM reference to him, confirming the private joke. Carpenter (*Secret Gardens*) suggests the reference shows 'Pooh has little self-centred concern with his own identity,' which seems to come straight out of *The Pooh Perplex*.
WWWVY Texas has a presentation copy with both signatures. It was originally sold for 42/-. By 1926 copies were quoted in London

for £53 and in NY for $225. 'No book of our time has so quickly attained the status of a classic' as one ad. had it. The ordinary London 1st edn was quoted at the same time for between $26 and $35 (different dealers). Good unsigned first editions can now fetch over £100.

Milne's royalty From Dutton's it was 10 per cent for the first 3,000 and 15 per cent thereafter. Dutton's also did a limited edition of 500 copies bound in 'colored boards.' Among many others, AAM gave a copy to Daphne's aunt Bessie de Sélincourt 'from Billy Moon who cannot write yet. Christmas 1924.'

illustrations AAM's Methuen contract dated 10 April 1924 says 'suitably illustrated at their own expense', i.e. Methuen's.

'the next day' EHS speaking in 'Mr Milne and Mr Shepard', Andrew Holmes's film for Weston Woods.

263 'By the end of the year' The binders ran out of the navy blue cloth before Christmas so that the fifth impression comes in both navy and kingfisher blue.

264 'John Drinkwater's review' *ST*, 23 Nov. 1924.
Geoffrey Grigson, *The Contrary View* (1974) The original article was written in 1958. He was apparently influenced by the effect of the poems on children made to recite them. 'We cringed with embarrassment when made to recite them to visiting friends and relations and *loathed* Christopher Robin. My sister can still do her party pieces 50 years later.' Jane Grigson to me, 8 April 1989.

266 Roald Dahl (b. 1916) 'The authentic voice for today's child' is on record as having called *WP* 'the best' and AAM an 'expert writer', distinguished most for the excellence of his dialogue.
Compton Mackenzie, *Literature in my Time* (1933).

267 Bruno Bettelheim, *The Uses of Enchantment* (1976).
'packers' strike' R. H. Havercroft, letter to MM-R, 13 March 1982. The 1925 strike was 'part of a concerted action by the Paperworkers' Union to improve pay and conditions throughout the industry. Once again the clerical staff helped to break the strike; the existing packing staff were sacked and replaced by new workers.' See Maureen Duffy, *A Thousand Capricious Chances: a history of the Methuen list* (1989)

268 'enthusiasm of Macrae's son' according to his father, 15 Oct. 1927, and again in 1935, promoting a cheap edition (Dutton). In fact *WWWVY* took off very quickly after a slow start. AAM to FS (25 Feb 1925): 'the book went into 18 editions in America in 9 weeks' (i.e. before the end of Jan.). It sounds as if Dutton's were consistently underestimating demand and printing new impressions in small quantities (see letter to EVL p. 269).
Fan letters from Dutton.

269 Edwin Samuel, later 2nd Lord Samuel (1898–1978).
NY Herald Tribune, 8 March 1925.

270 Philip Larkin (*New Review*, Autumn 1978), reviewing the Amis anthology, disputes whether Auden's reference was necessarily 'a good word.' 'A poetic situation made up of singing robes on the one hand

and A. A. Milne on the other . . . was plainly intolerable' to Auden, Larkin wrote.

essay on Calverley   from *Year In*, Dec. Another section of this apologia is quoted in Ch. 4 (p. 97).

'Neither Auden nor Amis'   AAM is omitted from most of the popular anthologies, e.g. Michael Roberts's *Faber Book of Comic Verse*, William Cole's *Fireside Book of Humorous Poetry*, J. M. Cohen's *Comic and Curious Verse* and Gavin Ewart's *Penguin Book of Light Verse*.

271 The rhymes from Drinkwater come from a letter to KJM.

272 Harold Fraser-Simson (1872–1944)   Walford Davies composed some 'glees and quartets' (AAM to CB, 15 Feb. 1925, Texas). CB archives in 1938 list four poems he set to music for Novello: 'The Christening', 'Disobedience', 'Bad Sir Brian Botany' and 'The Mirror'. Many of Fraser-Simson's MSS of AAM songs were sold at Sotheby's in Dec. 1987, e.g. MS of the songs for *The Hums of Pooh* for £1,000.

The book of *The Maid of the Mountains* was written by Frederick Lonsdale.

'thick with royalty'   EVL had helped Princess Marie Louise to form the library for the Queen's Dolls' House. 'I may say that E. V. Lucas contributed a great deal to my life, and our mutual friendship was, I think, as precious to him as it was to me.' Marie Louise in *My Memories of Six Reigns* (1956).

273 'second book'   *Teddy Bear* and other songs (1926).

Stephen Spender   letter to me, 15 July 1987.

Mussolini – murderer   *BTL* note on 'The Neutral'. Milne said this in 1926, soon after the death of Giacomo Matteotti, the leader of the Italian Socialist Party.

274 'collection of the cartoons'   *Lions and Lambs* by Low, with interpretations by Lynx (1928). *Nation* review, 6 Oct. 1928 in *BWI*. In his autobiography, Low describes AAM as 'a gentle, likeable man . . . just what the father of CR should be'.

Chapter 12   The Beginnings of Pooh

275 'trying to write'   four pieces by KJM in *Punch* in 1925, four more between 1926 and his death in 1929.

'reading for Methuen'   Duffy op. cit. (note to p. 267) makes no mention of KJM's reading but suggests AAM was a regular reader in the 1920s. I have no evidence of this, although EVL would consult him from time to time.

276 AAM to Maud   K. Fam. (*BMJ* = *British Medical Journal*).

FS in *Figures in the Foreground* describes Frankau (1884–1952) as someone who 'laughed, drank and flirted during hot nights in Havana' and Arlen (1895–1956) as someone who similarly appealed 'to the appetite for smartness'. They were both popular novelists at this time. *Four Plays* had no introduction, very unusually for AAM. To FS, 6

Dec. 1925 (in DM's hand): 'I keep tearing them up. I am in a state of being bored to death, not with writing plays, but with talking about them . . . and, in fact, having anything to do with them after I've written them.'

'Letters like yours' to Marie Meloney, 12 Jan. 1925, Columbia.

Kipling letter, 20 Aug. 1925, U. of Sussex.

278 Lady Desborough letter, 7 Jan. 1925, Herts County Record Office.

279 'most weekends' When they missed Denis Mackail's birthday party in June 1928 he wrote (*Life with Topsy*, 1942) that it was because of their 'ineradicable habit of week-ending at their country cottage'. But AAM would sometimes go to Somerset to see KJM.

'She responded' EP.

280 'in a novel' *Two People*.

282 'It was just the right width' EP.

'Poohsticks' In the MS at Trinity, Cambridge the game is quite clearly written without the 'h' and originally seems to have been called 'Poobridge' – which sounds quite natural, bridge being a game. Mary Keeys feels sure she remembers playing the game with CRM long before the story was published in 1928. It is interesting that in her letter to me she spelt the game Poosticks, as AAM does in the MS. Her father was a local builder, who did a good deal of work at Cotchford and her mother used to push her in her pram from the village to take her father's sandwiches. She remembered Nanny's 'long black skirts' and picnics in the Forest.

'some suggestion' In *Woman* (9 April 1966), in an article which rewrites history to some extent, DM: 'He began it all, as it was he who first brought Pooh to life through pretending to speak for him. One day when actor Nigel Playfair was visiting us, CR growled: "What a funny man. What a funny red face . . ." '

283 'a drooping neck' DM (op. cit.): 'a perfectly ordinary donkey until the wire in his head broke. Then he came to life as an individual through the way his head fell forward.'

AAM had parodied the *Just-So Stories* long before. 'How the *Granta* got its name.' *Granta*, 18 Oct. 1902, and two more in the same series.

'called Winnie' after Winnipeg, the home town of the soldier who bought the bear cub in White River, Ontario.

'sculpture' statue of a bear cub by Lorne McKeane, presented by the Trustees of the Pooh Properties, unveiled by CRM, 23 Sept. 1981.

'Canadian regiment' Princess Pat's Canadian Regt., 9 Dec. 1914.

Enid Blyton in *Teacher's World*, 1 Oct. 1926. This interview appeared before AAM's introduction, so it was obviously a story he told, but which she, perhaps, embroidered.

284 Irving's *Times* letter 14 Feb. 1981. Information from Brian Sibley, who researched the question for an article in the *London Zoo Magazine* in 1981, and from an unpublished autobiography of L. Irving from his son, John Irving and letters from J. Irving to me.

DM in *Woman* (op. cit.) has another version: 'One day a bee alighted on Winnie's nose and CR thought he heard him say "ther-pooh!" to blow it off.'

Pamela Irving (now Ingle-Finch) has no memory of the expedition. Some confusion was caused by AAM's use of 'polar' in the introduction to *WP*. 'He goes to where the Polar Bears are.' Winnie was certainly 'brown and furry', as AAM says.

'I gave it to him'   CRM to me, 1989.

'a child psychotherapist'   Adam Phillips, now at Great Ormond Street Hospital in London. Eric Partridge, *Dictionary of Slang and Unconventional English* (8th rev. ed. 1984).

285   'AAM himself'   in the introduction and Chapter I of *WP*.

286   'greatest children's book since Alice' (*The Times*); 'a classic!' (James Douglas in the *Sunday Express*.)   Both quoted on jackets and advertisements.

Pforzheimer   It seems that he began his collection in 1925, buying the fair copies of the poems prepared for the publisher, and in 1928 added the 'original pencil sketches' of the drawings, and finally in 1945 acquired the autograph MSS. On 2 April 1925 AAM wrote to the dealer Owen Winters of NY that the MS was 'a transcript of the original and sent with a typed copy of the verses to Dutton'. He had sold the MS of *WWWVY* even earlier and said he had forgotten about the Dutton copy. 'I didn't know this one was in existence, but I seem now to remember writing it out again for the American publisher.' In 1945 he wrote to Pforzheimer himself: 'If I was a little vague in 1925, I am not a very good witness in 1945.' This material is now in the Pierpont Morgan Library in NY.

286   *A Gallery of Children* was later reissued in a cheaper edition illustrated by A. H. Watson (1939).

'a recent critic'   Swann.

'more verses'   The poems which would eventually be in *NWA6* appeared in England in the *Royal Magazine* between Feb. and Oct. 1927. In America, they were in *Harper's* between Feb. 1926 and May 1927 and in *Collier's* in March and April 1927.

287   Letter to EHS, 9 Oct. 1925   supplied by Pickering and Chatto Ltd., later sold at Sotheby's.

'Everyone was wanting'   For instance, C & W had suggested EHS illustrated a selection of three or four of the more popular adult plays, but AAM was not keen on that idea.

288   'It seemed that'   *The Ivory Door* was written June 1925. Undated statement sold at Sotheby's in 1986 with MS of the play.

289   'a completely contemptible mix-up'   letter to Iona and Peter Opie, 11 Jan. 1951, copy at Bodleian.

'one story'   CRM did not remember listening to this story and indeed hardly remembers his father reading them to him after they were published. See CRM, *EP*, ch. 10.

290   'Wardrobe Mistress'   Ian Wallace, Toad at the Queen's Theatre in the early 1960s, told me: 'Mrs Milne visited me in my dressing-room

afterwards and commented favourably on my green silk tights, but was non-committal about the performance.'

292 The programme went out remarkably late for small children; it was obviously aimed at a general audience.

'Binker' at this stage was 'Dinkie', *Pears' Annual*, 1925. Proof at V & A with AAM's own alterations for *NWA6*.

'most famous' *Best-selling Children's Books* by Jean Spealman Kujoth (1973).

Chapter 13 *Winnie-the-Pooh*

293 *The Secret* AAM regretted this collection, explaining later that he had in 1929 'a transitory bibliographical value' (note to *Birthday Party*). At that stage, as Swann suggests, AAM could have published a rhyming grocery list and someone would have happily printed it in leather covers.

294 'Milne's instructions' Rawle Knox in *The Work of EHS*, ch. 4.

'I always had to start again' EHS in Weston Woods film, *Mr Shepard and Mr Milne* (Andrew Holmes), 1973, and interview in *ST Magazine*, 2 Nov. 1969.

'I think you must come here' V & A.

295 'CR's legs' EHS quoted in *ES*, 19 Sept. 1959.

'the juxtaposition' CRM, *EP*.

John Macrae publicity material at time of first cheap editions (1935), Dutton.

296 Miss Pearn letters copies at V & A.

Royal Magazine June-Dec. 1926 (seven chapters).

contracts Correspondence with CB in 1929 over *The Christopher Robin Reader* shows how scrupulous AAM was in his financial dealings with EHS. EHS had accepted 10 per cent of AAM's share of the royalties, but AAM said he was entitled to 15 per cent. Letter from CB to EHS, 25 June 1929, CB, London.

297 Texas has a copy of an agreement dated 6 Jan. 1930 between AAM and Stephen Slesinger of NY, granting SS 'the sole and exclusive right, license and privilege to use in any and every manner except as hereinafter expressly forbidden the following works *WWWVY*, *WP*, *NWA6* and *HPC* and of any literary works dealing with characters contained in them.' At some stage Slesinger must have sold these rights to Walt Disney. Walt Disney will not reveal the terms of their contracts but this would explain why EHS illustrated greeting cards can have a Walt Disney credit. On March 1926 AAM signed a contract with Dutton's to prepare an edition of *Mother Goose Rhymes*, to be illustrated by EHS and delivered before 1 Feb. 1927. This was never fulfilled, though *Ladies Home Journal*, Dec. 1930, used what would have been part of that book. Contract CB, London. Letter at V & A, AAM to EHS (8 March 1926) refers.

298 'He was a different man' EHS in Weston Woods film.
Gills Lap 'In the book it is Galleons Lap but otherwise it is exactly as described,' CRM, *EP*, ch. 8. There is now some confusion about the real name. *Walks in Ashdown Forest* by Hilary Longley-Cook (1973) adopts AAM's name: 'The higher one is Galleons Lap, the highest point on the forest and the group of trees in the Enchanted Place in *HPC* by AAM. The illustration by EHS still compares. Gills Lap and its car park can now be seen to the north-west under a mile away. The track back to Gills Lap goes off to the left just before you reach Galleons Lap.'
'a memorial' 'Here at Gills Lap are commemorated AAM 1882–1956 and EHS 1879–1976 who collaborated in the creation of "Winnie-the-Pooh" and so captured the magic of Ashdown Forest and gave it to the world.'
Mary Shepard Knox quoted in *The Work of EHS*.

299 'dog games' CRM, *EP*.
'less structured games' AAM tore some muscles 'playing the fool with Billy on Sunday', to EVL, 6 July 1926, Texas.
Brenda Tasker (now McCallum) writing to me, 12 Dec. 1988.
Olive Brockwell *ST*, 8 Aug. 1965 and *Washington Post*, 26 Sept. 1965. 'It was like a real tragedy for all of us. For days we all searched . . . I don't think I ever stopped looking for him till the day I left.'
'tree-climbing' AAM to KJM, Texas.

300 Chris Powling *Books for Keeps*, Nov. 1986: 'the stories can survive.' They also had to survive a sad deterioration in EHS's illustrations, particularly of CR. Compare the boy in the coloured pictures added to *The World of Pooh* and *The World of CR* in 1958 with the boy thirty years earlier.
'simple language' As early as 1912 (*Punch*, 'The Truth about Home Rails', in *OW, TWTD*) AAM had said he had always flattered himself he could explain 'in perfectly simple language anything which a child wants to know'.

301 Benedict Nightingale on *The Pooh Perplex* in the *Guardian*, 18 March 1964.
Alison Lurie 'Back to Pooh Corner', *Children's Literature*, vol. 1 (Journal of the MLA seminar on Children's Lit. and the Children's Lit. Assoc.), Temple U., Philadelphia, 1972, and in 'Now we are Fifty', *NY Times* Book Review, 14 Nov. 1976.

302 Humphrey Carpenter *Secret Gardens*, 'AAM & WP' (1985).
Richard Adams 'Some Ingredients of *Watership Down*' in *The Thorny Paradise*, ed. Blishen (1975).
John Rowe Townsend *Written for Children* (rev. edn. 1974).
Peter Hunt A. A. Milne in *Writers for Children*, ed. Jane M. Bingham (1988).

303 Alison Lurie op. cit.; Humphrey Carpenter op. cit.

Carol Stanger 'Winnie the Pooh through a Feminist Lens' in *The Lion and the Unicorn*, vol. II, no. 2, 1987.

Roger Sale *Fairy Tales and After* (1978). Sale actually says that the end of *HPC* can still bring tears to his eyes.

Margery Fisher 'Classics for Children and Young People', *Signal* (1986).

AAM to EVL 6 July 1926, Texas.

The MS of *WP* appeared in facsimile in 1971. *The Economist* complained that 'the deletions are frustratingly black' but I discovered not only Kanga's original masculinity, but also that at one point AAM had written 'Billy', obviously thinking of CR, but then deciding it would be funnier to repeat 'Eeyore' (facing page 126).

304 '*WP* was dedicated' *HPL* has a similar dedication to DM, paying tribute to her part in the books.

Ronald Bryden *Spectator*, 27 Nov. 1959.

'When I am gone' Brenda Jones in *ST* (2 Nov 69) seems to have printed this rhyme for the first time, shown it by *EHS*. Her suggestion that it was in the first American edition of *WP* has been much repeated, but it was not printed there. CRM thinks it unlikely the verse was written in the twenties.

305 *EN* article reprinted in the *Author*, April 1926.

308 Clara Hawkins *The Bookman* (US), vol. LXIV, Sept. 1926–Feb. 1927.

309 Wolsey underwear request AAM to Pinker, 1 Oct. 1939, Berg. Mackail, *Life with Topsy*.

310 'I loathe clubs' PGW to Usborne (1956) quoted in Frances Donaldson's *PGW* (1982).

311 'two bantams' etc. and conversation in letters to KJM at Texas. 'the necessary assumption' *Book Window*, W. H. Smith, Christmas 1928.

312 Enid Blyton (1897–1968) in *Teacher's World*, 1 Oct. 1926. She became probably the most prolific, most successful and most despised children's writer of all time. Thirty years or so later CRM made the decision not to stock her in his Dartmouth bookshop. For his reasons, see *Path*, ch. 7.

312 'numerous interviews' I have not written about the reporters CRM mentions in *EP*.

313 JVM to Biddie Warren, 1 Feb. 1927, CRM. Tony Milne did indeed win a scholarship to Westminster and was the only one of the four to become Captain. (Tim: I. I. Milne).

314 Howard Coster (1885–1959). The exhibition of his photographs at the National Portrait Gallery in 1985 was advertised by his photo of CRM, AAM and Pooh. CRM told Michèle Field the picture was posed and not natural. Other photos taken at the same sitting are in NPG archive at Lewisham.

'Years ago' in *Book Window*, Christmas 1928.

When We Were Rather Older illustrations by Jefferson Machamer.

315 Lord Bridgeman 1st Viscount Bridgeman of Leigh (1864–1954), First Lord of the Admiralty 1924–29, President of the MCC.
Hon. John Collier (1850–1934) trained at the Slade, wrote *The Art of Portrait Painting*.
'a sober veracity' from *DNB*.
William Joynson-Hicks Viscount Brentford (1865–1932): 'Conservative in politics and evangelical in religion' according to *DNB*, in 1922 he had 'made a formidable attack' upon the administration of AAM's old friend, E. S. Montagu, Secretary of State for India. As Home Secretary in this year Joynson-Hicks had to deal with the General Strike.

316 Brenda (Tasker) McCallum writing to me, 1988.

317 'Spleak painly' The US edition kept AAM's original Spoonerism until 1961 when it was also 'corrected'. The discrepancy was noticed by a Mrs Anne E. Knight of San Antonio, Texas, who wrote to Dutton's about it (24 Aug. 1978).
NY Herald Tribune 17 Oct. 1926.

318 *Churchman* 12 June 1926.

Chapter 14 The End of a Chapter

319 'one of Piglet's floods' *WP*. CRM had other floods, see *EP*, ch. 10.
'a new Pooh story' The first Pooh story for the second book appeared in *EN* (23 Dec. 1926), again with the main headline on the front page. 'STORY FOR CHILDREN: BY A. A. MILNE. See page 9. As with the very first one the year before, it was not illustrated by EHS but by J. H. Dowd.

320 Edwin Pugh (1874–1930) has a solid list of 33 books in the Cambridge bibliography. His last book, *Empty Vessels*, was published later that year, 1926. Vincent Brome included him in his 1965 British Council pamphlet *Four Realist Novelists*. A letter at Texas to Thomas Burke (19 Jan. 1927) seems to refer to this case. AAM wrote: 'Can you get 10 people to give £25 each – and will that be enough? Also what about the Literary Fund and the Author's Society Pension Fund? One always contributes to these things and they never seem to help anybody one knows.' He was told £15 each would be sufficient and responded (22 Jan. 1927). 'Giving money is easy; it is what *you* are doing that counts.'
Athenaeum AAM belonged to both the Beefsteak and the Savile. The Garrick continued to be the club he used most.
Chatto plays The plays were also all produced in cheap acting editions by Samuel French and these sold in very large quantities.
DM to Pforzheimer 19 July 1928, sold with MS at Sotheby's.

321 DM's receipt from NY 3 Oct. 1928.
Telephone conversation from AAM to KJM (undated), Texas.
An undated letter from AAM to *The Times* about the Children's

Country Holiday Fund was for sale in 1989 by David Holmes of Philadelphia at $1,500.

322 Toc H appeal   duplicated letter to Clayton dated 18 Jan. 1925; hospital letter dated 1 Dec. 1927 (Birmingham Public Lib. Ref. Dept.). This letter was commended in *Advertising and Selling* (27 May 1931) 'as an example of a good sales letter written by a man outside the advertising profession'.

323 'lacey things'   *Two People*. AAM's purchases from Tatyana Peppé, from conversation with DM.
PGW to Bill Townend   26 July 1928, in *Performing Flea*.
Viola Tree   in *Woman's Pictorial*, 10 Dec. 1927.

324 'suddenly stop'   See, e.g., *Michael and Mary*, Act II, and 'A Group of Silver Birches', *Saturday Review*, 4 Dec. 1926, *BWI*.
'One of Ken's children'   Angela Killey, writing to me.
'Each child lay on its front'   'The Road to Knowledge', *Sphere*, 24 Jan. 1920, *IIM*.

325 'wrote to Shepard'   undated, V & A.

326 Canadian paper   *Sunday Pictorial* (BC), C & W.
Granta   30 April 1926.

327 one reviewer   H. M. Walbrook, *Play Pictorial*, vol. III, no. 313, 1928.
'the lady bantam'   see 'Little Black Hen' in *NWA6*.

328 'Milne looked back'   letter to KJM, Texas.

329 'One of CRM's cousins'   Angela Killey.
two records?   CRM may have sung 'The Friend' only at the Pooh party.
'boys in the next study'   CRM *EP*, Epilogue.

330 '*Pooh* party'   It is interesting to compare AAM's account written at the time with CRM's memories about forty-five years later. His description in *EP* of Veronica bursting the balloon is particularly vivid. The party was on 17 March and given in aid of Queen Charlotte's Hospital. *NY Times*, 19 March 1928, reported CR somewhat improbably: 'It is fun being famous, but sometimes it is a nuisance. Wait and see how Father likes the poems I write about him.'
Information about pageant from programme of the event. Mackail, *Life with Topsy*.

331 Dorothy Parker   (1893–1967) was in 1927 at the height of her fame. It was the time when people would go to the Algonquin Hotel on W 44th St, NY, simply to have a glimpse of her lunching at the famous Round Table (otherwise known as the Vicious Circle). *Enough Rope*, her first volume of poems, was a current bestseller.

333 'Gon Out Backson'   *HPC*, ch. V.
The inscription in Anne's copy of *HPC* on her ninth birthday suggests that she and AAM had their own games and jokes. Part of it goes: 'This copy of *The House at Pooh Corner* belongs to my much-loved aunt Anne Darlington from her affectionate nephew, A. A. Milne. (Author and Owner of Race-horses)'. (Inscriptions to Anne Darlington from Peter Ryde).

333   WAD 'Moon's Toys', *Blackwood's*, April 1979.
'Christopher's nanny' *ST*, 8 Aug. 1965 and *Washington Post*, 26 Sept. 1965.

334   DM letter 9 Oct., no year, Temple U, Philadelphia (May Lamberton Becker collection).
May Lamberton Becker article *Dutton's Newsletter*, Oct. 1928, Dutton.
John o'London's Weekly, 21 April 1928.

336   *Punch*, 24 Oct. 1928; *Saturday Review*, 8 Dec. 1928; *TLS*, 13 Dec. 1928.
New Yorker, 20 Oct. 1928 It is interesting that the hum that naus-eated Dorothy Parker was singled out by Roger Sale, in his rather sad piece (op. cit.) about his adult reactions to the book, as one of the things his students most enjoy, among 'the parts of the books that are most relaxed, lazy and cosy'.

337   'In 1929' 'The End of a Chapter', *BWI*.

338   'the distinction' Carmen Blacker told me she remembered clearly as a four-year-old in 1928 being told by her nanny that CR was 'a real little boy'. She was amazed that there could be any question about it. The small child has little comprehension of fiction.
'both despised and loved' CRM makes his ambivalence clear in *EP*. As a child he had certainly 'quite liked being CR and being famous.' (ch. 14).

339   For Clare, see *Path, passim*.

341   Max Pemberton had once played football for HH where his brother was a pupil. Marjorie, KJM's daughter, had once worked for him.
The Perfect Alibi (The Fourth Wall) opened 27 Nov. 1928 at the Charles Hopkins Theater, NY and ran for 255 performances, 36½ weeks.

342   'I feel like Wolfe' Wolfe, having taken Quebec, is reported to have said he would have rather have written Gray's 'Elegy in a Country Churchyard'.
AAM to JVM K. Fam.
'article in *EN*' Prof. Charles J. Sisson, 3 April 1929: 'Which of our novelists will be read twenty or a hundred years hence? A professor of literature knows better than most people the risks of prophecy in such matters. But . . . I will tip two certain winners, Conrad and Mr A. A. Milne's *House at Pooh Corner*.'

343   KJM's obituaries *Punch*, 29 May 1929; *Times*, 25 May 1929.
Affirmations edited by Dr Percy Dearmer of King's College, U of London, assisted by a committee chaired by the Bishop of Liverpool. AAM's fellow writers included Hugh Walpole, Sybil Thorndike and Revd. G. A. Studdert-Kennedy. AAM said (30 Aug. 1927) 'I thought the Bishop would "curse me".' *The Times* said that in *The Ascent of Man* 'although he denounces Christianity, he espouses Christian values.' The pamphlet had extremely small sales, none at all in 1929

after the initial sales; it was not finally remaindered until 1941 (CB, London).

344 AAM to Irene Vanbrugh   26 June 1929, Harvard.

Chapter 15   *Toad of Toad Hall* and America

346 AAM to Curtis Brown is taken from *Contacts*, CB's autobiography. Angela Baddeley's name is a blank.

347 'note to Francis Lister'   17 April 1929, Texas.
'to delight and titillate'   Swann. 'Whimsical' is a very odd word. The basic dictionary definition may be neutral: 'full of odd fancies', 'fantastic, fanciful, actuated by whim or caprice', and it may still sometimes be used as praise. A review of David Lodge's *Write On* in *ST*, 10 July 1988, ended: 'He occasionally achieves a splendid whimsy.'

348 JMB on *Ivory Door*   quoted by AAM in letter to St John Ervine, 23 April 1929, Texas.
'The clown wants to play' *NZ Herald*, 20 April 1929.

349 Charles Morgan   *The Times*, 18 April 1929.
AAM to EVL   28 April 1929 (Texas).

350 *Yorkshire Weekly Post*   9 Feb. 1929.
Sunday Sun, 31 March 1929; *Era*, 27 March 1929; *Evening Telegraph*, 2 Feb. 1929.
TLS   1929; *New Yorker*, 29 Oct. 1927 (Charles Brackett).
Letters to Ervine   adapted and cut, Texas.

351 AAM always felt that criticism should be addressed to the public, not to the author. 'Certainly a BBC critic is not addressing a million listeners-in just on the off-chance that the author has a wireless set and is not having a bath.' Letter to *Times*, 15 Nov. 1929.
'often returned to'   e.g. interview in *NY Herald Tribune*, 15 Nov. 1931.

352 'Every dramatist'   Preface to *Michael and Mary*.
AAM to JVM   K. Fam.

353 'swanning along'   Angela Killey talking.
'closest relationships'; 'Maud was always a little in love with Alan'   Maud's children in conversation with me.
Reginald McKenna had been Chancellor of the Exchequer 1915–16.

354 original will   K. Fam.
'My trouble now'   *Everyman* interview, 15 Jan. 1931.

355 *Times*, 3 Feb. 1930: 'He flings himself at Michael's feet and, unless our eyes deceived us, kisses his hand.'

356 Frank Lawton   quoted in *North China Sunday News*, 12 Oct. 1930, C & W.
'I think modern women'   *New York Sun*, 31 Oct. 1931.

358 'marginally in love'   TP.
quotations on marriage from plays – *Ariadne, Gentleman Unknown*.
interview *NY Sun*   31 Oct. 1931.

359 'praise is what an author' *Everyman*, 15 Oct. 1931.
The quotations from *TP* are slightly adapted.

361 *Toad of Toad Hall* originally kept the name *The Wind in the Willows*
– certainly as late as 1925 when A A M was first adapting the stage
directions for publication.
'loving and efficient' Eric Shorter, *Daily Telegraph*, 28 Dec. 1965.
'one of the very few classics' Chris Dunkley, *Financial Times*, 1980.

362 *Tales of Pooh* Methuen, 1930 (Modern Classics).
'china' Mary Mackail (now Oliphant) still possesses some pieces of
the set A A M gave her. It was made by Ashtead Potters, who were in
business only between 1926 and 1936. A set was apparently presented
to the royal children, Princess Elizabeth and Princess Margaret Rose.
'year after year at Christmas' A A M explained to Elspeth Grahame
in 1938 (Bodleian) why *Toad* never made any money: 'Christmas
holidays only last four weeks: the week before Christmas is never any
good: and parents are apt nowadays to keep children away from
theatres in the week before they go back, so as to avoid the risk of
infection. We used to find the play only made money for a fortnight:
a profit balanced by the losses of the other weeks.' Peter Green,
Kenneth Grahame (1959), repeated in *Beyond the Wild Wood* (1982).

363 'It seemed clear to me' A A M in his introduction.
A A M on *Alice Year In*, Jan.
'When he and Mrs Grahame' Introduction to 1951 edition of *Wind
in the Willows*; (Methuen) version in Limited Editions Club edition
(N Y, 1940).

364 'Basil Dean's version' See Dean's autob., *The Mind's Eye* (1973). In
England the play was *The Fourth Wall* and the film *Birds of Prey*.

365 *Play Pictorial* July 1929.
Picturegoer Weekly 12 March 1932
'one could almost sniff' *N Y Times*, 13 March 1932.
letter to Ervine 23 Sept. 1929, Texas.
Hollywood Spectator March 1932.
another film *Four Days' Wonder*, was directed by Sidney Salkow for
Universal Pictures and first shown 24 Dec. 1936.
letter to Arthur Ransome 17 March 1948 at Leeds. *Missee Lee*
(1941).

366 Copy of letter sent to Committee of Authors' Society 24 March
1930, Illinois.
letter to H G W 25 March 1930. The 'troublesome collaborator' was
Hugh P. Vowles, see pp. 359–63 of the Mackenzies' *The Time Traveller: Life of H. G. Wells* (1973).

367 Denis Mackail, *Life with Topsy*.
Letters to CTS 3 April 1930, Dec. 1930, Jan. 1931, Cheltenham.

369 'a long article' *Everyman*, 15 Jan. 1931, already quoted from. In the
magazine Cracker is described as C R M's pony but he wrote to me:
'It belonged to a man called (I believe) Mr Higgs who lived near
Holtye and gave riding instruction.'

370 'O Lord our God, arise' *Times*, 14 Feb. 1931.
'Can you imagine' *NY Times*, 8 Nov. 1931.

371 'Mr Milne shrank into himself' Ishbel Ross in *NY Herald Tribune*, 28 Oct. 1931.
Vanity Fair, March 1932.

372 *Time*, 16 Nov. 1931.
PGW 14 Sept. 1931 in *Performing Flea* (1953).
'some damn good stuff' PGW's literary taste was hardly reliable. He thought *Tom Jones* 'lousy', 'had never so much as opened a book of Thomas Hardy's' and was never 'able to get through *Lucky Jim*.' See Frances Donaldson, *P. G. Wodehouse* (1982).

373 *NY Times Magazine* interview with S. J. Woolf, 8 Nov. 1931.

374 'looking very grown-up' Fanny Butcher, *Chicago Tribune*.
'Pooh sheds a tear' Interview in *Parents' Magazine*, April 1932, DM as told to Sara J. Wardel.
'going to the theatre'; 'English and American Audiences' *Theatre World*, Dec. 1932.

375 Mackail, *Life with Topsy*.
Parents' Magazine party *NY Times*, 3 Dec. 1931.
Dutton's party *NY Herald Tribue*, 15 Nov. 1931.
Norman Thomas was then Leader of the Socialist Party of America.
AAM to May Lamberton Becker Temple U.
Elmer Rice *Minority Report* (1963).

377 *Saturday Review*, 12 Nov. 1932.
'Christopher Robin' *Theatre World*, August 1933.
Theatre Arts Monthly Ivor Brown, reprinted in *Drama*, Dec. 1932.
'Chopkins' AAM quoted in CB, *Contacts*.

378 'memories of days' *Tribune*, April 1932.
NY Times, 11 April 1932.
'A more recent critic' Swann.
'He wrote two plays' *NY Herald* reported that the Theatre Guild would produce *Sarah Simple*, but it seems to have come to nothing. *H for Helena* at Texas is undated but seems to be post-1931 – the vintage given in the play for a glass of water.
AAM to JVM 20 April 1932, K. Fam.

379 John Milne's memory of what happened is very different. He wrote to me (12 March 1987): 'Alan gave £5,000 each to his Father and two brothers in anticipation of the legacies in his Will. His Father had already made a Will disposing of what little estate he had, either actually or effectively (in view of Ken's subsequent death) in my father's favour, so he had no need to refer subsequently to the £5,000 which was caught up automatically in the residuary bequest. Alan entirely unreasonably (as I told my father at the time) didn't see why Barry should benefit by this additional £5,000 – though it in no way affected Alan who had already parted with it – and to avoid family "dispute" my father, who wound up my grandfather's estate, returned

the £5,000 to Alan.' JVM left £6,562.8s. If Barry *did* return the £5,000, he certainly did not avoid a family dispute.

380 AAM to HGW 23 March 1928, Illinois. Barry died in 1942.

Chapter 16 The Thirties

381 AAM to Macrae quoted by Macrae in a letter to Wallace T. Atwood, President of Smith, who quoted it in an Armistice Day speech. (Dutton archive).
AAM to Drinkwater 23 Jan. 1934, Yale.
AAM to Raymond C & W.

382 *Punch*, 29 Aug. 1934.
letter to Marjorie env. dated 5 Aug. 1934, K. Fam.

383 Doris Lessing sent her regular publisher Cape a novel under a pseudonym and they turned it down.
Angela Killey writing for me, 1987.
NY Post, 26 Oct. 1937.

384 'someone who knew her well' Tatyana Peppé writing for me, 1988.
Fabia Drake talking to me, 1988.
Elmer Rice, *Minority Report*. His first marriage was to Hazel Levy in 1915; his second to Betty Field in 1942; his third in 1966. Born in 1892, he died in 1967.

385 'one of Milne's nieces' Angela Killey.
'friend' Tatyana Peppé.
'rhymed letter' dated 29.x.35, but actually November, Yale.
'in a play' *Gentleman Unknown* (1938) MS, Texas.

386 'Leonora Corbett behaved' Ivor Brown, *Drama*, Dec. 1932.
Griffith Jones and Godfrey Kenton letters to me, 1988.
AAM to Irene Vanbrugh 27 March 1938, Harvard.

387 Garrick lunch party from *Life with Topsy*.
Angela Killey writing for me.

388 H. F. Ellis writing to me, 28 March 1988.

389 'or, for that matter, parent' but CRM recalls various AAM interventions; see *EP*, ch. 15.
Letters to EVL Texas.

390 Pooh translations By 1938 into German, Danish, Dutch, Bohemian, Swedish.
Accounts 27 Nov. 1933, CB archives.

391 *Spectator* review Sylvia Norman, 3 Nov. 1933.
'not a detective story' The confusion has persisted. *A Reader's Guide to the Classic British Mystery* by Susan Oleksiw (1988) lists *Four Days' Wonder* as well as *The Red House Mystery*.
PGW inscription from Edward Cazalet.
Copy of Raymond letter, 25 Aug. 1933, C & W.

393 AAM letter to the *Spectator* 1 Dec. 1933.

395 *Living Age*, March 1934.

396 'I taught the dog to beg' Unpublished (?), MS, Texas.

AAM to HGW   12 June 1919, Illinois.

Oxford Union vote   9 Feb. 1933.

News Chronicle article reprinted in an undated pamphlet (presumably 1933), *King and Country* by AAM, by the Friends' Peace Committee.

398   AAM to Drinkwater   19 June 1932, Yale.

AAM to Ponsonby   29 Dec. 1934, Bodleian.

1st Baron Ponsonby (1871–1946), son of a General, diplomat, Liberal and later Labour MP. Chancellor of the Duchy of Lancaster.

'If everybody reads the book'   *Peace with Honour*, ch. 2.

AAM to EVL   24 April 1934, Texas.

399   'Roxburgh'   John Fergusson Roxburgh (1888–1954), distinguished headmaster of Stowe School. Like AAM, he had been at Trinity College, Cambridge and was a member of the Athenaeum.

Parents' Magazine, May 1933.

400   AAM to EVL   10 April 1938.

'more hopeful'   letter to H. M. Tomlinson, 5 Dec. 1934, Texas.

Times, 28 Sept. 1934.

401   'But Milne said'   preface to 4th edn., *Peace with Honour* (1935).

Liddell Hart material King's.

AAM to EVL   19 Oct. 1934, Berg.

402   Comments on schools from letters to Turley Smith (Cheltenham), Tomlinson (Texas) and Ponsonby (Bodleian).

Letter from Queen of Roumania, 27 Jan. 1936, CRM.

403   'letters from Communists'   'A Creed for a Crisis', MS, Texas.

David Spreckley, letter to me 21 Feb. 1989.

'in spite of Dick Sheppard'   *Time and Tide* essay, *c.* 1944, MS, Texas.

404   'the British Empire'   letter to *Times*, 21 Oct. 1937.

405   Carruthers Brothers' song   MS, Texas.

408   V. Woolf in her diary   5 Feb. 1935.

'like a cat in fly-paper'   *Time and Tide*, 9 Feb. 1935.

Gilbert Murray to AAM   16 Nov. 1934, Bodleian.u

AAM *Times* letter   16 Nov. 1934.

'Dawson's wall'   Robert Graves and Alan Hodge in *The Long Weekend* draw attention to the way newspaper editors censored letters in the 1930s – 'a picked selection confirming the general editorial policy'.

409   *Mein Kampf* letter   Murray to AAM, 30 Sept. 1935, Bodleian.

AAM to Murray on 'insatiable ambitions'   4 Oct. 1935, Bodleian.

410   AAM in *Time and Tide*   20 July 1935.

411   John Macrae   publicity release, Dutton.

412   *Times* letter   14 March 1936.

Troops entered Rhineland 7 March 1936   letter to CTS, 18 March 1936, Cheltenham.

414   'as much maturity as CR'   *PM* (US), 18 Nov. 1940.

Charles Morgan   *NY Times*, 23 May 1937.

415   *Times*, 5 May 1937.

415 J. C. Trewin writing to me, 14 Jan. 1988.
Angela Killey writing for me, 1988.

416 Dorset holidays from CRM, *EP* and 'notes towards a memoir' by Angela and Tony (K. Fam.).

417 Hitler's announcement   2 Aug. 1934.

418 'gloomy lunch'   Denis Mackail, *Life with Topsy*. It was 27 Sept. 1938.

Chapter 17   Hitler's War

419 *Atlantic Monthly*   April, May, June, 1939.

420 Fabia Drake talking to me, 1988.
Mackail, *Life with Topsy*.
'drink and fornication'   *Year In*, Aug.
Times, 17 Nov. 1938.

421 'out for a duck'   *Sunday Dispatch*, 2 Nov. 1952.
'My father had always hoped'   *Path*, ch. 1.

422 AAM to Alison (Brierly)   in her possession.
Denis Compton, Len Hutton and the West Indian Sonny Ramadhin were all famous Test cricketers of the time.

423 'a foundation stone'   *Path*, ch. 11.
advance on *Autob*, Foyles Book Club, Chamberlain letter, etc., Methuen archives.
TLS, 30 Sept. 1939.
NY Herald Tribune, 5 and 8 Oct. 1939.

424 *NY Post*, John Mason Brown, 5 Oct. 1939.
New Statesman, 11 Nov. 1939.
Charles Graves   22 Nov. 1939, quoted in John Adlard, *Owen Seaman* (1977).
Spectator, 6 Oct. 1939.

425 'It is not easy'   *War Aims Unlimited* (1941).

426 Letter to *Times*, 4 Sept. 1939   One of the letters in response to this letter was from John Middleton Murry. AAM's reply, 10 Sept. 1939: 'I think that all that any of us can do is to go on writing – letters and articles – in the hope of keeping some sort of idealism alive' (Texas).
'another letter'   *Times*, 5 Sept. 1941.
Joseph Kennedy   *Times*, 2 Dec. 1940.

427 'an American in London'   Albert H. Robbins, *Times*, 8 Sept. 1941.
Liddell Hart and AAM's reply, King's.

428 *Time and Tide* column   from undated MS at Columbia.
'I am afraid I am not with you'   letter (1 Dec. 1939) at Imperial War Museum – unidentified recipient.

429 'going into Europe'   MS, Texas.

430 *Evening News*   30 May 1946.

431 AAM to Chamberlain   24 May 1940, Methuen archives.

433 Denis Hayes, *Challenge of Conscience*, 1949.
'condemn the unconscientious fighter'   after 'The Objector' in *BTL*.

434 'the children of Europe' e.g. in *War with Honour*.
'He has a woman's capacity' *War Aims Unlimited*.

435 Peter Tasker talking to me, June 1988.
D M's friends talking to me: Tatyana Peppé, Esmé Squarey, Gina Hall.

436 'lending their Chelsea house' letters to Mrs Grahame, 26 July 1944 (Bodleian) and FS, 20 Oct. 1946 (Arkansas).
golf at Holtye CRM to Dave Singleton (Holtye Golf Club), 19 June 1987.

437 'Army barber' after 'Guests' in BTL.
Brenda (Tasker) McCallum writing to me from New Zealand, 8 Dec. 1988.
'terribly thin' AAM to Marjorie Murray-Rust, 24 Dec. 1942, K. Fam.
'Shall we have no one' 'Guests', *BTL*.
Angela Killey writing for me.

438 Letter to Tony Milne 10 Oct. 1940, K. Fam.
Chamberlain letters Methuen archives.

439 'How did one become a Sapper?' and 'What does a father do' *Path*, ch. 2.

440 AAM to Marjorie Murray-Rust, K. Fam.
AAM to Mrs Grahame, 26 July 1944, Bodleian.
'Tristram' in *Birthday Party and other stories*, MS at Texas.

441 AAM to MM-R 9 June 1943, K. Fam.
Denis Mackail, *Life with Topsy*. In her biography of PGW, Frances Donaldson says: 'In August of 1941 the broadcasts were repeated on long wave to England, this time not by the Foreign Office but by Goebbels Propaganda Ministry'. Before them PGW was heard saying why he gave them and that they had 'caused violent attacks on me in England . . .'
'My reason for broadcasting' PGW introd. to fourth talk, Frances Donaldson, *PGW*, ch. 11.
'Of course, I ought to have had the sense' PGW to Townend, 11 May 1942, *Performing Flea* (1953).
Auberon Waugh *Daily Mail*, 8 Oct. 1981.

442 Duff Cooper's views from his son John Julius Norwich, 18 March 1981, quoted in *Wodehouse at War* by Iain Sproat (1981).
Tony Milne writing for me, 1987.

443 Auberon Waugh *Daily Mail*, 8 Oct. 1981.
'Milne wrote' *Daily Telegraph*, 15 July 1941.

444 Denis Mackail and Leonora Cazalet Donaldson, *PGW*, ch. 12.
Compton Mackenzie *My Life and Times: Octave Eight* (1969).

445 Richard Usborne and PGW's comment Donaldson, *PGW*, note on ch. 12.
Tony Milne, writing for me and being very objective about his uncle, but not thinking PGW's conduct at Tost, as revealed in his Camp Diary, as above reproach: 'I can just imagine what Alan would have made of it – this mean, self-interested behaviour from a propagator

of public-school ethics. He would, I think have tackled it in the way he liked best – creatively.' A. K. Milne, then, for his own amusement, had a shot at it himself, imagining Mike and Psmith were in the camp with PGW (unpublished).

446 Muggeridge *Tread Softly for you Tread on My Jokes* (1966).
PGW to Mackail 27 Nov. 1945; Donaldson, *PGW*, ch. 15.
PGW to Townend 20 Nov. 1946, *Performing Flea*.

449 *William the Pirate* (1932).
Mary Cadogan *Richmal Crompton, The Woman Behind William* (1986).
'a critic' John Rowe Townsend on AAM in *Twentieth-Century Children's Writers*, ed. D. L. Kirkpatrick (1978).

450 FS *The Georgian Literary Scene*, Everyman's Library, 1938.

451 Penguin *Four Plays* Discussion about it had begun as early as 1936. H. Raymond to AAM, 18 Nov. 1936 (C & W). The book was published in 1939.

452 Sales of children's books (Methuen):

	Jan.–June 1940	Jan.–June 1941
WWWWVY	9,115	11,198
WP	8,052	11,114
NWA6	5,950	8,554
HPC	6,647	10,794

'increasing popularity' Randall Jarrell, letter, 25 March 1943: 'You don't know how pleased I was with my *WWWVY* – the perfect book for the soldier, this soldier anyway.' Pilot Officer Paul Mayhew (later killed in a flying accident) on receiving a parcel of books while interned in Ireland in 1940: 'Who was responsible for *WP*? Thank you – a real stroke of genius, as was Fisher's *History of Europe*.'
'I only hope' Chamberlain to AAM, 3 Sept. 1941, Methuen archives.
'One day during the war' and 'requisitioning field' MS, Texas. *Year In*, Jan.

454 *NY Times Magazine*, 25 July 1943.
Obituary note on Hon. Robert Lyttelton (6th son of 4th Baron) *Times*, 11 Nov. 1939.
'a tiny anemone' *Path.*

455 'Salerno inferno' AAM to Chamberlain, 17 Oct. 1943, Methuen archives.
Times letter in praise of infantry 24 April 1945.
ST review 'A Minor Classic', 30 July 1944.
Letter to Mrs Grahame, Bodleian.

456 CRM and Winwood Reade *EP*, ch. 20.
snake-charmer story *Year In*, Oct. CRM quotes it in *EP*, ch. 22.

457 letter to Mrs Grahame 7 Aug. 1944, Bodleian. (the Sea Rat is in *The Wind in the Willows*).
AAM to Chamberlain 19 Oct. 1944, Methuen archives.

458 'helped to loosen the bonds' *Path*, Interlude-Hedda.

459 AAM continued his support for the atomic bomb as a deterrent until the end of his life. He infuriated the pacifists by claiming still to be one when he wrote in the *Daily Mail* (23 Aug. 1950) in support of Duff Cooper and his insistence on the bomb's role in Britain's defence. On 25 Oct. 1950 he wrote to *The Times* supporting the Paris Peace Appeal, based on the Pasteur doctrine. 'Fifty years ago Pasteur prophesied that a day would come when war would kill itself by threatening a universal destruction in which there could be neither victors nor vanquished. With the atom bomb, that day is here.' In Jan. 1952 AAM was amazed in *The Times* that there was any cause for new horror: 'Long ago, common decency, coupled with a little imagination, could have expressed horror at the "conventional weapons" of war. Between 1914 and 1918 they destroyed ten million lives, as blindly as any atom bomb.'

Chapter 18   The Last Years

460 'communism, socialism' It is difficult in the 1980s to appreciate how closely the democratic Labour Party was identified with the Communist Party in the 1940s. A great deal of opposition to Labour was entirely because of the fear of Communism. Christopher Sykes on Evelyn Waugh: 'Socialists he feared and hated as people in a conspiracy to introduce Communism into Britain by means of a bloody revolution.'
'essential tyranny' *Times*, 31 Dec. 1947.
'Our Lib (or Rad)' and 'I doubt if we have ever had', unpublished (?) MSS, CRM.

461 Letters to *The Times* 4 Oct. 1947 and 1 Oct. 1951.

462 'If everybody can't have it' *Year In*, Aug.
Mrs Wilson's grumbling, tolerated by Marjorie Murray-Rust on many drives into Tunbridge Wells after AAM's death.

463 'The Beast is dead!' 'The Bottle', BTL.

464 Nancy Spain *Why I'm Not a Millionaire* (1956).

466 'How does one know' *The Fourth Wall*.
TLS, 6 July 1946.
'never done a better piece' *Miami Herald*, Dutton.
EN, 30 May 1946; *Spectator*, 4 Feb. 1949.

467 RADA Royal Academy of Dramatic Art.
Rupert Hart-Davis talking to me, Jan. 1987.
AAM on Nellie Maugham note to *Times* obituary, 18 Oct. 1950.

468 Basil Boothroyd writing to me, 7 Jan. 1987.

469 CRM *EP*, Epilogue.
'One of Aubrey's pupils' Kate Ward, now Kavanagh, talking to me, 1987.

470 AAM to Maud K. Fam.
'to Berry: in farewell' *Punch*, 13 Feb. 1946; *Year In*, Jan.

472 'short stories' At dinner in Tokyo in July 1985 Edward Seidensticker, the distinguished translator and writer on Japan, said to me: 'A. A. Milne? He wrote some rather good short stories, didn't he?'
'The Rise and Fall of Mortimer Scrivens' (first published as 'Offer Withdrawn' in *Cosmopolitan*, March 1950), *TNB*.
'the story of a man who has once killed' 'A Man Greatly Beloved' (first published as 'Greatly Beloved', *Good Housekeeping*, Feb. 1950), *TNB*.
'As I have written' 'One Man's Week', MS, Texas.

473 Peter Ryde talking to me, 1988.

474 'To a writer' 'One Man's Week', MS, Texas.
'a women's magazine' *Weldon's Ladies Journal*, Jan. 1950.
Elliot Graham writing to me, 1985. The toys are now on view in the New York Public Library.

475 'No explanation' publicity hand-out, Dutton.
'I'm weary of this world' and 'I am now in a position' (29 June 1948) in possession of Alison (Murray-Rust) Brierly. Shinwell, Strachey and Cripps were in the government of the time.

476 Charlie Chaplin's autograph K. Fam. See p. 223.
'I don't know why' Alison Brierly.
'only out of deference' Swann.
The Norman Church published 15 Oct. 1948; £100 advance.
'few cared to attack him' Among the very few papers preserved by DM on AAM's death was one, written by him on 25 July 1952 and obviously never sent, in which he replied at length and very temperately to a woman who had condemned his opinions as 'soiled' and 'vicious'. CRM.

477 'I would have thought' CRM, *EP*, Epilogue.

478 'It is indeed an extraordinary age' *Year In*, Dec.
'letter to his great-niece' 20 Jan. 1952, in Alison Brierly's possession.

479 *Spectator*, 6 June 1952; *TLS*, 27 June 1952; *Times*, 4 June 1952.
'a young journalist' Letter to Derek Parker, 3 Aug. 1952, Yale.
NY Times, 2 Dec. 1952.
'autobiography in verse' 12 Oct. 1952.

481 'an article appeared' *Sunday Dispatch*, Nov. 1952.

482 AAM to Maud, 9 May 1955, K. Fam.
Will witnessed, 3 Oct. 1955.
Joan Fuller Scoones talking to me, 1987.

483 'our only sons' 'For God so loved the word that he gave his only begotten son, that whosoever believeth in him should not perish but have everlasting life.' John 3.16.
PGW letter 14 April 1954, seen at Sotheby's, 1986, bought by Richard Usborne.

485 'He never saw her again' When DM was dying, she refused to see CRM. She said she did not want him to see her 'looking like this', though to MM-R and her friends she seemed as immaculate and 'glamorous' as ever, right to the end.

485 DM to Maud K. Fam.
CRM uses the end of *HPC* as the epigraph to *EP*.
Time 13 Feb. 1956, 'A Man who Hated Whimsy'.
486 'That's not true' Suzanne's comments, reported by Liz Waterland,
in *Signal* 51, Sept. 1986.
American newspaper *Christian Science Monitor*, nd, Dutton.
Nation, 20 Nov. 1926, in *BWI*.

INDEX

The arrangement within entries is basically in numerical order of page references, with general entries being marked off from sub-headings by semi-colons. Page numbers following n. refer to notes; illustrations followed by a page number refer to those in the text. Plate numbers of illustrations are italicized.

Index

Index

Index

By arrangement wi
Mr. DION

WIT

ON MONDAY, JANUARY 5th,

MR. PIM

A Comedy in Thre

Geo. Marden, J.P.
Olivia, his Wife
Dinah, his Niece
Lady Marden, his Aunt
Brian Strange
Garraway Pim
Anne

PETE
Matin
a

ACT I.—Before Lunch.   ACT II.—A
SCENE.—The Morning I

The Play produced

Prece

MR. LES

In his Entert

Miss Irene Vanbrugh's dress by Mad

Business Manager
Stage Manager   } Mr

Press Representative
Musical Director

Business Manager
Acting Manager   } For the late Sir
and Mi

Programme